1991-1992
HOCKEY
Scouting Report

1991-1992

HOCKEY

Scouting Report

Frank Brown
Sherry Ross

Douglas & McIntyre
Vancouver/Toronto

Douglas & McIntyre Ltd.
1615 Venables Street
Vancouver, British Columbia V5L 2H1

Cover photograph by Bruce Bennett
Cover design by Robert MacDonald/MediaClones
Printed and bound in Canada

To my parents for their love and support. To my advisor, K.B., for her loyalty. To my silent partners, Cody and Jolie, for their fuzzy companionship. And to my best friend, for his intangibles.

—S.R.

Acknowledgements

When Michael A. Berger, who fathered this annual compilation six years ago, asked Frank and me if we were interested in adopting his baby, we leaped at the chance. The expression "Look before you leap" was not coined for its alliteration. It was a tremendous amount of work, and a learning experience for two veteran hockey writers who had fancied themselves experts.

The list of sources for their book would read like an NHL's Who's Who: General managers, assistant GMs, coaches, assistant coaches, player personnel directors, and players themselves. Their anonymity is guaranteed in exchange for their honest assessments of the players you will be reading about. Their help was invaluable, and we thank them again.

Thanks also to the NHL public relations staff, and the staffs of the 22 member clubs, who provided us with guides, stats, info, and encouragement.

As for you, Michael A., I don't know whether to thank you or throttle you. I just hope we prove to be fit parents.

Sherry Ross
West Orange, New Jersey
July 1991

Contents

About the authors:

FRANK BROWN, 39, published his first story in 1970, about five years after being bitten by the hockey bug. For the past eleven years he has been senior hockey writer and columnist for the New York *Daily News*, which he joined after a seven-year career as national hockey editor at the Associated Press. Brown remains devoted to studying the game, and every Monday night is reserved for goaltending with the New York Hockey Media All-Stars, also known as the Zeroes of Hockey. Brown lives in New York City with his wife, Rhoda, and the world's smartest dog, Chuck.

SHERRY ROSS was one of the first woman sportswriters to cover a major professional sports beat. She began her career in 1978, and in her rookie season followed the New York Rangers to the Stanley Cup final. Sherry worked for such newspapers as *Newsday* and *The National*, and her work has appeared in *The Sporting News* and *The Hockey News*. Her first sports hero was the thoroughbred racehorse Kelso, but Rod Gilbert ran a close second. Sherry lives in New Jersey and is currently secretary-treasurer of the Professional Hockey Writers' Association.

BOSTON BRUINS

RAY BOURQUE

Yrs. of NHL service: 12
Born: Montreal, Que., Canada; December 28, 1960
Position: Defenseman
Height: 5-11
Weight: 210
Uniform no.: 77
Shoots: left

Career statistics:

GP	G	A	TP	PIM
870	251	683	934	703

1990-91 statistics:

GP	G	A	TP	+/-	PIM	PP	SH	GW	GT	S	PCT
76	21	73	94	+33	75	7	0	3	1	323	6.5

LAST SEASON

Led team in scoring, one of four defensemen in NHL to be club scoring leader. Led in assists and shots on goal. Finished fourth in NHL in assists and third in shots. Finished second among league defensemen in points and assists, tied for fifth in goals. Assist total was career high. Goals total was four-season high. Point total was second-highest of career.

THE FINESSE GAME

What is so amazing about Bourque's ability is his combination of skills and strength. He can move a mountain like Tim Kerr out from in front of the net and stay with the NHL's best buzzsaw skaters. There have been few defensemen in history with that blend of power and finesse.

His skating is top-notch. He possesses great acceleration, balance and mobility. Bourque has scoring skills better than those of most forwards. He has an outstanding slapshot and an even better wrist shot. His skating ability enables him to lead rushes or follow plays and work as the trailer. If Bourque weren't as committed to the defensive aspects of his game, he would have buckets of points like the Coffeys and MacInnises of the NHL, but he is just as willing to sacrifice his body to make a hit as he is to terrify opposition goalies with his shot.

Put all of those physical skills with Bourque's dedication and hockey intelligence and you have the NHL defensemen most general managers can only dream about.

THE PHYSICAL GAME

Bourque works extremely hard to maintain his physical conditioning, and since he has to be dragged off the ice, he needs every ounce of energy. Bourque is a workhorse who is unfazed by any of the NHL's bigger or tougher players (it is a measure of Bourque's respect around the league that he is not challenged by many players—he seldom fights because who wants to mess with him?).

He reads rushes extremely well and can defend with stick checks or by playing the body. He will make the hits along the wall and in the corners. Much is expected of Bourque, but nobody is more demanding than Bourque himself.

THE INTANGIBLES

As elite a talent as he is, Bourque is the consummate team man, a captain who goes out of his way to treat the most marginal player as considerately as a fellow All-Star. Bourque is to his position what Wayne Gretzky and Mario Lemieux are to theirs. If it were possible to build an NHL defenseman from a blueprint, Bourque's would be the plan to follow. He is the best all-around defenseman in the world and ranks second to only Bobby Orr in league history.

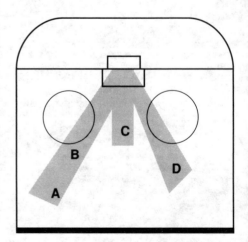

LYNDON BYERS

Yrs. of NHL service: 5
Born: Nipawin, Sask., Canada; February 29, 1964
Position: Right wing
Height: 6-1
Weight: 200
Uniform no.: 34
Shoots: right

Career statistics:

GP	G	A	TP	PIM
230	23	41	64	830

1990-91 statistics:

GP	G	A	TP	+/-	PIM	PP	SH	GW	GT	S	PCT
19	2	2	4	-2	82	0	0	0	0	20	10.0

LAST SEASON

Served a 10-game suspension. Byers suffered a broken left foot Dec. 16 and missed the remainder of the season. All totals were his lowest in four seasons.

THE FINESSE GAME

Byers can shoot a puck and has some offensive skills, but has never reached the next plateau where he could become a useful forward as well as a policeman. Much of that is mental. He sees himself in the enforcer role and doesn't envision much else.

Byers' skating is something he has to work on constantly, and since he is not a self-motivator, he has to be pushed by coaches into doing it. He has had a tendency to let things go and be contented as soon as he gets into the lineup rather than trying to improve his game. He is "pushable" and responds to coaching.

THE PHYSICAL GAME

Byers is one of the NHL's top fighters. He can stay with anyone in a fight and often initiates the proceedings. Byers does not control his emotions well when the battle is on, which makes him a little scary. There is no question he is valuable in an enforcer role.

He uses his body well but not wisely in checking. He keys on making the hit but can't see the game far enough ahead to figure out what comes next.

THE INTANGIBLES

In and out of the Bruins doghouse through his Boston career, Byers has never developed to what he showed in junior, where he combined some scoring ability with his physical prowess. Injuries have conspired to limit his ice time and it is likely Byers will never become more than a goon.

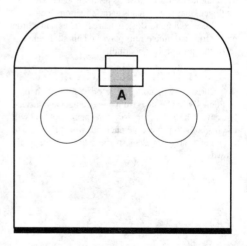

DAVE CHRISTIAN

Yrs. of NHL service: 11
Born: Warroad, Minn., USA; May 12, 1959
Position: Left wing
Height: 5-11
Weight: 195
Uniform no.: 27
Shoots: right

Career statistics:

GP	G	A	TP	PIM
862	316	392	708	231

1990-91 statistics:

GP	G	A	TP	+/-	PIM	PP	SH	GW	GT	S	PCT
78	32	21	53	+8	41	9	0	2	0	173	18.5

LAST SEASON

Second on club in goals, fifth in points, tied for third in power play goals. Goals and points totals two-season highs.

THE FINESSE GAME

Finesse has always been the key to Christian's game. He has lost some of his skating speed, especially the step to the outside that enabled him to beat the defense. He is not a power player or a grinder who can overpower people. Christian's style is to jump into the holes.

Christian has a good, quick wrist shot and one-times a puck well. He is patient, waiting for the goalie to commit. His biggest asset is his experience. He is an intelligent player who reads game situations well.

Since coming to Boston, Christian has had a little more room and time for his plays and his shots and has made the most of the opportunity.

THE PHYSICAL GAME

Christian will come back on defense and play positionally, but he shies from body contact and instead likes to use his stick to try to get the puck back. He will use his body to protect the puck but won't fight for it. He's not a lazy player, just one who likes to avoid crowds.

THE INTANGIBLES

Christian is a hard worker and a competent two-way player. His best scoring years may be behind him, but he can still produce offensively if he plays with linemates who can get him the puck.

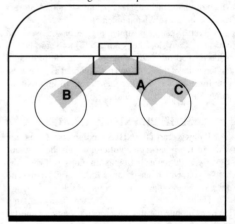

4

GARRY GALLEY

Yrs. of NHL service: 7
Born: Montreal, Que., Canada; April 16, 1963
Position: Defenseman
Height: 6-0
Weight: 190
Uniform no.: 28
Shoots: left

Career statistics:

GP	G	A	TP	PIM
452	52	157	209	478

1990-91 statistics:

GP	G	A	TP	+/-	PIM	PP	SH	GW	GT	S	PCT
70	6	21	27	0	84	1	0	0	0	128	4.7

LAST SEASON

Goals and assists totals were lowest in four years. PIM was career high.

THE FINESSE GAME

Galley is a former all-offensive defenseman who has really worked to become a solid overall player. His strengths are his ability to spot teammates breaking and making the pass to key a rush. He reads offensive situations well and jumps into the attack to become the fourth player. Galley works well on the point not because of his shot but because he has the poise and patience to control the play.

Galley is not a very strong skater, which limits his defensive strength, but he is agile and quick. He skates well with the puck but is more comfortable dishing off and trailing the play.

THE PHYSICAL GAME

Galley had to learn how to use his body and take players out, and had the mindset to do it. He is not a big player but he is willing to throw his body around. Galley has become a better player along the boards and corners although those are neighborhoods he is better off avoiding since he lacks the power to outmuscle players. Galley is better at riding an attacker to the outside with his positioning and skating, but the attacker usually maintains control of the puck.

THE INTANGIBLES

Galley is a consistent player and his willingness to bang compensates for his physical shortcomings. His game won't change much in the future. Galley is a proven commodity.

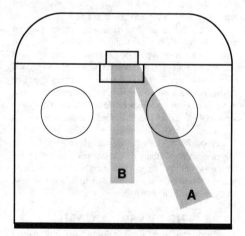

KEN HODGE JR.

Yrs. of NHL service: 1
Born: Windsor, Ont., Canada; April 13, 1966
Position: Center
Height: 6-1
Weight: 200
Uniform no.: 10
Shoots: left

Career statistics:

GP	G	A	TP	PIM
75	31	30	61	20

1990-91 statistics:

GP	G	A	TP	+/-	PIM	PP	SH	GW	GT	S	PCT
70	30	29	59	+11	20	12	2	4	0	137	21.9

LAST SEASON

First NHL season. Finished second among NHL rookies in goals and points and first in power play goals. Led club in shooting percentage and was fourth in NHL. Third on the club in goals, second in power play goals and fourth in points.

THE FINESSE GAME

Hodge may be one of the top faceoff men in the league. The Bruins wasted little time in recognizing his talents on the draw and had the rookie taking many crucial faceoffs in the defensive zone.

Hodge has a good scoring touch from medium range, both with his wrist and slap shots, which are powerful. He is not a pure goal scorer, but one who will get what he does through hard work. He has good offensive instincts around the net but is not good in traffic. Hodge needs to improve in that area and should as he gains more experience. He is a clever playmaker who could make a living off of give-and-gos.

Hodge needs to improve his skating and takes power skating lessons during the off-season. He has gotten quicker and there should be improvement in this area now that he has made a mental commitment to hockey. Until last season, Hodge didn't know how badly he wanted an NHL career.

THE PHYSICAL GAME

Hodge has good size but doesn't use it to his full advantage. He has worked on his conditioning to improve his skating and strength. He is learning to finish off around the net and take hits and be responsible defensively. As his skating improves, he will be able to use his body more effectively. Hodge could become a very effective grinding forward, since he is not blessed with real speed and quickness.

THE INTANGIBLES

Hodge is the son of former Bruins great Ken Hodge, and it took him some time to adjust to bearing the responsibility of the family name. Now that he has started to establish his own name in the NHL, his future will be limited only by his willingness to work.

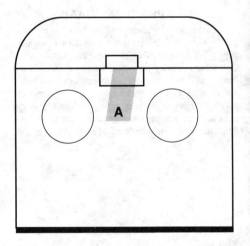

6

CRAIG JANNEY

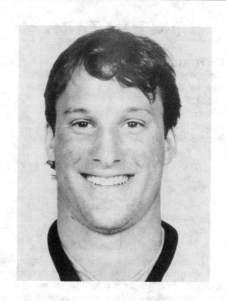

Yrs. of NHL service: 4
Born: Hartford, Conn., USA; September 26, 1967
Position: Center
Height: 6-1
Weight: 190
Uniform no.: 23
Shoots: left

Career statistics:

GP	G	A	TP	PIM
209	73	159	232	24

1990-91 statistics:

GP	G	A	TP	+/-	PIM	PP	SH	GW	GT	S	PCT
77	26	66	92	+15	8	9	1	5	0	133	19.5

LAST SEASON

All point totals were career highs. Second on the club in points and assists, tied for third in power play goals.

THE FINESSE GAME

Janney may be the best pure passer in the NHL. He is creative and unorthodox. No one (except for linemate Cam Neely) has any idea what he is going to do with the puck. If a teammate can get to a hole, Janney will find a way to get the puck to him. He can pass to either side and has a soft touch.

He is not a powerful skater, but he gets there, and has more moves than an eel. He sees the whole ice. Janney is always dangerous when he has the puck and less so when he doesn't—as Edmonton realized in the 1990 finals when they assigned Esa Tikkanen to shadow him.

He has tremendous patience with the puck, biding his time and drawing defensemen to him while the ice opens up for his teammates. Janney has a good shot that he doesn't use nearly often enough.

THE PHYSICAL GAME

Janney has size, but little upperbody strength. His knock is on defense, since he has trouble getting the puck back. He is not strong on his skates in grinding situations and is easily knocked off the puck. He positions himself well defensively, playing zone instead of man-to-man, where he can be beaten.

He is good in traffic offensively. He will take a hit to make a play and playing with Neely buys him a little extra room. Janney has to learn to develop more strength (through weights and off-ice programs), if only to avoid injuries.

THE INTANGIBLES

Janney is quietly developing the confidence that should take him to a new level. He has always been one of the best players at whatever level he has played (he is an excellent athlete in other sports as well), but needs a smidgen more self-motivation to become a true game-breaker. He is not far from that stage now.

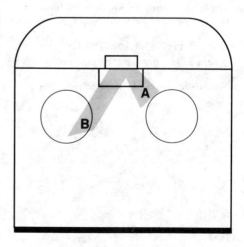

JEFF LAZARO

Yrs. of NHL service: 1
Born: Waltham, Mass., USA; March 21, 1968
Position: Left wing
Height: 5-10
Weight: 180
Uniform no.: 14
Shoots: left

1990-91 statistics:

GP	G	A	TP	+/-	PIM	PP	SH	GW	GT	S	PCT
49	5	13	18	+7	67	1	1	1	0	73	6.8

LAST SEASON

Signed as a free agent, Sept. 26, 1990.

THE FINESSE GAME

Lazaro is a buzzsaw skater, a small player with very good defensive instincts. Speed is his biggest asset. He is a tireless skater with the quickness to get in fast on the defense and the smarts to fall back to mind his own defensive duties.

Lazaro has limited finesse skills, but can play on both special teams because of his skating. He will chip in key goals here and there, but he will never be a big scorer. Most of his goals come from beating the defense in deep and wristing from the slot. He can shoot well on stride. Because he is not a strong player, he lacks a powerful shot.

THE PHYSICAL GAME

There is enthusiasm and life whenever Lazaro is on the ice. He will always be limited physically, but plays the kind of aggressive shifts that can change the momentum of a game. He will always be the kind of player who is on the bubble, and will always work hard.

THE INTANGIBLES

Lazaro came from nowhere (specifically, a free agent tryout camp) to earn a regular role with the Bruins at mid-season. He could be one of the great success stories of the NHL. He played defense at the University of New Hampshire and will be valuable as a player who can swing into either position.

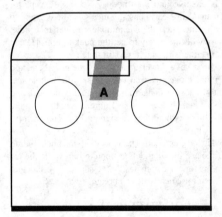

STEPHEN LEACH

Yrs. of NHL service: 4
Born: Cambridge, Mass., USA; January 16, 1966
Position: Right wing
Height: 5-11
Weight: 198
Uniform no.: 21
Shoots: Right

Career statistics:

GP	G	A	TP	PIM
246	43	54	97	322

1990-91 statistics:

GP	G	A	TP	+/-	PIM	PP	SH	GW	GT	S	PCT
68	11	19	30	-9	99	4	0	1	0	134	8.2

LAST SEASON

Goal production dropped by seven from prior season.

THE FINESSE GAME

Leach is not gifted with great hockey sense. It seems at times he goes to an area because the coach told him to, rather than because he understood the hockey concept which mandated his arrival there.

He is not without tools. Leach can skate, he can blow a shot past a goalie from the top of the circles in. He can drive to the net. But he can also miss the net when he should be on target; he doesn't always sense when he should drive to the net or walk out of the corners with a puck he has fought to win. He doesn't read defensive situations that well, so he gets caught flatfooted.

THE PHYSICAL GAME

Leach scraps in the corners, keeps his legs churning and keeps the puck in play. He's strong. He pays a physical price. He is a grinding, bumping, disturbing kind of player who is capable of success in a physical role, as long as his responsibilities are clearly—and narrowly—defined.

THE INTANGIBLES

Leach is determined at times, but not every night. Games on consecutive nights wear him down, because of the physical toll extracted by the driving, grinding style he plays. He has occasional problems with success; when he scores a goal or two, he tries to score more instead of being the third-line, fourth-line checking guy the team needs him to be.

Boston Garden should be good for Leach. He can simply bounce off people in the more-confined area there and should prosper by not having to cover as much acreage as Capital Centre's pond. Smaller ice also requires quicker decisions, however, and his ability to make them bears close scrutiny.

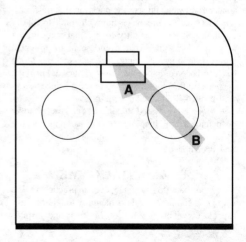

ANDY MOOG

Yrs. of NHL service: 10
Born: Penticton, B.C., Canada; February 18, 1960
Position: Goaltender
Height: 5-8
Weight: 170
Uniform no.: 35
Catches: left

Career statistics:

GP	MINS	GA	SO	GAA	A	PIM
379	21129	1185	13	3.37	17	90

1990-91 statistics:

GP	MINS	GAA	W	L	T	SO	GA	S	SAPCT	PIM
51	2844	2.87	25	13	9	4	136	1307	.896	20

LAST SEASON

Fourth among NHL goalies in goal-against average, which was his best in three seasons. Career-high four shutouts tied for second in league. Missed 10 games with strained knee ligaments.

THE PHYSICAL GAME

Moog is a quick player who relied on his reflexes to get him into the NHL, then on his improving technique to propel him to the top ranks of the goaltending brotherhood. He challenges shooters aggressively and is a good, balanced skater who is tough to fake. He will wait for the shooter and won't commit himself.

His weaknesses are his glove hand and five-hole. He had very quick feet, so he is adept at handling low shots. And while he is also fast on the draw with his glove, he can be beaten over his left shoulder. He concentrates well and sees the puck through traffic.

His small stature makes him vulnerable to crease-crashing, and opponents try to use that tactic to get Moog off his game. That would seem to prompt a protest from him for stronger net magnets. But Moog has also become one of the slyest goalies at knocking the puck off the mooring to stop play, and since he's so well-padded, he'll take the trade-off.

Moog is not a good stickhandler and prefers to let his defense do the lugging. He is remarkably adept at guiding his rebounds to his teammates to help turn the flow back up ice.

THE MENTAL GAME

Moog hates to get beaten, even in practice. He is a very good competitor who is mentally tough. Moog is capable of winning games on his own and inspires great confidence in his teammates. His off nights are rare, and when they come, they are forgotten the next day. He keeps himself in top physical shape, and has tremendous self-confidence.

THE INTANGIBLES

Moog is probably one of the top five goalies in the NHL in consistency. His intelligence, drive and skills should result in another top season.

CAM NEELY

Yrs. of NHL service: 8
Born: Comox, B.C., Canada; June 6, 1965
Position: Right wing
Height: 6-1
Weight: 210
Uniform no.: 8
Shoots: right

Career statistics:

GP	G	A	TP	PIM
564	272	231	503	1043

1990-91 statistics:

GP	G	A	TP	+/-	PIM	PP	SH	GW	GT	S	PCT
69	51	40	91	+26	98	18	1	8	0	262	19.5

LAST SEASON

Second in NHL in goals. Led team in goals and power play goals. Third in assists and points. Second-highest plus-minus on team. PIM seven-season low. Point and goals totals second highest of career. Missed five games with stick suspension.

THE FINESSE GAME

Neely is a finisher, perhaps second only in the NHL to Brett Hull in terms of his ability to get a shot away quickly, on target, and like a missle. He lacks solid puckhandling skills and won't make plays, but he will make the utmost of his scoring chances. Neely seldom gets in prolonged slumps because he doesn't try to do anything pretty.

He is a sturdy skater who can apply the jets. He is all but impossible to stop once he has built up a head of steam. More than one NHL defenseman has separated a shoulder by sticking one arm out and trying to slow Neely down. He is not very quick laterally but does have a good driving inside move—one step, and he's gone. He likes to skate in on his off-wing and fire a low, far-side shot that is deadly.

He is an excellent power play man who thrives in the slot. He is difficult to budge from in front because of his skating balance and strength. Neely is an on-ice leader who has matured into one of the game's best.

THE PHYSICAL GAME

Neely is a Mack truck. He has tremendous upper-body strength and is probably the top power forward in the league. He will go through anyone to get to the net to score a goal. He will patrol the corners and boards and dole out punishing checks. Neely's got a genuine streak of mean in him, but has worked at controlling his temper since he is much more valuable to the Bruins in front of the net than in the penalty box studying the advertising on the Garden boards. He is among the game's best fighters.

Neely is unquestionably the best in the league at offensive-zone hits. He has to play a hard, hitting game and gets a little lost on those rare nights when the Bruins play a more dainty game.

THE INTANGIBLES

Neely has established himself as one of the NHL's top right wings and experience will only continue to improve his game. He is a willing and dedicated player, an intense performer who puts a lot of pressure on himself and wants to be on the ice when the game is on the line.

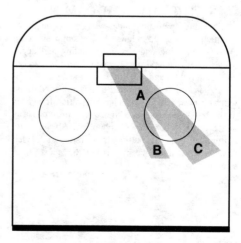

CHRIS NILAN

Yrs. of NHL service: 11
Born: Boston, Mass., USA; February 9, 1958
Position: Right wing
Height: 6-0
Weight: 205
Uniform no.: 30
Shoots: right

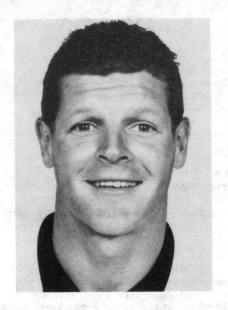

Career statistics:

GP	G	A	TP	PIM
632	104	108	222	2783

1990-91 statistics:

GP	G	A	TP	+/-	PIM	PP	SH	GW	GT	S	PCT
41	6	9	15	+4	277	0	0	2	0	41	14.6

LAST SEASON

Despite missing half the season with ankle surgery, led club in PIM. PIM and games played totals were three-season highs.

THE FINESSE GAME

Nilan is an intimidating player, but he has been effective in the NHL because he does have above-average skills for a player of his type. He has a good shot but not a very quick release and needs some time to get it off (his reputation has earned him a bit of breathing room).

He is an average skater but he has worked exteremely hard at making himself a two-way player and can be valuable as a checking forward. Nilan checks hard and plays with enough intelligence to maintain his position.

Nilan is fairly good with the puck in traffic, and is willing to fight for the puck in front of the net. He is an opportunistic scorer from close range.

THE PHYSICAL GAME

Nilan is a punishing hitter who can put on a last-minute burst of speed to hurt. He keeps himself in top physical condition and has good skating and upper body strength. He is strong along the boards. Nilan is a very good fighter and will not be intimidated.

Nilan knows that in order to stay in the NHL, he will have to stay away from cheap penalties. If he goes to the box, he has to take someone with him. He is pretty good at nettling the opposition. If he starts hurting his team by putting them into shorthanded situations, Nilan will be in street clothes most of the season.

THE INTANGIBLES

Nilan knows his role and he's like an aging gunslinger awaiting the challenge from the next young whippersnapper. His career is winding down but he can still be a useful player as long as his body holds out.

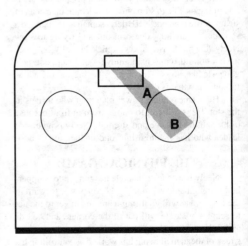

DAVE POULIN

Yrs. of NHL service: 8
Born: Timmins, Ont., Canada; December 17, 1958
Position: Center
Height: 5-11
Weight: 190
Uniform no.: 19
Shoots: left

Career statistics:

GP	G	A	TP	PIM
530	175	264	439	340

1990-91 statistics:

GP	G	A	TP	+/-	PIM	PP	SH	GW	GT	S	PCT
31	8	12	20	+5	25	0	2	0	0	60	13.3

LAST SEASON

Missed 49 games with a variety of injuries (groin pull, broken jaw, fractured left shoulder blade and flu). Games played and all point totals were career lows.

THE FINESSE GAME

Poulin's game is all in his head. He is utterly determined to get the puck, make the pass, or kill the penalty and whatever it takes to accomplish that, he will do. His tenacity is a big part of what makes him a superior penalty killer. His skating ability is good, with quick, shifty movements. He has lost some of his straightaway speed.

Poulin is not overly blessed with skills. Most of what he has done in the NHL has been the result of hard work. He does have some playmaking abilities, especially down low and in traffic. He also has a fairly good wrist shot. He has very strong arms and that helps him digging the puck out of skates or from scrums in the corner.

Poulin is a good overall athlete who combines average hockey skills with excellent hockey sense and intuition.

THE PHYSICAL GAME

Don't let the choirboy looks and the gentlemanly off-ice demeanor fool you; Poulin is a tough competitor who will do anything within the rules and many things outside of them to win. He can be sneaky-dirty, but that's not an insult. It's just one of the ways a little gritty guy can even the odds.

Poulin is devil-may-care and will throw his body at people and at shots. His unselfishness accounts for his injuries. The hurts have taken their toll, but don't expect Poulin to change his style. He will still give a team everything he's got. It's just that he has less and less to give as the years and the injuries mount.

THE INTANGIBLES

Poulin is one of the game's ultimate competitors and an inspirational on-ice leader. His future contributions will be limited by his physical capacity.

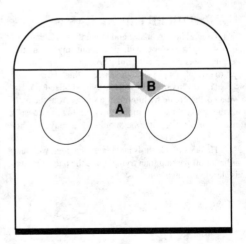

STEPHANE QUINTAL

Yrs. of NHL service: 3
Born: Boucherville, Que., Canada; October 22, 1968
Position: Defenseman
Height: 6-3
Weight: 215
Uniform no.: 21
Shoots: right

Career statistics:

GP	G	A	TP	PIM
109	4	11	15	140

1990-91 statistics:

GP	G	A	TP	+/-	PIM	PP	SH	GW	GT	S	PCT
45	2	6	8	+2	89	1	0	0	0	54	3.7

LAST SEASON

Games played, PIM and points career highs.

THE FINESSE GAME

Quintal has some excellent offensive skills which have not been put to their full use yet in the NHL. He has very soft hands and a wide variety of shots. He can shoot accurately and powerfully and may have a future as a point man on the power play. He rushes well with the puck and is a good stickhandler.

Quintal moves like a brontosaurus (well, like we imagine a brontosaurus would skate). He is a slow, plodding skater with good balance but without much quickness. He has concentrated on positional play to compensate for his lack of skating ability and has shown improvement in the mental aspect of the game.

THE PHYSICAL GAME

Quintal has great size and strength, and is capable of fighting toe-to-toe with just about anyone in the league. He is not a pushy, bully type, however, and has yet to establish a physical presence in the NHL.

He ties his man up without tying himself up. He protects the goalie by moving the screen from the path of the puck. Since his mobility is limited, he doesn't make the big take-outs he should for a player of his size.

He does block shots and clears the puck well and is better off passing than trying to lug the puck. Quintal is alert in his own zone.

THE INTANGIBLES

Quintal is a happy-go-lucky sort who has been slow to develop. He has yet to put all of his ingredients together on a consistent basis and remains a borderline NHL regular. His game would suit Boston Garden beautifully if he can step things up a notch.

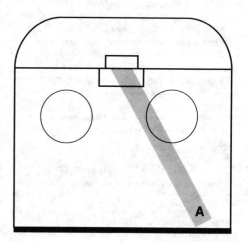

VLADIMIR RUZICKA

Yrs. of NHL service: 2
Born: Most, Czechoslovakia; June 6, 1963
Position: Center
Height: 6-3
Weight: 212
Uniform no.: 38
Shoots: left

Career statistics:

GP	G	A	TP	PIM
54	19	14	33	29

1990-91 statistics:

GP	G	A	TP	+/-	PIM	PP	SH	GW	GT	S	PCT
29	8	8	16	+1	19	4	0	0	0	51	15.7

LAST SEASON

Acquired from Edmonton Oct. 22, 1990, for Greg Hawgood. Suffered an ankle injury Dec. 29 and missed most of the second half of the season with recurring ankle tendinitis.

THE FINESSE GAME

Ruzicka is one of those big, smooth players who does everything so effortlessly that the first impression is how lazy he is. There is some truth to that. Ruzicka's weakness is in his defense. He gets mesmerized by the puck and trapped in the offensive zone. He does not play well without the puck—in fact, he is fairly useless without it.

But when he has the puck, and when he is interested, he is a dazzling puckhandler. He is a dangerous offensive player who can be a real threat on the power play. Ruzicka does not finish plays as well as he should for someone of his size and obvious ability.

Ruzicka is a good skater, but he has slowed in recent years and can't sustain the bursts of energy needed for a full night's work.

THE PHYSICAL GAME

Ruzicka is a perimeter player who doesn't use his body well in any zone. He can be intimidated, and when the intensity of the game increases—as in the playoffs—he does not make the plays that require any sort of physical sacrifice. He is solely a finesse player.

THE INTANGIBLES

For a team that can afford a power-play specialist, Ruzicka is the man for the job. His lack of defensive efforts make him a liability for a full-time forward.

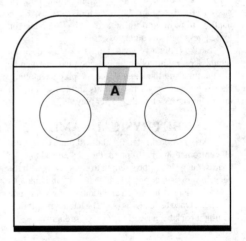

15

PETRI SKRIKO

Yrs. of NHL service: 7
Born: Laapeenranta, Finland; March 12, 1962
Position: Right wing
Height: 5-10
Weight: 175
Uniform no.: 18
Shoots: right

Career statistics:

GP	G	A	TP	PIM
500	176	216	392	433

1990-91 statistics:

GP	G	A	TP	+/-	PIM	PP	SH	GW	GT	S	PCT
48	9	18	27	-5	17	1	1	5	0	120	7.5

LAST SEASON

Acquired from Vancouver for second round draft pick in 1991, January 16, 1991. Games played and all point totals career lows.

THE FINESSE GAME

Skriko is a class act with a high skill level. His skating is the strongest part of his game, even though he has slowed a bit. He still possesses good speed and Quarterhorse quickness.

Skriko's great scoring years are behind him. He has an effective snap shot that fools goalies. He is unafraid to wade into traffic and is able to pounce on loose pucks with his quickness.

Skriko is not a very good playmaker. He does not see the ice well although he is a good passer when he has the time and the room to see the play developing. He has good hockey sense and his ability as a finisher makes him an asset on the power play.

THE PHYSICAL GAME

Skriko works his tail off and will plunge into a lot of confrontations in front of the net and along the boards, but he lacks the strength to come away with the puck in most situations. He is better off in situations where he can use his speed and nimble moves to elude checkers. Once he loses the puck, he has a difficult time getting it back because of his lack of strength.

THE INTANGIBLES

Skriko benefited from the change of scenery last season and adapted well to the lower tempo game played by the Bruins. If he is able to sustain that energy he could be a useful player, but he needs to add a defensive facet to his game.

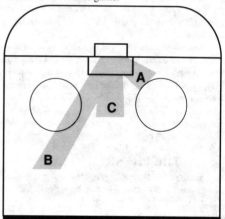

BOB SWEENEY

Yrs. of NHL service: 4
Born: Concord, Mass., USA; January 25, 1964
Position: Center
Height: 6-3
Weight: 200
Uniform no.: 42
Shoots: left

Career statistics:

GP	G	A	TP	PIM
319	75	98	173	401

1990-91 statistics:

GP	G	A	TP	+/-	PIM	PP	SH	GW	GT	S	PCT
80	15	33	48	+12	115	0	1	2	0	116	12.9

LAST SEASON

One of two Bruins to play in all 80 games. Point, PIM and assist totals career highs.

THE FINESSE GAME

Sweeney has size and range, a nice scoring touch for someone who is considered a checking center. Sweeney likes to skate in one-on-one and try to beat the defenseman. He has a nice, sweeping move and loves to bring the puck to his backhand for a shot.

Sweeney doesn't have an overpowering shot but he has a good snap shot that he doesn't use often enough. He frequently hangs onto the puck too long and is not a very good playmaker.

Sweeney is a lumbering skater who does not go from zero to 60 in the blink of an eye. It takes him some time to build up speed, but once he does he is a fairly fluid skater with long strides. He lacks quickness but has good balance and lateral movement. His skating ability is a definite drawback because Sweeney has offensive skills that could be put to better use—even on the power play—if he weren't such a poor skater.

THE PHYSICAL GAME

Sweeney can be pitted against many of the NHL's power forwards because of his good size. He has good balance and with his long arms can get in other people's way defensively. He is also willing to fight for the puck to score a goal. Sweeney will also drop his gloves if he has to, although he will seldom be the aggressor.

THE INTANGIBLES

Sweeney is a steady journeyman center who will always be able to find work as a third-line center if he can keep his intensity level up.

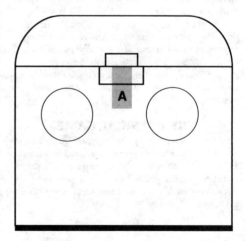

DON SWEENEY

Yrs. of NHL service: 2
Born: St. Stephen, N.B., Canada; August 17, 1966
Position: Defenseman
Height: 5-11
Weight: 170
Uniform no.: 32
Shoots: left

Career statistics:

GP	G	A	TP	PIM
171	14	23	37	145

1990-91 statistics:

GP	G	A	TP	+/-	PIM	PP	SH	GW	GT	S	PCT
77	8	13	21	+2	67	0	1	3	0	102	7.8

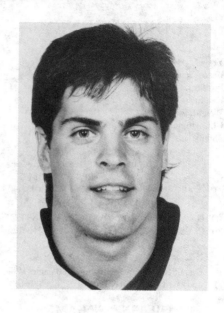

LAST SEASON

Games played and all point totals were career highs.

THE FINESSE GAME

Sweeney doesn't do any one thing particularly well, but he has worked hard to get to the NHL and has an effective if unspectacular package of talent. His strongest suit is his skating. He is very quick with good mobility, but attacking forwards have learned to go wide on him because he will lose them on the boards. His instincts are not good enough to make him a good rushing defenseman.

Sweeney can play the point when the first unit tires. He is intelligent in the offensive zone but had a limited repertoire of shots. He is a good playmaker and his puckhandling ability is one of the better parts of his game. Sweeney is usually back on his heels when the rush is coming at him and does not have the confidence to step up into the play.

THE PHYSICAL GAME

Sweeney will always be restricted by his lack of size. He is knocked off the puck easily and lacks reach. He can be overpowered by bigger players. He is stocky and strong for his size and will play as well as he can physically, but his determination can't always overcome his small stature.

THE INTANGIBLES

Sweeney's willingness is the reason why he is in the NHL and the reason why he will continue to improve. He lacks the qualities to be an impact player, but he can continue to be a solid everyday defenseman.

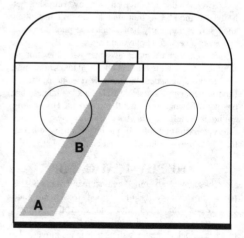

WES WALZ

Yrs. of NHL service: 1
Born: Calgary, Alta., Canada; May 15, 1970
Position: Center
Height: 5-10
Weight: 180
Uniform no.: 13
Shoots: right

Career statistics:

GP	G	A	TP	PIM
58	9	9	18	32

1990-91 statistics:

GP	G	A	TP	+/-	PIM	PP	SH	GW	GT	S	PCT
56	8	8	16	-14	32	1	0	1	0	57	14.0

LAST SEASON

First NHL season.

THE FINESSE GAME

A lot of ability in a little package. Much was expected of Walz (who has one of the better nicknames: "Tennessee") after the Bruins got a glimpse of him two seasons ago. But that was like a great trailer for a bad movie.

Not that Walz is a washout. No one should give up on a 21-year-old, especially when the high expectations were not his fault. Unlike Theoren Fleury (who took some time in the minors to develop), Walz has some quickness but is not blindingly fast. His shot is not spectacular, but he can be accurate and deceptive. Walz has a bad habit of turning away from the puck, which calls his desire into question.

Walz' greatest liability is his defensive play. Since he has not been able to post the kind of gaudy numbers that could make you overlook some lapses, Walz needs to develop into a better two-way player. The Boston organization has never had much tolerance for forwards who won't backcheck.

THE PHYSICAL GAME

Walz is not very strong on his skates and needs to develop better quickness and balance to avoid bigger checkers. So far, he has not shown much ambition.

THE INTANGIBLES

Walz has some raw talent but not enough to coast. He is a young player to watch and with the proper work ethic will make it as an NHLer.

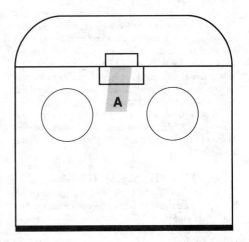

GLEN WESLEY

Yrs. of NHL service: 4
Born: Red Deer, Alta., Canada; October 2, 1968
Position: Defenseman
Height: 6-1
Weight: 195
Uniform no.: 26
Shoots: left

Career statistics:

GP	G	A	TP	PIM
314	46	124	170	256

1990-91 statistics:

GP	G	A	TP	+/-	PIM	PP	SH	GW	GT	S	PCT
80	11	32	43	0	78	5	1	1	0	199	5.5

LAST SEASON

One of two Bruins to play in all 80 games. Second among team defensemen in all point totals. All point totals two-season highs.

THE FINESSE GAME

Wesley is a very good skater with speed, balance and quickness in tight. He is better than most young defensemen in reading plays and knows when to step up into the flow.

He has a good, quick shot from the point—his wrist shot is his strongest weapon. He is a good point man on the power play because he can either take the shot or make a pass and he is a very good puckhandler who sees the ice well and can spy an open teammate. Wesley has a very good sense of when to pinch and when to back off the play. He can carry and control the puck with assurance and speed.

Wesley has shown very good poise under pressure (playing alongside Ray Bourque has no doubt helped his schooling). He is mentally tough and doesn't come unglued.

THE PHYSICAL GAME

Wesley was a gifted offensive defenseman who developed the courage to go into the corner and hit. The next step is for him to add more strength and power to enable him to pin players along the wall. Right now, he can't match up against the NHL's heavyweights. He is a good open ice checker because of his skating ability.

THE INTANGIBLES

Wesley has matured quickly into a solid everyday performer, but the potential is there for him to do even more. With his good hockey sense and willingness to improve his strength, he could move out of the middle echelon of defensemen and into the star ranks.

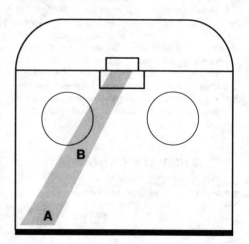

JIM WIEMER

Yrs. of NHL service: 4
Born: Sudbury, Ont., Canada; January 9, 1961
Position: Defenseman
Height: 6-4
Weight: 208
Uniform no.: 36
Shoots: left

Career statistics:

GP	G	A	TP	PIM
246	27	58	85	244

1990-91 statistics:

GP	G	A	TP	+/-	PIM	PP	SH	GW	GT	S	PCT
61	4	19	23	+3	62	0	0	1	0	86	4.7

LAST SEASON

All point totals two-season lows.

THE FINESSE GAME

Wiemer has some offensive abilities in all areas, but none is particularly overwhelming. He can score the odd goal or two and make a good pass and his strength is in his experience. He is a deliberate player who won't be rushed into making a bad pass.

He is a slow skater with a big stride, who can cover a lot of ground without picking up much speed. Wiemer has very slow reflexes and lateral moves and can be beaten one-on-one when he gets back on his heels.

THE PHYSICAL GAME

For his size, Wiemer is not much of a presence. He has never played tough and when he takes out an opposing player it will be more a rubout than a check. He is not a fiery competitor and not combative. He will fight only when absolutely necessary to defend a teammate.

THE INTANGIBLES

There are horses for courses and men for the Garden. It's unlikely Wiemer would be in the NHL if he played for any other team. He suits the Bruins in Boston and is useful mainly as a sixth defenseman to spell Ray Bourque.

BUFFALO SABRES

DAVE ANDREYCHUK

Yrs. of NHL service: 9
Born: Hamilton, Ont., Canada; September 29, 1963
Position: Left wing
Height: 6-3
Weight: 220
Uniform no.: 25
Shoots: Right

Career statistics:

GP	G	A	TP	PIM
631	278	341	619	445

1990-91 statistics:

GP	G	A	TP	+/-	PIM	PP	SH	GW	GT	S	PCT
80	36	33	69	11	32	13	0	4	3	234	15.4

LAST SEASON

Led team in goals and shared team lead in power-play scores. Of his 36 goals, nine were "clutch" (two in overtime, seven others in the third periods of close games).

THE FINESSE GAME

A truly terrible skater, though he is better now than when he first came to the league. The man certainly is not going to win many foot races and there is not a chance in the world of him carrying the puck the length of the ice to buzzbomb a shot past the goalie from the left-wing circle. Aware of his limitation, though, Andreychuk has turned himself into a short-game specialist and uses the assets of his size and strength and smarts to great advantage.

There are good hands at the end of those long arms, which provide Andreychuk with a subtle passing touch and a quick release for the snap shot he favors and he can handle the puck in traffic as well as anybody. His size also provides a considerable reach, which Andreychuk uses well on a favored play—coming out from behind the net for a stuff shot.

When the puck is on his stick in the slot, Andreychuk eagerly wades into the traffic and simply fires at the net. He doesn't try to be fancy or pick corners, he just wants a hard shot that will miss the goalie and hit mesh—or cause a rebound he can poach.

Focused at all times, Andreychuk will keep hacking away at the puck if he has been knocked down. Even on his knees, Andreychuk will shoot if he can get his hands free and will score a share of his goals from that position.

THE PHYSICAL GAME

Though not quick, Andreychuk is especially adept at using his body to protect the puck along the boards and in front of the net. Along the wall, he will bend at the waist and stick his rump in an opponent's belly; unless the opponent has an exceptional reach, Andreychuk will keep control of the puck and will always keep his body between the opponent and the puck. That tactic also is effective in the slot, as it keep Andreychuk's stick free to attempt deflections and to reach rebounds. He also uses it on faceoffs, which he wins

frequently. In the attack zone, Andrechuk will sweep the puck to the boards or the point, then wheel and plant that rump in the path of the opposing center—delaying access to the point.

Andreychuk willingly takes a hit, though he does not stand in the slot as a Rick Vaive does and leave defensemen no alternative but to take their best shot. Andreychuk moves into the slot, then out. Though he gets knocked down a fair amount for so large a player, he gets right back up from the ice and starts over again.

Perhaps because he is so imposing a specimen, Andreychuk almost never fights; when you're his size, with his seniority, you aren't often challenged. He hits with some authority, but without menace or mean streak.

THE INTANGIBLES

Andreychuk is a player who seems to shine when the crunch is on and there are precious few players on his team who can make that claim. The Sabres won three overtime games last regular season and his goals won two of them, against divisional opponents, which underscores his value.

He's never going to be a good skater, he's never going to be a finesse threat. His game is a strength game, though, and part of a strength game is running people over once in a while.

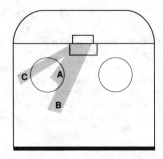

DOUG BODGER

Yrs. of NHL service: 7
Born: Chemainus, B.C., Canada; June 18, 1966
Position: Defenseman
Height: 6-2
Weight: 210
Uniform no.: 8
Shoots: Left

Career statistics:

GP	G	A	TP	PIM
489	59	231	290	462

1990-91 statistics:

GP	G	A	TP	+/-	PIM	PP	SH	GW	GT	S	PCT
58	5	23	28	-8	54	2	0	0	0	139	3.6

LAST SEASON

Injuries, including a separated shoulder, cost him 22 games. Games-played was a career-low, as were his totals for assists and points. Plus-minus dropped by eight.

THE FINESSE GAME

Bodger is a defensemen who doesn't do anything with brilliance, but can do anything well: He can skate, he can pass and he will use either of those skills to move the puck out of the zone. He will play the man, kill penalties, escort the rush up ice, anything. But if a teacher were grading last season, Bodger would have to receive an "incomplete" because of the injury.

Bodger is a fluid, acceptable-to-good skater who does a nice job of carrying the puck from the zone but who just as often makes smart passes to get it out as a result. He is more effective when his ice time is closely monitored and he is kept fresh.

Bodger had been a perfect complement to Phil Housley when Housley ran Sabres' power play, but he struggled somewhat last season under the burden of being top gun. And the injury didn't help. He is wonderfully gifted, though, at taking hard shots off the pass. Positioned at the right point, which opens his forehand for the one-timer, Bodger gets his bottom hand over quickly to keep the drive low—makes the goalie use his feet, often creating rebounds and scrambles.

THE PHYSICAL GAME

Bodger doesn't shy away from contact. He does what needs to be done and uses his strength in tying up opponents in front of net.

With very good one-on-one skills, Bodger rarely gets beaten in those confrontations and often will finish the play by guiding the opponent to the boards. The times he struggles, though, come when he plays the puck instead of the man and ends up tackling air.

THE INTANGIBLES

Bodger stays calm at all times on ice, especially in his defensive zone. He keeps the bench loose. He laughs and jokes and enjoys the game without sacrificing intensity and desire to win. He is a calming influence on his teammates.

It seems, though, that Bodger could make better use of his size and it seems just as doubtful, after this long, that he will. Also unresolved is whether he can handle the role he inherited with Housley's departure, whether his career has reached a hold point or whether Bodger can keep it moving forward.

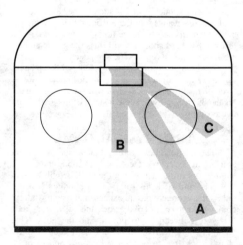

MIKE HARTMAN

Yrs. of NHL service: 5
Born: Detroit, Mich., USA; February 7, 1967
Position: Left wing
Height: 6-0
Weight: 198
Uniform no.: 20
Shoots: Left

Career statistics:

GP	G	A	TP	PIM
225	34	25	59	890

1990-91 statistics:

GP	G	A	TP	+/-	PIM	PP	SH	GW	GT	S	PCT
60	9	2	11	-10	204	2	0	1	0	65	13.8

LAST SEASON

Produced eight fewer assists than in prior season.

THE FINESSE GAME

You wouldn't know it to look at last year's numbers, but Hartman has offensive skills that feature good hands and a good shot. In practice, when he's relaxed, he'll put nice, fat, juicy saucer passes to a guy's stick, he'll use peripheral vision to spot a guy coming in late and displays nice offensive instincts.

Since no team ever gained two points for winning a practice, however, Hartman has some improving to do mentally to maximize those offensive talents under game conditions.

He should learn to relax in the defensive zone, as well. A good defensive player has to learn not to leave his position to hit a guy because, invariably, the puck goes to the player he should be covering. Search-and-destroy won't work and enthusiasm still carries Hartman around the corner of sensibility.

Possibly the team's best-conditioned athlete, he's bright, knows what he has to do, which is to channel that intensity into productivity. Trying to do too much can be as damaging as not doing enough.

THE PHYSICAL GAME

Hartman does all the physical stuff. He's very aggressive, very tough. He'll fight, he'll crash the net, follow through on every hit—no matter who the opponent is.

Hartman learned early in his junior career that if he played tough, he can make it in the big show. Now, the challenge is to transform a tough guy's intensity, every shift, into a balanced-player's control.

THE INTANGIBLES

Hartman wants to win. Last year he was a fourth-line player on a three-line team, but he has the goods to move up. He has the goods to be a 20-goal scorer, the instincts to make a lot of good plays.

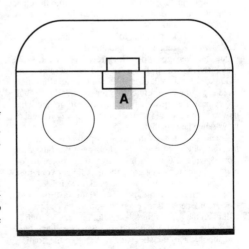

DALE HAWERCHUK

Yrs. of NHL service: 10
Born: Toronto, Ont., Canada; April 4, 1963
Position: Center
Height: 5-11
Weight: 185
Uniform no.: 10
Shoots: Left

Career statistics:

GP	G	A	TP	PIM
793	410	608	1019	510

1990-91 statistics:

GP	G	A	TP	+/-	PIM	PP	SH	GW	GT	S	PCT
80	31	58	89	2	32	12	0	1	1	194	16.0

LAST SEASON

Used 20-goal second half to lead team in scoring and marked ninth season of 30-plus goals after career-low 26 in prior campaign. Fell short of 90 points for second straight season after eight straight with 90 or more, but plus-minus improved by 13 and penalty minutes dropped by 38.

THE FINESSE GAME

While there are players who go out of their way NOT to get the puck, Hawerchuk wants it on his stick all the time, in every area of the ice—whether he's tired or fresh, whether he has four points already that night or if he has none—and always wants to use his one-on-one skills to dictate the terms of play.

Not one to go end-to-end, Hawerchuk will rattle opponents more with short bursts of skating and will seem to dart from one spot to the next; he will go from Point A to Point B, rather than from A to Z. Hawerchuk has only adequate speed. He won't break into the clear and pull away from many defensemen, but he is shifty and difficult to hit.

Hawerchuk prefers to skate against a right defenseman, make a backhand-forehand fake sequence, then go wide. He rarely makes the same move twice, which keeps defenders guessing, and modulates his speed, so a defenseman can think he's lined up—then be clutching air when Hawerchuk drives past. He knows where he wants to go and what he wants to do to get there and stays calm on breakaways when he gets them.

Hawerchuk sees the ice exceptionally well. His favored play is to carry the puck over the blue line, slow down and wait for his wings to get open. If you play wing for him, just go to the net and get your stick on the ice, because he'll get the puck to you.

His shot is more accurate than fast or hard; Hawerchuk depends more on deception than power. He will open the face of his stickblade, fake a shot high to the goalie's glove side, then turn his bottom hand over and shoot low to the stick side or between the goalie's legs.

On defense, Hawerchuk uses his experience to read the play. He looks around now, where he might not have in the past. He's alert for an open man.

THE PHYSICAL GAME

Willing and able to stand up for himself, Hawerchuk will get feisty and defend his turf. He occasionally will initiate contact, but this is not a guy who's going to bowl someone over.

Hawerchuk is somewhere in the middle of the pack on faceoffs, which is odd, as his hands certainly are quick enough to do better. And while he hardly is an imposing physical specimen, Hawerchuk would seem to own enough upper-body strength and leg drive to win more draws than he does.

THE INTANGIBLES

This is a durable, dependable athlete who has missed only seven regular-season games in his 10 seasons. Despite an uncertain start that could have been expected after the change in scenery and teammates, it did not take Hawerchuk long to earn respect with his enthusiasm for the game and his enjoyment of it. As usual, he produced over a point per game and now, with the benefit of a full season in Buffalo, can be expected to flesh out that production.

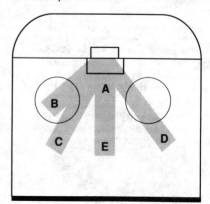

BENOIT HOGUE

Yrs. of NHL service: 3
Born: Repentigny, Que., Canada; October 28, 1966
Position: Center
Height: 5-10
Weight: 190
Uniform no.: 33
Shoots: Left

Career statistics:

GP	G	A	TP	PIM
184	45	66	111	273

1990-91 statistics:

GP	G	A	TP	+/-	PIM	PP	SH	GW	GT	S	PCT
76	19	28	47	-8	74	1	0	2	2	134	14.2

LAST SEASON

Added 31 games played, 61 shots and eight goals to prior season's totals. Set NHL career highs for games played and points.

THE FINESSE GAME

When he's on his game, when he's interested and motivated and feeling his oats, Hogue has great speed, which he still is learning to use to his advantage. He has the ability to get to an opening, get the puck and take off.

Hogue makes a crisp pass and he may have the hardest wrist and snap shots on the team, but is not keen on the deep attack-zone penetration that would make those weapons more effective. He tends to stay on the perimeter, on the fringe of the attack, which gives goalies a chance to time his shot. In tight, he seems to hear footsteps. And that leaves Hogue a just-above-average finisher, rather than a scoring threat, although 18 even-strength goals is a decent-enough season.

THE PHYSICAL GAME

Hogue has strength and, when he's into the game, delights in hitting along the boards. He gets on top of the puck and will punch the face of any opponent who asks him to give it up.

But for his strength, it is confounding to see Hogue allow so many opponents to take physical advantage. He accepts much more abuse than he should, than he used to; word travels fast in the NHL and lots of people gain courage when they play against Hogue.

THE INTANGIBLES

Benoit Hogue does not realize how good he can be. This may just be the case of a player who constantly needs a kick in the britches to keep his attention, because he seems to play his best hockey when the trade rumors are the loudest.

Still, Hogue is one of the truly confounding Sabres. Some nights, he's one of the best players on the ice; other nights, he's missing in action—doesn't hit, doesn't skate, doesn't chase the puck...is little more than a scratch with a sweater on.

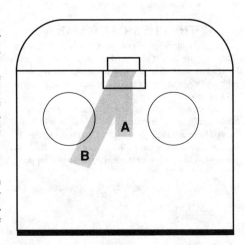

DEAN KENNEDY

Yrs. of NHL service: 8
Born: Redvers, Sask., Canada; January 18, 1963
Position: Defenseman
Height: 6-2
Weight: 190
Uniform no.: 26
Shoots: Right

Career statistics:

GP	G	A	TP	PIM
505	19	83	102	803

1990-91 statistics:

GP	G	A	TP	+/-	PIM	PP	SH	GW	GT	S	PCT
64	4	8	12	5	119	0	0	2	0	46	8.7

LAST SEASON

Missed 10 games due to injuries, six others while management looked at other defensemen. Goal total was a four-season high and his plus-minus improved by 17.

THE FINESSE GAME

Skating and quickness are significant drawbacks, but Kennedy compensates by not trying to do too much, too often. He is not going to bring the puck up ice with speed, but he will move the puck out of the zone with a smart pass. He won't be a guy to join a rush, but Kennedy is an appealing passing target once the puck has gotten into the zone, for when he has time to get it off, Kennedy has one of the heaviest shots in the game.

The trouble is, he inflicts as much damage on the endboards and glass as he does on other goalies.

It is the defensive end where Kennedy is more at home and more of a standout. He is a very steady, consistent stay-at-home defenseman who sees the ice well and tends to make the correct decisions.

THE PHYSICAL GAME

Every team wants an element of grit in its lineup; Kennedy provides it readily. He bangs and hits and hacks. You might beat him to the outside, but you'll be rubbing some spot from the two-hander you're going to get as a reward.

Kennedy's aggressiveness is visible especially on penalty killing, an aspect of the game at which he excels. Kennedy likes to be aggressive on the back side of box. He picks a target, hits it, then gets back in position. And he's one of the league's better scrappers.

THE INTANGIBLES

Dean Kennedy has not played this long because he is pretty to watch. He has not played this long because he is great at what he does. He has played this long because he is intelligent, because he gives a team toughness and character and commitment and steadiness of effort, steadiness of performance. Every building needs girders or it will collapse; Kennedy is a girder.

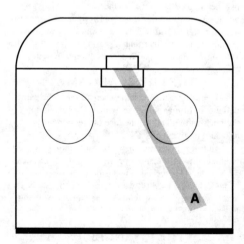

UWE KRUPP

Yrs. of NHL service: 5
Born: Cologne, West Germany; June 24, 1965
Position: Defenseman
Height: 6-6
Weight: 235
Uniform no.: 4
Shoots: Right

Career statistics:

GP	G	A	TP	PIM
319	23	78	101	358

1990-91 statistics:

GP	G	A	TP	+/-	PIM	PP	SH	GW	GT	S	PCT
74	12	32	44	14	66	6	0	0	2	138	8.7

LAST SEASON

Set career highs in goals, assists and points, shared team lead in plus-minus.

THE FINESSE GAME

A strong, powerful stride and solid strength on his stick give Krupp the wherewithal to carry the puck from one end to other. It takes some time, but once he gets all 235 pounds moving forward, Krupp also shows very good speed and mobility, light feet, for someone so large.

Sometimes in the offensive zone, Krupp develops tunnel vision and does not look for teammates who might be in better scoring position. He has a good knack for one-timing point shots, which is a plus because there is a hitch in his slap shot. Krupp's slapper is a bomb that bruises goalies to the bone, but it takes him a long time to load and fire, which makes him susceptible to blocks.

Those long arms provide a whopping reach which Krupp uses to advantage more on the defensive end of one-on-one confrontations than on offense. He isn't as likely to hold off a defenseman with one arm, carry the puck with the other and drive to the net, though he certainly is strong enough to do so.

Krupp doesn't quite have all the answers when it comes to reading the rush and making the smart, safe play out of the zone. He'll force an outlet pass into the middle or go cross-ice with the puck—mental errors that almost guarantee a turnover. On penalty killing, however, he really uses his range to his advantage; it's never a surprise to see him near the top of the circle or at the far boards.

THE PHYSICAL GAME

The knock against Krupp is that he doesn't hit enough or play mean enough for a guy his size, but that is the big man's burden. Players who are 6-3 and over have to kill people or they get dumped on for being a waste of height and weight. When Krupp does hit, he buries guys; but he remains more the gentle giant, tolerating more abuse than he should. That approach extends to the front of the net. Krupp will clear the front of the net at times, but tends more to tie up an opponent's stick.

Krupp brings a sense of desperation to his penalty killing role, though, and will do whatever is needed to get the job done. He stays in motion while killing penalties and does not leave his feet to block shots because it takes too long to recover and regain position. Instead, Krupp wisely uses his anticipation and his long reach to pick off passes.

THE INTANGIBLES

Krupp is just learning he can control entire games by himself. Now he needs to take the next step up. One can only wonder what would happen if he did some weight training, punched a few faces and played the game with more of a chip on his shoulder.

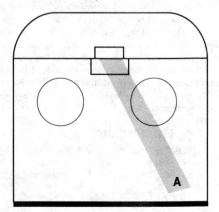

GRANT LEDYARD

Yrs. of NHL service: 7
Born: Winnipeg, Man., Canada; November 19, 1961
Position: Defeseman
Height: 6-2
Weight: 200
Uniform no.: 3
Shoots: Left

Career statistics:

GP	G	A	TP	PIM
433	50	124	174	444

1990-91 statistics:

GP	G	A	TP	+/-	PIM	PP	SH	GW	GT	S	PCT
60	8	23	31	13	46	2	1	1	1	118	6.8

LAST SEASON

Goal total was second-highest of his career, though 18 of the games he missed were by coach's decision. Plus-minus improved by 11 goals, which made him plus-25 over 71-game span bridging two seasons.

THE FINESSE GAME

Ledyard is a credible defender who in recent years has done a solid job of elevating his defensive skills to match his offensive talent. Formerly a one-zone player who might have been better-known as an "offense-man" because of the wicked slap shot that remains his main weapon, Ledyard is a strong skater with a quick stride, good mobility and acceptable balance.

Ledyard tends to join a rush, rather than lead it. He keeps the gap to the forwards tight as he moves up ice with the play, so if a teammate gains the blue line with some speed and leaves a drop pass, Ledyard can step up and nail it. If he has good support from a forward, Ledyard also will work the puck deeper with a stop-then-go move; but there also are times—too many, some nights—when he overhandles in those situations and gets caught after the turnover.

Skating ability gets Ledyard out of some of those jams. He can fly in a straight line, which enables him to catch some players from behind or at least eliminate an opponent from the counterattack. He'll fish for the puck at the defending blue line, but backs up that poke check by staying prepared to use his body if the poke check is unsuccessful. His skating skill helps there, too, as Ledyard has the agility to make the recovery turn quickly and accelerate.

THE PHYSICAL GAME

Though physical play is not a natural extension of his game, solid hits by Ledyard tell you the nights his game is fully at its strongest. He can play tough and physical and has the upper body strength to do so, but seemingly has to remind himself—convince himself—of the benefits. There isn't a player in the league who plays worse when he is more involved in more aspects of the game; Ledyard is no different.

THE INTANGIBLES

Ledyard's game is still improving, his approach is team-oriented and his confidence is filling in, but he still has some trouble differentiating between doing all the things he is capable of doing and trying to do too much. When he simply plays at his capabilities, in all areas, in a clearly defined role, Ledyard can compete for virtually any defense in the league.

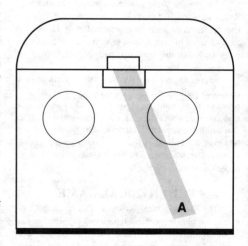

CLINT MALARCHUK

Yrs. of NHL service: 8
Born: Grande Prairie, Alta., Canada; May 1, 1961
Position: Goaltender
Height: 6-0
Weight: 187
Uniform no.: 30
Catches: Left

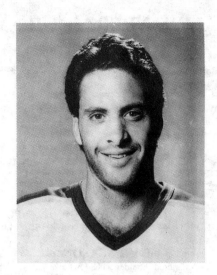

Career statistics:

GP	MINS	GA	SO	GAA	A	PIM
309	17,391	998	12	3.44	14	128

1990-91 statistics:

GP	MINS	GAA	W	L	T	SO	GA	S	SAPCT	PIM
37	2131	3.35	12	14	10	1	119	1090	.891	19

LAST SEASON

Added eight games played, and more than 500 minutes, to prior season totals, yet still matched prior-season's goals-against average.

THE PHYSICAL GAME

Malarchuk is a standup goaltender who makes good use of his angles, lets the puck hit him and gets back on his feet quickly on the occasions he drops to his knees. He challenges the shooters aggressively, rarely retreats inside the curve of the crease and makes use of his experience to anticipate the way the play will go.

An upright stance keeps him from planting too much weight on the inner edges of his skates. By staying balanced on his edges, Malarchuk is able to kick to either side when he needs to and also is able to move with the shooter.

Malarchuk is a good skater who can reach the pucks drilled hard around the endboards and he's getting better at handling it, getting it out of danger in a hurry. He is not stick-happy, from a puck-shooting standpoint, but is very alert for passes coming out from the corners and uses his stick to block any he can reach.

He goes post-to-post well enough when the puck is passed behind him, but is not lightning-fast laterally. He relies more on positioning and experience than quickness and agility to make the last-second, emergency saves.

Alert to the pace of the game, Malarchuk knows when to smother a rebound for a play stoppage and when to kick it in the corner so that play can continue. He plays a very controlled game—doesn't flop and flail. He plays a steady style that keeps things calm.

THE MENTAL GAME

Malarchuk has more than made peace with the goalie's biggest enemy: The mental wars, the ins and outs, ups and downs of confidence and security that all goalies face. He wants to play all the time but accepts the fact that he can't or doesn't. He keeps the weak goals to a minimum, rarely beats himself and spends many more nights giving his team a chance to win.

THE INTANGIBLES

Malarchuk has that rare ability to sit for four or five games, then come off the bench and stand on his head. He is a perfect No. 2, because he can give the other guy a breather and keep the coach confident the team has a chance. And should an injury require him to play a stretch of games, Malarchuk is more than up to the task. There were times last season when he was the only reason the team got a point or two on a given night.

Malarchuk played last year with cracked vertebrae and bulging discs. He couldn't turn and couldn't move the puck without pain, but he never complained. He works hard in the gym, stays in shape, stays ready to play and is a quiet leader.

ALEXANDER MOGILNY

Yrs. of NHL service: 2
Born: Khabarovsk, Soviet Union; February 18, 1969
Position: Left wing
Height: 5-11
Weight: 195
Uniform no.: 89
Shoots: Left

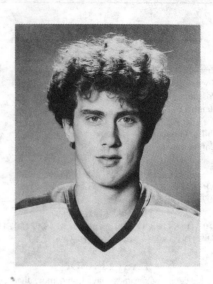

Career statistics:

GP	G	A	TP	PIM
127	45	62	107	32

1990-91 statistics:

GP	G	A	TP	+/-	PIM	PP	SH	GW	GT	S	PCT
62	30	34	64	14	16	3	3	5	0	201	14.9

LAST SEASON

An injured shoulder, a charley horse and a variety of other ailments cost him 18 games—three more than his rookie season. Yet Mogilny doubled his goal production, led the team in game winners, tied for the team lead in plus-minus and finished second on the team in shots on goal.

THE FINESSE GAME

His skates look about the same as everyone else's (blades, boots, laces), but few players in the league wear them as well or do as much with them. Mogilny has about five speeds, starting with fast, and can shift into any of the overdrives in a stride or two. He has speed, he has agility, he has balance—and uses them all to set his other skills into operation. It is one thing to skate fast and carry the puck, another thing to skate fast and make moves with it, still another thing to skate fast and make the moves Mogilny makes.

He will put the puck between a defenseman's skates. He will put it between their sticks and their skates. He will take any defenseman one-on-one and make them scramble with an almost-unmatched acceleration. Once he has the defensemen where he wants them, Mogilny prefers the inside route to the net for a strong wrist shot. He might get pounded with the occasional crosscheck while taking the more dangerous inside route (which slows him to warp speed), but it takes a lot more strength and effort to win outside—and the rewards are not as great.

Mogilny has passing skills and a sly mind. He will go behind the net, moving from his right to his left, making it seem he is planning to come out at the goalie's right. Then he will make a backhand pass that comes out at the goalie's left, against the flow. More often, though, Mogilny seems to want to pass only after he has stickhandled through the entire opposing team at least once. His idea of a perfect assist would be to fake past five guys, then feed a teammate at the goalmouth. While penalty killing, he will cheat into the neutral zone and look for a breakaway pass.

THE PHYSICAL GAME

Though not heavily muscled, Mogilny has exceptional lower-body strength. He is strong on his feet and very tough to push off the puck. He skates through checks and has surprised more than a few defensemen, who figured they'd crush him—only to end up on their backs.

Mogilny continues his adjustment to the more physical aspects of the North American game. Because he is an offensive threat and a newcomer, opponents make sure to get a piece of him whenever they can and Mogilny has at times been thrown off by the attention. Still, he is not scared to go into the corners; he'll go after the puck and get his nose dirty. He'll accept getting hit, but is not the team's most durable soul.

THE INTANGIBLES

Mogilny must use his linemates better, he's got to show up more nights with fire in his heart. Once he gets that figured out, once he matures, once he gets used to North America and the league, superstardom may not be out of reach.

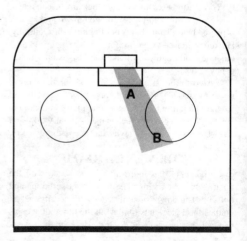

DAREN PUPPA

Yrs. of NHL service: 5
Born: Kirkland Lake, Ont., Canada; March 23, 1963
Position: Goaltender
Height: 6-3
Weight: 205
Uniform no.: 31
Catches: Right

Career statistics:

GP	MINS	GA	SO	GAA	A	PIM
158	8701	476	5	3.28		

1990-91 statistics:

GP	MINS	GAA	W	L	T	SO	GA	S	SAPCT	PIM
38	2092	3.38	15	11	6	2	118	1029	.885	6

LAST SEASON

Missed 25 games due to a back injury that troubled him all season and a groin pull that cost two more weeks.

THE PHYSICAL GAME

Puppa is a butterfly goalie who presents a forbidding obstacle when he is in proper position. With his size and long legs, Puppa takes away the low corners well. And his glove is quick enough to protect against some shots, but not all; he has major problems when people fake a shot, get him to drop, then fire high.

Other problems inherent to the style trouble Puppa. Because he's so tall and it is such a long time before his knees hit the ice, a triangle of space opens between the legs as he drops and more than a few NHL shooters can fill that hole with a puck. Also, once he's down in the butterfly, Puppa is susceptible to the deke.

Then there is the matter of recovery. There are times after he has gone down that Puppa ends up on the seat of his pants, vulnerable again. And, once down, Puppa needs time to regain his footing.

But he is by no means all downside. Puppa's feet are extremely quick and he can reach any number of pucks from the more conventional, standup approach. Puppa also is good with his stick on the poke check. Forwards breaking in on him have to keep their heads up, as he'll dive out with that long reach and knock the puck loose.

Puppa uses his pads well and controls his rebounds well. He has good mobility and reasonable quickness for a big man, which allow him to reach the hard-arounds. He has trouble deciding how to play the puck, though, which leads to cross-ups with the defensemen.

THE MENTAL GAME

When he's 'on,' Puppa is extremely tough to beat. When he isn't on, Puppa's confidence flags and he battles himself.

Puppa's approach has improved considerably, though. He keeps his concentration that rare time when he permits a soft goal and is doing a better job of handling adversity—heaven knows, he had enough practice at handling it last season.

Not a hugely confident individual, Puppa could fight himself a bit less, but is always ready to make the big save, play the big game.

THE INTANGIBLES

For a team that plays 40 games a season in a small rink and makes regular visits to the miniature pond in Boston, a goalie who could handle the puck would be a huge asset. The puck would be in his zone less and he would face fewer shots if Puppa added that dimension to his game.

MIKE RAMSEY

Yrs. of NHL service: 12
Born: Minneapolis, Minn., USA; December 3, 1960
Position: Defenseman
Height: 6-3
Weight: 195
Uniform no.: 5
Shoots: Left

Career statistics:

GP	G	A	TP	PIM
812	68	234	302	837

1990-91 statistics:

GP	G	A	TP	+/-	PIM	PP	SH	GW	GT	S	PCT
71	6	14	20	14	46	0	0	1	0	87	6.9

LAST SEASON

Goal total was a four-season high.

THE FINESSE GAME

In those rare moments when he isn't thinking strictly defense, Ramsey is a good man in the offensive zone. He is more capable on the attack than even he thinks and can surprise people by cheating into the slot and taking advantage of the fact that nobody sees him as a threat.

Ramsey isn't going to lead a rush, but is underrated in his ability to join one late, read a seam in the opposing defense and take advantage of something. He sees the ice well and has a decent shot from the point.

Not a marvelously fast skater, Ramsey uses a change of pace to make things happen. He will hang back, trailing a rush, so that a checker will pay attention to someone else; then he will sprint to a hole. And when he does it, he does it on a high-percentage basis—a smart basis. He will forgo the opportunity if there is even a slight chance that a turnover would leave his partner vulnerable to a quick two-on-one.

Another byproduct of his thinking defense before offense, Ramsey often moves the puck when he could or should skate with it. He is an average puck-handler, when he bothers.

THE PHYSICAL GAME

Ramsey is so courageous about blocking shots, so willing to sacrifice, and perhaps is the best in the league at this unenviable task. He will do it in the third period of a 9-0 game in November just as readily as he would in second overtime of the playoffs.

Ramsey can be a nasty, but generally clean, open-ice cruncher. He still uses the traditional hip check when the opportunity avails and if it comes from the blind side, that's somebody else's problem. Still he will finish and eliminate more than go for the big bang.

On penalty killing, he will leave Uwe Krupp in charge in front and barge to either corner when he feels the need. He also will return the favor when Krupp wants to move around and challenge.

THE INTANGIBLES

Mike Ramsey bleeds Sabre blue every game and will do anything to help his team win. He is the epitome of a professional athlete and team man. There may not be a handful of NHL players more revered and respected by teammates than this guy—on and off the ice. He is very focused on what he does best, which is defend his goalie, and gives all he has to doing it every night.

ROB RAY

Yrs. of NHL service: 2
Born: Belleville, Ont., Canada; June 8, 1968
Position: Left wing
Height: 6-0
Weight: 210
Uniform no.: 32
Shoots: Left

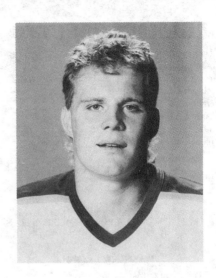

Career statistics:

GP	G	A	TP	PIM
93	10	9	19	447

1990-91 statistics:

GP	G	A	TP	+/-	PIM	PP	SH	GW	GT	S	PCT
66	8	8	16	-11	348	0	0	1	0	54	14.8

LAST SEASON

Games played more than doubled from his rookie season. Goal, assist, point and PIM totals were career highs.

THE FINESSE GAME

Ray got more ice time last season as his game evolved to one that included playing with the gloves ON occasionally. He played a fairly regular shift because of his toughness and his speed, which gave the Sabres a solid forechecking threat. He hits you, then he wants to hit you again, which makes it very aggravating for defensemen who want time to simply go back, get the puck and turn it up ice unbothered.

Actually improved his hands and his touch, which is his key to survival. Teams can't afford any longer to dress people whose only skill is fighting; if nobody fights them, they're a waste of a uniform. Ray is better off when he isn't fighting because he gets to play more and he gets to hit more. He is a punishing hitter and he gets to you in a hurry because he is very mobile and very fast for a guy 210 pounds.

THE PHYSICAL GAME

Because he will hit anywhere, Ray is probably the best player on his team for creating turnovers in the attacking zone and he's a favored linemate for the finesse guys who transform turnovers into goals. Aside from that, his less-rugged linemates get a little extra time and space when Ray is out there; when he is on the ice, enough players are mentally and physically intimidated by him that loose pucks abound.

THE INTANGIBLES

Ray will do anything he is asked to do. What he has to ask himself to do is continue to improve. People see 20-goal potential in him but that might be optimistic when a guy spends nearly six games in the penalty box just by doing his job. And that minus 11 makes grim reading.

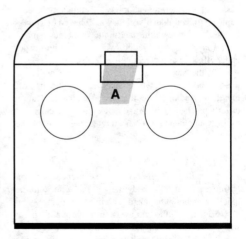

CHRISTIAN RUUTTU

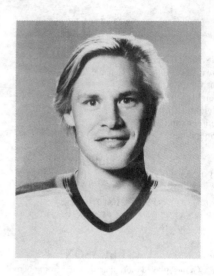

Yrs. of NHL service: 5
Born: Lappeenranta, Finland; February 20, 1964
Position: Center
Height: 5-11
Weight: 194
Uniform no.: 21
Shoots: Left

Career statistics:

GP	G	A	TP	PIM
368	97	209	316	361

1990-91 statistics:

GP	G	A	TP	+/-	PIM	PP	SH	GW	GT	S	PCT
77	16	34	50	-6	96	2	3	1	1	155	10.3

LAST SEASON

Point total and assist totals were NHL career lows, goal total was his second worst while penalty minutes were within two of career high.

THE FINESSE GAME

Somewhere between Ruuttu's head and his hands in the attacking zone, the message gets scrambled. He handles the puck well, but also overhandles it to the extent that linemates get tired of waiting/hoping for passes. Ruuttu creates all kinds of opportunities to score, but hits the goalie or the glass more than he hits the net. This is not a finisher, especially in close.

A gifted skater with light feet, good speed/quickness and substantial endurance, Ruuttu's defensive game is stronger than his offensive. Relieved of a puck-handler's responsibilities, Ruuttu combines smarts with a laudatory work ethic, which makes him especially effective as a penalty killer.

Of the faceoffs he wins, many come while his team is shorthanded, which helps eat valuable time off the clock. And after the disc has been cleared, Ruuttu eagerly pursues the puck and harries the puck carrier—expertly angling him to less-threatening areas of the ice.

THE PHYSICAL GAME

With Ruuttu's energy and exuberance comes a willingness to use the body; he will make noise in the quiet zones along the boards and in the corners.

Sometimes, though, away from the wall, Ruuttu will have a mental lapse that leads to an unnecessary penalty. He'll be right with an opponent, then for some reason the opponent will get a step on him and Ruuttu has to hook or trip the guy to prevent a scoring chance.

THE INTANGIBLES

Ruuttu comes to play every night. You know he's going to work. The disappointing thing is, the numbers he puts up don't match the effort he puts forth, so he doesn't get the rewards for his labor and his team doesn't reap the benefits. Some players simply get it in their minds that defense, not scoring, is their whole game; when their offensive game slides, though, the whole team suffers.

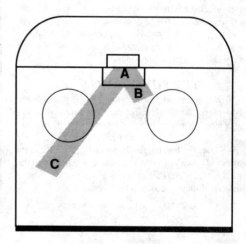

DARRIN SHANNON

Yrs. of NHL service: 2
Born: Barrie, Ont., Canada; December 8, 1969
Position: Left wing
Height: 6-2
Weight: 200
Uniform no.: 16
Shoots: Left

Career statistics:

GP	G	A	TP	PIM
54	10	13	23	16

1990-91 statistics:

GP	G	A	TP	+/-	PIM	PP	SH	GW	GT	S	PCT
34	8	6	14	-11	12	1	0	0	1	56	14.3

LAST SEASON

Split season between Buffalo and Rochester (AHL).

THE FINESSE GAME

It is difficult to determine whether Shannon doesn't shoot much because he doesn't shoot well or that he doesn't shoot well because he doesn't shoot much. Confidence seems to be an issue. Shannon doesn't snap the puck as he should when it's bouncing around the slot, which is a waste. He's in the slot traffic a lot, often with the puck on his stick, and he's strong enough to poach more than he does. Still, a goal every seven shots isn't all that bad.

Skating is a weakness, but he has the capacity to improve. He has a good stride, but his supply of leg power is lacking.

THE PHYSICAL GAME

One of the good cornermen in the league. When he wants the puck in the corners, which is regularly, he's going to knock somebody off it. Shannon keeps puck down low, takes the hits, then makes the play from the corner that gets it into scoring position.

Anybody who tries to knock him off it generally is making a futile attempt, because he is not knocked down easily. Although he is not a ruggedly aggressive physical player, he is one strong individual.

THE INTANGIBLES

Some people are born with confidence, some need to develop it; Shannon seems in the latter group. He has the size and the instincts to get a grinder's job done; more assertiveness would make him more effective.

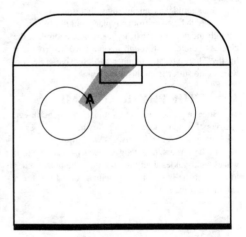

DAVE SNUGGERUD

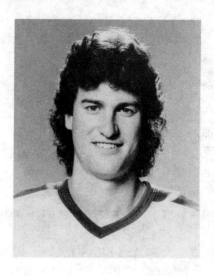

Yrs. of NHL service: 2
Born: Minnetonka, Minn., USA; June 20, 1966
Position: Right wing
Height: 6-0
Weight: 190
Uniform no.: 18
Shoots: Left

Career statistics:

GP	G	A	TP	PIM
160	23	31	54	73

1990-91 statistics:

GP	G	A	TP	+/-	PIM	PP	SH	GW	GT	S	PCT
80	9	15	24	-13	32	0	4	2	0	128	7.0

LAST SEASON

Goal production dropped by five and his plus-minus dropped by 21.

THE FINESSE GAME

Wonderful anticipation, strong stride and above-average speed help make Snuggerud a solid checker and penalty killer, as he likes to hound the puck carrier and his legs more than enable him to accomplish the objective.

Snuggerud has an average shot (he favors the snap), which he takes from anyplace, but doesn't shoot enough and doesn't finish anywhere near enough of the chances he creates through his hard work, drive and hustle. There are any number of defensive-style forwards who suffer from this affliction.

THE PHYSICAL GAME

Snuggerud does not classify as a physical player. He takes his man, doesn't back down, but he doesn't hit. Rather, he's a harrier, always working.

In the corners, he's a digger. He's persistent. He'll whack your ankles with his stick until the puck comes loose, then he'll scoot away with it and look for a teammate at the net.

THE INTANGIBLES

Pretty well-rounded on the mental side, Snuggerud knows the game, where he's supposed to be. Though aware he has maturing to do, there is leadership potential—if not scoring potential—in this player.

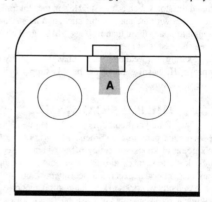

PIERRE TURGEON

Yrs. of NHL service: 4
Born: Rouyn, Que., Canada; August 29, 1969
Position: Center
Height: 6-1
Weight: 200
Uniform no.: 77
Shoots: Left

Career statistics:

GP	G	A	TP	PIM
314	120	195	315	115

1990-91 statistics:

GP	G	A	TP	+/-	PIM	PP	SH	GW	GT	S	PCT
78	32	47	79	14	26	13	2	3	0	174	18.4

LAST SEASON

Point total represented a 27-point drop from prior season, though he surpassed 30-goal plateau for third consecutive year. Assist total was three-year low, but plus-minus tied for team lead.

THE FINESSE GAME

Turgeon has thick legs, which he uses for good drive, strength of stride and speed that may not be exceptional but certainly gets him where he wants to go—when he wants to get there. Skating, however, is one weapon Turgeon rarely uses to his advantage and that often gets in the way of deploying his other wondrous skills.

Turgeon has fine one-on-one moves, soft hands for passing and good vision of the ice. He can make a lead pass, thread a needle or carry the puck into the zone and feed a teammate heading to the net. One of his favorite offensive plays is to hide behind the net, then materialize at the side of the cage to the goalie's left. On his off-wing that way, Turgeon is available for a stuff play on a pass across the crease.

An advocate of the snap shot—one of his real strengths—Turgeon's primary targets are the sweet spot between the goalie's shins or low rockets to the stick side. Those shots come right to the net, as Turgeon rarely fakes a shot and does something else, but it is more accurate than overpowering.

THE PHYSICAL GAME

Turgeon is strong on his stick and strong on his skates, which makes him difficult to move off the puck. But he hates the physical stuff. He does not take the puck into traffic and he will not go in there to get it, unless it is on his terms. He will turn away from any check possible.

The mere chance of a collision will stop his legs from moving, which is especially damaging when he has the puck on the attacking-zone boards; he fails to get the puck deep, it turns over and he's behind on the transition.

THE INTANGIBLES

Turgeon had some trouble adjusting to a role that was revised when Dale Hawerchuk came and took over as the team's top playmaker. And he struggled further against the added physical/checking attention 106-point scorers receive. Turgeon plays the game at an extremely high level, but would reach an even higher one—and receive more respect—with a little more speed, a little more muscle, a little more anger, a little more nerve.

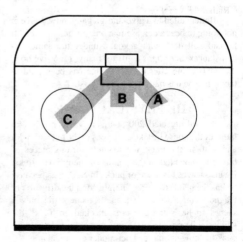

RICK VAIVE

Yrs. of NHL service: 12
Born: Ottawa, Ont., Canada; May 14, 1959
Position: Right wing
Height: 6-0
Weight: 200
Uniform no.: 22
Shoots: Right

Career statistics:

GP	G	A	TP	PIM
931	466	377	843	1679

1990-91 statistics:

GP	G	A	TP	+/-	PIM	PP	SH	GW	GT	S	PCT
71	25	27	52	11	74	9	0	3	1	155	16.1

LAST SEASON

Improved power-play goal total by one, though his shots-on-goal total dropped by 40 from prior season's total. Played 70-plus games for ninth time in his 12 campaigns.

THE FINESSE GAME

Year after year, Vaive returns to the front of the net to absorb more slashes, more crosschecks—to scramble for more rebounds, to tip more point shots, to tie up more defensemen. Just as there are players who make their living in the corners, Vaive earns his in front of the net.

Vaive spends more time there now because he has lost at least a step on his stride and a couple of miles-per-hour off the slap shot he used to blow past netminders after driving down the right side. He doesn't handle the puck much, doesn't have the breakaway speed, but his release from the slot remains quick and accurate when a teammate gets him the puck. He is a scorer, not a worker.

Better suited to a give-and-go game now, Vaive is not going to beat a defenseman one-on-one . . . though he can still deal with a goalie under the same circumstances. Scoring is a gift for many; for Vaive now, the goals come after a higher price has been paid in labor than he has had to pay in the past.

THE PHYSICAL GAME

A well-muscled 200-pounder, Vaive needs that bulk for the abuse he takes. He goes to the net well with and without the puck and has left various pieces of himself embedded in the boards of many NHL rinks. He also leaves his share of pucks in NHL nets because he has the hands to work "in tight" and the drive to put the puck in the scoring area. Considers the play a success if he is the guy crosschecked on top of the goalie while one of his teammates is burying a loose puck the now-submerged netminder can't reach.

This is a player with good hockey sense, a reliable player because he is able to keep his brains and his legs working at the same time—a tall order for some of his counterparts. One bodycheck is not enough to stop him; Vaive knows if you keep your feet moving, you get hooked or held or tripped or punched in the head. Then your team gets a power play and you can score. He knows low shots in tight create rebounds, which create havoc.

THE INTANGIBLES

There were a lot of nights last season when Vaive was not used very much more than five or six shifts, yet he still produced a respectable amount of goals, still was vocal in the dressing room, still came to the rink every night ready to win and provide for the younger players an example of an over-30 player willing to take the pounding to survive and succeed as his twilight days proceed.

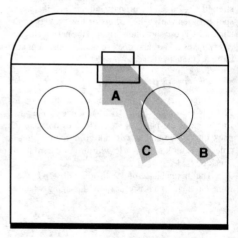

JAY WELLS

Yrs. of NHL service: 12
Born: Paris, Ont., Canada; May 18, 1959
Position: Defenseman
Height: 6-1
Weight: 210
Uniform no.: 24
Shoots: Left

Career statistics:

GP	G	A	TP	PIM
774	40	181	221	1845

1990-91 statistics:

GP	G	A	TP	+/-	PIM	PP	SH	GW	GT	S	PCT
43	1	2	3	-18	86	0	0	0	0	36	2.8

LAST SEASON

Broken ankle dropped his games played to figure that matched career low with Los Angeles in 1979-80.

THE FINESSE GAME

From a skating standpoint, Wells is better backwards than forwards; he doesn't get where he has to quickly enough at times. In today's game, with so much speed, a slow defenseman has to be very clever, because he has to challenge at the blue line; a guy who's slow has to cheat a bit and maybe concede room he can't afford to spare. Then, one on one, he ends up thinking more than reacting. Wells anticipates the defensive play well, though, and doesn't make many mental mistakes.

At the other end, Wells has a decent shot from the point and can make an intelligent pass.

THE PHYSICAL GAME

Wells is a strong player who will move the people in front of the net like a bouncer handles unruly customers. He gives them the heave-ho. When he plays very, very aggressively he can still compete at the NHL level. Wells also does a good job killing penalties.

THE INTANGIBLES

A very hard-working guy who comes to play, Wells faces strong job competition this season through the emergence of Ken Sutton and Kevin Haller, who are younger and have more skills to offer. The funny thing about prospects, though, is they tend to get a chance in the early part of the season, then make it clear they need more time to mature, and the guy who is in the press box while they're playing ends up back in the lineup. So don't write Wells off entirely.

CALGARY FLAMES

PAUL FENTON

Yrs. of NHL service: 5
Born: Springfield, Mass., USA; December 22, 1959
Position: Left wing
Height: 5-11
Weight: 180
Uniform no.: 12
Shoots: left

Career statistics:

GP	G	A	TP	PIM
351	89	79	168	165

1990-91 statistics:

GP	G	A	TP	+/-	PIM	PP	SH	GW	GT	S	PCT
78	14	21	35	-5	28	2	2	2	0	133	10.5

LAST SEASON

Acquired from Washington for Ken Sabourin, January 24, 1991. Played for three different teams (Winnipeg, Toronto and Calgary) in 1990-91.

THE FINESSE GAME

Fenton is a tenacious checker who plays the role of a defensive forward very well. He is a good penalty killer and an irritant because he is always in the face of whoever he is shadowing.

His end-to-end skating is not a threat, but he is quick enough to pounce on loose pucks and will score more "Look what I found" goals than ones on pretty or creative plays. What Fenton is lacking in hand skills he makes up for in determination. He is useful on the power play unit because he will jam the front of the net, looking for bang-ins. Fenton scores his goals the old-fashioned way: he earns them.

Fenton is a very smart player and a good fore-checker because of his anticipation and bulldoggedness. He is never out of position and will usually be the first forward back defensively.

THE PHYSICAL GAME

Fenton plays clean and hard for his size. Slap him down and back he comes, loath to be out of the play. He finishes his checks and plays much bigger than he is, but is also smart enough to avoid crashing head first into brick walls and can outwit most opponents.

THE INTANGIBLES

Fenton is one of the role players who can't seem to get comfortable anywhere (witness all of his changes of address last season). He scored 32 goals with Winnipeg last season, which now looks to be a bit of a fluke, but his future appears to be as a checking forward who can bag the odd key goal.

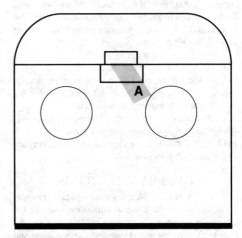

THEO FLEURY

Yrs. of NHL service: 2
Born: Oxbow, Sask., Canada; June 29, 1968
Position: Center
Height: 5-6
Weight: 160
Uniform no.: 14
Shoots: right

Career statistics:

GP	G	A	TP	PIM
195	96	108	204	339

1990-91 statistics:

GP	G	A	TP	+/-	PIM	PP	SH	GW	GT	S	PCT
79	51	53	104	+48	136	9	7	9	0	249	20.5

LAST SEASON

Tied with Marty McSorley for NHL's best plus-minus. Tied for second in NHL in goals. Second in NHL in shorthanded goals. Tied for third in NHL in game-winning goals. Led team in goals, points and shooting percentage. Career highs in all point categories.

THE FINESSE GAME

Fleury became the smallest 50-goal scorer in NHL history last season. He did it with a blend of his fabulous skills and playing like a little big man. Fleury is an excellent skater, especially in tight and also on the breakaway.

For a small player, he has an overpowering shot. He is dangerous from the circles in and has very good deking ability to go with his quickness and balance. He loves to shoot and is always on the move to put himself in good scoring position.

Fleury gets to the net in a hurry. He sees the ice well, but is not a clever playmaker. He uses his speed and his puck skills more than he uses other people, although he certainly has the stickhandling and passing skills to put his teammates to better use.

His defensive game is good, although it is overshadowed by his offensive game. He anticipates well and his speed makes him a shorthanded threat. He does a very good job checking.

THE PHYSICAL GAME

Since he was 16, Fleury was always taking runs at the bigger guys (which means almost everyone on the ice) and he didn't stop when he went from challenging boys to challenging men. He is absolutely fearless and can't be intimidated or dissuaded from his game. He is so quick that it's almost impossible for someone to retaliate and catch him to put a physical pounding on

him. He agitates with his style of play, with his demeanor and vocally. He will take dives and run at people to get the retaliation penalty. If he doesn't, he'll take another run. Fleury's not happy until he gets under the skin of the other team's skill players. His only weakness are situations where he has to go one-on-one in a muscle contest: he loses because of size and strength, not because of heart. Fleury is not shy about using his stick as an equalizer.

THE INTANGIBLES

Fleury is a complete player who comes to the top when the game is on the line. His 50-goal season was no aberration. Fleury seldom takes a night off and he is one of the game's most charismatic players.

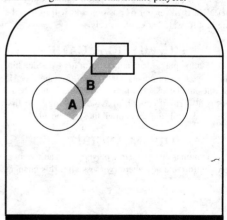

DOUG GILMOUR

Yrs. of NHL service: 7
Born: Kingston, Ont., Canada; June 25, 1963
Position: Center
Height: 5-11
Weight: 185
Uniform no.: 39
Shoots: left

Career statistics:

GP	G	A	TP	PIM
612	219	392	611	504

1990-91 statistics:

GP	G	A	TP	+/-	PIM	PP	SH	GW	GT	S	PCT
78	20	61	81	+27	142	2	2	5	0	135	14.8

LAST SEASON

Goal total was career low. Assist total was two-season low. Point total was six-season low. PIM was career high.

THE FINESSE GAME

Gilmour is a danger from the red line in. He can do the damage himself,or use others with his excellent playmaking skills. He is a smart, selective shooter who is very adept at using a screen and picking his shot. As a passer, he uses either wing equally well and he senses the plays well enough that he will lead a play in, put pressure on the defense, turn and feed a trailer for a good scoring chance. He has very good hands and the puck seldom bounces on him.

He is not a speed demon on skates, but he does have enough speed to outrace people to the puck. His anticipation and positioning help him here.

Gilmour is a good penalty-killer, since he is among the best face-off men in the NHL. By winning a draw, a center can kill off 20 seconds of a penalty. Offensively and defensively, he has nice hockey instincts.

THE PHYSICAL GAME

Gilmour is a hard worker and a very durable player who will play a very aggressive, physical game—he plays bigger than he is. He takes a pretty good pounding since he lacks the speed to escape some of the more vulnerable positions, but he seems to bounce back after every hit. He's not an agitator (although Los Angeles coach Tom Webster, who punched him last season, might disagree). He does his job quietly.

THE INTANGIBLES

With all of the finishers on the Flames, a play-maker like Gilmour is invaluable. He is a dedicated and consistent player and an on-ice leader who has been a captain or alternate almost everywhere he has played.

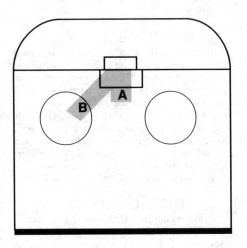

JIM KYTE

Yrs. of NHL service: 8
Born: Ottawa, Ont., Canada; March 21, 1964
Position: Defenseman
Height: 6-5
Weight: 220
Uniform no.: 4
Shoots: left

Career statistics:

GP	G	A	TP	PIM
498	14	35	49	1052

1990-91 statistics:

GP	G	A	TP	+/-	PIM	PP	SH	GW	GT	S	PCT
43	0	9	9	+10	155	0	0	0	0	29	0.0

LAST SEASON

Acquired from Pittsburgh on December 13, 1990, for Jiri Hrdina. Games played career low. Assist, point and PIM totals two-year highs.

THE FINESSE GAME

Kyte has very limited skills, especially when it comes to skating. He has tried to compensate somewhat by playing a smarter, positional game, but he is really in the wrong division because he is simply outmatched in high-tempo games.

Kyte has an adequate point shot but because of his slowness seldom minimizes his offensive involvement, preferring to stay close to home. He is fairly good at headmanning the puck. He has worked hard to overcome some of his deficiencies, but can't overcome all of his flaws.

THE PHYSICAL GAME

Kyte developed the reputation of being a good fighter, but went AWOL for awhile and seemed to develop a pacifist nature. That didn't stop others from challenging him and when he came out on the short end of a bout last season with Bob Probert, it became very apparent that Kyte just doesn't have the heart for it. He will come to the rescue of teammates, but he won't initiate anything, and that reduces his effectiveness as a physical force. Kyte will hit and use his body to clear the crease but, again, his skating limits his ability to be more effective in other areas of his zone.

THE INTANGIBLES

As long as his other skills remain in such short supply (and he has shown no indication of any real improvement), Kyte can survive in the NHL only by his toughness. When that is gone, his career will follow. Kyte deserves a ton of respect for overcoming a hearing handicap to make it to the NHL, however, and merits additional praise for his hockey work with hearing-impaired youngsters.

AL MACINNIS

Yrs. of NHL service: 8
Born: Inverness, N.S., Canada; July 11, 1963
Position: Defenseman
Height: 6-2
Weight: 195
Uniform no.: 2
Shoots: right

Career statistics:

GP	G	A	TP	PIM
606	154	455	609	711

1990-91 statistics:

GP	G	A	TP	+/-	PIM	PP	SH	GW	GT	S	PCT
78	28	75	103	+42	90	17	0	1	1	305	9.2

LAST SEASON

Led NHL defensemen in all scoring categories. Third in NHL in plus-minus. Led team in assists and shots. Second on team in points and power play goals. Goal total tied career high. Assists and points career highs.

THE FINESSE GAME

MacInnis has long been acknowledged as having the hardest, most accurate shot in the game and he has improved it. Boy, and you thought Stephen King knew a thing or two about scaring people. Now goalies have to sleep with the (red) lights on.

Where MacInnis once used to have a predictable skate, stop and shoot pattern, he has developed more tools, such as the best is-he-going-to-pass-or-shoot fake in the NHL. Defensemen are forced to react even quicker to him, because if they go down to block the shot (those foolhardy enough to do so), he keeps his head up and will spot the open man. MacInnis is like a pitcher who throws 99 m.p.h. fastballs and now has a killer curveball.

MacInnis has improved his game in other areas as well, particularly his skating. He has made a conscious effort to concentrate on his defensive responsibilities, perhaps in reaction to the criticism that he is a one-way defenseman. He will not get beaten in one-on-one situations as often as he used to and he will sacrifice an offensive chance to maintain a better defensive posture.

THE PHYSICAL GAME

MacInnis is a fair-sized defenseman who is starting to play bigger as he uses more energy and effort in his own zone. He is willing to scrap along the boards and in front of his net and once he gains control of the puck can move it out quickly because of his superior finesse skills. He is mentally tough.

THE INTANGIBLES

If the Flames need something to happen, MacInnis can do it. There has been a definite maturing process over the past two or three seasons and what used to be cockiness is changing to confidence. MacInnis has become a solid professional and a team leader whose overall game keeps getting better.

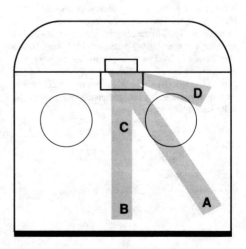

47

JAMIE MACOUN

Yrs. of NHL service: 8
Born: Newmarket, Ont., Canada; August 17, 1961
Position: Defenseman
Height: 6-2
Weight: 197
Uniform no.: 34
Shoots: left

Career statistics:

GP	G	A	TP	PIM
549	60	172	232	611

1990-91 statistics:

GP	G	A	TP	+/-	PIM	PP	SH	GW	GT	S	PCT
79	7	15	22	+29	84	1	1	0	0	117	6.0

LAST SEASON

All point totals were three-season lows.

THE FINESSE GAME

Macoun is no Tinkerbell on the ice, but he is a better than average skater for his size. He skates well enough to get involved offensively to a degree, but his primary job is staying back on defense and he is a very steadying influence on the blueline. He has very good quickness and mobility.

Macoun headmans the pass very well and has a good point shot. He will seldom venture in deep.

He is a very intense player and a key to the Flames defense. He is a very good penalty-killer, aided by his ranginess and his alert skating. He has good hand-eye coordination and can be used to take face-offs.

THE PHYSICAL GAME

Everyone knows when Macoun is on the ice, because they usually come away with a souvenir hit. He is not a big open-ice hitter but is very effective along the wall and in the corners. Macoun is not a dirty hitter or a fighter (note his modest PIM total), just a very honest defensive defenseman. He likes to play physical and is very good at blocking shots. Macoun doesn't run around, but he will never miss an chance to hit someone. He won't put them in the fifth row, but he will make solid contact.

THE INTANGIBLES

Macoun is the kind of defenseman every team would like to have. He gets little attention on the Flames because of their scoring stars, but he is a great asset to the team because of his consistency and hard work.

SERGEI MAKAROV

Yrs. of NHL service: 2
Born: Chelyabinsk, Soviet Union; June 19, 1958
Position: Right wing
Height: 5-8
Weight: 175
Uniform no.: 42
Shoots: left

Career statistics:

GP	G	A	TP	PIM
158	54	111	165	99

1990-91 statistics:

GP	G	A	TP	+/-	PIM	PP	SH	GW	GT	S	PCT
78	30	49	79	+15	44	9	0	5	0	93	32.3

LAST SEASON

Led NHL in shooting percentage. Third on team in goals. Tied for third in power play goals. Fifth on team in points. Goals and points two-season career highs. Missed two games due to personal matters.

THE FINESSE GAME

Of all the older Soviets who came in the first invasion, Makarov is the only one to have made a significant contribution. His skills are world-class, especially his hand and stick skills. He has almost too much talent. There are nights when he will beat five defenders, then circle around and try to beat them all again before getting right on top of the goalie and looking for a pass. That may be the heritage of Soviet training, in which skaters were taught to set up for the perfect shot and not just whale away at the goalie with lesser scoring chances.

Makarov is a tremendous skater and a very accurate, quick shooter. Like most Soviets, he doesn't have an overpowering shot, but from the top of the circles in, he can either make a creative passing play or flick off a tricky wrist shot, his shot of choice. He could definitely get more selfish and shoot more—check his shooting percentage and his low number of shots. He is excellent on the power play.

Makarov's game is flawed defensively. He either never understood his defensive responsibilities or didn't care to venture too deeply into his own zone, waiting instead for the chance to go on the attack.

THE PHYSICAL GAME

Makarov will not get involved physically, especially defensively. He will take or make a hit in the offensive zone and is so sturdy on his skates that he will usually end up with the puck and his balance. He uses his stick for any of the checking that he does and he has very quick, strong wrists.

THE INTANGIBLES

Makarov plays with very little emotion and erratic intensity. He pulls the chute in pressure situations, like the Stanley Cup playoffs, and has very little taste for the more physical North American style of play. Despite his NHL success, it wouldn't be surprising to see him leave to play in Europe.

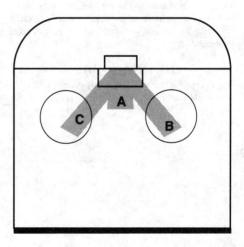

STEPHANE MATTEAU

Yrs. of NHL service: 1
Born: Rouyn-Noranda, Que., Canada;
September 2, 1969
Position: Right/left wing
Height: 6-3
Weight: 195
Uniform no.: 23
Shoots: left

Career statistics:

GP	G	A	TP	PIM
78	15	19	34	93

GP	G	A	TP	+/-	PIM	PP	SH	GW	GT	S	PCT
78	15	19	34	+17	93	0	1	1	0	114	13.2

LAST SEASON

First NHL season.

THE FINESSE GAME

Matteau skates with very good mobility and balance for a big forward. He can score in a variety of ways but his best efforts come from close in to the net, where he uses his good size and reach to complete plays. Matteau is very good in traffic with or without the puck. He stickhandles, passes and receives the puck well.

Matteau anticipates well, is a solid backchecker and can play either wing. He needs to improve his defensive play, but has shown desire and attitude and has the reputation for being a fast and willing learner.

THE PHYSICAL GAME

Matteau loves to get involved physically. He plays to his size and is not allergic to any of the busy areas of the ice. He will drive to the net to score and will wage war along the boards and in the corners for the puck. Matteau will not be intimidated. He is more interested in playing the game than in fighting, but he will go if challenged.

THE INTANGIBLES

Except for missing the mean gene, Matteau is capable of becoming a Shayne Corson-type forward for the Flames. He has good skills to go with his size and intensity and could develop into a 25-30 goal scorer in his sophomore season. Another winner for the Calgary scouting staff.

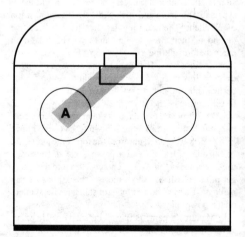

FRANK MUSIL

Yrs. of NHL service: 5
Born: Vysoke Myto, Czechoslovakia;
December 17, 1964
Position: Defenseman
Height: 6-3
Weight: 215
Uniform no.: 3
Shoots: left

Career statistics:

GP	G	A	TP	PIM
338	21	60	81	707

1990-91 statistics:

GP	G	A	TP	+/-	PIM	PP	SH	GW	GT	S	PCT
75	7	16	23	+12	183	2	0	1	0	73	9.6

LAST SEASON

Acquired from Minnesota on October 26, 1991, for Brian Glynn. Points career high. Goals, assists and PIM three-season highs. Missed one game with shoulder injury.

THE FINESSE GAME

The trade to the Flames was to Musil's liking. Their system of short, crisp passing suits his style. He doesn't like to get involved in the offensive flow. Although he has better than average puck ability, he prefers to headman the puck to get himself out of trouble and does a good job of starting things up-ice.

Musil is a solid, strong defenseman with a good read of plays coming at him, a good penalty killer and a key defensive player. He is a good skater, with good agility and lateral quickness and balance. He doesn't have a very good slap shot, so most of his goals come from his occasional forays in deep. He could easily contribute more offensively.

THE PHYSICAL GAME

Musil has good size and is a physical presence without being a real intimidating factor. He shuts off the ice well. He won't bang players around; he uses his size to stop things, not to punish anybody. Musil is difficult to get past. He will block shots but it is apparent that it doesn't come naturally to him. He is not intimidated and is very difficult to take off his game.

THE INTANGIBLES

Musil plays a common-sense game with little of the flash and dash most people associate with European players. He is a journeyman defenseman whose skills indicate he could be even better. He seems content, however, to play at the level he has shown the past few seasons. Playing with a stronger team could bring out the talents that have been hidden in his past four seasons.

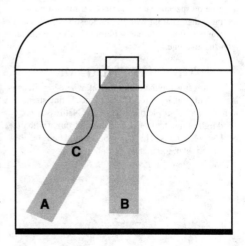

RIC NATTRESS

Yrs. of NHL service: 9
Born: Hamilton, Ont., Canada; May 25, 1962
Position: Defenseman
Height: 6-2
Weight: 210
Uniform no.: 6
Shoots: right

Career statistics:

GP	G	A	TP	PIM
438	20	106	126	285

1990-91 statistics:

GP	G	A	TP	+/-	PIM	PP	SH	GW	GT	S	PCT
58	5	13	18	-1	63	0	0	1	0	81	6.2

LAST SEASON

Missed eight games with knee injury, four games with neck injury and two with flu. Goals and points were four-season highs.

THE FINESSE GAME

Nattress has no particular skills that stand out, but in Calgary he is part of a good nucleus of defensemen where his capable skills make him a useful member as a fifth or sixth defenseman.

He has fairly good movement for a big man, although his mobility is quite limited and that makes him vulnerable in the one-on-one situations. He won't challenge shooters because he is afraid of getting caught out of position, so his basic game is trying to force the skaters to go wide.

Nattress has average hand skills and doesn't get ice time on special teams. He is better off just moving the puck than skating with it. He doesn't get involved deep in the offensive zone, seldom venturing in too far over the blue line.

THE PHYSICAL GAME

Nattress is tough around the net, where he will use his stick to punish people. He lacks the skating strength to really move people out effectively. Nattress is not a good fighter and doesn't go looking for trouble with the NHL's tough guys. He won't be intimidated, but he doesn't frighten too many other people either.

THE INTANGIBLES

Nattress will be playing a competent game when—all of a sudden—the lights go out and he will have a shift or a period where nothing seems to work and he can't get himself back into the groove. As his confidence grows, he is having fewer of these walkabouts, but they still plague him.

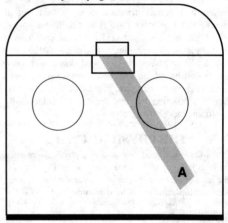

JOE NIEUWENDYK

Yrs. of NHL service: 4
Born: Oshawa, Ont., Canada; September 10, 1966
Position: Center
Height: 6-1
Weight: 195
Uniform no.: 25
Shoots: left

Career statistics:

GP	G	A	TP	PIM
319	197	163	360	125

1990-91 statistics:

GP	G	A	TP	+/-	PIM	PP	SH	GW	GT	S	PCT
79	45	40	85	+19	36	22	4	1	0	222	20.3

LAST SEASON

Led team in power play goals. Second on team in goals and points. Assist and point totals two-season lows. Missed one game with a charley horse.

THE FINESSE GAME

Nieuwendyk is more a goal-scorer than a play-maker. He is not very clever but uses his linemates better than, say, his teammate Theo Fleury. He is very adept at carrying the puck and shooting it. Nieuwendyk drives to the net well and has a very good wrist shot. He has great hand-eye coordination and is very good at tipping pucks—especially those bullets fired by Al MacInnis. He uses his size, strength and hockey sense to wedge his way into places to get in position for the tip. Nieuwendyk is exceptionally dangerous on the power play because of this talent.

For a big center, Nieuwendyk has great agility, mobility and speed. He has a very strong stride and, while he won't come down the ice on many breakaways, his skating serves him well in all of the traffic areas where he does his best work.

Nieuwendyk is very good on draws, where hand skills come into play. He is a very good penalty killer and a shorthanded threat. He is not shy about shooting.

THE PHYSICAL GAME

Nieuwendyk is not a physical force, but he will bump and go into the corners. Coming from a college program (Cornell), the grinding part of his game has not come naturally. He will drive to the net for a shot and use his muscle in the offensive zone. He checks well and willingly, especially in cramped quarters. He will not be intimidated.

THE INTANGIBLES

Nieuwendyk was expected to miss half the season with a knee injury suffered in the 1990 World Championships. He missed only one game with a minor injury unrelated to the knee. His determination and work ethic were only enhanced by his successful rehabiliation and he has continued to play with the same enthusiasm he demonstrated before the injury.

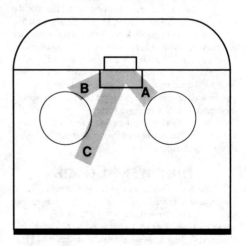

JOEL OTTO

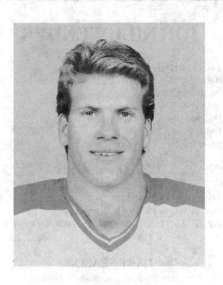

Yrs. of NHL service: 6
Born: St. Cloud, Minn., USA; October 29, 1961
Position: Center
Height: 6-4
Weight: 220
Uniform no.: 29
Shoots: right

Career statistics:

GP	G	A	TP	PIM
449	116	182	298	1111

1990-91 statistics:

GP	G	A	TP	+/-	PIM	PP	SH	GW	GT	S	PCT
76	19	20	39	-4	185	7	1	4	1	109	17.4

LAST SEASON

Goals, points and PIMs were two-year highs. Missed two games with a charley horse. Missed one game with the flu. Missed one game with a concussion.

THE FINESSE GAME

Looking at a monster like Otto, the question that usually crops up is why doesn't this guy score more by brute force? Otto scored 25 goals in his rookie season, but his other years have hovered around the 20-goal mark. He certainly seems to have the tools to be a consistent 30-goal scorer. Otto has been known to take the night off now and then and that may be why his production has lagged behind his apparent abilities. Most of his goals will come from his work in front of the net, banging at rebounds and tipping shots.

Otto has very average passing skills. He sees the ice well but plays a basic, straight-ahead game with few frills. He is a very good skater for a player of his size and thus makes an effective and intimidating checking center. His forechecking will create lots of scoring chances for his team. He is a good penalty killer because of his skating and defensive awareness and can also be used on power plays to screen and tip in front of the net. Otto is very tough to budge.

Otto is another good face-off man (the Flames seem to have no shortage of these) who can be used to tie up the opposing center.

THE PHYSICAL GAME

Otto is very seldom involved in fisticuffs, probably because so few opponents are willing to tangle with him. Who can blame them? Otto is thus left alone to wreak havoc in front of the net at both ends of the ice. His good skating adds some mustard to his hits. He is always in the hunt for the puck and forging his way through traffic.

THE INTANGIBLES

Otto is a very tough player who will fill a defensive, checking role and still be able to contribute big goals in special situations. His name gets mentioned in trade rumors only because every other team would like an Otto.

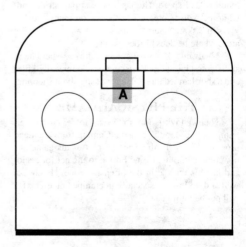

PAUL RANHEIM

Yrs. of NHL service: 2
Born: St. Louis, Mo., USA; January 25, 1966
Position: Left wing
Height: 6-0
Weight: 195
Uniform no.: 28
Shoots: right

Career statistics:

GP	G	A	TP	PIM
124	40	44	84	27

1990-91 statistics:

GP	G	A	TP	+/-	PIM	PP	SH	GW	GT	S	PCT
39	14	16	30	+20	4	2	0	2	0	108	13.0

LAST SEASON

Missed 41 games with a broken ankle.

THE FINESSE GAME

Ranheim has tremendous breakaway speed, not just quickness, and can beat the majority of NHL defensemen in a foot race. He uses his good size to help drive past the defensemen. Ranheim has the hand skills and intelligence to keep up with his speed, which is what makes him so dangerous from the blue line in. He can score in a variety of ways, especially off the fly.

You won't find Ranheim along the boards. His milieu is the open ice. That's not to say he lacks courage, he just likes to position himself where he can be off the to races, although he will power his way to the net if that's his better option. He will not chicken out and stay on the perimeter.

Ranheim's skating ability and hockey sense combine to make him a good defensive player positionally. He also is a good power play man and should continue to improve in that area as he gains experience.

THE PHYSICAL GAME

Ranheim doesn't go around looking to make hits. When he does it's to get possession of the puck and he is capable of fairly solid checks because of his skating speed and balance. He is a finesse player who avoids the rough stuff whenever possible.

THE INTANGIBLES

Ranheim is the kind of player who creates a sense of relief for the opposing coaches when he's not in the lineup. Since he missed half of last season, the challenge for Ranheim will be to return to his superb rookie form of two seasons ago. He has game-breaker potential.

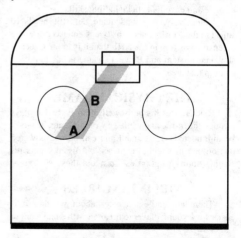

ROBERT REICHEL

Yrs. of NHL service: 1
Born: Most, Czechoslovakia; June 25, 1971
Position: Center
Height: 5-10
Weight: 170
Uniform no.: 26
Shoots: left

Career statistics:

GP	G	A	TP	PIM
66	19	22	41	22

1990-91 statistics:

GP	G	A	TP	+/-	PIM	PP	SH	GW	GT	S	PCT
66	19	22	41	+17	22	3	0	3	0	131	14.5

LAST SEASON

First NHL season. Missed four games with an injured tailbone.

THE FINESSE GAME

Reichel is another of those agile Europeans skaters, not only straightaway fast but with the kind of quickness in a 15-foot turning radius where he can turn on a dime and give a nickel change.

He has good hands and passes well. Like most Europeans, he has to be encouraged to shoot more. Reichel can handle himself in traffic because of his balance and excellent stickhandling skills.

Defensively, he is adequate but still needs to adjust to the North American style. Center is more of a defensive position in the NHL than it is in the Czechoslovakian system and Reichel's game needs improvement in that area.

THE PHYSICAL GAME

Reichel uses his body well offensively. He plays through the traffic and while he won't initiate, he won't be intimidated. He is small and can be overpowered one-on-one in strength contests, but usually puts his skating ability to good use to avoid those situations.

THE INTANGIBLES

There are endless debates about whether it is easier for a young player to break in with a bad team or a good one. Reichel has a strong supporting cast in Calgary, but the Flames obviously knew they had to make room for him (at a crowded position) and he looks as if he has the potential to keep developing.

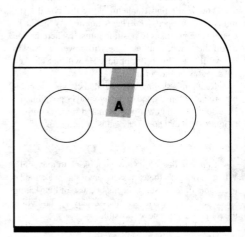

GARY ROBERTS

Yrs. of NHL service: 4
Born: North York, Ont., Canada; May 23, 1966
Position: Left wing
Height: 6-1
Weight: 190
Uniform no.: 10
Shoots: left

Career statistics:

GP	G	A	TP	PIM
335	101	105	206	1091

1990-91 statistics:

GP	G	A	TP	+/-	PIM	PP	SH	GW	GT	S	PCT
80	22	31	53	+15	252	0	0	3	0	132	16.7

LAST SEASON

Led team in PIM. PIM was three-season high. Goals, assists and points two-season lows. Only Flame to appear in all 80 games.

THE FINESSE GAME

Roberts is a solid, grinding forward with more offensive gifts than most players of his ilk. He can accept a pass, give a pass, handle the puck well and shoot. He is the top cornerman on the Flames and might be one of the best in the league. He has very good skating ability, making up in mobility what he lacks in outright speed. Roberts is not a dynamic skater, but he gets to where he needs to go and he has very good balance.

Roberts sees the ice well, so that when he does start motoring into the zone he can spot his teammates and make the smart offensive play. Most of his goals are scored by crashing the net, as he lacks a really good wrist or slap shot.

Because of his size (and he plays even bigger than he is) and hitting, he brings good forechecking presence to the line he is playing with. Roberts is very physical and does a good job positionally.

THE PHYSICAL GAME

Roberts is very strong and physical and will do all of the grunt work along the boards and in the corners. He plays with a lot of intensity and he'll occasionally become undisciplined and hurt his team by taking bad penalties, although not often enough for it to be considered a bad habit. He is a legitimate tough guy who will drop his gloves without a written invitation.

THE INTANGIBLES

Roberts is an under-rated member of a rock-solid team. He plays with a great deal of intensity and can be used on a line of finesse players to feed them the puck or work on a hard-nosed unit where he will try to do the scoring himself. He is a valuable character player.

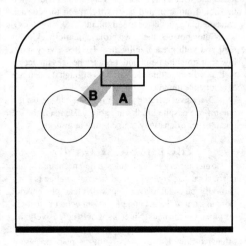

GARY SUTER

Yrs. of NHL service: 6
Born: Madison, Wisc., USA; June 24, 1964
Position: Defenseman
Height: 6-0
Weight: 190
Uniform no.: 20
Shoots: left

Career statistics:

GP	G	A	TP	PIM
441	89	327	416	612

1990-91 statistics:

GP	G	A	TP	+/-	PIM	PP	SH	GW	GT	S	PCT
79	12	58	70	+26	102	6	0	1	0	258	4.7

LAST SEASON

Missed one game with tailbone injury. Second among team defensemen in all point categories. Second on team in shots. Third on team in assists. Goal total was a four-season low.

THE FINESSE GAME

When the topic of pure offensive defensemen arises, Suter's name has to be near the top of the list. He may be one of the best skating defensemen in the NHL, in all categories—flat-out speed, acceleration, balance and, especially, mobility. His confidence in his skating allows him to gamble in the offensive zone and he has the hand skills to finish off the play or set up a teammate with a pass. Suter is very smart about when he should move in and he has the speed to get back when he makes an error in judgment.

Suter powers the power play, quarterbacking it well and with great intelligence. He has a very hard, low shot from the point and, because he sees the ice so well, is a threat to thread a soft pass through the defense to an open teammate.

Defensively, Suter is average and can be beaten one-on-one despite his skating ability. He reads the ice much better offensively than coming at him.

THE PHYSICAL GAME

Suter is very much a finesse defenseman. He has fairly good size and very good strength, but he is not a naturally physical player. He will clear players out from in front of the net and plays with good intensity in his pursuit of the puck. Suter's strength defensively lies in getting the puck and getting it (and himself) into the offensive flow. He can skate with the puck or pass it equally well.

THE INTANGIBLES

What? Gary Suter is still a Flame? Yes, trade rumors continue to hound Suter, yet he was able to maintain his offensive production and overcome the loss of his steady defensive partner, Brad McCrimmon. Suter has enough defensive flaws that he needs to be paired with a stay-at-home type; he is gifted enough offensively to be able to overlook the weaknesses. Suter rates as one of the all-time great draft steals (180th overall in 1984).

TIM SWEENEY

Yrs. of NHL service: 1
Born: Boston, Mass., USA; April 12, 1967
Position: Left wing
Height: 5-11
Weight: 180
Uniform no.: 7
Shoots: left

1990-91 statistics:

GP	G	A	TP	+/-	PIM	PP	SH	GW	GT	S	PCT
42	7	9	16	+1	8	0	0	4	0	40	17.5

LAST SEASON

First NHL season.

THE FINESSE GAME

Apparently the Calgary Flames are ahead of the rest of the NHL in cloning. They have come up with the replacement for Joe Mullen, right down to the nationality, uniform number, university background (Boston College) and size (Mullen lists at the same weight, just two inches shorter). Now if only Sweeney can duplicate on the ice what Mullen did in posting four 36-or-more goal seasons for the Flames.

Sweeney is an excellent shooter with a good wrist shot and is poised with the puck. He wants the puck in key situations (as shown by his four game-winning goals in just half a season of play). His first NHL goal was scored in overtime.

He is a good, shifty skater and works well on the penalty-killing unit. He has good playmaking capabilities.

THE PHYSICAL GAME

Sweeney is not a physical player and his defensive work has yet to match NHL standards. He is not a big player but so far has played even smaller than he is and needs to improve his upper body strength.

THE INTANGIBLES

Sweeney played very little in the second half of the season and was assigned to the minors in January.

The Flames seldom rush their prospects. With more seasoning, we'll see if Sweeney can truly become the next Mullen.

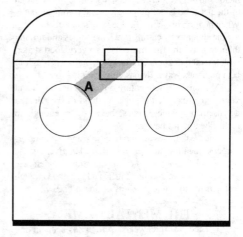

MIKE VERNON

Yrs. of NHL service: 6
Born: Calgary, Alta., Canada; February 24, 1963
Position: Goaltender
Height: 5-9
Weight: 170
Uniform no.: 30
Catches: left

Career statistics:

GP	MINS	GA	SO	GAA	A	PIM
292	16408	903	4	3.30	21	112

1990-91 statistics:

GP	MINS	GAA	W	L	T	SO	GA	S	SAPCT	PIM
54	3121	3.31	31	19	3	1	172	1406	.878	8

LAST SEASON

Second in NHL in wins. Has 30 or more wins in four of last five seasons. Games and minutes played were three-season highs. GAA was three-season high.

THE PHYSICAL GAME

Vernon has reflexes equal to those of any goalie in the NHL. His game has always been limited by the size factor and he recognizes that he just can't cover enough of the net if he is not playing a sound technical game. When he is on his game, he does. He's smart, challenging the shooters by cutting down the angles and forcing them to make the first move. He is a very good skater, with lateral quickness and fast feet, and he is tough to beat on breakaways. He has good anticipation.

Vernon does not venture out of his net much and doesn't over-handle the puck. With all of the talented defenseman on the Flames, he is smart enough to realize he doesn't have to.

His weaknesses are the five-hole and in the upper corners when the shooter is in tight. He gives up the occasional cheap goal when his attention wanders. He sees the puck well through traffic and has good enough instincts to block a lot of shots he doesn't see.

THE MENTAL GAME

For the past three years, Vernon has been among the NHL's top goalies, but there is a sense he is losing his battling edge. There are some games when he has suddenly and bewilderingly gone into the tank, in pointed contrast to his usual confidence and consistency. Vernon doesn't bounce back from bad efforts as well as he used to. When he is sharp, he is still capable of winning games on his own.

THE INTANGIBLES

Playing behind a strong, talented hockey club is not always as easy as it looks, but Vernon has handled the pressure well until last season—and that was only a small chink that showed. Vernon will be 29 this season and certainly has several prime seasons left.

RICK WAMSLEY

Yrs. of NHL service: 11
Born: Simcoe, Ont., Canada; May 25, 1959
Position: Goaltender
Height: 5-11
Weight: 185
Uniform no.: 31
Catches: left

Career statistics:

GP	MINS	GA	SO	GAA	A	PIM
387	22078	1211	12	3.29	9	50

1990-91 statistics:

GP	MINS	GAA	W	L	T	SO	GA	S	SAPCT	PIM
29	1670	3.05	14	7	5	0	85	762	.888	0

LAST SEASON

Games and minutes played were career lows. Missed 11 games with a broken bone in his left hand.

THE PHYSICAL GAME

Technical skill is the foundation of Wamsley's game. He lacks the quick feet and hands of most reflex goalies, so he concentrates on playing the angles to maximize his size and minimize the net the shooters get to see. He is much better than average technically. He challenges shooters very well.

Wamsley is lacking in several skills. He is not a very good skater, especially laterally, and is weakest on bang-bang plays. Wamsley does see the puck well in traffic and is good at making the first save, but his reflexes usually aren't quick enough to bail him out on the rebounds.

He does not handle the puck well and usually leaves it for his defense to handle. He is a smart goalie with good anticipation.

THE MENTAL GAME

Wamsley is unflappable and is a calming influence on his team when he is in the net. This is not characteristic of most goalies, who are lively holler guys. Because Wamsley is so economical in his playing style, he doesn't seem to get physically involved in most games. That's also true mentally and on nights when he isn't busy (behind the Calgary defense, it can happen), his concentration will lapse.

THE INTANGIBLES

Wamsley has a great attitude and disposition, an ideal No. 2 goalie who has enough talent, skill and confidence in himself (if no one else has it) to push the No. 1 goalie without being a disruptive influence. Wamsley keeps himself prepared for games and will always produce a workmanlike effort.

CAREY WILSON

Yrs. of NHL service: 7
Born: Winnipeg, Man., Canada; May 19, 1962
Position: Center
Height: 6-2
Weight: 205
Uniform no.: 33
Shoots: right

Career statistics:

GP	G	A	TP	PIM
488	154	239	393	269

1990-91 statistics:

GP	G	A	TP	+/-	PIM	PP	SH	GW	GT	S	PCT
57	11	18	29	-13	18	4	0	2	0	79	13.9

LAST SEASON

Acquired from Hartford for Mark Hunter on March 5, 1991. Missed one game with a knee injury. Games played and all points categories were two-season highs.

THE FINESSE GAME

Wilson has excellent skills from the blue line in, but has very little interest in what's going on anywhere else. He will use his size offensively around the net, where he can use his above average finesse skills.

Wilson is a very good skater and passer, although he prefers to carry the puck in and try to beat the defense one-on-one. He has fine lateral movement and balance, especially in deep, and will bury a goal with a strong wrist shot. When he is playing well, he will push his way to the right areas of the ice and get past smaller defensemen. The bigger ones will intimidate him.

His skills make him a good man to have on the ice for a power play. He sees the ice well and knows when to make the pass or take a shot. He is not a very good defensive player, although his size and skating ability would seem to mark him as a natural. He is not aggressive enough as a checker to do a good job here, however.

THE PHYSICAL GAME

Wilson is a big player who doesn't play big. He won't bash anyone and he hates to get hit himself, especially in the defensive zone. But he handles the puck well in traffic. On the nights when he is willing, he will work hard along the boards and in the corners, but he is inconsistent with those efforts.

THE INTANGIBLES

Wilson is a player of above average skills and size who has never put all the ingredients together with sufficient consistency to earn himself a regular spot in anyone's lineup. He wears out his welcome quickly in each new city because he never delivers what his talents promise. He may fare better with the Flames, who can afford to carry an in-and-out player more than some other teams can. Wilson will put together spurts where he is a force on the ice.

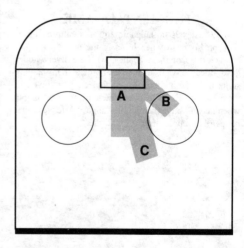

CHICAGO
BLACKHAWKS

ED BELFOUR

Yrs. of NHL service: 1
Born: Carman, Man., Canada; April 21, 1965
Position: Goaltender
Height: 5-11
Weight: 182
Uniform no.: 30
Catches: Left

Career statistics:

GP	MINS	GA	SO	GAA	A	PIM
97	5275	244	4	2.78	4	40

1990-91 statistics:

GP	MINS	GAA	W	L	T	SO	GA	S	SAPCT	PIM
74	4127	2.47	43	19	7	4	170	1883	.910	34

LAST SEASON

Earned Vezina Trophy as NHL's most valuable goaltender, adding Calder Trophy as Rookie of the Year and first all-star (and rookie) team honors as well. Set rookie records for games played and won

THE PHYSICAL GAME

Belfour plays his angles very well, commits himself early and establishes his position in anticipation of where puck will be shot. He's on his knees a lot, but he times the drops well, and he's back on his feet very quickly. Those who think they can beat him high have their hopes dashed regularly by Belfour's tremendous glove hand.

He is very economical in his motions. Belfour is up, he's down, he's on his side, but he's not flipping and flailing.

In traffic and screens, Belfour has an almost uncanny knack of spreading out, covering as much area as he can and letting the puck hit him. It's like he's made of sponge; the puck hits him and falls dead. He smothers and controls everything he can reach.

Belfour does not use the stick much for blocking passes, but he handles the puck so well, so intelligently, and is a strong enough skater to be confident ranging far from his net. Belfour is so much in control with the puck, he can check off to a second option. If an opponent is closing off the forehand boards, Belfour simply reverses it on his backhand—which requires wrist strength, skating balance and stick control.

Belfour's puck-handling skills are useful for penalty killing and for helping his defensemen on the smaller Chicago Stadium pond. Moreover, he communicates extremely well with his defensemen.

THE MENTAL GAME

Part of being a competitor is being emotional, and Belfour is a competitor. He hates to get pulled out of a game and will never get used to it, despite the amount of practice Mike Keenan has given him. But he is not high strung and moody about it. His approach is, "I wanted to finish this game, but I can't wait to start the next one."

Belfour concentrates very well. He is mentally tough and rarely beats himself. He gives his team a chance to win every night, keeping it in the games those nights when the offense takes until the second period to get rolling.

THE INTANGIBLES

Belfour works extremely hard in practice. He is dedicated athlete (and triathlete) whose demeanor is one of aggressive confidence. He isn't cocky, he is defiant. He says, "Beat me, shooter." The players like him and play for him. Unmistakably, Belfour is prime beef.

KEITH BROWN

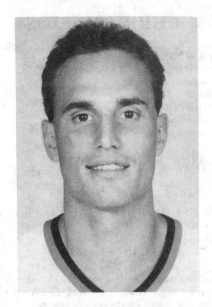

Yrs. of NHL service: 12
Born: Cornerbrook, Nfld., Canada; May 6, 1960
Position: Defenseman
Height: 6-1
Weight: 192
Uniform no.: 4
Shoots: Right

Career statistics:

GP	G	A	TP	PIM
722	56	250	306	746

1990-91 statistics:

GP	G	A	TP	+/-	PIM	PP	SH	GW	GT	S	PCT
45	1	10	11	9	55	0	0	0	0	71	1.4

LAST SEASON

Missed nearly half the season because of shoulder surgery. Goal total was seven-season low.

THE FINESSE GAME

An efficient skater with a powerful stride and excellent speed in both directions, Brown has performed with remarkably quiet elegance for a dozen seasons. He is like a good referee; his most successful nights are the ones where you barely notice him.

Brown passes well because he has good hands and a good read of the ice. On the strength of his shot from the point, Brown is used on the second-unit point.

He is a good penalty killer because he doesn't cough up the puck under pressure. Brown is skilled at carrying the puck up ice, but he tends to play one-on-one a little more than management prefers.

THE PHYSICAL GAME

Though there may be no greater devotee of the Blackhawks' weight room, Brown is much more a finesse player with size than a physical player with gentle skills. Brown eliminates opponents, but doesn't bang. He will go as far as wrestling with an occasional opponent, but rare is the night when he is mad enough or out of control enough to fight.

THE INTANGIBLES

A dedicated, consistent athlete, Brown plays the same way every game. A character player who hates losing, Brown does nothing flashy, but gets the job done.

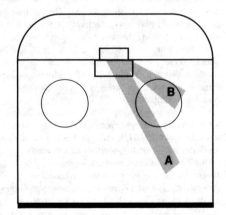

CHRIS CHELIOS

Yrs. of NHL service: 7
Born: Chicago, Ill., USA; January 25, 1962
Position: Defenseman
Height: 6-1
Weight: 186
Uniform no.: 7
Shoots: Right

Career statistics:

GP	G	A	TP	PIM
479	84	289	373	975

1990-91 statistics:

GP	G	A	TP	+/-	PIM	PP	SH	GW	GT	S	PCT
77	12	52	64	23	192	5	2	2	0	187	6.4

LAST SEASON

Played 71 or more games and collected 11 or more goals for fourth time in five seasons. Collected 50 or more assists for second time in three seasons and third time in his career. Penalty minutes were a career high.

THE FINESSE GAME

Few defensemen, if any, read the situation better than Chelios. Heady, confident and cool with the puck, he will skate it through the heavy going and out of danger, then make a crisp outlet pass. He will quarterback the power play very effectively, using his strong slap shot or working the puck to the open man.

Chelios makes excellent use of his stick and his skates. There are times when it appears he's been beaten to one side, but he will stay with the play and battle to recover, often using a diving poke check to defuse a pending crisis.

Chelios owes much of his speed and balance, while moving in either direction, to the good skating stance he maintains. He is shifty; he has a way of being the first to a puck in the corner with a player on his tail, but he'll make a head feint and come away with the puck while the checker goes into the boards.

And he is smart. Chelios is not going to go lunging for the puck or leaving his position for open-ice hits.

His 12 goals last season were okay, but that he needed 187 shots to score them suggests Chelios could use more mustard.

THE PHYSICAL GAME

Chelios is deceivingly strong in front, and chippy/mean at times. His defensive positioning usually is excellent, especially in the corners and in front of the net.

From the faceoff circles, he angles players to bad ice, gets in their way rather than being physically confrontational. But he will chop you and talk trash; he is easy to hate because he chirps at you, rubs his glove in your face, yet rarely fights.

THE INTANGIBLES

Chelios loves playing in his home city. He exudes confidence and a "We haven't even STARTED to play yet" attitude, then backs it up.

He is happy-go-lucky when he can afford to be, dead serious when the game starts. Chelios is mature, but there's still a lot of kid in him. He is a different kind of leader in the dressing room, but a genuine one nonetheless because he is team-oriented.

Chelios basically, has a green light to play however he wants, but he will spend an entire evening getting the puck to the red line and dumping it in if that is what the team needs. He isn't a spotlight hog, which makes him an extremely popular man in the dressing room.

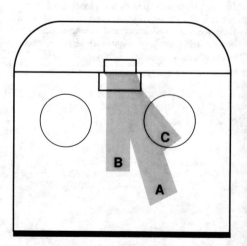

ADAM CREIGHTON

Yrs. of NHL service: 6
Born: Burlington, Ont., Canada; June 2, 1965
Position: Center
Height: 6-5
Weight: 210
Uniform no.: 22
Shoots: Left

Career statistics:

GP	G	A	TP	PIM
367	111	139	250	645

1990-91 statistics:

GP	G	A	TP	+/-	PIM	PP	SH	GW	GT	S	PCT
72	22	29	51	0	135	10	2	6	0	127	17.3

LAST SEASON

Had club's third-highest shooting percentage, though his shot total was tenth on team.

THE FINESSE GAME

One thing Creighton lacks is skating ability. He especially struggles changing directions and needs a lot of room for turns. Curves really slow him down, and he isn't that fast to begin with. There are times when he gets too upright, which throws his balance off. But on a straight line, he can move—though it takes a while to get going.

Creighton uses his whopping reach to his advantage, however. He is able to hold the puck way out and use his body to fend off opponents. In fact, he will tease with the puck a bit and lure a guy into challenging the reach, then move it to a player who isn't checked.

Creighton uses the reach more on offense, especially in the small rinks where he only needs about two strides to move from the corners to the slot, or to come out from behind the net and stuff the puck. The reach becomes an effective defensive tool, especially on penalty killing, because he can pick off so many passes with his wingspan.

Creighton has good hands for a big guy and uses them for fair success on faceoffs. He also has a just-okay slap shot, which diminishes in effectiveness the further from the net it is taken.

THE PHYSICAL GAME

He doesn't have speed or moves, but Creighton uses his size and strength well, makes use of the tools he was given. He will walk out from the corners and carry people with him. And around the net, he's an octopus. Some way or the other, he's going to get a shot off, or he is going to plant himself in front and make himself virtually impossible to move.

THE INTANGIBLES

Creighton still is young enough to keep improving and reach more of the potential people saw when Buffalo drafted him 11th overall in 1983, but his thought processes are flawed. He does not own great hockey sense and he does not read very well.

He is a likeable person, but is laid back in his approach to the game. You cannot tell from one night to next whether he's into the task at hand. The way you keep him quiet is to leave him alone; knock him on his butt and you wake up a guy you don't want to deal with.

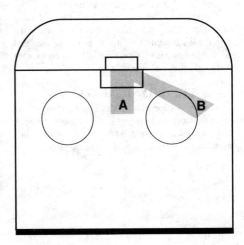

GREG GILBERT

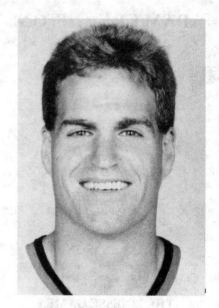

Yrs. of NHL service: 8
Born: Mississauga, Ont., Canada; January 22, 1962
Position: Left wing
Height: 6-1
Weight: 191
Uniform no.: 14
Shoots: Left

Career statistics:

GP	G	A	TP	PIM
571	115	178	293	436

1990-91 statistics:

GP	G	A	TP	+/-	PIM	PP	SH	GW	GT	S	PCT
72	10	15	25	6	58	1	0	0	0	98	10.2

LAST SEASON

Games played total was his highest in three seasons and was third highest of his career.

THE FINESSE GAME

Gilbert is a good, dependable, steady checking wing who can cover the mistakes of all-offense linemates. He is good along the boards and seems to get the puck out every time.

He's a good skater for balance and strength, but lacks speed. Still, Gilbert is very good defensively. He reads the play well and is a high-percentage player who makes the smart, safe play in the defensive zone.

Gilbert has an average shot, which he doesn't use much because he lacks finishing skills; but he also probably doesn't finish because he doesn't shoot enough. He had that one good scoring year (31 goals in 1983-84), but a season like that can hurt more than it helps, because Gilbert is not a finisher.

Gilbert is no playmaker; he'll get the puck deep and go after it, then work the puck in traffic and in the corners. He's the guy you use to protect a one-goal lead, a player who is strong enough defensively to work the second penalty-killing unit.

THE PHYSICAL GAME

Gilbert is strong along the boards. He uses his weight well and uses his feet well to control the puck when his arms are pinned. Although he is a tenacious player, his penalties are mostly restraining fouls.

THE INTANGIBLES

Gilbert is very demanding of himself, his biggest enemy. He gets down, and it shows up in his play. But he's a character player and works his way out of those slumps.

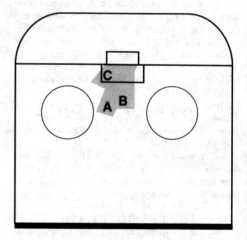

MICHEL GOULET

Yrs. of NHL service: 12
Born: Peribonka, Que., Canada; April 21, 1960
Position: Left wing
Height: 6-1
Weight: 195
Uniform no.: 16
Shoots: Left

Career statistics:

GP	G	A	TP	PIM
895	487	528	1015	687

1990-91 statistics:

GP	G	A	TP	+/-	PIM	PP	SH	GW	GT	S	PCT
74	27	38	65	27	65	9	0	1	1	167	16.2

LAST SEASON

Goal total was three-season high, point total was tops since 1987-88.

THE FINESSE GAME

Goulet is a good playmaker and fine goal scorer. He still has an accurate shot, and he always finds a way to get the puck to the net. More often than not, he still follows the shot to the cage, in case a rebound should pop loose.

For someone of such tenure, he remains extremely conscientious about his defensive-zone play and has been a plus player virtually his entire career. He stays in the defensive zone until the puck is clear of the blue line and is smart in his defensive anticipation.

Goulet doesn't zip around quite as he used to—which might be expected, after a dozen years on the circuit—but he has some range. He isn't anchored to the wing slot like some plastic player on a table hockey game; he gets around the ice, goes where the action is.

THE PHYSICAL GAME

Goulet can hold his own along the boards and in the corners. He's able to take a check and make a play. When he gets the puck in the corner, he's looking in front of the net or at the points, sizing up the best option for a pass.

THE INTANGIBLES

A low-key old pro whose nonchalance should not be mistaken for lack of concern, Goulet brings experience and savvy to the dressing room. He doesn't panic; he stays cool, doesn't rush. Now that the end is near, he seems to be using these concluding seasons to play for the fun as much as the money. He enjoyed the taste of team success in Chicago after years in the downward spiral at Quebec.

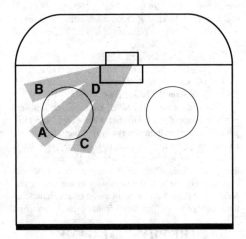

DIRK GRAHAM

Yrs. of NHL service: 7
Born: Regina, Sask., Canada; July 29, 1959
Position: Left/right wing
Height: 5-11
Weight: 198
Uniform no.: 33
Shoots: Right

Career statistics:

GP	G	A	TP	PIM
501	163	195	358	595

1990-91 statistics:

GP	G	A	TP	+/-	PIM	PP	SH	GW	GT	S	PCT
80	24	21	45	12	86	4	6	7	0	189	12.7

LAST SEASON

Goal total tied for third highest of his career, but point total was lowest since 1984-85. Led the team in shorthanded goals.

THE FINESSE GAME

Graham is an excellent skater with excellent speed, balance and strength, all of which which he uses on the breakaways he creates by driving to open ice when the percentages favor him. Aggressive penalty killing is his forte, thanks to his Selke-caliber smarts, his ability to read the play and his constant state of preparedness.

There never is a doubt in a teammate's mind which player Graham is picking up. Graham is disciplined enough to stay with his man, rather than leave his check to go after a puck some other Blackhawk has a better chance of reaching.

Graham complements his defense by being an annual 20-goal scorer, so he's consistent at both ends of the ice. His scoring skills deserve credit, as he doesn't get much time on the power play.

He is an unselfish and efficient passer, but you better be heading toward the net if you expect to get the puck, because Graham always moves the puck ahead. He seems genuinely to hate moving the puck back toward his own net for any reason—to the extent that in the attack zone, when he has the puck behind the opposing net, he will forego a pass to the slot or the point; instead he will throw an outlet to a teammate in the other corner and go to the front of the net himself.

THE PHYSICAL GAME

Graham makes the most of his size and never saw a loose puck he didn't want to win. He will bang and scrap in the scrums along the boards, and is a respected fighter.

THE INTANGIBLES

A consummate leader, Graham takes charge and isn't afraid to say what needs to be said in the dressing room. He leads by the example of his efforts and is respected by his teammates.

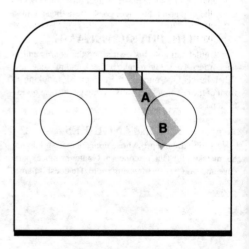

DOMINIC HASEK

Yrs. of NHL service: 1
Born: Pardubice, Czechoslovakia; January 29, 1965
Position: Goaltender
Height: 5-11
Weight: 165
Uniform no.: 34
Catches: Right

Career statistics:

GP	MINS	GA	SO	GAA	A	PIM
5	195	8	0	2.46	0	0

1990-91 statistics:

GP	MINS	GAA	W	L	T	SO	GA	S	SAPCT	PIM
5	195	2.46	3	0	1	0	8	93	.914	0

LAST SEASON

First in the NHL.

THE PHYSICAL GAME

Hasek plays a very unconventional style which he is still customizing to the challenges of NHL competition. He stays deep in his net, a reflection of his upbringing in the international arena, and gets away with using his reflexes.

Hasek has exceptionally quick legs and feet, and is so limber, he seems to be part rubber, part jelly, like a taller version of the Devils' Chris Terreri. Hasek's skating skills make him outstanding laterally. But he has been known to leave the big rebounds.

Hasek challenges the play and rarely commits himself too early. He comes out to meet the play, then backs in with the shooter, and is viper-strike quick with his catching hand.

His puck handling needs a lot of work, as international goalies rarely are called upon for it. It will have to come around in Chicago, though, as the Blackhawks emphasize stick skills for their goalies.

THE MENTAL GAME

Hasek brings a youthful enthusiasm to practice and an all-business approach to the games. He is confident in his skills and dedicated to improving those needed to make him credible in his NHL peer group.

THE INTANGIBLES

Hasek appears committed to the project of learning the language and playing hockey in North America. He may be the rare goalie capable of surviving the trip across the Atlantic Ocean, across hockey cultures. Forwards have come over and succeeded, defensemen have come over and succeeded; but no goaltender, really, has yet had that type of NHL impact.

STEVE KONROYD

Yrs. of NHL service: 11
Born: Scarborough, Ont., Canada; February 10, 1961
Position: Defenseman
Height: 6-1
Weight: 195
Uniform no.: 5
Shoots: Left

Career statistics:

GP	G	A	TP	PIM
720	34	155	189	687

1990-91 statistics:

GP	G	A	TP	+/-	PIM	PP	SH	GW	GT	S	PCT
70	0	11	11	11	40	0	0	0	0	93	.0

LAST SEASON

Plus-minus was fourth among Chicago defensemen.

THE FINESSE GAME

Konroyd is under-rated for his passing, his physical strength and, probably, his effectiveness. He is steady and skilled and smart and consistent, and he makes his partners better.

Konroyd has nice balance and a good stride. He can take the puck off the corner boards well with a nice, tight turn-and-stride. Konroyd especially uses his range while killing penalties: he will challenge all the way to the top of the circles at times, but will be smart about picking the right time to go.

Konroyd is savvy; he can read an offensive chance and move into the play. He will pass the puck up ice rather than carry it, and will keep his thought processes compact. He selects a course of action, finds an open forward with a pass and makes the play before he gets to the attacking blue line.

THE PHYSICAL GAME

Konroyd blocks shots very well and uses his strength in an effective, but understated, manner. He is a willing hitter, but not a fighter.

THE INTANGIBLES

The rest of the league may not appreciate Konroyd as much as the Blackhawks do. Konroyd does not play a flashy game, but the whole is made up of the sum of many parts, executed successfully by a player who keeps the game simple.

Every team, especially a contending team, needs a steadying influence of this type.

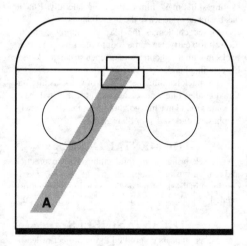

STEVE LARMER

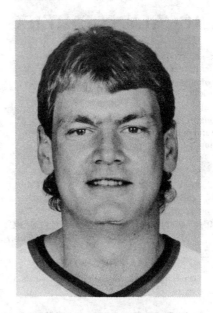

Yrs. of NHL service: 9
Born: Peterborough, Ont., Canada; June 16, 1961
Position: Right wing
Height: 5-11
Weight: 189
Uniform no.: 28
Shoots: Left

Career statistics:

GP	G	A	TP	PIM
727	342	437	779	362

1990-91 statistics:

GP	G	A	TP	+/-	PIM	PP	SH	GW	GT	S	PCT
80	44	57	101	37	79	17	2	9	0	231	19.0

LAST SEASON

Stretched streak of consecutive games played to 720 while leading his team in scoring for third successive season. Goal total was his highest in six seasons and just two short of career best, set in 1984-85.

THE FINESSE GAME

Steve Larmer is one of the best 'wrong-shooting' wings in the league. As a left-hand shot on the right side, his back frequently is to the play when he's trying to handle the puck along the boards, which means he cannot always see who's coming. Larmer makes the chore look easy, though he does get smeared occasionally. He also has the ability to accept a pass with his skates and kick it to his stick, which also comes in handy on the off-side.

Though his skating is a trifle unorthodox, Larmer never wastes a step—or an ounce of energy—and he cuts to the net very well. He uses remarkable balance to slip checks; people get a piece of Larmer, but his vision of the ice allows him to see the man coming and roll with the impact.

Larmer's shots are hard, accurate and varied. He is especially skilled at deceiving goaltenders; they read the position of the puck on his stick and anticipate he will shoot toward one spot—only to have him open or close the face of the blade and shoot toward another hole.

A solid defensive player and a top penalty killer with great anticipation, Larmer reads the play, anticipates well and makes an extremely quick transition from defense to offense. This is especially true when he is killing penalties; Larmer intercepts a lot of passes and does smart things with them. He is always in an opponent's way, in position—between the Chicago goal and his man. Either his body or his stick is always in the passing lane that forces the opposition to make a flip pass, which is much more difficult to one-time.

THE PHYSICAL GAME

Larmer won't run from physical play, but he never fights and doesn't wander toward the rough stuff while it's in progress.

He scraps efficiently for the puck, weasles away with it, brings it toward the net and gets off a strong snap shot.

THE INTANGIBLES

Larmer literally never takes a night off. And plays the same way every time, each game a virtual photocopy of its predecessor.

A durable, consistent player who works hard for his teammates, Larmer is the guy players listen to during the between-periods jaw sessions. Larmer is a humble, professional athlete. He takes great pride in excelling. Hockey is his job. He is not a hockey player, he is a hockey worker. He comes to the rink way early, but once the job is done, he's the first one out the door, back with his family.

And he made it very clear, last season, that he was not a guy who simply lived off playing with Denis Savard; it is time, retroactively, to give him the credit he has deserved for years.

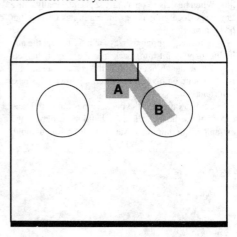

JOCELYN LEMIEUX

Yrs. of NHL service: 4
Born: Mount Laurier, Que., Canada;
November 18, 1967
Position: Right wing
Height: 5-10
Weight: 200
Uniform no.: 26
Shoots: Left

Career statistics:

GP	G	A	TP	PIM
217	31	29	60	363

1990-91 statistics:

GP	G	A	TP	+/-	PIM	PP	SH	GW	GT	S	PCT
67	6	7	13	-7	119	1	1	2	0	89	6.7

LAST SEASON

Games played and penalty minute totals were career bests.

THE FINESSE GAME

Lemieux is a strong skater—shifty, but not big on dekes or finesse. He gets up to top speed fairly quickly, has only one objective—to get to the net. He will be happy to knock you over if you're in his way.

Lemieux has a hard slap, which he fires off the wing, and always is willing to test the goalie's pain threshold. Lemieux will never drive a puck completely through a goalie, but that doesn't mean he isn't going to try.

Jocelyn is at his antagonizing best against the opposition's top wing, who is in for a long night—unless it's his brother, New Jersey's Claude, who is still the more annoying member of the family.

THE PHYSICAL GAME

Lemieux hits people and hurts people with his hits. When he gets in on a defense, he can really cause turnovers. Jocelyn is not as infuriating as Claude, but he is chippy.

A hustler, Lemieux always will try to beat the guy he hit (or who hit him) back into the play. If he gets whacked in the corner or along the boards, Lemieux is right back up on his feet and churning toward his next confrontation.

Lemieux digs for the puck, comes out with it and carries it to the net. He is a bulldozing player and extremely entertaining to watch in a John Tonelli mold.

THE INTANGIBLES

Lemieux is always trying to go 100 miles per hour, which is good and bad. It is good because all that motion keeps him from thinking—and Lemieux is at his best when he is sailing along without a thought in his head. It is bad because there often are times when Lemieux could maximize his performance by down-shifting one gear. So often, Lemieux is like a puppy after a ball; racing toward it, missing it and tumbling tail over paws.

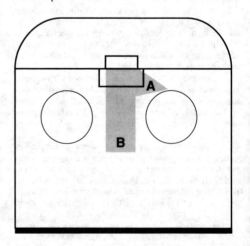

DAVE MANSON

Yrs. of NHL service: 5
Born: Prince Albert, Sask., Canada; January 27, 1967
Position: Defenseman
Height: 6-2
Weight: 202
Uniform no.: 3
Shoots: Left

Career statistics:

GP	G	A	TP	PIM
330	39	88	127	1177

1990-91 statistics:

GP	G	A	TP	+/-	PIM	PP	SH	GW	GT	S	PCT
75	14	15	29	20	191	6	1	2	0	154	9.1

LAST SEASON

Goal total was within four of career high, PIM was three-season low and a drop of 112 from 1989-90.

THE FINESSE GAME

A deep pushoff and good knee bend make Manson a strong skater with good balance. From that strength stems the power game coveted by so many general managers.

Manson may have the hardest shot in the league—ask all the Blackhawks forwards who have gotten their heads out of its path at the last second. He can beat a goalie to the top corner from the blue line, but also is the reason many Chicago forwards wear face shields.

Not a flexible thinker in his passing options, Manson will pick one target out of a crowd and will stick with the choice whether the receiver remains open or not. More often than not, he gets the puck to the target; but he takes high risks and seems oblivious to the consequences.

The same is true of his playmaking and his reads on defense. Manson has the skills to beat the first forechecker, but then gets into an overhandling mode. While he's trying to stickhandle, his teammates have to stop at the blue line to wait for his arrival.

On defense, Manson may misread the play, make the wrong decision and look bad. He will never play the game conservatively; his aim should be to play it consistently.

THE PHYSICAL GAME

Manson possesses good, bordering on great, physical skills. He uses his size constantly and is very aggressive. He bangs, he punches. He can be mean every shift; there is a very rough edge on his game.

Manson is just so spontaneous and energetic and unpredictable, he constantly evokes terror and creates space simply by approaching certain players. Nobody knows what to make of him; a night against Manson is like a night in the lion's cage at the circus.

THE INTANGIBLES

Manson is working to control his emotionalism, to add a little maturity to the recipe so he ends up spending less time in the penalty box—and Brian O'Neill's office. He doesn't vent his emotions as often, or as noticeably, as he used to, but you simply never know when his aggressiveness will become explosive.

He MUST work to maintain his skills, but Manson must never work at playing the game, because thinking on the ice slows him down; he has to be on auto-pilot to play his best hockey.

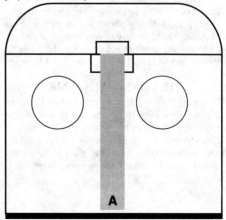

TROY MURRAY

Yrs. of NHL service: 9
Born: Calgary, Alta., Canada; July 31, 1962
Position: Center
Height: 6-1
Weight: 195
Uniform no.: 19
Shoots: Right

Career statistics:

GP	G	A	TP	PIM
654	196	287	483	678

1990-91 statistics:

GP	G	A	TP	+/-	PIM	PP	SH	GW	GT	S	PCT
75	14	23	37	13	74	4	0	2	0	130	10.8

LAST SEASON

Goal total was NHL career low, point total was seven-season low.

THE FINESSE GAME

Murray remains one of the league's stronger defensive/two-way centers because he still has the speed which is the primary asset of his game. He combines the speed with innate enthusiasm and, presto, comes up with the range he uses to pursue every puck with vigor.

The pursuit becomes vital in Murray's role as a penalty killer, and his devotion to conditioning adds endurance; he can chase and harry for his full shift. He will see where his opponent intends to take the puck and get there first, so the other guy has to change directions or slow down or do something he does not want to do.

Murray also sees faceoffs as a challenge. He takes pride in winning them and makes certain to lock off the opposing center after the puck has been dropped.

His puckhandling skills are not on a par with his puckchasing skills; Murray is very average at dishing off the puck and springing his wings for plays. But his snap shot and wrist shot remain strong and accurate.

THE PHYSICAL GAME

Murray likes to jolt people with his bodychecks and gets a little extra drive from his legs an instant before contact to further boost the energy transference. He sees his role as that of a person who finishes his checks with authority, wants the night to be a long, wearying one for the center against whom he is matched.

THE INTANGIBLES

Murray scored 45 goals his Selke Trophy season (1985-86) and has paid an emotional price for it ever since. He still is struggling to find his scoring identity and putting too much pressure on himself to match the output of that Selke campaign—even though he was a right wing with Denis Savard and Al Secord then and is a center with more checking responsibilities now.

Murray is steady, well-liked, a solid citizen and he scores enough.

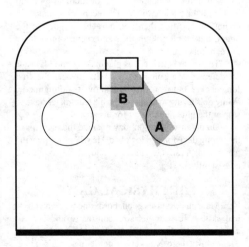

MIKE PELUSO

Yrs. of NHL service: 1
Born: Pengilly, Minn., USA; November 8, 1965
Position: Left wing/defenseman
Height: 6-4
Weight: 200
Uniform no.: 44
Shoots: Left

Career statistics:

GP	G	A	TP	PIM
55	6	1	7	335

1990-91 statistics:

GP	G	A	TP	+/-	PIM	PP	SH	GW	GT	S	PCT
53	6	1	7	-3	320	2	0	0	0	29	20.7

LAST SEASON

First season in the league.

THE FINESSE GAME

No club will turn its back on someone versatile enough to try two positions, mean enough to give the team bus a concussion, trustworthy enough to be on the ice with two shifts left in the game and his team up a goal. Mike Peluso is more than a pair of fists.

His skating needs work, though. His stride is too rigid, too straight-legged, so he loses balance easily. Peluso is adequate going backwards, doesn't stumble, and in fact might actually be better going in reverse.

Peluso reads the play pretty well and doesn't gamble. He plays it conservative because he knows he doesn't yet skate well enough to get fancy. As a left wing, Peluso is just a dump-in guy: he gets the puck to the center line, dumps it in, goes hellbent after it. As a defenseman, he's forced to find an outlet pass, but has decent success doing so.

THE PHYSICAL GAME

As his five hours in penalties might suggest, Peluso finishes his bodychecks hard and mean. He likes being the tough guy; it was his ticket to the pros, his path to an NHL salary, and he knows it.

THE INTANGIBLES

Peluso is not going to be a Cam Neely or a Rick Tocchet, who turned into fine players after arriving as scrappers. As soon as he thinks he can play, without using the physical tools that got him a contract, he's in trouble.

But there is a player in this guy someplace. A fitness freak, he has shifted from Body-by-Jay Caufield weight training to a more hockey-specific regimen. He made the team, stuck with it, he's popular in the dressing room and can improve to something better than a goon. Peluso knows to stay within his limits, which is most of the battle.

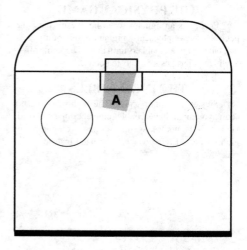

WAYNE PRESLEY

Yrs. of NHL service: 5
Born: Detroit, Mich., USA; March 23, 1965
Position: Right wing
Height: 5-11
Weight: 180
Uniform no.: 17
Shoots: Right

Career statistics:

GP	G	A	TP	PIM
354	93	93	186	495

1990-91 statistics:

GP	G	A	TP	+/-	PIM	PP	SH	GW	GT	S	PCT
71	15	19	34	11	122	1	0	3	0	141	10.6

LAST SEASON

Penalty minutes were pro career high. Goal production jumped by nine.

THE FINESSE GAME

Presley has the big slap shot that hits the corners or goes in off the goal posts. He can score on shots that draw oohs and aahs, like at the NBA Slam Dunk competition.

But he needs to be surrounded by more physical, better talented players, because of the general inconsistency of his finesse game. He has hockey sense and intelligence, some foot speed and quickness, but he seems to be without focus.

THE PHYSICAL GAME

Presley is an agitator when he doesn't have the puck. He is not physically big and he is not a fitness nut, but he yaps and jabbers until the gloves come off—at which point Presley elects to behave.

THE INTANGIBLES

Presley is a pure scorer. The nights he doesn't score, you might have trouble remembering he played. He had 34 points last season, so there were too many nights when "Elvis" was at Graceland instead of the rink.

He's a fourth-line player on a good team, a nice fit as a third right wing on most other clubs. If he's your second-line right wing, your team has a depth problem.

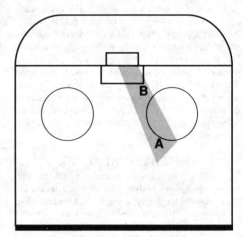

JEREMY ROENICK

Yrs. of NHL service: 2
Born: Boston, Mass., USA; January 17, 1970
Position: Center
Height: 6-0
Weight: 170
Uniform no.: 27
Shoots: Right

Career statistics:

GP	G	A	TP	PIM
177	76	102	178	138

1990-91 statistics:

GP	G	A	TP	+/-	PIM	PP	SH	GW	GT	S	PCT
79	41	53	94	38	80	15	4	10	1	194	21.1

LAST SEASON

All offensive stats were career highs. Plus-minus was third best in league.

THE FINESSE GAME

Roenick never stops skating. Without the puck, he's always in motion—which means he's never caught flat-footed, he always has a head start toward a faster speed, he's always closer to the place he needs to be, he's always involved. Roenick also uses every opportunity to set a skating screen, to interfere legally and buy a teammate more time with the puck.

He has excellent speed, breakaway speed; he has a lovely, long stride and glide. Roenick uses his edges brilliantly, which provides excellent balance plus a splendid, instant change of direction.

He can stop and start with quickness and agility, and his decision-making is excellent. He knows where he's sending the puck before he even has received it and can make moves at extremely high speed, which makes the moves more effective.

Scores from everywhere with every kind of shot, including the deflection, at which he is expert.

Roenick's passing skills should not be overlooked. His speed creates space, buys him time, which he uses to spot teammates in the clear.

THE PHYSICAL GAME

Has absolutely no respect for his body and the things in it that tend to break, split or bleed. There always seems to be a cut on his nose or stitches on his chin or a shiner in various shades of purple, and he comes by them all honestly, because he goes where the puck is.

And when he has the puck, he takes it where the goal is. If there is a defenseman or a goalie or a goal post in the way, that's their problem. Roenick dishes out the big hits, takes them, throws himself into the boards, whacks his face against the glass, then gets up and chases the puck some more.

Has to work on his upper body, though. Has to grow as big as he plays. His hunt for the puck often leads him into the Land of the Giant Wing, and 170 or so pounds leaves him at physical risk. He's getting away with speed and youthfulness, but he's getting hit. Hard.

THE INTANGIBLES

Jeremy Roenick does not consider it an official game until he has been wiped out for the first time. It helps him figure out who he's playing and how he's going to beat them. He scores at key times in big games, and he met the challenge extremely well after inheriting (creating?) the top center's job via the trade of Denis Savard.

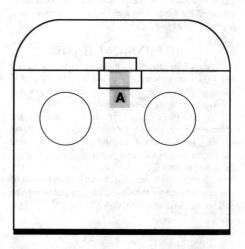

STEVE THOMAS

Yrs. of NHL service: 7
Born: Stockport, England; July 15, 1963
Position: Left wing
Height: 5-11
Weight: 185
Uniform no.: 32
Shoots: Left

Career statistics:

GP	G	A	TP	PIM
381	149	163	312	481

1990-91 statistics:

GP	G	A	TP	+/-	PIM	PP	SH	GW	GT	S	PCT
69	19	35	54	8	129	2	0	3	0	192	9.9

LAST SEASON

Was unable to play all games on schedule for seventh time in his career. Goal total was personal NHL low for season of more than 30 games.

THE FINESSE GAME

Thomas has remarkable skating speed, and may be the quickest on the team at reaching top speed from a standing start. Given that, he should have the patience to wait until the puck has been cleared safely before he leaves the zone. Instead, Thomas gambles on defense, Brett Hull-style, and leaves the zone before the 50-50 loose pucks are secured in the corners; then he has to skate like crazy to get back and find his man.

On offense, Thomas has SOME moves, but they don't work often enough to be a steady factor in his game. He is more a pure shooter than anything else. Thomas wrists the puck well and his slap shot is an asset. He shoots it a ton and uses it coming off left wing more than anything.

But he starts to get in trouble when things don't go right. When his hot streaks turn cold, Thomas starts overhandling the puck and aiming his shots at the net, instead of just blasting away.

THE PHYSICAL GAME

A good forechecker, Thomas uses his speed and his body, turning himself into a human bowling ball. For a smallish player, he uses the body a lot and is exceptionally strong, especially along the boards.

A dual-threat player in the physical battles, Thomas uses his upper-body strength during scraps for the puck and wins his share. And a soccer background (he played with Peter Zezel in Toronto) helps him use his feet to control the puck.

Thomas will fight, even enjoys it at times. But he lost most of a season to shoulder surgery after one scrap and is a touch more careful now.

THE INTANGIBLES

Thomas has a fine work ethic and intensity, but a confidence level that should not be as erratic as it is. His performance depends on his confidence, but Thomas is a bundle of nerves.

If his first shot of the game goes in, he'll be on fire all night. If it hits the post and bounces away, he starts to press, then to brood, then to slump, then to worry and battle himself because he feels he's letting the team down—letting down the guys who force passes to him to get him going again. It becomes an own-worst-enemy type of thing.

He needs a chill pill. Teammates get mad at him because he gets so mad at himself.

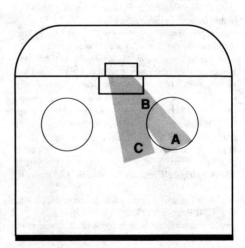

JOHN TONELLI

Yrs. of NHL service: 13
Born: Milton, Ont., Canada; March 23, 1957
Position: Left wing
Height: 6-1
Weight: 200
Uniform no.: 27
Shoots: Left

Career statistics:

GP	G	A	TP	PIM
976	322	500	822	860

1990-91 statistics:

GP	G	A	TP	+/-	PIM	PP	SH	GW	GT	S	PCT
71	14	16	30	3	49	2	0	5	0	84	16.7

LAST SEASON

Totals for goals, assists and points all were career lows. Games played was lowest since 1980-81, when he played a career-low 70. Though he played only two fewer games than prior season, he took 79 fewer shots.

THE FINESSE GAME

Tonelli is all arms and legs as a skater, and all that effort doesn't get him around as quickly as it used to. He remains relentless, nonetheless, and puts fear into opponents who know they cannot match his persistence, his endurance.

Tonelli is strong on his feet, yet his balance seems to betray him at times. The sheer effort of his strivings often leaves him on his belly or his bottom, and often he will drop in an attempt to draw a penalty; but other times, he goes down off incidental bumps that should not have such effect.

He still has a tremendous shot from the wing, but was not asked to use it much last season in Los Angeles. The Kings scored 340 goals without much help from him, but the Blackhawks' puny 284 might benefit from a Tonelli transfusion.

THE PHYSICAL GAME

Tonelli has tremendous strength and leg drive, which plays perfectly into his game along the boards. If he gets bored with carrying a defenseman to the left, he pauses for a moment, then starts carrying the defenseman in the other direction.

He is extremely useful on faceoffs, because he takes the draw, then takes his man out of the play with great authority. Tonelli will drive his stick between his rival's legs and bury his shoulder in the man's face, paralyzing his foe. He also uses his feet beautifully to control the puck; while tying up his opponent's arms, he will kick the puck to a teammate or kick it ahead, then step around his man to regain possession and drive to the net.

Tonelli also camps in front of the net and pays whatever price needs to be paid to score a goal or help create one.

THE INTANGIBLES

Tonelli's game is suited perfectly to the friendly confines of Chicago's little pond. He will live in the corners there, his enthusiasm will make him an instant hit with the fans and he does have those four Stanley Cup rings to show off in a dressing room which needs precisely that ingredient. If you want to win, you need winners; Tonelli may not have much left, but that one intangible will never leave him and the Blackhawks will benefit greatly by his presence.

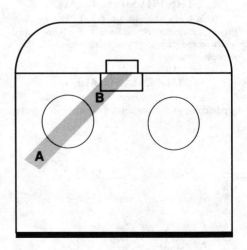

DOUG WILSON

Yrs. of NHL service: 14
Born: Ottawa, Ont., Canada; July 5, 1957
Position: Defenseman
Height: 6-1
Weight: 187
Uniform no.: 24
Shoots: Left

Career statistics:

GP	G	A	TP	PIM
938	225	554	779	806

1990-91 statistics:

GP	G	A	TP	+/-	PIM	PP	SH	GW	GT	S	PCT
51	11	29	40	25	32	6	1	1	0	162	6.8

LAST SEASON

Slow start was due to ankle surgery that kept him out of the early season. Has missed at least 10 games in each of past five seasons.

THE FINESSE GAME

Though known for his monster slap shot—big, heavy and fast—Wilson is under-rated as a defenseman because he is extremely difficult to beat one-on-one. He is a fine skater with speed, quickness, agility, above-average lateral mobility and a good ability to read the play. He knows which loose pucks he will reach and which he will not.

Wilson has poise without the puck and with it. Wilson can stickhandle with the puck until he spots an outlet pass, then can get the puck to the target. Experience tells him when to bust a pass up the middle to send teammates in on breakaways, and guts—plus hands— enable him to do it.

THE PHYSICAL GAME

Wilson is extremely strong and takes opposing players out quietly, but authoritatively. When paired with a more outwardly physical defenseman, his effectiveness in maximized.

THE INTANGIBLES

The only factor against Wilson is his age. His conditioning is exceptional for a 34-year-old player and he is a responsible leader in the clubhouse, but the Blackhawks are extremely concerned about the increasing age of their defense.

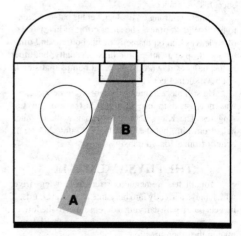

TRENT YAWNEY

Yrs. of NHL service: 3
Born: Hudson Bay, Sask., Canada;
September 29, 1965
Position: Defenseman
Height: 6-3
Weight: 192
Uniform no.: 8
Shoots: Left

Career statistics:

GP	G	A	TP	PIM
215	15	55	70	290

1990-91 statistics:

GP	G	A	TP	+/-	PIM	PP	SH	GW	GT	S	PCT
61	3	13	16	6	77	3	0	0	0	52	5.8

LAST SEASON

Goal and assist totals were three-season low, but plus-minus improved by 12 goals.

THE FINESSE GAME

Yawney is conservative, almost to a fault, in his approach to the game. He can handle the puck, can run the point on the power play and he skates well enough—with a strong, balanced stride—to keep the gap to the forwards closed as he follows the play up ice.

All things being equal, Yawney prefers to let the other Blackhawks take care of the puck-carrying and stick-handling stuff. He will get the puck to the red line, drive it deep in the attack zone, then get ready for the next emergency, because defense comes first. He will take the occasional shot (good enough that it should be used more often) just to keep the goaltenders honest.

Yawney reads the play well, picks up his man and doesn't strand his partner. If he were a Boy Scout, Yawney would get a merit badge for defensive comportment.

THE PHYSICAL GAME

Yawney is a contact player, an efficient takeout player, but not a banger. Really, his mind is his strength.

THE INTANGIBLES

Coach Keenan reportedly was on Yawney like ugly on a monkey at varying times last season. How many players can you name that Keenan wasn't on? He wants the best from his players, and Yawney can be more assertive than he was last season.

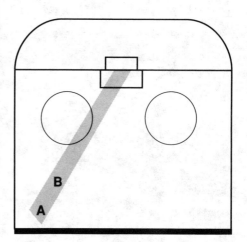

DETROIT RED WINGS

DAVE BARR

Yrs. of NHL service: 8
Born: Toronto, Ont., Canada; November 30, 1960
Position: Right wing
Height: 6-1
Weight: 195
Uniform no.: 22
Shoots: Right

Career statistics:

GP	G	A	TP	PIM
491	114	179	293	406

1990-91 statistics:

GP	G	A	TP	+/-	PIM	PP	SH	GW	GT	S	PCT
70	18	22	40	19	55	2	2	2	1	98	18.4

LAST SEASON

Second on team in plus-minus. Goal total was second highest of his career; he had 27 in 1988-89.

THE FINESSE GAME

Barr understands the nature and responsibilities of defensive hockey, comprehends that even the Steve Yzermans of the world—who seem to have the puck all night—in reality spend more time without the puck than they do with it. Barr has made himself an asset to the Red Wings by gaining a mastery of that far more challenging aspect of the sport; you can't coach scoring, but precious few players want to learn to check.

Barr will do a good job in that checking role and also will score in double figures every season, which makes him a premium player. He is solid on his skates (decent speed) and does a good job pressuring the puck when the other team has it; he is strong enough to hold off a defenseman and move the puck.

His goal production is noteworthy for two reasons: First, he shoots so little; second, his shot is only average at best. But he puts it at the goalie as well as on net. Barr has the hand-eye coordination to one-time a pass to the goalmouth and has the smarts to get in scoring position when the percentages favor him.

THE PHYSICAL GAME

Barr is a physical player. He is not a banger, but he plays tough and stands up for himself. No foul goes unavenged—unless the score is close and retaliation would hurt more than it might help. His physical nature has played a significant role in his survival these many years.

THE INTANGIBLES

Barr has never been a spotlight guy. He plays a quietly efficient game, does unremarkable things remarkably well, and does them three times in four nights when the schedule calls for him it.

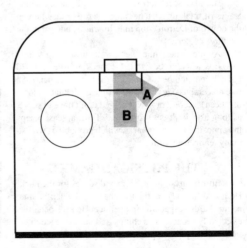

SHAWN BURR

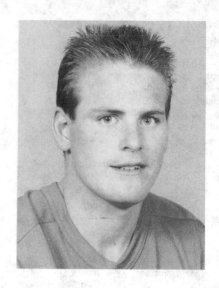

Yrs. of NHL service: 5
Born: Sarnia, Ont., Canada; July 1, 1966
Position: Left wing
Height: 6-1
Weight: 180
Uniform no.: 11
Shoots: Left

Career statistics:

GP	G	A	TP	PIM
407	103	137	240	482

1990-91 statistics:

GP	G	A	TP	+/-	PIM	PP	SH	GW	GT	S	PCT
80	20	30	50	14	112	6	0	4	0	164	12.2

LAST SEASON

Reached 20-goal mark for third time in five full Red Wings seasons. Played all 80 games for only second time. Point total was six short of prior season's career-high. Plus-minus was second highest on team.

THE FINESSE GAME

Burr's skating skills leave a bit to be desired and, by extension, leave his game a bit short of where it could be—given his eager approach to the game and his hockey IQ. If he skated better, he would kill penalties better, he would reach the puck that much faster and he would be more of a threat for a shorthanded goal.

But the acceleration is not quite there, which leaves Burr taking what he can get: a role somewhere in the crowd of Detroit's top nine forwards, but not in the top three centers.

At the same time, he is one of the very few forwards who can be handed a checking role and still put a decent number of pucks in the net. Once handed a role that emphasizes defense, people get in that mindset of "I can't score," or—worse—"I don't have to score, as long as I don't get scored on." Burr, at least, keeps the opposition people honest, which probably is why so many teams want him.

THE PHYSICAL GAME

Burr bangs in the corners and scraps for the puck. He takes the body on the forecheck and when he hits, he hits hard—especially in open ice. He kills penalties effectively because he's chippy and has good ice intelligence. He reads the play properly and reacts correctly.

THE INTANGIBLES

He is intense enough; what you see is just about what you get—a consistent effort, consistent numbers, consistent work. The Red Wings had any number of centers dispatched to the flank last season because of their all-star crowd up the middle, but while many of them hoped for a trade that would ease the congestion, Burr has become a significant contributor in a new role. This is a sound wing.

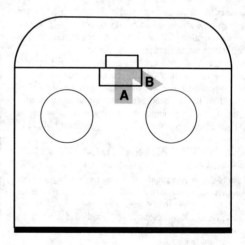

JIMMY CARSON

Yrs. of NHL service: 5
Born: Southfield, Mich., USA; July 20, 1968
Position: Center
Height: 6-1
Weight: 200
Uniform no.: 10
Shoots: Right

Career statistics:

GP	G	A	TP	PIM
352	183	188	371	139

1990-91 statistics:

GP	G	A	TP	+/-	PIM	PP	SH	GW	GT	S	PCT
64	21	25	46	3	28	5	1	4	2	175	12.0

LAST SEASON

Shoulder injuries caused the bulk of the games lost due to injury. Goal total tied for career low, set in 1989-90.

THE FINESSE GAME

Carson will drive to the center of the attack zone, between the tops of the circles; he will fake a shot, then move to his right on the forehand and try a snap shot. He also will try a move favored or popularized in the international game: moving behind the net, from the goalie's right to the goalie's left, Carson will throw a pass against the grain, back out at the goalie's right, for a quick shot by a teammate that can catch netminders by surprise.

With skills and instincts such as those, Carson could be counted on for much more production than he compiled last year—playing much of the time in pain from an injured shoulder. He is a short-game player who scores from the faceoff dots and closer.

Carson has good skating speed but not great balance. To get where he needs to go, Carson could use a little more knee-bend and a little less foot elevation.

THE PHYSICAL GAME

Carson is not strong or physical, but he is smart. He is expert at using his body to shield the puck from harm, but is not expert at using his body to nullify the other center after a faceoff. This problem afflicts most of the other Detroit centers as well.

THE INTANGIBLES

Carson is in such a difficult position, given the office addresses of Steve Yzerman and Sergei Fedorov. He isn't going to get a lot of minutes, isn't going to be the top dog—when there are so many NHL teams with empty kennels. Detroit may be his home town, but it may not be his hockey home much longer, unless life as a right wing agrees with him. The Wings have so many centers on the flanks as it is, Carson may be the next one tried there.

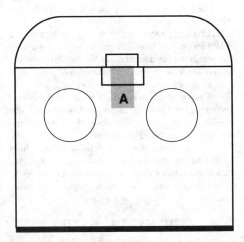

TIM CHEVELDAE

Yrs. of NHL service: 2
Born: Melville, Sask., Canada; February 15, 1968
Position: Goaltender
Height: 5-10 1/2
Weight: 180
Uniform no.: 32
Catches: Left

Career statistics:

GP	MINS	GA	SO	GAA	A	PIM
95	5337	324	0	3.64	6	4

1990-91 statistics:

GP	MINS	GAA	W	L	T	SO	GA	S	SAPCT	PIM
65	3615	3.55	30	26	5	2	214	1716	.875	2

LAST SEASON

Was third in the league in victories, behind Chicago's Ed Belfour (43) and Calgary's Mike Vernon (31). His games played total was second only to Belfour's 74. Games played more than doubled his prior personal best, victory total was three times his prior career figure.

THE PHYSICAL GAME

Cheveldae plays a very controlled, standup game. He is extremely economical in his motions, which helps conserve energy and keep him fresh for the later stages of the game and season. He does not sprawl on his side; only on the rarest occasions are his shoulders perpendicular to the ice for emergency saves. Thus he usually is in exceptional position for a second shot off a rebound (he doesn't permit many) or a bang-bang play.

Cheveldae is an angle goalie with perhaps the best stance in the league. He is a bit more upright than most, but is balanced perfectly on his skates, which keeps to a minimum the five hole between his knees and allows him maximum freedom to move his feet. His catching hand—which helps govern balance—is waist-high, open at all times and extremely quick.

When he drops to his knees, Cheveldae recovers his footing quickly and is in good position for the next challenge. A fine skater, he moves well side-to-side and across the crease on odd-man attacks.

Cheveldae always is alert for passes coming from behind the net or the corners and is active in using his stick to try to block them. He gets to most of the pucks behind the net and is working to improve his puck-handling.

THE MENTAL GAME

Cheveldae concentrates extremely well. Even if he is set for a shot that is deflected, Cheveldae is in such control of his body that he can adjust to the puck's new direction.

Some goalies also make a "big" save, then get so emotionally overwhelmed by the accomplishment that a simple followup beats them. It isn't only a bad goal that can be a distraction good plays can have a similar effect, but Cheveladae remains cool and calm. As soon as he makes the big save, it's already forgotten—and the same is true of the rare bad goal he permits or bad game he plays.

THE INTANGIBLES

Cheveldae does not lose his confidence or his hope. For someone so new to the NHL experience, he has an excellent disposition about the position and its demands. He does not wear himself down mentally or physically, which makes HSR believe he can play the game in this league—and play it very well—for a lot of years to come.

It would be stupid to hand him laurels, as he hasn't won anything. But the door to elite NHL status is open for Cheveldae. And there is every indication he will walk through it.

STEVE CHIASSON

Yrs. of NHL service: 5
Born: Barrie, Ont., Canada; April 14, 1967
Position: Defenseman
Height: 6-0
Weight: 202
Uniform no.: 3
Shoots: Left

Career statistics:

GP	G	A	TP	PIM
248	32	93	125	473

1990-91 statistics:

GP	G	A	TP	+/-	PIM	PP	SH	GW	GT	S	PCT
42	3	17	20	0	80	1	0	1	0	101	3.0

LAST SEASON

An ankle that was broken, then re-broken just as he was about to return to action, limited Chiasson to his fewest games-played since 1986-87.

THE FINESSE GAME

You don't want to watch Chiasson's choppy strides if you want to watch pretty skating, but he will get where he wants to go. The place the Red Wings want him to go is someplace where there is an open shot, because the guy has got a cannon, heavy and hard, that can drive a goalie backward. He can overpower a netminder.

Chiasson's shot is a key component for the power play, and the Red Wings really suffered for his absence from it. The only small point is a shortage of lateral mobility that limits his options at the point. The better point men, such as the Rangers' Brian Leetch or the Flames' Al MacInnis, use their mobility to "slide" across the blue line, change the setup, open a new shooting angle or a new option and proceed from there. Though working on it, Chiasson has not quite climbed that mountain.

He sees the ice well and moves the puck quickly from his defensive zone. He looks to join the rush and will work his way in front from the point to score from short range if the opportunity arises.

THE PHYSICAL GAME

Chiasson has a mean streak. He will fight, but he's not a fighter; he is a mean and competitive player who does what is necessary to make his point. He is an aggressive penalty killer, strong in the corners and in front of the net.

THE INTANGIBLES

When, and if, the lateral mobility makes its appearance, Chiasson can be a top defenseman—assuming, also, that accidental good health would allow him to surpass his one-season career-high of 67 games-played.

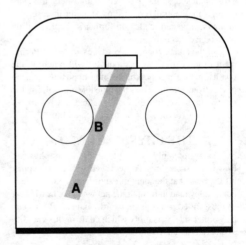

DOUG CROSSMAN

Yrs. of NHL service: 10
Born: Peterborough, Ont., Canada; June 30, 1960
Position: Defenseman
Height: 6-2
Weight: 190
Uniform no.: 39
Shoots: Left

Career statistics:

GP	G	A	TP	PIM
779	93	316	409	482

1990-91 statistics:

GP	G	A	TP	+/-	PIM	PP	SH	GW	GT	S	PCT
74	8	29	37	-23	48	4	0	0	0	108	7.4

LAST SEASON

Obtained Feb. 20 from Hartford for Doug Houda. Plus-minus was worst on the team, though only minus 6 of it came over his 17 games with Detroit. He was minus 4 in 16 games with the Islanders and minus 13 in 41 games with Hartford.

THE FINESSE GAME

Crossman's real asset is the ability to get the puck out of the defensive zone and into the attacking zone. He has nimble-enough hands, strong-enough feet and clear-enough ice vision to skate the puck out of the defensive zone or make a sensible first pass to a teammate who has some open ice in which to work.

Once the defending blue line has been gained, Crossman keeps the gap tight and ushers the play through the neutral zone, riding shotgun in case of a turnover, prepared to step up further if there is a drop pass to be collected.

In the attack zone, it takes takes an Act of Parliament to get Crossman to shoot. He will pinch up the boards, does a nice job of keeping opposing clearing passes from getting across the blue line and will fire the occasional rocket toward some goalie. But Crossman's better offensive days appear to be behind him.

THE PHYSICAL GAME

Does not apply to this player. He is not physical. He will not skate through checks. He will send the puck off the boards at the mere threat of body contact. He is not a happy man in front of the net when the traffic is at its most furied. He is not outwardly intense. But he can play either side, versatility which confirms his viability as an NHL defenseman.

THE INTANGIBLES

Yes, that minus 23 is a turn-off, but he played last season for three teams who were a combined minus 130 in goal differential. If the way he plays is such a turn-off, how come so many clubs with poor team defenses trade to get him? Because they feel he's going to make them better. Because he gets the puck out. If more people had the skill Crossman has, he wouldn't be playing; but he is playing.

Crossman wasn't physical with the Blackhawks or Flyers, he wasn't physical with the Islanders or the Whalers. And he isn't physical for the Red Wings. Who will he not be physical for next?

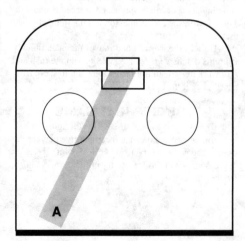

BOBBY DOLLAS

Yrs. of NHL service: 3
Born: Montreal, Que., Canada; January 31, 1965
Position: Defenseman
Height: 6-2
Weight: 220
Uniform no.: 8
Shoots: Left

Career statistics:

GP	G	A	TP	PIM
128	3	13	16	104

1990-91 statistics:

GP	G	A	TP	+/-	PIM	PP	SH	GW	GT	S	PCT
56	3	5	8	6	20	0	0	1	0	59	5.1

LAST SEASON

Games played and goal totals were NHL career highs. Assist total matched career high.

THE FINESSE GAME

When he and Brad McCrimmon were paired so successfully against Brett Hull in the St. Louis series last spring, Dollas' speed, mobility and agility were the counterpoints to McCrimmon's strength, positioning and steadiness.

Dollas can make a play out of the defensive zone as well as anybody on Detroit's defense and is more than trustworthy against the other team's second and third lines. In the neutral zone, though, the transition game gives him some difficult moments; he might not see the occasional wing gaining speed away from the puck.

Dollas has some nice finesse tools, which include a powerful skating stride, solid passing skills and a strong shot from the blue line. He takes a while to fire, however, which leaves him vulnerable to being blocked.

THE PHYSICAL GAME

Dollas will bump his man, ride him out of the play, but won't hit anybody with the hammer. He is a finesse player with a bit of size and no mean streak.

In front of the net, for a large player of acceptable strength, Dollas does not scare people. Neither will he be intimidated.

THE INTANGIBLES

Dollas earned respect from his teammates—and a contract from the Red Wings—for playing, and playing hard. He basically was a walk-on with the Red Wings, but he showed enough grit to earn a job and make a responsible contribution.

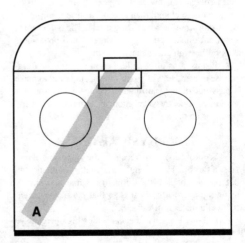

SERGEI FEDOROV

Yrs. of NHL service: 1
Born: Pskow, Soviet Union; December 13, 1969
Position: Center
Height: 6-1
Weight: 191
Uniform no.: 91
Shoots: Left

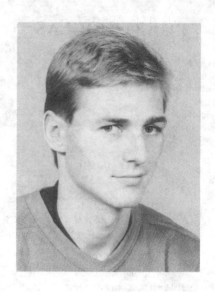

Career statistics:

GP	G	A	TP	PIM
77	31	48	79	66

1990-91 statistics:

GP	G	A	TP	+/-	PIM	PP	SH	GW	GT	S	PCT
77	31	48	79	11	66	11	3	5	1	259	12.0

LAST SEASON

First season in NHL. Finalist for Rookie of the Year award.

THE FINESSE GAME

Fedorov is so phenomenal a skater that he seems to be gliding ABOVE the ice, not on it. He is gifted with exceptional agility, a nice change of speed, plus the balance and wrist strength to make tight pivots in the corners with the puck on his backhand.

His lateral mobility borders on the wondrous. He takes a defenseman wide on the backhand, shifts inside to open the forehand, then gets off a strong, surprising wrist shot from the right wing circle. The defenseman starts out thinking he's got Fedorov lined up, then is lucky if he even gets a piece of him.

Just as he is ultra-agile, Fedorov also is an ultra-finesse player. He will go into traffic, but only to make a pass out of it to an unchecked teammate—a play made possibile by very good awareness of players' positions on the ice.

THE PHYSICAL GAME

Fedorov does not lock off the opposing center after a faceoff. He will hit if the contact is incidental, but prefers to play the geometric game and simply angle a player to the boards so that the player essentially eliminates himself.

Fedorov is a stick checker with a high percentage of his penalty minutes owed to restraining fouls or incautious whacks of the wood. He skates past players, rather than hit them or even bump into them.

THE INTANGIBLES

Fedorov had a splendid freshman season in the NHL, but elite Soviet players are just as vulnerable to sophomore slump as any North Americans. Virtually none of the 1989-90 Soviet arrivals had a glittering second season. It is up to Fedorov to start a trend the other way.

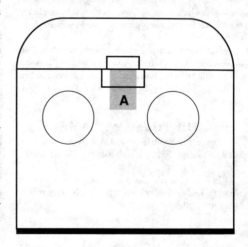

BRENT FEDYK

Yrs. of NHL service: 2
Born: Yorkton, Sask., Canada; March 8, 1967
Position: Right wing
Height: 6-0
Weight: 195
Uniform no.: 14
Shoots: Right

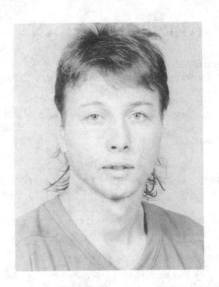

Career statistics:

GP	G	A	TP	PIM
101	19	24	43	46

1990-91 statistics:

GP	G	A	TP	+/-	PIM	PP	SH	GW	GT	S	PCT
67	16	19	35	21	38	0	0	1	0	74	21.6

LAST SEASON

Plus-minus and shooting percentage were best on team. First full season in NHL.

THE FINESSE GAME

Fedyk was the Red Wings' best checking forward last season, a player who got the playing time and made the most of it. On any team, the second right wing should be a strong finisher, the third right wing should accentuate the defensive while adding an occasional goal; Fedyk filled the bill, and then some, at the No. 3 spot.

Given the chance to show his stuff as a regular, Fedyk used his strong skating skills to pursue the puck and exploited his ability to read the play properly. He virtually never caused his team to face an odd-man situation through the neutral zone, which afforded his defensemen the luxury of standing up to the play as it approached the Detroit blue line.

On attack, Fedyk uses a quick release to launch a strong, albeit infrequent, shot. He scored 40 goals in the minors, 42 his last year of juniors, so the hands skills are there—as is the potential for exceptional two-way play.

THE PHYSICAL GAME

Fedyk rides his check out of the play, angles his man to bad ice, but he is not a banger, aggressive or a physical player, which to an extent diminishes his impact as a checking wing. Good checking wings also are extremely annoying to play against; Fedyk uses less guile and more skill.

THE INTANGIBLES

Fedyk took barely one shot per game and scored on one of every five—without the benefit of a single shift on the power play—yet he had essentially a weak year when it came to finishing his scoring chances. Simple mathematics would suggest 30-goal potential if he improved his scoring skills beyond the merely opportunistic and wasted an occasional shot.

The other thing with Fedyk is, this is the first time he has come to training camp with a job. All the other years, he had to earn one.

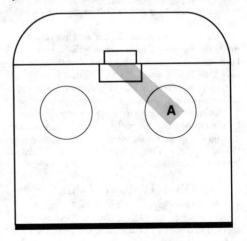

GERARD GALLANT

Yrs. of NHL service: 6
Born: Summerside, P.E.I., Canada; September 2, 1963
Position: Left wing
Height: 5-10
Weight: 185
Uniform no.: 17
Shoots: Left

Career statistics:

GP	G	A	TP	PIM
427	189	218	407	1225

1990-91 statistics:

GP	G	A	TP	+/-	PIM	PP	SH	GW	GT	S	PCT
45	10	16	26	6	111	3	0	1	0	82	12.2

LAST SEASON

Lost a load of playing time to back trouble which required surgery in March. Games played was a six-season low, as were totals for goals, assists and points. Had been assessed at least 215 PIM in each of prior five seasons.

THE FINESSE GAME

Has the physical tools to play wing for Steve Yzerman, but also has the smarts that send him to the holes Yzerman invariably causes with his whirlybird rushes. As Yzerman creates the chaos with his spins and swerves, Gallant calmly breaks to the openings—often to find a gift-wrapped Yzerman pass waiting patiently on the doorstep or at the left-wing dot. Clearly, the guy has finishing skills, as last season marked the first time in five Gallant mustered fewer than 34 goals.

Gallant is somewhat suspect as a backchecker, ironic for a guy who spent so much time getting his back checked last spring. But most offensive players have their lapses, and Gallant's downfall has been a difficulty identifying the man he is supposed to pick up in the transition to defense.

Gallant's skills are very blunt, no-nonsense ones. He is no speed merchant, but he gets where he wants to go, and that is nearest the most recent Yzerman pass. He will make a strong pass himself, and Gallant's heavy wrist shot throws lots of rebounds up for grabs.

THE PHYSICAL GAME

An up-and-down wing with great hockey sense, Gallant's injury was severe enough doctors were shocked he could play even a single shift, much less 45 games.

Gallant is one ornery, mean, chippy, dirty, competitive individual on the pond. He is a Kevin Dineen-style forward with rather less skating ability. He comes to play, and a night against him is not a party with cake and hats. Anybody who touches Yzerman gets a free conference with Gallant, who then—too often—ends up with a free misconduct penalty.

THE INTANGIBLES

A back is a back. You may feel better one day, be in traction the next. As training camp approached, Gallant was telling friends the back was stronger than ever.

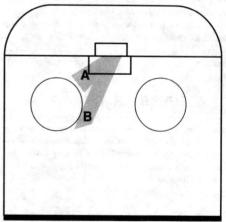

JOHAN GARPENLOV

Yrs. of NHL service: 1
Born: Stockholm, Sweden; March 21, 1968
Position: Left wing
Height: 5-11
Weight: 183
Uniform no.: 15
Shoots: Left

Career statistics:

GP	G	A	TP	PIM
71	18	21	39	18

1990-91 statistics:

GP	G	A	TP	+/-	PIM	PP	SH	GW	GT	S	PCT
71	18	21	39	-4	18	2	0	3	0	91	19.8

LAST SEASON

First season in NHL.

THE FINESSE GAME

Garpenlov has some strength on his skates, some balance, and uses it. When on his game, he can beat a man back into the play from the boards, get tripped to his knees but still control the puck and finish the play by regaining his footing and getting off a strong snap shot. He will take the puck to the net, North American-style.

When he heads to the net, however, more often than not it is with the intention of passing, rather than shooting. If Garpenlov can score once every five shots, as he did last season, imagine the dramatically greater impact if he watched some tapes of Tomas Sandstrom and commuted to the 150-shot neighborhood.

THE PHYSICAL GAME

Garpenlov certainly is not intimidated, but he is not a physical player. Overall physical strength affects the skating, puckhandling and shooting skills—all of which Garpenlov owns, all of which he needs to improve if he is to survive the rigors of 80-plus games.

THE INTANGIBLES

Good players are always around the puck, the puck is always around good players. The puck wasn't around Garpenlov enough last season, but he would not

be the first rookie import about whom that claim would be made, and he would not be the first Red Wing who had to adjust to the newness of the wing after spending lots of time in the middle.

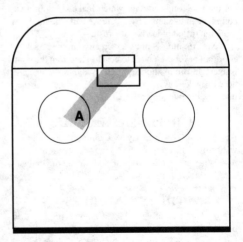

BRAD MCCRIMMON

Yrs. of NHL service: 12
Born: Dodsland, Sask., Canada; March 29, 1959
Position: Defenseman
Height: 5-11
Weight: 197
Uniform no.: 2
Shoots: Left

Career statistics:

GP	G	A	TP	PIM
890	68	269	337	1033

1990-91 statistics:

GP	G	A	TP	+/-	PIM	PP	SH	GW	GT	S	PCT
64	0	13	13	7	81	0	0	0	0	43	.0

LAST SEASON

Games played was NHL career low.

THE FINESSE GAME

If experience makes the best teacher, then McCrimmon has a graduate's degree. He understands his position and the game very well, is alert for every edge in body positioning and stick positioning. He makes a simple, direct and accurate first pass out of the zone and keeps the game extremely safe.

McCrimmon is not a puckhandler. He prefers to get the puck and move it, which makes him an ideal complement to an offensive defenseman who might be more interested in leading the rush.

McCrimmon is not very creative in the attacking zone, but never pretended to be. His shot from the point is average. But his hockey sense is above average and he will make the occasional unexpected pass or play that catches everyone off-guard.

every partner with whom he has been paired. Age is an issue; he is slowing down, giving up more ice than he would like. But he is a solid team leader; he wants to be pushed to be better—which is a high compliment for someone of his tenure.

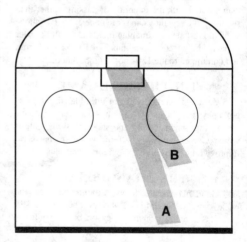

THE PHYSICAL GAME

Forwards have to pay McCrimmon's price if they want to win position in the corners or the front of the net. When the coast is clear, McCrimmon delivers some crunching crosschecks.

THE INTANGIBLES

A dedicated athlete, McCrimmon works hard in practice to perfect and maintain a no-frills game that has helped every team for which he has played—and

RANDY MCKAY

Yrs. of NHL service: 2
Born: Montreal, Que., Canada; January 25, 1967
Position: Right wing
Height: 6-1
Weight: 185
Uniform no.: 29
Shoots: Right

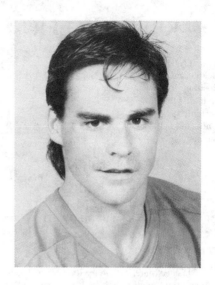

Career statistics:

GP	G	A	TP	PIM
83	4	13	17	234

1990-91 statistics:

GP	G	A	TP	+/-	PIM	PP	SH	GW	GT	S	PCT
47	1	7	8	-15	183	0	0	0	0	22	4.5

LAST SEASON

PIM and assist totals were a career high.

THE FINESSE GAME

All McKay's non-fighting skills are just average and his defensive game is below average. He has adequate speed, alright balance and agility; but he does not turn well and his upper body does not seem in synch with his lower body when McKay is skating on a straightaway. His arms stay very close to his body, which limits his stride and range.

The skating problem directly inhibits his hitting game, as by the time McKay gets there to hit somebody, his target has left the area. On offense, hand quickness is an issue even though he scored 29 one year in the minors. Defensively, there is work to be done.

THE PHYSICAL GAME

McKay's penalty minutes are more telling of his role. He is not a dirty player, but he goes to the net hard and he stands up for his teammates.

And he fights the heavyweights. He knows where to grab and where to hold.

THE INTANGIBLES

Desire would lead the list of McKay's intangibles. He wants to be a player, he works hard, tries to improve his ability.

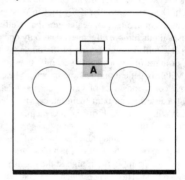

KEVIN MILLER

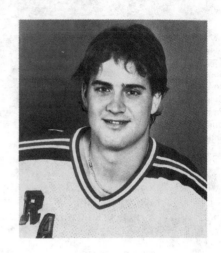

Yrs. of NHL service: 2
Born: Lansing, Mich., USA; September 2, 1965
Position: Right wing/center
Height: 5-10
Weight: 191
Uniform no.: 23
Shoots: Right

Career statistics:

GP	G	A	TP	PIM
114	25	38	63	71

1990-91 statistics:

GP	G	A	TP	+/-	PIM	PP	SH	GW	GT	S	PCT
74	22	28	50	-3	67	1	3	3	0	136	16.2

LAST SEASON

Obtained March 5 from the Rangers, with Dennis Vial and Jim Cummins, for Joe Kocur and Per Djoos.

THE FINESSE GAME

Miller has light feet and quick acceleration to breakaway speed: a stride or two and it's bye-bye. He always gains speed through the neutral zone so he can attack the blue line at top flight. Uses the same spin-o-rama his less-gifted brother Kelly tries in Washington, but makes a much tighter, neater turn than Kelly does and uses it much more effectively—as only one of his tricks. He will do it at the top of the circle, as Kelly does, or in traffic, which Kelly generally does not.

Miller is patient and lets the opponent beat himself. He commands a lot of space from most defensemen, because he can burn them either with speed or moves. When they back off, he lets them, then takes advantage of the room they concede.

He has good hands and can pick off passes by batting them out of the air and finish plays any number of ways, preferring to fire it high to the goalie's catching-glove side. Has a nice touch in tight, will fake forehand and go backhand.

To those assets, Miller adds good ice vision. He sees a teammate streaking to the net and gets the puck to him nicely with pass that is as hard as it needs to be.

THE PHYSICAL GAME

Though not a big player, Miller uses what size he has to play a rugged game. And he does have a mean streak. He will click out. He will fight. He will hit hard.

He will be confrontational. He will hack and crosscheck and elbow.

THE INTANGIBLES

Miller's talents are much more suited to center than right wing, but Red Wings are loaded there. His effectiveness will be limited on the flank, although it always is an advantage to have a right wing with a center's skills, shiftiness, speed and sense.

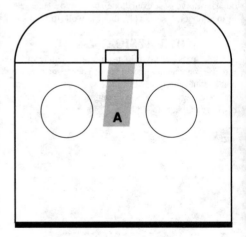

KEITH PRIMEAU

Yrs. of NHL service: 1
Born: Toronto, Ont., Canada; November 24, 1971
Position: Center
Height: 6-4
Weight: 220
Uniform no.: 55
Shoots: Left

Career statistics:

GP	G	A	TP	PIM
58	3	12	15	106

1990-91 statistics:

GP	G	A	TP	+/-	PIM	PP	SH	GW	GT	S	PCT
58	3	12	15	-12	106	0	0	1	0	33	9.1

LAST SEASON

First in NHL.

THE FINESSE GAME

Primeau is a strong skater over long distances, but his first three or four steps need work. Balance is not a problem, though; Primeau gets his drive from a powerful knee bend and a solid stride, which allow him to stickhandle around and through people. The drive, balance and size also help on faceoffs.

For so young a player, such a newcomer to NHL play, Primeau has relatively good hockey sense. He played out of position at left wing, which limited his options but also limited the amount of ground he had to cover, and regularly picked the proper passing target.

Though he played on the wing and spent much of his time as a grinder, Primeau retained his puck-handling ability and his precise passing skills. His shot was something of a downside; Primeau does a good job of driving wide, but has a slow release. He doesn't get the puck to the net quickly enough.

THE PHYSICAL GAME

Primeau's physical game matches up well with his size. He loves to hit and he plays the same size at home and on the road. He relishes one-on-one battles for the puck and wins his share

THE INTANGIBLES

After being a dominant player in junior hockey, Primeau spent his first pro season as a minnow swimming in a giant lake of much bigger fish. He survived by doing the simple things well and can be expected this year to show greater signs of matching the potential that caused him to be drafted third overall.

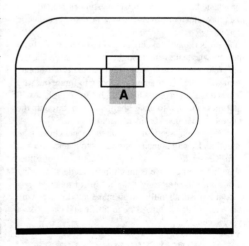

BOB PROBERT

Yrs. of NHL service: 6
Born: Windsor, Ont., Canada; June 5, 1965
Position: Right wing
Height: 6-3
Weight: 215
Uniform no.: 24
Shoots: Left

Career statistics:

GP	G	A	TP	PIM
265	73	82	155	1247

1990-91 statistics:

GP	G	A	TP	+/-	PIM	PP	SH	GW	GT	S	PCT
55	16	23	39	-3	315	4	0	3	0	88	18.2

LAST SEASON

Missed start of season due to league suspension, yet games played figure was three-season high and goals scored figure was second only to his 29 in 1987-88.

THE FINESSE GAME

Probert boasts fairly amazing finesse skills for so large and physical a player.

Not the least of those talents are the skating skills so many other big men fail to master. Probert has surprising agility, good balance and monstrous skating strength. He can make a tight turn in close quarters, even with the puck on his backhand. He owns some speed and has an improving, powerful first step toward the puck after a turnover or when the chase is on in the corners.

Probert unmistakably gets some extra room from players who fear even the slightest collision, and he has the good sense to use that extra room to his advantage. And while the defensemen are trying to figure out who has enough courage to challenge his rush, Probert will at times attempt to split them and go through the middle—he is that confident with the puck.

His hands seem more suited to punching than shooting. He will launch some pucks to the net quickly, Tim Kerr-style, but takes lots of time to get off other shooting attempts. He is much more facile at creating the chance than at converting it. Still, Probert does a nice job of stickhandling, can make good moves with the puck while wading through traffic and can make a very acceptable pass.

THE PHYSICAL GAME

Your team is much better off leaving him alone. You don't want him mad at you, unless there's an ambulance in the lobby, because he will break your face—or go down trying to. A lot of the league call him, "Mr. Probert, sir."

Yet this guy is not a gym rat, not a weightlifter, not an all-world physique.

THE INTANGIBLES

Probert has put a lot of effort into overcoming the obstacles his lifestyle placed in the way of his career. It is a battle he appears to be winning; he and the team should be commended for undertaking it. But it is not over, and it will never will be.

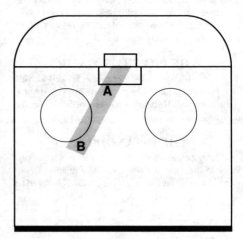

YVES RACINE

Yrs. of NHL service: 2
Born: Mutane, Que., Canada; February 7, 1969
Position: Defenseman
Height: 6-0
Weight: 185
Uniform no.: 33
Shoots: Left

Career statistics:

GP	G	A	TP	PIM
90	11	49	60	56

1990-91 statistics:

GP	G	A	TP	+/-	PIM	PP	SH	GW	GT	S	PCT
62	7	40	47	1	33	2	0	1	1	131	5.3

LAST SEASON

Joined team in December after being called up from Adirondack (AHL). All offensive figures were career highs.

THE FINESSE GAME

Racine is a nice skater, and pairs the foot skills with hand skills. He can take the puck off the boards and make a turn on his backhand. He can control the puck well, use his body to shield the puck and his arm to fend off a forechecker.

Racine uses his reach to sweep or poke pucks off opponents' sticks at the defensive blue line. If the check fails, Racine stays prepared to back up the effort with his body. If it succeeds, Racine is quick to start the transition game; he gets the puck moving quickly out of the zone.

Racine has the vision and the hand skills to do some of his best passing in the center zone—sending the puck cross-ice to someone breaking for a hole.

THE PHYSICAL GAME

A hard hitter, especially along the boards, Racine knows how to take the body and finish a check. He is not a heavyweight banger—at 185 pounds, he simply is not strong enough—but when he hits, people stay hit and they don't hurry back into the play.

THE INTANGIBLES

Time is on Racine's side. This will be only his second full season and HSR is a staunch believer in giving defensemen five years to fulfill their promise.

He needs to fill out, get stronger and cut down on the times when he overhandles or mishandles the puck under pressure. He is promising enough, though that the Red Wings gladly will live with those few mistakes.

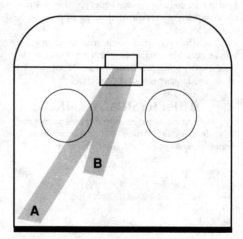

PAUL YSEBAERT

Yrs. of NHL service: 2
Born: Sarnia, Ont., Canada; May 15, 1966
Position: Left wing/center
Height: 6-1
Weight: 190
Uniform no.: 21
Shoots: Left

Career statistics:

GP	G	A	TP	PIM
72	20	27	47	22

1990-91 statistics:

GP	G	A	TP	+/-	PIM	PP	SH	GW	GT	S	PCT
62	19	21	40	-7	22	6	0	1	0	128	14.8

LAST SEASON

Obtained November 27, from New Jersey, for Lee Norwood. Games played and all offensive totals were career highs.

THE FINESSE GAME

Ysebaert's skating skills are somewhat surprising, as he utterly explodes to top speed with his first four steps off the mark. He complements the ready-set-go speed with some outside speed, which he uses at times to beat people wide.

Like the Rangers' Darren Turcotte, Ysebaert is useful at the point on the power play because of his acceleration. He is that much quicker to pucks cleared down the ice and in that much better position to deploy his sound defensive skills if there is a break by the shorthanded team.

Ysebaert's production stems from the short game, with an occasional blast from the wing thrown in. He has a scorer's touch, but from in close. He has a quick release and his shot is hard and accurate.

THE PHYSICAL GAME

Ysebaert has added considerable bulk to his upper body since joining Detroit, but will need more to handle the rigors of NHL life along the wall.

THE INTANGIBLES

Another of the centers who have become Wing wings, Ysebaert handled the adjustment easily, produced, and earned himself the job the Devils, in their finite wisdom, could not give him.

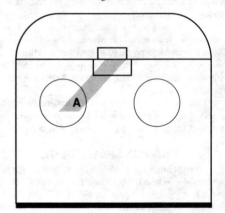

STEVE YZERMAN

Yrs. of NHL service: 8
Born: Cranbrook, B.C., Canada; May 9, 1965
Position: Center
Height: 5-11
Weight: 183
Uniform no.: 19
Shoots: Right

Career statistics:

GP	G	A	TP	PIM
594	342	458	800	368

1990-91 statistics:

GP	G	A	TP	+/-	PIM	PP	SH	GW	GT	S	PCT
80	51	57	108	-2	34	12	6	4	1	326	15.6

LAST SEASON

Led team in all offensive categories. Tied for second in NHL goal scoring, fifth in shorthanded goals, second in shots. Goal and assist totals were personal three-season lows.

THE FINESSE GAME

Exceptional skating skills open so much of Yzerman's game. His sharp stops and turns, his curls and pivots, his straightaway acceleration and corner shiftiness all are of premier caliber. He has superior balance and weight transfer and light feet but a powerful stride. He has very good speed with the puck, especially after he has skated through a turn. Yzerman complements these tools with wrist and upper-body strength plus a fine field of vision that allows him to make Magic Johnson-style, no-look passes.

Strength allows Yzerman to come out from either side of the goalie and attempt to stuff pucks. The forehand, coming out from the goalie's right, is his preference. But Yzerman's many wheely-deely, spin-o-rama cuts into and through the slot continually reaffirm his control of the puck on the backhand.

For a center, Yzerman doesn't spent a great deal of time in the middle. Without the puck, he gravitates to the left wing, keeping his forehand open and available should a pass come his way. While stickhandling, he will use the right-wing side of the ice. Many players use their bodies to shield the puck, but Yzerman goes that one better by driving into a confined space, such as the corner, and use the BOARDS to shield it. That way, he can only be attacked from his left side for the most part.

He will pull up short at the top of the right wing circle, lure the defenseman into a challenge, then sprint down the boards, stop short again in the corner and try to curl into the slot on his backhand—which causes the chaos Yzerman wants by luring the opposition out of position. If teammates are ready, there are goals to be had from his passes; if they aren't, Yzerman is always prepared to take one of his hard, heavy, accurate shots.

Yzerman overhandles at odd times, he isn't dominant on faceoffs—unless it's an emergency—and for someone who played just about every power play for 80 games, 12 power-play goals really isn't much. But he still is an "A+" forward in the NHL academy.

THE PHYSICAL GAME

Yzerman will bump. He will participate in a physical game. He thrives in traffic, especially with the puck, and does not lose a lot of strength matchups.

THE INTANGIBLES

He is the man who makes the Red Wings go. He is their spirit, their emblem player, their elite, electrifying element.

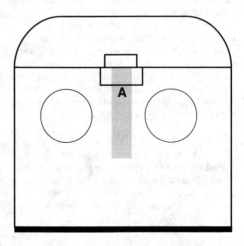

RICK ZOMBO

Yrs. of NHL service: 5
Born: Des Plaines, Ill., USA; May 8, 1963
Position: Defenseman
Height: 6-1
Weight: 195
Uniform no.: 4
Shoots: Right

Career statistics:

GP	G	A	TP	PIM
350	14	73	83	429

1990-91 statistics:

GP	G	A	TP	+/-	PIM	PP	SH	GW	GT	S	PCT
77	4	19	23	-2	57	0	0	0	0	68	5.9

LAST SEASON

Games-played tied for career high.

THE FINESSE GAME

Zombo is a rather unorthodox-looking skater, kind of herky-jerky, because he makes very short, sharp stops and tends to dart around the defensive zone. But he moves extremely well and at times is reminiscent of James Patrick for his "happy feet."

Zombo has a strong stride, good balance, excellent agility and lateral mobility. He really gets drive and power from his hips, which helps generate marvelous acceleration to top speed. Zombo uses skating range to great advantage while killing penalties—he's aggressive, challenges to the boards and well into the faceoff circles—and has tremendous confidence stepping up to a play because he has a better-than-even chance of using his speed to recover.

There are times he overdoes it and a pass goes right to the area he just left. And for a player who is more than able to do it, Zombo virtually never steps up into the rush, doesn't see the ice too well offensively and his production stats consistently underwhelm because of an only-average shot.

On defense, though, Zombo is much more than adequate. He understands the position. He doesn't get hypnotized by the puck, because he is continually alert, aware, keeping his head on a swivel to see who is where. He holds his position well. He'll block shots and he will start the transition game with a crisp pass, because Zombo always seems to know what he's going to do with the puck when he gets it.

THE PHYSICAL GAME

Zombo is a very aggressive penalty killer who will get involved with clearing the crease and tying up the man in front. At the corners and sideboards, he is more an eliminator than a crushing hitter. His one-on-one strength is suspect, but that can be improved.

THE INTANGIBLES

Zombo is a hustler who works every shift, plays like he wants to get the most out of himself, and from the red line back, he does just that. From the red line up to the attacking goal, though, Zombo remains a puzzle.

Aside from his skills, Zombo has perhaps the best hockey name since Bart Crashley. Zombo SOUNDS like a hockey player. He's a good one, who could be better.

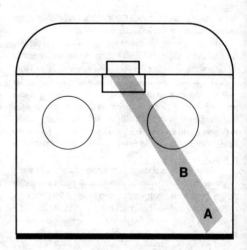

EDMONTON OILERS

GLENN ANDERSON

Yrs. of NHL service: 11
Born: Vancouver, B.C., Canada; October 2, 1960
Position: Right wing
Height: 6-1
Weight: 190
Uniform no.: 9
Shoots: Left

Career statistics:

GP	G	A	TP	PIM
828	413	483	896	771

1990-91 statistics:

GP	G	A	TP	+/-	PIM	PP	SH	GW	GT	S	PCT
74	24	31	55	-7	59	8	0	4	0	193	12.4

LAST SEASON

Second time in three years, also second time in his entire career, Anderson scored fewer than 30 goals. Reduced penalty minutes by 48.

THE FINESSE GAME

Anderson's skating game remains his premier asset. He is blindingly fast and able to makes plays while at top speed. Anderson still is among the best in the game at cutting in from his off-wing, driving to the net and making a play. His slap shot isn't bad, but more of his goals come on close-in moves, as Anderson's thoughts and hands are as quick as his feet.

He is versatile enough offensively; Anderson will create goals of his own, or will use his knowledge of how to get open to play off his linemates for scoring rushes.

A dependable defensive player, Anderson will not leave the zone early and think offense before the defensive job is done. He will hold his position in the zone and be there for the outlet pass when the defenseman has to rap it around the boards. And, of course, there isn't a soul he can't catch from behind.

THE PHYSICAL GAME

Anderson is a feisty player. After all the accomplishments, all the championships, a fire still burns inside him. He hits, he yaps. He absolutely will not take a backward step. Cross him, you'll pay.

THE INTANGIBLES

Anderson is one of the fine clutch scorers in team history. He comes up with the big play at the proper time and probably never gets enough credit for his level of play.

Anderson essentially is an unflappable individual. Not too many things bother him, but contract hassles last season may have been a distraction and a partial explanation for his 10-goal dropoff in scoring plus his dramatic reduction in penalty time.

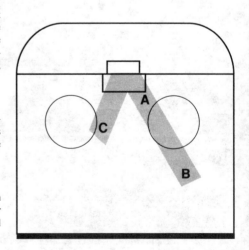

CRAIG BERUBE

Yrs. of NHL service: 3
Born: Calahoo, Alta., Canada; December 17, 1965
Position: Left wing
Height: 6-1
Weight: 205
Uniform no.: 17
Shoots: Left

Career statistics:

GP	G	A	TP	PIM
235	16	26	42	848

1990-91 statistics:

GP	G	A	TP	+/-	PIM	PP	SH	GW	GT	S	PCT
74	8	9	17	-6	293	0	0	0	0	46	17.4

LAST SEASON

Obtained from Philadelphia May 30 with Craig Fisher and Scott Mellanby for Dave Brown, Corey Foster and the rights to Jari Kurri. Kurri's rights were traded, with Jeff Chychrun, to Los Angeles for Steve Duchesne, Steve Kasper and a fourth-round draft choice in 1991.

THE FINESSE GAME

Berube is at his best as a straight-ahead skater, though his acceleration leaves plenty to be desired. He needs a lot of strides to reach top speed, and once he's there, even a slight change in direction can give him difficulty. Berube stops short well enough, but those first two or three steps going the other way—though improving—are in need of dramatic upgrade.

Though known more for his physical game, Berube can play the game with his gloves on. He remains within his limitations, knows better than to try beating goalies from long range. His goals are going to come from rebounds or turnovers, and certainly Berube has the muscle, and the balance, to remain upright in the slot traffic.

Berube knows where to go; the issue, again, is getting there. He is an asset in a dump-and-chase game; the sight of him bearing down on a defenseman can be imposing, indeed, and will cause a share of turnovers. The trouble starts when the defenseman has an extra second to make a move; too often Berube has forechecked too enthusiastically and then is tackling air as the defenseman moves past him.

THE PHYSICAL GAME

Of course, if he were a completely terrible skater, Berube would not be the effective fighter that he is. He has the balance to handle all the wrestling and tugging and shoving designed to throw an opponent off-balance. He has strength to go with his size, can throw them over and under when he gets his right hand free.

Berube also hits anyone he can reach and eagerly will do so.

THE INTANGIBLES

Berube made solid strides last season. He still fought constantly, of course, but also scored some nice goals, made some intelligent plays and did some good forechecking. Certainly, he remains a role player, and we all know what that role is; but there were a lot of nights last season when Berube was among his team's most effective players, so he cannot be dismissed as a thug-for-hire.

Berube wants to play, wants to win, and he needed a change of scenery. More good things can be expected if he isn't overwhelmed by playing in his home province. He is never going to combine his physical attributes with finesse skills to the level of a Bob Probert, but he is one of the very few players in the league who can win a fight yet not hurt the team at even strength.

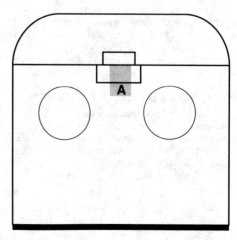

JEFF BEUKEBOOM

Yrs. of NHL service: 5
Born: Ajax, Ont., Canada; March 28, 1965
Position: Defenseman
Height: 6-4
Weight: 215
Uniform no.: 6
Shoots: Right

Career statistics:

GP	G	A	TP	PIM
266	12	52	64	655

1990-91 statistics:

GP	G	A	TP	+/-	PIM	PP	SH	GW	GT	S	PCT
67	3	7	10	6	150	0	0	0	0	48	6.3

LAST SEASON

PIM increased by 64. Goal total was three-season high.

THE FINESSE GAME

While it improved last season, Beukeboom's skating still is about what you would expect from a player his size. Though he is strong on his skates, skating is not a strong point in his game. On a straight-line basis, Beukeboom's skating is fine. His mobility is not bad, but he is a little on the slow side; to compensate, Beukeboom has done a lot of work to improve at angling players to bad ice. He still gets beaten to the outside occasionally, but far less so than earlier in his career.

Just as his reads are improving at both ends of the ice, Beukeboom is gaining confidence in carrying the puck. He knows where he is going to go with it and no longer hurries the plays as he did. Now, he waits that extra second or half-second and moves the puck at the correct time, to the correct person, with a good pass. He is gaining confidence with the puck and may carry it increasingly this season, which should provide the further improvement his passing game needs.

His shot from the point, when he really gets a hold of one, is heavy, hard and fairly accurate. Beukeboom also is smart at the point; if the slap shot is not an effective play, he simply will snap a shot to the net to set up a deflection or a rebound.

THE PHYSICAL GAME

Beukeboom has splendid size and strength for his position and uses it at every opportunity, which makes him extremely useful in defensive situations. He can make a solid open-ice hit and he will hurt people along the boards, where he takes them out hard and knocks them down when he can.

If his game is "on," Beukeboom can be dominant in his defensive zone. That is significant, as he often is matched against the opposition's most threatening offensive line. He can intimidate people with his size and strength, can crush them with a hit and use superb balance to remain perpendicular to the ice after it.

THE INTANGIBLES

Beukeboom improved significantly last season and his stock rose markedly during the playoffs. He played more and benefited from the experience, gaining confidence in a variety of pressure situations; every time he made the right play, the confidence increased.

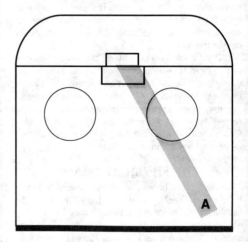

KELLY BUCHBERGER

Yrs. of NHL service: 3
Born: Langenburg, Sask., Canada; December 2, 1966
Position: Left wing
Height: 6-2
Weight: 210
Uniform no.: 16
Shoots: Left

Career statistics:

GP	G	A	TP	PIM
204	11	16	27	643

1990-91 statistics:

GP	G	A	TP	+/-	PIM	PP	SH	GW	GT	S	PCT
64	3	1	4	-6	160	0	0	2	0	54	5.6

LAST SEASON

PIM declined for third consecutive season.

THE FINESSE GAME

Buchberger still is working at putting the pieces together. He will work and work to win a puck in a corner, and generally will have the right idea about what to do with it next, but somehow will end up holding the puck too long to make the play work—basically wasting the effort he made in the first place.

On the back end of the play, Buchberger will get the occasional goal by hacking at a bouncing puck in front, but otherwise has no appreciable scoring skills. Though an enthusiastic puppy in the attacking zone, the puck-handling skills are not there yet and his shot is erratic enough that it sends members of both teams ducking for cover.

Buchberger's skating improved significantly last season, to the point where he has a fair amount of quickness, agility and strength on his skates.

THE PHYSICAL GAME

If the puck is shot into his corner, Buchberger will grind and battle for it as long and as ruggedly as is needed to win it. At times, it doesn't take long at all; defensemen look over their shoulder for him when Buchberger is the first man on the puck, and he forces a fair number of turnovers because he is a constant hitting threat.

He also is a constant punching threat. If you need somebody to fight for your team, Buchberger is your man.

THE INTANGIBLES

His instincts are coming along. The more he plays, the more he will come to grips with the complexities of forechecking. There must be defensemen who have nightmares about a forechecking line with Buchberger on the right side and Craig Berube on the left.

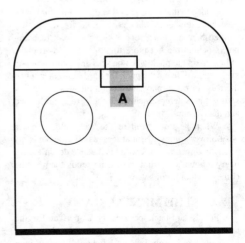

GRANT FUHR

Yrs. of NHL service: 10
Born: Spruce Grove, Alta., Canada;
September 28, 1962
Position: Goaltender
Height: 5-10
Weight: 186
Uniform no.: 31
Catches: Right

Career statistics:

GP	MINS	GA	SO	GAA	A	PIM
423	23910	1470	9	3.69	36	54

1990-91 statistics:

GP	MINS	GAA	W	L	T	SO	GA	S	SAPCT	PIM
13	778	3.01	6	4	3	1	39	380	.897	0

LAST SEASON

Returned February 18 from suspension for substance abuse and collected shutout in first game back, against New Jersey.

THE PHYSICAL GAME

Except for his well-chronicled five-hole problems and occasional trouble pushing away from the dinner table, there may be no more complete goalie in the game than Grant Fuhr. He is an exceptional skater with excellent balance, his reflexes are remarkable (he can kick out at full-windup shots from 10 feet), his feet are lightning-quick and he is strong with both gloves.

Added to that is his puck-handling skill, for which Fuhr probably does not get enough credit. He has worked hard at getting out of the net more, reaching pucks behind the net more to stop the hard-arounds. Fuhr can zip the puck when he sees an open teammate available, will leave the puck for his defensemen when there is no other play and communicates extremely well with his defensemen when their backs are turned and their vision is limited.

When he does drop to the ice, Fuhr recovers position very quickly. But at least as remarkable is his ability to direct the puck with his feet. He doesn't leave many rebounds in front, rather, he sends them to the corners, out of harm's way.

THE MENTAL GAME

Fuhr's laid-back personality is perfect for the pressures and rigors of his business. He has great confidence in his ability—as he should, having won virtually every significant recognition—and is able to take pressure off his teammates by accepting it on himself.

He is extremely tough when the game is on the line. He will never, ever, give up the goal that takes you out of the game, and dozens of times has made the saves that have kept his team in the game.

It bothered Fuhr to share ice time with Bill Ranford last season, and vice versa, but that steams from the competitive nature of each player. Fuhr wants to play every game.

THE INTANGIBLES

If you need a big save in a big game, no goalie in the NHL has a better track record for providing it than Grant Fuhr. He knows what it takes to win and provides it for his teammates.

MARTIN GELINAS

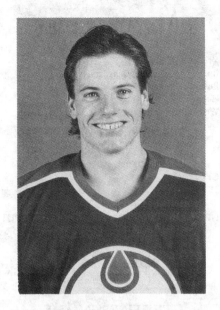

Yrs. of NHL service: 2
Born: Shawinigan, Que., Canada; June 5, 1970
Position: Left wing
Height: 5-11
Weight: 195
Uniform no.: 20
Shoots: Left

Career statistics:

GP	G	A	TP	PIM
125	38	30	68	64

1990-91 statistics:

GP	G	A	TP	+/-	PIM	PP	SH	GW	GT	S	PCT
73	20	20	40	-7	34	4	0	2	1	124	16.1

LAST SEASON

Goals increased by three, assists by 12 over prior season. Penalty minutes were career high. Plus-minus worsened by seven.

THE FINESSE GAME

Not a natural goal scorer, Gelinas spends more time muscling pucks into the net than finessing them in with pretty moves and plays. He is a stocky, strong player with enough speed to beat a defenseman wide, enough balance and power to push him toward the net. Once there, he can score on in-close moves, but also will plant himself in front for the occasional deflection or rebound goal.

Gelinas has hard-to-handle slap and wrist shots. He gets a lot of opportunities because of his speed, but does not finish especially well—owing, probably, to a lack of experience and a lack of variety in his attack. The give-and-go game would maximize his talents, but Gelinas is not one of its more proficient students; he makes the same move repeatedly, rather than throw a new wrinkle at a defenseman.

Still to be gained is a conviction that work on his defensive game will get him the puck quicker. If he comes farther back for it, he will be that much closer to it when people are looking to pass from the defensive zone; if he "hangs" well up ice, it becomes too difficult to reach him with the puck, so people look for other teammates.

THE PHYSICAL GAME

Thick through the upper body, Gelinas is not at all afraid of getting into the corners and grinding for the puck. Generally, his speed will get him there first; more than generally, because of his strength and his aggressiveness, he will come out of the corner with the puck. Gelinas has the power to run over or through people if his speed will not carry him past them.

THE INTANGIBLES

Gelinas is an energetic, determined player who wants to win and wants to succeed, but who still needs the polish only experience can provide.

Youthful enthusiasm carried him to prominence during the Oilers' winning run in the 1990 playoffs, but youthful inexperience cost him at times last season because he remained uncertain of which player to pick up during scrambles in his defensive zone. He didn't always know where to be, but that can be corrected.

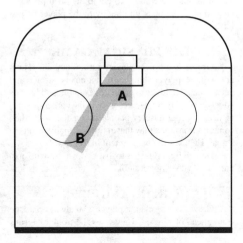

ADAM GRAVES

Yrs. of NHL service: 3
Born: Toronto, Ont., Canada; April 12, 1968
Position: Center
Height: 5-11
Weight: 185
Uniform no.: 12
Shoots: Left

Career statistics:

GP	G	A	TP	PIM
217	23	37	60	331

1990-91 statistics:

GP	G	A	TP	+/-	PIM	PP	SH	GW	GT	S	PCT
76	7	18	25	-21	127	2	0	1	0	126	5.6

LAST SEASON

Plus-minus declined by 26 goals. Assist total was career best.

THE FINESSE GAME

Speed is the name of Graves' game, as his hand skills—passing and shooting—lag behind the quickness, strength and power his foot skills provide.

Graves passes okay and shoots okay, but should score more, given the types of chances he creates off the forecheck. He is not confident one-on-one, again probably because his hands let him down at times. When he gets all of a puck, the shot is hard and heavy, but more of his goals are going to come off loose pucks and deflections.

On defense, Graves is still learning the game, is getting better at identifying the open man and getting to him. He remains vulnerable to youthful mistakes in his reading of the play, however; he will see an open man and leave his check to try to get to the open player—only to have the puck go directly to the player he just left.

THE PHYSICAL GAME

Graves is a power player, not a fancy one. He is not a large player, but he is extremely strong and determined. He loves to grind, loves to hit, and his hits knock people flying. Graves goes in the corners, cycles in deep, he outmuscles people along the wall, then comes in front for a play that at times actually results in a goal. He takes the punishment in front.

He will fight if he has to, backs down from no one, but Graves does not go looking for that sort of action.

THE INTANGIBLES

Graves is a worker, a player who always puts the team ahead of himself. He causes the trouble he runs into, though, by putting a tremendous amount of pressure on himself. After a super playoff, almost out of the blue, in 1990, Graves expected himself to take off from there and never look back—rather like trying to hit a three-run homer with only one man on base.

He probably will be a very good third-line center, though, if he can learn to relax and start getting some points. Teams want 50 or 60 points from their No. 3s, and barely half that won't cut it.

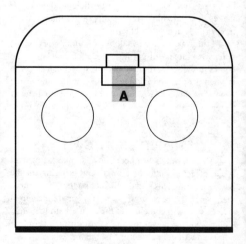

112

CHRIS JOSEPH

Yrs. of NHL service: 2
Born: Burnaby, B.C., Canada; October 10, 1969
Position: Defense
Height: 6-2
Weight: 210
Uniform no.: 2
Shoots: Right

Career statistics:

GP	G	A	TP	PIM
117	9	30	39	131

1990-91 statistics:

GP	G	A	TP	+/-	PIM	PP	SH	GW	GT	S	PCT
49	5	17	22	3	59	2	0	0	0	74	6.8

LAST SEASON

Totals for goals and games played were career highs.

THE FINESSE GAME

Joseph has solid skating skills forward and backward. He can skate and stickhandle with the puck or pass it out of the defensive zone. He joins the rush effectively because of his speed.

The offensive reads and offensive pace remain a rough edge. At times, he will hold the puck while a teammate is open, then force a pass after the player is checked. A lack of ice time will cause those problems in a player; you sit and sit, and know you don't want to make a mistake when you get out there—then you end up making a mistake precisely because you tried so hard to avoid it.

Still, Joseph has shown the ability to beat people in one-on-one meetings. He simply needs to learn when to force those matchups and when not to.

As a shooter, Joseph is maybe a bit above average, and that is a problem with the Oilers so desperate for a point man on their power play. He isn't going to overpower any goalie with his shot.

THE PHYSICAL GAME

Strength and aggressiveness are a problem. Joseph wouldn't hurt a fly, which doesn't make him a bad person but makes for difficulties in front of his defensive net when he should be knocking people down. He has trouble in traffic.

THE INTANGIBLES

The Oilers have been without an honest-to-goodness point man for the power play since Paul Coffey was traded. They have auditioned all kinds of people for the job and none has been overly successful. Joseph, who has most of the skills to fulfill the role, may get the next chance.

The unknown is whether he is ready for it, whether he wants it and whether he wants to use all his assets every night. Another question is whether now is the time to be placing so much responsibility on his shoulders. Not every defenseman is ready for those extra challenges at age 22; the position is challenging enough, especially with limited ice time.

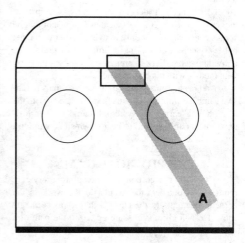

PETR KLIMA

Yrs. of NHL service: 6
Born: Chaomutov, Czechoslovakia;
December 23, 1964
Position: Left wing
Height: 6-0
Weight: 190
Uniform no.: 85
Shoots: Right

Career statistics:

GP	G	A	TP	PIM
426	194	149	343	333

1990-91 statistics:

GP	G	A	TP	+/-	PIM	PP	SH	GW	GT	S	PCT
70	40	28	68	24	113	7	1	5	0	204	19.6

LAST SEASON

Totals for goals and points were personal one-season bests. Plus-minus improved by 33 goals. Penalty minutes were career-high

THE FINESSE GAME

Klima has breathtaking finesse skills and super-star talent. He skates so well, is so agile and light on his feet to either side, it seems he barely is touching the ice. He accelerates to top speed in a flash, and that top speed is breakaway speed.

He has marvelous hands, quick and deft, and a panic point hours past that of most other players in his category. In close quarters, he will hold the puck and hold the puck and let defensemen dive and flop; he will let the goalie go down, get up and go down again before scoring.

Klima needn't depend on hands and in-tight moves for scoring. He's got a cannon of a shot that he sprays everywhere, not only to every corner of the net but every corner of the rink. Klima simply prefers the individual game, likes to embarrass defensemen—toy with them—with his one-on-one fakes.

And, as his plus-minus indicates, Klima's defensive game has improved. In his first full season with the team, Klima learned the system, became a better positional player and worked to bear down so he wouldn't get caught as often.

THE PHYSICAL GAME

This is not a cornerman. Except for very rare moments, Klima lets the grunts do the work in the corners, then cuts to the chase—the offensive magic show. He will eliminate, skate up ice in the path of a player whose team has the puck, will initiate a very occasional piece of body contact, but is more on the fringes of the fray until the puck squirts loose.

THE INTANGIBLES

Klima reads the play well and has a very good head for the game. His stomach for it is another matter; Klima gets satisfied with nice numbers, even if they aren't close to the great ones he would produce if he made maximum use of his skills.

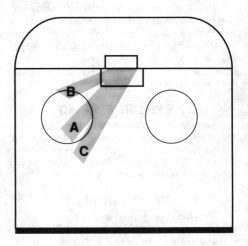

MARK LAMB

Yrs. of NHL service: 3
Born: Ponteix, Sask., Canada; August 3, 1964
Position: Center
Height: 5-9
Weight: 180
Uniform no.: 7
Shoots: Left

Career statistics:

GP	G	A	TP	PIM
140	20	33	53	89

1990-91 statistics:

GP	G	A	TP	+/-	PIM	PP	SH	GW	GT	S	PCT
37	4	8	12	-2	25	1	0	1	0	41	9.8

LAST SEASON

Games played and offensive totals experienced dramatic drop-off from prior season's career-high 58, 12-16-28. Plus-minus also decreased by 12 goals.

THE FINESSE GAME

Lamb has decent skating skills, with hands and instincts better suited to defense than the attack. He uses his quickness on the forecheck to harry a puck carrier and force the opponent to make a play quicker than he wants to. It isn't that Lamb is going to blast anybody with a check, more that he is going to swarm the opponent and force a turnover if the puck is not moved quickly.

Should that occur, Lamb tends to look for an open man rather than try to haul the mail in front. He will use the element of surprise to come in front occasionally, but prefers to make use of a nice passing touch.

Lamb can be counted on only for an occasional goal, but over the past two seasons, three of his 16 tallies have been game-winners.

THE PHYSICAL GAME

Lamb plays way bigger than his size, using anticipation and hockey sense to make up for an absence of stature. He is not at all afraid of being hit, and he is persistent; he refuses to take a larger player's "no" for an answer.

He does tend to get lost in a stampede of larger players, though, and his ice time must be handed out judiciously as a result.

THE INTANGIBLES

Intangibles are key components of Lamb's game. His job security always seems to be hanging by a fingernail, he always seems to be a half-step away from a seat in the press box or a spot in the waiver draft. Yet when push comes to shove and the crunch is on, there is Lamb, winning an important faceoff in the defensive zone.

Though his mental toughness and survival skills flag occasionally, they remain worthy of respect. At times, his precarious position weighs Lamb's spirits down; yet he tends to make the most of his time in the lineup.

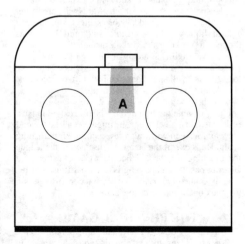

KEVIN LOWE

Yrs. of NHL service: 12
Born: Lachute, Que., Canada; April 15, 1959
Position: Defenseman
Height: 6-2
Weight: 195
Uniform no.: 4
Shoots: Left

Career statistics:

GP	G	A	TP	PIM
911	71	288	359	1057

1990-91 statistics:

GP	G	A	TP	+/-	PIM	PP	SH	GW	GT	S	PCT
73	3	13	16	-9	113	0	0	0	0	51	5.9

LAST SEASON

Goal total was five-season low. Assist and point totals were career lows. Plus-minus declined by 27 goals.

THE FINESSE GAME

Lowe is to the Campbell Conference what Buffalo's Mike Ramsey is to the Wales Conference—the steady, experienced, shot-blocking, all-defense defenseman who loves the game and loves to play it. Lowe also is an expert penalty killer, the type who can be trusted when two teammates are in the box because of his smarts and his ability to read the situation.

On defense, Lowe's stick is his best friend and he uses it intelligently to expand his range; it is a hedge against a lack of blazing speed. One of his favorite plays is to dive on his belly, the stick fully extended, to take away the pass—and part of the shot—on two-on-Lowe breaks. He is always prepared to use the poke check or the sweep check, and also is expert at extending the stick against opposing forwards who are trying to beat him to the outside. Those skaters who succeed against him will fake a shot, wait until Lowe has dropped to his knees, then skate around him.

Lowe's agility is an under-rated part of his game. He turns very well, very smoothly, and does not take long to reach full speed once he has shifted directions. His mobility laterally is not bad at all.

As his point totals indicate, Lowe's shot from the point is not what got him into the NHL. He will make a rush or two in a given game, he might even beat the odd player wide, then will wait a few games before rushing again. He is one of the better defensemen in the league for pinching up the sideboards to block attempted clearing passes. His passing is not what it used to be, but it is eminently serviceable when it comes to getting the puck out of the defensive zone.

THE PHYSICAL GAME

In Lowe's case, the physical game pertains to the bruises on his legs, the casts on his hands, the zippers in his face from his commitment to defense and whatever that may entail. He rubs people out along the boards and in front, but is not by any means a punishing hitter.

It simply is not his nature to hurt; he doesn't have to prove anything to anyone about his physical prowess. He plays a thoroughly efficient game, but respects his fellow athletes and that respect is returned unanimously by the rest of the league. People do not get stupid with Kevin Lowe.

THE INTANGIBLES

Kevin Lowe has given so much to his team. He has thrown his body in front of a million shots, has played despite severe pain, has been the ultimate leader, the keeper of the team's spirit. If Messier is the emblem Oiler for the offense, Lowe unmistakably is the emblem for the defense. He is selfless, relentlessly positive, a champion. His number belongs on the Northlands Coliseum roof when his playing days are done.

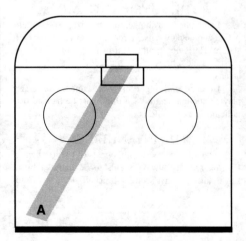

CRAIG MACTAVISH

Yrs. of NHL service: 10
Born: London, Ont., Canada; August 15, 1958
Position: Center
Height: 6-1
Weight: 195
Uniform no.: 14
Shoots: Left

Career statistics:

GP	G	A	TP	PIM
690	161	194	355	466

1990-91 statistics:

GP	G	A	TP	+/-	PIM	PP	SH	GW	GT	S	PCT
80	17	15	32	-1	76	2	6	1	0	113	15.0

LAST SEASON

Second time in six seasons MacTavish failed to score at least 20 goals. Assist total was NHL full-season career low. Plus-minus worsened by 14 goals.

THE FINESSE GAME

Craig MacTavish is the player you depend on in the tough defensive situations—the key you put out for the faceoff in your defensive zone with 30 seconds left in the period, the person you count on to be in the proper position and make the proper play.

In penalty killing situations (he is among the best in the league), MacTavish reads the play extremely well and virtually never is caught out of position. He doesn't quite have the speed to be darting all over the ice, but his sense of anticipation is strong, as is his discipline.

Yet from this defensive mindset springs some excellent offensive instincts, supported largely by a strong skating stride and rather surprising agility. He can score spectacular goals because of his ability to deke. He twists and turns quickly and still manages to control the puck, and some of his goals come at critical stages of the game.

One downside: he tends to stickhandle with his head down, which brings him up short when it comes to spotting other teammates and getting the puck to them.

THE PHYSICAL GAME

MacTavish always is there for his teammates when things get rude, though his truly scrappy days are well behind him. His bumps and shoves come more in the corners and along the boards, where he mucks for the puck. MacTavish also stakes out his territory in the scoring area between the faceoff circles, and does a good job of gaining position on defensemen in front.

THE INTANGIBLES

Two items that are the first to "go," the legs and the desire, have not gone yet on Craig MacTavish. He has not lost a step, he is in great condition and he loves to play. MacTavish still wants to pay the price, and that attitude can be contagious. He is very well-liked by his teammates.

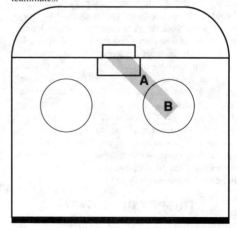

SCOTT MELLANBY

Yrs. of NHL service: 5
Born: Montreal, Que., Canada; June 11, 1966
Position: Right wing
Height: 6-1
Weight: 205
Uniform no.:
Shoots: Right

Career statistics:

GP	G	A	TP	PIM
355	83	114	197	694

1990-91 statistics:

GP	G	A	TP	+/-	PIM	PP	SH	GW	GT	S	PCT
74	20	21	41	8	155	5	0	6	0	165	12.1

LAST SEASON

Obtained from Philadelphia May 30 with Craig Fisher and Craig Berube for Dave Brown, Corey Foster and the rights to Jari Kurri. Kurri's rights were traded, with Jeff Chychrun, to Los Angeles for Steve Duchesne, Steve Kasper and a fourth-round draft choice in 1991.

THE FINESSE GAME

Mellanby is a grinder with a fine scoring touch who has the potential to produce 30-35 goals. Hands are the least of Mellanby's worries. He can be fine enough to score from in-close or strong enough to score from the top of the circles.

As a skater, he is something of a workman, so getting into position to score is more difficult than it should be. And Mellanby falls somewhat short in imagination away from the puck—one of the last lessons most pros learn and perhaps the most difficult. He needs to get to the holes quicker and create a few of his own if that scoring potential is going to be fulfilled.

Foot skills are limited to straight-ahead power; this player does not have the agility yet to cut inside people or dart outside people and sprint to the net. Mellanby will get to a spot when he gets to it, which also cuts into his usefulness as a forechecker; to forecheck, he has to get there and turn the puck over, not watch forlornly—or put his head down and try to catch up—when the puck has passed him in the other direction because he got there late.

THE PHYSICAL GAME

Limited areas and limited responsibilities are more suited to his game, which is why Mellanby does some of his best work in the confined areas along the boards and in the corners. There, the game slows to a crawl more suited to his speed, and there he can scrum for the puck—using the strength in his upper and lower body to significant advantage.

Mellanby will throw his shoulder into people, will reveal a mean streak and will fight if things sink to that

THE INTANGIBLES

There were people in the Flyers' organization who projected Mellanby as a better player than Rick Tocchet when both were in the infant stages of their careers. That projection so far has proven monstrously inaccurate.

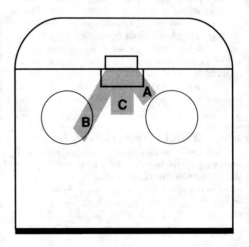

MARK MESSIER

Yrs. of NHL service: 12
Born: Edmonton, Alta., Canada; January 18, 1961
Position: Center
Height: 6-1
Weight: 210
Uniform no.: 11
Shoots: Left

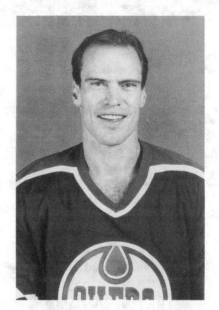

Career statistics:

GP	G	A	TP	PIM
851	392	641	1033	1122

1990-91 statistics:

GP	G	A	TP	+/-	PIM	PP	SH	GW	GT	S	PCT
53	12	51	63	15	34	3	1	2	0	109	11.0

LAST SEASON

Missed large portion of schedule due to knee injury and chipped bone in thumb. Games played was an NHL career low. Goal total tied career low of his rookie season. Assist total was six-season low.

THE FINESSE GAME

So big, so strong, so fast, so much of a threat. Come up with three ways to stop him, he'll find a fourth way to beat you with a big hit, a big goal, a big play, a new level of speed with or without the puck.

Massive physical strength energizes his game from head to toe. Messier has tremendous leg strength, which fuels his speed and balance and power, qualities which allow him to hold off a defender with one hand and pass the puck with the other. He has granite for an upper body, which makes him an intimidating, bruising hitter and also puts the snap in a superior snap shot, which he uses with exceptional accuracy and which can overpower goalies because he gets it away so quickly. Hand-eye coordination make him a dominant competitor on faceoffs, though a chipped thumb hampered him in that area late last season.

Good vision of the ice and fine anticipation help Messier make decisions quickly, experience helps him make the right choice a high percentage of the time. He'll lure a defender to him, then hook a pass to an unchecked teammate; the mere threat of that happening also buys Messier extra time and space, so he can keep the puck and make a one-on-one play if he wants.

THE PHYSICAL GAME

Messier is a power player, a power forward. He hits shoulder-to-shoulder, shoulder-to-chest and people lose their balance or their footing or both and the puck comes loose. Then Messier, who virtually never goes down, claims the disc and looks up immediately. He is the definition of a heads-up player. From deep in the zone, in the corners or behind the net, he will look first to bring the puck in front, and clearly is strong enough to do it.

In fact, he is more than strong enough to bury you in any physical aspect. He will make the whopping hit, he'll fight, slash or simply run you over—while he has the puck or when he is going after it.

THE INTANGIBLES

Injuries left Messier unable to dictate terms as much as he liked last season. He is 30 years old and he has played a staggering amount of pressure hockey, demanding of himself every molecule of power and touch. You wonder how much water is left in the well; so will the other GMs, who need to know if Messier can give them back what they will have to pay to obtain his leadership, his commanding presence.

He remains Edmonton's emblem forward—the one who puts fear in people, the one who comes through in the important games. His desire to win is no less strong; his ability to carry a team through 100 games again is a question he will be challenged to answer.

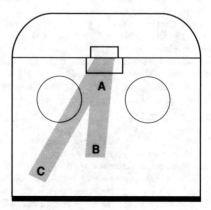

CRAIG MUNI

Yrs. of NHL service: 5
Born: Toronto, Ont., Canada; July 19, 1962
Position: Defenseman
Height: 6-3
Weight: 200
Uniform no.: 28
Shoots: Left

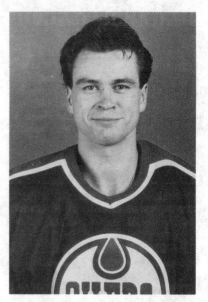

Career statistics:

GP	G	A	TP	PIM
386	22	73	95	397

1990-91 statistics:

GP	G	A	TP	+/-	PIM	PP	SH	GW	GT	S	PCT
76	1	9	10	10	77	0	0	0	0	47	2.1

LAST SEASON

Totals for goals, assists and points all were full-season NHL lows. Plus-minus declined by 12 goals.

THE FINESSE GAME

Muni plays an exemplary defensive game and is a player his coach can use with confidence in any defensive situation. He very seldom gets beaten one-on-one, he kills penalties well and can be trusted when his team is two players short. Muni knows which player to take after a defensive-zone faceoff, and can be matched any night against the opposition's top offensive line.

His defensive game is as solid as his finesse game is weak. He is not much of a skater. Some players simply do not have a good stride and simply never will, and Muni seems to be one of those players. His turns from forward to backward skating are average, his mobility is average and, laterally, he is not going to get beat wide if he really works. But straight-ahead, well, he is not going to catch anyone from behind.

Muni does not handle the puck well; his passing is only average, but it is better than his skating, so Muni tends to pass the puck out of the defensive zone. His shots hit a lot more shin guards than goalies because he takes so long to launch, which may be the reason Muni often passes up the shot entirely; if there is no clear shooting chance, he will just drill the puck around the boards to a forward behind the net. In fairness, he plays the off-side, which makes it difficult to tee up the forehand and leaves available the threat that the shot will be blocked.

Muni does have a long reach, which he uses to advantage—especially when standing up to challenges at the defensive blue line.

THE PHYSICAL GAME

Muni hurts people with his hits and may be the most controversial defenseman in the NHL because of open-ice hip checks that have blown out some fairly famous opposing legs. The Kings' Tomas Sandstrom was one victim in the playoffs last spring, and Bob Kudelski went out in the same series. Whether the check is legal or not, the mere threat of it serves a significant purpose: players keep their heads up when Muni is lurking on the ice like some crocodile on a shoreline, ready to feed on a forward. In the corners, he is more a take-out guy than a blaster.

Muni also plays very strong in front of his net and along the boards and does not hesitate to block shots. He times the blocks well; he does not drop too soon.

THE INTANGIBLES

Last season may have been a reputation season for Muni. He became notorious because of those people he sent to the hospital. Hey—there are only so many ways of gaining attention when you're a defensive defenseman who, though solidly efficient, still tends to fade into the background. It's a lot easier to negotiate a contract when you're known for SOMETHING.

JOE MURPHY

Yrs. of NHL service: 4
Born: London, Ont., Canada; October 16, 1967
Position: Right wing
Height: 6-1
Weight: 190
Uniform no.: 8
Shoots: Left

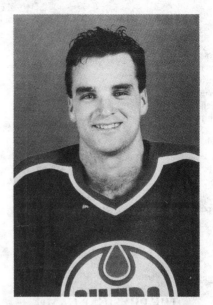

Career statistics:

GP	G	A	TP	PIM
232	48	71	119	162

1990-91 statistics:

GP	G	A	TP	+/-	PIM	PP	SH	GW	GT	S	PCT
80	27	35	62	2	34	4	1	4	1	141	19.1

LAST SEASON

All offensive totals surpassed prior career totals.

THE FINESSE GAME

Agility, balance and quickness to either side provide confidence in the moves that set up Murphy's scoring plays.

Murphy has fine speed (with and without the puck), a good passing touch and a very effective wrist shot. He is beginning to use those weapons on a more regular basis—and to fulfill the goal-scoring potential that was seen in him. Murphy complements the wrist shot with a strong slap shot, which he unloads quickly and which arrives at the net with speed and power.

The overall speed of his finesse game improved last season and his numbers improved as a direct result.

THE PHYSICAL GAME

Murphy's speed also is an asset for forechecking and he is aggressive in his pursuit of the puck. He will grind on occasion, will win a corner, but is more of a bumper than a banger.

Murphy has a mean streak when things get nasty, but he keeps it well hidden.

THE INTANGIBLES

Murphy is maturing, making forward strides now, is becoming more of the player people predicted he would be. All the pressure and adversity at the start of his career seems to have helped forge a mental toughness, and playing for such a mentally-tough team may have helped, as well.

The next step is consistency. Last season was the first in which Murphy played all 80 games and he had some difficulty focusing on so long a campaign. He disappeared for certain stretches of the schedule, then resurfaced, went from the being one of his team's best players in a given game to being a non-factor in the next.

The skills are there, though. Murphy will be as good as he wants to be.

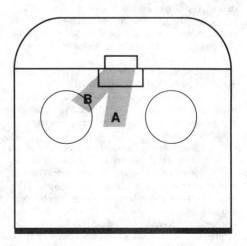

BILL RANFORD

Yrs. of NHL service: 5
Born: Brandon, Man., Canada; December 14, 1966
Position: Goaltender
Height: 5-10
Weight: 170
Uniform no.: 30
Catches: Left

Career statistics:

GP	MINS	GA	SO	GAA	A	PIM
196	10830	585	5	3.24	9	34

1990-91 statistics:

GP	MINS	GAA	W	L	T	SO	GA	S	SAPCT	PIM
60	3415	3.20	27	27	3	0	182	1705	.893	6

LAST SEASON

Games played and minutes played were career highs, as were victories and decisions.

THE PHYSICAL GAME

Ranford belongs high on the list of elite NHL goalies because he does well at so many of the important functions. He skates well, so he stays on his feet nicely while moving across the slot with a shooter. He does a good job of keeping the five-hole between his knees closed, keeping that vulnerable area protected with his stick while moving with a puckhandler.

Excellent balance keeps him on his feet as much as possible, but when he drops to his knees or makes a kick save to either side, Ranford has excellent leg strength which pushes him right back up into his stance. He recovers extremely well; the few times he buys a first fake, Ranford can regain enough position to challenge the second fake. He does not give up; the play is not over unless he has controlled the puck or it's in the net.

Ranford plays a confident, aggressive style and is out on the curved rim of his crease—at minimum—to reduce the shooting angle. Quick and compact in his movements, Ranford always is coiled and ready to explode toward a shot. His catching glove is extremely quick, as are his feet.

There are four weaknesses though. Sometimes, he loses track of where the net is. Sometimes, he has trouble controlling his rebounds. Sometimes, he gets tired of staying in his stance, waiting for a shot. The seat of his pants goes too far backward, his shoulders and stick lean too far forward, and Ranford can't move in time on the low shots. Ranford also has a nervous habit of tapping his catch glove on his blocking glove while taking short steps side to side; this lifts his stick off the ice for a fraction of a second and leaves him vulnerable between the skates.

THE MENTAL GAME

Ranford is very well focused. When he steps onto the ice, he is ready to play to win. His work ethic is exceptional; Ranford may not bark or beg, but he works like a dog at practice.

He is a competitor. He wants to play, wants to win and is doing a better job of recovering from the bad goal or bad game.

THE INTANGIBLES

Ranford is a player who responds extremely well to adversity. When the going gets tough, etc., etc. The team has 100 percent confidence in him.

ANATOLI SEMENOV

Yrs. of NHL service: 1
Born: Moscow, Soviet Union; March 5, 1962
Position: Center/left wing
Height: 6-2
Weight: 190
Uniform no.: 19
Shoots: Left

Career statistics:

GP	G	A	TP	PIM
57	15	16	31	26

1990-91 statistics:

GP	G	A	TP	+/-	PIM	PP	SH	GW	GT	S	PCT
57	15	16	31	17	26	3	1	1	0	101	14.9

LAST SEASON

First in NHL.

THE FINESSE GAME

This is a highly-skilled idividual.

Semenov passes extremely well, sending out those big, fat, juicy "saucer" passes to open ice and allowing a teammate to skate into them with speed. Semenov reads the play well and has an excellent shot.

He also has a vast assortment of moves and boasts the marvelous agility to make them thanks to the strong skating stride and balance characteristic of his country's training.

Semenov adds to those qualities a good sense of anticipation on defense and a reasonable dose of killer instinct/finishing instinct on offense. He likes to beat people one-on-one with speed, then he drives right to the net for a better scoring opportunity before he shoots.

THE PHYSICAL GAME

Semenov plays well in traffic, goes to the corners and battles. He takes the bumps and gives one of his own every once in a while. He is fairly strong, but he is not a physical player; a few more pounds of muscle would not be the worst thing to happen to him.

THE INTANGIBLES

Semenov had a little trouble with his first 80-game season with new teammates and a new system and a new language and a new league. He might be expected to rebound in his second NHL season, with his greater familiarity of the league and his surroundings, but hockey players seem prone to second-year slumps.

It would not be too great a shock to see him on right wing this year, as he probably plays that side better than the left side and it would open his shooting angles coming in off the wing.

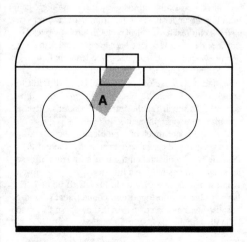

CRAIG SIMPSON

Yrs. of NHL service: 6
Born: London, Ont., Canada; February 15, 1967
Position: Left wing
Height: 6-2
Weight: 195
Uniform no.: 18
Shoots: Right

Career statistics:

GP	G	A	TP	PIM
449	187	176	363	509

1990-91 statistics:

GP	G	A	TP	+/-	PIM	PP	SH	GW	GT	S	PCT
75	30	27	57	-8	66	15	0	5	0	143	21.0

LAST SEASON

Point total was lowest in his three-plus seasons with Oilers. Reduced penalty minute total by 111. Goal total was second on team to Petr Klima's 40.

THE FINESSE GAME

Simpson is a scorer, not a skater. He has no speed to the outside; he doesn't carry the puck much, doesn't go in the corners to win the puck much. But when it's hopping around in the slot or the goalmouth, when there are missiles headed goalward from the point, Simpson puts them in the red rectangle, and his teammates know that, depend on it.

He very rarely shoots from more than 20 feet, but he can be devastating in his chosen scoring area, can fire the puck under the crossbar from in tight. Simpson also uses his reach to control bouncing, rolling pucks in traffic and is an able passer. He can get the puck to open people when defensemen are double-teaming him.

Simpson gets his feet wide apart when camping in front and makes use of his balance. He is difficult to knock down; when he ends up on his belly, it is generally as much for the referee's benefit as it is a compliment to his opponent's strength.

Range is not much of a problem in the attacking zone. He gets to the scoring area and stays there. But in the defensive zone, and on the transition from offense to defense, things happen a little too quickly. Simpson is not much of an acceleration player, so he ends up lagging behind on opposing counter-attacks more because he cannot keep up than that he doesn't want to keep up with the play.

THE PHYSICAL GAME

Simpson certainly takes the punishment in front of the net. He goes into traffic and willingly makes himself a candidate to get splattered with a crosscheck in order to maintain position for a rebound or a deflection.

Simpson's acceptance of the contact gets the Oilers a lot of power plays, and so does his assortment of theatrical dives. Simpson also is an annoying opponent, to the point of being obnoxious; something about his yapping makes people want to—like to—punch him, which gains more power plays.

THE INTANGIBLES

Simpson loves to play, has a great will to win and he plays a fascinating role on his team. To look at him off the ice, Simpson appears more of a sniper than a mud-wrestler who wades through the slop in front of the net and pays so high a price for his goals. He looks like a guy who would score on a shot off the rush, not a guy on the receiving end of the punishment. Few scorers pay as high a price for 30-goal seasons as Simpson.

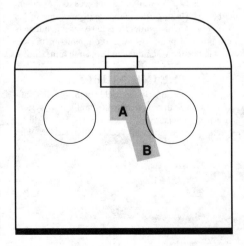

GEOFF SMITH

Yrs. of NHL service: 2
Born: Edmonton, Alta., Canada; March 7, 1969
Position: Defenseman
Height: 6-3
Weight: 200
Uniform no.: 25
Shoots: Left

Career statistics:

GP	G	A	TP	PIM
133	5	23	28	107

1990-91 statistics:

GP	G	A	TP	+/-	PIM	PP	SH	GW	GT	S	PCT
59	1	12	13	13	55	0	0	0	0	66	1.5

LAST SEASON

Assist total was career high. Missed playing time due to bad back.

THE FINESSE GAME

Geoff Smith may be the best skater on the Oilers, which is quite a claim as long as Mark Messier wears blue and orange. Smith has light feet, turns extremely well, has nice lateral movement and virtually never is beaten to the outside as a result. He also is exceptionally quick backward.

Smith teams those quick feet with good hands. He is skilled at carrying the puck and finding the open man with a pass while on the move. He can beat a player one-on-one if he gets the room; and if he tried it more, Smith probably would gain confidence in those endeavors. Once he does get past an opponent, Smith generally makes a smart play or takes a shot at the net, though his slap shot is weak.

Confidence may also be an issue in the pinching game. Though he has the wheels to recover if the puck squirts past him, Smith is not aggressive in his thinking about that play. Likewise, Smith foresakes a few passes too many, seemingly for fear they will be intercepted—though, again, he is quick enough to recover. Sometimes, he simply will air-mail a turnover to the net, just to get the puck deeper, when his skills could support a more daring play.

THE PHYSICAL GAME

Smith can take out a man and not get in trouble, but generally, he lacks aggressiveness—possibly because he lacks the upper-body strength that would help his physical play and also probably would help his shot. He does not use his size to advantage.

THE INTANGIBLES

Last season may have witnessed Smith's second-year blahs; this season should witness Smith's stride toward reaching his potential. He has a little more experience and he has the skills to be a good, sound, offensive defenseman in the NHL—if he hikes up the assertiveness.

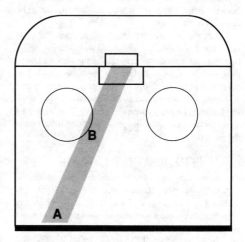

STEVE SMITH

Yrs. of NHL service: 6
Born: Glasgow, Scotland; April 30, 1963
Position: Defenseman
Height: 6-4
Weight: 215
Uniform no.: 5
Shoots: Left

Career statistics:

GP	G	A	TP	PIM
385	46	172	218	1080

1990-91 statistics:

GP	G	A	TP	+/-	PIM	PP	SH	GW	GT	S	PCT
77	13	41	54	14	193	4	0	2	0	114	11.4

LAST SEASON

Goal total was career high, assist total was within two of career high (1987-88), point total within one of career high, set same season. Penalty minutes increased for third consecutive season.

THE FINESSE GAME

Big men are not expected to skate as well as Smith does. He has light feet and a smooth stride, is agile enough to turn well to either side and use his whopping reach to advantage as players test him to the outside. Smith also can handle the inside move with a quick crossover that leaves the puck carrier very few options.

On offense, Smith endures some big-man struggles, as offense often is the last aspect defensemen master. Though an excellent skater, he does everything at the same speed. Though he has a very strong shot from the point, Smith often takes too long to fire, so he hits a lot of shinguards.

And though he is a smart player, he doesn't always see a play beyond burying his head and shooting, when he would have more success faking the shot and stepping past his check. In fairness, because Smith is a defensive player with offensive talents, he does sacrifice some offensive chances for defensive responsibility; knowing he hasn't won the gamble if he fakes past a guy and makes a play but gets caught on transition if the puck turns over.

THE PHYSICAL GAME

Smith has exceptional size and uses it intelligently. In the playoffs two seasons ago, Smith was matched against Boston's Cam Neely and very clearly won the matchup against one of the league's premier power forwards.

In the corners, all Smith has to do is lean on a player to nullify him. In front of the net, Smith raises the level of his physical play and is almost always as menacing a hitter as he could be.

THE INTANGIBLES

This is the time for Steve Smith to be moving toward that next step up from very good to excellent, and quickness—mental, as well as physical—will determine whether he makes that step. The consistency must emerge and the confidence must double, along with the eagerness to accept responsibility for performances as big as his body.

That is a tremendous amount to ask over 80 games plus playoffs, but it is within Smith's capabilities to accept the challenges.

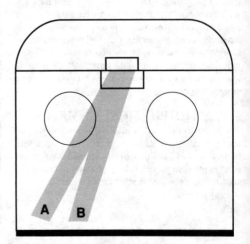

ESA TIKKANEN

Yrs. of NHL service: 6
Born: Helsinki, Finland; January 25, 1965
Position: Left wing
Height: 6-1
Weight: 200
Uniform no.: 10
Shoots: Left

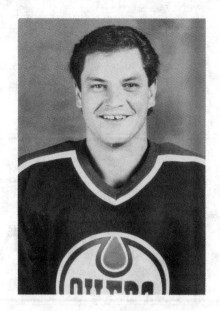

Career statistics:

GP	G	A	TP	PIM
416	152	223	375	639

1990-91 statistics:

GP	G	A	TP	+/-	PIM	PP	SH	GW	GT	S	PCT
79	27	42	69	22	85	3	2	6	0	235	11.5

LAST SEASON

Plus-minus was second best on team. Goal total dropped three from prior season, assist total jumped nine.

THE FINESSE GAME

Gifted with exceptional speed and skating agility that allows him to change direction in an eyeblink, Tikkanen also has the hockey smarts, anticipation and vision of the ice to change his mental direction as well. Accordingly, he can run a power play nicely from the right point and can help create scoring plays with extremely efficient passes.

Extensively skilled also in the defensive aspect, Tikkanen will stick to an opposing forward as though stitched to the guy's shoelaces. Any star rival forward better be prepared to carry 200 extra pounds all night when playing against one of the league's truly effective checking forwards, an annual Selke Trophy candidate.

Tikkanen has the physical strength to take a faceoff, tie up the opposing center and kick the puck to the point. He has the touch and finishing skills—a steel-hard slap shot, released quick as a rocket—to outscore the people he has been assigned to check; and he does so on a regular basis. The shot is supplemented by good in-tight moves for an overall package with very few weaknesses.

THE PHYSICAL GAME

Tikkanen can evoke anger from even the most passive opponent. He has a face that begs to be punched, and he all but sticks out his chin and dares you to do it. Of course if you swing at him, he'll be down and writhing before the punch lands, and you'll be in the penalty box or the dressing room—if not this time, then the next time. He'll keep trying until he has gotten you to do something stupid.

But when it comes down to pure, physical hockey, Tikkanen handles himself extremely well. He will hit and accept being hit, he will go in the corner. He will throw himself in front of a shot.

THE INTANGIBLES

Tikkanen is a character player—a big-game, big-play player who loves pressure and wants the puck when the games is on the line. An extremely calculating player, Tikkanen always knows what he's doing and why he's doing it. He is Edmonton's Most Valuable Pest.

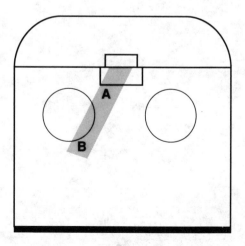

HARTFORD
WHALERS

MIKAEL ANDERSSON

Yrs. of NHL service: 5
Born: Malmo, Sweden; May 10, 1966
Position: Center
Height: 5-11
Weight: 185
Uniform no.: 34
Shoots: left

Career statistics:

GP	G	A	TP	PIM
190	21	64	85	32

1990-91 statistics:

GP	G	A	TP	+/-	PIM	PP	SH	GW	GT	S	PCT
41	4	7	11	0	8	0	0	0	0	57	7.0

LAST SEASON

Games played and all point totals two-season lows.

THE FINESSE GAME

Andersson is a tremendously gifted skater whose speed is well above the NHL average. Most of that speed goes to waste because Andersson is missing the other ingredients needed to become an effective scorer or playmaker. He has a very good release on his wrist shot but hardly ever uses it. When he does, he is effective because he disguises the shot well and the goalie doesn't expect it.

Andersson has poor timing when it comes to passing and overhandles the puck. He has stayed in the league mainly because of his agility, which makes him in demand as a finesse checker: a player who will be able to pounce on loose pucks even though he can't do much with them once he gets them.

THE PHYSICAL GAME

Andersson has failed to adapt to the NHL level of physical play. He is not strong and is unwilling to battle in the corners and along the boards. He is easily outmuscled one-on-one despite his skating strength. His lack of involvement lowers the consistency and level of his play, despite his obvious skills. Andersson also lacks the mental toughness needed to succeed in the NHL.

THE INTANGIBLES

Andersson is a skilled player whose recent offensive production has not compensated for his deficiencies in his overall play. He will continue to be an in-and-out player whose apparent lack of interest in paying the price will keep him from playing in the NHL on a regular basis.

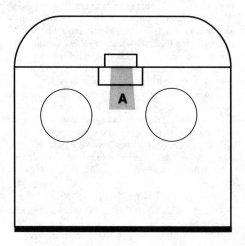

ROB BROWN

Yrs. of NHL service: 4
Born: Kingston, Ont., Canada; April 10, 1968
Position: Right wing
Height: 5-11
Weight: 185
Uniform no.: 4
Shoots: left

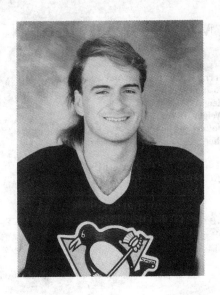

Career statistics:

GP	G	A	TP	PIM
268	130	167	297	371

1990-91 statistics:

GP	G	A	TP	+/-	PIM	PP	SH	GW	GT	S	PCT
69	24	34	58	-7	132	12	0	2	0	126	19.0

LAST SEASON

Acquired from Pittsburgh for Scott Young, December 21, 1990. Goals matched four-year career low. Assists and points were three-year lows. Penalty minutes were career high.

THE FINESSE GAME

Brown is a charismatic goal scorer. He is always buzzing around the net, working to get into position for the shot. Brown is also effective at trailing the play and coming in as the late man to one-time a shot. He doesn't have a very hard shot, but it is very quick and accurate (as shown by his good shooting percentage). All of these opportunistic tendencies make him an excellent man to have on the ice on a power play. Brown thrives with that extra open ice.

Although he is known as a goal scorer, Brown is also one of the NHL's most underrated playmakers. He has very good hand skills and possesses the ability to draw two or three defenders to him and then dish the puck off to a teammate. If he did this more often he could shed the image he has as a selfish player.

Brown has very good hockey instincts, both offensively and defensively. The problem with his defensive work is that he lacks the skating speed to get back into position after penetrating so deeply into the attacking zone. Brown does have very good balance, which helps him in traffic. He is not very intense without the puck or along the boards.

THE PHYSICAL GAME

Brown is not afraid to take a hit in order to make a play. His intensity depends on the game situations. He will work hard and be aggressive when the score is close, but will vanish on other occasions. He is not very strong because of his stature and his lack of skating ability. Brown is an agitator who is able to infuriate opponents—especially goalies—with his yapping. He was one of the NHL's softest players, physique-wise, at the start of last season, but has improved his off-ice training somewhat. It wouldn't hurt his game to step that up another notch.

THE INTANGIBLES

Brown's lack of intensity led to his departure from Pittsburgh. He can be a game-breaker because of his offensive instincts, but because he does not work hard at a consistent level, the lows of his game stand out in stark contrast to the highs and that has resulted in the bad rap of Brown being an overrated player. A better description would be an unfulfilled player, because the NHL hasn't seen Brown at his best yet.

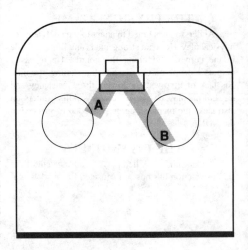

ADAM BURT

Yrs. of NHL service: 2
Born: Detroit, Mich., USA; January 15, 1969
Position: Defenseman
Height: 6-0
Weight: 195
Uniform no.: 6
Shoots: left

Career statistics:

GP	G	A	TP	PIM
110	6	15	21	174

1990-91 statistics:

GP	G	A	TP	+/-	PIM	PP	SH	GW	GT	S	PCT
42	2	7	9	-4	63	1	0	1	0	43	4.7

LAST SEASON

Missed 20 games with ligament damage to his right knee.

THE FINESSE GAME

Burt moves with good agility and balance and is a finesse player who concentrates on his defense. He is not flashy and his offensive instincts aren't on a par with his talents. He has a powerful slap shot, handles the puck fairly well and sees some time on the power play. Rather than rush the puck, he will start a play with a good outlet pass.

With increased confidence, Burt could play more of an offensive role. He plays a smart defensive game. He is a better than average skater, possessing the mobility to be a defenseman who can challenge skaters at the blue line. Burt sees the ice well and can dish off equally effectively to his right or left. He has a nice passing touch and also a good slap shot. He could develop into a good point man on the power play, given the playing time and some added confidence.

Every indication is that Burt's skills have been untapped. He has shown flashes of his ability, but not enough on a consistent basis.

THE PHYSICAL GAME

Burt uses his body effectively in clearing players from in front of the net. He will take and give hits and is willing to play a tough game along the boards and in the corners. Burt can be overpowered by some of the NHL's bigger skaters and needs to improve his upper body strength for his body to be able to do what his instincts tell him to. He is not a fighter. His skating agility and balance help his checking game and he plays a smart game positionally.

THE INTANGIBLES

Burt's major drawback has been his lack of confidence. He has a strong competitive spirit and work ethic. With more concentration on his strength and conditioning, he could become a solid everyday performer.

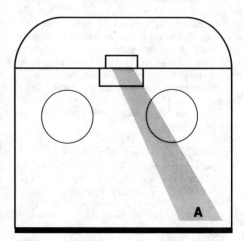

SYLVAIN COTE

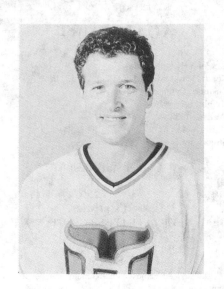

Yrs. of NHL service: 6
Born: Quebec City, Que., Canada; January 19, 1966
Position: Defenseman
Height: 5-11
Weight: 185
Uniform no.: 21
Shoots: right

Career statistics:

GP	G	A	TP	PIM
382	31	61	92	147

1990-91 statistics:

GP	G	A	TP	+/-	PIM	PP	SH	GW	GT	S	PCT
73	7	12	19	-17	17	1	0	0	0	154	4.5

LAST SEASON

All scoring and games played totals were two-year highs as Cote played only 28 games in 1989-90 due to a succession of injuries. Worst plus-minus on team.

THE FINESSE GAME

Cote has some good tools but lacks a blueprint. His hockey instincts lag behind his talents, which makes most of his abilities all but useless to the team, except where he succeeds on his raw talents.

The best part of Cote's game comes from his skating ability. He can put on a quick burst of speed forward and backward and has very good lateral mobility and balance.

Cote rushes the puck but he can't make a move with it. He can handle the puck on an individual basis, but can do very little with it when he's on the move and trying to make a play. He's just not a quick thinker. He has a good shot and likes to skate in near the top of the circles to snap it. Cote's better plays will come from making a quick pass out of his own zone and gives the offense a jump, but he usually tries to take the puck out himself, and that cuts down the team's options because of Cote's lack of playmaking sense.

He is very competitive, well-conditioned and loves the ice time.

THE PHYSICAL GAME

Cote is very strong for his size (but he is small by NHL standards for a defenseman). He plays on his physical ability but he is not a real banger or big hitter. He will finish off his checks. Cote is better at tying opponents up. He gets into trouble because he doesn't read plays well and often starts running around out of position. He has the skating ability to recover from some of his mistakes, but usually realizes the correct play much too late. Cote seldom takes bad or cheap penalties and he is not a tough guy.

THE INTANGIBLES

Cote is limited by his lack of hockey sense. He will be able to improve his game through experience and hard work. He is a very willing player who will stick around the NHL through his strength and hard work.

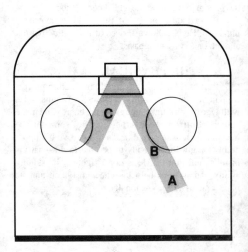

JOHN CULLEN

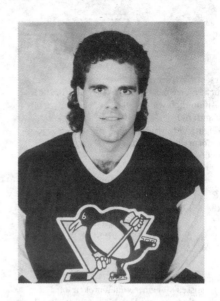

Yrs. of NHL service: 3
Born: Puslinch, Ont., Canada; August 2, 1964
Position: Center
Height: 5-10
Weight: 185
Uniform no.: 15
Shoots: right

Career statistics:

GP	G	A	TP	PIM
229	83	168	251	360

1990-91 statistics:

GP	G	A	TP	+/-	PIM	PP	SH	GW	GT	S	PCT
78	39	71	110	-6	110	14	0	3	1	205	19.0

LAST SEASON

Acquired from Pittsburgh with Zarley Zalapski and Jeff Parker for Ron Francis, Ulf Samuelsson and Grant Jennings, March 4, 1991. Led team in assists (63 scored with Pittsburgh) and points (94 scored with Pittsburgh). Second on team in power play goals. Goals, assists and point totals were career highs.

THE FINESSE GAME

Cullen is excellent at moving the puck. He's not a great skater but he has a great head and that makes him a topnotch playmaker.

He has great vision and is willing to get into the areas where his vision is very effective for him. Where some smaller players might not get in front of the net or into the corner, he will. When he does, his vision is so good that he will trap one or two defenders with a pass.

Cullen is very good in traffic, where his skating quickness (not speed) gains him a precious step on larger defenders who can often look lumbering in their pursuit of the darting center. Cullen has a good wrist and snap shot and he is very good at going after loose pucks in front of the net.

He is not a very good defensive player. While he has improved in that area, his small size will prevent him from being a force in the defensive zone. Cullen plays well positionally because of his good hockey sense.

THE PHYSICAL GAME

Cullen is small, but plays bigger, especially in the offensive zone. He will take or give a hit to get the puck and will sacrifice his body to make a play. He is feisty and unafraid, a real terrier who will launch himself at larger players. Cullen will get outmuscled in the close-in confrontations, but he won't give up his chase after the puck.

THE INTANGIBLES

Cullen is a small, competitive player with great on-ice leadership qualities. He will be thrust into a new role now in Hartford, where he becomes the No. 1 center instead of Mario Lemieux's caddy. He proved during Lemieux's absence from the Penguins that he could help carry a team. He will have even more of a burden on him now with the less talented Whalers and last season's numbers will be tough to equal.

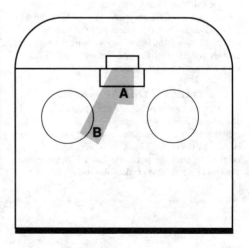

RANDY CUNNEYWORTH

Yrs. of NHL service: 7
Born: Etobicoke, Ont., Canada; May 10, 1961
Position: Left wing
Height: 6-0
Weight: 190
Uniform no.: 7
Shoots: left

Career statistics:

GP	G	A	TP	PIM
419	126	139	265	686

1990-91 statistics:

GP	G	A	TP	+/-	PIM	PP	SH	GW	GT	S	PCT
32	9	5	14	-6	49	0	0	1	0	56	16.1

LAST SEASON

Missed 40 games with a broken left fibula. As as result, all totals were lowest since his first full season.

THE FINESSE GAME

You won't notice Cunneyworth taking off on many breakaways, but you will see him bulling his way through traffic in front of the net to score and doing whatever it takes in his own zone to backcheck. He has excellent balance and strength, both lower and upper body.

Cunneyworth is not a gifted goal scorer but he does have better than average hand skills and likes to score from close in. He is a good passer and likes to work the give-and-go in deep where he will pass to a teammate and then drive to the net for a return pass or in search of the rebound.

He can play a fairly high tempo game because he remains poised under pressure. He does have the odd game where his aggressiveness gets the better of him, but he has matured and those incidents are getting rarer. Cunneyworth is a reliable forward and a coach knows what he's getting when he's on the ice.

THE PHYSICAL GAME

Cunneyworth has fair size and he uses it to his best advantage. He is a very aggressive player who will lay the body on in all three zones. Since he has very good hockey instincts, his checking is augmented by his good skills with the puck. He has the mobility and strength on his skates to make solid contact and he will block shots.

THE INTANGIBLES

Cunneyworth is one of the valuable role players, the consistent grinders, that a team might not notice until he's gone, as Cunneyworth was for half of last season. The only question will be if the recovery from his injury will slow him down. He seemed to rebound just fine in the last half of last season.

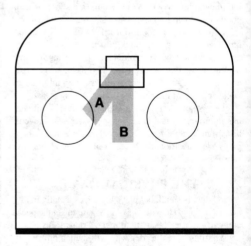

KEVIN DINEEN

Yrs. of NHL service: 7
Born: Quebec City, Que., Canada; October 28, 1963
Position: Right wing
Height: 5-11
Weight: 195
Uniform no.: 11
Shoots: right

Career statistics:

GP	G	A	TP	PIM
473	210	230	440	1008

1990-91 statistics:

GP	G	A	TP	+/-	PIM	PP	SH	GW	GT	S	PCT
61	17	30	47	-15	104	4	0	2	0	161	10.6

LAST SEASON

Missed a total of 19 games with a variety of ailments: hip pointer, bruised shoulder and a flare-up of Crohn's disease. Goal total was career low. Assist totals was two-season high. Point total was six-season low. Worst plus-minus on team among forwards.

THE FINESSE GAME

Dineen might be the biggest 180-pound player in the game. His No. 1 asset is his intensity. He depends on his enthusiasm for the game to make things happen.

Dineen is an excellent skater, quick and strong, and with great balance that powers his kamikaze style. He will act as a power forward in front of the net or work along the boards and behind the net to free up the puck.

His skills with the puck are average at best. He has a good wrist shot with a quick release, which he doesn't use often enough. Dineen overhandles the puck at times. Since he is so good in traffic, he should be firing away more often and then following up for the rebound. He is a good passer and can carry the puck at a good speed.

THE PHYSICAL GAME

When Dineen's enthusiasm is at a high level, he becomes an impact player. Because of his size, he can't carry that stature all the time. He's getting older, too, and the years and the illness he has battled (Crohn's disease) sometimes take their toll on him. Dineen works hard to keep himself in good condition.

Dineen will try to tackle anybody to do what he has to do. His skating ability gives him good mobility and the balance to keep his feet after most hits.

THE INTANGIBLES

Dineen is a leader who wants to be on the ice in critical situations, but he often gets frustrated and wants to do everything himself. He gets himself into trouble by trying to play an individual game and not using his teammates for support. He means well—he wants the team to succeed, but going it alone isn't always the way to do it.

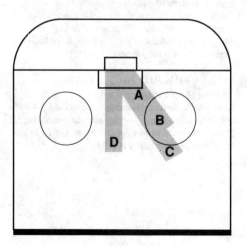

DEAN EVASON

Yrs. of NHL service: 6
Born: Flin Flon, Man., Canada; August 22, 1964
Position: Center
Height: 5-10
Weight: 180
Uniform no.: 12
Shoots: left

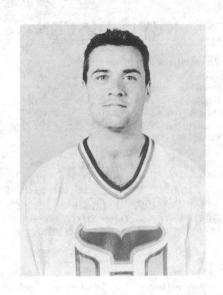

Career statistics:

GP	G	A	TP	PIM
451	90	152	242	621

1990-91 statistics:

GP	G	A	TP	+/-	PIM	PP	SH	GW	GT	S	PCT
75	6	23	29	-6	170	1	0	0	0	85	7.1

LAST SEASON

Goals total was career low. Point total was two-year low.

THE FINESSE GAME

Evason brings to the ice a package of modest skills wrapped in a fiercely competitive nature. He is an average skater whose speed and agility match almost equally. He is very good darting into holes when he opts to play a small man's game.

His shooting skills are fair. He is a checking forward who can contribute offensively with his good wrist shot and some opportunistics rebounds. He can be used on the power play, although he is becoming almost purely a defensive forward. It's unlikely he will score more than 20 goals (as he did in 1986-87) again.

He does a fair job on faceoffs. Evason also has average hockey sense. He is smart enough to know what has to be done, but it is really his huge heart and character that get the job done.

THE PHYSICAL GAME

Strong for his size and willing to pay the price, Evason nonetheless is simply outmuscled when it comes to going mano-a-mano with the team's bigger players. He wants to do more than his body will let him, but it's just not physically possible.

THE INTANGIBLES

Evason scores strongest in intangibles. He is a gritty, hustling forward who is limited by his lack of size, but does his best to overcome it. He is an excellent team man.

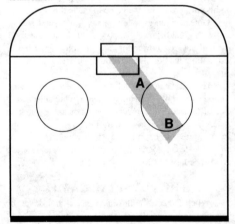

BOBBY HOLIK

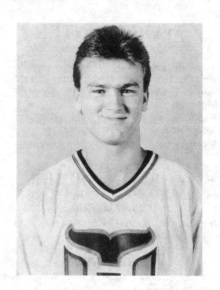

Yrs. of NHL service: 1
Born: Jihavla, Czechoslovakia; January 1, 1971
Position: Left wing/center
Height: 6-3
Weight: 210
Uniform no.: 24
Shoots: right

Career statistics:

GP	G	A	TP	PIM
78	21	22	43	113

1990-91 statistics:

GP	G	A	TP	+/-	PIM	PP	SH	GW	GT	S	PCT
78	21	22	43	-3	113	8	0	3	0	173	12.1

LAST SEASON

First NHL season. Second among NHL rookies in shots. Fifth among NHL rookies in power play goals.

THE FINESSE GAME

Holik can wrist the puck very well and needs to shoot it more. He has the ability to be a better playmaker than most people gave him credit for in his rookie season. Once he gets settled and confident in the league, his vision skills and his ability to move the puck will advance another level. Holik has the ability to be more than a good "B" player. He can be an "A" player.

Holik is a strong skater but needs to improve his acceleration since other players can get a jump on him. This hurt him defensively and he was moved to the wing from his natural center position because of some of his defensive shortcomings.

Holik's skills make him an excellent power play man. He should be even more dangerous this year as he becomes more comfortable in the NHL.

THE PHYSICAL GAME

Holik's style is not that of the stereotypical European. He is a big forward who likes to play the body and he has the skating strength to win most battles. He is not afraid of getting hit and went out of his way to show that he would not be shy about getting involved. That may be one reason why he did not do as many things with his vision as he is able. Once he has established himself as a player who can't be intimidated, his finesse skills will come to the fore.

THE INTANGIBLES

Holik plays with a lot of enthusiasm and gives the same level of drive every night. He wants to succeed in the NHL and should not suffer from a sophomore slump.

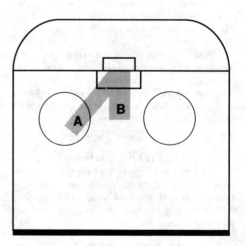

MARK HUNTER

Yrs. of NHL service: 10
Born: Petrolia, Ont., Canada; November 12, 1962
Position: Right wing
Height: 6-0
Weight: 205
Uniform no.: 26
Shoots: right

Career statistics:

GP	G	A	TP	PIM
558	203	158	361	1253

1990-91 statistics:

GP	G	A	TP	+/-	PIM	PP	SH	GW	GT	S	PCT
68	14	18	32	+2	165	7	0	0	0	110	12.7

LAST SEASON

Acquired from Calgary for Carey Wilson, March 5, 1991. All totals were two-year highs, as Hunter missed all but 10 games of the 1989-90 season with a knee injury and subsequent surgery.

THE FINESSE GAME

Hunter is well-named because he loves to hunt for goals. He would much rather shoot than pass. Since he lacks good playmaking skills, he is at his most effective playing with someone creative who can get him the puck. Hunter doesn't fool around once he gets it, but fires away with a fairly good wrist or slap. Unfortunately, he will often overlook teammates in better shooting position. He scores most of his goals from 15 feet in.

Hunter skates fairly well, with speed and acceleration ahead of his lateral movement and balance. Hunter understands the game well defensively, but with the great depth on the Calgary Flames, did not get much playing time in those situations because of the players who were far ahead of him in defensive ability.

He does not see the ice very well.

THE PHYSICAL GAME

Hunter is a good grinder. He has good size and the streak of nastiness that keeps players around him on the alert. He will work very hard in the corners and along the boards and sacrifices willingly in all zones. He is somewhat injury prone.

THE INTANGIBLES

Hunter's work ethic has been called into question in the past and may have contributed to his departure from Calgary. At Hunter's age, it was difficult to come back from his serious knee surgery and it's not likely he'll be the effective player he was two and more seasons ago. Hunter did have a clutch playoff performance for the Whalers and it looks like he will still be able to contribute.

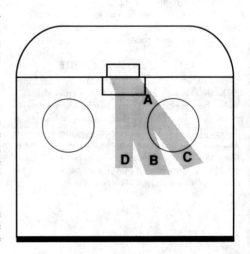

ED KASTELIC

Yrs. of NHL service: 4
Born: Toronto, Ont., Canada; January 29, 1964
Position: Right wing
Height: 6-4
Weight: 215
Uniform no.: 22
Shoots: right

Career statistics:

GP	G	A	TP	PIM
195	10	7	17	658

1990-91 statistics:

GP	G	A	TP	+/-	PIM	PP	SH	GW	GT	S	PCT
45	2	2	4	-7	211	0	0	0	0	15	13.3

LAST SEASON

Second on team in PIM despite not playing in 35 games. Missed a total of 13 games with suspensions. Missed seven games with a rib injury.

THE FINESSE GAME

Kastelic has very little hockey ability. He is not a bad skater, at least straightaway and after he's had a few strides to build up a head of steam, but his agility is poor.

Kastelic can shoot a puck when he is in very tight, but he takes a very long time on his release. He needs all kinds of time to do it, so he doesn't get involved in the game. His passing skills are minimal and, again, his reaction time is slo-mo.

Kastelic hasn't established himself physically enough to buy enough room to do those things, like a Joe Kocur has. With Kastelic, defenders stay close and figure he'll run out of room. And he does.

THE PHYSICAL GAME

Call him Gentle Ed. Kastelic is a big bear of a man without a mean streak. He doesn't know how strong he is and maybe that's what keeps him from being a fierce force on the ice. If he had a little angry in him, Kastelic would be much more effective. Once in a while he gets wound up; when he does, he can fight anybody in the league. But he doesn't do it often enough to merit much respect.

As a checker, he is a willing hitter but his lack of skating ability severely limits his range.

THE INTANGIBLES

Kastelic stays in the league because of his size and strength. Anyone his size can be an insurance policy for some of the smaller guys on the ice. But his hockey skills remain minimal and so does his impact as a real enforcer.

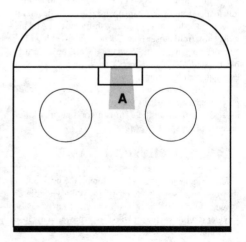

TODD KRYGIER

Yrs. of NHL service: 2
Born: Northville, Mich., USA: October 12, 1965
Position: Left wing
Height: 5-11
Weight: 180
Uniform no.: 17
Shoots: left

Career statistics:

GP	G	A	TP	PIM
130	31	29	60	147

1990-91 statistics:

GP	G	A	TP	+/-	PIM	PP	SH	GW	GT	S	PCT
72	13	17	30	+1	95	3	0	2	3	113	11.5

LAST SEASON

One of only two fulltime forwards on the team with a plus ranking. Games played and assist totals were two-year career high. Goals were two-year low. Points total matched rookie campaign.

THE FINESSE GAME

Krygier is a speed demon whose arsenal is limited to one weapon but it is an effective one: he likes to jet ahead with his good straight-on speed, set the defenseman back on his heels and fire off a slap shot from the wing.

Unfortunately for Krygier, that move can be rapidly mapped out by opposing teams. He has little lateral movement so he can't put on any shifty moves. And his wrist shot, from closer range, is not effective. It would be more dangerous if he could use it while he's skating, but he can't. Krygier is not a very good playmaker, especially at high tempo.

Krygier is a converted defenseman and reads plays well coming back. He is always aware of his defensive responsibilities. He is a good penalty killer because of his speed.

THE PHYSICAL GAME

Krygier will work hard along the boards in his defensive zone and is good at chipping the puck out of the zone because of his tenacity. He is not very big or strong and can be knocked off the puck fairly easily. Krygier is a finesse player who is overpowered in close confrontations.

THE INTANGIBLES

Krygier is a self-made player who really wants to make the NHL. He knew he had to bulk up to compete with this level of competition and he did it. His weaknesses may overcome his desire, however. Unless he can add an element or two to his offensive game, he will never be more than a 20-goal scorer.

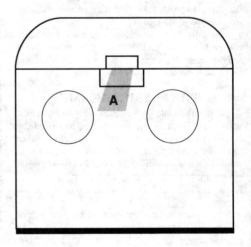

RANDY LADOUCEUR

Yrs. of NHL service: 9
Born: Brockville, Ont., Canada; June 30, 1960
Position: Defenseman
Height: 6-2
Weight: 220
Uniform no.: 29
Shoots: left

Career statistics:

GP	G	A	TP	PIM
606	23	97	120	929

1990-91 statistics:

GP	G	A	TP	+/-	PIM	PP	SH	GW	GT	S	PCT
67	1	3	4	-10	118	0	0	0	0	44	2.3

LAST SEASON

Games played total eight-season low. Missed 10 games with a sprained ankle.

THE FINESSE GAME

Ladouceur is a veteran who gets by mostly on his experience. He is an average skater who doesn't get involved offensively and prefers to stay at home. He won't carry the puck (or perhaps can't), preferring instead to dump and hope. He doesn't see the ice well and is not good at headmanning.

Ladouceur will seldom journey into his team's offensive zone. He has an average slap shot that nets him a goal or two a season.

His skating is hampered by his poor mobility and agility. It is easy for opponents to put a fake on him so Ladouceur must concentrate on his positioning and forcing the skater wide. He is a very hard worker but his talents are unremarkable. His attitude is a plus.

THE PHYSICAL GAME

Ladouceur has good size, even by today's standard for mutant NHL defensemen, but he doesn't play up to it. He prefers to use his skating agility to play a positional game, then use his long reach to knock the puck away. He doesn't like to play the body and, with a body like his, that's a waste.

THE INTANGIBLES

Ladouceur is a competent, journeyman defenseman who survives on his experience. He will have a stretch every season of 15 games or so where he moves his game up to another level, but it is never sustained over an entire season.

BRAD SHAW

Yrs. of NHL service: 2
Born: Cambridge, Ont., Canada; April 28, 1964
Position: Defenseman
Height: 5-11
Weight: 170
Uniform no.: 32
Shoots: right

Career statistics:

GP	G	A	TP	PIM
150	7	62	69	63

1990-91 statistics:

GP	G	A	TP	+/-	PIM	PP	SH	GW	GT	S	PCT
72	4	28	32	-10	29	2	0	1	0	129	3.1

LAST SEASON

Second among defensemen on team in scoring. Goals in second full NHL season were career high; assists and points were two-year lows.

THE FINESSE GAME

Shaw is a very smart player with or without the puck and with improved skating ability could become a controlling defenseman. Shaw moves the puck very well, passing well as he starts a rush when he dictates the tempo. He is very good at spying the openings and his passes lay down on the recipient's stick. However, he can't play the game at a high speed with his legs as well as he does with his head and hands.

Shaw is an agile skater but not a fast skater. His first few strides are quick but he can be caught after that. Speed is not his major asset.

He is very good on the power play. He has good vision and a good shot. His slap shot is deceptive and on the net or he can make a pass off the shot. Because of his lack of speed, he will not pinch in offensively. His scoring comes from the blue line.

THE PHYSICAL GAME

Shaw is not strong physically but is strong mentally. He stays out of the physical confrontations because he's smart, but when he's in them, he is willing to take a hit and willing to try to take a guy out of a play. Shaw tries to avoid these situations by his puck control and positional play.

THE INTANGIBLES

Shaw worked a long time in the minors to get to the NHL and his No. 1 asset is his desire to play. He has heart. He could use more upper body strength to improve his chances in the tight spots.

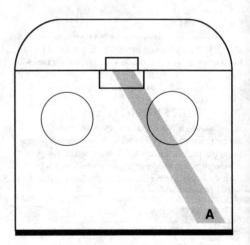

PETER SIDORKIEWICZ

Yrs. of NHL service: 3
Born: Dabrowa Bialostocka, Poland; June 29, 1963
Position: Goaltender
Height: 5-9
Weight: 180
Uniform no.: 30
Catches: left

Career statistics:

GP	MINS	GA	SO	GAA	A	PIM
143	8351	464	6	3.33	8	10

1990-91 statistics:

GP	MINS	GAA	W	L	T	SO	GA	S	SAPCT	PIM
52	2953	3.33	21	22	7	1	164	1284	.872	6

LAST SEASON

Games and minutes played were career highs. GAA was two-year best. Missed five games with a sprained ankle.

THE PHYSICAL GAME

Sidorkiewicz has very good fundamentals. He approaches the game with good understanding and plays his angles well. He does not rely on his instincts. He focuses on the angles, the positioning of his glove, the positioning of the puck. . .a complete mental checklist.

When he is standing up and facing the play, he is a very good goaltender. He is a good skater, adept at getting out of his net and stopping the puck, leaving it for his defensemen or moving it up the boards to a teammate. He does not overhandle the puck. Sidorkiewicz communicates well with his defense and they like to play in front of him because he is workmanlike.

He is not as good on short-range play, since his reflexes are not outstanding. Although he concentrates well, he has trouble with change of direction plays.

THE MENTAL GAME

Sidorkiewicz lacks the mental toughness to be a No. 1 goalie. He inherited the job almost by default in Hartford. If he can get himself stronger mentally and not be so concerned about the downside of his game when things aren't going so well, he could become one. He has shown poise in pressure situations, but not consistently. He prepares himself well for games.

THE INTANGIBLES

Sidorkiewicz goes into the season with a virtual lock on the No. 1 job again. Maybe another year in the position will improve his confidence. He is very close.

MIKE TOMLAK

Yrs. of NHL service: 2
Born: Thunder Bay, Ont., Canada; October 17, 1964
Position: Left wing
Height: 6-3
Weight: 205
Uniform no.: 28
Shoots: left

Career statistics:

GP	G	A	TP	PIM
134	15	22	37	103

1990-91 statistics:

GP	G	A	TP	+/-	PIM	PP	SH	GW	GT	S	PCT
64	8	8	16	-9	55	0	1	0	0	69	11.6

LAST SEASON

Goal and PIM totals were two-year career highs. Assists and point totals were two-year lows.

THE FINESSE GAME

Tomlak is a purely defensive forward, very smart and a strong positional player without the puck. He helps his defense down low, getting into position for a pass, and he works hard. That is his forte.

Tomlak is a better skater than people give him credit for. He's an average skater without a lot of speed, but he is strong on his skates and has a good stride and a lot of stamina.

On the whole, his skills are very average. He is a strong forechecker because of his intelligence and most of his goals will come from forcing turnovers and giveaways. He is a good penalty killer and good on faceoffs, because even when he loses them, he will be sure to pick up his man.

THE PHYSICAL GAME

Tomlak is strong because of his size, not strong because he is a physical player. He uses his size well in certain situations when he can get there—his skating doesn't always let him. If he could get a little more aggressive he would be a better player.

THE INTANGIBLES

Tomlak is one of the NHL's more underrated checking forwards. There is little indication he will add any other dimensions to what he does, but he plays his role very well.

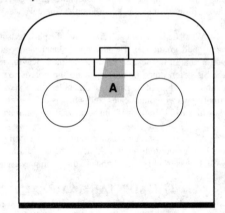

PAT VERBEEK

Yrs. of NHL service: 8
Born: Sarnia, Ont., Canada; May 24, 1964
Position: Right wing
Height: 5-9
Weight: 195
Uniform no.: 16
Shoots: right

Career statistics:

GP	G	A	TP	PIM
623	257	235	492	1417

1990-91 statistics:

GP	G	A	TP	+/-	PIM	PP	SH	GW	GT	S	PCT
80	43	39	82	0	246	15	0	5	1	247	17.4

LAST SEASON

Only player in NHL to lead his team in goals and PIM. Also led team in power play goals, game-winning goals and shots; second on team in points. Only Whaler to appear in all 80 games. Goals, assists and points all two-year lows.

THE FINESSE GAME

Play word association with almost anyone in the NHL and the first reaction to the name Verbeek is "feisty." He gives a team on-ice leadership and an aggressive game that creates most of his scoring opportunities.

There are few downsides to his game. He has very good anticipation and is always buzzing around the net for loose pucks, rebounds and tips. He has very strong wrists and can flick goals in with one hand while he is holding off a defender with the other. He will give not just the second effort, but the third and fourth.

Verbeek is good on power plays, with his willingness to stand in front and scrap. He is not a very good playmaker (although he came up through junior as a center). There is nothing fancy about him. He plays a power game.

He is not a particularly fast skater, although he can put on a quick burst in a little bit of space. He does have some breakaway speed when he gets a jump at neutral ice with his good anticipation. Verbeek is a fairly good defensive player.

THE PHYSICAL GAME

Verbeek is willing to pay the price in front of the net and along the boards. He has a low center of gravity and is surprisingly strong for a short player (we can't say small, because of Verbeek's husky build). He has to play physical to be effective. Verbeek will seldom be outworked, especially in the attacking zone, where he is ferocious in his pursuit of the puck. He can be outreached, but because his balance is so much better than most of the players he goes up against, he can knock others off the puck before they get a chance to tie him up. Verbeek has the ability to give a big hit.

Because he is so aggressive, Verbeek spends too much time in the penalty box as a result of bad penalties.

THE INTANGIBLES

Verbeek has firmly established himself among the NHL's premier right wings. Another 40-45 goals season should be expected from this consistent and hardworking forward.

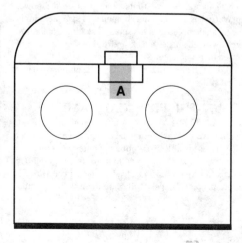

ZARLEY ZALAPSKI

Yrs. of NHL service: 3
Born: Edmonton, Alta., Canada; April 22, 1968
Position: Defenseman
Height: 6-1
Weight: 210
Uniform no.: 3
Shoots: left

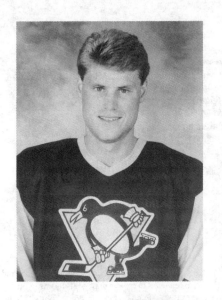

Career statistics:

GP	G	A	TP	PIM
201	36	105	141	166

1990-91 statistics:

GP	G	A	TP	+/-	PIM	PP	SH	GW	GT	S	PCT
77	15	39	54	+8	65	8	1	1	0	156	9.6

LAST SEASON

Acquired from Pittsburgh with John Cullen and Jeff Parker for Ron Francis, Ulf Samuelsson and Grant Jennings, March 4, 1991. Led team in plus-minus (he brought a plus-15 rating with him from Pittsburgh). Led team defensemen in goals, assists and points. Goals, assists and points all career highs.

THE FINESSE GAME

Zalapski has still not developed the defensive insight to make him a good two-way defenseman so he remains a highly skilled player whose contributions are all offensive.

He is an excellent skater in all areas—dead-ahead speed, acceleration, agility and balance. He can move well in all directions and his ability gives him the confidence to challenge at both blue lines. Zalapski can handle the puck while he's doing all of these maneuvers, which makes him very dangerous when armed. He is better at moving with the puck than he is moving it.

Zalapski is a first-rate point man on the power play. He has a good point shot but will also pressure in deep, again because of his superior skating. He likes to get involved in the attack and follows the play well when he is not leading it.

He can also kill penalties because of his speed and hand skills.

THE PHYSICAL GAME

Zalapski is a finesse defenseman who is not aggressive and dislikes contact. He has good size but doesn't use it well. He is not a big hitter, but prefers to use his stick skill and speed to move the puck out. He needs to be paired with a steady defenseman who will scare people. Zalapski will scare them with his skills.

THE INTANGIBLES

Even Paul Coffey gets down and dirty when he has to. Zalapski has some world-class ability, but hasn't yet shown the desire that would nudge him into the top echelon of defensemen.

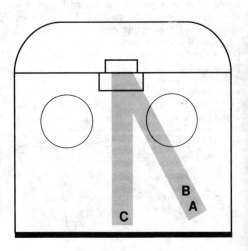

LOS ANGELES KINGS

BRIAN BENNING

Yrs. of NHL service: 5
Born: Edmonton, Alta., Canada; June 10, 1966
Position: Defenseman
Height: 6-1
Weight: 195
Uniform no.: 2
Shoots: Left

Career statistics:

GP	G	A	TP	PIM
341	42	136	178	548

1990-91 statistics:

GP	G	A	TP	+/-	PIM	PP	SH	GW	GT	S	PCT
61	7	24	31	12	123	2	0	1	0	120	5.8

LAST SEASON

Penalty minutes were a career high. Plus-minus improved by 14 goals.

THE FINESSE GAME

Benning is a skater of style and substance. He may not be as quick or agile as the now-traded Steve Duchesne, but he gets the job done in a similar fashion. Benning's natural instinct is to get involved in the offense, and he does it intelligently; he sees the ice well, goes to the right places and maximizes his effectiveness with strong passing and shooting skills.

Benning sends his shots accurately to the net, but not until he has looked in front to see if any teammates might be in a better position to score. He will wind up to fake the shot and freeze people, then slide a pass to a teammate at the side of the net.

He improved as a defenseman last year because he played more consistently. Benning reads his partner well, and made a nice complement last season for Rob Blake; when one went up on the attack, the other stayed back.

THE PHYSICAL GAME

Benning is not a large player. He gets out-muscled at times, and gets in trouble in strength confrontations in the corners or in front of the net. He is willing to take the players on, he makes sure to grab an opponent's stick or get a piece of him some way, but sometimes simply is shoved aside.

Benning is not afraid of any confrontation and when people try to take undue advantage, Benning unmistakably has a mean streak, which can express itself with a crosscheck directly to the nose—as Vancouver's Gino Odjick can attest.

THE INTANGIBLES

Benning's emergence as an offensive force was one reason the Kings felt they could trade a player of Steve Duchesne's prowess. Of course, Duchesne scored three times as many goals, but having Benning, Rob Blake and Duchesne made things a bit crowded on the power-play point.

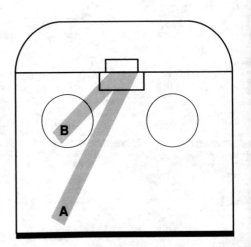

DANIEL BERTHIAUME

Yrs. of NHL service: 5
Born: Longeuil, Que., Canada; January 26, 1966
Position: Goaltender
Height: 5-9
Weight: 151
Uniform no.: 36
Catches: Left

Career statistics:

GP	MINS	GA	SO	GAA	A	PIM
162	8957	530	5	3.55	3	32

1990-91 statistics:

GP	MINS	GAA	W	L	T	SO	GA	S	SAPCT	PIM
37	2119	3.31	20	11	4	1	117	1086	.892	10

LAST SEASON

Obtained from Minnesota September 6, 1990, for Craig Duncanson. Games played, minutes played and victory total all were three-season highs. Goals against average was lowest since 3.17 in 31 games his rookie season.

THE PHYSICAL GAME

A goaltender who moves with extreme quickness, Berthiaume is an entertaining acrobat in the net. He stays a little deep and dares the shooters to beat him, using his butterfly agility to take away the low corners, his anticipation and ultra-quick glove to protect against high shots.

Being a very good skater helps Berthiaume move smoothly side-to-side; he handles plays across the goalmouth very well. Berthiaume also recovers position well after dropping to the ice and is ready for the second shots when they come.

Handling the puck is not one of his real strengths. He doesn't have exceptional skill at getting behind the net to stop the hard-arounds, and he doesn't have a very good shot. He does, however, use his stick whenever possible to block passes to the goalmouth.

THE MENTAL GAME

Berthiaume is gaining mental toughness and emotional control, working to get off the roller coaster of overconfidence when he's playing well, underconfidence when he is struggling. Consistency, in practices and games, is the aim.

He is getting better at leaving bad goals behind him, is better-prepared to play when his turn comes in the rotation. He makes the big saves in the big games.

THE INTANGIBLES

Berthiaume did the best he could to accept second billing at the end of last season. You can't have a solid one-two punch without somebody being the "2."

ROB BLAKE

Yrs. of NHL service: 1
Born: Simcoe, Ont., Canada; December 10, 1969
Position: Defense
Height: 6-3
Weight: 215
Uniform no.: 4
Shoots: Right

Career statistics:

GP	G	A	TP	PIM
75	12	34	46	125

1990-91 statistics:

GP	G	A	TP	+/-	PIM	PP	SH	GW	GT	S	PCT
75	12	34	46	3	125	9	0	2	0	150	8.0

LAST SEASON

First in the NHL. Voted to NHL all-rookie team.

THE FINESSE GAME

Blake is a thinking man who doesn't fall into the big man's trap of trying to be overwhelming every shift. He plays with a purpose. He thinks. Blake uses his peripheral vision and view of the ice, is creative within a framework of positional discipline. It all ties into a very nice package.

He has light feet, can change direction well and can cover ground rapidly. Blake will step up with the play, but not when his offense is not needed; he is more likely to activate in the third period, when his team is down a goal. Mostly, though, Blake makes a quick evaluation of the offensive options when he has the puck; if nothing is available, other than a high-risk play, he simply makes a safe pass or gets the puck deep.

A good point man for the power play, Blake has a quarterback's poise and uses his teammates. He will fake the big windup, lure an opponent into dropping to the ice, then will beat the player to the outside. Other times, though, he will take the big windup from the point and take so long to fire, the shot will blocked.

On defense, Blake generally extends himself; he uses his reach, uses the pokecheck and the sweepcheck to challenge the attack. He also will place himself in defensive peril at times, going for the poke but not recovering his balance if the opponent steps around him.

and thus can fulfill his role by getting an efficient job done quietly. If all that's needed is a puck driven around the boards, or a point shot flipped lightly at the net so that a teammate can tip it, that is what Blake does—accomplishing more by doing less, by picking his spots.

Blake will make an occasional unforced error (a blind reverse for a turnover behind his net, a poor decision about pinching off the boards), but such events serve to remind people last season was his first in NHL. Because in so many other ways, Blake played like a veteran.

THE PHYSICAL GAME

Blake is not a crushing hitter. He finishes, uses his strength along the boards and in the corners and in front, and he uses physical pressure intelligently.

THE INTANGIBLES

Blake has big-play potential, but has enough maturity to know he plays on a team of big-play players

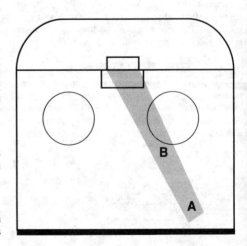

150

JEFF CHYCHRUN

Yrs. of NHL service: 3
Born: LaSalle, Que., Canada; May 3, 1966
Position: Defenseman
Height: 6-4
Weight: 215
Uniform no.:
Shoots: Right

Career statistics:

GP	G	A	TP	PIM
199	3	17	20	606

1990-91 statistics:

GP	G	A	TP	+/-	PIM	PP	SH	GW	GT	S	PCT
36	0	6	6	1	105	0	0	0	0	25	.0

LAST SEASON

Obtained from Philadelphia, May 30, 1991, with rights to Jari Kurri, in exchange for Steve Kasper and Steve Duchesne.

THE FINESSE GAME

For a 215-pound player, Chychrun skates fairly well but is not especially mobile in either direction and can be beaten one-on-one. He will try to take the play wide and angle the forward to a place where he can hit, but lacks the range necessary to do it effectively.

To compensate, Chychrun does a good job of getting the puck and moving it up ice quickly, so it is out of danger and the pressure is relieved.

Chychrun has a fairly good shot—though you wouldn't know it from last year's numbers—and can make a play if he has a lot of room. But his preference is to get rid of the puck; he does not relish carrying it.

THE PHYSICAL GAME

Chychrun simply does not know how to fight defensively. He is all offense—will land some solid shots—but he has taken some fearful punches in the last few seasons, and a person can get really tired of being pounded like that. His aggressiveness is not innate; he is not innately mean, and a strictly physical/fighting role simply may not hold appeal to him.

THE INTANGIBLES

Chychrun made room for himself by playing as physically as he did his first three season. The question entering this campaign is whether Chychrun still is ready and willing to remain a physical, fighting presence. If Chychrun is not going to fight and be a menace, he is going to have to get by on an extremely limited amount of skill.

MIKE DONNELLY

Yrs. of NHL service: 2
Born: Detroit, Mich., USA; October 10, 1963
Position: Left wing
Height: 5-11
Weight: 185
Uniform no.: 23
Shoots: Left

Career statistics:

GP	G	A	TP	PIM
149	21	24	45	111

1990-91 statistics:

GP	G	A	TP	+/-	PIM	PP	SH	GW	GT	S	PCT
53	7	5	12	3	41	0	0	2	0	76	9.2

LAST SEASON

Obtained from Buffalo, September 30, 1990, for Mikko Makela.

THE FINESSE GAME

Things didn't work for Donnelly as a scorer in his first two NHL stops with the New York Rangers and Buffalo Sabres; he didn't really have the size or the inclination/hunger to drive to the net. The Kings put him in a checking role, allowed him to use his speed that way, and Donnelly showed some good signs.

Donnelly can win an end-to-end foot race, has agility and is very quick off the mark, all of which help make him useful in a penalty killing role. He has good anticipation, and uses it to stay ahead of plays and situations.

Sometimes, offensive instincts can return from a defensive posture. Donnelly handles the puck well—his passing being more noteable than his shooting at the moment—and should be expected to at least double his output with regular ice time.

THE PHYSICAL GAME

Donnelly is not real strong on the puck, which may be why he doesn't carry it much. Donnelly uses his speed to reach the puck, then uses his quick hands to move it someplace. Still, he accepts being hit; he can take a hit and stay in the play, and on the rare occasion will initiate some contact.

THE INTANGIBLES

Donnelly may finally have found a home, a place where he can play his game and have it fit into a framework that can support it. He never had much of a chance with the Rangers or Sabres; but he might be able to stick with the Kings if he becomes more assertive.

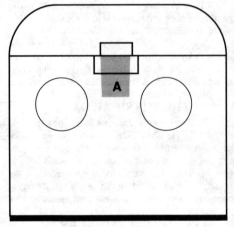

TONY GRANATO

Yrs. of NHL service: 3
Born: Downers Grove, Ill., USA; July 25, 1964
Position: Left wing
Height: 5-10
Weight: 180
Uniform no.: 21
Shoots: Right

Career statistics:

GP	G	A	TP	PIM
202	78	85	163	418

1990-91 statistics:

GP	G	A	TP	+/-	PIM	PP	SH	GW	GT	S	PCT
68	30	34	64	22	156	11	1	3	0	197	15.2

LAST SEASON

Goal total improved by 18, plus-minus improved by 23 goals, shot total jumped by 77 though his games played was up only 12. Penalty minutes were a career high.

THE FINESSE GAME

Granato is a hornet on skates, buzzing here, buzzing there, always looking to sting somebody. His speed and quickness are assets at both ends of the rink; so much of his offense stems from those mile-a-minute legs, as does so much of his ability to forecheck and pressure the puck carrier.

On offense, Granato has a nose for the net. He likes to weave into the slot—near enough for a wrist shot or snap shot, far enough away that defensemen can't get a good piece of him. Granato also uses the element of surprise: the times he drives to the net, he will try to get a shot off even if he has only one hand on his stick. At other times in traffic, he will switch hands and transform himself from a right shot to a left shot and try to catch a goalie napping.

At still other times, Granato is too slow making his decisions at the offensive blue line. He uses speed to get the defensemen to concede the line, but causes lots of offsides by failing to move the puck when the opening is there. He also will be guilty of cheating without the puck; he will drive to the line at top speed on timing plays, then be hopelessly offside if the passing lane closes.

On defense, Granato uses guile and smarts against larger, stronger opponents. He loses a lot of strength mismatches, as might be expected, ends up on the seat of his pants a lot, but he still tries to lift an opponent's stick off the puck or block a shot or make whatever contribution he can.

THE PHYSICAL GAME

Granato knows the key to his survival is not backing down, not allowing anyone to intimidate him.

So he starts a lot of the confrontations, knowing a bigger player can't win strategically by picking on a smaller one. Granato stands up for himself, gets back up when he is knocked down and comes right back for more.

Granato annoys opponents into penalties by working harder than they do and by being pesky. He hits, he hooks, he slashes, he is always trying something to get an edge.

THE INTANGIBLES

Granato pays a physical price for playing the game as he does, but has very impressive resiliency. It takes much more than fatigue to get him out of the lineup, because his fire keeps the pot boiling, his grit adds pepper to the stew.

WAYNE GRETZKY

Yrs. of NHL service: 12
Born: Brantford, Ont., Canada; January 26, 1961
Position: Center
Height: 6-0
Weight: 175
Uniform no.: 99
Shoots: Left

Career statistics:

GP	G	A	TP	PIM
925	718	1424	2142	422

1990-91 statistics:

GP	G	A	TP	+/-	PIM	PP	SH	GW	GT	S	PCT
78	41	122	163	30	16	8	0	5	2	212	19.3

LAST SEASON

Surpassed the 2,000-point milestone, scored at least 40 goals and 100 assists for the 12th consecutive season, led NHL scorers for the ninth time in his career. In addition to setting a club record, the assist total was Gretzky's highest in five seasons. The penalty-minute total, meanwhile, was his NHL career low.

THE FINESSE GAME

Gretzky wears out checkers, defensemen and goalies because he makes them think so much, forces them to make so many decisions, makes them do what they absolutely hate doing. He sets up the office behind the net because goalies despise it when the puck is back there. If the goalie watches the puck, they can't see who is moving into position in front; if they look in front, they know Gretzky will come out for a stuff shot on the forehand or backhand.

Gretzky uses his edges so well. He can make a backhand pass, then change edges and be on his forehand—ready for a return pass—before his teammate even receives the puck. And you can't use the backhand as much as Gretzky does without skating strength and balance. Carrying on the backhand, especially carrying to the net on the backhand, is a lot more difficult than he makes it look; this guy throws in a tight turn or a 360-degree swivel that would screw the rest of the league into the ice.

Gretzky never looks at the goalie; he looks at the hole the goalie leaves, and the goalie always leaves something because Gretzky's backhand is as much a threat as Gretzky's forehand—for passes as well as shots. More than shooting speed and strength, Gretzky depends on the accuracy of the shots he always sends back against the grain. You know he'll carry to his left across the top of the circles, then shoot back to his right. Goalies know it but still can't cheat; if they leave some long side, Gretzky will put the puck in it.

The backhand allows him to use his body to protect the puck, forcing a defenseman to reach in—which leaves Gretzky at least two options: he can dive to the ice, "held," or he can step past the defenseman while the defenseman regains his balance.

Gretzky holds the puck, daring defensemen to rush toward him so there will be all kinds of open ice into which he can put the puck. Space is the name of his game; creating it and filling it are his art.

THE PHYSICAL GAME

Gretzky isn't asked to work in the ditches, down low, scrumming for the puck. If he stays up high, to challenge the point men, he remains a threat even on defense, because he can spring the transition game in an eyeblink. One good outlet pass and he's gone, or he's one-touched it ahead for a fast-breaking teammate.

Still, specific strength is a significant part of Gretzky's game. When he's on the fringe of the battles, waiting for the puck, Gretzky keeps a strong grip on his stick—which allows him to cradle softly even the hardest desperation pass. The stick is always on the ice, too, always in position to accept the puck or shoot it. The respect he receives for his passing and playmaking and scoring are well-earned, but he may never get enough credit for simply executing fundamentals.

Does he have flaws? Sure. He's rotten on breakaways. A scrawny upper body is a liability on faceoffs. He doesn't/can't carry people to the net and he doesn't like getting hit.

Big deal.

THE INTANGIBLES

One cannot put a dollar value on the significance of having won, of being a winner, of knowing what it takes to win. Gretzky knows all those things, makes his team better by showing them and sharing them. After all he has achieved, he still has one of the top work ethics on the team. If the Greatest One can ride the bike extra after practice, how can some ordinary teammate dare not to?

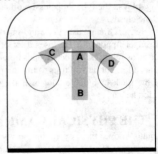

KELLY HRUDEY

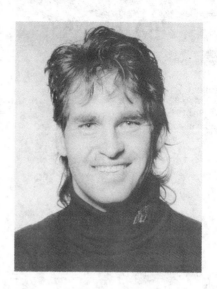

Yrs. of NHL service: 8
Born: Edmonton, Alta., Canada; January 13, 1961
Position: Goaltender
Height: 5-10
Weight: 180
Uniform no.: 32
Catches: Left

Career statistics:

GP	MINS	GA	SO	GAA	A	PIM
356	20183	1160	12	3.45	10	139

1990-91 statistics:

GP	MINS	GAA	W	L	T	SO	GA	S	SAPCT	PIM
47	2730	2.90	26	13	6	3	132	1321	.900	14

LAST SEASON

Played in five fewer games than 1989-90, but reduced goals against average from 4.07 and improved save percentage from .873. Loss total was career low, as was goals against total. Shutouts tied one-season high. Played 41 or more games for seventh consecutive season.

THE PHYSICAL GAME

Hrudey uses his instincts and reactions more than a strict butterfly or standup style.

He plays some low shots with his hands, which is unorthodox to say the least. Usually, goaltenders divide the net behind them into four sections that correspond to the areas behind their feet and hands. They don't often use their hands to stop shots their feet should handle any more than they do the reverse. But Hrudey gives himself an edge on the control aspect of things by gloving certain low shots; thus he controls/limits/denies rebounds and can direct pucks where he wants. It doesn't work for everybody, but it seems to help Hrudey.

Hrudey moves well, if a bit scrambly side-to-side. He reacts quickly on passes from the corners to the slot and not only stops those shots but controls and smothers the rebounds they cause. He is very alert, very quick, sees the puck very well.

But Hrudey has a fundamental flaw or two. He doesn't always get his stick to the goalpost first when he's moving to the post at his left; that leaves him vulnerable to stuff shots and to shots from the slot off passes from behind the net, which he should be blocking. And though he does a consistently excellent job of keeping the catching hand high, a key to balance and mobility, you know he's struggling when he surrenders that glove side.

Hrudey likes to play the puck, likes to catch the opponents napping and make the occasional long pass to a breaking teammate in the neutral zone.

THE MENTAL GAME

Hrudey plays his best when he is emotionally involved. He battles. He's intense, but under control, calm in the clutch. He keeps his head clear, looks forward, never backward. It's the next save that matters.

THE INTANGIBLES

The decision to rotate Hrudey with Daniel Berthiaume last season may have reduced Hrudey's playing time, but it kept him fresher—and that was important, as Hrudey is an extremely emotional competitor who drains himself in a game and can't always sustain high-level play over a long stretch of games.

BRAD JONES

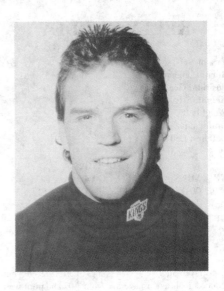

Yrs. of NHL service: 2
Born: Sterling Heights, Mich., USA; June 26, 1965
Position: Center
Height: 6-0
Weight: 195
Uniform no.: 47
Shoots: Left

Career statistics:

GP	G	A	TP	PIM
100	18	21	39	78

1990-91 statistics:

GP	G	A	TP	+/-	PIM	PP	SH	GW	GT	S	PCT
53	9	11	20	11	57	0	1	1	0	47	19.1

LAST SEASON

Games played and all offensive totals were career highs.

THE FINESSE GAME

One of the pure speed skaters in the league—straight ahead, end-to-end, the fastest player on his team—Jones needs to come out of his shell completely if he is going to be a relevant player.

He uses his speed to a degree, but does not use it much in tight because he also is not nearly as aggressive as he could be. Speed is less effective when a player is reluctant to use it to carry him to war for the puck, and that is a drawback of Jones' game.

He is working on that deficiency, however. Jones is stepping out of the perimeter and into the slot, accepting some hits, but still must improve if his credentials are to be respected. Until then, he will be used mostly in penalty-killing situations, so his speed at least can be used in pursuit of the puck.

Jones does have some scoring skill. He has an extremely hard and accurate snap shot, but he does not use it enough. Again, the snap is best used close-in, and Jones doesn't penetrate that often. It is fairly difficult not to get one shot per game, even by accident, but Jones succeeded in that endeavor last season

THE PHYSICAL GAME

Not a physical presence. Jones wants no part of the rough stuff, of bumping a guy off the puck, of winning a puck in the corner and bringing it to the net, of camping in front for a deflection or a screen.

THE INTANGIBLES

Jones' skills are well known. The question is whether he will go to the next plateau and use them to their maximums in order to secure regular ice time with an NHL team. It won't come without an acceptance of the physical nature of his profession and a commitment to rounding out his game.

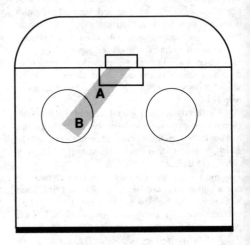

BOB KUDELSKI

Yrs. of NHL service: 3
Born: Springfield, Mass., USA; March 3, 1964
Position: Right wing
Height: 6-1
Weight: 200
Uniform no.: 37
Shoots: Right

Career statistics:

GP	G	A	TP	PIM
174	47	30	77	120

1990-91 statistics:

GP	G	A	TP	+/-	PIM	PP	SH	GW	GT	S	PCT
72	23	13	36	9	46	2	3	3	0	137	16.8

LAST SEASON

Games played total improved by 10. Goal, assist, point, power-play goal and game-winning goal totals all matched prior season's figures. Shot total went up by two, penalty minute total dropped by three, plus-minus improved by 16.

THE FINESSE GAME

Kudelski's outstanding attribute is his ability to shoot the puck off the pass. He is among the league's best in that department and complements the bomb with a sneaky-strong wrist shot.

He isn't going to blind anyone with his speed. Kudelski is an above-average skater, but it is not on a par with his shot.

If there is a quickness other than the release of his shot, it is in his mind. Kudelski is improving at getting himself open for a pass on offense, and he reads the defensive situation very well. That helps his center, who can take more chances knowing Kudelski has the defensive smarts to protect against a break the other way.

Versatility also is an asset. Kudelski played some center in college and is an effective faceoff man, which helps flesh out his penalty-killing skills and makes him an effective "second center" for power-play draws when the first center is thrown out of the circle.

THE PHYSICAL GAME

Kudelski doesn't play a grinding game, doesn't hit enough, but he gets involved—under control, with a purpose. He takes opponents off the puck along the boards, will go into traffic if the puck is there.

THE INTANGIBLES

Kudelski has a lot of talent, but at times is just a uniform with a body in it—he just is someplace else mentally, just putting in the shifts because the coach sends him out there. He is a confounding puzzle to teammates who feel he would achieve a great deal more if he made a greater commitment to improving his skills and conditioning.

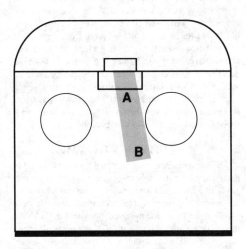

JARI KURRI

Yrs. of NHL service: 10
Born: Helsinki, Finland; May 18, 1960
Position: Right wing
Height: 6-0
Weight: 183
Uniform no.:
Shoots: Right

Career statistics:

GP	G	A	TP	PIM
754	474	569	1043	348

LAST SEASON
Played in Italy.

THE FINESSE GAME
A fluid skater who sees the ice extremely well, whose mental agility matches his skating agility, Kurri is one of the truly elegant players of his generation. Exceptional vision maximizes his two-way skills. He sees the openings, uses his speed and quickness to drive for them on offense; he sees dangers emerging and acts to prevent them on defense. And he does each with equal skill.

In fact, he transacts every element of finesse play at the highest possible level. Instant acceleration can drive him in any direction, at top speed or near it. The speed and accuracy of his slap shot and wrist shot are surpassed only by the quickness of their release. Kurri can take a pass in stride and fire off the rush; he can one-time the puck, can drive to the goalmouth for redirections. From the circles in, Kurri's magnificent hands and touch allow him to score from anywhere.

All those aspects make Kurri a high-level special-teams player who can handle the traffic but whose excellence is accentuated the more open ice there is available. While killing penalties, Kurri can sense when to sneak into the clear for a breakaway pass, can accept the pass in soft hands and can use pull-away speed to leave the defense well behind.

THE PHYSICAL GAME
His experience, mental toughness and strength make Kurri an extremely imposing player. You are not going to intimidate him as much as he can intimidate you with his skills and intellect and success. He gets involved, he fights for the puck, he wins the puck and then makes a strong play with it. Kurri reads off other players so well and has such one-step quickness; he can spring off a hit near the boards, be away with the puck and make a pass to a teammate before opponents can react

THE INTANGIBLES
A winner, a success, a player of achievement and character, Kurri would make any team dramatically better. But to be back with Wayne Gretzky makes Los Angeles the ideal place for him. The two of them are comfortable together as an old sweatshirt and a pair of jeans. They don't have much time left, but they will spend it making hockey magic.

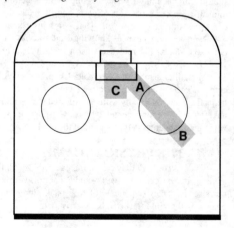

JOHN MCINTYRE

Yrs. of NHL service: 2
Born: Ravenswood, Ont., Canada; April 29, 1969
Position: Center
Height: 6-1
Weight: 180
Uniform no.: 44
Shoots: Left

Career statistics:

GP	G	A	TP	PIM
128	13	20	33	257

1990-91 statistics:

GP	G	A	TP	+/-	PIM	PP	SH	GW	GT	S	PCT
69	8	8	16	6	140	0	1	0	0	33	24.2

LAST SEASON

Obtained from Toronto, November 9, 1990, for Mike Krushelnyski. Goals, assists and penalty minutes were career bests.

THE FINESSE GAME

McIntyre's forte is the defensive aspect of the game, which is fine with a Los Angeles team that is heavily laden with offensive talents. He doesn't much have the hands for scoring, but the rare goals he does contribute come from hard work—slamming in a rebound, tipping shots—more than from a straight shot or a deke play.

McIntyre is projected as a solid player, one who is going to kill penalties and fill out to be a commanding presence on faceoffs in all three zones. Already effective on draws, McIntyre likes to scoop the puck on his forehand, then follow through with his body—planting his butt in the opposing center's way and buying his teammates time to reach the puck or to move it.

Skating is a bit of a problem. His stride gets very choppy as he digs his feet into the ice and churns away, so his speed is only average and is not the equal of his balance, which he uses to advantage when tying up an opponent in front of the net.

THE PHYSICAL GAME

McIntyre is a big, strong, extremely physical presence, a good grinding player who is honest, hard-working and always on the scene when things get nasty. If they aren't nasty, he will initiate. McIntyre plays big and likes to hit, which is not a bad thing.

THE INTANGIBLES

McIntyre is working on his skating, shooting and faceoffs. He studies the game, sees what other centers do; so, because he is only 22, projections can remain rosy for a while.

If he reaches potential, the Kings may have themselves a Guy Carbonneau/Troy Murray-type player who will produce 20 goals from a defensive posture.

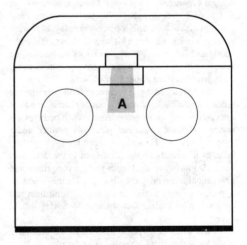

159

MARTY MCSORLEY

Yrs. of NHL service: 8
Born: Hamilton, Ont., Canada; May 18, 1963
Position: Defenseman
Height: 6-1
Weight: 225
Uniform no.: 33
Shoots: Right

Career statistics:

GP	G	A	TP	PIM
449	56	110	166	1779

1990-91 statistics:

GP	G	A	TP	+/-	PIM	PP	SH	GW	GT	S	PCT
61	7	32	39	48	221	1	1	1	0	100	7.0

LAST SEASON

Shared NHL lead in plus-minus with Calgary's Theoren Fleury; plus-minus jumped 46 goals. Assist total was career high, penalty-minute total dropped by 101.

THE FINESSE GAME

McSorley has one speed—trudge—and it takes a while to reach that. Once he is moving in one direction, it will be a very long time before he can change the route. He does not turn well.

Generally, he passes to skates or shinguards before finding a teammate's sticktape, the exception being a very nice eye and touch from the point, where he takes a very strong shot or spots the open man and gets him the puck for a high-percentage play. McSorley also has a quick release on his wrist shot in traffic and a good head for the safe play; the pucks he reaches, he smacks to the wall and out of danger—gets them as far away from his team's goal as possible.

On defense, McSorley screens off players who are pressuring the puck, buying his partner some time for a rush up ice. But for those occasions when he helps his partner, McSorley also can place his partner under extreme pressure. He seems to need his stick for balance, as it is rarely on the ice—even in the defensive zone. He pinches up the boards at the wrong times and gets caught when the puck slips past. He misjudges an opponent's speed as the rush comes at him, then can only watch his partner face the man McSorley should have had.

And when he is panic-stricken in the defensive zone, McSorley takes himself out of the play by flopping to the ice, trying to block shots—only to have forwards step right past him for a scoring chance.

THE PHYSICAL GAME

McSorley, of course, is a physical threat. He gets a piece of an opponent at every possible opportunity, though his range is so limited, he cannot reach as many players as he would like.

McSorley is mean in front of his net, and just about everywhere else—a reputation which gains him skating room. McSorley uses that edge to his advantage, as it provides the extra time he needs to make a decent play. Like that nasty shark in the old Jaws movies, he keeps people on edge, they never know if he's just out for a swim or if he wants a snack.

THE INTANGIBLES

One thing is certain: all McSorley's mistakes, and there are many, are of comission, not omission. He has tremendous pride and is always trying to make the most of his eminently finite skills.

With barely a handful of finesse skills, McSorley was plus 48 last year. No matter what you think of the stat, plus 48 is a major-league number and it is not something you do with mirrors. He has learned his position and is learning how to minimize the situations where his vulnerabilities can be exploited.

JAY MILLER

Yrs. of NHL service: 6
Born: Wellesley, Mass., USA; July 16, 1960
Position: Left wing
Height: 6-2
Weight: 210
Uniform no.: 29
Shoots: Left

Career statistics:

GP	G	A	TP	PIM
379	36	37	73	1474

1990-91 statistics:

GP	G	A	TP	+/-	PIM	PP	SH	GW	GT	S	PCT
66	8	12	20	9	259	1	0	0	0	35	22.9

LAST SEASON

Goal total was second best of career. Shooting percentage was over 22 per cent for third straight year. Penalty total was four-season high. Plus-minus improved by 15 goals.

THE FINESSE GAME

Jay Miller has a better offensive touch than it is possible to imagine, given the fact fighting is his job and he enjoys doing it.

He can score. Miller has 25 goals on 109 shots over three seasons, a 22.9 per cent shooting percentage. He has some moves in front. He has hands, yes, even with his gloves on; he has a very hard shot.

Miller rarely shoots because he rarely has the puck. He still has something of a tough-guy mentality that tells him he doesn't have to score, that his role is to fight and that it is others' jobs to score.

But he can do it. He can skate a bit, shows it most when he skates to the net from the outside and forces the defensemen to turn and stay with him. He has balance, though he depends more on strength than speed—of which he has none—to carry him inside the scoring area.

THE PHYSICAL GAME

Miller remains a premier tough guy in the league. He will still fight the tough guys, relishes the challenge. He is a good athlete and competitor who makes intelligent reads of situations. But he usually is placed in a role where he is asked to do one thing and one thing only: punch face.

THE INTANGIBLES

Miller seems satisfied with his role and the Kings seems satisfied with his performance of it, as they signed him to a new contract at very nice money. Which is worse—that he got eight goals on 35 shots for the Kings or that Gino Cavallini got eight on 131 shots for the Blues?

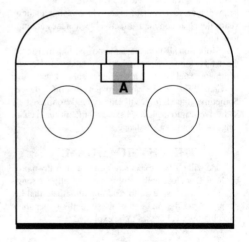

LARRY ROBINSON

Yrs. of NHL service: 19
Born: Winchester, Ont., Canada; June 2, 1951
Position: Defenseman
Height: 6-4
Weight: 225
Uniform no.: 19
Shoots: Left

Career statistics:

GP	G	A	TP	PIM
1328	205	740	945	756

1990-91 statistics:

GP	G	A	TP	+/-	PIM	PP	SH	GW	GT	S	PCT
62	1	22	23	22	16	0	0	0	0	70	1.4

LAST SEASON

Goal total was career low, assists total was lowest in 18 seasons. Plus-minus improved by 15 goals.

THE FINESSE GAME

Robinson still covers acres with his stride, leads an occasional rush and makes a fine lead pass. He has splendid hands and a brilliant hockey mind, which is one reason he has lasted this long and may last even longer.

Few defenseman have the skill Robinson does at keeping the puck and the man away from the net. He is so strong and has such a long reach, which he uses to significant advantage. He intercepts crossing passes, keeps players to the outside as best he can after all these years, then leans on them effectively when they attempt to cut in.

Robinson also is a master at positioning in front of the net. He knows every trick and uses them all. He will tie up your stick, he will give you the subtle knee or the "invisible" jab at the ankle to get you off balance. Sometimes, he simply will lean strongly on his stick and drive it into a player's skates—the ultimate challenge of that player's balance.

THE PHYSICAL GAME

He will not win every strength matchup any more, but he will not lose many. Robinson is so tall, so strong, so fit, so smart, so able to read and anticipate that he simply steers the plays into his strengths rather than allowing his weaknesses to be exploited.

THE INTANGIBLES

Robinson still can help, but he will need to be paced and spotted if coach Tom Webster is to get as much out of him as he did last season. Robinson is 40 years old, he has played 20 years, and he still enjoys it more than anybody; he's like a rookie who thinks hockey is the best job in the world. It will not be his much longer.

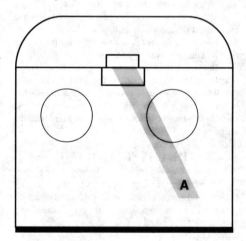

LUC ROBITAILLE

Yrs. of NHL service: 5
Born: Montreal, Que., Canada; February 17, 1966
Position: Left wing
Height: 6-1
Weight: 190
Uniform no.: 20
Shoots: Left

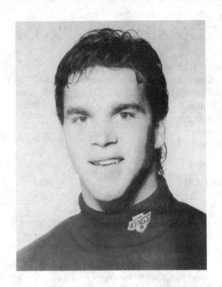

Career statistics:

GP	G	A	TP	PIM
393	241	244	485	281

1990-91 statistics:

GP	G	A	TP	+/-	PIM	PP	SH	GW	GT	S	PCT
76	45	46	91	28	68	11	0	5	1	229	19.7

LAST SEASON

Fifth straight season of 45 goals or more, fourth straight season of 90 points or more. Plus-minus jumped by 20 goals.

THE FINESSE GAME

Robitaille's overall speed and quickness pale in comparison to his exceptional hands, shooting skills and goal-scoring ability—assets he maximizes with a number of finesse skills.

On the skating end, Robitaille may not be fleet, but he makes himself faster by using his head—by deciding where he is going to shoot or pass almost before he gets the puck, by using his vision of the ice and read of the play to sense which is the optimal scoring position.

On the shooting end, Robitaille retains the element of surprise by varying the selection and location of his shots. Robitaille has an accurate snap shot off the rush and a quick release on the slap shot. He will go high, then low, but always will put it where he wants because his stick control is extremely good. That also helps significantly on deflections, an expert aspect of his game because his hand-eye coordination is so good.

Robitaille also is accepting more defensive responsibilities, working to make himself more complete.

THE PHYSICAL GAME

Robitaille is a very determined player, a second- and third-effort scorer who goes to the net to try to screen the goaltender or attempt a deflection. He keeps his legs driving and regains his footing quickly when he is knocked down. He will go into the traffic areas, handle the contact and win his share of loose pucks.

THE INTANGIBLES

Robitaille is maturing, growing into a better player than just a pure goal scorer. He wants the team to go farther in the playoffs and wants the responsibility for that progress on his shoulders. He is changing from someone who played for fun to someone who takes a serious approach to the profession.

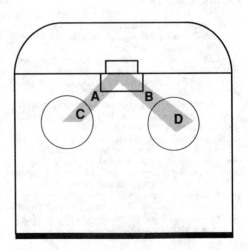

TOMAS SANDSTROM

Yrs. of NHL service: 7
Born: Jakobstad, Sweden; September 4, 1964
Position: Right wing
Height: 6-2
Weight: 200
Uniform no.: 7
Shoots: Left

Career statistics:

GP	G	A	TP	PIM
403	231	271	502	697

1990-91 statistics:

GP	G	A	TP	+/-	PIM	PP	SH	GW	GT	S	PCT
68	45	44	89	27	106	16	0	6	1	221	20.4

LAST SEASON

Goal and point totals were career highs, shooting percentage improved from 12.9. Power-play goal production improved by nine, game-winning goal production doubled. Plus-minus improved by 38 goals. Games played was a five-season low.

THE FINESSE GAME

A player of commanding size and range, imposing strength and intimidating determination, Sandstrom's game approaches the unstoppable most nights. He has a splendid, explosive first step that jump-starts his acceleration to top speed. He has an immense, powerful stride and upper-body strength that helps put the sizzle in his overwhelming slap shot. Only a dope of a defenseman would play the body on a Sandstrom rush; even if you play the body, you may slow him, but you have to be very strong to stop him.

A whimsical player with the puck, Sandstrom will use his finesse skills and imagination. Just for the heck of it, he will make a 360-degree turn with the puck and sweep a backhand at the net on the mere chance it might create a rebound he can convert. From center ice, he will shoulder-fake, as though he is going to drive the puck around the boards, then drill a shot on net to keep the goalie honest.

But there also are finer strokes on the canvas; Sandstrom has moves in tight. He can feather the puck between a defenseman's skates and use his agility to step around, reclaim it and snap or wrist a shot to the net. And now, with Gretzky, he has a center who challenges him to get open—plus a center intelligent enough to get open in return, which forces Sandstrom to be crafty both with the puck and without it.

A harrier on defense, Sandstrom will use his reach to attempt a sweep check. He is alert, picks up a man; he will come back and lift an opponent's stick from behind to steal the puck.

THE PHYSICAL GAME

Sandstrom hits whenever he can, and is strong enough to punish people physically. He is chippy, aggressive, brash at times, mean at others, but has no problem with being a target on the ice. He never disappears or hides; if you want him, you know where to find him.

Sandstrom uses his strength to scrap along the boards, uses his skating power and balance to beat his check back into the play after contact. Sandstrom has no regard whatever for his physical well-being. He does not hesitate to drive to the net and place himself at physical risk in order to get a scoring play finished. Keeps his legs moving, even when being held, driving through checks and carrying whatever opponents he can to the scoring area.

THE INTANGIBLES

This guy plays with broken bones. You have to tie him to the bench to stop him. Maybe it never would have happened in New York, maybe he never would have become the player he is now, but the Rangers very certainly would like to know.

Can you imagine a more imposing set of right wings than Tomas Sandstrom and Jari Kurri? A more imposing line than Sandstrom, Gretzky and Kurri if everyone stays healthy?

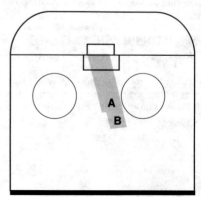

DAVE TAYLOR

Yrs. of NHL service: 14
Born: Levack, Ont., Canada; December 4, 1955
Position: Right wing
Height: 6-0
Weight: 190
Uniform no.: 18
Shoots: Right

Career statistics:

GP	G	A	TP	PIM
953	411	607	1018	1449

1990-91 statistics:

GP	G	A	TP	+/-	PIM	PP	SH	GW	GT	S	PCT
73	23	30	53	27	148	6	0	2	1	122	18.9

LAST SEASON

Games played was a five-season high, PIM was a career high, plus-minus improved by 10 goals.

THE FINESSE GAME

Taylor only knows one way, and that is top-speed, full-out, every shift. Top speed never exceeded the legal limit, and now it is more persistence and consistence than insistence. He is the ideal "third man high" in the attack zone, uses his anticipation to maximize his still-sharp defensive instincts.

Twenty-three goals is a very acceptable output for a fellow who played with Charlie Simmer and Marcel Dionne. He remains strong in the slot, picking up his goals in about a 15-foot radius of the net. Balance remains a strength; he can drive into dense traffic for loose pucks and can make plays in a crowd.

To compensate for declining speed, Taylor has built an exceptional conditioning base. He may be fitter now than ever, and can still get the job done from the offensive and defensive standpoints.

THE PHYSICAL GAME

Taylor's all-time high penalty figure suggests more overt emotionalism than ever, in addition to the physical skills he always was willing to use. He hits as hard and as often as possible, still makes the plays out of the corners, still goes to the trouble spots and sticks his nose in—even if there's a plastic shield in front of it now.

THE INTANGIBLES

Taylor always demands more of himself that anyone else ever could demand of him. He needs more nights off now, because he gets tired and can't handle 100-plus games per season, but he can still do it skillwise and his experience is of great benefit to younger players.

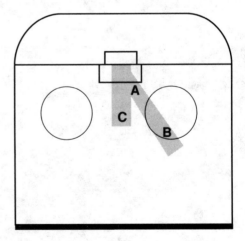

165

MINNESOTA
NORTH STARS

BRIAN BELLOWS

Yrs. of NHL service: 9
Born: St. Catherines, Ont., Canada; September 1, 1964
Position: Left wing
Height: 5-11
Weight: 195
Uniform no.: 23
Shoots: left

Career statistics:

GP	G	A	TP	PIM
673	312	335	647	496

1990-91 statistics:

GP	G	A	TP	+/-	PIM	PP	SH	GW	GT	S	PCT
80	35	40	75	-13	43	17	0	4	0	296	11.8

LAST SEASON

Led team in shots. Second on club in goals, power play goals and points. Only North Star to play in all 80 games. Worst plus-minus on team.

THE FINESSE GAME

Bellows has developed into a very solid all-around player. All of his skills are above average, yet none of his skills stands out above the others.

Bellows is a very good skater, strong and with excellent balance. He can drive to the net as well as any of the NHL's best power forwards. He is not very fast on open ice but he is nimble in traffic. Bellows doesn't have many lace-trimmed moves. He prefers traveling the shortest distance between himself and the net.

Bellows has tremdendous hand skills and can pick the puck out of a tangle of sticks and skates. He is a good passer but the real beauty of his game lies in his shot. He can shoot in tight or rifle a one-timer from the circle. Bellows is an excellent power play quarterback, and even when other teams try to key on him and shut him down, he can play through it.

Bellows is not a good checker although he plays responsibly and is better than he used to be.

THE PHYSICAL GAME

Bellows has incredible strength and he uses every ounce of it. he will grind along the boards and in the corners. He will use his body to bump defensemen off the puck and, when he doesn't get back defensively, will sacrifice himself. He won't be intimidated. Bellows knows the Stars need more than goals from him. He has to crash the net and check.

THE INTANGIBLES

The knock on Bellows in past years has been his inconsistent efforts, but Bellows quieted those critics with an outstanding playoffs. Bellows took nothing for granted during the regular season as he proved himself to a new coach and GM. And when crunch time came in the playoffs, Bellows was there.

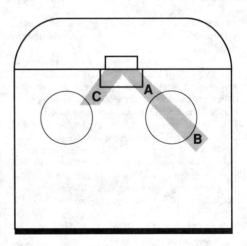

NEAL BROTEN

Yrs. of NHL service: 10
Born: Roseau, Minn., USA; November 29, 1959
Position: Center
Height: 5-9
Weight: 170
Uniform no.: 7
Shoots: left

Career statistics:

GP	G	A	TP	PIM
772	229	500	729	419

1990-91 statistics:

GP	G	A	TP	+/-	PIM	PP	SH	GW	GT	S	PCT
79	13	56	69	-3	26	1	2	0	1	191	6.8

LAST SEASON

Led team in assists. Fourth on team in points. Goal total was three-season low. Assists and points were two-season lows.

THE FINESSE GAME

Broten has tremendous finesse skills and intuition. He has had to be urged to shoot more through most of his career. He still prefers to pass rather than shoot, but at this stage in his career he will recognize when his shot is the best option and will take it. But his playmaking skill is exceptional. He can thread passes through traffic or skim a hard pass to break out a teammate. He is very artistic and has to play with alert teammates because he can make a scoring opportunity out of a seemingly impossible situation. The North Stars have a rule on their power play: when in trouble, get the puck to Broten, and he'll find a way to get things started.

He is a great skater with great balance and is really tough to knock off the puck. Broten is very deceptive. He can get himself or his teammates into scoring position by his activity in the zone. Broten has very good acceleration and is agile. Checkers have to keep close tabs on him because he is a quiet sort who can suddenly disappear and reappear in a dangerous area.

To top off all of his skills, Broten has terrific hockey sense. He sees the ice very well, which makes him an excellent quarterback on the power play, especially because of his passing skills. Broten is underrated defensively and is very good down low.

THE PHYSICAL GAME

Broten is not a physical player and is at his best when the ice opens up. He is a very hard worker, and willing, but he does not have the strength to out-muscle bigger players. He prefers to dart in and out with the puck. It's a smart game for a player of his small size.

THE INTANGIBLES

Broten is the real heart of the North Stars. Age is creeping up on him (he will be 32 shortly after the season begins), but it has not diminished his work ethic. Broten has so many strengths and is so valuable to the team that his value can't be measured in goals.

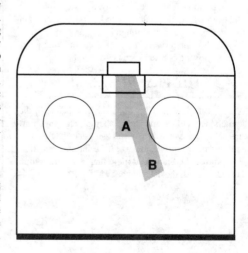

JON CASEY

Yrs. of NHL service: 4
Born: Grand Rapids, Minn., USA; March 29, 1962
Position: Goaltender
Height: 5-10
Weight: 155
Uniform no.: 30
Catches: left

Career statistics:

GP	MINS	GA	SO	GAA	A	PIM
213	11702	630	7	3.23	6	58

1990-91 statistics:

GP	MINS	GAA	W	L	T	SO	GA	S	SAPCT	PIM
55	3,185	2.98	21	20	11	3	158	1,450	.891	22

LAST SEASON

Fourth in NHL in minutes played.

THE PHYSICAL GAME

Casey's style is unorthodox, a result of his breaking into the NHL as a scrambling, reflexive goalie, and then taking more than two years in the minors to develop a classic, play-the-angles style. Casey is unafraid to venture out of his net to challenge shooters. He does more than challenge them with his aggressiveness—he often startles them, especialy on breakaways or one-on-ones. He is a small goalie, but because of his effectiveness at cutting down the angles, he plays bigger than he is. He doesn't surrender much of the net, and few goals come cheaply.

When Casey does get caught out of his net, he doesn't panic and flop about like a beached fish. He keeps skating, chasing a player like a defenseman if he has to, anything to force the issue. He will knock a player down if he has to. Casey is capable of making some amazing recoveries from disastrous situations.

Casey does not stickhandle well, although he uses his stick to poke check around the net. He has a very quick glove hand and is capable of grabbing pucks that appear to have gotten past him.

THE MENTAL GAME

Casey is a shy and quiet man, but an intense competitor who proved in the playoffs that he is capable of winning games on his own. He concentrates well and is not fazed by bad goals or games. He doesn't need a coach to point out his flaws. Casey knows the game well enough to know what he's done wrong and the next game can't roll around fast enough. His confidence does falter on occasion, but the funks don't last long.

THE INTANGIBLES

It's hard to believe the North Stars signed Casey to a termination contract three years ago. Where would they be without him? After several seasons of playing well for an unsuccessful team, Casey got to strut his stuff during the Stars' amazing run to the Stanley Cup final. He is a proven No. 1 goalie now, and the only question is if that undisputed status will rob him of any of the drive to prove himself. Casey has demonstrated enough maturity to indicate that shouldn't happen. He has been a winner at every level he's played.

SHANE CHURLA

Yrs. of NHL service: 3
Born: Fernie, B.C., Canada; June 24, 1965
Position: Right wing
Height: 6-1
Weight: 200
Uniform no.: 27
Shoots: right

Career statistics:

GP	G	A	TP	PIM
162	6	11	17	879

1990-91 statistics:

GP	G	A	TP	+/-	PIM	PP	SH	GW	GT	S	PCT
40	2	2	4	+1	284	0	0	0	0	32	6.3

LAST SEASON

Despite missing half the season with a separated shoulder, Churla led the team in PIM.

THE FINESSE GAME

Churla has average skills for an NHL police-man—good enough to keep him in the lineup, but not so good that he can start thinking of becoming the next Bob Probert.

Churla has pretty good hands and scored a couple of big goals for the Stars in the playoffs. His reacton time is slow and because he is a bit of a slug as a skater, he has difficulty getting in good position for a shot. He needs to be casting his shadow on the goalie.

He has worked to improve his skating, but he lacks any speed or mobility. His desire to get the job done ranks higher than his skating skill. Churla played pretty responsible defense last season.

THE PHYSICAL GAME

Churla has become a more effective enforcer because he can play a disciplined style when necessary. To carry through a stat we showed you last year: for every NHL goal he has scored, Churla has accumulated 146.5 minutes in penalties. But in the playoffs, when the Stars needed him to play smart, Churla scored two goals and had "only" 90 PIM, without losing any of his toughness. Churla doesn't have much range, but he will hit whatever crosses his path. And he is a legitimate heavyweight fighter.

THE INTANGIBLES

Churla's value to the Stars is for his toughness on the ice and his heart and soul in the dressing room. He protects his smaller teammates and will do whatever the coaching staff asks of him.

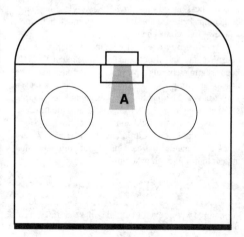

MIKE CRAIG

Yrs. of NHL service: 1
Born: London, Ont., Canada; June 6, 1971
Position: Right wing
Height: 6-0
Weight: 180
Uniform no.: 20
Shoots: right

Career statistics:

GP	G	A	TP	PIM
39	8	4	12	32

1990-91 statistics:

GP	G	A	TP	+/-	PIM	PP	SH	GW	GT	S	PCT
39	8	4	12	-11	32	1	0	2	0	59	13.6

LAST SEASON

First season in NHL. Second worst plus-minus on club. Missed games with a broken right hand.

THE FINESSE GAME

Craig is a creative player with an ability to produce offensively in a number of ways. An indication of his ability is that he was used as a linemate for Eric Lindros in the 1991 World Junior Championships. Craig sees the open man and times his plays very well. He has good hockey sense and plays unselfishly.

Craig plays intelligently around the net. He has a good wrist shot that he gets away quickly. His offensive instincts make him a natural for the power play. He has very good hands.

Craig skates with good speed, acceleration and balance. He needs to work on the defensive aspects of his game.

THE PHYSICAL GAME

Craig is a banger, an aggressive forechecker. He angles his man off the puck by anticipating the play well. Craig is gentlemanly, but will not shy from the physical game. He will stir things up and has a good work ethic.

THE INTANGIBLES

Craig was moved in and out of the lineup down the stretch and in the playoffs because of his inconsistency, but he may be ready to step into a regular role this season.

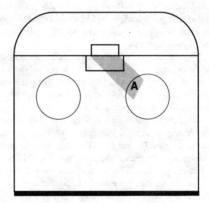

ULF DAHLEN

Yrs. of NHL service: 4
Born: Ostersund, Sweden; January 12, 1967
Position: Right wing
Height: 6-2
Weight: 195
Uniform no.: 22
Shoots: left

Career statistics:

GP	G	A	TP	PIM
268	94	82	176	112

1990-91 statistics:

GP	G	A	TP	+/-	PIM	PP	SH	GW	GT	S	PCT
66	21	18	39	+7	6	4	0	3	0	133	15.8

LAST SEASON

Goal total was two-season high. PIM was career low.

THE FINESSE GAME

In what might be an unusual description for a Swedish player, Dahlen is among the best cornermen in the NHL, and is assuredly the most unsung. Dahlen has excellent balance, which is the strongest part of his overall good skating ability. He has little speed and no flash. He takes a hit, rolls with it and keeps going with the puck. He has John Tonelli-like tenacity, and doesn't just go in banging. He plots out his play and has the hand skills to execute.

One of Dahlen's favorite moves is to carry the puck in down the wing and turn sideways as he comes along the defense. This way he protects the puck with his body and he is impossible to knock off the puck because of his skating strength.

Dahlen has an accurate wrist shot, but doesn't shoot enough. Like most Europeans, he prefers to work as a set-up man. He has great patience with the puck, sometimes too much, when he gets into lulls of overhandling. Dahlen is in and out of the lineup because of his inconsistent play, but he always seems to come back strong after a benching.

THE PHYSICAL GAME

Dahlen has good size but doesn't always play to it. He was criticized once this season for being a 198-pound player in a 208-pound body. He is not a very aggressive player except in the pursuit of the puck—meaning he doesn't play as well as he should without it. Dahlen has to be judged by harsher standards because of his capabilities. He could become a tremendous two-way player but needs to develop a more forceful game.

THE INTANGIBLES

Dahlen was supposed to be ticketed for the West Coast in part of the complicated deal between the Stars and the expansion Sharks, but some quick manuevering kept him in Minnesota. GM Bob Clarke's interest in keeping Dahlen is a testament to his importance, largely as a team man. He is very well liked by his fellow Stars.

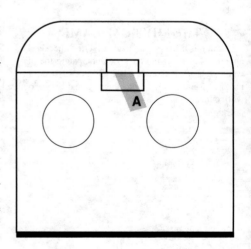

GAETAN DUCHESNE

Yrs. of NHL service: 10
Born: Les Saulles, Que., Canada; July 11, 1962
Position: Left wing
Height: 5-11
Weight: 200
Uniform no.: 10
Shoots: left

Career statistics:

GP	G	A	TP	PIM
743	140	199	339	434

1990-91 statistics:

GP	G	A	TP	+/-	PIM	PP	SH	GW	GT	S	PCT
68	9	9	18	+4	18	0	0	1	0	100	9.0

LAST SEASON

Games played and point totals were career lows.

THE FINESSE GAME

Is Duchesne well-respected as a defensive forward? Just consider the assignment he was given in the playoffs: shut down Brett Hull, the NHL's leading goal scorer. Mission accomplished.

Duchesne routinely plays against the other team's top forwards. He is a very good skater and accents that with excellent vision. Most of his scoring chances come when he intimidates puck carriers with his skating and uses his good anticipation to pick off passes. He doesn't have great hands and he needs a lot of time to get his shot away. His goals will come from short-range wrist shots and scrambles around the net. Despite his great vision, he is not a good playmaker either, because he does not pass the puck well.

Duchesne is an excellent penalty killer but is not a shorthanded scoring threat because of his lack of offensive skills.

THE PHYSICAL GAME

Duchesne will sacrifice himself for the team. He is of average height but very solid, and by playing smart and positioning himself well he can avoid getting into trouble in situations where he will be outmuscled by bigger players. He will initiate contact in all zones in his checking role.

THE INTANGIBLES

Duchesne sticks to what he does best, the checker's role, and does it well. He plays with the energy and effort of a man who knows there's always someone younger and faster, with more scoring potential, and stays in the lineup because it is going to take that younger person years to learn what he already knows.

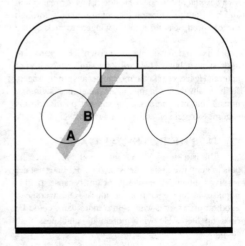

TODD ELIK

Yrs. of NHL service: 2
Born: Brampton, Ont., Canada; April 15, 1966
Position: Center
Height: 6-2
Weight: 190 Uniform no.:
Shoots: left

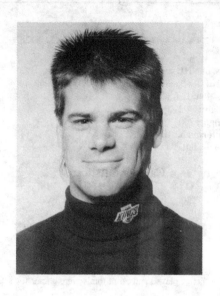

Career statistics:

GP	G	A	TP	PIM
122	31	60	91	99

1990-91 statistics:

GP	G	A	TP	+/-	PIM	PP	SH	GW	GT	S	PCT
74	21	37	58	+20	58	2	0	4	0	153	13.7

LAST SEASON

Acquired from Los Angeles for Randy Gilhen, Charlie Huddy, Jim Thompson and a fourth-round draft choice in 1991 (Alexei Zhitnik), June 22, 1991. Games played and all point totals career highs.

THE FINESSE GAME

Elik is a predominantly offensive player with good speed, balance and agility. He handles the puck well and has a good shot. Although he is not a natural scorer, he does score, and in a number of different ways. He can shoot well enough with his wrist shot or he can use his speed to drive to the net, beat a defender and score.

As a center, Elik is more a driving force than a playmaking force. He sometimes doesn't utilize his wingers at the right times, even when it would be in his own best interest to do so. He doesn't have great vision and he'll put pressure on the defense mainly through use of speed, leaving it to his wingers to pick up the pieces.

Elik is defensively inconsistent. He seems to understand it, but it's hard work for him because it's not natural. He likes to stay in motion because of his speed, so he's always swinging, and sometimes swinging himself out of a defensive or support position in his eagerness to get something going offensively.

THE PHYSICAL GAME

Elik is a strong player with good size, which he puts to good use in the offensive zone. He does not get involved much defensively, again because of his impulses to get the jump on the attack. He is average to good on draws, and with a little more work could be right up there. He wins more with quickness than strength.

THE INTANGIBLES

Elik is unreliable when it comes to crunch time. Although he has developed and matured, there is still much room for growth in that area. Inconsistency has also plagued him, especially defensively—if coach Bob (Selke Trophy) Gainey can't cure that, who can?

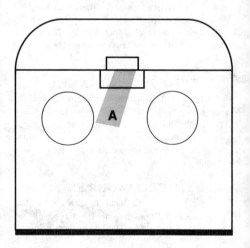

DAVE GAGNER

Yrs. of NHL service: 5
Born: Chatham, Ont., Canada; December 11, 1964
Position: Center
Height: 5-10
Weight: 180
Uniform no.: 15
Shoots: left

Career statistics:

GP	G	A	TP	PIM
358	134	150	287	374

1990-91 statistics:

GP	G	A	TP	+/-	PIM	PP	SH	GW	GT	S	PCT
73	40	42	82	+9	114	20	0	5	2	223	17.9

LAST SEASON

Led club in goals, points, power play goals and plus-minus. Third on club in assists. Goal total matches career high. PIM was career high. Served a one-game stick suspension.

THE FINESSE GAME

Gagner is a skilled player, but all of his skills are based on his determination and grittiness. Gagner has a good shot from the top of the circle, but he won't blow it by anyone. He is better in tight, where he works hard and uses his good mobility and balance. He will go to the net and stick his nose in. Gagner has found the balance between patience with the puck and a quick release - he consistently makes the best shot selection.

He is a very intelligent player who has great vision, but he is not a playmaker. He is a finisher, but one who will get the puck himself if he has to.

Gagner is not a great skater but he has the quickness to get around people, and that makes the defense tentative. He is very strong on his skates and his powerful stride earns him that extra step. He is quick to move to open space, although he is not afraid to go in traffic.

Gagner is not an outstanding defensive player, but he is adequate and has worked to improve that part of his game.

THE PHYSICAL GAME

Gagner plays to about twice his size. He knows he has to survive in the NHL by hard work, so he doesn't let up, even for one shift. He is aggressive and fearless, and he will go after bigger players. He is feisty and will take or make hits to make plays. He will use his stick (as evidenced by his suspension).

THE INTANGIBLES

Gagner was on the scrap heap a few seasons back and was planning on leaving the NHL to play in Europe. His wife talked him out of it, and the Stars should give her a playoff bonus. Gagner is a team leader on the ice (he is less vocal off it, leaving that to holler-guys Basil McRae and Shane Churla). He is enthusiastic and a competitor.

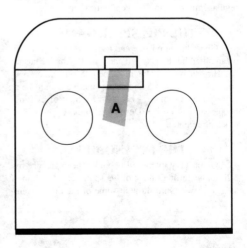

BRIAN GLYNN

Yrs. of NHL service: 2
Born: Iserlohn, West Germany; November 23, 1967
Position: Defenseman
Height: 6-4
Weight: 215
Uniform no.: 6
Shoots: left

Career statistics:

GP	G	A	TP	PIM
143	13	26	39	189

1990-91 statistics:

GP	G	A	TP	+/-	PIM	PP	SH	GW	GT	S	PCT
66	8	11	19	-5	83	3	0	0	0	111	7.2

LAST SEASON

Acquired from Calgary for Frank Musil, October 26, 1990. Games played was three-season high. Goal total was career high. Point total matched career high.

THE FINESSE GAME

Glynn is a big defenseman with a cannon shot and he likes to jump up and get involved in the offense. He will be the fourth man on a rush, and the Stars gave him the license to do it. He could develop into a very good point man on the power play.

Glynn has fairly good speed, which allows him to get into the attack flow, but has to concentrate on his positional play because his lateral movement is not first-rate.

Glynn has had a tough time sticking in the NHL because of his inconsistent defensive play. Given a regular shift, his game will continue to improve.

THE PHYSICAL GAME

Glynn has good size and uses it well. He is not a mean hitter, but he is tough and will do what he has to do. He can overwhelm most people on one-on-one contests. He is so big and strong that he should be a more punishing hitter - not to the extent of chasing people around the ice. Despite his bulk, Glynn is not much of a fighter.

THE INTANGIBLES

Glynn has a lot of ability but has been plagued by self-doubts through most of his spotty career. Minnesota stuck with him through some of his inconsistent play and that show of confidence and his playoff performance should give his game a real boost. He is still young and could prove to be a late bloomer.

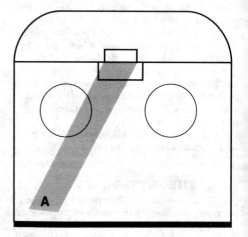

JIM JOHNSON

Yrs. of NHL service: 6
Born: New Hope, Minn., USA; August 9, 1962
Position: Defenseman
Height: 6-1
Weight: 190
Uniform no.: 8
Shoots: left

Career statistics:

GP	G	A	TP	PIM
434	15	104	119	758

1990-91 statistics:

GP	G	A	TP	+/-	PIM	PP	SH	GW	GT	S	PCT
68	1	14	15	+6	123	0	0	0	0	83	1.2

LAST SEASON

Acquired from Pittsburgh with Chris Dahlquist for Larry Murphy and Peter Taglianetti, December 11, 1990. Games played, goal and point totals were three-season lows.

THE FINESSE GAME

Johnson's game is all in his head. He understands the game and recognizes his abilities and limitations, and plays accordingly. He is an active rather than a reactive player, forcing plays at the blue line and challenging shooters.

He does not get involved offensively, but stays back and works well paired with an offensively minded partner. He is a good skater who can get back quickly (although he's never far up ice). Johnson's skating ability helps him positionally and as a checker, since his moving targets have trouble eluding him.

While Johnson does not rush the puck, he will pass it crisply out of his zone and most of his assists come from rushes he generates on breakouts. He sees the ice well, knows where his teammates are and seldom is forced into a bad pass.

THE PHYSICAL GAME

Johnson is an honest competitor who won't be intimidated. He isn't mean but he is intense and will do all the right things to clear out his end of the ice. He plays positionally, finishes his checks and checks hard. He won't be intimidated and will fight if he has to, but is smart enough to not go looking for trouble. He has become a solid defensive defenseman.

THE INTANGIBLES

Johnson was a missing link in the Stars' firmament, a stay-at-home defenseman who allowed defense partners like Mark Tinordi and Brian Glynn to get involved offensively. He has been underrated through most of his career, but has found a happy home in his native state.

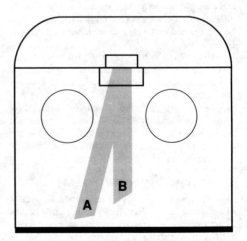

CRAIG LUDWIG

Yrs. of NHL service: 9
Born: Rhinelander, Wisc., USA, March 15, 1961
Position: Defenseman
Height: 6-3
Weight: 215
Uniform no.: 17
Shoots: left

Career statistics:

GP	G	A	TP	PIM
672	27	119	146	696

1990-91 statistics:

GP	G	A	TP	+/-	PIM	PP	SH	GW	GT	S	PCT
75	1	8	9	-24	77	0	0	0	0	46	2.2

LAST SEASON

Acquired from New York Islanders for Tom Kurvers, June 22, 1991. Plus-minus was lowest on Islanders.

THE FINESSE GAME

Ludwig is a very experienced, defensive defenseman who had to learn a new defense system when he came to the Islanders after eight seasons with Montreal. Montreal defensemen learn to protect the middle of the ice, sag, let the shooter take the shot and then play the rebound. The Islanders (under coach Al Arbour) want tight gap control, with the defenseman staying within two stick-lengths of the shooter and forcing him to make the play. Ludwig made the transition with some difficulty at first, then had a solid first half. Inexplicably, he reverted back to his Montreal tendencies in the second.

His mobility is below average, but he makes up for that by his experience and his ability to read plays, which is excellent. He is mentally tough and is always poised under pressure.

Ludwig moves the puck well but does not get involved offensively. He is a classic stay-at-home defenseman. He would be more effective paired with a good offensive defenseman, but the Islanders did not have one last season.

THE PHYSICAL GAME

Although Ludwig is wiry and strong, he usually ties players up rather than hits. Once in a while he gets a burr under his saddle and does start punishing people, and he can be a mean hitter. He keeps players in front of him and anyone trying to invade his turf will pay a price, as Ludwig is not shy about using his stick.

Shot blocking is his forte and he will throw himself fearlessly in front of the hardest slapper.

THE INTANGIBLES

Ludwig is a hard-working player who sticks to the basics and knows his limitations. He will be reunited with former Canadiens teammate Bob Gainey in Minnesota. His attitude, however, is not great—or wasn't in New York.

BASIL MCRAE

Yrs. of NHL service: 7
Born: Beaverton, Ont., Canada; January 5, 1961
Position: Left wing
Height: 6-2
Weight: 205
Uniform no.: 17
Shoots: left

Career statistics:

GP	G	A	TP	PIM
383	43	61	104	1816

1990-91 statistics:

GP	G	A	TP	+/-	PIM	PP	SH	GW	GT	S	PCT
40	1	3	4	-8	224	0	0	0	0	44	2.3

LAST SEASON

Missed half the season with surgery to repair torn stomach muscles. Despite the layoff, finished second on the team in PIM.

THE FINESSE GAME

McRae works hard at both ends of the ice, but in both cases his work is undone by his modest hockey skills. He has better hands than one might expect for the player of his penalty minutes total. He can handle the puck and make a play and since he gets a lot of space he has time and can be careful with his play selection. He doesn't have much of a shot, but will muck from close in for a rebound or deflection.

He is an average skater, with fairly good speed that helps his forechecking. He can play an effective checking role. Although he will be outclassed by the league's better skaters, he can keep up most of the time. His hockey instincts are not bad.

Most important is McRae's physical presence. He can stir things up and disturb the other team's skilled players.

THE PHYSICAL GAME

The NHL's penalty leader in 1989-90, McRae adds legitimate toughness to the Stars. He had a difficult time coming back from his surgery, since his workouts were limited by the nature of the injury. He worked hard at his rehab, however, and was key to Minnesota's drive to the finals.

When McRae, Shane Churla and Mark Tinordi are all on the ice at the same time, the more faint of heart among the opposition start wondering why they didn't take up golf instead of hockey. McRae will do anything for a teammate, anything to win. He opens up huge ice for anyone he plays with. He is a willing but not good fighter, but his real scariness comes from his crunching checks.

THE INTANGIBLES

McRae loves the game and loves to compete, and his enthusiasm rubs off on his teammates. It may not be a coincidence that the Stars got off to such a miserable start after McRae was injured in pre-season. Even while he was recuperating, coach Bob Gainey would pack him along on road trips, because of what McRae can do for the attitude in the dressing room. His emotion and enthusiasm more than make up for any of his finesse deficiencies. And for a player of his type, McRae's overall game is above average.

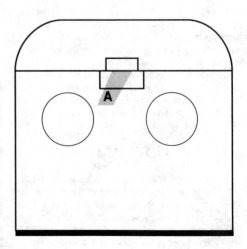

MIKE MODANO

Yrs. of NHL service: 2
Born: Livonia, Mich., USA; June 7, 1970
Position: Center
Height: 6-3
Weight: 190
Uniform no.: 9
Shoots: left

Career statistics:

GP	G	A	TP	PIM
159	57	82	139	128

1990-91 statistics:

GP	G	A	TP	+/-	PIM	PP	SH	GW	GT	S	PCT
79	28	36	64	+2	65	9	0	2	2	232	12.1

LAST SEASON

Third on team in goals, tied for third in power play goals, fifth in points and assists. All point totals lower than his rookie season. Tied for third on team in power play goals.

THE FINESSE GAME

Modano is charisma on skates and most of his dynamic talent stems from his exceptional skating ability. Modano has outstanding speed, acceleration, agility and balance. He can stop and start quickly, and uses his feet to control the puck as well as his good stickhandling.

Modano has terrific hands. He releases the puck quickly and doesn't have to be urged to shoot. He has good puck control, especially in a crowd, where he protects the puck well from a checker. He can pass equally well forehand and backhand, and can accept a pass on either side of his blade.

Modano has good enough vision that he is capable of playing the point on the power play, and he spots the open man well. He is a very creative player and one that the opposition has to always be aware of. He can draw one or two players to him and open up ice for his linemates.

Modano was benched for one game early in the season when coach Bob Gainey was unhappy with his intensity. Gainey was a player who took few nights off and it must annoy him to watch someone with Modano's gifts play so in and out.

THE PHYSICAL GAME

Modano is a big kid who doesn't play to his size. He's shown improvement and he will angle opponents to the boards to squeeze them out of the play, but he won't hit hard. He has good balance and a long reach,and is difficult to separate from the puck. The Stars often play him with one of their enforcers to limit other teams taking runs at him, but that wastes some of Modano's playmaking skill.

THE INTANGIBLES

Modano's game remains inconsistent. He floats one night and breaks a game wide-open the next. He is a dynamic player who can lift fans out of their seats (now that the North Stars have fans), because they are never sure what they are going to see. Modano has suffered through some frustrating slumps and, with his sensitive nature, took critcisms to heart. Critics seemed to neglect the fact that Modano was only 20 years old during the season. He has some growing up to do, but should mature into one of the game's true stars.

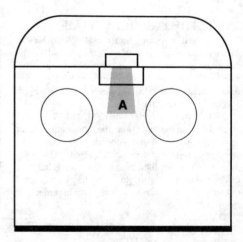

ALLEN PEDERSEN

Yrs. of NHL service: 5
Born: Edmonton, Alta., Canada; January 13, 1965
Position: Defenseman
Height: 6-3
Weight: 210 Uniform no.:
Shoots: left

Career statistics:

GP	G	A	TP	PIM
333	4	31	35	408

1990-91 statistics:

GP	G	A	TP	+/-	PIM	PP	SH	GW	GT	S	PCT
57	2	6	8	+15	107	0	0	0	0	34	5.9

LAST SEASON

Acquired from Boston in expansion draft. Second among Bruins defensemen in plus-minus.

THE FINESSE GAME

Pedersen's playing style reminds you of a giraffe. He might look gawky and slow, but he only needs a long stride or two to get to where he's going because he covers so much much ground. He is hard to beat one-on-one because of his size and range, even though his mobility is limited.

Pedersen has limited skills, but possesses more offensive capabilities than he has shown—or even tried to show. His has been a career of self-doubt and with some encouragement he could become more of an all-around player than the one-dimensional defenseman he is now. He does not overhandle the puck and makes quick, accurate outlet passes. Pedersen is not very creative, but he can handle the basics. He seldom tries to rush the puck.

THE PHYSICAL GAME

Because of his size, Pedersen is an intimidating factor. He concentrates on playing his position and won't go pell-mell looking for a hit, but when a skater comes into his zone, Pedersen will make the big check. He clears the front of the net well and is a goalie's best friend: a willing shot-blocker who eats the puck (a goalie playing behind Pedersen would never seen the puck were it to get through).

THE INTANGIBLES

Pedersen's game will always be handcuffed by his lack of agility, but he is a reliable stay-at-home defenseman. If he could improve his self-confidence a notch, he could become more valuable to his team.

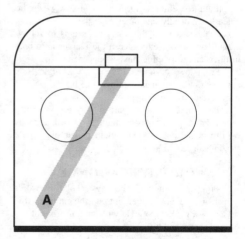

BRIAN PROPP

Yrs. of NHL service: 12
Born: Lanigan, Sask., Canada; February 15, 1959
Position: Left wing
Height: 5-10
Weight: 195
Uniform no.: 16
Shoots: left

Career statistics:

GP	G	A	TP	PIM
883	398	535	933	849

1990-91 statistics:

GP	G	A	TP	+/-	PIM	PP	SH	GW	GT	S	PCT
79	26	47	73	+7	58	9	0	1	0	171	15.2

LAST SEASON

Games played total was eight-season high. Goals total was two-season high and assist and point totals were three-season highs. Tied for third on team in power play goals.

THE FINESSE GAME

Propp has always been a top offensive player and experience has helped him in areas where his age might have slowed him down a step. Propp is not a fast skater but he is opportunistic. His good hockey sense helps him find the openings, especially down low, where he unleashes a deadly one-timer from the side. Propp is one of those players that the puck seems to follow around, but of course that doesn't just happen. Propp's instincts and work ethic make it happen.

Propp loves to shoot, and he is very accurate. He's not much of a playmaker and most of his assists will come off his own scoring efforts.

Propp has developed into a very good penalty killer. He is a power play specialist, however, and was on fire in the playoffs with eight power play goals (leading all scorers).

THE PHYSICAL GAME

Propp is not known for his physical play. He won't punish anyone, but he'll accept punishment himself if he senses a goal playoff. He will stand in front of the net and screen and tip.

THE INTANGIBLES

Propp played like a very young 32-year-old, with the same high intensity every night that would put most younger players to shame. He wants to play another season or two, but he will be hard-pressed to match his production of last season.

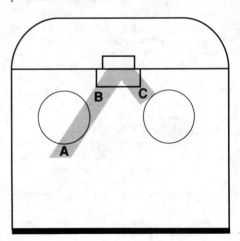

ROB RAMAGE

Yrs. of NHL service: 12
Born: Byron, Ont., Canada; January 11, 1959
Position: Defenseman
Height: 6-2
Weight: 200
Uniform no.:
Shoots: right

Career statistics:

GP	G	A	TP	PIM
915	130	404	534	673

1990-91 statistics:

GP	G	A	TP	+/-	PIM	PP	SH	GW	GT	S	PCT
80	10	24	34	+2	173	5	0	2	0	169	5.9

LAST SEASON

Acquired from Toronto in expansion draft. Only Maple Leaf to play in all 80 games. Goal total was four-season high. Assist and point totals were two-season lows. He was the only Maple Leaf regular with a plus rating.

THE FINESSE GAME

Ramage has average skating speed, but it is his other skating qualities - balance and lateral mobility—that make him such a good offensive defenseman.

Ramage has a great point shot that gets through and hits the net 85-90 percent of the time. He doesn't gamble in deep as often as he once did, but he will get involved offensively and not get trapped because of his sound hockey judgment. He is a very smart passer and can clear his own zone when he is in trouble. He can also set up a teammate with a pass for a good scoring chance.

Ramage never neglects his defensive duties and is better in his own zone than most defensemen with the "offensive" label.

THE PHYSICAL GAME

Ramage has played a lot of games and logged a lot of miles, but despite the wear and tear remains a durable player. Ramager will play a solid physical game, using his size and strength well, especially in clearing the front of his net. He takes the man and finishes his checks, and can play it mean when he has to. He is a well-respected bodychecker. Ramage will fight if provoked, but he's not terribly good at it.

THE INTANGIBLES

Ramage's acquisition was curious, since the Stars seem to be well stocked with both offensive and veteran defensemen. Ramage's character may be what GM Bob Clarke was interested in, since he is a team leader and an exceptional guy to pair with a younger defenseman.

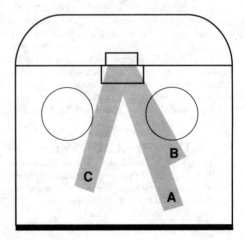

BOBBY SMITH

Yrs. of NHL service: 13
Born: North Sydney, N.S., Canada; Febuary 12, 1958
Position: Center
Height: 6-4
Weight: 210
Uniform no.: 18
Shoots: left

Career statistics:

GP	G	A	TP	PIM
964	343	635	978	798

1990-91 statistics:

GP	G	A	TP	+/-	PIM	PP	SH	GW	GT	S	PCT
73	15	31	46	-9	60	7	0	2	1	121	12.4

LAST SEASON

Acquired from Montreal for a 1992 fourth-round draft pick on August 7, 1990. All point totals two-season highs.

THE FINESSE GAME

Smith demonstrated that not all of his offensive skills have eroded as he enjoyed a successul season in his return to Minnesota.

Smith is a fine skater, a graceful goer with deceptive speed and a stride that seems to take him two strokes to cross the ice. One-on-one, with his reach and lateral movement, he can still burn many a defenseman. Smith can still gear it up for an end-to-end rush.

His hockey sense and hand skills are excellent. He has one of those rare weapons—a strong backhand shot—and he also likes to pass off his backhand.

Smith is a very good man on the power play because of the combination of hockey sense and skills. He has good hand/eye coordination and takes key defensive faceoffs, and he ties up the opposing center if he does lose it. He is strong in his own end of the ice and is a sound defensive player with far better than average offensive skills.

THE PHYSICAL GAME

Smith's balance and wingspan make him a difficult player to check off the puck. Smith himself doesn't like to play a physical game, but he is very strong and he will absorb a hit although he won't initiate.

THE INTANGIBLES

Coach Bob Gainey (Smith's former Montreal teammate) tried to shoehorn his old buddy into a strictly defensive role and it just didn't work. While Smith has slowed a step and no longer can carry a team with his offense, he is a good two-way center who can still contribute with his skills and experience.

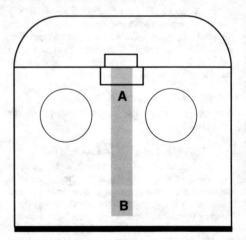

MARK TINORDI

Yrs. of NHL service: 3
Born: Deer River, Alta., Canada; May 9, 1966
Position: Defenseman
Height: 6-4
Weight: 205
Uniform no.: 24
Shoots: left

Career statistics:

GP	G	A	TP	PIM
206	11	39	50	588

1990-91 statistics:

GP	G	A	TP	+/-	PIM	PP	SH	GW	GT	S	PCT
69	5	27	32	+1	191	1	0	2	0	92	5.4

LAST SEASON

Led team defensemen in assists, points and PIM. Games played and all point totals career highs. Missed 10 games with a suspension for leaving the penalty box during an exhibition game.

THE FINESSE GAME

In an amazing transformation, Tinordi has evolved from the one-dimensional goon he was when he started his career with the New York Rangers to a dominating defenseman for Minnesota. Tinordi is a triple threat: a defenseman who can play positional defense, contribute offensively and play the tough, physical game with equal ability. The latter half of his season was Norris Trophy caliber, as was his performance throughout the playoffs.

Tinordi's confidence shows most in his involvement in the offensive play. Not only will he be the fourth man joining the play—frequently he will be the second, skating through the middle of the ice and boring his way to the net. Tinordi used to be gangly and awkward, but his skating has improved awesomely.

He was an integral part of the almost unstoppable Minnesota power play in the playoffs. He can move the puck, move into the play, take the shot or work the pass in deep. The Stars went out and got several important stay-at-home defensemen to free Tinordi's game, but who ever suspected it could get this good?

THE PHYSICAL GAME

Tinordi is a true heavyweight. He will take on all comers and win more than his share. He has matured into a player who won't go looking for trouble for trouble's sake, but will fight when his team is challenged. He won't waste his time with the NHL's punks.

Tinordi used to worry about making a bad play, then would make matters worse by not doing anything at all. No more. He hits with authority and plays well positionally.

THE INTANGIBLES

Tinordi has to keep a mental picture of the kind of defenseman he should be - more Ray Bourque than Al MacInnis. If Tinordi gets too taken with his offensive success, he will lose the edge he gets from playing such a physical game. He has worked so hard to get to where he is and the Stars have helped him by assembling a stronger supporting cast. Tinordi was Minnesota's MVP.

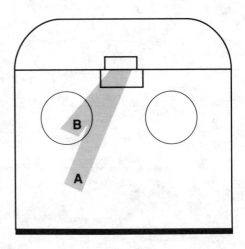

MONTREAL
CANADIENS

GUY CARBONNEAU

Yrs. of NHL service: 9
Born: Sept-Iles, Que., Canada; March 18, 1960
Position: Center
Height: 5-11
Weight: 180
Uniform no.: 21
Shoots: right

Career statistics:

GP	G	A	TP	PIM
700	185	268	453	516

1990-91 statistics:

GP	G	A	TP	+/-	PIM	PP	SH	GW	GT	S	PCT
78	20	24	44	-1	63	4	1	3	1	131	15.3

LAST SEASON

Point total was three-season low. Goal total was two-season high.

THE FINESSE GAME

Carbonneau reads plays quicker than Evelyn Woods. He has excellent instincts in all zones, but his forte is in the offensive zone, where Carbonneau has carved out his niche as one of the game's outstanding forecheckers.

Carbonneau may have lost a half step, but he is still one of the best skaters in the NHL. He has speed, quickness, acceleration, agility and outstanding balance. Carbonneau is the beginning and end of most discussions of defensive forwards.

But Carbonneau has terrific offensive skills to supplement his defensive play. He can produce a steady 20-25 goals a season and is always a threat to score shorthanded. He has excellent hands and uses his teammate well. He has a strong wrist shot from the circles or in tight.

Carbonneau has few equals on the draw.

THE PHYSICAL GAME

Carbonneau uses all of his small frame to block shots, and his skating ability helps him line up checks. Then his hand skills comes to the fore, and he comes away with the puck. He plays well positionally, not letting his mark get a step on him towards the net, and he will bang along the baords and in front of the net. He will use his stick to hook and whack.

THE INTANGIBLES

Carbonneau has lost a step and a contract squabble with the Habs last season took some of the edge off his competitive nature. He played out his option and was not a happy Habitant.

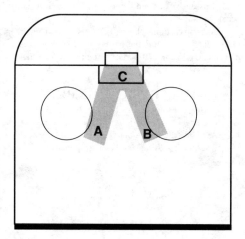

ANDREW CASSELS

Yrs. of NHL service: 1
Born: Bramalea, Ont., Canada; July 23, 1969
Position: Center
Height: 6-0
Weight: 190
Uniform no.: 15
Shoots: left

Career statistics:

GP	G	A	TP	PIM
60	8	19	27	22

1990-91 statistics:

GP	G	A	TP	+/-	PIM	PP	SH	GW	GT	S	PCT
54	6	19	25	+2	20	1	1	3	0	55	10.9

LAST SEASON

First full NHL season.

THE FINESSE GAME

Cassels has been tested as a linemate for Denis Savard, and may find success there as Cassels likes to come into the play late and would be the perfect foil for Savard's curl-and-pass. Cassels releases a wrist shot quickly and accurately. He anticipates well and finds the holes.

He is also a good passer, with quick hands and a soft touch. He was not very successful on the power play last season, but neither was anyone else on Montreal. Cassels skates with good balance, agility and acceleration.

Like most young players, Cassels needs to work on his defensive game, but he has good hockey sense and should develop that part of his game over the next season or two.

THE PHYSICAL GAME

Cassels does not use his body willingly and needs to get stronger. He won't be intimidated easily and because of his balance is not easy to move off the puck. He is a solid face-off man and can kill penalties.

THE INTANGIBLES

Cassels has been given a taste of the NHL for the past two seasons and wants it badly. He has the desire and work ethic to earn a regular role this season.

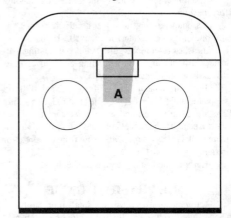

TOM CHORSKE

Yrs. of NHL service: 1
Born: Minneapolis, Minn., USA; Sept. 18, 1966
Position: Right wing
Height: 6-1
Weight: 204
Uniform no.: 31
Shoots: right

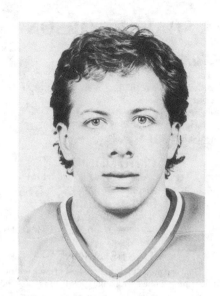

Career statistics:

GP	G	A	TP	PIM
71	12	12	24	34

1990-91 statistics:

GP	G	A	TP	+/-	PIM	PP	SH	GW	GT	S	PCT
57	9	11	20	-8	32	3	0	1	0	82	11.0

LAST SEASON

First full NHL season.

THE FINESSE GAME

Chorske is a good skater with long, powerful strides. He goes to the net well and can reach top speed in a few strides. He doesn't lose speed when carrying the puck.

He is confident around the net and scores most of his goals from close range. He has strong, quick hands and shoots well off the pass. Chorske has a good snap shot that he gets off quickly and accurately.

Chorske is a good passer but not a creative playmaker. He has a soft touch with the puck.

THE PHYSICAL GAME

Chorske does not use his good size as effectively as he should. He has worked hard to improve his upper body strength and that, combined with his skating, may turn him into a good power forward. He protects the puck well with his body when driving to the net and he will take a hit to make a play.

THE INTANGIBLES

Chorske has been a good scorer at every level he has played (university, U.S. national team and minors)

but he has yet to carry that ability to the NHL level.

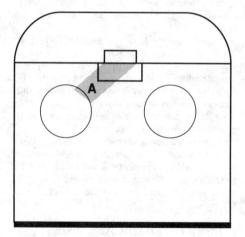

SHAYNE CORSON

Yrs. of NHL service: 5
Born: Barrie, Ont., Canada; August 13, 1966
Position: Center
Height: 6-0
Weight: 175
Uniform no.: 27
Shoots: left

Career statistics:

GP	G	A	TP	PIM
356	104	130	234	773

1990-91 statistics:

GP	G	A	TP	+/-	PIM	PP	SH	GW	GT	S	PCT
71	23	24	47	+9	138	7	0	2	1	164	14.0

LAST SEASON

Goal and point totals were lowest in three seasons. Missed nine games with injury. Will miss first four games of this season with suspension incurred in playoffs.

THE FINESSE GAME

Corson's game comes down to basics. He works up and down his wing with nothing creative, but he uses his skating strength and speed to clear a path for himself.

Corson sees the ice well, is aware of his best play options and he has the skills to follow up. He doesn't like to play dump and chase (he's really not crazy about crashing into the boards after a puck, although he will). He likes to carry the puck in and run over people, since he lacks the agility to get around them. He will head for open ice or pass off to a teammate down low. He forechecks well and forces turnovers.

Corson has very good hands and has the patience to wait for a good opening. His shot is quick and accurate, and he is a finisher who takes his punishment to score a goal. Corson is good on the power play, where he will forge to the net for rebounds and deflections.

THE PHYSICAL GAME

Corson has a mean streak a mile wide and his opponents know he can be goaded into taking bad penalties—meaning that Corson often goes off with a player of lesser ability and hurts his team because of it. He is very strong on his skates and is a solid hitter.

THE INTANGIBLES

Corson has been named in several trade rumors, and with a contract dispute brewing and a well-publicized off-ice incident in his past, we think Corson will be wearing a new jersey this season. His trade value is at a maximum after his strong playoff performance.

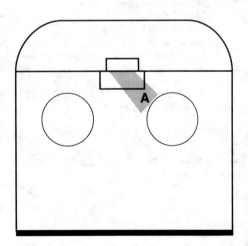

RUSS COURTNALL

Yrs. of NHL service: 7
Born: Duncan, B.C., Canada; June 2, 1965
Position: Right wing
Height: 5-11
Weight: 180
Uniform no.: 9
Shoots: right

Career statistics:

GP	G	A	TP	PIM
523	165	227	392	314

1990-91 statistics:

GP	G	A	TP	+/-	PIM	PP	SH	GW	GT	S	PCT
70	26	50	76	+5	29	5	1	5	1	279	9.3

LAST SEASON

Led team in assists, points and shots. Third on team in goals. Assist and point totals were career highs.

THE FINESSE GAME

Courtnall is an electrifying player with great skating ability who lifted his game to a new level last season. The little dynamo can motor at full speed and has some spry moves and excellent puckhandling skills that enable him to do moves like pull the puck through a defenseman's legs and keep going for the net. He really loves that trick, and it's fun to watch, unless you're the defenseman.

And Courtnall will keep going as long as there's open ice. He's made centering passes from one knee, and blindly, because he has an awareness of where his linemates are. Courtnall won't power to the net because he lacks the size to physically challenge anyone, but he sets the defense back on their heels because of his intimidating speed and that opens up plenty of room for him. He is a constant breakaway threat.

Courtnall has a wonderful wrist shot and he can one-time a shot with the best of them. With Guy Carbonneau, he formed one of the better penalty killing forward duos, and he can rag a puck all night long.

He skated better than ever last season, was a mainstay on the power play and is developing into a two-way player.

THE PHYSICAL GAME

Courtnall will always be limited by his size, but he plays a tough game and his skating speed puts extra oomph into his checks. His hand skills help him come away with the puck and he has the acceleration to get out of jams quickly. He won't be intimidated. He has good hockey courage.

THE INTANGIBLES

Courtnall was called into Serge Savard's office early in the season and was told the team wanted him to be a team leader. Nobody had ever asked that of Courtnall, or maybe he wasn't mature enough to respond before. As one of the more experienced Canadiens, Courtnall tried his best to do what didn't come naturally. He is a charismatic player who has become a complete one.

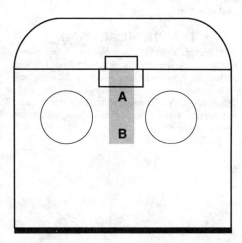

J.J. DAIGNEAULT

Yrs. of NHL service: 6
Born: Montreal, Que., Canada; October 12, 1965
Position: Defenseman
Height: 5-11
Weight: 185
Uniform no.: 48
Shoots: left

Career statistics:

GP	G	A	TP	PIM
323	22	90	112	227

1990-91 statistics:

GP	G	A	TP	+/-	PIM	PP	SH	GW	GT	S	PCT
51	3	16	19	-2	31	2	0	0	0	68	4.4

LAST SEASON

Games played and all point totals were three-season highs.

THE FINESSE GAME

Daigneault is an excellent skater who has breakaway speed. He can carry the puck at a high tempo and moves the puck at the right time without telegraphing his plays.

Daigneault will come in deep because he has the skating ability to recover defensively. On the attack, he plays with poise and confidence and reads the plays well. He is not as astute when reading rushes coming at him.

Daigneault has very strong arms and can wrist a good shot from almost out near the blue line. This makes him valuable on the point because he can get a low and accurate shot on net quickly. He also has a good slap shot.

THE PHYSICAL GAME

Daigneault remains a one-dimensional player who doesn't do the little things a defenseman needs to do, like finish his checks. He will never be a physical player because of his size limitation, but too frequently Daigneault plays even smaller than he is. He is quick with his stick and thus a good poke checker. He is not tough or aggressive

THE INTANGIBLES

Although he is offensively gifted, Daigneault is too much of a defensive liability and will be on the bubble wherever he plays.

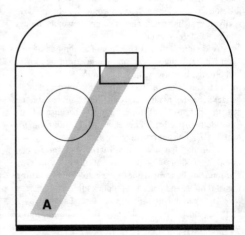

ERIC DESJARDINS

Yrs. of NHL service: 3
Born: Rouyn, Que., Canada; June 14, 1969
Position: Defenseman
Height: 6-1
Weight: 200
Uniform no.: 28
Shoots: right

Career statistics:

GP	G	A	TP	PIM
153	12	44	56	104

1990-91 statistics:

GP	G	A	TP	+/-	PIM	PP	SH	GW	GT	S	PCT
62	7	18	25	+7	27	0	0	1	0	114	6.1

LAST SEASON

Tied for best plus-minus among team defensemen. Games played and all point totals were career highs.

THE FINESSE GAME

Although Desjardins has concentrated on his defensive work, he has very good offensive instincts and has the skills to get involved in the attack.

He skates well with balance and acceleration, moves to his right or left equally well and he has a small turning radius. He also skates well backwards and is agile for a big man.

Desjardins will pick his spots to jump into the attack. When he doesn't, he's not afraid to penetrate down the middle and work down low, but he will not do this unless he feels the play is secured defensively. He passes crisply and accurately and keeps his options open. He one-times the puck well from the point. He can work well on both special teams.

THE PHYSICAL GAME

Desjardins has worked hard to improve his upper body strength (and he has added about 15 pounds of muscle in the past two seasons). This has added an extra dimension to what was already a sound positional game. Desjardins can cover a lot of ice and doesn't panic even when faced with a two-on-one, even when one of the two is Wayne Gretzky. He plays a sound, clean, no-nonsense game. He clears the front of his net, clears rebounds and blocks shots.

THE INTANGIBLES

Desjardins rebounded from a disappointing sophomore season to establish himself as the steadiest blueliner among the young Montreal defense corps. He is a collected player who is maturing into a very steady blueliner who can also get involved offensively. He is a defenseman worth keeping an eye on.

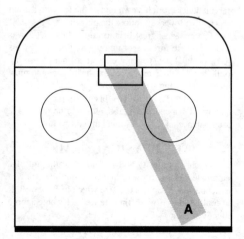

BRENT GILCHRIST

Yrs. of NHL service: 3
Born: Moose Jaw, Sask., Canada; April 3, 1967
Position: Center
Height: 6-1
Weight: 190
Uniform no.: 41
Shoots: left

Career statistics:

GP	G	A	TP	PIM
157	23	40	63	54

1990-91 statistics:

GP	G	A	TP	+/-	PIM	PP	SH	GW	GT	S	PCT
51	6	9	15	-3	10	1	0	1	0	81	7.4

LAST SEASON

Missed 19 games with a broken finger. Missed additional games with eye and shoulder injuries. Games played and all point totals were two-season lows.

THE FINESSE GAME

Gilchrist is one of those minor league scoring whizzes whose finesse skills never translated into NHL scoring success. Gilchrist has developed into more of a checking center, who may be a possible successor to Guy Carbonneau, although he lacks both Carbonneau's exceptional skating ability and hockey sense. He can start an attack from his own end of the ice with a good pass and will work to follow the play up.

Gilchrist has great balance around the net and is aggressive. He forces scoring opportunities not by his playmaking skills (which are minimal) but by driving to the net. He does not have a powerful shot and must generate his offense near the goal.

Thus far Gilchrist has been hampered by his skating. His speed is average, although he does have good balance and shows some jump down low.

THE PHYSICAL GAME

Gilchrist is feisty and will jump to the aid of a teammate, not by throwing punches, but by getting in someone's face. He has fair size which he uses well. If he could improve his skating, he would become a more effective hitter.

THE INTANGIBLES

Gilchrist is a hard-working, intense competitor who ran into injury woes last season. He is a journeyman center, but adds zest to the fourth line.

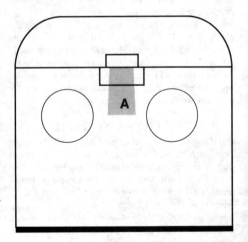

MIKE KEANE

Yrs. of NHL service: 3
Born: Winnipeg, Man., Canada; May 28, 1967
Position: Right wing
Height: 5-11
Weight: 175
Uniform no.: 12
Shoots: right

Career statistics:

GP	G	A	TP	PIM
216	38	57	95	197

1990-91 statistics:

GP	G	A	TP	+/-	PIM	PP	SH	GW	GT	S	PCT
73	13	23	36	+6	50	2	1	2	0	109	11.9

LAST SEASON

Point total was a career high. Missed seven games with a lacerated kneecap.

THE FINESSE GAME

Keane has good acceleration and is one of those sneaky-fast skaters who can slip in behind the defense and take a pass. He has the hand skills to pull a backhand to his forehand in tight, and he can do it at a pretty good clip.

He has good hockey sense and thinks fast, but there is little creative to his game. Keane just keeps going to the net, and when he can't go, he'll shoot. He has a good one-timer. Keane dishes and accepts passes equally well on his forehand or backhand, but he doesn't have a backhand shot.

THE PHYSICAL GAME

He's not the biggest specimen we've seen on ice, yet Keane derives his offense by bowling his way to the net. He's tough and physical and worms his way through crowds around the net. He is a willing checker and, though he is on the small side, his skating and intensity power his checks. Keane will block shots and he won't be intimidated.

THE INTANGIBLES

There should always be room on a roster for a player with Keane's work ethic, but as his performance lags behind his potential, his job will always be in jeopardy.

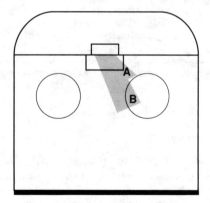

STEPHAN LEBEAU

Yrs. of NHL service: 2
Born: St.-Jerome, Que., Canada; February 28, 1968
Position: Center
Height: 5-10
Weight: 180
Uniform no.: 47
Shoots: right

Career statistics:

GP	G	A	TP	PIM
131	37	52	89	37

1990-91 statistics:

GP	G	A	TP	+/-	PIM	PP	SH	GW	GT	S	PCT
73	22	31	53	+4	24	8	0	2	0	108	20.4

LAST SEASON

Tied for second on club in assists. Fourth on team in points. Second on team in power play goals. Games played and all point totals career highs.

THE FINESSE GAME

Lebeau has fabulous, soft hands and he shoots first and asks question later. Lebeau is an amazingly accurate shooter (his average over two NHL seasons is 19.8 per cent). Lebeau has good skating ability—both quickness and outright speed—and he is a darter going for the openings with his quick release.

Lebeau is more of a shooter than a playmaker and has to play with a winger who will get him the puck. Lebeau lacks the size to tackle most NHL defensemen along the boards and he is better off coming in as the trailer. When he carries the puck in leading the rush, he won't go to the net but will pull up at the blue line and wait for help.

Lebeau is exceptional on the power play, when he has the extra ice to maneuver. He is defensively aware.

THE PHYSICAL GAME

Lebeau is a small player who tries to play big, but there are some situations where he just doesn't have a chance. Last season, the Canadiens sometime scratched Lebeau from games in smaller buildings, like Boston Garden, because they feared the pasting he would get.

THE INTANGIBLES

Lebeau is willing, but his frame will always limit just how effective a player he can be. Maybe after Theo Fleury's 51-goal season, Lebeau can convince his coaches there is room for a small man in this game.

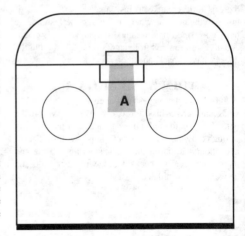

SYLVAIN LEFEBVRE

Yrs. of NHL service: 2
Born: Richmond, Que., Canada; October 14, 1967
Position: Defenseman
Height: 6-2
Weight: 200
Uniform no.: 3
Shoots: left

Career statistics:

GP	G	A	TP	PIM
131	8	28	36	91

1990-91 statistics:

GP	G	A	TP	+/-	PIM	PP	SH	GW	GT	S	PCT
63	5	18	23	-11	30	1	0	1	0	76	6.6

LAST SEASON

Worst plus-minus on team. All point totals topped rookie season.

THE FINESSE GAME

Nothing about Lefebvre's game is exceptional. He has a good foundation with his skating, with a strong stride and some speed. He puts these abilities together with a pretty smart game, although he had his defensive lapses last season as part of a very young Montreal defense—probably the youngest defense in the NHL.

Lefebvre is best described as a stay-at-home defenseman. He does not get involved in the offensive flow. He is a good passer and prefers headmanning the puck to rushing with it.

Lefebvre has limited offensive skills. His shot from the point is average. He will get time on the power play because he sees the ice well.

THE PHYSICAL GAME

Lefebvre is tall and rangy but needs to develop more upper body strength. He loses some of the one-on-one battles. He is a solid checker and plays well positionally. He does not fight.

THE INTANGIBLES

Lefebvre was given a great deal of ice time and responsibility last season due to injuries and shouldn't be judged by his plus-minus alone. He can be a reliable, journeyman defenseman.

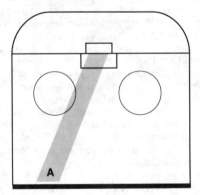

MIKE MCPHEE

Yrs. of NHL service: 8
Born: Sydney, N.S., Canada; July 14, 1960
Position: Left wing
Height: 6-1
Weight: 200
Uniform no.: 35
Shoots: left

Career statistics:

GP	G	A	TP	PIM
503	146	147	293	518

1990-91 statistics:

GP	G	A	TP	+/-	PIM	PP	SH	GW	GT	S	PCT
64	22	21	43	+6	56	2	0	4	0	123	17.9

LAST SEASON

Points total three-season high. Games played and assist totals two-season highs. Missed 16 games with a groin injury.

THE FINESSE GAME

Talk about your lunchpail forwards. There is nothing fancy about McPhee. He is an underrated, understated winger whose game is powered by his strong skating.

McPhee is another one of those big guys with deceptive speed. He also has experience and anticipation, which makes him one of the NHL's better forecheckers. He will intimidate with his size and quickness and force turnovers deep in the zone.

McPhee don't have really fine hands and doesn't have much natural scoring ability, but he works hard around the net and capitalizes on other's mistakes. He has a knack for scoring big goals. McPhee scores few goals away from the net. He is a good playmaker, opportunistic if not creative a la Denis Savard.

McPhee is a very good penalty killer because of his speed and reads.

THE PHYSICAL GAME

McPhee's nagging groin injury has robbed him of some of his speed and it could continue to affect him. If it does, McPhee's play will suffer, because it is mostly his skating balance and power that makes him such a reliable workhorse along the boards. He is a good checker who remains upright when others try to bowl him over. McPhee has a strong upper body to go with his skating strength.

THE INTANGIBLES

For three consecutive seasons, McPhee has been nominated as Montreal's choice for the Masterton Trophy for sportsmanship and dedication to hockey. He has Susan Lucci's luck when it comes to winning (but she's been nominated for 12 daytime Emmys and hasn't collected, so McPhee has a way to go to catch her). The nominations illustrate how valuable McPhee is to his team in his self-effacing way.

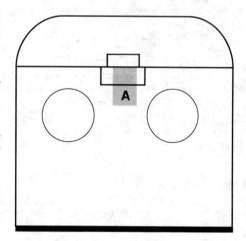

LYLE ODELEIN

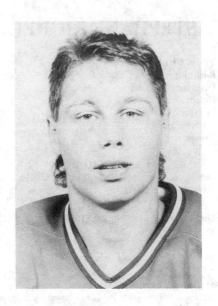

Yrs. of NHL service: 1
Born: Quill Lake, Sask., Canada; July 21, 1968
Position: Defenseman
Height: 5-10
Weight: 205
Uniform no.: 24
Shoots: left

Career statistics:

GP	G	A	TP	PIM
60	0	4	4	292

1990-91 statistics:

GP	G	A	TP	+/-	PIM	PP	SH	GW	GT	S	PCT
52	0	2	2	+7	259	0	0	0	0	25	0.0

LAST SEASON

First full NHL season. Led team in PIM.

THE FINESSE GAME

Odelein has used his modest finesse skills and stocky frame to become one of the steadier Montreal blueliners. Odelein is a good skater with some balance and quickness, but little outright speed. He won't win many races to the puck, so he compensates by playing a contained game.

Odelein will not jump into the offensive flow and will work best paired with a more offensive defenseman who can go with the puck. Odelein is a fair passer who is intent on getting the puck safely out of the zone.

THE PHYSICAL GAME

Odelein is an aggressive player who doesn't back down from a challenge, although he doesn't win many fights. Fighting doesn't seem to come naturally to him, but hitting does, and he can play a sound physical game in his own end, sticking with his man and playing his angles well. He has a tendency to get excited, both by physical play and by watching the puck and getting lured out of position.

THE INTANGIBLES

Odelein was the biggest surprise of the Montreal season. The Canadiens need a defenseman with physi-cal presence and with more seasoning, and Odelein might fit the bill. He is a willing player with a reputation as a team man.

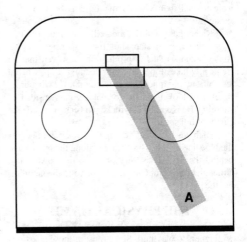

STEPHANE RICHER

Yrs. of NHL service: 6
Born: Ripon, Que., Canada; June 7, 1966
Position: Right wing
Height: 6-2
Weight: 200
Uniform no.: 44
Shoots: right

Career statistics:

GP	G	A	TP	PIM
390	198	168	366	362

1990-91 statistics:

GP	G	A	TP	+/-	PIM	PP	SH	GW	GT	S	PCT
75	31	30	61	0	53	9	0	4	1	221	14.0

LAST SEASON

Led team in goals and power play goals. Second on team in points. Third on team in assists. All point totals two-season lows. PIM two-season high. Missed five games with the flu.

THE FINESSE GAME

Richer's production was a huge disappointment off his 50-goal season of a year ago. Things got so bad for Richer that he was booed by schoolchildren who were treated to a visit to the Forum for a practice session.

Richer has good skating skills and, most of all, a huge, heavy, hard slap shot for a scoring weapon. Richer's shot is such a production, however, that he frequently takes too much time loading it up, when a less splashy but quicker shot would do. He will sometimes also look too hard to make a pass instead of shooting. He is a good playmaker and can give and take passes at full speed.

Richer is better off getting the puck before he hits the blue line than he is working it along the boards and behind the net. He is very good on the power play, although he will not consistently drive to the net without the puck.

THE PHYSICAL GAME

There are questions about Richer's heart and his willingness to play hurt. Since most of those questions have been raised by his coach, that made for an uncomfortable season for the sensitive forward.

There is no doubt Richer can play a physical game. He's got size, strength and balance, but little inclination to go crashing around the boards, at least not constently. Richer is very good in traffic and will protect the puck with his body.

THE INTANGIBLES

Richer was benched for part of Montreal's last playoff game against Boston and has feuded with coach Pat Burns. Expect more fireworks on and off the ice from Richer.

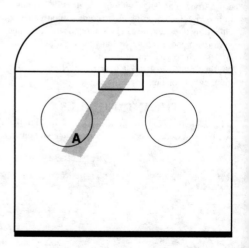

PATRICK ROY

Yrs. of NHL service: 6
Born: Quebec City, Que., Canada; October 5, 1965
Position: Goaltender
Height: 6-0
Weight: 175
Uniform no.: 33
Catches: left

Career statistics:

GP	MINS	GA	SO	GAA	A	PIM
289	16695	779	13	2.80	19	34

1990-91 statistics:

GP	MINS	GAA	W	L	T	SO	GA	S	SAPCT	PIM
48	2835	2.71	25	15	6	1	128	1362	.906	6

LAST SEASON

Second in NHL in save percentage. Third in league in goals against average. GAA was three-season high. Win total was three-season low. Missed 14 games with torn ankle ligaments; missed several starts after that due to soreness from the injury. Missed games in mid-season with knee injury.

THE PHYSICAL GAME

There is a book on Roy and every shooter knows it: Roy drops to his knees quickly, so beat him high. If he's so vulnerable there, and if it's no secret, how does he stay among the NHL's elite goalies in wins, saves and GAA?

Heaven knows it's not the defense he plays behind, which last year was made up of kids too young to remember Ken Dryden. Roy takes away low, but bounces back up as quickly, and uses his lightning-fast glove to rob the rest. If Roy has developed any susceptibility lately, it is the five-hole, and that should disappear as soon as the stiffness from Roy's knee and ankle injuries get worked out during the off-season.

Roy is well balanced and quick on his feet. He will stop the puck behind the net but he does not play it often, and he is not a good stickhandler.

Roy has never played his angles well. He has gotten a little better technically but why tinker with success?

THE MENTAL GAME

Mental toughness is where Roy has the edge over most NHL goalies. He knows he can turn a game around with one save, and since he has toiled for years for a low-scoring team, he knows his team knows it. Roy has very good concentration and is always checking his position by smacking his glove and stick against the posts. Roy talks to his defense, talks to his posts and gets the shooters talking to themslves. He intimidates them with his very presence.

THE INTANGIBLES

Rare is the goalie who gets a team to design its style of play around him, but Roy is one of those goalies. Since he came into his own (starting in 1985-86), the Canadiens have designed their defense so that their blueliners stand up and let Roy take the first shot, then concentrate on clearing rebounds. He did not play as well in the playoffs last season as we are accustomed to because of lingering effects from his ankle injury. Remember, Roy is only 26. He has plenty of prime time left.

DENIS SAVARD

Yrs. of NHL service: 11
Born: Pointe Gatineau, Que., Canada; Febuary 4, 1961
Position: Center
Height: 5-10
Weight: 175
Uniform no.: 18
Shoots: right

Career statistics:

GP	G	A	TP	PIM
806	379	693	1072	880

1990-91 statistics:

GP	G	A	TP	+/-	PIM	PP	SH	GW	GT	S	PCT
70	28	31	59	-1	52	7	2	0	0	187	15.0

LAST SEASON

Second on team in goals and tied for second in assists. Third on team in points. Led club in short-handed goals. Games played and goal totals were three-season highs. Point total was career low. Missed 10 games with an assortment of injuries, including strained thumb ligaments.

THE FINESSE GAME

Savard has always thrived on his skating, but he has lost some of the zip, and those famous spin-o-rama moves have been less and less frequent.

Savard is still quick and shifty with amazing peripheral vision. He can turn a defender inside out, but Savard needs a trailing winger to move to the openings he creates. Savard is most effective with his wrist shots from close range. He lacks the velocity to beat the goalie from long range, yet the Canadiens kept putting Savard out on the point on the power play. It wasn't for Savard's shot, but for his slick fake shot/pass and his vision of the attacking plays.

Savard is a genius with his stick. He can carry it at high speeds, curl, accelerate and slip into the middle of the ice for his shot.

As for backchecking, forget it. Savard is a role player, and his role is shooting star.

THE PHYSICAL GAME

Savard avoids contact at all costs, even to the point of rushing a pass to bail out of an impending hit. He stalks the perimeter and, with his hockey sense and skating quickness, avoids the gridlocked areas of the ice.

THE INTANGIBLES

Savard and Montreal seemed like such a natural, but the magic one is having his troubles in his new town. Savard may seem like an easy center to play with—who couldn't score playing alongside such a creative playmaker?—but Savard takes some getting used to. He seldom does the same thing twice, and he does things only he knows he's going to do. Savard is not a great support player. He is a brilliant individualist who is at his finest one-on-one. He didn't have the supporting players in Montreal as he did in Chicago and the search will continue this season for wingers who can figure him out.

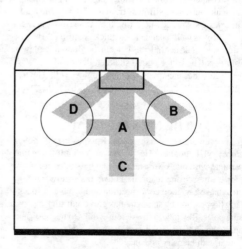

MATT SCHNEIDER

Yrs. of NHL service: 2
Born: New York, N.Y., USA; June 12, 1969
Position: Defenseman
Height: 5-11
Weight: 180
Uniform no.: 18
Shoots: left

Career statistics:

GP	G	A	TP	PIM
117	17	34	51	90

1990-91 statistics:

GP	G	A	TP	+/-	PIM	PP	SH	GW	GT	S	PCT
69	10	20	30	+7	63	5	0	3	0	164	6.1

LAST SEASON

Led team defensemen in goals and points. Tied for best plus-minus among team defensemen. Games played and all point totals were career highs.

THE FINESSE GAME

Schneider is a finesse defenseman whose game is founded on his superb skating—agility, acceleration and balance are all present in equal doses. Schneider is a shifty change-of-pace skater who can move to his right or left equally well. He lacks straightaway speed, but uses his intelligence and quickness to overcome that weakness.

He is an offensive force who will become even stronger with more experience and confidence (remember he has less than a season and a half of playing time). He has very soft hands and is a good passer. He shoots well off the one-timer. Schneider has faced a lot of pressure as a power play quarterback and hasn't quite lived up to expectations yet. He has a good shot and sees the ice well. He maintains his poise when the pace heats up.

Schneider has the talent and the desire to become an impact defenseman.

THE PHYSICAL GAME

Schneider's mental toughness and concentration compensate for his small size. He will try to move guys from the front of the net, but he is better at the Canadiens' style of defense, which is to let the goalie see the first shot, and then clear the rebound. With his quickness, Schneider can beat almost anyone to the loose puck. He will move the puck out smartly, rather than try to lug it himself. Schneider will lose most of the one-on-one confrontations in close quarters because he lacks upper body strength. He has always played against players bigger than himself and his aggressiveness isn't forced, it's natural.

THE INTANGIBLES

Schneider was cursed with the label of the "next Chris Chelios" following the latter's departure to Chicago in 1990. From all indications, Schneider might yet match Chelios skill-wise, although he lacks the orneriness and size of Chelios. Chelios won the Norris Trophy in his fifth season. Check Schneider's progress in three more years. He might not win the trophy, but he could be garnering a few votes.

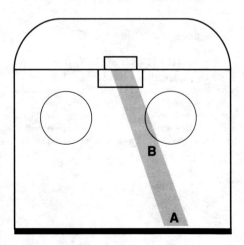

BRIAN SKRUDLAND

Yrs. of NHL service: 6
Born: Peace River, Alta., Canada; July 31, 1963
Position: Center
Height: 6-0
Weight: 185
Uniform no.: 39
Shoots: left

Career statistics:

GP	G	A	TP	PIM
410	70	133	203	501

1990-91 statistics:

GP	G	A	TP	+/-	PIM	PP	SH	GW	GT	S	PCT
57	15	19	34	+12	85	1	1	2	0	71	21.1

LAST SEASON

Led team in plus-minus. Best shooting percentage on team among regulars. Games played was career low. Goals total was career high. Missed 15 games with a broken foot.

THE FINESSE GAME

Skrudland is a muscular skater with a low center of gravity, making it tough for checkers to knock him off the puck. He is an excellent forechecker because of his balance and agility. Although he is not fast, he anticipates plays well and forces mistakes in the offensive zone. He is always back defensively to help out in his own end.

Skrudland is not a natural goal scorer (he should contribute 20 a year if he stays healthy), but he works hard for what he gets. Almost all of his goals result from rebounds and loose pucks in front of the net.

Skrudland is a solid two-way player who plays equally hard at both ends of the rink. Playing with Russ Courtnall allows that skater the freedom to play his dynamic offensive role, and gives Skrudland better scoring chances as well.

THE PHYSICAL GAME

Skrudland sets himself a very broad base with his wide skating stance and is difficult to budge from in front of the net. He is aggressive and quick in tight spaces and he loves to drive to the net with or without the puck. He is one of the best crease-crashers around, but he is able to disguise it by looking like the helpless victim of a hook.

THE INTANGIBLES

Skrudland has an excellent work ethic and delivers a consistent, high intensity level of play every game.

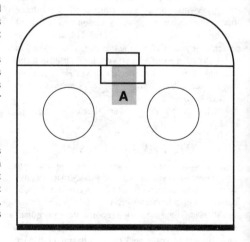

PETR SVOBODA

Yrs. of NHL service: 7
Born: Most, Czechoslovkia; February 14, 1966
Position: Defenseman
Height: 6-1
Weight: 170
Uniform no.: 25
Shoots: left

Career statistics:

GP	G	A	TP	PIM
476	34	174	208	667

1990-91 statistics:

GP	G	A	TP	+/-	PIM	PP	SH	GW	GT	S	PCT
60	4	22	26	+5	52	3	0	1	0	67	6.0

LAST SEASON

Led team defensemen in assists. Missed 20 games with a fractured foot. Goals total was five-season low. Assist total was three-season low. Point total was four-season low.

THE FINESSE GAME

Even coming back from his foot injury, Svoboda is an excellent skater in all departments. He is lacking only in strength (something he could work on), but he is quick and agile, with great mobility and balance.

Svoboda can rush the puck from his own zone to get out of trouble and he likes to get into the offensive flow. He is a good point man on the power play and one of his better moves is his glide into a one-timer in the middle of the blue line. He has a low, accurate slap and a strong wrist shot which he can unleash from the blue line.

Svoboda is not as effective a playmaker at even strength, because he doesn't seem to read plays well and can't always seem to find the open man. He is improving his play defensively and his speed helps him recover from errors in judgement at the other team's blue line.

THE PHYSICAL GAME

Svoboda is a light, aggressive player who will use his stick to compensate for not having the strength to clear the front of his net. Svoboda will take a hit to make a play, but he gets bounced around easily and should develop some upper body strength to go along with his considerable finesse skills.

THE INTANGIBLES

Svoboda vowed he would not return to the Canadiens this season, but a fat new contract changed his mind. Montreal could use a healthy, interested Svoboda, since he showed signs last season of continuing his development as a solid two-way defenseman.

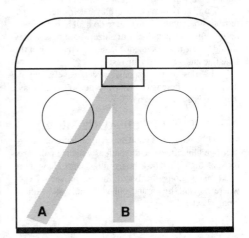

SYLVAIN TURGEON

Yrs. of NHL service: 8
Born: Noranda, Que., Canada; January 17, 1965
Position: Left wing
Height: 6-0
Weight: 195
Uniform no.: 16
Shoots: left

Career statistics:

GP	G	A	TP	PIM
461	213	173	386	467

1990-91 statistics:

GP	G	A	TP	+/-	PIM	PP	SH	GW	GT	S	PCT
19	5	6	11	-2	20	1	0	1	0	41	12.2

LAST SEASON

Missed 33 games following off-season groin surgery. Missed 23 games with with fractured right kneecap. All totals career lows as a result of injuries.

THE FINESSE GAME

Turgeon is a pure offensive player with terrific skating and scoring skills - the prototypical goal scorer. He has very good outside speed and quickness. He likes to go for a big slap shot, but he will go to the net as well. As a hockey player, Turgeon loves to score goals.

Turgeon gets his shot away quickly and accurately. He is a second-effort guy who won't just admire his shot but will follow it up in case of a rebound.

Turgeon is limited as a playmaker. He is not a terribly smart player, and tries to do it all himself. He is either selfish or just doesn't realize what the best play would be. He needs someone to get him the puck at the blue line and let him do the rest.

He tries to be responsible defensively, but he doesn't have defensive instincts, doesn't read plays well and is a defensive liability,

THE PHYSICAL GAME

Although he has good size, Turgeon prefers not to sacrifice himself, especially defensively. He will carry his stick high when he is being roughed up. He will not make plays along the boards unless he sees a spot where he can slip in and out with the puck without being checked.

THE INTANGIBLES

Injuries wiped out Turgeon last season. The Canadiens hope to play him alongside Denis Savard. The pairing would be a defensive nightmare but a wonderful and charismatic show. They could revive the gloried tradition of the Flying Frenchmen. Turgeon needs to show some consistency in his intensity level, which has been sporadic thus far in his career.

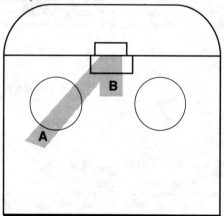

NEW JERSEY DEVILS

LAURIE BOSCHMAN

Yrs. of NHL service: 12
Born: Major, Sask., Canada; June 4, 1960
Position: Center
Height: 6-0
Weight: 185
Uniform no.: 16
Shoots: left

Career statistics:

GP	G	A	TP	PIM
864	212	321	533	2,043

1990-91 statistics:

GP	G	A	TP	+/-	PIM	PP	SH	GW	GT	S	PCT
78	11	9	20	-1	79	0	1	1	0	91	12.1

LAST SEASON

Acquired Sept. 6, 1990, from Winnipeg for Bob Brooke. Goal total was three season high. Assist and point totals were career lows. Missed two games with a bruised left shoulder.

THE FINESSE GAME

Boschman's skating ability is deceptive, because he isn't fast or flashy. He is very agile, however, and very strong on his skates. What he has lost in speed over the years he has compensated for by playing an intelligent game.

He seldom plays with linemates who are finishers, so his playmaking abilities, which are average at best, usually pass unnoticed. Boschman is not a fancy scorer, but will bang some in from short range as a result of his hard work around the net. As his primary responsibility is that of a checking center, Boschman is more concerned about preventing goals than scoring. He once scored 32 goals with the Jets, but those days are long gone and he has realized his role is that of a defensive forward.

Boschman has also gotten smarter about penalties without losing any of his feistiness. His PIM total was low (lowest since his rookie season), but you'll still see him anger opponents with some of his stick work. He is very good without the puck, always in good position and anticipates well.

THE PHYSICAL GAME

Boschman is a most annoying player to play against—there may be no better player in the league at holding an opponent's stick and pretending that he's the one being held (Boschman still draws his share with his sly acting ability). He is very wiry and tenacious, and seldom loses any one-on-one battles for the puck. The second effort is still there even after a dozen years in the league. He is a durable player.

The toughest part for a purely defensive player, which Boschman is now, is the mental aspect, since it is a job that goes largely unnoticed except on a night when he draws a checking assignment against a Mario Lemieux or a Wayne Gretzky. Boschman has adjusted well to this role. He has lost little quickness on faceoffs, where he is consistently above .500, winning most of his draws outright.

THE INTANGIBLES

Boschman is a quiet leader with experience, no rah-rah man but a player who is well respected by his teammates. His own game was freshened last season by his exodus from Winnipeg (at his request) and the effect of playing for a contending team took some of the years off. He is mentally tough.

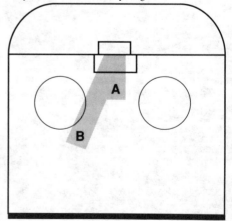

DOUG BROWN

Yrs. of NHL service: 4
Born: Southborough, Mass., USA; June 12, 1964
Position: Right wing
Height: 5-11
Weight: 180
Uniform no.: 24
Shoots: right

Career statistics:

GP	G	A	TP	PIM
264	57	58	115	55

1990-91 statistics:

GP	G	A	TP	+/-	PIM	PP	SH	GW	GT	S	PCT
58	14	16	30	18	4	0	2	2	1	122	11.5

LAST SEASON

Scored 14 goals for the third time in his four-year career. Assist and point totals were two-year lows. Tied for three-way club lead in shorthanded goals. Led all team forwards in plus-minus. Missed two games with a bruised foot.

THE FINESSE GAME

Because Brown is always hustling, he gives the impression of being a very fast skater. He's not—at least not straight-ahead, although he does have real quickness side-to-side. He is sometimes too fast on his feet and wipes out frequently after losing his edges. Brown gets a lot of breakaways because of the quick jumps he gets on the opposition. Unfortunately, he lacks the offensive skills to finish off the play.

Brown is not a big scorer or a big checker, but he does give a coach a consistent level of play night after night. He always attains his level of play but seldom surpasses it, which is why coaches are always giving other players ice time ahead of him early in the season, before going back to the reliable Brown after the newcomer fails to show the same reliability.

He will produce about 15 goals a season, but probably never more than 20. Brown is an excellent, aggressive penalty killer and will get the odd short-handed goal with a shot that can surprise a goalie because he gets it away quickly. He also never quits around the net and scores with stuffs and tip-ins.

THE PHYSICAL GAME

Brown is not a strong player but he is one of the better grinders along the wall, since he will hang in and keep the puck alive along the boards with his stick and his feet. He will let opponents get away, however, because he lacks the strength to tie up bigger players. He is not a fighter (another reason he sometimes has trouble getting into the lineup), but he is tough and will play hurt.

The key to Brown's game is his maturity and responsibility. Give him the role to play, and he'll play it. He seldom takes bad or lazy penalties, because quickness and intelligence keep him in position.

THE INTANGIBLES

Because his game will never rise beyond a certain level, Brown is always going to have to battle for a job and he knows it (the Devils exposed him in the expansion draft, but he was not taken). He keeps himself in good physical shape and is a hard worker who enjoys the game. He is the typical journeyman, but as long as he maintains his quickness and drive, he will be a valuable role player.

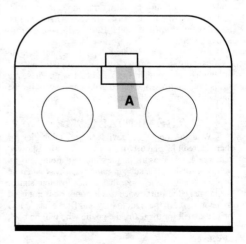

SEAN BURKE

Yrs. of NHL service: 4
Born: Windsor, Ont., Canada; January 29, 1967
Position: Goaltender
Height: 6-3
Weight: 205
Uniform no.: 1
Catches: left

Career statistics:

GP	MINS	GA	SO	GAA	A	PIM
162	9,063	552	4	3.65	4	116

1990-91 statistics:

GP	MINS	GAA	W	L	T	SO	GA	S	SAPCT	PIM
35	1,870	3.59	8	12	8	0	112	875	.872	18

LAST SEASON

Games and minutes played were fewest for a full NHL season, while his GAA was lowest. Missed three games with knee injury, one game with back spasms.

THE PHYSICAL GAME

Burke is a big goalie whose agility is always questioned, but he is very quick for his size. He has sharp reactions and reflexes, and excels on the bang-bang plays, the one-timers and rebounds. Because he is big and strong, he is able to take a pounding around the net.

Burke has a good glove hand, but let in some odd goals off his glove last season, which may have been more the fault of the equipment than the goalie. When he is on his game, he stands up well, but his best work comes when he fills the net with slides across to block low shots.

Burke's game has several flaws, most notably the blatantly bad goals he will allow on breakaways and long shots, especially to the stick side. He is weak around his feet (as many tall goalies are) and struggles most when he has the most time to think. Burke underwent knee surgery during training camp in 1990 and it forced him to alter his style somewhat, since he lost flexibility in his V-style. He is still having problems adjusting.

For a big goalie, Burke is a poor stickhandler. He has difficulty stopping hard-arounds behind the net and although he is strong, he is not a good passer. These are skills that could be improved with hard work, but he has not shown an inclination to work on them.

THE MENTAL GAME

When he joined the Devils after the Olympics for their incredible playoff run of 1988, Burke showed remarkable composure in pressure situations and an ability to shake off a subpar game. That was when he was the No. 1 goalie. Now that he has lost that status, the mental edge Burke once had is gone. He is not used to having to earn the right to play and Burke has to feel he is the man for the team, the goalie who will be back in the nets for 60-70 games a season, in order to be effective.

Focus and concentration used to be very strong aspects of his game, but those have eroded with his confidence. Where his teammates once relied on him to win games almost single-handedly, they now seldom win in front of him, even when he turns in a winning performance. Much of this is due to the momentum-deflating goals he allows. His better saves in close quarters are less obvious.

THE INTANGIBLES

It may be impossible for Burke to live up to the hype that surrounded his splashy NHL debut. It's also impossible to think that Burke, at 24, can't be a better goalie than he has shown the past few seasons. Trade rumors have surrounded Burke for two years and a change of scenery could be the best thing for him. Burke played out his option last season and that pressure may have also had an effect on him.

ZDENO CIGER

Yrs. of NHL service: 1
Born: Martin, Czechoslovakia; October 19, 1969
Position: Left wing
Height: 6-1
Weight: 190
Uniform no.: 33
Shoots: left

Career statistics:

GP	G	A	TP	PIM
45	8	17	25	8

1990-91 statistics:

GP	G	A	TP	+/-	PIM	PP	SH	GW	GT	S	PCT
45	8	17	25	3	8	2	0	1	0	82	9.8

LAST SEASON

First season in NHL.

THE FINESSE GAME

Ciger has explosive lateral speed, but his straight-away skating is hampered by a bad habit that is proving hard to break: Ciger skates with a herky-jerky motion when carrying the puck, because he has to move the stick at the same time he is moving his feet. He will often lose the puck with nobody on him because of this quirk.

Ciger has an excellent wrist and slap shot, but seldom uses it because he is looking to make a pass rather than take the shot. He is a perimeter player, usually pulling to the outside rather than trying to penetrate the defense and cut to the net. Unless Ciger learns to drive to the net (and he has to want to pay the price to do it), his scoring potential may go unrealized.

Because of his tentative offensive style, Ciger often turns over the puck and is a defensive liability. Even though left wing is the defensive forward position in the Czechoslovakian system, it is not as physical as North American checking. He is a reaction player, but has the raw talent and fundamental skills to make him a genuine offensive threat.

THE PHYSICAL GAME

Ciger is big, strong and powerful on his skates, but those attributes go to waste when a player is unwilling to put them to use. Ciger spent some time in the minors last season because of his lack of hitting. He is a player with awesome potential, but the adjustment to the North American style of game may take some doing.

Ciger showed little interest in off-ice conditioning last season and will have to step up his intensity in that department if he wants to stay in the NHL. An upper-body regimen would help him immensely.

THE INTANGIBLES

This year will be a big one for Ciger. Will he be the kind of scorer that he has the skills to be? Or a case of promise unfulfilled? His teammates were unhappy with the lack of commitment Ciger showed last year (he also spoke hardly any English, which didn't help matters), and if he doesn't start demonstrating some kind of commitment this could be a very difficult season for him.

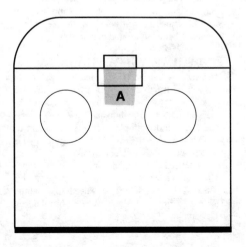

TROY CROWDER

Yrs. of NHL service: 1
Born: Sudbury, Ont., Canada; May 3, 1968
Position: Right wing
Height: 6-4
Weight: 215
Uniform no.: 25
Shoots: right

Career statistics:

GP	G	A	TP	PIM
69	6	3	9	205

1990-91 statistics:

GP	G	A	TP	+/-	PIM	PP	SH	GW	GT	S	PCT
59	6	3	9	-10	182	0	0	0	0	46	13.0

LAST SEASON

First full season in NHL

THE FINESSE GAME

Crowder earned a reputation with quick early season KOs of toughies like Bob Probert and Jeff Chychrun, so any discussion of Crowder's hockey skills will be as brief as most of his bouts. Crowder is so huge that he looks like he is lumbering on the ice, but he actually is faster than he looks. He has no lateral quickness at all, but has average straight-line speed.

He has very good hands (when they aren't swollen from fights), good hand-eye coordination and showed some surprising dexterity on a couple of goals. He has a good wrist shot and could develop into a Probert-type scorer if he can improve his game to where he could skate a regular shift.

Crowder's greatest liability is his defensive play. He does not read plays well and frequently misses his checking assignments. If he does not improve that aspect of his game, he will never get the ice time to develop into a better all-around player.

THE PHYSICAL GAME

Crowder is an absolutely fearless fighter, a puncher with destructive ability. He is, in fact, afraid to battle smaller players and they have learned to take advantage of him by hitting him and knowing he won't hit back. Crowder doesn't play dirty and seldom instigates a fight. His effectiveness is often negated by his lack of aggression—if you don't wake Crowder up, you won't notice he was in the game.

Crowder needs to hit more with his body, not his hands. He has no "dark side" and he needs to get a little meaner and hungrier to make the kind of hits that can help his team.

THE INTANGIBLES

Crowder was off to a strong start last season, but got self-satisfied in the middle of the year and has to apply himself more. He shouldn't be content with what he has done so far (i.e., earning a part-time job in the NHL, which he could easily lose when the next gunslinger comes along), because he could do so much more by earning a steady shift.

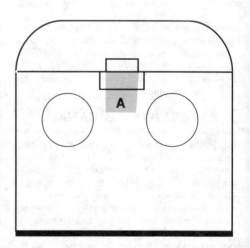

KEN DANEYKO

Yrs. of NHL service: 7
Born: Windsor, Ont., Canada; April 17, 1964
Position: Defenseman
Height: 6-0
Weight: 210
Uniform no.: 3
Shoots: left

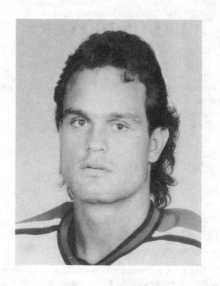

Career statistics:

GP	G	A	TP	PIM
449	23	69	92	1,300

1990-91 statistics:

GP	G	A	TP	+/-	PIM	PP	SH	GW	GT	S	PCT
80	4	16	20	-10	249	1	2	1	0	106	3.8

LAST SEASON

Led team in PIM. Had worst plus-minus among team defensemen. Was one of only two Devils to play in all 80 games.

THE FINESSE GAME

Daneyko has good agility for his size but often looks awkward because he still has difficulty with his play selection. Daneyko will attack a player and make a wrong read and be left reading the back of the opponent's sweater as he motors past him—for a physical defenseman, this is a dreadful flaw. He has to become more than one-dimensional and learn when to wait, when to poke-check or when to line up a skater for a hit.

Daneyko does several things very well. He is an excellent shot-blocker and has improved his skills in moving the puck. Where he used to panic and ice the puck or throw it blindly to where an opponent was waiting, he now looks for a headman pass or dumps the puck to where a teammate can pursue it.

An emotional player, Daneyko has also cut down on his bad penalties without losing any of his toughness. He has developed into a good penalty-killer. Daneyko has also showed improvement offensively and is much better at timing his rushes. His slap shot is not potent, but he is accurate with his shot. He has the skills to be more than a one-dimensional defenseman.

THE PHYSICAL GAME

Daneyko seldom loses a player along the boards. He is excellent in take-outs and his skating ability and size add up to crunching checks. He is also willing to drop his gloves to help out a teammate. Daneyko loves to bang and could develop into a very steady backliner if he can cut down on the mental errors. He is a hard worker and always keeps himself in top physical shape. He has tremendous all-around strength.

THE INTANGIBLES

Daneyko is maturing but he is still an inconsistent defenseman who tries to do too much and ends up being all over the ice. He was cursed by being drafted by a weak franchise and was rushed to the majors before his game was complete. He had showed steady progress until last season, when he levelled off. Off-ice problems may have affected his game, since he is such an emotional player.

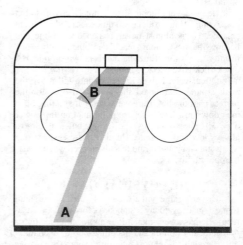

BRUCE DRIVER

Yrs. of NHL service: 7
Born: Toronto, Ont., Canada; April 29, 1962
Position: Defenseman
Height: 6-0
Weight: 185
Uniform no.: 23
Shoots: left

Career statistics:

GP	G	A	TP	PIM
434	50	205	255	321

1990-91 statistics:

GP	G	A	TP	+/-	PIM	PP	SH	GW	GT	S	PCT
73	9	36	45	11	62	7	0	2	0	195	4.6

LAST SEASON

Led team defensemen in points and assists; second among defensemen in plus-minus. Goal total was three-season high. Missed seven games with a fractured rib.

THE FINESSE GAME

Until he started to wear down physically late in the season, Driver was probably the team's best all-around defenseman for most of the year. Despite his size, which makes him a relative lightweight among most NHL blueliners, Driver was tops on the team in takeouts because of the precision of his checks and his astute positioning. You seldom see Driver scrambling back defensively because he sees the ice well and anticipates and doesn't get caught asleep. Driver is a student of the game and is always conscious of who he is playing against and what their tendencies are. Coaches will usually have him on the ice against the opponent's top forward line because Driver makes few mistakes.

He is a very good skater, not overly fast but possessing a fluid stride, good quickness and excellent balance. He is almost never beaten one-on-one and because he has a long reach combined with quick reactions, he's sometimes hard to beat two-on-one. His quick-flick poke check is almost an art form.

Offensively, Driver is patient and will move the puck around sharply on the point and wait for the perfect pass or shot. He is very good at spotting open men down low and is a solid point man on the power play. His shot is not overpowering, but it is almost always low and accurate. He also possesses a strong wrist shot and is not afraid to sally in deep when he has the opportunity.

THE PHYSICAL GAME

Driver's game will always be limited by his small frame (small by today's standards for NHL defensemen). He has a very meticulous approach to his nutrition and conditioning and maximizes all of his natural gifts through his almost scientific approach. Unfortunately, he still can be beaten along the boards and in physical battles around the net because his upper-body strength simply can't match up to many of the bigger NHL grinders. Driver's strength tends to ebb as the long season wears on and he becomes vulnerable to injury.

He has a quiet toughness that he showed when he took a scary 41-stitch cut around his right eye in mid-season but never missed a game because of it.

THE INTANGIBLES

Could someone get this man a copy of "The Power of Positive Thinking?" Driver is overly modest in his personal assessments and if he set his sights a little higher and saw himself as a more commanding player, his game could improve several notches. He will never be a Paul Coffey-type scorer, but he could go from 50 points to 70 or so without losing any of his defensive effectiveness. He is one of the most underrated two-way defensemen in the league since he lacks the gaudy point totals to draw some attention to his play.

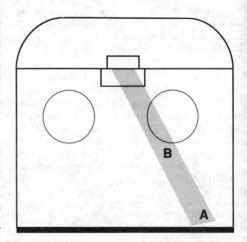

VIACHESLAV FETISOV

Yrs. of NHL service: 2
Born: Moscow, Soviet Union; May 20, 1958
Position: Defenseman
Height: 6-1
Weight: 205
Uniform no.: 2
Shoots: left

Career statistics:

GP	G	A	TP	PIM
139	11	50	61	114

1990-91 statistics:

GP	G	A	TP	+/-	PIM	PP	SH	GW	GT	S	PCT
67	3	16	19	5	62	1	0	0	0	71	4.2

LAST SEASON

All offensive totals were career lows. Missed nine games with bronchial pneumonia.

THE FINESSE GAME

All of Fetisov's game is finesse, now that age has robbed him of speed. There will be one or two moments a game when Fetisov makes a threadneedle pass to a breaking forward that few other defensemen in the world could make, but the problem is his insistence on trying to make the home run play now that his reflexes have slowed. When those plays go wrong, they are easily intercepted by opponents and turned into scoring chances against him. His adjustment to North American hockey this late in his career has been another drawback, as he is still sometimes surprised by the speed and intensity of the other team's forechecking.

Fetisov carries the puck like a forward and is a very creative player. He still sees himself as the general he was when the Soviets ruled the hockey world and wants to take the responsibility for the game and be placed in a leadership role. His desire to lead often outstrips his abilities, which often makes his game somewhat depressing to view.

A good shot blocker who is strong on his skates, Fetisov also is very good at reading plays and seeing the ice, as he demonstrates when he kills penalties, but his physical capabilities are not what they once were and he is frequently deceived by his own instincts into making the wrong play (what would have been the right play back when he was 25). If he could start doing the obvious and not trying for the world-class play, he would have an easier time of it. His teammates have started to become more used to his creativity and sometimes anticipate the unusual pass, but as the Soviet habits are ingrained in Fetisov, so are the North American habits deeply etched into his teammates' styles.

THE PHYSICAL GAME

Fetisov still appears stunned when body-checked by an opponent. Not a physical player himself, Fetisov will often use his stick in defense or retaliation, but he is loath to drop his gloves. He was a frequent target of opponents in his first NHL season and took a battering.

Opponents still believe that Fetisov can be taken out of a game with enough punishment, but he has started to adapt. He has started working more on his upper body conditioning, knowing it will be necessary for him to work harder to remain in the NHL. Although he is fairly strong, Fetisov does not take out opposing players with much authority. Possibly as a throwback to his international days, Fetisov often is fishing for the puck when he should be taking the man who is next to him.

THE INTANGIBLES

Fetisov has clearly been frustrated by his North American experience. Off the ice, he is very happy living in the USA. But he does not accept defeat well and it is difficult for him to believe his coaches when they tell him he's not capable of doing certain things anymore when at times he is. Clearly the greatness is gone from Fetisov's game, but if he can accept a new role, he could still be a valuable NHL player—just not the all-world player he once was. It is a genuine shame glasnost came too late for NHL fans to watch Fetisov in his prime.

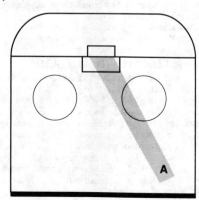

ALEXEI KASATONOV

Yrs. of NHL service: 2
Born: Leningrad, Soviet Union; October 14, 1959
Position: Defenseman
Height: 6-1
Weight: 210
Uniform no.: 7
Shoots: left

Career statistics:

GP	G	A	TP	PIM
117	16	46	62	92

1990-91 statistics:

GP	G	A	TP	+/-	PIM	PP	SH	GW	GT	S	PCT
78	10	31	41	23	76	1	0	3	0	122	8.2

LAST SEASON

Best plus-minus on team. Led defensemen in goals and was second among defensemen in points.

THE FINESSE GAME

Kasatonov is a blue-collar Soviet, if there could be such a thing. Where most Soviet players have graceful, seamless games, Kasatonov is a worker. He is a powerful skater, very wide-based, and his "railroad" stance makes him a very difficult player to knock off his skates. He is not fluid, but he does have good speed, quick lateral movement and great anticipation. Kasatonov's skills simply are far less obvious than many of the other Soviet skaters.

Kasatonov is a good offensive player because of his experience and passing skills. He is an excellent stick-checker and is able to turn the flow back quickly the other way and jump into the play offensively. He does not like to carry the puck—a legacy of the Soviet system—although he has the ability. He prefers to make the quick pass and he can hit the tape. Kasatonov can play on the power play, although he is not creative. Nor does he disguise his shot well, which is why many are blocked.

He is an excellent penalty killer, aggressive without losing his position. His enthusiasm for the game shows, but his emotions seldom affect him in a negative fashion. Coaches never have to worry about his intensity level, because he brings a consistent desire to excel to the rink every game.

Kasatonov is a very intelligent player and sees the ice well. He is not rattled in pressure situations.

THE PHYSICAL GAME

One of the highlights of Kasatonov's season was probably the fight he won with Ron Francis. Not that Francis is a heavyweight, but Kasatonov finally struck a blow for all of the Soviets who are constantly "tested" by NHL bullies. Kasatonov even took some sparring tips from his teammates during the season and has proven he can't be intimidated. In fact, Kasatonov has shown a taste for the rough stuff.

He is a very physical player, but will not check hard. He will take an opponent out, but let him off the hook. Many of Kasatonov's marks are able to get back into the play offensively because he takes them out so gently. He has to learn to crunch, because he has the size and especially the skating strength to do so.

THE INTANGIBLES

Timing is everything and Kasatonov's was even better off the ice than it is on. He benefited by coming to the NHL after the 1989-90 season was in progress, when the focus was on the other Soviet pioneers, like his teammate Viacheslav Fetisov. Expectations for Kasatonov were not as high and he had time to adjust to the NHL in relative peace. Now the secret is out. Kasatonov was the team's best defenseman over the long haul last season, showing real improvement late in the year. He is still at his best when paired with Fetisov, because the two had played together for years in the Soviet system, but he shows every sign of being to adapt successfully to the North American style of play.

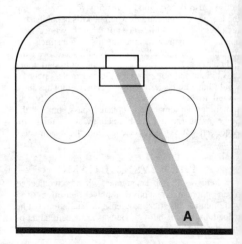

CLAUDE LEMIEUX

Yrs. of NHL service: 5
Born: Buckingham, Que., Canada; July 16, 1965
Position: Right wing
Height: 6-1
Weight: 215
Uniform no.: 22
Shoots: right

Career statistics:

GP	G	A	TP	PIM
359	127	109	236	681

1990-91 statistics:

GP	G	A	TP	+/-	PIM	PP	SH	GW	GT	S	PCT
78	30	17	47	-8	105	10	0	2	0	271	11.1

LAST SEASON

Acquired Sept. 4, 1990, from Montreal for Sylvain Turgeon. Goals were one short of career high. Assists were second-lowest total of career. Second on team in goals, fifth in points. Missed two games with an eye injury.

THE FINESSE GAME

Lemieux rebounded from abdominal surgery, which forced him to miss more than half the 1989-90 season, with a spectacular offensive show in his first season in New Jersey. He combines speed with a booming shot and can one-time the puck as well as almost anyone in the NHL. Speed is also Lemieux's problem—he is frequently too far ahead of the play and when the puck is where he should have been, he's already somewhere else. Lemieux also loves to attack so much that he will make unwise forays deep into the offensive zone and enable the opposition to break out easily.

Lemieux is almost as powerful a skater as he is a personality. Everyone knows when Lemieux is on the ice. If he could channel all of his energies into his game, he could become even more of a force. But yapping and irritating the enemy is as much a part of Lemieux's game as his wrist shot. Lemieux gets into trouble when he lets his high-test energy get the better of him and begins playing with reckless abandon. Lemieux needs to slow his game down on occasion to make the best use of his shots, but patience is not one of his virtues. He has excellent outside speed and is at his most dangerous when he is bearing down for a shot off the wing.

Lemieux needs to play with forwards who can get the puck to him. He is not much of a playmaker, but he's a tremendous finisher. He is an excellent man to have on the ice during the power play, since he is unafraid to pay the price for scoring a goal in front. He is gifted physically and makes the most of his talents.

THE PHYSICAL GAME

Lemieux is a warrior who doesn't handle failure (of his own or his team's) gracefully. He seems to let a lot of his feelings out, but he still holds a lot inside.

Hitting and agitating the opposition isn't just an assignment for Lemieux, it's the best way for him to get involved in the game.

Lemieux likes playing the game and he works hard at it—on the ice. He is not big on off-ice conditioning, but his natural strength and willingness have worked for him, so most coaches are happy to let him go his own way. Lemieux's game is power and he needs to maintain his strength to be effective.

THE INTANGIBLES

Lemieux brought his game to a higher level last season after his departure from Montreal, where he had a difference of opinion with coach Pat Burns and where the pressure was intense for the French-Canadian. He brought a new level of consistency to his game and the question this season will be to ascertain if he has developed the maturity to channel his considerable energy and repeat his steady and often spectacular performance.

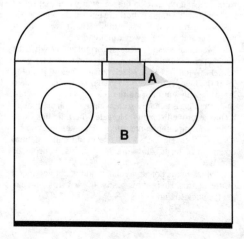

JOHN MacLEAN

Yrs. of NHL service: 8
Born: Oshawa, Ont., Canada; November 20, 1964
Position: Right wing
Height: 6-0
Weight: 200
Uniform no.: 15
Shoots: right

Career statistics:

GP	G	A	TP	PIM
546	217	224	441	785

1990-91 statistics:

GP	G	A	TP	+/-	PIM	PP	SH	GW	GT	S	PCT
78	45	33	78	8	150	19	2	7	2	292	15.4

LAST SEASON

Goals and PIM were career highs. Fifth in league in shots and power play goals. Led team in goals, points, shots and power play goals. Missed two games with a stomach contusion.

THE FINESSE GAME

MacLean's game is incredibly simple: he goes to the net, he shoots the puck, he scores. At least, that's MacLean's game when he's going well. He gets into slumps when he abandons that simplicity and tries to make the pretty plays and his attention is distracted by all of those nasty players who won't let him do it. Of course, MacLean is going to draw checking attention because of his great goal touch, but when MacLean is focused and driving, he never even notices he's getting hacked and held, because he lets nothing stop him. He has to learn he doesn't have to be tough and to retaliate in his own way—by scoring goals—because he doesn't do his team any favors by sitting in the penalty box.

MacLean has all the shots: a slap shot, a one-timer (from a waiting position or on the fly), a wrist shot and a snap shot. He is best from the slot, but he will shoot from almost anywhere on the ice, at any time, and even his "impossible angle" shots are hard and accurate. He has one of the best shots in the NHL. It is just overpowering and he fires away quickly.

MacLean wasn't successful right away when he made the jump from junior and he works hard for what he gets. What has kept MacLean just below the elite level (he has yet to score 50 goals) is the inconsistent lapses he runs into during the season. He is not a fast skater and he is actually somewhat awkward although he has improved steadily. He gets where he has to go and his anticipation in the offensive zone makes up for his slow feet. He isn't what one could call a natural talent, since he has to work hard at his game to be effective.

MacLean is not a playmaker and is not very good off the boards. He is at his best with forwards who can get the puck to him.

THE PHYSICAL GAME

As MacLean has matured, he has paid more attention to his physical fitness and he is a much stronger player because of that. He is not very big by NHL standards and is not a particularly punishing hitter although he will taken the body. He is unafraid to go to the net to score and will absorb abuse to get the goal. He has good balance, with a wide stance when he's going through traffic. He is very durable.

Defensively, MacLean plays a pretty smart game and he is sometimes used to kill penalties.

THE INTANGIBLES

If there were a statistical category for "most stupid penalties by a player of all-star caliber," MacLean would lead the NHL. On the plus side, MacLean gets into his own little world when he is playing really well and he never knows if there are 20 minutes or 20 seconds left in a game, because he will work with the same poise and determination no matter what the game situation. MacLean is reaching his physical peak and is capable of a monster year if he can maintain his consistency.

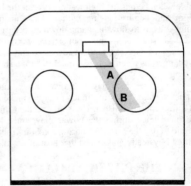

DAVID MALEY

Yrs. of NHL service: 5
Born: Beaver Dam, Wisc., USA; April 24, 1963
Position: Center/left wing
Height: 6-2 **Weight** 205
Uniform no.: 8
Shoots: left

Career statistics:

GP	G	A	TP	PIM
294	31	51	82	680

1990-91 statistics:

GP	G	A	TP	+/-	PIM	PP	SH	GW	GT	S	PCT
64	8	14	22	9	151	1	0	3	0	67	11.9

LAST SEASON

Tied with two other players for best plus-minus among team forwards. Tied career high in goals. Missed 11 games with a sprained ankle. Missed two games with a fractured hand.

THE FINESSE GAME

Maley's slow reaction times hamper his offensive skills. He has a good shot, but gets it away slowly. Shooting does not come naturally to him under pressure. He does have some nice moves and can carry the puck, but sometimes so slowly that you can tell what he's thinking just by watching.

He skates like a shark—he must keep moving and circling because he can't stop and start with any quickness. He is strong on his skates, however, and when he has to get someplace, he will do it mostly on sheer desire.

THE PHYSICAL GAME

If you needed someone to protect you in a dark alley, Maley would be the player to choose. He is an honest enforcer, not a bully, but a powerful fighter with a real desire to protect his teammates. His feistiness gives him some room, which is useful because he needs the extra time to make plays.

Maley is better than average on faceoffs, with the strength to tie up the opposing center. Goalies love him because he always stops to see if his goalie is set before moving in for the draw (you would be surprised to see how many faceoff men don't). He also uses his strength well on the wall, where he is a grinder and reads the play well. Defensively, he is very responsible.

THE INTANGIBLES

If Maley works hard at the offensive part of his game (the defensive part is already very sound), he could become a solid, two-way physical center. He is developing a better work ethic and is respected by his teammates.

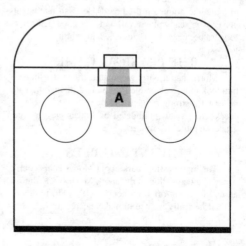

JON MORRIS

Yrs. of NHL service: 1
Born: Lowell, Mass., USA; May 6, 1966
Position: Center
Height: 6-0
Weight: 175
Uniform no.: 20
Shoots: right

Career statistics:

GP	G	A	TP	PIM
77	15	28	43	35

1990-91 statistics:

GP	G	A	TP	+/-	PIM	PP	SH	GW	GT	S	PCT
53	9	19	28	9	27	1	0	1	0	44	20.5

LAST SEASON

First full season in NHL. Missed four games with rib injury. Tied with two other players for best plus-minus among team forwards.

THE FINESSE GAME

Grace is the first word that comes to mind about Morris' game. He is a highly skilled puckhandler and playmaker and makes everything look easy. Unfortunately, some of his moves are compromised by his lack of skating quickness.

Morris has great hands and his biggest failing is his unselfishness. He will look too hard to make a play when the shot is his for the taking and he has the skills to put some points on the board. He is an intelligent player who reads plays well and is a good defensive forward because of his stick-checking ability.

THE PHYSICAL GAME

Morris has a wiry, greyhound frame that makes him look more vulnerable than he is. Although he will never be a strong enough player to make big bodychecks, he is not intimidated by bigger players—he gets even more determined.

THE INTANGIBLES

The big question mark about Morris is his confidence and dedication to the sport. Morris took almost an entire season off from hockey (1988-89) to determine if he really wanted to make a career of it, so his commitment is questionable. Morris does enjoy playing the game and if he wants to pay the price, he has the potential to develop into a top playmaker.

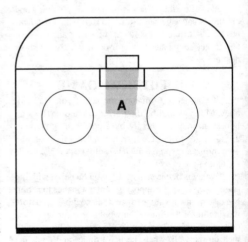

KIRK MULLER

Yrs. of NHL service: 7
Born: Kingston, Ont., Canada; February 8, 1966
Position: Center/left wing
Height: 6-0
Weight: 205
Uniform no.: 9
Shoots: left

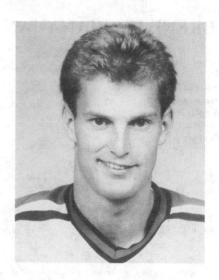

Career statistics:

GP	G	A	TP	PIM
556	185	335	520	572

1990-91 statistics:

GP	G	A	TP	+/-	PIM	PP	SH	GW	GT	S	PCT
80	19	51	70	1	76	7	0	3	1	221	8.6

LAST SEASON

One of two Devils to appear in all 80 games. Led team in assists, second in points, which were the lowest total since his rookie season (as were his goals).

THE FINESSE GAME

Muller works best in traffic, since he has a quick but not a great shot. It's just that he's more willing than most other players to make the effort to get the puck. Muller is also good at taking shots off the wing, but is reluctant to do it. He basically scores within a 10-foot radius of the goalmouth.

Muller is not a gifted, natural athlete with flowing moves. When he skates hard up-ice, he looks like he's skating hard, as if he's straining with every stride. He is not a good open-ice playmaker, but will work well in cramped quarters to get a pass to a teammate.

Desire and determination have always been the hallmarks of Muller's game. He doesn't relax until the final buzzer and few are better than he at scoring in the waning seconds. Muller sometimes is too intense, putting too much pressure on himself to carry the team.

THE PHYSICAL GAME

Muller is one of the best forwards in the league along the boards. He is almost as good with his feet as his stick (he was a good soccer player and the training shows) and he's a striver. He'll go through a door without bothering to check if it's locked, or even if it's open. Muller could save a little wear and tear on himself if he did stop trying to go through opponents, but because he lacks confidence in his skating ability, he prefers trying to overpower people.

He is a tiger on faceoffs. He is not the quickest, but he ties up opposing centers very well and battles for the loose puck. His play without the puck is excellent and he works well on both specialty teams.

THE INTANGIBLES

Muller's drive makes him an outstanding on-ice leader. He needs a more talented supporting cast to be more of an offensive force. Muller played most of his junior career at center and still wants to play there, but his style will bring him the most success on the left wing.

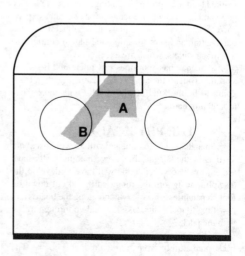

BRENDAN SHANAHAN

Yrs. of NHL service: 4
Born: Mimico, Ont., Canada; January 23, 1969
Position: Right wing
Height: 6-3
Weight: 205
Uniform no.: 11
Shoots: right

Career statistics:

GP	G	A	TP	PIM
281	88	126	214	524

1990-91 statistics:

GP	G	A	TP	+/-	PIM	PP	SH	GW	GT	S	PCT
75	29	37	66	4	141	7	0	2	3	195	14.9

LAST SEASON

Goals were one shy of his career high. Third on team in goals and points, second in assists, tied for third in power play goals. PIM were career high. Missed five games with surgery to repair a fractured sinus.

THE FINESSE GAME

Shanahan has excellent hands and a nice release on his shot. He has the inner drive to want to be the kind of player who is relied on when the chips are down. Shanahan was rushed into the NHL and it has taken him time to mature and find his way around the league. He also faced a crisis of confidence when he struggled making the adjustment from junior. Now that he has, he is willing to assert himself on the ice and take respnsibilty for what may be a very successful pro career.

He is a strong skater but not very quick. He gets off to an awkward start and is not fluid, but he has worked hard to improve his skating. His passing is very good and he is seeing the ice better as he gains experience. Shanahan is sometimes too deliberate in his playmaking and shot selection and has to continue to trust his instincts, which are excellent.

Shanahan has enormous raw talent and he is just starting to put all the pieces of his game together. He is going to be the kind of player who will make those around him better.

THE PHYSICAL GAME

Shanahan likes to fight and will go with just about anyone in the league, but now that his skills have proven to be so valuable, he will have to develop the discipline to ignore the rough stuff and cut down on foolish penalties. He is very good along the boards and is willing to make hits, take hits and go through traffic with the puck.

He has no fear, as he demonstrated when he came back prematurely from a fractured cheekbone. The injury came as a result of an accidental deflection of a teammate's shot and Shanahan practiced for his return by standing in the identical spot and working on tip-ins of the same teammate's slapshot. This is one tough kid.

THE INTANGIBLES

Shanahan has improved and matured with each season. He has cut down on unnecessary penalties while losing little of his toughness. Though his defensive game still needs work, this could be the breakthrough year for him to establish himself among the NHL's best all-around wingers. The Devils are notoriously tight with a buck and since Shanahan has played out his option, he could well be in another uniform by the time the season opens.

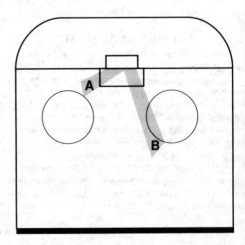

PETER STASTNY

Yrs. of NHL service: 10
Born: Bratislava, Czechoslovakia; September 18, 1956
Position: Center
Height: 6-1
Weight: 200
Uniform no.: 29
Shoots: left

Career statistics:

GP	G	A	TP	PIM
826	400	716	1,116	756

1990-91 statistics:

GP	G	A	TP	+/-	PIM	PP	SH	GW	GT	S	PCT
77	18	42	60	0	53	4	0	3	0	177	15.4

LAST SEASON

Fourth on team in points with lowest career marks in all offensive categories. Missed two games with the flu.

THE FINESSE GAME

Age has robbed Stastny of his skating speed and shot. At one point, Stastny was among the world's elite offensive players, but his big output years are past. He can't do all the things he did before, although he can still provide a consistent level of solid play and maturity and professionalism to a team badly in need of them.

Stastny is still a very good skater with tremendous lateral quickness. Most of his game is in his head and he has the edge over almost any opponent in how he sees the ice. He can still outskate players in a straightaway situation because of his determination, but the stamina isn't always there.

Stastny still has considerable playmaking abilities, but sometimes he wants to carry the puck and make the play himself, when he should start using his wingers to do more of the work. Stastny's passing work is wonderful to watch down low, especially on the power play as he threads passes right through his opponents. His best shots come off the backhand (a skill virtually ignored by most North American forwards) and the wrist shot.

THE PHYSICAL GAME

Stastny's game is all finesse, but as he makes the transition to a more defensive forward, he will have to use his body more. He is a very strong skater, but is at his best in open ice. He does not work well along the boards or in traffic, but he is willing to run the gauntlet in the offensive zone when he senses a scoring opportunity.

He remains one of the league's best faceoff men, with great anticipation, hand-eye coordination and an utter hatred of not winning more than his share.

THE INTANGIBLES

Stastny is adjusting well to his different role and is aware he can still contribute. He will learn to pace himself—to not expend the same energy on every shift but to recognize the big opportunity when he can surprise an opposing defenseman with a burst of speed and an accurate shot.

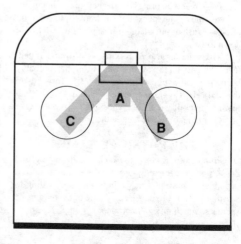

PATRIK SUNDSTROM

Yrs. of NHL service: 9
Born: Skelleftea, Sweden; December 14, 1961
Position: Center
Height: 6-0
Weight: 200
Uniform no.: 17
Shoots: left

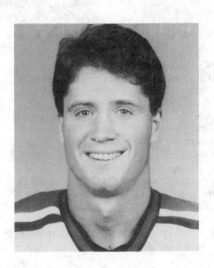

Career statistics:

GP	G	A	TP	PIM
662	218A	366	584	341

1990-91 statistics:

GP	G	A	TP	+/-	PIM	PP	SH	GW	GT	S	PCT
71	15	31	46	7	48	4	1	1	0	96	15.6

LAST SEASON

Lowest goal output in three seasons, fewest assists and points since since his rookie year. Missed five games with groin injury. Missed one game with hip pointer. Missed one game with hand injury.

THE FINESSE GAME

Sundstrom has never been a flashy scorer, but he is one of the top two-way forwards in the league when healthy. He has enough polish and style to make the game look easy, but he is a very hard worker. There is no one aspect of Sundstrom's game that stands out from any other. He is a good skater in all departments: straightaway speed (although he is starting to lose a step), lateral mobility and balance.

Sundstrom can handle the puck well in traffic and seldom makes a bad pass because he reads the situations well and never panics. His shot is quick but not powerful and he is more interested at this stage of his career in setting up his teammates. Sundstrom is a support player who brings out the best in his linemates. He can move the puck up ice himself to start on offensive rush or put a tape-to-tape pass through traffic down low.

His value as a penalty-killer is also underrated. Over the past three seasons, Sundstrom has probably been among the top half-dozen defensive forwards in the NHL. He is aggressive in his pursuit of the puck and his skating ability and poke-checking skills don't give point men much time to handle the puck.

THE PHYSICAL GAME

Sundstrom is very big-boned and sinewy and doesn't give an impression of size or strength. He is a deceptively strong player, willing to hit and willing to sacrifice his body to make a play (one of the reasons he spends so much time in the trainer's room). He is not a fighter by any means, but he is very tough in his own way.

Sundstrom blocks shots as well as most defensemen, and his fearlessness seems almost foolhardy. Sundstrom gets tremendous respect from his teammates for the price he is willing to pay to win a game.

THE INTANGIBLES

If he had played for better teams than the Canucks and Devils through his NHL career, this atypical Swede would have singlehandedly dispelled the myth of what a European player plays like. Injuries have taken their toll, so this very quiet leader may never get his proper due. He knows the game as well as (perhaps better than) any coaches he plays for and will remain an asset to any team as long as his body holds out. In fact, when his career is over, he would make an excellent coaching prospect.

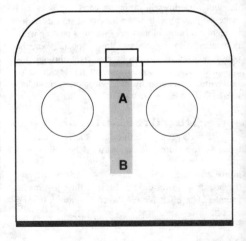

CHRIS TERRERI

Yrs. of NHL service: 2
Born: Providence, R.I., USA; November 15, 1964
Position: Goaltender
Height: 5-9
Weight: 160
Uniform no.: 31
Catches: left

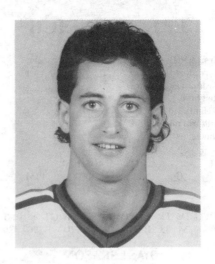

Career statistics:

GP	MINS	GA	SO	GAA	A	PIM
103	5,591	293	1	3.14	3	2

1990-91 statistics:

GP	MINS	GAA	W	L	T	SO	GA	S	SAPCT	PIM
53	2,970	2.71	24	21	7	1	144	1,348	.893	2

LAST SEASON

Games played, minutes played and wins were two-year career highs. GAA was seventh-best in NHL. Missed one game with flu.

THE PHYSICAL GAME

Terreri earned the nickname "scary" with some of his heart-stopping saves early in his career. He is still an acrobatic goalie, but he has learned to play his angles better and conserve his energy, which is important because of his frame. Terreri is small and looks skinny, but he is very wiry and strong, and devoutly follows his nutrition and conditioning guidelines.

Because of his size, Terreri is a target for crease-crashing teams (Devils coaches in the past have opted for the bigger Sean Burke against teams with a reputation of crowding the net), but Terreri will stand in to the best of his ability. He sees the puck very well through a crowd.

Terreri has a very good glove hand and because of his last-gasp quickness, he is a goalie who can really intimidate the opposition. Terreri is at his best in games when he gets a lot of shots. He is not a shutout goalie (he never was at any level of his career) and will let in a soft one now and then, but he rarely beats himself.

He is a good skater and stops hard-arounds behind the net with complete assurance. He has learned to control his rebounds better, which has cut down on the scrambles in front. When he does lose one, his reflexes are so quick he is able to recover. Terreri has matured with the added responsibilty he has been given and his more relaxed attitude shows in his game.

THE MENTAL GAME

When Terreri is hot, there is almost a tangible cockiness to some of the saves he makes. This is also where he can get into trouble. When Terreri gets too overconfident, he will over-anticipate shooters instead of making the basic plays. The same overconfidence creeps into his stickhandling, which has improved terrifically in the past season due to his hard work. Terreri would love to be the next goalie to score a goal, but he has to make sure he doesn't get too excited and err in making a risky pass up the middle.

Terreri has earned the confidence of his teammates. He can win a game by himself with his quickness and competitive personality. He is excellent at stopping breakaways and penalty shots.

THE INTANGIBLES

Terreri had seemed destined to spend his Devils career as a backup to Sean Burke, but with his talent and dedication took over the No. 1 spot. Terreri has all the tools and is limited only by his size. He will wear down over the course of a season and coaches have to be careful not to play him on too many consecutive nights. He is very upbeat, personable and coachable—a good player to have on the ice or in the dressing room.

ERIC WEINRICH

Yrs. of NHL service: 1
Born: Roanoke, Va., USA; December 19, 1966
Position: Defenseman
Height: 6-1
Weight: 210
Uniform no.: 5
Shoots: left

Career statistics:

GP	G	A	TP	PIM
97	6	41	47	59

1990-91 statistics:

GP	G	A	TP	+/-	PIM	PP	SH	GW	GT	S	PCT
76	4	34	38	10	48	1	0	0	0	96	4.2

LAST SEASON

First full season in NHL. Tied for third among NHL rookies in assists. Third best plus-minus on team.

THE FINESSE GAME

Weinrich is a big player who is a finesse defenseman. He is a good skater, with lateral ability, but he needs to develop more strength in his skating to be more of a factor along the boards. He is very quick with his feet, but his balance is terrible. He will bump with a player 30 pounds lighter and Weinrich will be the one to fall down. He needs to learn better technique.

He has excellent passing skills and has a promising future as a point man once he starts to read plays better. His shot from the point is good—low, hard and accurate, and he gets it away fairly quickly. What Weinrich can't do yet (because of his lack of skating ability) is get into the offensive flow with any confidence.

Weinrich doesn't do anything flashy. He needs to develop a more consistent game, but his future as a solid everyday defenseman doesn't seem far off, if he can raise his skating a notch.

THE PHYSICAL GAME

The aerobic part of Weinrich's game is fine: he is in good shape and can skate all day. But he needs to work more on his lower body strength. He is not a fighter, but he does have hockey courage and he will go back at a player, he just won't initiate.

Weinrich has fairly good hockey instincts. He is cool under fire and has learned to take a more commanding role with the puck in his own zone. He rushes the puck well and is learning to do things more smoothly and easily. Weinrich doesn't read plays well coming at him, however.

THE INTANGIBLES

Weinrich is an introspective player who needs frequent reassurance from his coaches. He is gaining confidence with experience and is becoming more vocal. He has leadership qualities that will start to emerge more and more in the next season.

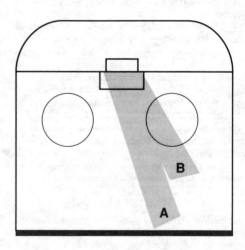

NEW YORK
ISLANDERS

KEN BAUMGARTNER

Yrs. of NHL service: 4
Born: Flin, Flon, Man., Canada; March 11, 1966
Position: Defenseman/left wing
Height: 6-1
Weight: 200
Uniform no.: 24
Shoots: left

Career statistics:

GP	G	A	TP	PIM
222	5	17	22	981

1990-91 statistics:

GP	G	A	TP	+/-	PIM	PP	SH	GW	GT	S	PCT
78	1	6	7	-14	282	0	0	0	0	41	2.4

LAST SEASON

Led club in PIM. Career high in assists.

THE FINESSE GAME

Although he has worked hard to improve his skating, it remains the weakest aspect of Baumgartner's game. He has below-average speed and agility and to overcome this deficiency he has to work more diligently at the mental aspect of being a defenseman. He can help himself most by improving his reaction time. He reads a play well, but it takes a while for the message to get from his brain to his body and he will have to remain mentally sharp throughout a game to avoid getting beaten.

Discipline will be the key to any improvement in the defensive zone. Baumgartner is composed and well-positioned as the play enters the zone, but the longer the opposition controls the play and maintains pressure in the zone, the faster his composure crumbles. Baumgartner has little patience and starts thinking, "I want to hammer that guy," and there is where his game breaks down.

Baumgartner has a good wrist shot and a good slapshot—in practice. In game situations, he has a tendency to get too excited and doesn't set the shot up properly or get it away well. He needs to relax and use his offensive skills more. He is also capable of good breakout plays, but that's an area where he is not going to make a living and he is better off with the safe clears.

THE PHYSICAL GAME

Baumgartner is a punishing hitter and a willing (frequently initiating) fighter. His only weakness in this area is his over-aggressiveness, both in taking bad penalties and his checking. Baumgartner can actually hit a player too hard, bouncing him off the boards so that the player is able to rebound and get back inside Baumgartner and into the play. He has to learn to get just enough of the skater to take him out effectively.

Improved skating will be a necessity if Baumgartner is going to become a more competent checker.

THE INTANGIBLES

Maturity will be the key to any further development. Since some of the physical parts of Baumgartner's game are lacking, he will need intelligence to maintain his performance at an NHL level. Baumgartner is very hard working and aware of his flaws and another year of experience under coach Al Arbour should help him take the next step.

BILL BERG

Yrs. of NHL service: 1
Born: St. Catherines, Ont., Canada; October 21, 1967
Position: Left wing/defenseman
Height: 6-1
Weight: 190
Uniform no.: 4
Shoots: left

Career statistics:

GP	G	A	TP	PIM
85	10	16	26	77

1990-91 statistics:

GP	G	A	TP	+/-	PIM	PP	SH	GW	GT	S	PCT
78	9	14	23	-3	67	0	0	0	0	95	9.5

LAST SEASON

First full NHL season.

THE FINESSE GAME

A converted defenseman, Berg has been playing left wing for only a season and a half. He skates well, not fast, but is very strong and agile. He has good lateral moves.

He has average hands and his best scoring area is around the front of the net. Berg is not afraid to stand in traffic and get the garbage goals. If he is not open to get a pass, Berg is very good at setting an offensive pick to open up some up ice his teammates.

Because he played defense most of his career, Berg is very conscientious in his own zone and in backchecking. He sometimes worries so much about getting back, however, that he does not finish his checks in the offensive zone.

THE PHYSICAL GAME

Berg is willing to take a hit but he will seldom initiate. He does not use his size as well as he might, possibly because of the confusion of moving up to a forward position. Perhaps as Berg becomes more comfortable on the wing, his positioning and body-checking will improve.

THE INTANGIBLES

An honest player with marginal skills, Berg probably would not have made the majors if he had been with a stronger organization. He is making the most of the playing time he gets with the Islanders and could develop into a reliable checking forward, but his game will remain one-dimensional.

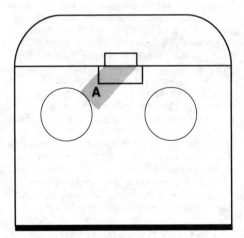

DAVID CHYZOWSKI

Yrs. of NHL service: 2
Born: Edmonton, Alta., Canada; July 11, 1971
Position: Left wing
Height: 6-2
Weight: 190
Uniform no.: 9
Shoots: left

Career statistics:

GP	G	A	TP	PIM
90	13	15	28	109

1990-19 statistics

GP	G	A	TP	+/-	PIM	PP	SH	GW	GT	S	PCT
56	5	9	14	-19	61	0	0	0	0	66	7.6

LAST SEASON

Worst plus-minus among team forwards. Games played was two-year career high.

THE FINESSE GAME

Chyzowski has a tremendous slapshot, which netted him 56 goals in his last year of junior, and the Islanders would like to see a lot more of it. The trouble is, Chyzowski hasn't yet adjusted to the time change between the WHL and the NHL, and that is that you don't get as much time to unleash it.

Chyzowski works hard to get himself into scoring position, but he lost confidence in his ability to shoot before getting checked. As a result, he became a little gun-shy and started looking to make plays. He was not made a No. 1 pick because of his playmaking ability. This kid is a finisher. His best move, his bread-and-butter play, is to just come down the wall and wire the puck. He will go into the corners and dig for the puck, but he is more deadly as an up-and-down winger, trailing the play and waiting for a drop or back pass. He uses a long stick and can whip a major league one-timer.

He has very good skating ability, combining quickness, agility and balance. Chyzowski is a good forechecker and can be used to kill penalties, but his real future lies as a power play specialist. He is an intelligent player whose poise will show when he has gained a little more experience and confidence.

THE PHYSICAL GAME

Chyzowski is a competitor who loves to play aggressively. He will hit and will fight (he was proud of holding his own against New Jersey's tough Troy Crowder last season). He is big and uses his size well.

Chyzowski's conditioning was a question mark, but he had some growing up to do and had to learn what it takes to stay in the NHL. He has applied himself more to off-ice training and practice sessions and coaches have been pleased with his improved attitude. The results show should show on the ice this season.

THE INTANGIBLES

Although he has struggled in his first two seasons in the NHL, Chyzowski is a winner who can be counted on at crunch time, as he has shown in international competitions at the junior level. He has great potential, but breaking in with a weak franchise may curtail his development. He could well struggle through this season as well. Chyzowski will be a late bloomer—a player to watch in the future.

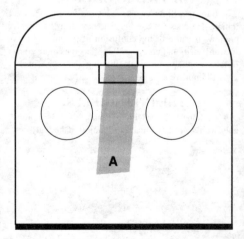

RAY FERRARO

Yrs. of NHL service: 7
Born: Trail, B.C., Canada; August 23, 1964
Position: Center
Height: 5-10
Weight: 185
Uniform no.: 33
Shoots: left

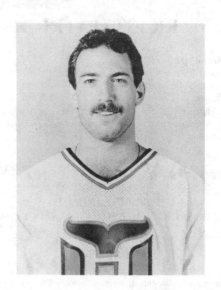

Career statistics:

GP	G	A	TP	PIM
503	176	210	386	485

1990-91 statistics:

GP	G	A	TP	+/-	PIM	PP	SH	GW	GT	S	PCT
76	21	21	42	-12	70	6	0	1	1	109	19.3

LAST SEASON

Acquired from Hartford for Doug Crossman, November 13. Six-year lows in goals, assists and points. Best shooting percentage on team.

THE FINESSE GAME

If Ferraro were a golfer, you could say he had a very good short game. Ferraro is at his best deep in the zone, in tight situations around the net and working snappy give-and-go passes. In a scrum in front of the goalie, he will fish the puck out of a crowd of skates and make a short pass to a teammate or get a shot on net. He thrives on pressure and really wants to get the goal. Ferraro really has amazing composure around the net, where he stays relaxed and has the vision to make the right play.

Ferraro has always been an offensive player and because he is always in so deep fighting to score, he is late getting back into the play defensively. Although he tries to be mindful of his defensive duties, that part of his game is below average. Ferraro's game is one-way, and that way is to the net.

He is strong on his skates, but takes choppy, short strides and doesn't have good end-to-end speed, although his balance helps him in traffic. Ferraro has a good wrist shot and gets it away with no wasted motion. He is average on faceoffs.

THE PHYSICAL GAME

If Ferraro doesn't play gritty, he doesn't play well. You can tell early in a game what kind of night it will be for him, because if he doesn't have a scrappy first shift or two, he will be invisible the rest of the night. Ferraro is not very big but he will take a hit to make a play, especially in the offensive zone. Ferraro wisely stays away from the boards, unless he is darting in to pounce on a loose puck.

THE INTANGIBLES

Ferraro's drawback has been his lack of intensity. If he comes to play every night, he is certainly capable of another 30-goal season. He is capable of adding real spark to a team, since he has a knack for scoring early goals on those nights when he does show up.

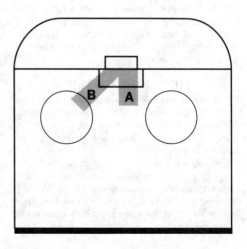

MARK FITZPATRICK

Yrs. of NHL service: 3
Born: Toronto, Ont., Canada; November 13, 1968
Position: Goaltender
Height: 6-1
Weight: 190
Uniform no.: 29
Catches: left

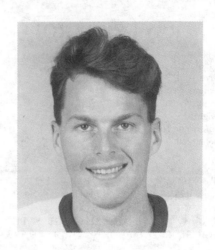

Career statistics:

GP	MINS	GA	SO	GAA	A	PIM
77	4,357	261	3	3.59	4	22

1990-91 statistics:

GP	MINS	GAA	W	L	T	SO	GA	S	SAPCT	PIM
2	120	3.00	1	1	0	0	6	60	.900	0

LAST SEASON

Fitzpatrick missed most of the season battling a career- and life-threatening condition called eosini-phila-myaligia syndrome, a disease which causes swelling of muscles and tissues.

THE PHYSICAL GAME

Fitzpatrick was showing his talents at the end of the 1989-90 season, but his illness put his career and development on hold. From what has been seen on Fitzpatrick so far in the NHL, he has tremendous tools to become a dominating goalie. His skating and balance are good.

He is a standup goalie who uses his size well to cut and cover his angles. Fitzpatrick has a quick glove, which he keeps low to the ice. He challenges well and is very good on breakaways and one-on-ones because he does not overplay the shot.

Fitzpatrick is a good skater with balance and is agile for a big goalie. He seldom strays far from his crease. Technically, he is weak on passing and stopping pucks behind the net. He must work to improve his stickhandling skills, because he has the strength to shoot the puck with some ginger.

THE MENTAL GAME

Ability to maintain his concentration is one area where Fitzpatrick needs to develop consistency. He has trouble following the puck through traffic, but that can improve through effort. When he is on his game, he handles rebounds very well.

Fitzpatrick loves to play big games, but he is competitive to the point where he has to watch his self-control. He challenges shooters well. He doesn't allow many bad goals and bad games don't keep him down long; he's a battler and wants to get back in the net as soon as possible.

THE INTANGIBLES

Fitzpatrick was supposed to be one of the star goalies of the future. A winner at the junior level, (he backstopped the WHL Medicine Hat Tigers to two Calder Trophy championships), Fitzpatrick showed tremendous courage in battling back from EMS. He has been hit by adversity and that can motivate him to become a better player because he has worked so hard to get back to an NHL level.

PATRICK FLATLEY

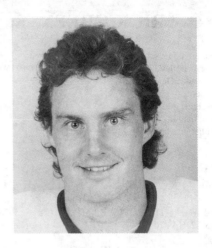

Yrs. of NHL service: 8
Born: Toronto, Ont., Canada; October 3, 1963
Position: Right wing
Height: 6-2
Weight: 195
Uniform no.: 26
Shoots: right

Career statistics:

GP	G	A	TP	PIM
429	112	194	306	493

1990-91 statistics:

GP	G	A	TP	+/-	PIM	PP	SH	GW	GT	S	PCT
56	20	25	45	-2	74	8	0	4	0	137	14.6

LAST SEASON

Tied for fourth on the team in points. Missed 20 games with a fractured finger on his left hand, yet had best goals output in five seasons and best point total in four seasons.

THE FINESSE GAME

Flatley is one of the best cornermen in the league. He has very good hands, is intense and is strong on his skates and on his stick. Although in open ice he is a choppy, graceless skater, along the boards he is tough to knock down and he will keep digging until he comes away with the puck.

Flatley likes to set up shop in front of the net and is hard to budge. He likes to go upstairs with his wrist shot and he has the touch and the patience to do it. He is also a banger and a whacker. He will keep slashing at the puck as long as it is loose in the crease.

Flatley is a good playmaker who sees the ice well. He gets into occasional slumps when he waits too long to look for an even better, prettier play than the one that's open to him. He is excellent at protecting the puck with his body.

Despite his lack of speed, Flatley is a very good penalty killer because he compensates with intelligence and hockey sense.

THE PHYSICAL GAME

One image of Flatley that time can't erase is a crunching check he threw against Rangers defenseman Barry Beck in the 1984 playoffs. The check ruined Beck's shoulder and he was never the same player again. Flatley is still a good hitter, but these days he is more likely to get hit, and badly injured. He made it back from full reconstructive surgery on his right knee in 1987 and hasn't played more than 63 games in a season since. Many of the injuries are a result of Flatley's unselfishness. He will leave himself vulnerable to a check in order to make a play.

Flatley is by nature a kamikaze who will keep making the dangerous play if it will help his team.

THE INTANGIBLES

Flatley is a leader by example, who is very well respected by his teammates and coaches. An intense player, Flatley hates to lose, and more important, loves to win. He will pay any price to do it.

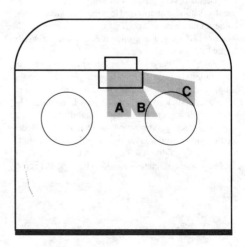

RICK GREEN

Yrs. of NHL service: 14
Born: Belleville, Ont., Canada; February 20, 1956
Position: Defenseman
Height: 6-3
Weight: 220
Uniform no.:
Shoots: Left

Career statistics:

GP	G	A	TP	PIM
841	43	220	263	588

1990-91 statistics:

GP	G	A	TP	+/-	PIM	PP	SH	GW	GT	S	PCT
65	2	14	16	10	24	0	0	0	0	36	5.6

LAST SEASON

Assist total matched his best in past four NHL seasons.

THE FINESSE GAME

Green covers ground very well. Though large players, especially large defensemen, tend to lumber, Green has rather light feet and a long, smooth stride. Good balance allows him to take a hit or give one and remain upright.

Positionally, Green is steady and solid, ready to clear the rebound or to skate it from harm's way. He is good with the puck and makes intelligent moves to get the puck out of the zone.

He does, however, concede a fair amount of space to an onrushing attacker. He meets the skater deeper in the zone than he would like, but uses his experience in dealing with the situation.

THE PHYSICAL GAME

Green is very physical in front of the net during penalty killing situations. He tends to jump to the corners, challenge, and get back to position in front; but when called upon for a one-on-one test of strength, Green handles himself well.

And he is very strong on his stick; some of his most quietly effective defense gets played when he simply uses his stick, and his strength, to pin an opposing player's stick to the ice as a pass is coming. The opposing player is nullified and immobilized.

Green gets good position on his man and reduces the opponent's options, taking away the inside path to the net while guiding the player into his reach. Along the boards, he eliminates more than he crushes people.

THE INTANGIBLES

Green is an efficient player and good leader for younger players, which should be a real boost to the underconfident bunch on the Islanders' back line. He replaces the Stanley Cup ring the Islanders traded (Craig Ludwig), and you never can have too many rings in your dressing room. Green has won, he knows what it takes and how it is done, and the Islanders seem long ago to have forgotten. So the relationship should be a positive one.

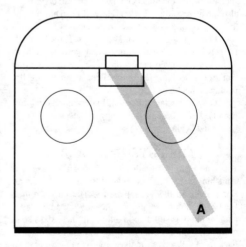

GLENN HEALY

Yrs. of NHL service: 4
Born: Pickering, Ont., Canada; August 23, 1962
Position: Goaltender
Height: 5-10
Weight: 175
Uniform no.: 35
Catches: left

Career statistics:

GP	MINS	GA	SO	GAA	A	PIM
175	9,815	627	3	3.83	6	55

1990-91 statistics:

GP	MINS	GAA	W	L	T	SO	GA	S	SAPCT	PIM
53	2,999	3.32	18	24	9	0	166	1,557	.893	214

LAST SEASON

Missed eight games with an injured left ankle.

THE FINESSE GAME

Healy is a pure reflex goalie. He sometimes goes down quickly, which he has to, as a small goalie, to cover the ice, but he can recover very fast and get back to his feet. He sees the puck well in traffic and is a scrapper who won't stop until the puck is across the line. He has a good glove and quick feet.

Healy's major weakness is his puckhandling ability. He is reluctant to leave the puck for his defenseman and there often are communication mixups with his backliners behind the net.

Healy also has to improve playing his angles. He relies so much on his reflexes that he gives the shooters a lot of net. He is a good skater with quick lateral movement that helps him on the post-to-post slides when the action is quick in deep.

Healy is vulnerable to leaving rebounds and makes a lot of games difficult for himself. Often, he has to make a great save on a second shot because he didn't do a good-enough job of making a good save on the first shot. He'll kick a point shot into the slot instead of to the corner, then have to make one of his acrobatic, desperation miracle plays to get a toe on the follow-up. He was guilty of that much more early in the season than at the end; either he got smarter or he got tired.

THE PHYSICAL GAME

Because of his small size and the acrobatic nature of his style, Healy can wear down and become dehydrated over the course of a busy game. Healy has to expend a lot of energy to play the way he does and is very conscious of his off-ice conditioning, so his physical recovery is usually quick. Crease-crashing is a problem for small goalie and Healy is frequently used

as a bowling pin. His mental toughness usually keeps this tactic from rattling him, although you can bet the referee will get an earful.

THE INTANGIBLES

Healy was to be relegated to a backup role with the planned emergence of Mark Fitzpatrick, but the young goalie's illness put the responsibilty back on Healy's shoulders. He took it gladly, and though he is a good team man, he may be affected if his ice time is cut drastically this season.

DEREK KING

Yrs. of NHL service: 4
Born: Hamilton, Ont., Canada; February 11, 1967
Position: Left wing
Height: 6-1
Weight: 200
Uniform no.: 27
Shoots: left

Career statistics:

GP	G	A	TP	PIM
229	58	106	164	108

1990-91 statistics:

GP	G	A	TP	+/-	PIM	PP	SH	GW	GT	S	PCT
66	19	26	45	-1	44	2	0	2	0	130	14.6

LAST SEASON

Tied for fourth on team in points, fourth in assists. Games played and goals were four-year career highs. Led team forwards in plus-minus. Missed four games with a separated right shoulder.

THE FINESSE GAME

All that talent, with none of the drive, King can be a coach's nightmare. He has the physical tools to be an above-average NHL skater and scorer, but motivation remains a big question mark.

King has very good hands, sees the ice well and is capable of making the big, home-run play. He is patient and composed in-tight. King has a very good slapshot but his best weapon is a quick wrist. He uses a stick that is barely legal, curved from the heel like a nine-iron, and it helps him get off a shot that can really takes goalies by surprise. King is clearly capable of a 40-goal season.

Although not a very good skater, when King is playing one of his involved games, this flaw is not as noticeable. He is mobile in close quarters.

THE PHYSICAL GAME

King is physically capable of playing a solid hitting game but, again, is not always willing. He has battled a weight problem, which will probably plague him through his playing career.

King is very intelligent and with his good sense can work well in traffic - he's at his best there. When he fails to penetrate but seems satisfied with being a perimeter player, it is going to be one of those games where King is very ineffective.

THE INTANGIBLES

King has played his best with linemates Brent Sutter and Patrick Flatley, two hard workers who demand the same from anyone they play with. King needs to be constantly driven and unless he is willing to make a commitment to the game, he will never be more than a fringe player.

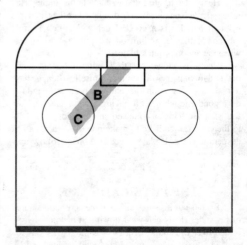

TOM KURVERS

Yrs. of NHL service: 7
Born: Minneapolis, Minn., USA; October 14, 1962
Position: Defenseman
Height: 6-0
Weight: 205
Uniform no.:
Shoots: left

Career statistics:

GP	G	A	TP	PIM
445	63	217	280	229

1990-91 statistics:

GP	G	A	TP	+/-	PIM	PP	SH	GW	GT	S	PCT
51	4	26	30	-25	28	3	0	0	0	99	4.0

LAST SEASON

Aqcuired from Minnesota for Craig Ludwig, June 22, 1991.

THE FINESSE GAME

Kurvers is an intelligent player with good stick-handling and passing skills. He is not an overpowering shooter or a blindingly fast skater—although he is one of those deceptively fluid skaters who covers a lot of territory with little evident effort.

Kurvers rushes the puck well and can do a change of pace. He likes to lead the rush from his own end to the other team's blue line, then break the team in on the attack while he waits at the point. He sets up well on the power play and will be a real asset to the Islanders there.

Kurvers is less secure in his own zone. He has played for defensively bad team in recent years (and comes to yet another one) so his defensive work is not as bad as his stats might indicate.

THE PHYSICAL GAME

Kurvers plays below his size, preferring instead to make the finesse plays. He will work best paired with a defensive defenseman who hits (Rich Pilon seems like an ideal partner). Kurvers sometimes needs a little time to make his plays and a physical partner would open up some skating room. But Kurvers best "partner" will be Pat LaFontaine (assuming LaFontaine plays for the Isles this season). It's been years since LaFontaine has played with a defenseman who will be able to hit him at mid-ice with a pass like Kurvers will.

THE INTANGIBLES

Kurvers desperately wanted to play for a U.S.-based team. While he might have been happier in his native Minnesota (he was a North Star only briefly in a three-way deal), he will get his share of ice time with the Islanders as their best offensive defenseman.

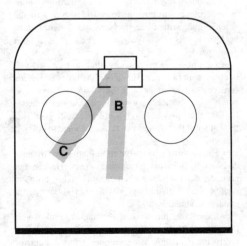

PAT LAFONTAINE

Yrs. of NHL service: 8
Born: St. Louis, Mo., USA; February 22, 1963
Position: Center
Height: 5-10
Weight: 175
Uniform no.: 16
Shoots: right

Career statistics:

GP	G	A	TP	PIM
530	287	279	566	309

1990-91 statistics:

GP	G	A	TP	+/-	PIM	PP	SH	GW	GT	S	PCT
75	41	44	85	-6	42	12	2	5	1	225	18.2

LAST SEASON

Led club in all major offensive categories: goals, assists, points, shots, power play goals and game-winning goals. Goals and points totals were the lowest in four years.

THE FINESSE GAME

LaFontaine is a brilliant individualist, and since his ability has been so far above most of the other players he has been teamed with throughout is career, he is used to doing it all himself. He doesn't utilize his teammates well in plays inside the blue line. If there is a best single LaFontaine play it is this: the pass comes off the wall out of the defensive zone, the darting LaFontaine accelerates in three or four strides, blows by the defense and, with three or four dekes, scores on a backhand. It is electrifying, since he does it at such great speed.

LaFontaine is gritty and willing to go to the net, but only with the puck. He can hit the holes and needs someone to get him the puck. Surprisingly, LaFontaine doesn't see the ice very well and is a much better finisher than playmaker. It's not necessarily selfishness: it's just that he's grown so accustomed to doing it himself.

He has terrific hand-eye coordination and tremendous strength in his hands and wrists. He can cut around a defenseman, switch the stick to his left hand while holding off the player with his right and get a good shot on net.

LaFontaine has worked very hard to improve on faceoffs. He has also become much more aware defensively and is making a concentrated effort to improve that part of his game.

THE PHYSICAL GAME

Despite his small size, LaFontaine is as tough and hard-nosed a player as you will find in the NHL. If he's in the right frame of mind (see below), he will take a beating and just keep going. He is a very strong player with a compact body that makes it difficult to move him off the puck because of his low center of gravity.

THE INTANGIBLES

About the last word we would use to describe LaFontaine is quitter, since throughout his career he has persevered through some of the worst punishment opposing defensemen could dish out without breaking stride or whining. But last season's contract dispute and eventual trade demand took some of the heart out of LaFontaine's game. If the Islanders don't move him (or if GM Bill Torrey and/or team owner John Pickett fail to remove themselves), LaFontaine may suffer through another subpar year. LaFontaine's bitterness is as genuine as his talent.

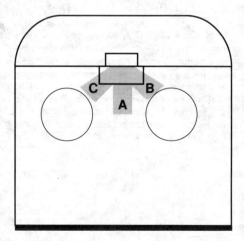

WAYNE MCBEAN

Yrs. of NHL service: 3
Born: Calgary, Alta., Canada; February 21, 1969
Position: Defenseman
Height: 6-2
Weight: 190
Uniform no.: 6
Shoots: left

Career statistics:

GP	G	A	TP	PIM
136	5	22	27	110

1990-91 statistics:

GP	G	A	TP	+/-	PIM	PP	SH	GW	GT	S	PCT
52	5	14	19	-21	47	2	0	0	0	93	5.4

LAST SEASON

Plus-minus was second lowest on team. Games played matched career high. Goals, assists and points were career highs.

THE FINESSE GAME

Although this will be his fourth NHL season, McBean had little continuous playing time until last season. He was rushed in the Los Angeles system as a youngster and since a trade to the Islanders has spent considerable time in the minors learning the pro game and restoring some shaken confidence.

McBean's physical skills will allow him to become very involved offensively. He is an excellent skater forwards and backwards. He accelerates quickly and pivots deftly. It is McBean's skating ability that covers up for some of his defensive lapses. He needs to improve his play selection and learn when to venture in deep on the attack and when to hold up. He has good hockey instincts in this regard, but doesn't seem to trust them. That is, he knows what he should have done, and what he did wrong, but under pressure he doesn't always do the right thing. McBean is a good learner so this defect can probably be overcome.

McBean has a very good one-timer, a good wrist shot and slap shot. He could develop into an excellent point man on the power play. He has outstanding passing and stickhandling abilities and is able to spot the open man. Assuming Pat LaFontaine remains an Islander, this could become a Montana-to-Rice combination.

THE PHYSICAL GAME

Finesse is more McBean's game, but he does not mind hitting because he wants to win. He won't back down, but he needs to develop more upper body strength. He plays fairly well along the boards and in the corners and is also a good poke checker. McBean is not a fighter, but he won't be intimidated.

THE INTANGIBLES

With all of his raw talent, McBean could be due for a big year if he can gain some measure of consistency to merit the ice time. He is very dedicated to making it in the NHL and is going to give himself the best chance. He is by nature a winner and the kind of player who wants the puck in a pressure situation to make the game-winning play.

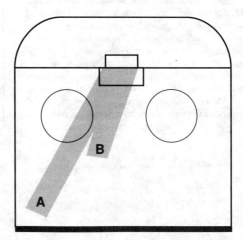

JEFF NORTON

Yrs. of NHL service: 3
Born: Cambridge, Mass., USA; November 25, 1965
Position: Defenseman
Height: 6-2
Weight: 195
Uniform no.: 8
Shoots: left

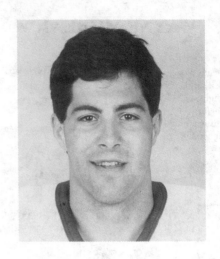

Career statistics:

GP	G	A	TP	PIM
188	9	110	119	169

1990-91 statistics:

GP	G	A	TP	+/-	PIM	PP	SH	GW	GT	S	PCT
44	3	25	28	-13	16	2	1	0	0	87	3.4

LAST SEASON

Served an eight-game suspension from a stick incident during the pre-season. Missed 25 games with three shoulder separations and subsequent surgery.

THE FINESSE GAME

Norton is a very good skater with excellent lateral movement and balance. He can look like a cartoon car snaking down a mountain, where the car's tires stay on the road yet the body hangs out over the chasm. Norton may be one of the best skating defensemen in the NHL.

He is a fairly good point man but he is an inconsistent shooter. Sometimes he will take his eye off the puck and fan, or he will lean back and get only part of the puck and shoot a harmless floater. He is good on a rush from his own end and likes lugging the puck up the left wing boards, staying wide, and finding an open guy cutting to the net.

THE PHYSICAL GAME

With all of that talent, what's the problem here? Mental toughness, for starters. Norton has a low threshhold of pain. He really hates to get hit, to the point where he will bail out of a play and leave his defense partner outnumbered. Norton does not play the man and will be mesmerized by the puck and try to play it rather than make the smart defensive play. He doesn't read the rush well and does very little right in his own end. Since he is such a strong skater, he has the capability to be a much better defensive player.

Norton gets very few even-strength points.

THE INTANGIBLES

Much more has been demanded of him than Norton has been able to deliver, and while not all of that may be his fault, Norton has to realize that with all his skills he has to produce more offensively to compensate for his defensive shortcomings. His commitment to the game is in question and this could be a critical year for him.

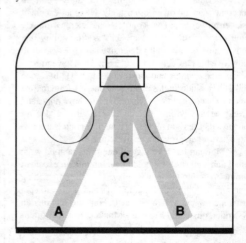

GARY NYLUND

Yrs. of NHL service: 9
Born: Surrey, B.C., Canada; October 23, 1963
Position: Defenseman
Height: 6-4
Weight: 210
Uniform no.: 36
Shoots: left

Career statistics:

GP	G	A	TP	PIM
579	31	140	171	1,182

1990-91 statistics:

GP	G	A	TP	+/-	PIM	PP	SH	GW	GT	S	PCT
72	2	21	23	-8	105	0	0	0	0	102	2.0

LAST SEASON

PIM was six-season low. Goal total was five-season low. Missed three games with a fractured left heel that required off-season surgery.

THE FINESSE GAME

Nylund is a good skater for his size and has a big shot that can get him a lot of assists from his teammates scoring on tip-ins and rebounds. He could shoot more, but he doesn't think of himself as an offensive defenseman and is sometimes reluctant to get involved in the play offensively.

Despite his skating ability, Nylund does not skate well with the puck and is better moving the puck by passing. He doesn't see the ice well when he is moving and he has a hard time finding people to pass to.

Nylund is very noticeable on nights when he is playing with poise and control. In those games, he can be one of the best defensemen on the ice, with solid take-outs and smart positional play. He has not yet developed the consistency to play at that level on a regular basis.

THE PHYSICAL GAME

Nylund is a punishing hitter who sometimes gets too excited about making a big check and ends up running around and getting out of position. He is intense and aggressive—again, he can be overly so, and he will sometimes start banging away at people while ignoring what is going on with the play. Nylund can get overexcited in the heat of battle and while he has come a long way in self-control and discipline, he still has a way to go.

THE INTANGIBLES

Nylund was a No. 1 draft pick by Toronto back in 1982 and it has taken a long time for him to disabuse himself of the idea that he can be a dominating defenseman. He doesn't have the tools for it. He can be a very capable journeyman and a physical presence.

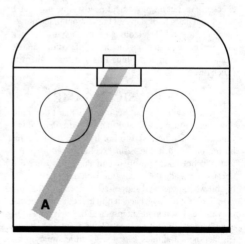

RICH PILON

Yrs. of NHL service: 3
Born: Saskatoon, Sask., Canada; April 30, 1968
Position: Defenseman
Height: 6-0
Weight: 200
Uniform no.: 47
Shoots: left

Career statistics:

GP	G	A	TP	PIM
136	1	21	22	399

1990-91 statistics:

GP	G	A	TP	+/-	PIM	PP	SH	GW	GT	S	PCT
60	1	5	6	-12	126	0	0	0	0	33	3.0

LAST SEASON

Missed 20 games with a left knee surgery. Scored first NHL goal.

THE FINESSE GAME

Pilon suffered a potential career-ending eye injury in 1989 but fought his way back. The injury still has a bit of an effect, since he will occasionally lose a puck, but his return to form has exceeded anyone's expectation.

Pilon's stickhandling and puck movement are average. He is a good skater with speed to jump up and join a rush, although he is by nature a stay-at-home defenseman. His skating speed, combined with his size and strength, is what makes him such a dangerous checker. His lateral movement needs to be improved.

Pilon has a hard slapshot but without much movement on it, and it seldom gets through to the net. Defensively, he is seldom caught out of position and he challenges skaters at the blue line and forces them to check or go wide.

THE PHYSICAL GAME

One drawback from his injury is that Pilon must now wear a face shield and that has curtailed Pilon's fighting, which he loved to do. It hasn't hindered his hitting one whit. Pilon is an excellent open-ice hitter and will not take himself out of position to make it because he reads the opposition well and goes for the big hit when he is well supported.

Teams will come back at him in retaliation but that only makes Pilon more intense, and the next hit will be even harder. He will not back down from a challenge (in fact, he sometimes gets a scary little smile on his face that really must unnerve other skaters). Pilon has sufficient physical presence to disrupt another team's game entirely.

THE INTANGIBLES

Pilon may be one of the only players who would play for nothing or even pay the NHL to let him play there. He is a genuine throwback, with a real love for the game, and there is no question about his dedication to making himself the best player he can be.

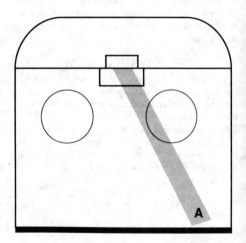

JOE REEKIE

Yrs. of NHL service: 4
Born: Petawawa, Ont., Canada; February 22, 1965
Position: Defenseman
Height: 6-3
Weight: 215
Uniform no.: 29
Shoots: left

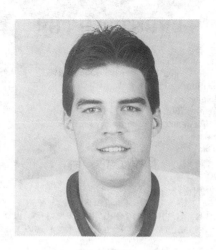

Career statistics:

GP	G	A	TP	PIM
201	7	39	46	329

1990-91 statistics:

GP	G	A	TP	+/-	PIM	PP	SH	GW	GT	S	PCT
66	3	16	19	17	96	0	0	2	0	70	4.3

LAST SEASON

Games played, goals, assists and points were career highs. Led club in plus-minus with a remarkable plus 17 (the next best among regulars was plus 1). Missed six games with a right eye injury.

THE FINESSE GAME

Reekie was probably the most improved player on the Islanders last season. Given the Isles' performance, that might not be saying much, but let's give credit where it's due.

His skating style is unorthodox. Reekie is a good skater for his size, with a choppy stride but good agility. He is surprisingly light on his feet for such a big man. He has very good anticipation and knows when to jump into a play and pick off a pass. He moves the puck well and is positionally sound, although he has a tendency to play the puck instead of the man. He has very good peripheral vision.

The biggest improvement in Reekie's game has been mental. Confidence has always been his biggest problem and he is not a player who handles criticism or praise well.

THE PHYSICAL GAME

For his size, Reekie is not a hard hitter. Call him economical. He will take out players along the boards and will keep the front of his net clear. His PIM total is low, and will not usually get involved in a fracas. However, he is quick to come to the aid of a teammate in trouble. Reekie would just rather stay on the ice.

THE INTANGIBLES

Reekie has shown continual improvement and will become an integral part of the team's defense if he maintains his mental sharpness and work ethic. After five seasons of bouncing between the NHL and the minors, Reekie might be a regular in the show at last.

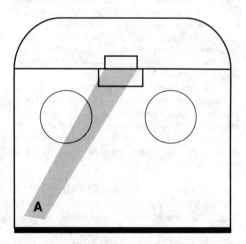

BRENT SUTTER

Yrs. of NHL service: 10
Born: Viking, Alta., Canada; June 10, 1962
Position: Center
Height: 5-11
Weight: 180
Uniform no.: 21
Shoots: left

Career statistics:

GP	G	A	TP	PIM
686	283	317	600	755

1990-91 statistics:

GP	G	A	TP	+/-	PIM	PP	SH	GW	GT	S	PCT
75	21	32	53	-8	49	6	2	4	1	186	11.3

LAST SEASON

Third on club in assists and points. Goals total was eight-year low, points was seven-year low. PIM was lowest of career. Missed five games with a right shoulder injury.

THE FINESSE GAME

If the six Sutter brothers ever held a skills competition, Brent would be the hands-down winner. He has excellent hand-eye coordination, which shows on his faceoffs and in his work in cramped quarters. He is very good on the short give-and-go and protects the puck well in the corners and coming out from behind the net. He uses a short stick to give him more control in small spaces, which is where he thrives.

Sutter has an accurate shot which isn't very hard, but he has a good release. He is not a very fast skater, but he has good balance and strength, which complement his hard work in traffic.

Sutter is an excellent special-teams player. On the power play, he is exceptional working low, skating in from the side and jamming the net or standing in front, screening and tipping. Killing penalties begins with his quickness on the faceoffs. He is very smart, reads plays well and what he lacks in speed he makes up for in brains.

THE PHYSICAL GAME

Sutter doesn't get as involved physically as he used to. He has had several injuries through the years that have taken their physical toll on him, but he never complained—he has often annoyed coaches by covering up the extent of the injury. He is still willing to make or take a hit in front of the net to score a goal.

THE INTANGIBLES

Sutter is a highly motivated leader and if the Islanders ever trade him, it will have to be for a more skilled player to make up for the qualities they will lose were Sutter to go. He despises losing and is able to motivate others with his own desire.

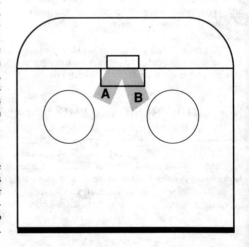

DAVID VOLEK

Yrs. of NHL service: 3
Born: Prague, Czechoslovakia; June 18, 1966
Position: Left wing
Height: 6-0
Weight: 185
Uniform no.: 25
Shoots: left

Career statistics:

GP	G	A	TP	PIM
234	64	90	154	122

1990-91 statistics:

GP	G	A	TP	+/-	PIM	PP	SH	GW	GT	S	PCT
77	22	34	56	-10	57	6	0	1	1	224	9.8

LAST SEASON

Second on club in assists and points. Goals, assists and points were two-year highs.

THE FINESSE GAME

Volek has extremely quick hands and feet, which may be attributed to his training in Czechoslovakia. He is agile and is good at darting in and out of holes with speed. He has good balance, very strong legs and is difficult to knock off the puck.

He has several weapons in his offensive arsenal. The best is his move/shot combo, where he makes a quick deke on the defenseman and then gets a quick wrist shot away. He also likes to come in on his backhand, make a quick shift to his forehand and wrist it, or make a quick curl to set up a teammate. He sees the ice well and is capable of more creativity than he has shown on a consistent basis. His slapshot is average. Volek has a good short game in traffic and is not shy about getting involved physically.

Volek has improved in his own end to where he can be considered an average NHL player defensively. He will still try to make a low percentage play in the defensive zone.

THE PHYSICAL GAME

Volek has a wiry strength that sometimes surprises opponents, because he looks so lean. He likes the rough going and won't be intimidated. He is mentally tough and will pay the price along the boards to get the puck. Volek does have to watch his nutrition and conditioning and guard against wearing down over the course of a long season because of his body type.

THE INTANGIBLES

Volek can be hard on himself and get down emotionally, but he is maturing and has not yet reached his potential. He will likely be a consistent 30-goal scorer.

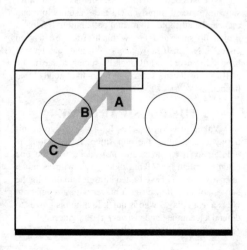

MICK VUKOTA

Yrs. of NHL service: 4
Born: Saskatoon, Sask., Canada; September 14, 1966
Position: Right wing
Height: 6-2
Weight: 195
Uniform no.: 12
Shoots: right

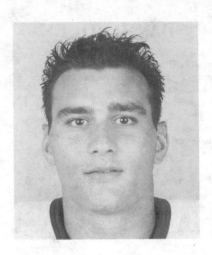

Career statistics:

GP	G	A	TP	PIM
201	9	14	23	847

1990-91 statistics:

GP	G	A	TP	+/-	PIM	PP	SH	GW	GT	S	PCT
60	2	4	6	-13	238	0	0	0	0	39	5.1

LAST SEASON

Second on team in PIM. Missed four games with a continuation of a suspension from the 1990 playoffs.

THE FINESSE GAME

Vukota's game still needs improvement in all the basic areas, especially in his skating speed, release of his shot and playing one-on-one situations. Vukota is a fairly fast, straight-ahead skater with little agility and that allows opposition skaters to avoid his checks. Vukota will battle along the boards, but lacks the hand skills to come away with the puck.

Vukota is not a good passer and his offensive contribution is usually limited to plays close to the net.

Vukota's defensive play backslid last season after showing marked improvement the season before and that can be attributed to mental preparation. If Vukota is mentally sharp and stays within his role, he can be an effective player. If he wanders from that role, he will have to improve his skill levels drastically to stay in the NHL. There doesn't seem to be much likelihood of that happening.

THE PHYSICAL GAME

Vukota was very successful a season ago in initiating and goading the opposition. Last season, he didn't play it as smart and instead he was the one caught retaliating. Vukota didn't play with as much intensity and may have fooled himself into thinking he had established himself as a player with a reputation. He is a team player who is quick to drop his gloves to defend a teammate and is a very good fighter.

THE INTANGIBLES

Vukota's role of enforcer is an obvious one, but he has to step up his intensity to that of a year ago and avoid hurting his team with bad penalties.

No one is expecting him to score 20 goals, but he has to make more productive use of his ice time.

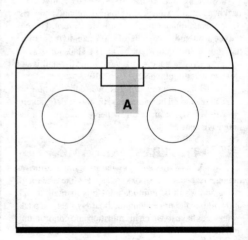

246

RANDY WOOD

Yrs. of NHL service: 4
Born: Princeton, N.J., USA; October 12, 1963
Position: Left wing
Height: 6-0
Weight: 195
Uniform no.: 11
Shoots: left

Career statistics:

GP	G	A	TP	PIM
258	86	71	157	212

1990-91 statistics:

GP	G	A	TP	+/-	PIM	PP	SH	GW	GT	S	PCT
76	24	18	42	-12	45	6	1	3	1	186	12.9

LAST SEASON

Second on club in goals. Goals total matched career high.

THE FINESSE GAME

Speed, speed, speed. Unharnessed, unvarnished, breakaway speed. That is the extent of Wood's game. He has very little agility, however, and his upper body strength exceeds that of his lower half, which makes him an unbalanced skater and one who can be easily knocked off the puck if the defensemen only gets a small piece of him as he tries to race past.

Wood lacks any hand skills to go with his speed. He basically tries to intimidate the goalie, by taking the defenseman wide to the right and then driving fearlessly to the net. Wood often follows the puck right into the net or the goalie. He is one of the best (or worst, depending on your point of view) crease-crashers in the NHL. He can be very streaky in his play and point production.

Wood has absolute tunnel vision when he has the puck. He does not see other players or look to make plays, which is why he seldom gets time on the power play. He doesn't take passes well, either. He will be used to kill penalties, but only because of his speed, not for his hockey sense. Wood's defensive ability is average.

THE PHYSICAL GAME

Because of his lack of skating balance, Wood is an ineffective hitter in open ice or along the boards and he is easily overpowered. Wood is often careless with his stick and in some Patrick Division dressing rooms is the most disliked Islander.

THE INTANGIBLES

Because his shooting skills are limited and his foot speed overpowers all other aspects of his game, Wood will never be more than a 25-goal scorer.

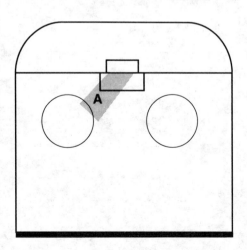

NEW YORK
RANGERS

JOE CIRELLA

Yrs. of NHL service: 8
Born: Hamilton, Ont., Canada; May 9, 1963
Position: Defenseman
Height: 6-3
Weight: 210
Uniform no.: 18
Shoots:

Career statistics:

GP	G	A	TP	PIM
617	57	183	240	1116

1990-91 statistics:

GP	G	A	TP	+/-	PIM	PP	SH	GW	GT	S	PCT
58	3	10	13	-27	111	0	0	0	0	82	3.7

LAST SEASON

Obtained January 17 from Quebec for Aaron Miller and a fifth-round pick in 1991 draft (Bill Lindsay). Plus-minus matched prior season, which puts him at -54 over his past 114 regular-season games.

THE FINESSE GAME

He gets ground covered thanks to skating skills that are a spot above average. He gets the puck out of the zone by using the boards, high or low, and keeping things simple—as he must, to succeed.

Under pressure, Cirella goes right to the nearest outlet if danger is brewing; but he doesn't always recognize the danger as the clouds gather on the horizon. He will step up to challenge a guy, or overload an area his teammates have contained, then be toasted as somebody sneaks behind him for a pass.

THE PHYSICAL GAME

Cirella is going to get a piece of you every chance he gets. He may not knock you through the boards, but he will tie you up in front, deliver the odd cheap shot, get involved in the odd fight.

Cirella is a fairly fearless shot blocker. He is an eager visitor to the corners, where he tends to tie up his man and free the puck for a teammate. He does things efficiently.

THE INTANGIBLES

Cirella was acquired as an insurance policy and ended up playing more effectively in the playoffs than most of the other defenseman. That says as much about him, at this advanced stage of his career, as it says about the Rangers' defense.

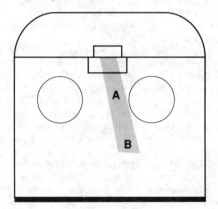

JAN ERIXON

Yrs. of NHL service: 8
Born: Skelleftea, Sweden; July 8, 1962
Position: Left wing
Height: 6-0
Weight: 196
Uniform no.: 20
Shoots: Left

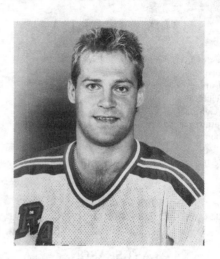

Career statistics:

GP	G	A	TP	PIM
465	44	139	183	153

1990-91 statistics:

GP	G	A	TP	+/-	PIM	PP	SH	GW	GT	S	PCT
53	7	18	25	13	8	0	3	0	0	40	17.5

LAST SEASON

Plus-minus was second on team. Shorthanded goal total led team and was career high. Missed 26 games due to sprained right knee and subsequent inflammation.

THE FINESSE GAME

Most checking players in the league have real trouble scoring and Erixon is no different. It's probably the reason he is a checker in the first place. Erixon works hard to pry the puck loose, his skating and hockey sense create so many turnovers and opportunities, and his ice IQ makes him the perfect complement for two all-offense linemates.

At the start of last season, Erixon scored on a breakaway or two, made some one-on-one moves that he finished with a pretty goal, and he made people think—"Ah! Finally! He's getting the touch." Then he got hurt and the jury had to leave again, to consider the evidence of another seven-goal season and another dozen nights when an Erixon goal off a turnover could have/would have/should have turned the tide in a close game.

Erixon has strength. He has balance. He is one of the best in the league at angling players to the boards, then beating them for the puck along the wood. He skates through hooks and hits and body slams, kicks the puck ahead to his stick while he is being held. When he has the puck, Erixon knows what to do and when to do it, but he simply does not finish.

THE PHYSICAL GAME

From the standpoint of abuse accepted, sacrifice made, strength along the boards and dedication to the checking arts, Erixon may be the most physical player the Rangers have. He is not going separate shoulders with a bodycheck, unless the shoulder is his own. He is not going to do much of anything, other than outwork your whole team for the puck, go one-on-five while killing penalties and keep his legs going while smeared along the boards by at least two opponents.

THE INTANGIBLES

Erixon's work ethic is universally respected in the dressing room. He is determined to do his job well, utterly without need of credit or recognition. A more selfish Erixon might be a more successful one.

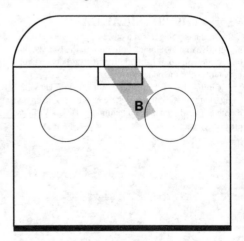

MIKE GARTNER

Yrs. of NHL service: 12
Born: Ottawa, Ont., Canada; October 29, 1959
Position: Right wing
Height: 6-0
Weight: 190
Uniform no.: 22
Shoots: Right

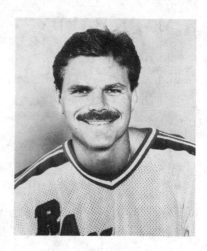

Career statistics:

GP	G	A	TP	PIM
929	498	460	958	863

1990-91 statistics:

GP	G	A	TP	+/-	PIM	PP	SH	GW	GT	S	PCT
79	49	20	69	-9	53	22	1	4	2	262	18.7

LAST SEASON

Goal total was second highest of his career, second highest in team history and fifth in NHL last season. Power-play goal total tied for second behind Brett Hull's 29 and marked second straight season with 20 or more PPG. Reached 30-goal plateau 11th consecutive season.

THE FINESSE GAME

Always a threat because of his speed and strong skating stride, Gartner is an excellent "stretch" man. Opposing defensemen have to back off the attacking blue line when he cheats toward it, knowing Gartner can be off and gone with a pass should his team gain possession. As a result, he helps "stretch" the ice lengthwise, creating space for his teammates. Gartner also uses his speed to stretch the ice width-wise; he loves to steam left-to-right at the attacking blue line, looking for a breakaway pass, and has a gift for accepting those hard passes on the backhand at full speed. He accelerates into the pass with such speed that linesmen call offside even when the play was good. For a player who scores lots of goals from his strength and power (shots from the wing off the rush), Gartner also has a nice touch in close when the situation calls for finesse over strength. He is expert at deflections, including one where he uses his own body as a screen, tips the puck with the heel of his stick and allows it to carom through his legs.

Rather than take what opponents give him, Gartner prefers to dictate the terms. He will wind up, faking the big slap shot from the right-wing circle, freezing the defensemen and, often the goalie; then—having changed the shooting angle, which the goaltender now must scramble to protect—Gartner will get off a shot as quickly as possibly, firing for the hole he has forced the goalie to give him. Other times, he uses the faked shot and cuts inside. If forced outside, Gartner often will keep the puck and circle the entire zone while deciding what to try next.

THE PHYSICAL GAME

There are times when defensemen read that faked shot, stand up and splatter Gartner with an open-ice hit. That doesn't bother him. He accepts all kinds of crosschecks and rabbit punches because he is a scorer, and he knows that taking the poundings in front makes the difference between a 30-goal season and a 50-goal season.

Gartner goes where the screens and the deflections are. He goes to the deep slot, where the rebounds bounce and the scrambles start. He walks out of the left-wing corner on his forehand and absorbs the punishment. He is enough of a pig to jab at any puck he can reach; if it goes in, no matter how, he has done his job.

And he is enough of a threat to draw at least one defenseman to him at all times; teammates read off that, use the space he has created for them. A defenseman may tie Gartner up, but the defenseman thereby also ties himself up—leaving the goalie one helper short should the puck squirt to an open man.

THE INTANGIBLES

Defense gives Gartner problems at times. Especially when the puck is in the quiet zones along the boards and behind the Rangers' net, Gartner gets hypnotized, staring at the disc, instead of keeping his head on a swivel and being alert for opponents coming into the play.

Still, Gartner does not shirk many duties. He is a responsible professional who plays hurt. He is a second- and third-effort player. He plays winning hockey, unmistakably, but plays it for teams that do not win when it counts—an irritating contradiction that wrongly glues a loser's tag to his jersey.

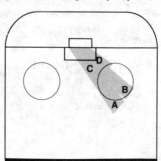

MARK HARDY

Yrs. of NHL service: 11
Born: Semaden, Switzerland; February 1, 1959
Position: Defenseman
Height: 5-11
Weight: 195
Uniform no.: 14
Shoots: Left

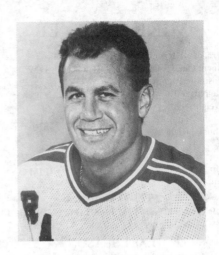

Career statistics:

GP	G	A	TP	PIM
792	60	282	342	1112

1990-91 statistics:

GP	G	A	TP	+/-	PIM	PP	SH	GW	GT	S	PCT
70	1	5	6	-1	89	0	0	0	0	63	3.7

LAST SEASON

Goal production improved by one over prior campaign, assist total dropped by 10.

THE FINESSE GAME

Three assets make Hardy valuable: he can skate, he has experience and he has a good handle on the game.

He may have lost some speed, compared to his younger, faster days. But Hardy is very smooth on his feet. He covers ground—he is not a chugger—so he can move the puck up and move ahead with the play. He can angle players to the corners because his straight-line speed is more than acceptable.

Hardy has some offensive skills. In his Los Angeles days, he was one of their top offensive point people. His role changed over the years, but Hardy knows what to do in the attacking zone. His shot isn't much. He isn't going to overpower people with it, but he gets it to the net fairly successfully. There will be occasions when his awareness falters, he shoots right off a guy's shinguards and is caught in a lurch when the opposing forward races past him; but those times are relatively rare.

THE PHYSICAL GAME

Hardy is mostly a finesse player, but he does not shy away from physical confrontations. He goes to the corner, he battles in front of the net. His fighting days appear to be over, but he plays the body and plays an efficient physical game.

THE INTANGIBLES

Hardy's play deteriorated over the second half of the season. He was doing well until slapped with a five-game suspension for a stick incident with Winnipeg's Doug Evans. And it may not have helped that he decided to play out the option season of his contract. It appeared to affect his play negatively.

He is not done yet. Hardy can still help a team, can be especially good for a young partner who can learn from his experience.

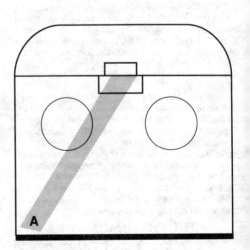

JODY HULL

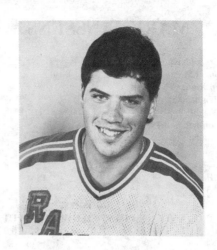

Yrs. of NHL service: 3
Born: Cambridge, Ont., Canada; February 2, 1969
Position: Right wing
Height: 6-2
Weight: 200
Uniform no.: 21
Shoots: Right

Career statistics:

GP	G	A	TP	PIM
145	28	36	64	61

1990-91 statistics:

GP	G	A	TP	+/-	PIM	PP	SH	GW	GT	S	PCT
47	5	8	13	2	10	0	0	0	0	57	8.8

LAST SEASON

Goal total was a career low. Game appearances were second to his 60 with Hartford in 1988-89

THE FINESSE GAME

Hull has some fine natural skills. His powerful skating stride is almost syrupy smooth. He has some range, he can skate with people, slow them down, pick off passes headed to them, and so forth.

His snap shot is heavy and effective, though he takes a while on the release. Hull was a goal scorer in junior, but people don't want to grow old waiting for the touch to return in pro.

There are times when it seems you can hear him thinking. He will cut into the middle at the blue line, then outguess himself on the proper play. Even if he has skating room and could take the puck closer to the net, Hull does not penetrate, drive the defense back and pull the goalie out to him.

Otherwise, he makes decent reads. If Peterborough gives you one thing over years in junior hockey, it is a degree in hockey sense

THE PHYSICAL GAME

Hull is rather a polite player. There is no mean streak to speak of, though he can be goaded into an occasional slash. So there is a pulse, but it rarely shows.

THE INTANGIBLES

Hull has a lot of ability he appears not to use. He does not show much expression on the ice and tends to fade into the background. Virtually nothing he does draws attention. He does more defensive things than offensive things, more things away from the net than near it.

Sometimes the game ends and you ask yourself, "Did Jody Hull play tonight?" And there are times when you cannot answer beyond, "I think so."

Hull can change all that by putting some salt in the soup, so to speak. The Rangers have too many right wings as it is; playing a quiet game and scoring five goals is not going to keep Hull in uniform.

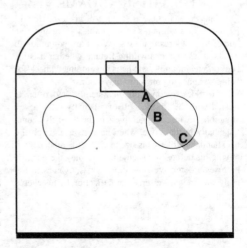

MARK JANSSENS

Yrs. of NHL service: 2
Born: Surrey, B.C., Canada; May 19, 1968
Position: Center
Height: 6-3
Weight: 215
Uniform no.: 15
Shoots: Left

Career statistics:

GP	G	A	TP	PIM
153	14	15	29	333

1990-91 statistics:

GP	G	A	TP	+/-	PIM	PP	SH	GW	GT	S	PCT
67	9	7	16	-1	172	0	0	1	0	91	20.0

LAST SEASON

Shooting percentage was second on team. Goal total was career-high.

THE FINESSE GAME

Janssens is rather a lumbering skater. He has some range, he covers ground, he gets places, but quickness of hand and foot are a problem, and he knows it—works on it as much as possible during the season and during the summer.

While he may not have great hands, Janssens can muscle a puck into the net and isn't afraid to stand in traffic. He isn't a bad defensive player, but he has a bit of a problem staying with the speedier players in the game.

THE PHYSICAL GAME

Janssens will take advantage of his size. He will jab at the puck while it's in the goalie's glove and give one of those glares that says, "What are you going to do about it?" He is a willing fighter, whether it is his beef or a teammate's, and he is developing a knack for being an annoying player to play against.

He does a good job on faceoffs, and often is trusted with the first faceoff of a penalty kill—a key situation, because it generally is in the defensive zone. Especially in that zone, when he wins a draw on the backhand, he will use his size to cut off the other center, buying his defensemen some time to play the puck. If he loses a defensive-zone draw, Janssens goes to the body and prevents a screen or deflection by his check.

Janssens scraps along the boards, uses his body mass to lean on people and finishes checks with authority whenever possible.

THE INTANGIBLES

There is leadership in this player. He is big and he stands up for his teammates. He doesn't like to lose. Something about his manner suggests a potential alternate captain a few years down the road.

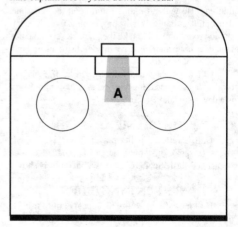

TIM KERR

Yrs. of NHL service: 11
Born: Windsor, Ont., Canada; January 5, 1960
Position: Right wing
Height: 6-3
Weight: 230
Uniform no.:
Shoots: Right

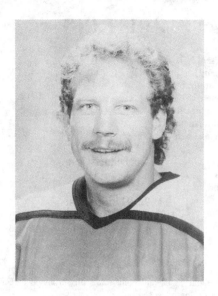

Career statistics:

GP	G	A	TP	PIM
601	363	287	650	577

1990-91 statistics:

GP	G	A	TP	+/-	PIM	PP	SH	GW	GT	S	PCT
27	10	14	24	-8	8	6	0	0	0	74	13.5

LAST SEASON

Obtained from San Jose for Brian Mullen and future considerations after the expansion draft, May 30. Injuries and a personal tragedy restricted him to the second-lowest figures in games played, goals, assists and points since 1982-83.

THE FINESSE GAME

This is the drill: Kerr's team gets a power play, Kerr goes on the ice. He camps in the slot, he tips in a point shot or buries a rebound, and that is that. A loose puck lands near him, he whips it under the crossbar or through the goalie's pads or through the goalie. That is what he does.

It may be all he does, and it may be the only thing he does faster than anybody in the NHL. Everything else is snail-slow. Kerr has hands. Magic hands. For the power play, he is a specialist. He has an amazing release, an amazing snap shot, amazing wrist strength, a very good reach and ridiculous foot strength.

Kerr is a short-game player, because he is a man of limited range, limited agility and exceptional balance. He is a 14-story building on skates and is just as difficult to move.

One way of stopping Kerr in the slot is to put both defensemen on his stick, like parrots on a perch. He isn't going to bother them much; he is going to stand just far enough from the net that a defenseman would have to leave his position to reach him—thus leaving open space for someone (Mike Gartner?) to walk out of the corner after decoying a pass. Or he will post-up against one or both of the defensemen and cause some chaos.

THE PHYSICAL GAME

Kerr is a very good-natured soul, so he accepts a lot of the abuse people hand him as part of the game. He does have a breaking point and when he reaches it, the target of his anger pays a painful price.

Kerr does not initiate a lot of contact; it seems to find him, though it doesn't have much effect. He's so big and strong, he seems barely to notice the hacks and slashes.

THE INTANGIBLES

At this stage of his career, the last thing Kerr needs to do is prove himself, but after all the injuries he has suffered, you just want him to get through a game without some body part falling off. After all the punishment his body and his heart have endured, Kerr does not give up; he comes back for more. Kerr is a quality individual, a proven point producer, a force on the power play. He can be a leader, even in his new surroundings. Younger players can benefit from being around him.

But it would be ludicrous for the Rangers to count on him for too many games or too many points; he's always hurt, everybody knows it. And he must be spotted at even strength, which means he will endure long stretches on the bench, because there is so little even-strength play. Kerr is a delightful luxury; as such, every game he plays and point he produces should be considered a bonus.

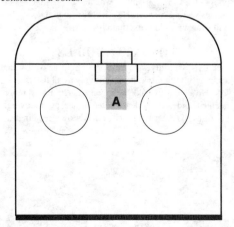

KRIS KING

Yrs. of NHL service: 3
Born: Bracebridge, Ont., Canada; February 18, 1966
Position: Left wing
Height: 5-11
Weight: 210
Uniform no.: 12
Shoots: Left

Career statistics:

GP	G	A	TP	PIM
198	20	24	44	612

1990-91 statistics:

GP	G	A	TP	+/-	PIM	PP	SH	GW	GT	S	PCT
72	11	14	25	-1	156	0	0	0	1	107	10.3

LAST SEASON

Shot total was more than double prior campaign's 49. Goal, assist and point totals all surpassed career totals prior to last season.

THE FINESSE GAME

King will not earn many style points for his skating. He is not quick to accelerate; it takes a while for him to reach top speed. He is a bit labored on the turns, takes a while to change directions.

But this ain't the compulsory figures. There are better skaters in the league who don't have the balance of skills King boasts. He skates better now than he did, shoots better than he used to, when he played well enough to be given away by the Red Wings and Washington Capitals. He can make a pass, he can make a play and he certainly can help his team win.

THE PHYSICAL GAME

King causes turnovers in the neutral zone. He can be a factor in the forecheck, because he takes the body—hard as possible, whenever possible—and creates scoring chances. He is a pretty good fighter who will show up even if overmatched.

THE INTANGIBLES

Kris King dives so much he might as well wear scuba gear to the rink; he is annoying as a blister.

He's no Esa Tikkanen, who is 20 times more talented and still at least three times as annoying, because Tikkanen ticks off even his own teammates.

But he is in that mold of the rugged left wing who antagonizes the other team's best right wing all night and who chips in with his share of goals.

King has worked to improve and is very much a team-oriented player from whom signs of leadership are emerging. But he can't get a big head about all that. He fought, grinded, dived and worked his way to regular ice time; only more of the same will keep the roll going.

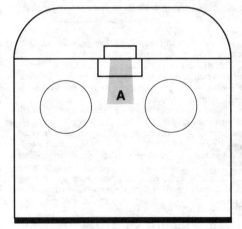

JOE KOCUR

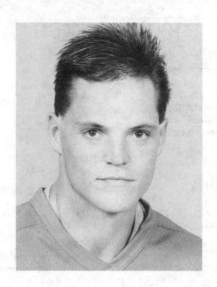

Yrs. of NHL service: 6
Born: Calgary, Alta., Canada; December 21, 1964
Position: Right wing
Height: 6-0
Weight: 194
Uniform no.: 26
Shoots: Right

Career statistics:

GP	G	A	TP	PIM
404	56	55	111	1758

1990-91 statistics:

GP	G	A	TP	+/-	PIM	PP	SH	GW	GT	S	PCT
57	5	4	9	-7	289	0	0	0	0	73	6.8

LAST SEASON

Obtained March 5 from Detroit, along with Per Djoos, for Kevin Miller, Dennis Vial and Jim Cummins.

THE FINESSE GAME

Kocur has some OK foot skills, strength probably being the main among them. He doesn't turn especially well; once he is going in one direction, it is not easy for him to stop and change course.

The other side of it is, once he is going in a specific direction, he can generate enough strength (and make use of enough balance) to drive directly through any player in his path.

The assumption is that his scoring returned to a more characteristic level last year because his hands (or at least his right one) were so messed up from all the fighting he has done over the years. Kocur underwent off-season surgery to tighten some tendons in the right hand, his power punching hand, so it remains to be seen whether his 16 goals of two seasons back can be replicated.

THE PHYSICAL GAME

Kocur can throw a lot of players off their games. He can hit, he can be aggressive, play tough at home or on the road and be a presence against such players as Rick Tocchet or Cam Neely.

He can finish fights in one punch, or at least should be able to again, if the surgery was successful.

THE INTANGIBLES

Kocur's toughness is legendary; his contribution to the Rangers last season was minimal, to be generous. He will have to prove this season that he was worth what he cost, and that should be a formidable challenge. It may take a solid half-season before he and his new teammates understand each other.

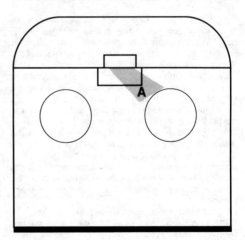

BRIAN LEETCH

Yrs. of NHL service: 3
Born: Corpus Christi, Tex., USA; March 3, 1968
Position: Defense
Height: 5-11
Weight: 185
Uniform no.: 2
Shoots: Left

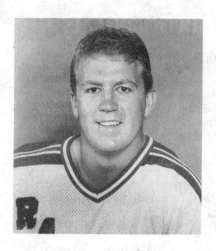

Career statistics:

GP	G	A	TP	PIM
237	52	177	229	118

1990-91 statistics:

GP	G	A	TP	+/-	PIM	PP	SH	GW	GT	S	PCT
80	16	72	88	2	42	6	0	4	1	206	7.8

LAST SEASON

Led team in scoring. Set club records for assists and points by a defenseman. Finished fourth league-wide in scoring by defensemen and third overall in power-play scoring with 52 points. Was only Ranger to play 80 games.

THE FINESSE GAME

Leetch has the skating strength and stickhandling ability to beat a first forechecker, then a second, with ease. Marvelous hand control and strength on his stick make it extremely difficult for checkers to separate him from the puck with stick checks; if you're going to stop his legs from moving, you've got to restrict his space, get a lot of your body in front of him and pin him along the boards.

With the puck, Leetch will envision his chance, create it and defy you to stop it; his confidence on the rush has grown now to the point where he will drive right into the retreating defense and try to split it if the Rangers really need a goal. Without the puck, he has an exceptional sense of anticipating where it will be; and he often intercepts the pass precisely at the spot where he predicted it would arrive. It can be a high pass, too; a good bunter back in his baseball days, Leetch can bat the puck out of the air with the best of them.

Likewise, he can control the point and run the power play with the league's finest. He will shift from the left point into the center of a one-two-two formation; on occasion, he even will call the shots from the left-wing boards; on others, he will slide over to the right point—opening his forehand for one-timer passes.

Yet his creative genius far surpasses his finishing skills. Leetch isn't good at all in tight and he will not overpower many goalies with his shot from the point. Far more of his success stems from splendid passing; he is always aware of where his teammates are, constantly makes the best decision for where the puck should go, and makes the play with passes that are accurate and easy to handle. Teammates can accelerate into the pass, gaining momentum for the rush.

THE PHYSICAL GAME

Leetch unmistakably has all-around skills, but he will not have an all-around game to challenge Ray Bourque's unless and until he adds a physical element to his play. Admittedly, he plays a great deal, which is a drain, and his involvement in the attack is a critical component of the Rangers' success. But there is such a thing as reaching for the next level, and the time seems to be right, as Leetch enters his fourth season, for the guy to extend himself.

Leetch gets involved physically. He eliminates people, ties them up in the corners. When he hits people, they stay hit; he just doesn't do it that much, and his laid-back nature suggests the requisite meanness is not part of his makeup. But he certainly has the range to reach people and the capability to be as feared in his defensive zone as he is in the attacking zone.

He never will be a fighter, but who cares? Still, would not kill Brian Leetch to do some upper body work—the upper body includes the head—and determine exactly how far he wants to take his career and how far he wants to carry his team.

THE INTANGIBLES

A lot of players would be very happy to be as very good as Brian Leetch; 21 other teams would love to have him. He now must decide whether good is enough, whether a "very good" Brian Leetch is enough to make Stanley Cup contenders of his team, whether Brian Leetch can win a Norris Trophy playing a 180-foot game on a 200-foot rink.

Leetch is an extremely humble person, critical of himself far more than any of the words printed here. He is respected by his teammates and is a quiet leader. There is no reason he can't be a noisier one on a team that comes dangerously close to accepting mediocrity as a sad and unchangeable fact of life.

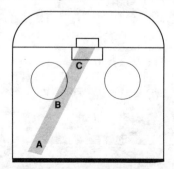

TROY MALLETTE

Yrs. of NHL service: 2
Born: Sudbury, Ont., Canada; February 25, 1970
Position: Left wing
Height: 6-2
Weight: 210
Uniform no.: 16
Shoots: Left

Career statistics:

GP	G	A	TP	PIM
150	25	26	51	557

1990-91 statistics:

GP	G	A	TP	+/-	PIM	PP	SH	GW	GT	S	PCT
71	12	10	22	-8	252	0	0	2	0	91	13.2

LAST SEASON

Cut penalty minutes by 53 from prior season's rookie club record. Plus-minus matched prior season. Goal production dropped by one, assist total by six. Missed eight games due to bumps and bruises.

THE FINESSE GAME

Mallette is not really a puckhandler. He has to get the puck and move it, because otherwise he tends to get the puck and hold it—gets paralyzed by having to make decisions faster than his so-very-limited experience permits.

Once in a while, Mallette makes a nice shoulder fake, then passes to an open teammate. But he also goes long, long stretches without points, tries to do too much instead of just throwing a puck at the net and seeing if it might hit somebody or some thing and go in.

He can skate some, but his balance is not great. His overall skills need work, which is what coaches are for.

THE PHYSICAL GAME

This kid loves to hit. He loves to get a nice running start, then jump up and hit people in the shoulders with his hips. In the span of 10 seconds, he happily will pinball off four opponents in the attacking zone, but he is still seeking the element of being under control during this chaos he is causing. He'll throw that one hit too many and get called for charging.

Mallette also has a really annoying habit of blasting a guy, then acting like he is going to drop the gloves and fight. The other player drops his gloves, then is left standing alone, because Mallette has skated away. Opponents remember players who start stuff they don't want to finish. Nobody likes to get shown up.

Maturity probably will wean Mallette away from 1) leaving his feet to hit people and 2) that faked fight thing.

THE INTANGIBLES

Mallette wants to play, he just doesn't know how yet; every area of his game needs polish. His development will require time—the sequence usually goes banger, then checker, then scorer—but the Rangers are not known for patience.

Still, physical left wings his size are a nice commodity to have; the Rangers could do plenty worse than to dump the puck in his corner and let the other team's best defenseman worry about ducking a Mallette missile.

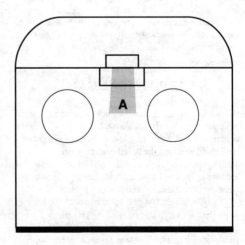

RANDY MOLLER

Yrs. of NHL service: 9
Born: Red Deer, Alta., Canada; August 23, 1963
Position: Defenseman
Height: 6-2
Weight: 207
Uniform no.: 24
Shoots: Right

Career statistics:

GP	G	A	TP	PIM
629	38	150	188	1302

1990-91 statistics:

GP	G	A	TP	+/-	PIM	PP	SH	GW	GT	S	PCT
61	4	19	23	13	161	1	0	0	1	75	5.3

LAST SEASON

Plus-minus tied for second on team. Missed 15 games with dislocated right shoulder.

THE FINESSE GAME

Moller's best finesse weapon is his head. He isn't going to overpower anybody with his shot from the right point, and he knows it, so he just feathers a glider to the net and lets the people in front do their work. The shot is accurate enough that if a screen does its job, the puck will get through the goalie and into the net. It is soft enough that a teammate in front can tip it and change its direction or momentum. It is almost as much of a pass as it is a shot, and it is an extremely effective tool at Moller's disposal.

There may be no better Ranger at firing a sizzling outlet pass from behind the net to the blue faceoff dot at center ice. A Ranger with speed, a Mike Gartner or a Darren Turcotte, will break into the clear and Moller will get them the puck with unfailing accuracy at least seven times in every 10 tries.

Moller has rather a choppy stride, but he gets to the corners pretty well and pivots pretty well. He doesn't have great speed to begin with, so the puck doesn't slow him down.

THE PHYSICAL GAME

Moller absolutely always makes some kind of contact with whoever has the puck or just had it in his coverage area. Whether it's a hack with the stick in the corner or smack with the glove in front of the net or a hard shoulder along the boards, the play isn't over until Moller has finished it to his satisfaction. He angles forwards to the boards, then finishes—hard, but clean—with all the authority he can muster.

Moller fought last year for the sake of showing up more than for any hope of winning. He plays a feisty game, and even though his shoulder was utterly ruined (it was a joke that he fought at all because he could not punch), Moller dropped the gloves when somebody reacted to a hit he had thrown or when one of his teammates had gotten abused beyond reason. He took 10 punches for every one he could throw, and mostly just wrestled around until the linesmen arrived.

THE INTANGIBLES

He's a team guy, a game, aggressive player. He just tries to do the job the best he can, which in Moller's case means accomplishing more by doing less—but doing it well. He improves the team's chances of winning because he is in the support role that best suits his game at this stage of his career. He might be able to handle spot duty on the top two pairs, but does a more effective job being spotted at No. 5 or No. 6.

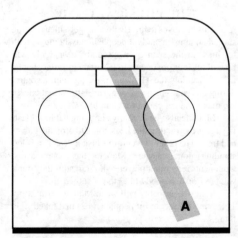

BERNIE NICHOLLS

Yrs. of NHL service: 9
Born: Haliburton, Ont., Canada; June 24, 1961
Position: Center
Height: 6-0
Weight: 185
Uniform no.: 9
Shoots: Right

Career statistics:

GP	G	A	TP	PIM
705	364	504	868	881

1990-91 statistics:

GP	G	A	TP	+/-	PIM	PP	SH	GW	GT	S	PCT
71	25	48	73	5	96	8	0	2	0	163	15.3

LAST SEASON

Missed five games due to shoulder separation, three due to league suspension and one due to coach's decision. Finished second in team scoring.

THE FINESSE GAME

An interesting, creative player when he feels like it, Nicholls does an extremely effective job as "side man" on the Rangers' remarkably potent power play. He acts as a second quarterback to Brian Leetch, setting up his office at the boards-side hashmarks of the left-wing circle. He can feed Leetch at the point, go cross-ice to whoever is in the right-wing circle, looking for a one-time pass. He creates space for himself in that little quarter of the zone by letting the defense think he's going to make a certain play, by holding the puck while they react to what they think he's going to do, then doing something else.

When the puck is at the left point, Nicholls will not screen the goalie by planting himself in front of the net, but will attempt a "field of vision" screen and skate through the goalie's line of sight just as the puck is arriving—a much more effective play, as the goalie sees the shot, then loses it, then has to react. When the puck is at the right point, Nicholls will curl away from the net, to a "rebound area" in the left-wing circle. Lots of times, goalies kick right-point shots into the left-wing circle, and Nicholls always is ready to drill in the carom in before they can react.

At even strength, Nicholls throws a nice "area" pass and lets his teammates skate into it with good speed. He attacks the blue line, then pulls up to buy time for his wings or a defenseman coming in late; he does the same thing in the left-wing corner, after sliding down the boards.

On faceoffs, the guy is a mystery. He's got nice hands. He can win one draw with ease, then not even contest the next one.

THE PHYSICAL GAME

Nicholls will pick up a man and backcheck. He even will get an occasional piece of an occasional opponent, even will bump and battle occasionally in the corners—usually on the power play. But generally, he is not very interested in the boards, and he generally is not eager to lock off the opposing center after faceoffs.

There is a truly obnoxious side to Nicholls' game, one that reaches full flower only if he has a heavyweight puncher on his line. There is a wild streak in him. He can be infuriating to opponents. He can be a filthy, chippy player who can be a real distraction and can win a mental war when he wants to.

THE INTANGIBLES

While his numbers are all right, Nicholls has not yet provided the Rangers with many of the qualities they thought they were obtaining when they paid so high a price (Tomas Sandstrom and Tony Granato) in a trade for him. His many moments of excellence are matched by long stretches of apparent lethargy; his moments of complete control often are matched by an utter lack of discipline.

So on a given game night, it is a question whether the coaching staff will get the best out of Nicholls or whether Nicholls will get the best out of himself. He clearly enjoys his life, enjoys the game, seems to love playing it and draws the top checkers, because he averages a point per game. But there were too many nights last season when he barely scratched the surface of his skills, too many nights when he simply did not work.

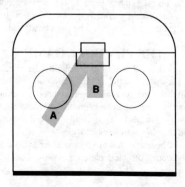

JOHN OGRODNICK

Yrs. of NHL service: 12
Born: Ottawa, Ont., Canada; June 20, 1959
Position: Left wing
Height: 6-0
Weight: 205
Uniform no.: 25
Shoots: Left

Career statistics:

GP	G	A	TP	PIM
854	379	406	785	236

1990-91 statistics:

GP	G	A	TP	+/-	PIM	PP	SH	GW	GT	S	PCT
79	31	23	54	15	10	12	0	4	0	250	12.4

LAST SEASON

Goal total was second on team to Mike Gartner's 49. Plus-minus led team.

THE FINESSE GAME

Ogrodnick very rarely beats a goaltender from the circles with a shot any more. His game has changed. He is much more a short-game guy, someone who scores from between the circles or the goalmouth.

To transact that business, Ogrodnick gets his feet wide apart for balance in the traffic areas, then accelerates well when the situation calls for speed. He especially likes to gain momentum through the neutral zone, so he can break across the blue line with speed and power.

In the attacking zone, Ogrodnick gets himself into position to score, which is his job. He will use a snap shot; on occasion, he will use the backhand with shocking success—given the peculiar pitch he puts on his stick blade. He will go for deflections, will follow his shot to the net in case there's a rebound, will jab at the loose pucks until somebody comes to hammer him, will gravitate at times to the right side, which opens his shooting angle.

He does rather an effective job in the neutral zone and probably should get more credit for his passes, which generally are sharp and accurate. Ogrodnick does, at times, get beaten back to the play from the boards; the defensive zone is not his strongest. But he led the team in plus-minus so he can't be all bad.

THE PHYSICAL GAME

Ogrodnick doesn't kill people, but he eliminates them. He will throw the odd shoulder along the boards, he will throw the very rare bomb of a bodycheck along the boards—he obliterated John Druce in the playoffs last year—but also will tie up or slow down a man behind the play in the neutral zone.

And he spends too much time along the back wall and the corners to be declared a non-physical player.

He goes in front, stakes out his territory, accepts the crosschecks while the point shots are on their way to the net. He cycles, grinds, pays a price, uses his size and his strength, tries for tip-ins or slam dunks or anything else that will put the puck in the net.

Despite all that, you don't tend to think of him when you think of physical forwards. Perhaps you should, starting now.

THE INTANGIBLES

Ogrodnick combined so well with Kelly Kisio and Brian Mullen; now they are in San Diego, and Ogrodnick, at 32, coming off a 31-goal season, is adjusting to new linemates. Very weird. It seems, after 74 goals in two seasons, his goal-scoring skills hardly have eroded, yet the organization has a very hard time giving him the respect he seems to merit.

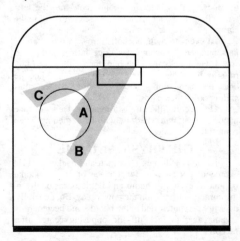

JAMES PATRICK

Yrs. of NHL service: 7
Born: Winnipeg, Man., Canada; June 14, 1963
Position: Defenseman
Height: 6-2
Weight: 204
Uniform no.: 3
Shoots: Right

Career statistics:

GP	G	A	TP	PIM
525	85	282	367	424

1990-91 statistics:

GP	G	A	TP	+/-	PIM	PP	SH	GW	GT	S	PCT
74	10	49	59	-5	58	6	0	2	0	138	7.2

LAST SEASON

Point total was eleventh best among defensemen in NHL and second highest of his career. Assists total was a personal best, but goal total was a four-season low.

THE FINESSE GAME

Patrick is one of the league's truly exceptional skaters. He is so fleet, so agile, so light on his feet, so mobile, he can carry the puck out of the zone going sideways or backwards—and has done both. But generally, Patrick doesn't carry the puck from the zone much; he passes to his partner, then trails his partner out, always keeping his forehand available for a pass if an emergency arises, or staying alert in case of a turnover.

Patrick will join a rush as support more than anything else. While Brian Leetch might join a rush with scoring on his mind, Patrick joins it because four men are tougher than three to check at the blue line.

When he does carry the puck, Patrick generates superb forward speed, skates through any number of slashes and hacks, and makes the safe play that gets the puck deep into the attacking zone. He does not gamble. Patrick also is a willing, able complement to Leetch on the power-play point; when Leetch slides over to the middle and turns the formation into an umbrella, Patrick eases to the top of the right-wing circle.

THE PHYSICAL GAME

The corner battles that Patrick wins are more on agility and fishing for the puck than victories of muscle and aggression. He tends to tie up the man and wait for support to come along and take the puck. In front of the net, he does what he can, but tends to use his reach and his stick or drop to one knee to break up plays rather than crunch people. He gets physically involved, but hardly is a physical defenseman.

THE INTANGIBLES

His entire career, Patrick has been a defense-first player with offensive skill, but always has been expected to play with those roles reversed because of the offensive reputation he brought to New York. As Brian Leetch has emerged, Patrick has been able to concentrate on what he likes to do—stay in the shadows, play the support role.

There is nothing wrong with playing that role. And certainly, there is nothing wrong with 10 goals. But, even factoring in the wrist injury that hampered Patrick's shooting last season, the feeling lingers that Patrick can get more out of himself—could take some risks, could put some anger into his game . . . break out somehow to make the rest of his game as elite as his skating.

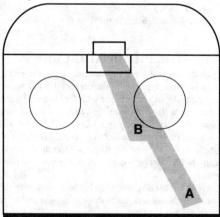

STEVEN RICE

Yrs. of NHL service: 1
Born: Kitchener, Ont., Canada; May 26, 1971
Position: Right wing
Height: 6-0
Weight: 210
Uniform no.: 10
Shoots: Right

Career statistics:

GP	G	A	TP	PIM
11	1	1	2	4

1990-91 statistics:

GP	G	A	TP	+/-	PIM	PP	SH	GW	GT	S	PCT
11	1	1	2	2	4	0	0	0	0	12	8.3

LAST SEASON

Spent last season with three Ranger teams—the New York Rangers (NHL), the Binghamton Rangers (AHL) and the Kitchener Rangers (OHL).

THE FINESSE GAME

Rice drives his legs with great power and balance. He gets where he wants to be, which generally is a place where he can blast the daylights out of the defenseman who has the puck in his corner of the ice. Rice is just so solid on his skates, so solidly built; he gets those feet wide apart and lowers the boom that unmistakably is the dominant aspect of his game... away from the puck.

With the puck, Rice also is gifted. He had 30 goals and 30 assists in just 29 games after being sent back to junior hockey last season, so clearly there are times when his stick is on the ice and in contact with the puck. And hitting isn't the only thing that got Rice on the World Junior Championships team. His shot is hard and accurate, he makes a fine pass from the corner after winning a battle for the puck, or he can carry the puck to the net himself, because traffic is not a problem for him.

THE PHYSICAL GAME

Rice has that innocent face and quiet demeanor, but he hits like dynamite in the corners. He just blasts people. He doesn't have to leave his feet and give it the extra show, as Troy Mallette does. Rice just bumps into people and separates their shoulders.

His style is better suited to give-and-go or dump-and-chase. It isn't at all that Rice can't handle the puck; clearly he can. But he is better when in motion, gaining momentum.

If he has to carry people on his back, Rice will. He is strong in the corners, keeps the legs moving and wins the wars down low.

THE INTANGIBLES

Still somewhat at the "Aw, shucks," stage. But he is going to force some very serious decisions from Rangers management, because if he isn't ready for regular NHL duty, he is very darn close. There were a lot of right wings in New York last season while Rice was getting more time in juniors and the American League. Another year of "seasoning" might make him stale.

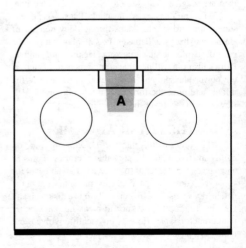

MIKE RICHTER

Yrs. of NHL service: 1
Born: Abington, Penn., USA; September 22, 1966
Position: Goaltender
Height: 5-10
Weight: 187
Uniform no.: 35
Catches: Left

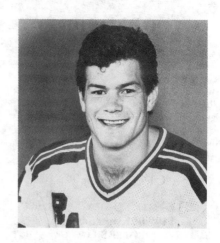

Career statistics:

GP	MINS	GA	SO	GAA	A	PIM
68	3916	201	0	3.08	4	4

1990-91 statistics:

GP	MINS	GAA	W	L	T	SO	GA	S	SAPCT	PIM
45	2596	3.12	21	13	7	0	135	1392	.903	4

LAST SEASON

Finalist for Vezina Trophy, voted by NHL general managers for league's most valuable goalie. Compiled 4-1-5 record when facing 40 shots or more and set club record with 59 saves in 3-3 tie at Vancouver Jan. 31.

THE PHYSICAL GAME

There are very few flaws in Richter's fundamentals. He sets in a solid stance that closes the five-hole between the knees, but allows complete freedom of movement to any of the four corners. He keeps his stick on the ice, his catching glove open, ready and waist high for superior balance. Richter stands up, plays the angles well and simply allows the puck to hit him. Excellent skating skills allow him to explode to the puck when he needs to use his body quickly. He forces the opponent to make a great shot—not just a good one—to score.

When he goes to his knees, his shoulders remain square to the puck and he is back on his feet very quickly and will stop his share of second shots. Occasionally he will get caught deep on an angle. But most of the time, if Richter is beaten it is because he was screened.

Richter is not hugely proficient in working with his stick from the standpoint of blocking passes to the slot from the corners or behind the net. Clearing the puck is not much of an issue, as under coach Roger Neilson's guidelines, the goalies are not supposed to be winging the puck around the boards all the time.

THE MENTAL GAME

Richter has not permitted many bad goals, barely has played a handful of truly bad games. When he does, he picks the appropriate time to be upset over such things—after the game, not during it—then moves on.

Richter is a big fan of practice. He likes to work hard and get the most out of it. That tells a lot about his attitude toward the sport and his role in it.

THE INTANGIBLES

Richter has poise far beyond his actual NHL playing experience, enough character and leadership-by-example that he can carry the team if asked. He certainly gives the appearance of a franchise goalie: he can come up with a big game on the road, can steal a point or two against a better team. On a rare night, his play will take them out of a game; on far, far many more nights, he will be the only reason they still have a chance to win.

NORMAND ROCHEFORT

Yrs. of NHL service: 11
Born: Trois Rivieres, Que., Canada; January 28, 1961
Position: Defenseman
Height: 6-1
Weight: 214
Uniform no.: 5
Shoots: Left

Career statistics:

GP	G	A	TP	PIM
566	39	117	156	525

1990-91 statistics:

GP	G	A	TP	+/-	PIM	PP	SH	GW	GT	S	PCT
44	3	7	10	10	35	0	0	0	0	34	8.8

LAST SEASON

Games played was a three-season high. Missed 22 games due to tendinitis in left knee, three because of a fractured index finger and eight due to fractured vertebra.

THE FINESSE GAME

Rochefort can handle the puck. He doesn't just throw the puck blindly around the boards; he'll hold it and see what space is available, then fill it with a precise pass. Other times, no matter the zone, he will make the safe, easy play. At still other times, he will sneak into the slot and be available for a shot. The guy knows what to do; the issue is getting his battered body to do it.

His skates are responsive, at least. Rochefort steps up into the play, meeting the opposing attack in the neutral zone as it approaches the blue line. He forces the forward to make a decision ("Can I beat this guy?"), then allows the forward to go ahead and try it

THE PHYSICAL GAME

Few things please Rochefort more than a tooth-rattling bodycheck. He loves to play the body, loves to crunch at the sideboards and at times will go way out of position just to drill somebody. He is very strong in front of the net, a fine penalty killer and—given his constantly broken body—far too willing a shot-blocker. His feet are sore from September to April.

THE INTANGIBLES

Rochefort flat-out loves the game, loves everything about it except rehab, which is where he always seems to find himself after his latest severe injury. His heart is monstrous; his body simply cannot handle all the demands he asks of it. One thing is sure, though: Rochefort never is cheated. He puts his all into every game and gets at least as much out of it.

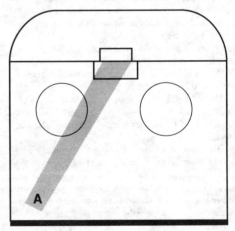

DAVID SHAW

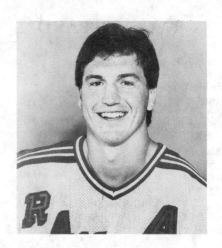

Yrs. of NHL service: 6
Born: St. Thomas, Ont., Canada; May 25, 1964
Position: Defenseman
Height: 6-2
Weight: 204
Uniform no.: 21
Shoots: Right

Career statistics:

GP	G	A	TP	PIM
397	24	94	118	457

1990-91 statistics:

GP	G	A	TP	+/-	PIM	PP	SH	GW	GT	S	PCT
77	2	10	12	8	89	0	0	1	0	61	3.3

LAST SEASON

Offensive stats matched his totals for 1989-90, when shoulder surgery limited his season to 22 games. Plus-minus ranked him third among Ranger defensemen.

THE FINESSE GAME

Shaw meets the rush confidently, reads the play well and makes a solid move to impose his will on the proceedings. From the hash marks of the circles back, he tightens the screws, making it increasingly difficult for the puck—or puck carrier—to advance. He spends a whole bunch of his time in this little quarter of the ice (from the hash marks to behind the net) It is his turf, where he is most able, most confident; the area in front of the net comes a close second.

He polices this territory with quite acceptable range. He uses his reach, he uses his body and makes the smart, simple pass to ease the puck out of the zone.

On the attack, Shaw has much more skill than he showed last season. He can fire from the right point. He keeps it low so that it can be deflected. He doesn't shoot enough; with Brian Leetch to his left, that is easy to understand.

THE PHYSICAL GAME

Shaw bangs, takes the body, rubs out in the corners. But the mean part isn't there as much as it was before he received that 12-game suspension for whacking Mario Lemieux in 1988-89. That seemed to take some starch out of Shaw, who was far scrappier before the incident occurred.

THE INTANGIBLES

Shaw is a very responsible player who seems to have toned down his play in order to be the complement Leetch needs. It is Shaw's heady, steady, unheralded play that frees Leetch to play his game so effectively.

But Shaw might be more effective with more responsibilities of his own. He has point skills he should be using. He is big and mobile and can be mean, and he was only a fraction of what he can be last season as Leetch dominated. It might be time for a change, at least of partners. Shaw needs to go back to being a leader instead of Leetch's babysitter.

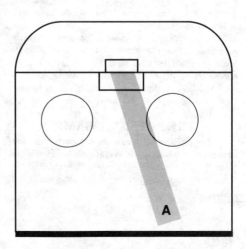

RAY SHEPPARD

Yrs. of NHL service: 4
Born: Pembroke, Ont., Canada; May 27, 1966
Position: Right wing
Height: 6-1
Weight: 182
Uniform no.: 23
Shoots: Right

Career statistics:

GP	G	A	TP	PIM
218	88	73	161	50

1990-91 statistics:

GP	G	A	TP	+/-	PIM	PP	SH	GW	GT	S	PCT
59	24	23	47	8	21	7	0	5	0	129	18.6

LAST SEASON

Missed 13 games due to sprained right knee, three more due to separated shoulder. Led team in game-winning goals. Ranked fourth on team in shooting percentage.

THE FINESSE GAME

On dozens of other pages in this book you will find players credited with deceptive speed. In fairness, then, we must call Sheppard deceptively slow—he looks slow, but isn't. His feet unmistakably are heavy; he does not look like he's covering much ground. If he was slow as he appears, though, people would have an easier time checking him.

Sheppard does not turn quickly, and his balance is not great, but he can curl out of the right-wing circle on his backhand and get into the slot, then shift to the forehand and get off a snap shot or wrist shot. That play requires agility poor skaters don't have. Sheppard keeps his feet moving, especially when checked, holds the defenseman with one hand and shovels a pass with the other. If he were a rotten skater, Sheppard wouldn't be able to do that, either.

He has a center's view of the ice, a center's eagerness to distribute the puck to a player in better scoring position. He has a short backswing and a quick release on his shots—the snap or wrist are preferred.

And he is at least responsible in his defensive zone, reading the play fairly well.

THE PHYSICAL GAME

Sheppard pays his dues in the corners, has size and strength and uses it to his advantage. He is not a big hitter; he rubs out. He gets mad, he stands up for himself, he does not get intimidated, but he does not fight.

THE INTANGIBLES

There is nothing about Ray Sheppard's game that makes the fans go wild, but they appreciate him as a workman. He does not cheat, does not take the easy way out. He gives an honest effort. The only even mild issue is that he does get hurt and he does miss playing time. Had he been healthy for the playoffs, the Rangers might have lasted much longer than they did.

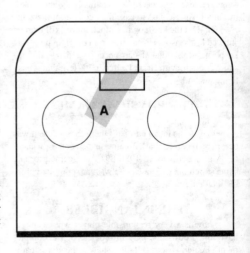

DARREN TURCOTTE

Yrs. of NHL service: 2
Born: Boston, Mass., USA; March 2, 1968
Position: Center
Height: 6-0
Weight: 185
Uniform no.: 8
Shoots: Left

Career statistics:

GP	G	A	TP	PIM
170	65	78	143	73

1990-91 statistics:

GP	G	A	TP	+/-	PIM	PP	SH	GW	GT	S	PCT
74	26	41	67	-5	37	15	2	3	1	212	12.3

LAST SEASON

Missed five games with bumps and bruises. Notched team's only hat trick for second consecutive season.

THE FINESSE GAME

Skills of hand and foot are this player's main strengths. Turcotte is agile and quick with the puck, absolutely a greyhound without it. Turcotte hits top speed in very few strides, and that top speed ranks with any in the league. He is the perfect point man in the last minute when his team's net is empty; he has the gifted hands and creativity to make a play if the faceoff is won, the speed to reach the puck down-ice and save valuable seconds if the draw is lost and the opposition clears the zone.

Turcotte is strong on the skates as well; he handles the puck nicely with his feet when circumstances dictate. Though he gets knocked down a fair amount, that is more a matter of a physical strength rather than an issue of balance or leg drive.

Excellent hand-eye coordination and fine shooting strength make him a devastating threat to shoot off the pass. And he has the scorer's greedy hunger to drive the puck through the goalie, through the back of the net, through the boards and out into the lobby. You don't teach that. Turcotte doesn't simply finish; he buries.

THE PHYSICAL GAME

Though more a finisher than a setup man, Turcotte can use his speed to drive a defense off its blue line, throw his shoulder into a defenseman's chest, shield the puck with his body, then hit a teammate with a nice pass.

But those events are only occasional. Turcotte seems intimidated by traffic. He will absorb a hit to make a play, but he rarely goes into traffic to get the puck. He almost never carries into a crowd to create some chaos, and isn't keen on going to the net for tangles with a defenseman who generally is larger and stronger.

While killing penalties, Turcotte will take a man by nullifying his stick but still uses his skating and counterattack skills as his biggest threats. He plays about to his size (though other players his size play bigger) but is widely accused of playing a "soft" game that calls for less grit and fewer stitches.

THE INTANGIBLES

In his rookie season, Turcotte was a scorer and a plus player (32 goals, plus 3). Last season, he was given the checking role against such elite centers as Wayne Gretzky, Mark Messier, Jeremy Roenick and Steve Yzerman/Sergei Fedorov. What will be asked of him this season?

Some people can fill both roles, can score AND check, but some people simply score, which is why checking wings have jobs—to cover the defensive liabilities of the scoring centers. A non-physical player with explosive speed and a lithe frame, Turcotte is better-suited to an offensive game that exacts a lighter physical toll. It may have been the team's fault more than his that Turcotte scored just nine times at even strength.

Turcotte accepted the defensive challenge, claimed he enjoyed it. But it will be difficult for him to proceed without knowing his hockey identity: checker? Scorer? Both?

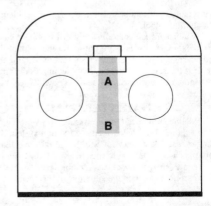

JOHN VANBIESBROUCK

Yrs. of NHL service: 7
Born: Detroit, Mich., USA; September 4, 1963
Position: Goaltender
Height: 5-9
Weight: 175
Uniform no.: 34
Catches: Left

Career statistics:

GP	MINS	GA	SO	GAA	A	PIM
356	20097	1186	10	3.54	21	171

1990-91 statistics:

GP	MINS	GAA	W	L	T	SO	GA	S	SAPCT	PIM
40	2257	3.35	15	18	6	3	126	1156	.891	18

LAST SEASON
Shutout total tied for third in league.

THE PHYSICAL GAME
Vanbiesbrouck is an extremely aggressive goaltender. He may get beaten, but it will not be from lack of effort. Vanbiesbrouck may charge out, lay flat on the ice and force an onrushing shooter well wide of the net. He may reach way out with his stick in a diving attempt at a poke check. But he isn't going to get beat because he was too deep in his net, unless it is on a stuff from the goalmouth off a pass from behind the net.

Post-to-post is one place where Vanbiesbrouck struggles. He is fine when it comes to reaching the post at his right, but he feels the need to drop to one knee as he moves to the post at his left, which leaves space at the top corner—space opposing forwards have filled in the past. He is a more-than-strong enough skater to get to the left without that extra lunge, which does get his stick across to block passes, but leaves him off-balance if the pass gets through.

Otherwise, Vanbiesbrouck plays the inverted V— knees together, feet planted firmly on his inside edges. Though it is difficult to move with his feet anchored as they are, Vanbiesbrouck does a good job of getting his skates on to shots to the corners when he has to. Up high, Vanbiesbrouck still doesn't always get his glove closed on shots to that side—a legacy, probably, of the surgery that repaired cut tendons after a household accident a few summers back.

Vanbiesbrouck is among the most mobile goalies in the game. He loves to go out to get the puck at the end boards and is much smarter now about winging the puck off the glass—or over it. Now, he moves the puck with more of a purpose and does it very well.

THE MENTAL GAME
Vanbiesbrouck has matured extremely well. There is no way he could have liked the rotation system the Rangers used last year, no way he could have liked being pushed somewhat to the side by Mike Richter's emergence. Outwardly, at least, Vanbiesbrouck kept an even emotional keel on the situation and seemed intent on making the best of it for the sake of the team, rather than going into a "Me first" sulk as he might have in his cockier years.

The enduring image of last season will be one totally bizarre late-season goal in Pittsburgh. Off the opening draw in overtime, Kevin Stevens whacked the puck off the endboards; Vanbiesbrouck turned to his left, faced the puck and stooped to scoop it up—then watched in horror as it bounced crazily from all the rotation, rolled up his catching glove, rolled down, and crossed the goal line. It was the low point of a frustrating year that saw him record three shutouts, but also saw him endure long stretches without a victory and another drastically sub-.500 season on the road (6-13-2).

THE INTANGIBLES
John Vanbiesbrouck is a literate individual. He can read the writing on the wall and the writing, for better or worse, right or wrong, says Mike Richter is coach Roger Neilson's man. There will be no rotation this year, which could change his name to John Van-bye-bye if the Rangers can trade him and get something good. Of course, they would have to get a goalie as part of the deal; if they put all their eggs in Richter's basket and the basket breaks, they're in big trouble.

PHILADELPHIA
FLYERS

KEITH ACTON

Yrs. of NHL service: 11
Born: Stouffville, Ont., Canada; April 15, 1958
Position: Center
Height: 5-8
Weight: 170
Uniform no.: 25
Shoots: Left

Career statistics:

GP	G	A	TP	PIM
813	209	326	535	952

1990-91 statistics:

GP	G	A	TP	+/-	PIM	PP	SH	GW	GT	S	PCT
76	14	23	37	-9	131	2	1	1	1	120	11.7

LAST SEASON

Games played was four-season high, goal total matched five-season high.

THE FINESSE GAME

Acton enjoyed an offensive rebirth last season. Fellow forecheckers created a number of opportunities and Acton converted more than his share by using his skating speed, smarts and a scoring touch that was thought to have abandoned him forever.

Because of his age, his experience and his virtually scientific study of the art of the faceoff, Acton was placed in a defensive role. As it ended up, people had to check him; he used his quickness and his hockey sense to reach the open man with a pass, then jump to a hole to get clear for a return at the goalmouth.

Still, defensive responsibility is the driving force of Acton's game. Few players in the league take faceoffs as seriously as he does and few do a more effective job of winning them. Acton uses his entire body on draws to gain the leverage that helps win control of the puck, then swivels into his opponent to box out the player.

Also, Acton tries never to use the same method on successive faceoffs, in order to keep his rival guessing and off balance mentally.

THE PHYSICAL GAME

In order to compensate for his lack of size, Acton looks for any possible edge he can gain. On faceoffs, he takes every inch of space, uses any method possible to distract the linesman and break the concentration of other center.

Acton yaps all night long, scraps all night long with any and all opponents, regardless of how much bigger they are. He has been punched in the face

enough times that another one or two won't make much difference if it helps get his team more involved and alert in both the physical and emotional elements of the game.

THE INTANGIBLES

Though he brings an angry demeanor to the opening draw, Acton is the class clown virtually until the contest begins. His antics keep the team loose when they need to be, pumped up when they need to be, which makes him valuable beyond his on-ice contribution.

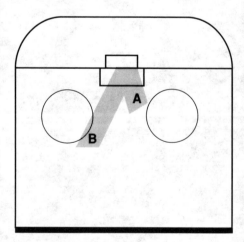

MURRAY BARON

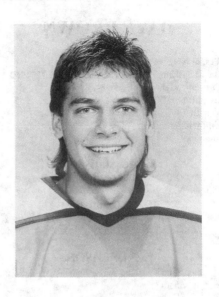

Yrs. of NHL service: 1
Born: Prince George, B.C., Canada; June 1, 1967
Position: Defenseman
Height: 6-3
Weight: 210
Uniform no.: 8
Shoots: Left

Career statistics:

GP	G	A	TP	PIM
83	10	10	20	86

1990-91 statistics:

GP	G	A	TP	+/-	PIM	PP	SH	GW	GT	S	PCT
67	8	8	16	-3	74	3	0	1	0	86	9.3

LAST SEASON

First in NHL.

THE FINESSE GAME

Baron's skating may be the best-kept secret in the division, the conference or the league. For pure speed on the straightaways, Baron may be the fastest big man on the circuit, and to that speed, he adds surprising agility plus endurance. The guy doesn't get tired. He skates as strongly in the last minute of a game as the first.

Baron has good enough vision and stick-handling ability to skate the puck up the ice on the power play when needed. He uses his skating ability to move up with every play. At even strength, he has the sense to get the puck and move it, rather than hold it.

Problems arise, however, in his manner of puck movement. Baron doesn't snap his passes, he pushes them. When the situation calls for a sharp, crisp first pass out of the zone, Baron instead will hoist a blimp to the neutral zone and hope someone will fair-catch it.

THE PHYSICAL GAME

Baron is not physical enough in the defensive zone. Just as he is not aggressive with the puck, he is not aggressive enough with his body on a regular basis. He has no visible mean streak; it takes a very long time for the fuse to set off his dynamite. He is not a force in front of his net, which rather wastes his gift of size.

It is unfair to blame Baron if a finesse player's mindset was placed in a power player's body, but he probably is not good enough to get by in the NHL as a pure finesse player, the way Paul Coffey can. A more physical Baron, who could catch you and hit you, would be a threat to an opponent.

THE INTANGIBLES

If track record is any indication, Baron is another season or two from becoming a very good, impact NHL player. He was a late bloomer at the Tier II level, took a couple of years to get a handle on the collegiate game at North Dakota and has some obstacles to surmount now with the Flyers.

Baron plays the toughest position to learn, especially against the elite skaters and clever minds he must face every night. But Baron should more than get by, despite the rough edges, until his game is polished to a shiny gleam by the buffing rag of experience.

DAVE BROWN

Yrs. of NHL service: 7
Born: Saskatoon, Sask., Canada; October 12, 1962
Position: Right wing
Height: 6-5
Weight: 205
Uniform no.:
Shoots: Right

Career statistics:

GP	G	A	TP	PIM
453	36	41	77	1402

1990-91 statistics:

GP	G	A	TP	+/-	PIM	PP	SH	GW	GT	S	PCT
58	3	4	7	-7	160	0	0	0	0	32	9.4

LAST SEASON

Goal total was three-season high, assist total was a four-season low.

THE FINESSE GAME

Brown always could play a little. He can skate a little, make a pass, win a puck along the boards, score off going to the net.

But his offensive figures speak for themselves. Skating a little means no sharp, quick changes of direction. Making a pass means having the time and the room to aim one at a teammate. Winning a puck along the boards mostly means intimidating someone into leaving it there.

If he were a complete waste, though, Brown would have been out of the game long ago. He can still find work because of his physical—fist-ical—attributes.

THE PHYSICAL GAME

Fighting is what got Brown into the NHL and fighting is what keeps him in the NHL. It is a wonder that after seven seasons of it the guy hasn't had enough yet.

It probably is more wondrous that a new trend is beginning: People no longer bother fighting the players whose only role is intimidation. The less you fight them, the less you create situations where a fight is called for, the more you keep these players on the bench. Thus, in a strange way, Brown could dress for a game, not play a shift, and get his job done effectively.

Another example: Brown and the Rangers' Joe Kocur are good friends. They are no more likely to scrap during the Rangers-Flyers series than Kocur and Bob Probert (buddies) would in Rangers-Red Wings games.

THE INTANGIBLES

Back "home" after his sojourn in Edmonton, Brown replaces Craig Berube, the fellow who will take over the menace role with the Oilers. Berube's game still improving, though, and he can be used in more situations than can Brown.

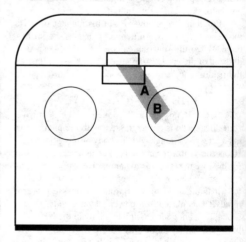

TERRY CARKNER

Yrs. of NHL service: 5
Born: Smiths Falls, Ont., Canada; March 7, 1966
Position: Defenseman
Height: 6-3
Weight: 215
Uniform no.: 29
Shoots: Left

Career statistics:

GP	G	A	TP	PIM
335	27	112	139	797

1990-91 statistics:

GP	G	A	TP	+/-	PIM	PP	SH	GW	GT	S	PCT
79	7	25	32	-15	204	6	0	1	0	97	7.2

LAST SEASON

Plus-minus declined by seven goals, penalty-minute total jumped by 37, goal production jumped by three to second-best career total.

THE FINESSE GAME

Carkner has worked countless hours in an attempt to improve his foot speed, to add some agility and quickness to his game. The results are evident; though his feet remain heavy, his turns rather labored, Carkner is a fairly fluid player—the pieces of his game forming a work still in progress.

He is above average laterally, and actually moves well for a big man, but he is not agile. Defensively, Carkner is a very well-rounded player who will make you beat him, as he will not beat himself; he is a solid positional player who is smooth going backward and who can move the puck while going in reverse.

Carkner also has a good mind for offense, knows when to jump into holes, knows when to shoot for a goal and when to set up a deflection. But there are times when he simply does not move the puck quickly enough—when he is too deliberate, tries to be too artistic or do too much. While he holds on, the game comes to a screeching halt.

When he keeps the game simple, though, Carkner is a very solid defensive citizen.

THE PHYSICAL GAME

Carkner is a volcano, never far from eruption. He hits at every opportunity and plays an extremely physical game. He is strong in the corners, mean in front of the net and uses his size to significant advantage. He goes to the corners expecting to win the puck, and he wins a high percentage of the time.

THE INTANGIBLES

All things considered, Carkner is in the upper echelon of big players who can provide an above-average total package while doing nothing remarkably well. The only overwhelming aspect of his game is his desire—to win, to improve, to make his team better.

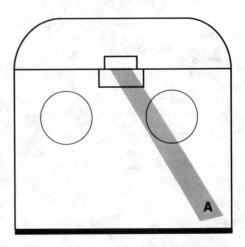

MURRAY CRAVEN

Yrs. of NHL service: 8
Born: Medicine Hat, Alta., Canada; July 20, 1964
Position: Left wing
Height: 6-2
Weight: 185
Uniform no.: 32
Shoots: Left

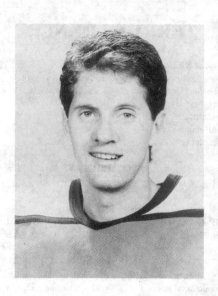

Career statistics:

GP	G	A	TP	PIM
557	153	280	433	319

1990-91 statistics:

GP	G	A	TP	+/-	PIM	PP	SH	GW	GT	S	PCT
77	19	47	66	-2	53	6	0	0	0	170	11.2

LAST SEASON

For sixth time in seven Flyers seasons, he played 72 or more games and scored 19 or more goals. Assist total was within three of his career high, set prior season.

THE FINESSE GAME

Craven is a solid two-way hockey player, extremely valuable to his team in either the offensive or defensive roles. He can run the point on the power play, kill penalties, win important faceoffs and use his skating speed to advantage in both ends of the rink.

When the Flyers are playing dump-and-chase, Craven is one of the most effective chasers because of his speed. He can get to the puck, get to the puck carrier, can use his reach to challenge the player and attempt to force a turnover.

When he has the puck, Craven uses his speed to intimidate the defense and his agility to dart past them after they have conceded too much ground. He has a smashing wrist shot, which he releases quickly and uses effectively.

While killing penalties, Craven will take faceoffs and eliminate his man efficiently, leaving the puck free for his defensemen and preventing the other center from going to the net for screens or deflections.

THE PHYSICAL GAME

Craven is big and strong enough to smear players along the boards. He is an effective, but not punishing hitter; he accepts contact in more cases than he initiates it.

THE INTANGIBLES

Craven is a proven, consistent, intelligent performer of middle-range skills and above-average versatility. He can work both special teams. He is one of the few speed forwards on the Flyers, which makes him an extremely important player for them.

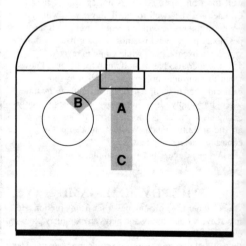

STEVE DUCHESNE

Yrs. of NHL service: 5
Born: Sept-Iles, Que., Canada; June 30, 1965
Position: Defenseman
Height: 5-11
Weight: 195
Uniform no.:
Shoots: Left

Career statistics:

GP	G	A	TP	PIM
382	95	197	292	397

1990-91 statistics:

GP	G	A	TP	+/-	PIM	PP	SH	GW	GT	S	PCT
78	21	41	62	19	66	8	0	3	0	171	12.3

LAST SEASON

Third consecutive season with 20 or more goals, 40 or more assists. Obtained from Los Angeles with Steve Kasper in the trade that sent the Kings Jeff Chychrun and the rights to Jari Kurri.

THE FINESSE GAME

Skating skill is a key component of Duchesne's game. He is a quick skater, agile and he covers a lot of ground laterally. Duchesne has excellent balance and can change direction instantly.

From those attributes comes others that make Duchesne a very gifted finesse player who will dramatically improve the Flyers in a number of areas. He can use his speed to skate the puck out of the defensive zone or can make a quick first pass after gaining control. Duchesne then will quickly step up with the play, available for a return pass.

He escorts the play up ice, keeping the gap to the forwards tight and staying ready to activate into the attack. But Duchesne does not overstay his welcome in the offensive zone; he assesses the play quickly and correctly most of the time, and anticipates well. If the puck turns over, he rarely is trapped too deep to recover; he reacts calmly to emergency situations or missed assignments by his teammates and always is mentally prepared with Plan B.

Duchesne gets the puck to the net quickly; he rarely wastes time. His game is speed, and rapid puck movement is a significant factor in playing to that strength. As a result, he is eminently capable of one-timing the puck and doing it accurately.

THE PHYSICAL GAME

Duchesne gets physically involved, but is not an eagerly combative player. He wins his battles through positioning rather than physical force, and would make a perfect complement to the more physical—less agile—Terry Carkner.

THE INTANGIBLES

Duchesne will lead the transition of the Flyers' defense into one with more speed and mobility, will use his scoring skills to make the team more potent at both ends of the ice and will provide the power-play anchorman that Mark Howe no longer is able to be.

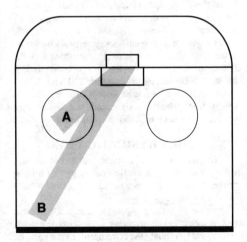

PELLE EKLUND

Yrs. of NHL service: 6
Born: Stockholm, Sweden; March 22, 1963
Position: Center
Height: 5-10
Weight: 175
Uniform no.: 9
Shoots: Left

Career statistics:

GP	G	A	TP	PIM
435	99	264	363	79

1990-91 statistics:

GP	G	A	TP	+/-	PIM	PP	SH	GW	GT	S	PCT
73	19	50	69	-2	14	8	0	4	0	131	14.5

LAST SEASON

Played 70 or more games for sixth consecutive season. Goal total was second-best of his career, his third straight season of 18 or more; assist total was within one of career-high. Plus-minus declined by nine goals.

THE FINESSE GAME

Eklund is the Flyers' best all-around player.

A masterful skater, agile and shifty, Eklund backs opposing defensemen off the blue line with his speed. Then he likes to carry the puck down the wing, stop short at the hash marks near the boards, buy some time and assess his options.

A bit too often, that option is a drop pass which frequently in the past has surprised teammates more than opponents. Otherwise, though, Eklund sees the smart play and makes it with the deft passing touch that brings him nearly three assists for every goal he scores. His thoughts are as quick as his hands, which are quick as his feet—which are not fast, but are very, very quick.

Eklund's exceptional hockey sense is useful on defense, as well. He effectively can shadow a Pat LaFontaine and is in strong-enough condition to double shift if LaFontaine double shifts. Eklund doesn't mind a defensive role, as he knows offensive chances emerge from defensive assignments, and he more than has the ability to convert turnovers or transition plays.

THE PHYSICAL GAME

Eklund may have a slight frame, but he is a willingly physical player. He accepts getting hit and thrives on the contact, because it keeps him more fully involved in the game.

However, nothing is going to change the fact that he is at a physical disadvantage in most of the run-ins. If it is clear he is going to get trampled, Eklund gets rid of the puck; but when it appears he is dodging a check, it is more a credit to his sensibility than a knock on his courage.

He does not retaliate when run by other players—partly because he is extremely disciplined, partly because he is a key player on the power plays that are created, so often, by fouls against him.

THE INTANGIBLES

Eklund plays 28-30 minutes a game, does virtually everything he is asked and does it well. He is eminently tough enough, mentally and physically, to handle NHL rigors with elegance and ease.

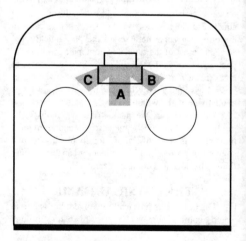

RON HEXTALL

Yrs. of NHL service: 5
Born: Brandon, Man., Canada; May 3, 1964
Position: Goaltender
Height: 6-3
Weight: 192
Uniform no.: 27
Catches: Left

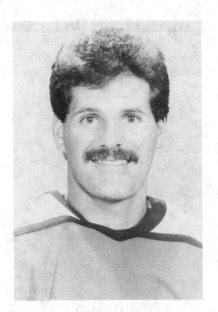

Career statistics:

GP	MINS	GA	SO	GAA	A	PIM
236	13569	735	1	3.25	11	345

1990-91 statistics:

GP	MINS	GAA	W	L	T	SO	GA	S	SAPCT	PIM
36	2035	3.13	13	16	5	0	106	982	.892	10

LAST SEASON

Saw limited playing time due to recurring groin injuries. Was under .500 for first time in his career. Goals against average was five-season low.

THE PHYSICAL GAME

Hextall's fundamental skills may have reached a low point last season, even if his goals against average was gaudy. He was very inconsistent and on the bad nights, Hextall was, quite simply, all over the place.

Hextall often left giant chunks of net available to the shooters. He flopped around, over-challenged. When he moved right-to-left on quick passes across the slot, Hextall at times would not even get his stick across to cover the monster space between his legs as he kicked. A significant portion of the time, Hextall was vulnerable on his catching glove side—usually a strength—because instead of having his catching hand open and ready for a shot, the glove was turned inward, toward his left knee.

Other nights, Hextall was calm, composed, dramatically more in control. He stood up extremely well, would drop to his knees but would not flop on his sides and would recover nicely if there was a rebound to confront. More noticeably, he was much more restrained in his puck-handling; instead of firing the puck around the left-wing boards, where an opponent always seemed to be waiting, Hextall made much smarter plays—accomplishing more by doing less.

Hextall also tries to use his stick to block passes from the corners to the slot. His reach is a giant advantage.

THE MENTAL GAME

Hextall's mental toughness seemed shaken last year. When he was successful, he projected an air of invulnerability on which the rest of the team fed. He was not convincingly invincible last year, and the team seemed to sense that as well.

THE INTANGIBLES

Injuries, suspensions and contract hassles have cost Hextall the better part of the past two seasons. He needs a strong, healthy, consistent campaign to make it clear he isn't simply living on the reputation built in the better days when he beat people by using his size, skating skills, positioning and anticipation.

Hextall may still be able to carry a team on his back, but he will have to show it.

MARTIN HOSTAK

Yrs. of NHL service: 1
Born: Hradec Kralove, Czechoslovakia;
November 11, 1967
Position: Center
Height: 6-3
Weight: 198
Uniform no.: 26
Shoots: Left

Career statistics:

GP	G	A	TP	PIM
50	3	10	13	22

1990-91 statistics:

GP	G	A	TP	+/-	PIM	PP	SH	GW	GT	S	PCT
50	3	10	13	1	22	1	0	0	0	64	4.7

LAST SEASON

First in NHL.

THE FINESSE GAME

The big question on Hostak is his foot speed and quickness, and whether either is up to the challenges of the big-league game. He will make a play if he has a lot of time, but otherwise, Hostak too often ends up behind the play.

A plodding, knock-kneed skater, he does not get into the play on time as the second man on the forecheck, and if he is the first man in, Hostak does not have a prayer of putting enough pressure on the puck when it is dumped into the attacking zone.

His hand skills salvage part of the equation. Hostak can stickhandle nicely and can control the puck in a crowd. He has a great release on the wrist or snap shots and he is very good close-in because he is very patient; but he rarely reaches the play.

THE PHYSICAL GAME

When he has the puck, Hostak is reminiscent of Minnesota's Ulf Dahlen. He is very strong on his feet and it is difficult to dislodge the puck from his grasp. But too often he is not willing to go to the corners to get the puck; or, by the time he arrives there, the puck has headed somewhere else.

Also, he will not touch a soul. This is not a physical player.

THE INTANGIBLES

Some of his problems last season may have been physical; if you're slow, you're slow. But Hostak also was said to have reported in miserable condition last season, and reportedly worked extremely hard this summer to avoid a repeat of that mistake. He knows what it takes to play now, knows the price that must be paid to get in shape and maintain it.

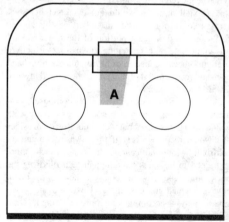

STEVE KASPER

Yrs. of NHL service: 11
Born: Montreal, Que., Canada; September 29, 1961
Position: Center
Height: 5-8
Weight: 175 Uniform No.:
Shoots: Left

Career statistics:

GP	G	A	TP	PIM
737	170	282	452	524

1990-91 statistics:

GP	G	A	TP	+/-	PIM	PP	SH	GW	GT	S	PCT
67	9	19	28	3	33	0	1	1	0	70	12.9

LAST SEASON

Goal and point totals were lowest since injury-shortened 1983-84 season. Obtained from Los Angeles May 30, with Steve Duchesne, for Jeff Chychrun and rights to Jari Kurri.

THE FINESSE GAME

Checking and defensive play remain Kasper's forte. Though among the league's smallest centers, Kasper is able to compensate through a number of means that turn his diminutive size into an asset.

Quick hands and anticipation that make him the equal, on faceoffs, of any center to whom he concedes tremendous advantages in height and weight. Kasper is shifty enough to dart around larger, clumsier players because of agility, balance and better-than-average speed. Kasper gets a low center of gravity, which heightens his balance and makes it difficult to knock him off the puck.

Also, he is able to control the puck well with his feet, which is useful after faceoffs. Kasper can use all his strength to tie up the opposing center, then use his skates to direct the puck to a teammate.

His offensive skills are skidding, but Kasper certainly is capable of scoring. He has a fine passing touch and a complete view of the ice, which combine to create scoring opportunities for his linemates. Kasper also has a solid wrist shot and a more than acceptable slap shot, which generally comes from close range (between the circles) and gives goalies trouble.

THE PHYSICAL GAME

He has played this long, so you know he can't be run out of the league. Kasper doesn't get hit much, but doesn't get into position to be hit much. His is more an open-ice game of persistence and pursuit, of clogging passing lanes, of staying between his man and the puck or his man and the net. These items require stamina and conditioning and wit, all of which Kasper possesses and brings to every game.

THE INTANGIBLES

Kasper can still kill a penalty, win an important draw during crunch time, shadow an offensive star. He and Keith Acton, both tenured NHL veterans, could become a defensive center platoon for the Flyers— giving the team a fresh checking ace every night during those stretches of four games in five nights.

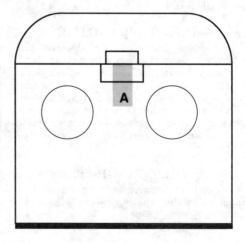

DALE KUSHNER

Yrs. of NHL service: 1
Born: Terrace, B.C., Canada; June 13, 1966
Position: Left wing
Height: 6-1
Weight: 195
Uniform no.: 10
Shoots: Left

Career statistics:

GP	G	A	TP	PIM
63	7	11	18	195

1990-91 statistics:

GP	G	A	TP	+/-	PIM	PP	SH	GW	GT	S	PCT
63	7	11	18	-4	195	1	0	0	0	59	11.9

LAST SEASON

First in NHL.

THE FINESSE GAME

A better-than-average skater with decent hands, Kushner seems to make a lot of things happen. He plays either wing, forechecks well, is good along the boards and is substantial defensively—never hurts you without the puck. Most of this stems from an eagerness and intensity, but it is supported by the leg strength and balance that get him to the puck on time instead of too late.

A few seasons in the minors seemed to polish Kushner's hockey sense. He knows what to do when he gets the puck, and it doesn't take all week for the messages from his head to reach his hands. Kushner can make a pretty fair pass and gets enough on his shot to score from the circle at times.

THE PHYSICAL GAME

Kushner is perfect for those 45-second chaos shifts that wake up everybody in the building. He can run around the attacking zone, banging everyone in sight, pressuring the puck, pinning a defenseman against the boards and setting up the faceoff that leads to a Flyers goal. He'll be on the bench when that puck goes in, so he doesn't get the point or the plus, but he will have had an instrumental—albeit indirect—role in the play.

THE INTANGIBLES

A locker-room cutup, Kushner has the ability to laugh at himself and with others, to keep his teammates relaxed. He wants to be better, wants to earn more respect for his finesse skills and is not at all in love with the scrappy, part-time role he is asked to play.

But he does it, does it well, and scores about every eight shots, which is not awful; the better scorers in the league score roughly once every four or five shots, and they get lots more ice time.

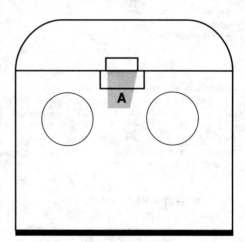

NORMAN LACOMBE

Yrs. of NHL service: 6
Born: Pierrefonds, Que., Canada; October 18, 1964
Position: Right wing
Height: 6-0
Weight: 210
Uniform no.: 36
Shoots: Right

Career statistics:

GP	G	A	TP	PIM
319	53	62	115	196

1990-91 statistics:

GP	G	A	TP	+/-	PIM	PP	SH	GW	GT	S	PCT
74	11	20	31	-1	27	1	0	1	0	101	8.9

LAST SEASON

Reached double figures in goals for only second time in his career. Assist total was career-high.

THE FINESSE GAME

Lacombe shows occasional quickness. He will see an opening and go to it, will make a smart move, an agile move, a quick move, and polish off an occasional scoring chance.

But he will not do it all the time. Lacombe does not assert himself, does not consistently make himself a force. He has good hands, but is not a great finisher; he skates pretty well, but sometimes seems uncertain of where to go.

Lacombe is adequate defensively; he identifies his check and does a decent job on a man-to-man basis.

THE PHYSICAL GAME

Lacombe hardly is a ferocious hitter, but he goes to the corners and uses his strength to dig the puck out. He grinds along the boards, gets involved and is the prototypical third-assist player: Some guy puts the puck away after two nice passes, but it was Lacombe's work along the wall that forced the turnover or poked the puck loose to start things.

THE INTANGIBLES

Intensity is an issue for this player. A first-round pick in 1983, Lacombe is playing for his third team and has not made a real impact on any of them. He has physical tools, but consistent insistence is lacking.

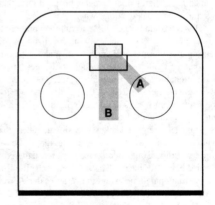

JIRI LATAL

Yrs. of NHL service: 2
Born: Olomouc, Czechoslovakia; February 2, 1967
Position: Defenseman
Height: 6-0
Weight: 190
Uniform no.: 11
Shoots: Left

Career statistics:

GP	G	A	TP	PIM
82	11	34	45	20

1990-91 statistics:

GP	G	A	TP	+/-	PIM	PP	SH	GW	GT	S	PCT
50	5	21	26	-19	14	1	0	0	0	81	6.2

LAST SEASON

Played 18 more games than in rookie season, but plus-minus worsened by 25 goals. Assist total was NHL career high.

THE FINESSE GAME

Latal has tremendous offensive ability. A marvelous skater with speed to burn, Latal can take a gamble on joining a rush or leading one, because he has more than enough wherewithal to regain his position if there is a transition break the other way.

Latal has the hockey sense to run the point on the power play. He has a nice passing touch but is still battling the international instinct to make a passing play rather than just take a shot at the net. In the international game, on the larger ice, you need an overnight courier service to get the puck to the net from the point; there is no such struggle in the NHL game, but certain habits die hard.

On defense, Latal takes occasional, rather than regular, advantage of his speed. He ranges to the corners at times, but often seems a bit too tethered to the area in front of the net. That, too, is a transition from the international game, where it is a $10 cab ride from the front of the net to the corners.

THE PHYSICAL GAME

The gritty moments in the defensive zone create problems for Latal, as he simply is not strong enough to handle some of the game's bigger players. He has not yet learned to use quickness and body position to compensate in the matchups of muscle and mettle.

THE INTANGIBLES

This is the year Latal tells us where his game is headed. He wants to play, the question is whether his body can stand up to the punishment. In just two seasons so far, Latal has battled significant injuries to his shoulder, ribs and knee.

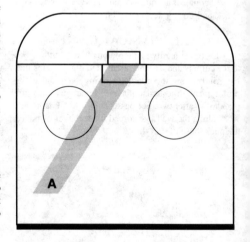

GORD MURPHY

Yrs. of NHL service: 3
Born: Willowdale, Ont., Canada; March 23, 1967
Position: Defenseman
Height: 6-2
Weight: 195
Uniform no.: 3
Shoots: Right

Career statistics:

GP	G	A	TP	PIM
230	41	89	130	221

1990-91 statistics:

GP	G	A	TP	+/-	PIM	PP	SH	GW	GT	S	PCT
80	11	31	42	-7	58	6	0	2	0	203	5.4

LAST SEASON

Point total was career high. Shot total increased by 43 from prior season.

THE FINESSE GAME

Though the Philadelphia defense has been known in the past for its brute strength and intimidating demeanor, Murphy is a symbol of the Flyers' new blue line: he is a player with foot and hand skills and a less-abrasive personality, a player solid at both ends of the ice.

Murphy is an impressively mobile, agile skater who turns well to either side and who can make a neat change of directions in a very small amount of space. He has the speed to join the rush, the strength to skate through checks, the balance to hold his own when trying to keep his goalie's crease clear.

He also has a nice touch with the puck in close quarters and a strong snap shot from the right point. Murphy's hand skills also complement his hockey sense; he doesn't get the puck and hold it, he gets the puck and moves it ahead.

Beyond that, Murphy uses his stick, reach and instincts well. It may look as though an opponent has beaten him wide, but Murphy will angle the player to bad ice or dive effectively to poke away the puck.

THE PHYSICAL GAME

For a 205-pound player, Murphy is not especially enthusiastic about making the most of his size. He gets in people's way, he's strong enough to get by, but he is not a force in the strength aspect.

THE INTANGIBLES

The arrival of Steve Duchesne could free Murphy from some of the offensive responsibilities and, accordingly, offensive pressures. Murphy won't necessarily have to play entire power plays, along with his regular shift, which could leave him more energy to add a physical element to his finesse skills.

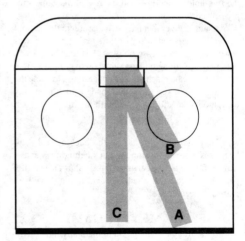

PETE PEETERS

Yrs. of NHL service: 12
Born: Edmonton, Alta., Canada; August 1, 1957
Position: Goaltender
Height: 6-0
Weight: 195
Uniform no.: 33
Catches: Left

Career statistics:

GP	MINS	GA	SO	GAA	A	PIM
489	27699	1423	21	3.08	14	212

1990-91 statistics:

GP	MINS	GAA	W	L	T	SO	GA	S	SAPCT	PIM
26	1270	2.88	9	7	1	1	61	623	.902	14

LAST SEASON

Posted goals against average under 3.00 for third time in four seasons, was over .500 for sixth time in seven seasons.

THE PHYSICAL GAME

Peeters was remarkably relaxed and poised when the Flyers handed him the job in the first half last season. His fundamentals were extremely strong. He may never have appeared more comfortable in his stance—his weight even on his skate blades, his feet ready to move, his catching glove open and at the perfect height for maximum balance, his stick covering the five-hole perfectly—and the rest of his game simply flowed.

Lateral movement has been a problem throughout Peeters' career and while it still isn't great, he was getting across the crease on plays last season. He was getting the job done on first shots, recovering for more rebounds than he reached in prior seasons. He made the big saves at the key times and made it look relatively easy, though he still struggled with in-close plays such as stuff tries from the side of the net or scrambles in front.

He is not going to handle the puck a great deal. Peeters is more apt to stop the puck behind the net and leave it for the defenseman or make a short, safe outlet pass. But the overall effect is control, and the Flyers reaped the benefits.

THE MENTAL GAME

If he struggles with goaltending's ups and downs, Peeters certainly hides it well. He seems persistently positive at this late stage of his career, on an even mental keel, and is giving up fewer of the weak goals he permitted when he was more outwardly intense. If he has a poor game, it is forgotten by the next day's practice. The ability to relax is one of the toughest to attain, but Peeters seems to have managed it.

THE INTANGIBLES

Peeters remains the ideal backup, the fellow who will play as much as he's asked and sit as much as he's told—without making waves. He never once complained or rocked the boat when he was banished to the bench or the press box following a November surge that kept the Flyers from falling into the Eric Lindros sweepstakes. The team, and the fans, responded to Peeters, who responded to the challenge.

MIKE RICCI

Yrs. of NHL service: 1
Born: Scarborough, Ont., Canada; October 27, 1971
Position: Center
Height: 6-0
Weight: 190
Uniform no.: 180
Shoots: Left

Career statistics:

GP	G	A	TP	PIM
68	21	20	41	64

1990-91 statistics:

GP	G	A	TP	+/-	PIM	PP	SH	GW	GT	S	PCT
68	21	20	41	-8	64	9	0	4	0	121	17.4

LAST SEASON

First season in NHL.

THE FINESSE GAME

Ricci can score from anywhere. Exceptional hand-eye coordination makes him an artist at deflections. Ricci also has enough of a touch to tuck a backhand shot in the upper corner of the net off a scramble and enough mustard and accuracy on his shot to score from longer-range.

Ricci does a good job of reading the play at both ends. He knows the game and is solid in a defensive role—perhaps more solid than any of his fellow Flyers centers. The hand-eye coordination that gives him such an edge on deflections also makes him extremely strong on faceoffs.

It is not inappropriate to expect 80 or 90 points per season from this young man, but Ricci will not challenge the 100-point milestone without improvement in his skating. He doesn't get places fast enough, doesn't get a good-enough jump on the puck, but Ricci will battle to get the most out of himself and that includes adding some jump to his step.

THE PHYSICAL GAME

Ricci plays a strength game in the areas where strength is needed, and should get stronger as his physical maturity proceeds. He goes along the boards, bumps and does the dirty work willingly. Likewise, he goes to the front of the net, though in each case, his lack of upper body bulk limits the amount of impact he can have.

THE INTANGIBLES

Mature beyond his years, Ricci has such innate leadership skills that virtually none of the players viewed him as a rookie after the halfway mark of last season. He is a character player who genuinely cares about the team and his contribution to it, one who puts pressure on himself to excel and who sets a solid example with his comportment.

This could be a breakout season for him.

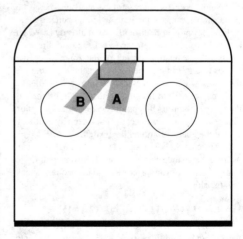

KJELL SAMUELSSON

Yrs. of NHL service: 5
Born: Tyngsryd, Sweden; October 18, 1958
Position: Defenseman
Height: 6-6
Weight: 235 Uniform No.:
Shoots: Right

Career statistics:

GP	G	A	TP	PIM
372	26	86	112	643

1990-91 statistics:

GP	G	A	TP	+/-	PIM	PP	SH	GW	GT	S	PCT
78	9	19	28	4	82	1	0	3	1	101	8.9

LAST SEASON

Goal total was a career high, assist total was second-best lifetime total, penalty minutes dropped to career low.

THE FINESSE GAME

Owner of the most remarkable wingspan in the game, it seems sometimes that Samuelsson could stand at the center faceoff dot, stretch out his arms and touch one hand to each sideboard. He complements that reach with a huge stride that covers a mammoth amount of territory; you just know it will be a warm winter night in Winnipeg before somebody beats him to the outside. Even if he doesn't break up the play, he changes its intended course—and buys himself time.

Samuelsson is successful because he keeps the game simple; most of the time he knows better than to make a play any more difficult than it already is. When he has the puck in the defensive zone, he sends the puck safely off the boards and out of the zone, or up the boards to a teammate; the times he gets in trouble are the times when he forces passes into the middle, as those passes tend to become turnovers. On offense, if there is no room as he approaches the attacking blue line, Samuelsson tries to get the puck deep by drilling a shot at the goalie or around the boards.

An extremely strong player, Samuelsson can overpower goalies with his shot from the point. He rarely shoots from anyplace else and is not one to sneak into the slot.

THE PHYSICAL GAME

Samuelsson is a pleasant, kind-hearted soul off the ice, but he's pretty nasty on it. He has no aversion to the obnoxious and is pointedly rude to countryman, and former teammate, Tomas Sandstrom. Samuelsson will slash and elbow, rub his glove in your face and yap all night at you. He reminds of a taller, gawkier Ulf Samuelsson in his attitude, though the two are not known to be related.

Samuelsson is all clutch-and-grab in front of his net. He can smother a player in the corners, at times to such an extent that the other player vanishes from sight.

THE INTANGIBLES

Samuelsson plays an awful lot of minutes. He plays a pretty physical, confrontational style and plays despite a lot of nagging nicks and bruises. Yet he is so big and strong and powerful, and he seems in such good shape, that he appears capable of at least another few seasons as an effective contributor.

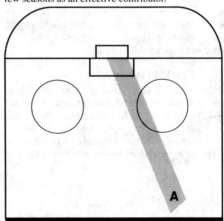

DERRICK SMITH

Yrs. of NHL service: 7
Born: Scarborough, Ont., Canada; January 22, 1965
Position: Left wing
Height: 6-2
Weight: 215
Uniform no.: 24
Shoots: Left

Career statistics:

GP	G	A	TP	PIM
494	80	87	167	338

1990-91 statistics:

GP	G	A	TP	+/-	PIM	PP	SH	GW	GT	S	PCT
72	11	10	21	0	37	0	1	2	0	100	11.0

LAST SEASON

Plus-minus improved by 15 goals from prior season. Goal total reached double figures for fifth time in his seven seasons.

THE FINESSE GAME

Smith's ability to skate powerfully enables him to keep up with the opposition's top right wing, and his checking skills make him a good bet to nullify that rival sniper. Right wings have become the home-run hitters in hockey, left wings have become the guys who dig the puck out for them on offense or try to keep it away from them on defense, and Smith is among the top few at the latter aspect.

He better be strong on defense, because his hands simply do not get the job done on offense; most nights, he is incapable of burying the most rudimentary scoring chance. Smith may be another prisoner of that very prevalent all defense, no offense mindset that afflicts checking players. They think defense, defense, defense, to the extent that their hands turn to marble when opportunities arise for passing or shooting.

Accordingly, Smith sticks to shadow work and penalty killing. He gravitates toward the boards, perhaps because when most of the ice is behind you, a player can get away with a lack of creativity. When the ice is in front of you, there are many more complicated decisions to make.

THE PHYSICAL GAME

Smith finishes every check he can. He scraps for the puck in the combat zones along the walls and in the corners, using his strenth and balance to withstand the initial collision and win the ensuing scrum.

THE INTANGIBLES

Smith is another graduate of the disciplined, no-nonsense, junior hockey "finishing school" they run in Peterborough, Ont. The players produced by the Petes are not the world's most colorful personalities—witness such as Bob Gainey, Doug Jarvis, Mike Ricci, Terry Carkner, John Druce, Kris King, Steve Yzerman and on and on. But they are extremely effective at what they do and their checking skills are positively first-rate.

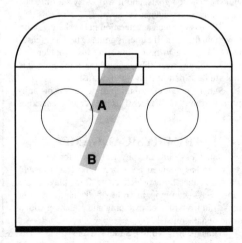

RON SUTTER

Yrs. of NHL service: 8
Born: Viking, Alta., Canada; December 2, 1963
Position: Center
Height: 6-0
Weight: 180
Uniform no.: 14
Shoots: Right

Career statistics:

GP	G	A	TP	PIM
555	137	223	360	854

1990-91 statistics:

GP	G	A	TP	+/-	PIM	PP	SH	GW	GT	S	PCT
80	17	28	45	2	92	2	0	1	0	149	11.4

LAST SEASON

Third straight season in which games played and assist totals have increased.

THE FINESSE GAME

There isn't much to it, really. There don't seem to be any natural, innate skills in Sutter's game, and any that he brings to the rink are the result of monstrous amounts of work.

He has a blocky stride that gets him places, but it is Sutter's hunger for the puck that seems to carry him closer to it, as though he is magnetized and the puck is metal. Sutter is going to get virtually all his scoring chances from forechecking, from forcing loose pucks and converting them into goals. He also will come up with shorthanded goals, and it was fairly startling last season that Sutter did not get any.

There isn't much acceleration in his skating, with or without the puck. If Sutter is going to beat a defenseman, it is going to be by lowering his shoulder and bowling the guy over. If he is going to get to a hole, it is going to be as part of a give-and-go rush.

Sutter's major contribution these days is his ability to win important faceoffs and play in a checking role

THE PHYSICAL GAME

Sutter has paid the physical price for so many years. He has endured back pain, jaw fractures and countless other hurts which come from playing the Sutter way—camping in front of the net, throwing himself in front of shots, yapping and punching with a world of antagonists.

Though fairly willing, Sutter is a lousy fighter. His physical game runs off the size of his spirit, not the size of his body.

THE INTANGIBLES

The defensive emergence of Mike Ricci, the Flyers' off-season acquisition of Steve Kasper, and the return of Keith Action seemed to leave Sutter, the team captain, in a lurch. Kasper and Acton are closer to the ends of their careers than is Sutter—for whom more also could be gained in a trade. As the off-season proceeded, it certainly appeared Sutter was headed either to the right wing, where the Flyers are weak behind Rick Tocchet, or to another uniform.

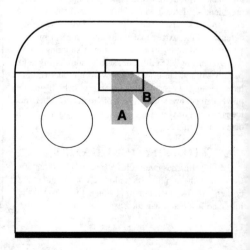

RICK TOCCHET

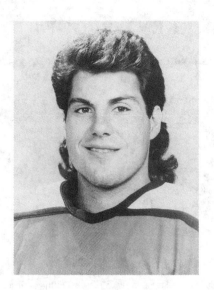

Yrs. of NHL service: 7
Born: Scarborough, Ont., Canada; April 9, 1964
Position: Right wing
Height: 6-0
Weight: 200
Uniform no.: 22
Shoots: Right

Career statistics:

GP	G	A	TP	PIM
489	202	231	433	1581

1990-91 statistics:

GP	G	A	TP	+/-	PIM	PP	SH	GW	GT	S	PCT
70	40	31	71	2	150	8	0	5	1	217	18.4

LAST SEASON

Goal total was second highest of his career, though power-play goal production dropped by seven. Games played marked second consecutive season he played as many as 70 games; he missed the others due to groin pull. Penalty minute total was career low. Led team in shooting percentage.

THE FINESSE GAME

Though not the world's greatest skater, Tocchet has worked to improve himself to a level above the straight-ahead loose cannon he was when he broke into the NHL. Tocchet remains at his best on the straightaways, but has added some agility to his drive and balance for better-rounded foot skills. He has some quickness, and his offensive instincts continue to improve.

In his early years, Tocchet concentrated on forechecking, throwing the big hits and fighting all comers. Now, he has added an open-ice element to his confined-ice eagerness, which gets him into scoring position more regularly.

Tocchet can manufacture goals by recognizing the holes and jumping to them. He works constantly on his slap shot and wrist shots; he can overpower goalies from the slot with his wrist shot and can score from the tops of the circles with the slap shot. Still, his hand skills are not yet such that he can be considered a top-level deker.

THE PHYSICAL GAME

The guy is a bull. He wants the puck and will do anything to get it, from lifting an opponent's stick to flattening him with a body check. Tocchet bangs with the best, fights with the best, can carry defensemen on his back out of the corners. And he follows an old-school honor code; it's all aggressive, it's all as mean as necessary, but it's all clean.

THE INTANGIBLES

Tocchet is a player for the last minute of every period, the player who scores a second-effort goal or a muscle goal 20 seconds before the buzzer to change momentum. He makes the big hit or the big play almost a routine event and gives everything he has to every Flyers activity.

He started out as a hot-head, now is something along the lines of an emotional player who has occasional instances of heart over head. If he can rein himself in even further, channel the energy even better, Tocchet will be elite-plus.

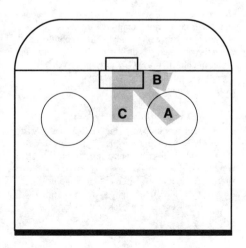

KEN WREGGET

Yrs. of NHL service: 6
Born: Brandon, Man., Canada; March 25, 1964
Position: Goaltender
Height: 6-1
Weight: 180
Uniform no.: 35
Catches: Left

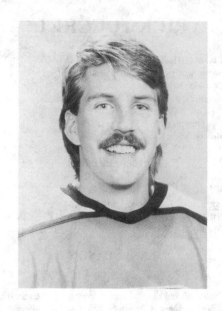

Career statistics:

GP	MINS	GA	SO	GAA	A	PIM
284	15498	1061	2	4.10	15	124

1990-91 statistics:

GP	MINS	GAA	W	L	T	SO	GA	S	SAPCT	PIM
30	1484	3.56	10	14	3	0	88	660	.867	6

LAST SEASON

Games played was three-season low, minutes played was lowest in seven seasons. Fifth consecutive season of at least 10 victories.

THE PHYSICAL GAME

Wregget is not a stylist. He stands up and plays the angles; he does not care if the save is pretty, he just wants to get some part of himself on the puck. Wregget will get caught too deep in the crease on occasion; at other times, he appears off balance—leaning, lurching and awkward. But in the final analysis, he does not give shooters much of the net.

The glove hand may be Wregget's strongest asset when it comes to reflex and reaction saves. Otherwise, he uses anticipation and positioning to put himself in the place where the puck arrives. This is especially true when the puck is behind the net or in the corners. Wregget is alert for passes from those areas, and tries to block them with his stick. But when he cannot reach them, Wregget simply turns his body to face the shot and repels a number of seemingly sure goals.

Wregget has enough range to reach the puck behind the net when it is drilled around the boards, but he does not play it much. Generally, he leaves it for the defensemen and allows them to stop behind the net to size up their options.

THE MENTAL GAME

Wregget is a competitor, but he doesn't always do the best job of reading the play. There are times a defenseman will dive in front of him to block a shot, taking away the "low" corners from the shooter; instead of standing up—if the shot is going to get through, it will have to be high—Wregget at times will drop to his knees and get beaten at the high side he vacated.

Generally, Wregget has a good disposition for goaltending. But he is a bit high-strung and has been known to pressure himself unduly.

THE INTANGIBLES

Wregget is not one of the great athletes of our time. He is not a big fan of the stationary bicycle or other conditioning tools, which may be the reason he seems to wear down a bit late in the game and give up the crushing goal.

PITTSBURGH
PENGUINS

TOM BARRASSO

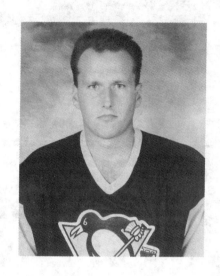

Yrs. of NHL service: 8
Born: Boston, Mass., USA; March 31, 1965
Position: Goaltender
Height: 6-3
Weight: 206
Uniform no.: 35
Catches: right

Career statistics:

GP	MINS	GA	SO	GAA	A	PIM
382	21917	1273	14	3.48	27	279

1990-91 statistics:

GP	MINS	GAA	W	L	T	SO	GA	S	SAPCT	PIM
48	2754	3.59	27	16	3	1	165	1579	.896	40

LAST SEASON

Led NHL goalies in assists and PIM. Fifth in NHL in wins. Victory total was five-season high. GAA was four-season low. Missed two games with finger injury. Missed three games with foot injury. Missed two games with groin injury.

THE PHYSICAL GAME

Barrasso is a big goalie with above average skills, and now that he has a Stanley Cup ring, he has shaken the last criticism that he is not a gamer. He is, as he proved through the playoffs battling back from nagging injuries.

If Barrasso didn't invent the idea of the stickhandling goalie, he took it to the next level. Barrasso can act like a third forward in coming out to get the puck and whipping it off the boards or up the middle of the ice (a dangerous play that costs him once in a while). He uses his stick and long reach to try to knock the puck away from the skater behind the net or to break up passes in front.

He is a very good skater with good balance and quickness. He will challenge shooters, and when he loses his angle he is still big and agile enough to recover and turn to get back into the play.

Barrasso covers a lot of net and when he learns to play his angles better will improve his game even more. He has one weakness in his tendency to go down too fast, but he has such good reflexes, especially with his feet, that it doesn't hinder him as much as it might another goalie.

And woe to any forward who trespasses in Barrasso's crease. He is likely to be welcomed with a blocker in the kisser.

THE MENTAL GAME

Barrasso showed much more consistency last season (even before the playoff run) than he ever had before. He is a battler who fights for the puck until the last chance. His feistiness sometimes gets him into trouble with penalties, but he keeps his cool and doesn't get distracted from his game.

THE INTANGIBLES

Barrasso had a difficult personal season in 1989-90 with the illness of his young daughter. Happily, she is doing well, and the upturn in her condition has reflected in Barrasso's more relaxed emotional state. Barrasso seems to have matured and the change in his attitude has been happily noted by his teammates.

PHIL BOURQUE

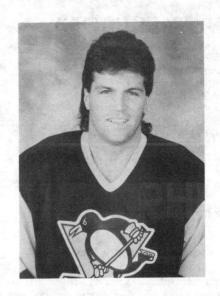

Yrs. of NHL service: 4
Born: Chelmsford, Mass., USA; June 8, 1962
Position: Left wing
Height: 6-1
Weight: 205
Uniform no.: 29
Shoots: left

Career statistics:

GP	G	A	TP	PIM
286	65	73	138	377

1990-91 statistics:

GP	G	A	TP	+/-	PIM	PP	SH	GW	GT	S	PCT
78	20	14	34	+7	106	1	4	0	0	122	16.4

LAST SEASON

Led club in shorthanded goals. Missed one game with wrist injury. Goals and points totals two-season lows.

THE FINESSE GAME

Bourque is a basic up-and-down winger whose skating is his most outstanding skill. Bourque has little agility and can't turn quickly, but he has a lot of strength and puts it to good use as a grinding forward.

Bourque liks to carry the puck and can do so with speed, but isn't too creative with the puck. He can't put any dekes on a defenseman, so he will try to overpower the defenseman to get a step to the outside if he can. Bourque doesn't see the ice well and doesn't use his linemates well.

Bourque's speed makes him a natural in short-handed situations. He is defensively aware and can score breakaway goals. He is a good forechecker because of his speed and tenacity. His hand skills are about average. If they were a little better Bourque would be on the scoreboard more. He is an honest player.

THE PHYSICAL GAME

Bourque likes to take the body and get involved—he is almost invisible on the nights when he doesn't get a few hits in early to get his blood circulating. He is excellent along the boards and in the corners, and is unafraid in traffic. He will fight, and will usually take someone good with him when he does, making it a good trade for the Penguins.

THE INTANGIBLES

Bourque will give a team a steady 20 goals (and he can play defense in a pinch), but his real assets are his attitude, experience and willingness to work and sacrifice for the team.

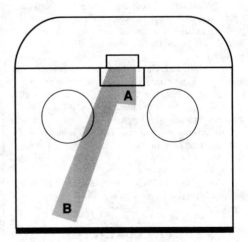

PAUL COFFEY

Yrs. of NHL service: 11
Born: Weston, Ont., Canada; June 1, 1961
Position: Defenseman
Height: 6-0
Weight: 200
Uniform no.: 77
Shoots: left

Career statistics:

GP	G	A	TP	PIM
809	307	738	1045	1204

1990-91 statistics:

GP	G	A	TP	+/-	PIM	PP	SH	GW	GT	S	PCT
76	24	69	93	-18	128	8	0	3	0	240	10.0

LAST SEASON

Second on team in assists and points. Tied for third among NHL defensemen in goals, third in points, fourth in assists. Missed three games with hip injury. All point totals three-season lows. Worst plus-minus on team.

THE FINESSE GAME

Whenever scouts start describing a young offensive defenseman, the prospect is usually painted as some shade of the next Paul Coffey. That alone should indicate in what high regard Coffey's offensive skills are held throughout the hockey world.

Coffey is probably the best-skating defenseman in the NHL, and few forwards come close. He has all the right components—speed, balance, agility and a teeny pivoting radius—and can tie opposing skaters into pretzels when they try to pursue him. He is also just plain fast.

His hand skills and his brain operate at the same high tempo as his skates. He can do an amazing variety of things at a quick pace. Coffey sees the ice very well and seldom are his outlet passes picked off. He has a feather-light touch with a pass.

Coffey can score from anywhere on the ice and with any kind of shot. He has the confidence in his skills to penetrate deep and he commands such respect that he has a lot of room to operate.

Coffey plays indifferent defense most of the season (see Intangibles), relying on positioning and stick checking.

THE PHYSICAL GAME

Coffey is a finesse player who uses his body as a last resort. He will sometimes neglect the front of his net and concentrates instead on trying to intercept a pass or stick-block a shot.

THE INTANGIBLES

Coffey takes a lot of heat for not being an involved player, but you don't get a Stanley Cup ring for each finger by being a perimeter player. Sure, Coffey is a finesse player during the regular season and takes some nights off, but when the money is on the line, Coffey is throwing his body and blocking shots. He played through most of the playoffs with an eye injury and a broken jaw. His courage is unquestioned. Grace under pressure, to steal a phrase.

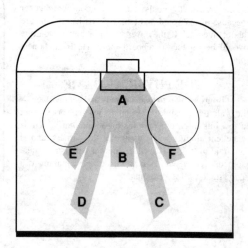

BOB ERREY

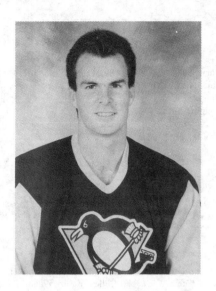

Yrs. of NHL service: 8
Born: Montreal, Que., Canada; September 21, 1964
Position: Left wing
Height: 5-10
Weight: 175
Uniform no.: 12
Shoots: left

Career statistics:

GP	G	A	TP	PIM
440	105	118	223	372

1990-91 statistics:

GP	G	A	TP	+/-	PIM	PP	SH	GW	GT	S	PCT
79	20	22	42	+11	115	0	1	2	0	131	15.2

LAST SEASON

Goal total matched previous season. Assist and point totals two-season highs.

THE FINESSE GAME

Errey is an outstanding support player, and the player he supports best is Mario Lemieux. Errey has the skating ability, especially the speed, to keep up with Lemieux, and he is a hard worker along the boards with his feet and his stick. He keeps the puck alive. Errey is not too quick at making plays, but since he is often on the ice with Lemieux and Kevin Stevens he gets some room, and time, to make his plays. He is an average passer.

Errey's speed sometimes gets him in too deep to do much with the puck, since he doesn't have very quick hands and doesn't shoot well when he's in tight. Errey will score most of his goals by knocking in loose pucks.

He is a very good penalty killer, especially when teamed up front with Mario Lemieux. He is a very good forechecker and plays well positionally.

THE PHYSICAL GAME

Errey is a scooter who plays much bigger than his vital statistics indicate. He flings himself at bigger players (it's a wonder he doesn't get hurt more often with the physical game he plays). He will block shots or do whatever it takes (legal or not) to get the job done.

THE INTANGIBLES

Think it's a no-brainer to play alongside Mario? It's tougher than it looks (where have you gone, Warren Young?) and Errey has complemented him as well as any other forward since Lemieux began his career. Errey is Lemiex's safety valve defensively, and doesn't hurt offensively.

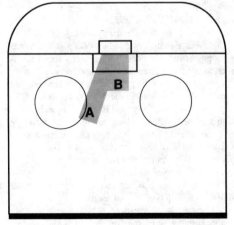

RON FRANCIS

Yrs. of NHL service: 10
Born: Sault Ste. Marie, Ont., Canada; March 1, 1963
Position: Center
Height: 6-2
Weight: 200
Uniform no.: 9
Shoots: left

Career statistics:

GP	G	A	TP	PIM
728	266	566	832	559

1990-91 statistics:

GP	G	A	TP	+/-	PIM	PP	SH	GW	GT	S	PCT
81	23	64	87	-2	72	10	1	7	0	174	13.2

LAST SEASON

Acquired from Hartford with Ulf Samuelsson and Grant Jennings for John Cullen, Zarley Zalapski and Jeff Parker, March 4, 1991. Only NHL player to appear in more than 80 regular-season games last season. Third on club in scoring. Goal total matched career low. Assist and point totals two-season lows.

THE FINESSE GAME

When it comes to combining offense and defense, there are few centers in the league the equal of Francis. He is a good positional player and is smart with and without the puck. Francis has a good head for the game, which is his No. 1 asset.

None of his skills merit headlines. He is is an above average skater because he works at it, but he has a choppy stride. He doesn't have much speed but is good in tight with lateral mobility and balance.

Francis moves the puck pretty well but he is not consistently committed in the aggressive areas of the game. He has good vision and is very calm and patient with the puck when looking for the open man. He probably doesn't shoot often enough. He has a good slap shot and wrist shot—both are hard and accurate—but he is a better playmaker than scorer.

Francis is good on faceoffs and is willing to adapt his role to the needs of the team. He can play in all situations and on both special teams.

Francis has an excellent attitude and leadership qualities (he was captain of the Whalers) and his acquisition was one of the keys to the Penguins' Stanley Cup championship.

THE PHYSICAL GAME

Francis has good size and his strength is O.K. He seems to be willing at times to go to the net and take a hit but he is not consistent with this move. He would be another level of player if he would.

THE INTANGIBLES

Francis was the Whalers during his tenure there. He takes a distinct back seat to Lemieux in Pittsburgh, but with the big man in delicate health, Francis is invaluable as a backup. While Lemieux is in the lineup, watch for Francis to develop into a better and better defensive center. His 100-point seasons are behind him, but Francis should still be able to contribute 30 goals.

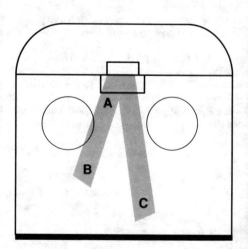

JIRI HRDINA

Yrs. of NHL service: 3
Born: Mlada Boleslav, Czechoslovakia;
January 5, 1958
Position: Center/left wing
Height: 6-0
Weight: 190
Uniform no.: 38
Shoots: left

Career statistics:

GP	G	A	TP	PIM
194	42	72	114	76

1990-91 statistics:

GP	G	A	TP	+/-	PIM	PP	SH	GW	GT	S	PCT
51	6	17	23	-6	17	1	1	0	0	66	9.1

LAST SEASON

Acquired from Calgary for Jim Kyte, December 13, 1990. Missed two games with flu. Missed six games with ankle injury. Games played and all point totals career lows for full season.

THE FINESSE GAME

Age has caught up to Hrdina, but he can still function as a part-timer with good skating and play-making skills. Hrdina prefers passing to shooting, and since most opponents have scouted this trend, defenders don't fall for his fake shot as often as they used to, and anticipate the pass. When Hrdina does shoot, he has an average wrist and snap shot from close range.

The Penguins like to use Hrdina for offensive zone faceoffs, especially on the power play. This not only relieves some of the strain on Mario Lemieux's injured back, but it leaves the big guy free for one-timers off the draw.

His overall game is inconsistent and he is a defensive liability.

THE PHYSICAL GAME

Hrdina does not get involved physically, at least not in the defensive zone. His good balance and foot skills help him in the traffic area offensively, but he is not very aggressive in this area.

THE INTANGIBLES

Hrdina might have been obtained as a baby-sitter for Jaromir Jagr, but he proved himself a key role player on special teams. At 35, he will be little more than a role player again this season.

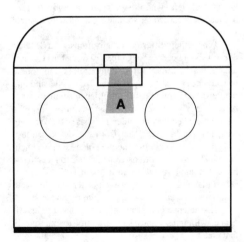

JAROMIR JAGR

Yrs. of NHL service: 1
Born: Kladno, Czechoslovakia; February 15, 1972
Position: Right wing
Height: 6-2
Weight: 200
Uniform no.: 68
Shoots: left

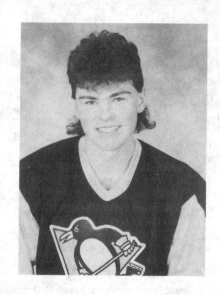

Career statistics:

GP	G	A	TP	PIM
80	27	30	57	42

1990-91 statistics:

GP	G	A	TP	+/-	PIM	PP	SH	GW	GT	S	PCT
80	27	30	57	-4	42	7	0	4	0	136	19.9

LAST SEASON

First NHL season. Third among NHL rookies in goals, fourth in assists and points. Third on club in goals. One of three Penguins to play in all 80 games.

THE FINESSE GAME

Look at Jagr streaking down the ice, and you think you're seeing a negative image of Mario Lemieux. Jagr shoots left, Lemieux shoots right; but given their physical resemblance and similar uniform numbers, the confusion is understandable. Both are mountainous yet graceful skaters whose styles are deceptively lazy because they can cover so much ground with a single stride.

Where they differ is in their offensive style. Jagr doesn't shoot nearly enough for a player of his extraordinary hand skills. But remember that the rookie needed one season to adjust to the NHL style, and that the European habit of being unselfish to a fault may not be as deeply ingrained in Jagr as it is in players who come here when they are older. Jagr has several scoring weapons, but his wrist shot from the slot is scariest.

Jagr likes to control the puck and is an excellent passer. He has good offensive instincts and likes to use his speed and strength to go to the net. He is a good power play man and will get even better as he learns to shoot more, he can shoot well off the fly and at speed.

His defense is a problem, but he has the intelligence, willingness and skating ability to improve in that area.

THE PHYSICAL GAME

In addition to looking like Lemieux, Jagr shares his strength. He can hold a defensive player off and still drive to the net to score. He will work behind the net and along the boards to get the puck, and he will use his body in all zones. He won't fight and he won't be intimidated.

THE INTANGIBLES

Jagr was the youngest player in the NHL last season, which made his successful leap to the majors even more amazing. He clearly has the skills to become a 50-goal scorer in the next season or two, and as he demonstrated with a key overtime goal in the playoffs, can be an impact player because of his combination of skill and size.

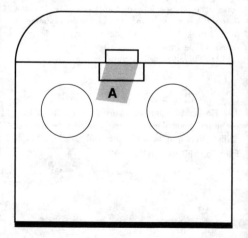

MARIO LEMIEUX

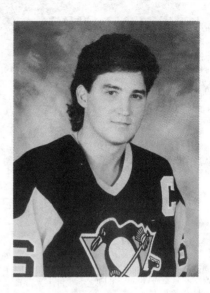

Yrs. of NHL service: 7
Born: Montreal, Que., Canada; October 5, 1965
Position: Center
Height: 6-4
Weight: 210
Uniform no.: 66
Shoots: right

Career statistics:

GP	G	A	TP	PIM
453	364	519	883	454

1990-91 statistics:

GP	G	A	TP	+/-	PIM	PP	SH	GW	GT	S	PCT
26	19	26	45	+8	30	6	1	2	0	89	21.3

LAST SEASON

Missed 50 games following off-season back surgery and subsequent viral infection (vertebrael osteomyelitis) that threatened his career. Missed one game each with groin, foot and eye injuries. His truncated season resulted in career lows in all offensive categories—still, he finished sixth on the team in scoring.

THE FINESSE GAME

Oh, we could write a book. And hey, we are! So let's get to those undisclosed flaws of Mario Lemieux: bad posture. And we hear sometimes he doesn't pick up after himself and steams uncancelled stamps off envelopes.

But seriously... One would really have to pick nits to find anything negative to say about Lemieux. Critics keep trying, but let's dwell on the positive. Lemieux is one of the those rare athletes in the history of sport, not just hockey, who can bend a game to his will.

Lemieux has the hands of a surgeon; even in plays when it looks like his body is too far beyond the puck to make a play, he will use his octopus reach to get the puck and shoot. He can put a lot of moves in a little space. He plays well at a high tempo and is a goalie's nightmare on a breakaway. He can score anywhere from the top of the circles in. He can takes passes on his backhand or forehand. And he is an excellent passer, especially when he sets up behind the net.

Lemieux wants the puck in key situations. He wants it all the time. Lemieux will shoot first and ask questions later and his goals per game average (.804) is the highest in NHL history among players with 200 or more career goals.

Lemieux kills penalties not because of his defensive ability, but because of his breakaway speed and moves. He loves the extra ice.

THE PHYSICAL GAME

Lemieux's strength comes from his size and skating, but he was never much of a hitter and will do even less of it following his back surgery. He is more willing in the offensive zone to go behind the net and into the traffic areas than he is to help out defensively, although he will ride his man off the puck. Lemieux prefers to be unfettered to be able to go on the attack.

He has a reputation for histrionics when he gets hit, but anyone who gets whacked and lassoed as much as Lemieux deserves a break now and then. Lemieux also dishes out his share of cheap stuff, which is more infuriating when it comes from such a big guy.

THE INTANGIBLES

Maybe President Bush doesn't know who he is, but the rest of the sporting world certainly does after Lemieux's playoff MVP performance in leading the Penguins to their first Stanley Cup. The only question about Lemieux was whether he had the heart and desire to be a winner. Question answered. If he can stay healthy, he will continue to cement his niche among the NHL's legends.

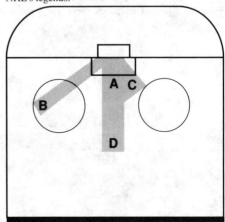

TROY LONEY

Yrs. of NHL service: 6
Born: Bow Island, Alta., Canada; September 21, 1963
Position: Left wing
Height: 6-3
Weight: 205 Unifrom no.: 24
Shoots: left

Career statistics:

GP	G	A	TP	PIM
374	54	68	122	754

1990-91 statistics:

GP	G	A	TP	+/-	PIM	PP	SH	GW	GT	S	PCT
44	7	9	16	+10	85	0	0	2	0	51	13.7

LAST SEASON

Missed 28 games rehabilitating his right knee after off-season surgery. Games played and point totals four-season low. Goal total three-season low.

THE FINESSE GAME

There are few surprises to Loney's game. What he brings to the ice is hard work and a typical grinding game along the boards.

He is not a great skater, at least not laterally. He can build up a fairly good head of steam once he starts churning, but he can't turn well and can be out-manuevered. He can't do much with the puck when he is heading straight-on to a defender.

Loney doesn't have a very good shot, and gets his 10-15 goals from a 10-15 foot radius of the net. His knee injury has made him even less mobile.

He has been put into the role of a checking forward and works hard defensively, although he doesn't have the greatest hockey sense.

THE PHYSICAL GAME

Loney has very good size and uses it at every opportunity. His lack of skating agility hurts him since he can't always catch up to people to hurt them, but he will sacrifice himself and block shots. He is not an especially mean player.

THE INTANGIBLES

Loney is definitely on the bubble, although the Penguins need his size and presence up front for now. His biggest assets are his attitude and reputation as a team man.

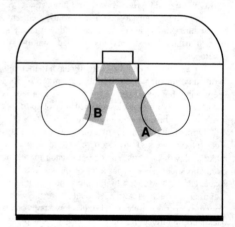

JOE MULLEN

Yrs. of NHL service: 10
Born: New York City, N.Y., USA; February 26, 1957
Position: Right wing
Height: 5-9
Weight: 180
Uniform no.: 7
Shoots: right

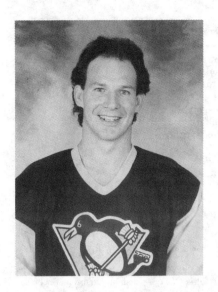

Career statistics:

GP	G	A	TP	PIM
693	358	404	762	146

1990-91 statistics:

GP	G	A	TP	+/-	PIM	PP	SH	GW	GT	S	PCT
47	17	22	39	+9	6	8	0	2	0	85	20.0

LAST SEASON

Games played and all point totals were eight-season lows. Missed 32 games with a neck injury; underwent surgery to repair a herniated disk.

THE FINESSE GAME

At almost every level where a coach has eyed Mullen dubiously, Mullen has opened those eyes with his skills and desire.

Mullen sees the ice exceptionally well. He anticipates the action well and has the vision to play well in tight quarters, which is where he likes to go. Mulllen likes to shoot and has a very strong wrist shot (also a bullet slapper from the circle), but he is unselfish and will make the proper pass.

His skating helps him in (and out of) tight situations. Although Mullen will battle anyone for the puck, he is more effective when he is on the move, jumping into and out of holes, with or without the puck. He is always in motion. He has excellent shot selection, which is reflected in his shooting percentage.

Mullen is a power play specialist, adept at working the puck down low.

THE PHYSICAL GAME

Mullen is 5-foot-9 and plays 6-foot-5. He is fearless in heavy going, and even with his neck brace on following his surgery was plunging into the slot and the corners. He will hit anyone in pursuit of the puck and since he is so keen with the puck once he gets it, he makes for a very tough cornerman. He will get outmuscled, but he won't get outworked.

THE INTANGIBLES

Mullen's health is a question mark because of the injury he suffered midway through the season. He came back big in the playoffs, but could be vulnerable again over the long haul. Don't count this tough New York City kid (at 34) out, however. He is a character player.

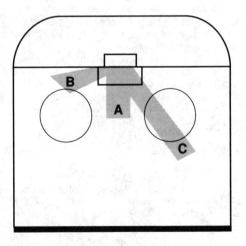

LARRY MURPHY

Yrs. of NHL service: 11
Born: Scarborough, Ont., Canada; March 8, 1961
Position: Defenseman
Height: 6-1
Weight: 210
Uniform no.: 55
Shoots: right

Career statistics:

GP	G	A	TP	PIM
860	160	512	672	711

1990-91 statistics:

GP	G	A	TP	+/-	PIM	PP	SH	GW	GT	S	PCT
75	9	34	43	-6	68	3	0	2	0	188	4.8

LAST SEASON

Acquired from Minnesota with Peter Taglianetti for Chris Dahlquist and Jim Johnson, December 11, 1990. Goal total was three-season low. Assist and point totals were seven-season lows. Missed five games with foot injury.

THE FINESSE GAME

Murphy is a mobile, rushing defenseman whose skills are most evident from the red line in—into the offensive zone, not his own. He is a very good skater. He can control the tempo with his change of pace skating and is quite agile and balanced.

Murphy has too much confidence in his skating, though, and will make ill-timed pinches into the offensive zone and get trapped. Since he tries to play the puck instead of the body, he frequently gives up odd-man rushes against his partners.

He has very good offensive skills. Murphy handles the puck well and likes to rush, but he can also pass well. He has a good shot from the point and will cheat down into the circle on the power play.

Murphy can play defensive hockey, he just has to be constantly reminded to do so because it doesn't come naturally to him. He is not an overly intelligent player.

THE PHYSICAL GAME

Murphy has good size but plays smaller than he is. He doesn't hit nearly as well as he should for a skater of his size and skating ability. Murphy is not very strong or determined in front of his own net. He will take out players, but not with authority.

THE INTANGIBLES

Joining a team with Paul Coffey probably took some of the pressure off Murphy, who knew he wouldn't be relied upon as the No. 1 scoring defenseman, but when Coffey suffered a rash of serious injuries in the playoffs, Murphy stepped in and ended up as the club's fourth-leading playoff scorer (and he tied for the club playoff lead in plus-minus).

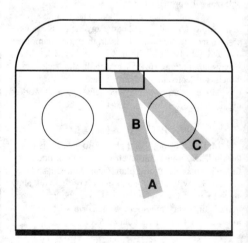

FRANK PIETRANGELO

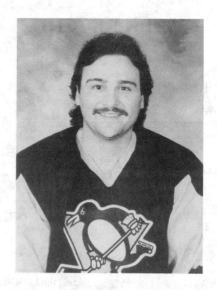

Yrs. of NHL service: 4
Born: Niagara Falls, Ont., Canada;
December 17, 1964
Position: Goaltender
Height: 5-10
Weight: 180
Uniform no.: 40
Catches: left

Career statistics:

GP	MINS	GA	SO	GAA	A	PIM
82	4253	288	1	4.06	1	28

1990-91 statistics:

GP	MINS	GAA	W	L	T	SO	GA	S	SAPCT	PIM
25	1311	3.94	10	11	1	0	86	714	.880	24

LAST SEASON

Games, minutes played and win totals were career highs. GAA was career low.

THE PHYSICAL GAME

Pietrangelo lives and dies by his reflexes. His glove hand is so quick that he appears to snatch pucks out of the air that are already past him, like a magician producing a silver dollar from behind his ear.

Because of his small size, Pietrangelo must work at playing his angles. When he's playing well, he is standing up and challenging shooters. When he's not, he starts backing into his net and flopping.

Pietrangelo does play the puck well. He is an average skater and wisely avoids roaming out of his net unless he has to.

THE MENTAL GAME

Pietrangelo is capable of sitting on the bench for a month or more, then getting into a game on a moment's notice and performing to the best of his ability. Pietrangelo remains focused and his confidence was bolstered by being in the nets for some of the Penguins' biggest games last season: when they clinched the division title with a win over Detroit and in games 6 and 7 against New Jersey in the first round of the Stanley Cup playoffs. He can handle the pressure.

Although he wants to play more often, Pietrangelo keeps the best interests of the team at heart and doesn't complain. He is a good team man.

THE INTANGIBLES

Concerned he wasn't going to get enough playing time, Pietrangelo had to be talked out of playing last season in Italy. Good thing for the Penguins he changed his mind, because he made some key appearances in the playoffs when Tom Barrasso was injured. Pietrangelo got a chance to prove his worth, but the bottom line he is a solid No. 2 goalie—maybe one of the best in that thankless role.

MARK RECCHI

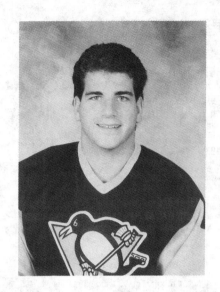

Yrs. of NHL service: 2
Born: Kamloops, B.C., Canada; February 1, 1968
Position: Right wing
Height: 5-9
Weight: 185
Uniform no.: 8
Shoots: left

Career statistics:

GP	G	A	TP	PIM
167	71	111	182	92

1990-91 statistics:

GP	G	A	TP	+/-	PIM	PP	SH	GW	GT	S	PCT
78	40	73	113	0	48	12	0	9	0	184	21.7

LAST SEASON

Tied for club lead in goals. Led club in assists, points and game-winning goals. Tied for third in NHL in game-winning goals. Tied for fourth in NHL in assists. All point totals career highs. Fifth in league in shooting percentage. Missed one game with shoulder injury. Missed one game with knee injury.

THE FINESSE GAME

Recchi thinks like a choreographer, which is what makes him such a first-rate playmaker. He opens up ice by drawing defenders to him, then spots the openings and directs his linemates to them. He has the footwork to get himself into the holes. Recchi has great agility and quickness, and is able to shift in mid-stride to another direction entirely, leaving his checker baffled. He has excellent hockey sense and vision. He is good under pressure with the puck and doesn't seem to notice if the game is in the first or last five seconds—he works regardless.

Recchi's skating style is graceless. He has an awkward, short stride, but he gets his legs going like pistons. Sometimes he gets going too fast and wipes out, losing his edges. He will build up some speed and get a good shot off while in motion. His best weapon is a strong wrist shot from the circle. Recchi is not very big, but he steps into his shot and puts everything he has into it. He is a very accurate shooter, picks his best spots and passes when a teammate has the better percentage play. Recchi pursues the puck and maintains the pursuit even if he loses control.

Recchi is a strong forechecker who anticipates well. He plays well positionally on defense and always comes back for the puck.

THE PHYSICAL GAME

Recchi is a spunky player, with a fireplug build, who plays pinball hockey in the corners. He has a huge heart and works hard every night. He will get outmuscled by bigger players, because he does not match up physically.

THE INTANGIBLES

Recchi is an intense competitor and a gamer, as he showed in the playoffs. Like Kevin Stevens, Recchi was shopping for a new contract during the off-season. The Penguins cannot afford to lose him. He has proven his stellar rookie season was no fluke.

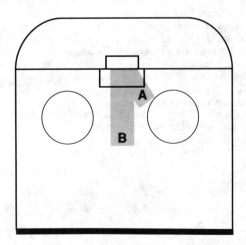

GORDIE ROBERTS

Yrs. of NHL service: 12
Born: Detroit, Mich., USA; October 2, 1957
Position: Defenseman
Height: 6-1
Weight: 195
Uniform no.: 28
Shoots: left

Career statistics:

GP	G	A	TP	PIM
900	53	319	372	1350

1990-91 statistics:

GP	G	A	TP	+/-	PIM	PP	SH	GW	GT	S	PCT
64	3	13	16	+17	78	0	0	0	0	24	12.5

LAST SEASON

Acquired from St. Louis for future considerations, October 27, 1990. Tied for best plus-minus on team. Games played career low. Point total four-year low. Missed two games with foot injury.

THE FINESSE GAME

Roberts survives in the NHL largely on his experience and his conservative game. He can't do that much skills-wise, so he doesn't try to put himself in precarious situations.

Roberts won't give you points, but he will give reliable positional play and a cool demeanor under pressure. Since he doesn't lug the puck and isn't a great passer, he works well with the Penguins forwards, most of whom come back for the puck. He is able to spring them for quick outlets and make the transition to offense, but won't be leading any rushes. Despite his lack of offensive involvement, Roberts was a plus 13 for the Penguins in the playoffs.

He is a good skater, with agility and good balance.

THE PHYSICAL GAME

Roberts plays a little taller and a little heavier than his stature. He is a willing if not punishing checker, very sturdy, and he moves men out from in front of the net. Since he can turn the play so quickly, he doesn't allow the opposition sustained pressure in the zone.

THE INTANGIBLES

Roberts was an unsung member of a glittering defense corps, and played a steady stay-at-home role. He has a strong work ethic and is a valuable fifth or sixth defenseman for the Pens.

ULF SAMUELSSON

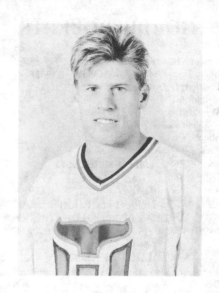

Yrs. of NHL service: 7
Born: Fagersta, Sweden; March 26, 1964
Position: Defenseman
Height: 6-1
Weight: 195
Uniform no.: 5
Shoots: left

Career statistics:

GP	G	A	TP	PIM
477	32	148	180	1147

1990-91 statistics:

GP	G	A	TP	+/-	PIM	PP	SH	GW	GT	S	PCT
76	4	22	26	+17	211	0	0	0	0	125	3.2

LAST SEASON

Acquired from Hartford with Ron Francis and Grant Jennings for John Cullen, Jeff Parker and Zarley Zalapski, March 4, 1991. Tied for best plus-minus on club. Led team in PIM, a career high. Games played three-season high. Point total two-season high.

THE FINESSE GAME

Samuelsson is a very good skater—an excellent one, really, for his size. In every phase, speed and acceleration, balance and quickness, Samuelsson's skating is world class. He reads plays well (better defensively than offensively) and challenges skaters coming at him. He will also try to pinch, often unwisely.

Samuelsson wants to do more offensively and tries too hard to jump into the plays to force something to happen. He gets into trouble and gets out of position. He also overhandles the puck. His offensive ability is limited and though he has been tried on the power play because of his good shot, he is not very effective there.

Samuelsson lacks fundamental concentration. He has trouble staying focused on what he should be doing and, as a result, he'll start to run too much and overload one side. He gets overanxious and hasn't developed the patience you like to see in a defenseman, especially when he doesn't have the puck.

He is a good penalty killer.

THE PHYSICAL GAME

As nasty as he wants to be. Samuelsson so tormented Boston forward Cam Neely (no wallflower himself) during the Stanley Cup semifinal that Neely refused to shake Samuelsson's proffered hand at the end of the series. His teammates love him, his opponents hate him. He has learned to play more disciplined but he is not happy unless he is antagonizing the other team's skill players.

Samuelsson is a big hitter (thanks to his skating) and will go after anyone. He doesn't fight, but he will use his sticks and elbows to intimidate. He blocks shots well.

THE INTANGIBLES

Samuelsson is a very willing player who loves the game. He remains a cut below the NHL's elite defensemen because of the mental aspect. Samuelsson can play a very intense 20 minutes, then play five where it looks like his brain has left the building. Until he can sustain his play, he will remain a good defenseman, but not a great one.

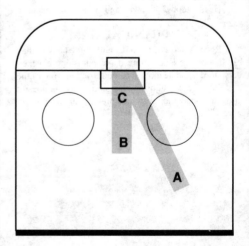

PAUL STANTON

Yrs. of NHL service: 1
Born: Boston, Mass., USA; June 22, 1967
Position: Defenseman
Height: 6-0
Weight: 190
Uniform no.: 22
Shoots: right

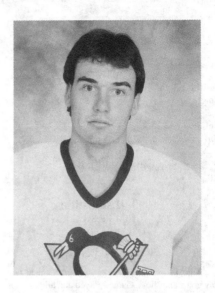

Career statistics:

GP	G	A	TP	PIM
75	5	18	23	40

1990-91 statistics:

GP	G	A	TP	+/-	PIM	PP	SH	GW	GT	S	PCT
75	5	18	23	+11	40	1	0	1	0	72	6.9

LAST SEASON

First NHL season.

THE FINESSE GAME

Stanton's game is founded on his skating. He is not breakaway fast, but he is very spry and has good foot speed. This helps him avoid some hits along the boards, which he is somewhat allergic to.

Stanton is not a very creative playmaker, but he is a good passer and likes to go for the home run play. He will get involved in the play offensively. He has a good point shot and reads offensive situations well. Stanton plays well positionally.

THE PHYSICAL GAME

A college product (University of Wisconsin), Stanton is a finesse player with no real taste for physical play. He will go along the boards and into the corners for the puck, but his objective is to move the puck quickly and then get the hell out of the way. Sometimes in his eagenress to get rid of the puck, he will make a bad pass through the middle of the zone instead of the safe play up the wall.

THE INTANGIBLES

Stanton came from nowhere to earn a regular spot on the Penguins defense. He has the finesse skills to play at the NHL level; now he has to learn to play to his size to lift his game another level.

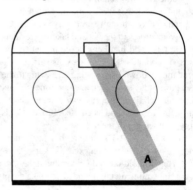

KEVIN STEVENS

Yrs. of NHL service: 3
Born: Brockton, Mass., USA; April 15, 1965
Position: Right wing
Height: 6-3
Weight: 220
Uniform no.: 25
Shoots: left

Career statistics:

GP	G	A	TP	PIM
196	86	92	178	331

1990-91 statistics:

GP	G	A	TP	+/-	PIM	PP	SH	GW	GT	S	PCT
80	40	46	86	-1	133	18	0	6	2	253	15.8

LAST SEASON

Tied for team lead in goals. Led team in power play goals and shots. Games played and all point totals career highs. One of three Penguins to play in all 80 games.

THE FINESSE GAME

Instead of the skating Penguin crest, Stevens could sport a cowcatcher. This man is a train, a relentless locomotive who seldom gets derailed and leaves blood on the tracks. Stevens combines intensity, power and speed to play a brutally productive game.

Stevens drives to the net and takes up residence in front. He has good hand-eye coordination for deflections and rebounds. Stevens can also drive wide (a favored move) down his off-wing and swing to the net. He is a power play specialist, and one-times the puck as well as any NHLer. Stevens has a fantastic scoring touch with a quick and accurate release. He is the prototypical winger of the 90s.

His skating is NHL calibre but he is not very quick. Stevens is very strong on his skates, and very patient. He will hold on to the puck and delay the pass until the right moment, taking the hit to make the play if he has to.

He is an intelligent player and needs only to work on the defensive aspects of his game (which have improved) to be a complete player.

THE PHYSICAL GAME

Stevens loves to hit. He can throw some real bell-ringers too, and will have to be one of the skaters careful about the crackdown on dangerous hits near the boards. He will fight when provoked, but has learned that he can be tough by responding with a goal instead of wasting time in the penalty box. He has an imposing physical presence.

THE INTANGIBLES

Stevens played out his option last season and with each successive and successful shift, we could hear the cash register ringing. He is still maturing and if he can maintain the attitude and positive habits he has shown in the past two seasons, he will be mentioned in the same sentence with Cam Neely, the ultimate power forward. Neely has shown his ability over the seasons. Now it's up to Stevens to match that consistency.

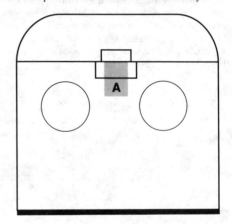

PETER TAGLIANETTI

Yrs. of NHL service: 4
Born: Framingham, Mass., USA; August 15, 1963
Position: Defenseman
Height: 6-2
Weight: 195
Uniform no.: 32
Shoots: left

Career statistics:

GP	G	A	TP	PIM
246	13	45	58	697

1990-91 statistics:

GP	G	A	TP	+/-	PIM	PP	SH	GW	GT	S	PCT
39	3	8	11	+16	93	0	0	0	0	25	12.0

LAST SEASON

Acquired from Minnesota with Larry Murphy for Chris Dahlquist and Jim Johnson, December 11, 1990. Missed one game each with neck and foot injuries. Missed nine games with a collapsed lung. Games played four-season low.

THE FINESSE GAME

Taglianetti is a stay-at-home defenseman who gets to bring in the mail and feed the cat while his partner Paul Coffey goes wandering all over creation. And last season Taglianetti was good in that role. Reliable and responsible.

Taglianetti is not a finesse player. There may be only one player on the Penguins less dangerous than Taglianetti on a breakaway—Tom Barrasso, and even that is a close call. Taglianetti will get into the play at the blue line although he will not penetrate the zone. He has a good low slap shot, which is how he gets his handful of goals every season.

Taglianetti is an average skater and doesn't have very good balance. He works well on the penalty killing unit by holding his position and forcing the attacker wide.

THE PHYSICAL GAME

Taglianetti is a pretty tough customer who plays a solid, physical game. Again, being paired with a finesse defenseman means he must do more than his share of banging, and Taglianetti is willing and able. He can be knocked off the puck, but he has good size and is very aggressive.

THE INTANGIBLES

Taglianetti was a key acquisition for the Penguins, giving them a defensively sound blueliner. He has a good work ethic and is a good team man. He plays beyond his skill level.

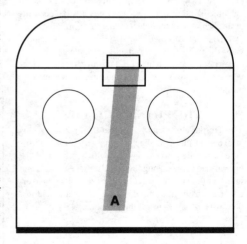

BRYAN TROTTIER

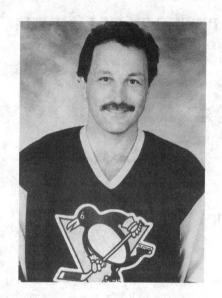

Yrs. of NHL service: 16
Born: Val Marie, Sask., Canada; July 17, 1956
Position: Center
Height: 5-11
Weight: 195
Uniform no.: 19
Shoots: left

Career statistics:

GP	G	A	TP	PIM
1175	509	872	1381	822

1990-91 statistics:

GP	G	A	TP	+/-	PIM	PP	SH	GW	GT	S	PCT
52	9	19	28	+5	24	0	1	0	0	68	13.2

LAST SEASON

Signed as free agent after his contract was bought out by New York Islanders. Missed 13 games with back injury. Missed 13 games with groin injury. Games played and goal totals career lows.

THE FINESSE GAME

Trottier a role player? Who would have believed it back in the early 80s when Trottier was helping lead the Islanders to four consecutive Cups. Now he has a fifth, after playing a minor but key role in the championship.

Trottier still can't break a pane of glass with his shot, yet he scored at least one critical playoff goal. All of his skills are intact, especially his quickness on faceoffs. Trottier's greatest asset has always been his desire, which was rekindled by the move to Pittsburgh.

His biggest asset is that he reads the situation, knows what he can and cannot contribute and has the expertise to know when to do it during the game. He is very good at protecting a lead and turns it on when he's needed.

THE PHYSICAL GAME

Trottier always played bigger than his size and is in excellent physical shape. He is very strong on his skates, unbelievably so, and he will win most of the one-on-one battles along the boards, in the corners and in front of the net. He has always been a bit cantankerous, and has been accused of dangerous hits. He just does what he has to to get the job done.

THE INTANGIBLES

Leaving the Islanders added at least a season, maybe two, to Trottier's career. He left the baggage of the four Stanley Cup seasons behind, where the memories of what he could do in his prime were still fresh. With Pittsburgh, he could fall into a more supportive role, and was appreciated for what he had done without being asked to do it again. It's too bad the Islanders bungled his departure so badly, because a graceful goodbye would have made the move one of the best things to happen to this future Hall of Famer.

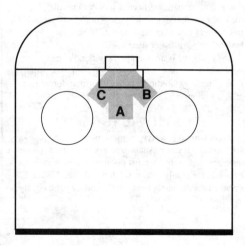

SCOTT YOUNG

Yrs. of NHL service: 3
Born: Clinton, Mass., USA; October 1, 1967
Position: Right wing/defense
Height: 6-0
Weight: 190
Uniform no.: 34
Shoots: right

Career statistics:

GP	G	A	TP	PIM
240	60	105	165	117

1990-91 statistics:

GP	G	A	TP	+/-	PIM	PP	SH	GW	GT	S	PCT
77	17	25	42	-6	41	6	2	5	0	210	8.1

LAST SEASON

Acquired from Hartford from Rob Brown, December 21, 1990. All point totals career lows for full season.

THE FINESSE GAME

Young is very good at getting the puck and he knows what to do with it when he does. He will score more points than the average defensive winger because of his superior skating and skills. He can one-time the puck, he can shoot on the fly or he can fend off a checker and bang a loose puck in from close range. Young is a better playmaker than shooter, and can fire or feather a pass.

Young is a very fast skater and will frequently outrace defensemen to the puck to negate icings. His is also a mobile and balanced skater, with good strength on his feet and quickness and lateral movement.

Young reads plays in all zones equally well, and has good anticipation. He plays well at a high tempo, and pays strict attention to his checking duties. His speed helps him as a forechecker and allows allows him to recover defensively.

THE PHYSICAL GAME

Young is not a very physical player. He will do what he has to do along the boards and in front of the net and is fairly strong—strong enough to win most of the one-on-one battles with all but the behemoths of the NHL. Since his hands skills are so developed, he can come away with the puck more often than not. He does not hit as well as he should for his size and skating ability.

THE INTANGIBLES

With the rosters being cut from 18 to 17 skaters, Young will be one of those rare valuable players who can play forward and defense almost equally well. He is hard-working and has a good attitude.

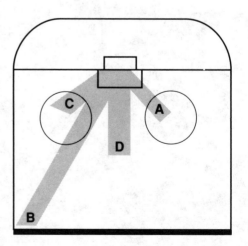

QUEBEC NORDIQUES

SHAWN ANDERSON

Yrs. of NHL service: 3
Born: Montreal, Que., Canada; February 7, 1968
Position: Defenseman
Height: 6-1
Weight: 200
Uniform no.: 37
Shoots: left

Career statistics:

GP	G	A	TP	PIM
134	9	36	45	87

1990-91 statistics:

GP	G	A	TP	+/-	PIM	PP	SH	GW	GT	S	PCT
31	3	10	13	+2	21	2	0	0	0	44	6.8

LAST SEASON

Games played and all point totals two-season highs.

THE FINESSE GAME

Anderson has all the right offensive instincts. He will jump into the play smartly and is a good enough skater in get involved that way. He reads situations intelligently when on the attack, but doesn't grasp the play well when it is coming back towards him.

His skating suits him better when he plays up front than back on defense. He has good speed and fairly good agility, but his turns are suspect and he is a below average skater for a defenseman.

Anderson will challenge at the blue line and try to meet the attacker, but he is more likely to make a stick check than take the body. He doesn't rush with the puck, but makes good outlet passes and sees the breaking play fairly well. He will panic when pressed, since he lacks confidence in his defensive-zone play. He also doesn't get as much time on the power play as he should because of his lack of confidence.

THE PHYSICAL GAME

Physical play is not Anderson's forte. He is a converted forward whose game is a finesse one. He is willing to take the body, but it is apparent that this part of the game does not come naturally to him. Anderson will seldom be on the ice in key defensive situations. With his size, he could have a more physical presence.

THE INTANGIBLES

Anderson is an offensive defenseman whose skills are not overwhleming enough to earn him an everyday role with a team. With the arrival of Mikhail Tatarinov, Anderson's role with the Nordiques will be even more diminished.

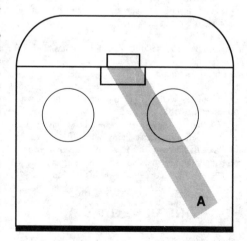

JACQUES CLOUTIER

Yrs. of NHL service: 7
Born: Noranda, Que., Canada; January 3, 1960
Position: Goaltender
Height: 5-7
Weight: 165
Uniform no.: 32
Catches: left

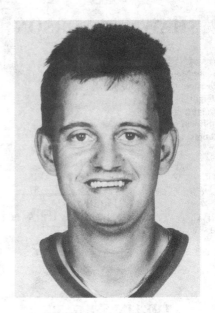

Career statistics:

GP	MINS	GA	SO	GAA	A	PIM
212	10851	656	3	3.63	7	30

1990-91 statistics:

GP	MINS	GAA	W	L	T	SO	GA	S	SAPCT	PIM
25	1231	4.14	5	11	2	0	85	701	.879	6

LAST SEASON

Acquired from Chicago for Tony McKegney, January 29, 1991. Games played, minutes played and win totals three-season lows.

THE PHYSICAL GAME

Cloutier had to make a big adjustment in his game after moving from the defense-conscious Blackhawks to the defense-be-damned Nordiques. In the first place, he faces many more shots. And to minimize their damage, he feels compelled to stickhandle more to help out his defense. Since this is not Cloutier's forte, he will get into trouble when he tries to do too much of the work. He is good at stopping the puck, but not great at moving it.

Cloutier is a small reflex goalie who has big first-save capacity but lacks the skating balance to recover well for the rebounds. Cloutier's weaknesses are high on his stick side and the five-hole because he does not set his angles well all the time and has his feet in motion at the wrong moment.

Cloutier is at his best when he's playing the angles. Goalies for weak teams have difficulty doing this, because they are worried not only about their own job but also about what the rest of the team is going to do. Cloutier must concentrate on his own task or his game will fall to pieces.

THE MENTAL GAME

Cloutier has had a reputation in the past for not being mentally tough. The Nordiques will test all of his inner strength, but he seems to be aware of the team's struggles and knows there are going to be a lot of long nights.

THE INTANGIBLES

Cloutier impressed his new teammates with his positive attitude and work ethic. He will work with all of the Nordiques young players, not just the goalies, and is a good influence. He is unselfish and understands his role as the No. 2 goalie but wants his ice time and will be ready when called upon.

STEVEN FINN

Yrs. of NHL service: 5
Born: Laval, Que., Canada; August 20, 1966
Position: Defenseman
Height: 6-0
Weight: 198
Uniform no.: 29
Shoots: left

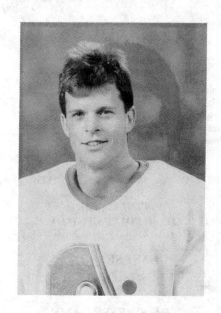

Career statistics:

GP	G	A	TP	PIM
340	16	41	57	937

1990-91 statistics:

GP	G	A	TP	+/-	PIM	PP	SH	GW	GT	S	PCT
71	6	13	19	-26	228	0	0	0	1	91	6.6

LAST SEASON

Tied for worst plus-minus on club. Led team in PIM. All point totals career highs. PIM two-season high.

THE FINESSE GAME

Because Finn has such an aggressive reputation and because he has toiled for an obscure team for several seasons, his finesse skills are often overlooked. He is above average in several categories and he makes the best of his natural gifts with his effort.

Finn doesn't have much lateral movement and can be beaten one-on-one in open ice. To counteract this, he concentrates on playing positionally and angling the attacker towards the boards, where he will get the edge with his strength. He plays a very conservative defensive game, to suit his skill level.

Finn has a low, accurate slap shot without a lot of zip on it. He doesn't get involved too much offensively (last season was his most productive). He lacks the hand skills to get very creative and doesn't rush well with the puck. With the Nordiques, he is playing with several forwards who are very eager to get their sticks on the puck and go, so he usually starts breakouts with a quick pass. Again, this is a case of being smart enough to realize what he can and cannot do.

THE PHYSICAL GAME

Finn is aggressive, hardnosed and doesn't like to see his teammates getting pushed around. He will initiate fights only when he thinks the other team is taking too many liberties, even though he is not one of the NHL's better fighters. He will try and go with anyone. He will take the body but doesn't make big hits. He is very good along the boards. Finn will overcommit at times.

He will also block shots.

THE INTANGIBLES

Finn is a hard-working defenseman who stretched his offensive talents just a little farther last season. We'd like to see him push the envelope just a little farther, but with the dearth of defensive defensemen on the Nordiques, Finn will probably concentrate on his duties in his own zone. He is a leader on the ice.

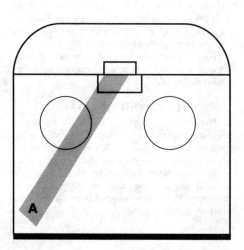

BRYAN FOGARTY

Yrs. of NHL service: 2
Born: Brantford, Ont., Canada; June 11, 1969
Position: Defenseman
Height: 6-2
Weight: 198
Uniform no.: 43
Shoots: left

Career statistics:

GP	G	A	TP	PIM
90	13	32	45	55

1990-91 statistics:

GP	G	A	TP	+/-	PIM	PP	SH	GW	GT	S	PCT
45	9	22	31	-11	24	3	0	2	0	107	8.4

LAST SEASON

Underwent treatment for alcohol abuse during the season.

THE FINESSE GAME

Fogarty is easily the most gifted defenseman on the Nordiques and has the talent to become one of the NHL's better defensemen if he can overcome his off-ice woes. Skating gives Fogarty his edge over most NHL players. He skates smoothly, forward or back, with solid balance and mobility. He accelerates well and loves to rush with the puck.

Fogarty has great patience and anticipation with the puck. Since he is equally comfortable carrying it or passing, opponents are not sure what he is going to do and he disguises his intentions well. Fogarty has very good hands and plays a polished and unselfish game.

His shot is not overpowering. He keeps it low and on target, which makes him a good point man on the power play. He also quarterbacks well with his good vision and passing. He will venture in deep and has a good shot from the top of the circles.

Fogarty's defensive play needs work, but he is willing to learn and he is able to overcome his errors with his skating.

THE PHYSICAL GAME

Fogarty is not overly tough although he has decent size. Rather than make a big hit, he will try to tie up his opponents along the boards. He shies away from the corners. Fogarty stick checks well and is able to make a transition to the attack very quickly. He is adjusting to positional play and when he does will make a very good finesse defenseman since he has shown the ability to play an intelligent game.

THE INTANGIBLES

Fogarty has to be wished all the best in his battle with alcoholism, not only for his personal life but for the kind of niche he will be able to carve himself in the NHL. Success can be a scary thing. He is in a difficult situation and needs the courage to face it.

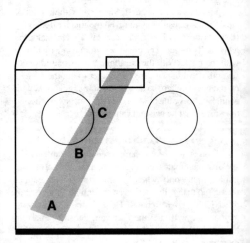

ALEXEI GUSAROV

Yrs. of NHL service: 1
Born: Leningrad, USSR; July 8, 1964
Position: Defenseman
Height: 6-2
Weight: 170
Uniform no.: 5
Shoots: left

1990-91 statistics:

GP	G	A	TP	+/-	PIM	PP	SH	GW	GT	S	PCT
36	3	9	12	-4	12	1	0	0	0	36	8.3

LAST SEASON

First NHL season.

THE FINESSE GAME

Gusarov has very good offensive skills, but in his first half-season in the NHL seemed to sit back and take everything in rather than take an active role in his team's attack. He will follow the offensive flow but won't lead, although he has the goods to do so.

He is a very good skater with good hand skills. He sees the ice well offensively and doesn't like to hang on to the puck too long. Sometimes he gets rid of it too quickly and makes those goalmouth passes that are a part of the Soviet system but anathema to North Americans.

Gusarov has so far been a perimeter player whose involvement is very limited. He has the capability to be more of a force and may be as he becomes more acclimated to the North American game.

THE PHYSICAL GAME

Gusarov is tall but lean and plays a strictly finesse game. Rather than play the body, he tries to reach around a skater (and Gusarov has a loo-o-ong reach) to flick at the puck with his stick. He has strong hands and wrists and can control the puck one-handed. He will position himself well defensively. On the down side, Gusarov doesn't work nearly as hard as he should in the defensive zone. Desire is always a question mark with the Soviet players and Gusarov has to answer that question.

THE INTANGIBLES

Gusarov was the only Soviet on the team last season and spoke little English. He will feel more at ease with fellow Soviets Valeri Kamensky and Mikhail Tatarinov, who are expected to join the Nordiques this season. He has shown his teammates a very easy going attitude, which has helped his acceptance by North American players.

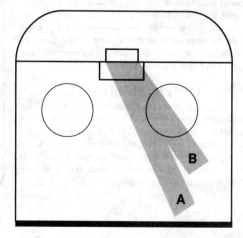

MIKE HOUGH

Yrs. of NHL service: 4
Born: Montreal, Que., Canada; February 6, 1963
Position: Right wing
Height: 6-1
Weight: 190
Uniform no.: 18
Shoots: left

Career statistics:

GP	G	A	TP	PIM
225	44	53	97	315

1990-91 statistics:

GP	G	A	TP	+/-	PIM	PP	SH	GW	GT	S	PCT
63	13	20	33	-7	111	1	1	1	0	106	12.3

LAST SEASON

Games played, assist and point totals were career highs. Goal total matched last season's career high.

THE FINESSE GAME

There is little finesse to Hough's game, yet he is at his best with finesse players like Joe Sakic and Mats Sundin as his linemates because he will do his best to get them the puck. He also has enough defensive sensibility to play with the more gung-ho offensive players and be their safety valve.

Hough will get his 10-15 goals a season by buzzing around the net. He gets his assists by his hard work on the boards. He is not a very creative player or a good passer and he doesn't move it especially quickly, but he seems to get the job done.

Hough is not a very fast skater either, but he plays a pretty smart game so his weakness there is not as glaring at it might be in some other players. He has good quickness in close quarters.

THE PHYSICAL GAME

Hough doesn't shy away from contact and his skating strength added to his good size makes him a solid hitter. He will go to the wall or the corners against bigger skaters and often come away with the puck. He plays a smart defensive game—compare his plus-minus to the rest of the team's. Considering the ice time Hough gets, it's an achievement.

THE INTANGIBLES

Hough is a consistent, hard worker who has been up and down to the minors in his past and now knows what it takes to stick in the NHL. He is the kind of forward coaches are always trying to replace, but they end up turning back to Hough because of his consistency and commitment.

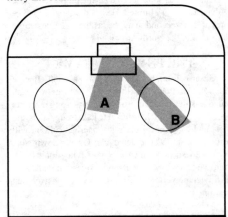

CURTIS LESCHYSHYN

Yrs. of NHL service: 2
Born: Thompson, Man., Canada; September 21, 1969
Position: Defenseman
Height: 6-1
Weight: 205
Uniform no.: 7
Shoots: left

Career statistics:

GP	G	A	TP	PIM
194	9	22	31	164

1990-91 statistics:

GP	G	A	TP	+/-	PIM	PP	SH	GW	GT	S	PCT
55	3	7	10	-19	49	2	0	1	0	57	5.3

LAST SEASON

Missed 25 games with a knee injury. Games total was career low as a result.

THE FINESSE GAME

Leschyshyn has a lot of good finesse skills for a player of his stature. He can skate equally well forwards and backwards and has good lateral movement. He is strong on his skates and has very good quickness.

He has excellent stick skills, with his passing getting a slight edge over his shooting. He has soft hands for passes to either side, but passes better when on the attack than when he is in his own zone and trying to get out of danger. Leschyshyn doesn't get as involved offensively as he should, given his skills, and seems to lack the leadership instinct necessary to take charge.

Leschyshyn has a good shot from the left point, low and accurate, and he has a good wrist shot when he gets in deep. He doesn't shoot as often as he should, often passing up a good shot to make a play, even when the better option is to shoot.

Leschyshyn is a willing learner with a good attitude and he works hard. He will do what it takes to win.

THE PHYSICAL GAME

Leschyshyn is not as physical as he should be for a player of his size and doesn't appear to have the temperament to play a hot and nasty game. He will move players out of the crease, and along the boards, but he doesn't scare anybody and thus doesn't have the imposing physical presence he might have to get himself more room. Since he needs time to make some of his plays in the defensive zone, he would benefit from the real estate.

THE INTANGIBLES

Leschyshyn has continued to develop under difficult circumstances. He would benefit by being paired with a steady, veteran defenseman who would be willing to teach by example (and would give Leschyshyn the confidence to get more involved in the attack flow). Unfortunately for Leschyshyn and his inexperienced fellow backliners, the Nordiques don't have anyone who fits that description. (Paging Kevin Lowe.)

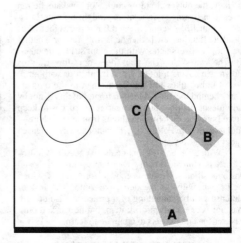

ERIC LINDROS

Yrs. of NHL service: 0
Born: London, Ont., Canada; February 28, 1973
Position: Center
Height: 6-5
Weight: 227
Uniform no.: 88
Shoots: Right

Career junior statistics:

GP	G	A	TP	PIM
82	88	97	185	250

1990-91 junior statistics:

GP	G	A	TP	+/-	PIM	PP	SH	GW	GT	S	PCT
57	71	78	149	74	189	19	10	16	2	270	26.3

LAST SEASON

Plus-minus set one-season Ontario Hockey League record, as did his total of game-winning goals. Point total was one short of team record shared by Tony Tanti (1980-81) and Scott McCrory (1986-87).

THE FINESSE GAME

Though Lindros has Mario Lemieux's size, he is not as smooth or deft with the puck as Lemieux; he is not a player with a 'touch,' although he handles the puck skillfully. Though he sees the ice extremely well and makes precise passes to both sides, taking a page from Wayne Gretzky's book, he is much more of a marauder in the attacking zone than is Gretzky, who is much more subtle.

Rather than favor the give-and-go game, Lindros is a straight-ahead, bowl-you-over sort of center more along the lines of a larger Mark Messier; in junior hockey, the players Lindros could not outskate, he ran over. His skating style is more straight-up than Lemieux's hunched-over profile and Lindros' height makes it difficult to judge whether he is truly fast or whether he simply covers acres with the giant strides he takes. But he can skate. The puck does not slow Lindros down. He covers a lot of ground with it or without it.

Lindros likes to beat defensemen to the outside, carry behind the net and feed in front, but that is not by any means his only play. He varies his rushes to keep from being predictable and shoots from everywhere— and to every area of the net. The shot, always released quickly, is heavy and hard.

With 29 special-teams goals last season, Lindros clearly is a threat on both power plays—his team's and the opposition's. He does a good job on faceoffs, which helps especially in the defensive zone. The rest of defense will be something of a project for Lindros; it has not been a high-priority item, but he worked on it last season and expects to continue to learn.

THE PHYSICAL GAME

Lindros is big enough, strong enough and willingly physical enough to at least generate thought that he could play an occasional shift on the wing if some situation calls for it. This is a skilled linebacker on skates who can nail you with a bodycheck or a punch.

Fearless of the corners and boards, Lindros will chase the puck anywhere and will use his physical assets to win it. He will camp in front of the net and challenge defensemen to move him; few can.

Lindros will fight, but as is the case with so many other elements of his game, his dominance of so many categories in junior play may not translate immediately into top billing against older, wiser, larger players.

And the physical aspect remains one semi-unknown. Lindros is not mentally fragile, but by hitting him constantly, opponents have gotten him to play more to his physical strengths than to his offensive strengths—which keeps the game closer.

THE INTANGIBLES

Often you have a skill player who is not aggressive, an aggressive player who is not skilled, a talented player who doesn't work, or a talented guy who is not a leader. When one player can combine more than a few of these qualities, he generates excitement. The player Lindros was in junior hockey is not necessarily what he will be as a pro. But Lindros has charisma, he has class. He's a leader. He has prepared himself to excel. When he's challenged, he responds. By the time he reaches his full maturity and full growth, he will dominate; don't expect that to occur immediately but be pleasantly surprised if it does.

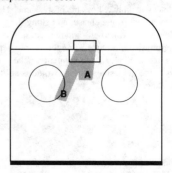

MIKE MCNEIL

Yrs. of NHL service: 1
Born: Winona, Minn., USA; July 22, 1966
Position: Left wing/center
Height: 6-1
Weight: 175
Uniform no.: 20
Shoots: left

1990-91 statistics:

GP	G	A	TP	+/-	PIM	PP	SH	GW	GT	S	PCT
37	4	7	11	+4	10	1	1	0	0	31	12.8

LAST SEASON

Acquired from Chicago with Ryan McGill for Paul Gillis and Dan Vincelette, March 5, 1991. First NHL season.

THE FINESSE GAME

McNeil is a peppery, pesky forward who is very annoying to play against. McNeil is an exceptional skater, probably the best skater on the Nordiques. He is speedy and quick and works extremely hard. He seldom takes a shift off.

McNeil was an amazing +5 in his 14 games with Quebec. Sure, it's only part of a season, but to have that kind of ranking on a team that played as poor team defense as Quebec did last season is saying something about McNeil's defensive play. His shot is good enough to net him 15-20 goals over the course of a full season, once he gets that chance. He is always driving for the net when on the attack, without losing sight of the overall game.

He is very good on faceoffs and is the kind of player who can be relied on in tight games to do his job. He might not win the game for you, but he won't lose it.

THE PHYSICAL GAME

McNeil is always hustling and making hits in all zones. He's not a punishing hitter, but he finishes his checks and is usually in good position to do something constructive with the puck. His good skating ability helps him, but he could add some upper body strength since he can be outmuscled no matter how hard he strives. Pesky as he is, he takes few bad penalties.

THE INTANGIBLES

McNeil could blossom into a very effective checking forward, given a full season of ice time. His skating ability and instincts should make him an effective penalty killer and he could be useful on the power play as well, although his shooting and passing skills are only average.

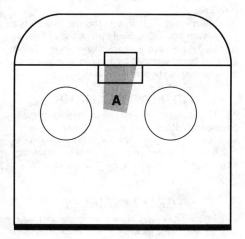

KIP MILLER

Yrs. of NHL service: 0
Born: Lansing, Mich., USA; June 11, 1969
Position: Center
Height: 5-10
Weight: 160
Uniform no.: 49
Shoots: left

1990-91 statistics:

GP	G	A	TP	+/-	PIM	PP	SH	GW	GT	S	PCT
13	4	3	7	-1	7	0	0	0	1	16	25.0

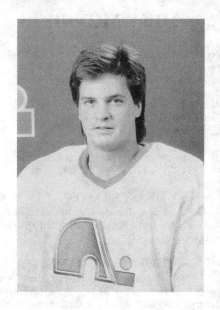

LAST SEASON

Joined team late in season after stint with Halifax (AHL).

THE FINESSE GAME

Line up the ducks, here's Miller to take his shots. Miller just loves to shoot and, if anything, is a little too selfish, but his wingers won't complain too often because he's such an accurate shooter. He has a very good snap shot and works to get into position for his scoring chances. When he does get creative, Miller can be an intelligent playmaker who works best down low, through traffic and on short give-and-gos. He doesn't have a heavy shot but is dangerous in tight. He scored 36 goals in 66 AHL games and looks ready to make the jump to the NHL.

Miller is a defensive liability, but is a smart player and should be able to play the NHL game with some experience.

Miller's skating ability could be improved. He is a shifty mover who can suddenly put on a good burst of speed and elude a pursuer in just a stride or two. He has excellent lateral mobility, but he is not very strong on his skates and can be parted from the puck.

THE PHYSICAL GAME

His small size will always limit his physical capabilities, but Miller will not shy away from a hit and will try to take the body and interfere with an opponent as best he can, with the annoying quickness and tenacity of a terrier. He is better off avoiding traffic. He has a good work ethic.

THE INTANGIBLES

Miller is a creative playmaker who has yet to get the ice time to show what he can do in the NHL. Should the Nordiques sign Lindros, Miller will be behind both Lindros and Sakic, and you have to wonder just how he will get any kind of opportunity in Quebec—unless, like his brother Kevin in Detroit, he gets shifted to the wing.

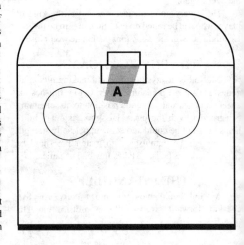

STEPHANE MORIN

Yrs. of NHL service: 1
Born: Montreal, Que., Canada; March 27, 1969
Position: Center
Height: 6-0
Weight: 175
Uniform no.: 25
Shoots: left

Career statistics:

GP	G	A	TP	PIM
54	13	29	42	30

1990-91 statistics:

GP	G	A	TP	+/-	PIM	PP	SH	GW	GT	S	PCT
48	13	27	40	+6	28	3	1	2	0	63	20.6

LAST SEASON

First full NHL season. Fourth on team in assists and points, tied for fourth in goals. Best plus-minus among forwards who played at least half a season. Missed games with a broken finger.

THE FINESSE GAME

Morin is a talented offensive player who is at home on special teams. A scoring star in the Quebec league, Morin had little trouble making the transition to the NHL. His skating is adequate, with fair acceleration and speed, and he sees the ice well. He is a heads-up playmaker who can pass equally well to either side. His offensive instincts make him a natural for the power play; he can also kill penalties and be a shorthanded scoring threat.

Morin plays well positionally (he had a decent plus-minus for this team) although he will not take the body.

THE PHYSICAL GAME

Morin does not like to get involved physically and lacks the upper body strength to get involved in any tussles in front of his net—so he doesn't. He is suspect on faceoffs.

THE INTANGIBLES

Morin made the most of his time last season before being injured, but will be caught in a numbers game at center if Nordiques get Lindros. Quebec might consider moving him to the wing to make use of his offensive skills.

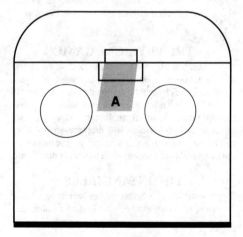

OWEN NOLAN

Yrs. of NHL service: 1
Born: Belfast, Northern Ireland; February 12, 1972
Position: Right wing
Height: 6-1
Weight: 195
Uniform no.: 11
Shoots: right

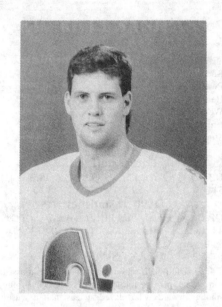

1990-91 statistics:

GP	G	A	TP	+/-	PIM	PP	SH	GW	GT	S	PCT
59	3	10	13	-19	109	0	0	0	0	54	5.6

LAST SEASON

First NHL season.

THE FINESSE GAME

Good skater, good passer, bad attitude.

Nolan sees the ice very well and anticipates. He is a good enough skater to force the play and with his size could be a more intimidating presence. He has good speed and good hand skills, although he is a better passer than shooter.

Nolan is a defensive liability and showed no inclination to work at trying to improve his game to the NHL level. He has some raw skills but without the head to go with it, any of Nolan's talent will go to waste. Of course, Nolan is very young and in no way should be considered a washout. But he needs someone to pick him up by the scruff of his neck and give him a good shake.

THE PHYSICAL GAME

Nolan can play feisty and physical when he's in the mood, but he's so inconsistent that you can't figure out what games he will be involved in or when he will be floating. He has the good size to be more of a power forward than he's shown and he can bounce off some pretty stiff checks. Nolan will drop the gloves when nettled (he is more reactive than active), but there were too many nights last season when he simply didn't care.

THE INTANGIBLES

It's debatable whether Nolan would have been better off spending another year in junior rather than making the premature jump to the NHL. He certainly came to training camp last year with the wrong attitude and it didn't improve as the season went along. Nolan has a lot of growing up to do.

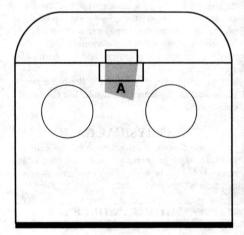

GREG PASLAWSKI

Yrs. of NHL service: 7
Born: Kindersley, Sask., Canada; August 25, 1961
Position: Right wing
Height: 5-11
Weight: 190 Uniform no.:
Shoots: right

Career statistics:

GP	G	A	TP	PIM
482	139	144	283	137

1990-91 statistics:

GP	G	A	TP	+/-	PIM	PP	SH	GW	GT	S	PCT
55	11	11	22	-6	14	1	0	2	0	75	14.7

LAST SEASON

Acquired from San Jose for Tony Hrkac, May 30, 1991. Games played and all point totals were three-season lows.

THE FINESSE GAME

Paslawski has fairly good skills but lacks the intensity to put them to work every night. He is a good skater with speed and mobility, but where he could put pressure on the defense as a forechecker, he seems content to stay back and let the play come to him.

He seems to have good vision, but his reaction time is not the quickest and by the time he makes a pass (or decides to jump into an opening for a shot), the window of opportunity is closed. He has a good shot, especially from the top of the circle in, but doesn't shoot often enough. Likewise, his passing is workman-like.

Paslawski seems to have the head but not the heart for the game.

THE PHYSICAL GAME

Paslawski has a burly build and will go in traffic in front of the net, but generally avoids the board and corner work. He prefers the open ice, and is not a physical player although he has improved in that area, especially in the defensive zone.

THE INTANGIBLES

Paslawski dwells in the comfort zone most nights, playing just to his level of ability. There are occasions when he turns the heat up a few degress, but he doesn't do it often enough (that might be why he changed teams four times in five months in 1991).

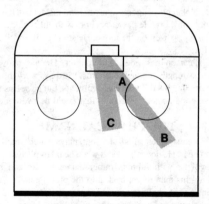

SCOTT PEARSON

Yrs. of NHL service: 2
Born: Cornwall, Ont., Canada; December 19, 1969
Position: Left wing
Height: 6-1
Weight: 205
Uniform no.: 22
Shoots: left

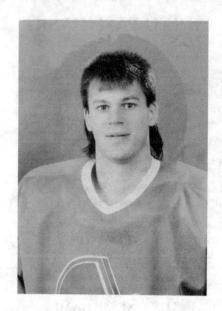

Career statistics:

GP	G	A	TP	PIM
97	16	15	31	196

1990-91 statistics:

GP	G	A	TP	+/-	PIM	PP	SH	GW	GT	S	PCT
47	11	4	15	-9	104	0	0	0	0	74	14.9

LAST SEASON

Acquired from Toronto with second round draft picks in 1991 and 1992 for Aaron Broten, Lucien DeBlois and Michel Petit. Games played and all point totals were career highs.

THE FINESSE GAME

Pearson has a pretty good finesse package of skating and shooting skills. He skates with a smooth stride, good speed and acceleration and good change of direction.

Nolan plays aggressively around the net and has a variety of shots. He passes accurately to either side and takes a pass well on the move. He stickhandles well in traffic.

Pearson has good anticipation. He has shown some strength along the boards. He pays very little attention to his defensive assignments, but he seems to have good hockey sense and that could be overcome.

THE PHYSICAL GAME

Pearson has good size but plays much smaller than he is. He doesn't hit and when he takes players out it will be with rubouts rather than takeouts and he allows his man to get back into the play. Pearson will stand up to a challenge but is not especially brave. He is very strong and could be more of a physical force.

THE INTANGIBLES

Have the Nordiques cornered the market on underachieving first-rounders? Pearson really has more talent than he has shown at the NHL level. He could be a real power forward if he had the inclination. So far, he hasn't shown it.

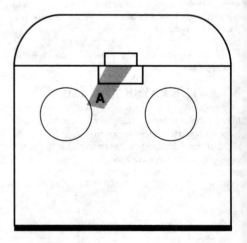

HERB RAGLAN

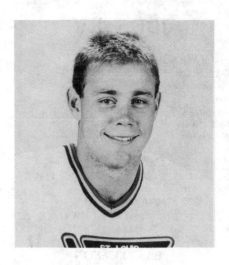

Yrs. of NHL service: 5
Born: Peterborough, Ont., Canada; August 5, 1967
Position: Right wing
Height: 6-0
Weight: 200
Uniform no.: 14
Shoots: right

Career statistics:

GP	G	A	TP	PIM
250	27	42	69	601

1990-91 statistics:

GP	G	A	TP	+/-	PIM	PP	SH	GW	GT	S	PCT
47	4	6	10	+5	82	0	0	1	0	48	8.3

LAST SEASON

Acquired from St. Louis with Tony Twist and Andy Rymsha for Darin Kimble, February 4, 1991. Games played and point totals were two-season highs after missing most of 1989-90 with a broken hand. Missed 11 games with a knee injury.

THE FINESSE GAME

The key is Raglan's game is his speed. He is very strong on his skates and gets to where he wants to go, but he doesn't have much agility so the cute little moves are out.

Raglan has a hard shot which he likes to use from 15-20 feet out instead of in close. He is not very agile in traffic and he needs a little time to get his shot off so he is not very effective in close. Raglan's hand skills are minimal. He doesn't carry or pass the puck well and that minimizes his board work. He will fight hard for the puck but can't do too much once he gets it.

Raglan is a good role player and is very good defensively—he learned well during his apprenticeship with St. Louis coach Brian Sutter. He is aware of his positions and recognizes game situations and knows what to do. He is a very determined checker.

THE PHYSICAL GAME

Raglan is feisty and physical. He has good balance and strength in tight. With his speed and balance he can really line up some teeth-jarring open-ice hits, although he can be outmanuevered. He has good size and with his intensity can get things stirred up in either zone. He will fight and he's an enthusiastic player other guys like to play with. Raglan's playing style leaves him vulnerable to injuries.

THE INTANGIBLES

Raglan continued to be hounded by nagging injuries. If he can stay in one piece, he will be valuable to a team because of his excellent attitude and work ethic. All he wants to do is win and he's not shy about stepping on a teammate's toes if that will help the team's cause.

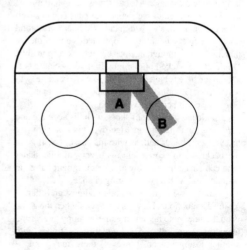

JOE SAKIC

Yrs. of NHL service: 3
Born: Burnaby, B.C., Canada
Position: Center
Height: 5-11
Weight: 185
Uniform no.: 19
Shoots: left

Career statistics:

GP	G	A	TP	PIM
230	110	163	273	75

1990-91 statistics:

GP	G	A	TP	+/-	PIM	PP	SH	GW	GT	S	PCT
80	48	61	109	-26	24	12	3	7	1	245	19.6

LAST SEASON

Led team in all scoring categories, including power play goals, shorthanded goals and shots. His plus/minus rating tied for worst on team. One of three players on team to play in all 80 games. Goals and points career highs.

THE FINESSE GAME

Sakic is blessed in every area of skills. Primary among them is his stickhandling ability. Sakic can hang on to the puck forever, drawing checkers like a top junior prospect attracts scouts. Then, with his exceptional view of the ice, he will find an open man for the pass. His hand-eye coordination is excellent (this helps him on face-offs, which he will take in all zones) and he is a creative playmaker. He can throw in several moves in a very tiny area of ice. Sakic can pass equally well off his forehand and backhand. He has very good hockey instincts, better in the opponent's end of the ice than in his own, although he does backcheck responsibly. Don't let the wicked plus-minus fool you—Sakic gets a lot of ice time for a terrible team, but is a capable two-way center. Obviously, he is a top power play man, but he can also kill penalties very well.

Sakic has a variety of shots, with his accurate and hard wrist shot having an edge over his slap shot. He has very soft hands and, as with his passing, will go to the backhand to score. Sakic is a very mobile skater who can shake his shadow and seem to materialize in open ice and with a good scoring chance.

Sakic has shown his mental toughness and character in key situations. He wants the puck when the game is on the line (note his seven game-winning goals for a team that won only 16). If Quebec continues with another losing season, however, there may come a point when the constant team failures wear on him.

THE PHYSICAL GAME

Sakic is not very big and does not try to play a big man's game. He will force his man off the play when he is not outmuscled and he will not be intimidated. He is very tenacious in traffic, where his excellent balance is put to good use. He is a very well-conditioned athlete.

THE INTANGIBLES

Sakic has been Quebec's undisputed on-ice leader for the past two seasons, getting the lion's share of ice time and attention. Should Eric Lindros sign with the Nordiques, the question will be: is this ville big enough for the both of them?

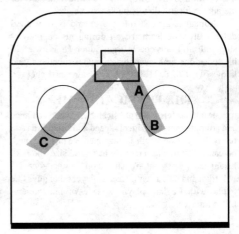

EVERETT SANIPASS

Yrs. of NHL service: 4
Born: Big Cove, N.B., Canada; February 13, 1968
Position: Left wing
Height: 6-2
Weight: 204
Uniform no.: 21
Shoots: left

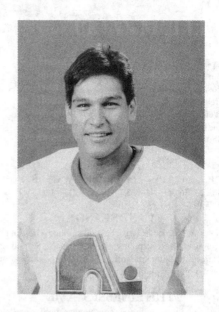

Career statistics:

GP	G	A	TP	PIM
164	25	34	59	358

1990-91 statistics:

GP	G	A	TP	+/-	PIM	PP	SH	GW	GT	S	PCT
29	5	5	10	-15	41	1	0	0	0	38	13.2

LAST SEASON

Goal total matched last season's output. Sanipass has yet to play more than 57 games in a season. Missed eight games with a back injury.

THE FINESSE GAME

Sanipass gets his shot away quickly and with a fair degree of accuracy. His hands are average, but he positions himself to maximize his scoring chances and has a good selection of shots. He is a good passer who is aware of his options and he is a good player on the power play because of this.

Sanipass is an average skater with a big stride and limited mobility.

All of his skills are mitigated by his general lack of effort and hockey sense. He does not play well defensively. His work ethic and attitude don't help him.

THE PHYSICAL GAME

Sanipass is big and strong and occasionally will battle for the puck along the boards and in the corners. He will take punishment in the slot to score and will take a check to make a play in his offensive zone. He doesn't play as well defensively and he doesn't do anything consistently to make his size a factor in his game.

THE INTANGIBLES

Sanipass has been a player on the bubble for the last four seasons. As the Nordiques strengthen their lineup with more skilled players, it is not likely he will get much playing time this season unless his desire matches his potential. He is another first-rounder (by Chicago in 1986) gone sour.

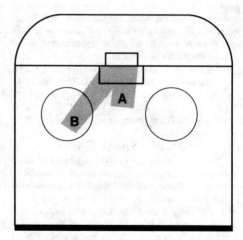

MATS SUNDIN

Yrs. of NHL service: 1
Born: Sollentuna, Sweden; February 13, 1971
Position: Right wing
Height: 6-3
Weight: 185
Uniform no.: 13
Shoots: right

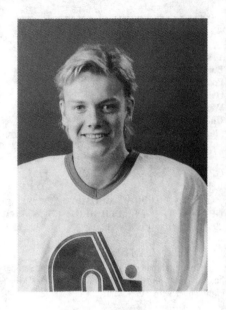

Career statistics:

GP	G	A	TP	+/-	PIM	PP	SH	GW	GT	S	PCT
80	23	36	59	-24	58	4	0	0	1	155	14.8

LAST SEASON

First season in NHL. Second among NHL rookies in assists, third in points, fourth in goals. Second on team in all point categories. One of three players on team to play in all 80 games.

THE FINESSE GAME

Sundin is a big, rangy winger with excellent finesse skills. He has good speed with impressive skating agility.

Sundin is very strong with the puck. He has an average shot from medium range and is most dangerous in close, where his superior hand skills allow him to thread the puck through skates and sticks. Sundin occasionally lacks patience, especially when going to his backhand (which he loves to do) and he ends up rushing his shot. He is very hard to knock off the puck because of his good balance. He won't stand his ground in front of the net, but he will dart through the slots and front of the net for his chances.

Sundin needs work on his defensive game but he will come back into the zone to help out his defense. He uses his very long reach to knock the puck away from opponents. He is willing to listen and learn and is adapting to the North American style of play.

THE PHYSICAL GAME

Sundin is feisty and doesn't like getting knocked around—and, gee, do you think anyone in the NHL takes runs at Europeans? Well, they'll think twice with Sundin. He is not overly physical, but he will come back—and he will use his stick to get his point across. Sundin is very strong on his skates and does not get inimidated. He is good in traffic because of his hand skills.

THE INTANGIBLES

A 40-goal season is not far in Sundin's future—this season, most likely - and it would be no shock to see him net 50 in seasons to come. Sundin gives an honest account of himself every night. He is definitely one of the league's brightest young stars.

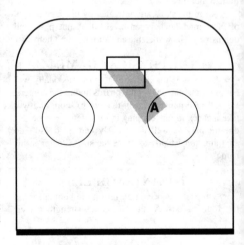

MIKHAIL TATARINOV

Yrs. of NHL service: 1
Born: Irkutsk, Siberia; July 16, 1966
Position: Defenseman
Height: 6-1
Weight: 185
Uniform no.:
Shoots: Left

Career statistics:

GP	G	A	TP	PIM
65	8	15	23	82

1990-91 statistics:

GP	G	A	TP	+/-	PIM	PP	SH	GW	GT	S	PCT
65	8	15	23	-4	82	3	1	1	0	145	5.5

LAST SEASON

Began season with Dynamo Moscow of Soviet Elite League, joined Capitals October 20. Traded by Washington to Quebec June 22, 1991, for Nordiques' second choice in the entry draft.

THE FINESSE GAME

Tatarinov has a monster shot from the blue line and a fine head for offensive finesse, but to succeed in his new NHL surroundings, he must upgrade the tempo at which he acts. He sees the open man and passes accurately, with authority ... eventually ... because he is used to having more time on a larger ice surface. He has the offensive tools—good play-reading skills, an offensive mindset, the ability to jump to holes—but struggled in his adjustment to the quicker tempo, the need for gettting his shots and passes in motion more rapidly.

The defensive adjustment will take more time, because Tatarinov does not seem as interested in it. Tatarinov does not have anything resembling great speed, so he falls a step behind at inconvenient times. He is quick the first couple of strides and covers a lot of ground with them, but the top-end speed is not there; whatever speed he has reached after those first few strides is what he has. But he will make a smart, creative breakout pass to a player breaking for space in the neutral zone.

Tatarinov is very good backward—perhaps better than forward—and very good laterally. He can throw a solid hip check and has fine mobility and agility.

THE PHYSICAL GAME

Tatarinov takes a hit and gives one, will play a scrappy game and will throw his body in front of shots. He will not back down, will not be intimidated. But contact is not instinctive in certain defensive situations; he does not restrain an opponent from breaking away. That, too, might be related to his experience on larger surfaces, where there always seems to be time and space to catch up with a player if he has eluded you once or twice already.

THE INTANGIBLES

Fine tuning and NHL experience are all that is needed. If he adds some leg strength, learns to get the puck and move it, starts to shoot lower from the point and takes more interest in his defensive game, Tatarinov should be a significant improvement for a Quebec defense that needs all the help it can get.

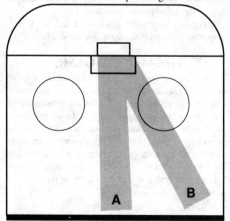

RON TUGNUTT

Yrs. of NHL service: 3
Born: Scarborough, Ont., Canada
Position: Goaltender
Height: 5-11
Weight: 150
Uniform no.: 1
Catches: left

Career statistics:

GP	MINS	GA	SO	GAA	A	PIM
123	6774	462	0	4.09	4	4

1990-91 statistics:

GP	MINS	GAA	W	L	T	SO	GA	S	SAPCT	PIM
56	3145	4.04	12	29	10	0	212	1853	.866	0

LAST SEASON

Fifth among NHL goalies in minutes played. Games played, minutes played and wins all career highs.

THE PHYSICAL GAME

Tugnutt is small and he uses his angles well to cover as much net as he can. He has very good reflexes to back his game up and, unlike most goalies for bad teams, has not fallen into the trap of trying to do too much. He concentrates on his own job, which is difficult enough without trying to be a third defenseman.

Tugnutt is limited in handling the puck. He communicates well with his defensemen and they know he expects them to do the work.

He comes out of the net to challenge shooters and his good skating helps him moves quickly on close-in plays. He has good balance and recovers quickly for the second shot (unfortunately, the Quebec defense usually allows a third, fourth and fifth shot).

He has a very good glove hand and quick feet. Opponents try to go to his stick side to beat him.

THE MENTAL GAME

Tugnutt seems to have resigned himself to the fact that he will get a lot of work behind the inexperienced Nordiques defense (which allowed an average of 33 shots against when Tugnutt was in the net). Tugnutt earned a tie last season with an incredible 70-save performance against Boston. Tugnutt seems capable of making the big saves, but his team was overwhelmed on so many nights there were few chances to prove it. He is a battler and does not give up even on the worst nights.

THE INTANGIBLES

Tugnutt may face a challenge in goal from young Stephane Fiset this season, but he earned the No. 1 spot with his attitude and ability. It will be interesting to see how Tugnutt fares if/when the Nordiques improve their team defense.

RANDY VELISCHEK

Yrs. of NHL service: 8
Born: Montreal, Que., Canada; February 10, 1962
Position: Defenseman
Height: 6-0
Weight: 200
Uniform no.: 27
Shoots: left

Career statistics:

GP	G	A	TP	PIM
471	19	73	92	379

1990-91 statistics:

GP	G	A	TP	+/-	PIM	PP	SH	GW	GT	S	PCT
79	2	10	12	-19	42	0	0	0	0	47	4.3

LAST SEASON

Acquired from New Jersey as future considerations from Peter Stastny trade, August 13, 1990.

THE FINESSE GAME

Velischek is a player of limited skills, skills that are enhanced by his work ethic and intelligence. Velischek does all the little things necessary to get the job done. He doesn't skate fast and has limited mobility, so he will seldom get himself in situations where he is forced to scramble. He will chip in offensively, but infrequently. His slapshot is accurate but doesn't have much velocity.

Velischek does not rush the puck, but he will skate the puck out slowly and since he sizes up the ice well, can start an attack with a good pass. He prefers to stay at home but tries not to let too big a gap with his forwards.

Velischek is a hard worker and doesn't give up easily. He is a very good penalty killer because of his smarts and his solid positional play.

THE PHYSICAL GAME

Velischek is a willing hitter, but his skating deficiencies limit his range. He is fairly strong along the boards and in front of the net, but is not a hard hitter. He is not a fighter or a dirty player.

THE INTANGIBLES

Velischek has superior mental talents that make him an ideal fifth or sixth defenseman. He makes an ideal partner for a skilled but inexperienced defenseman trying to develop his NHL skills, because Velischek will help a young player improve.

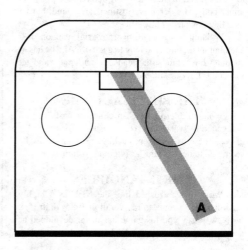

CRAIG WOLANIN

Yrs. of NHL service: 6
Born: Grosse Pointe, Mich., USA; July 27, 1967
Position: Defenseman
Height: 6-3
Weight: 205
Uniform no.: 6
Shoots: left

Career statistics:

GP	G	A	TP	PIM
376	21	78	99	568

1990-91 statistics:

GP	G	A	TP	+/-	PIM	PP	SH	GW	GT	S	PCT
80	5	13	18	-13	89	0	1	0	0	109	4.5

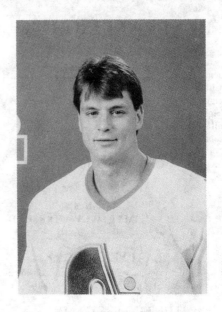

LAST SEASON

One of three players on team to play all 80 games. Goal total was highest in three seasons.

THE FINESSE GAME

A player of contradicitions.

Wolanin was blessed with all of the physical gifts an NHL defenseman could ask for, but rarely uses them.

He has enough average skating ability to be in the right position, but lacks quickness. He does not have good balance and looks awkward on the ice, almost top-heavy, as if his legs aren't big enough to support his upper body. His defensive instincts are sound, but he uses them inconsistently.

Wolanin has a huge, overpowering cannon of a shot, but it takes him too long to get it off. And he has to shoot it from a standstill, because he can't move and get the shot off in one smooth motion.

THE PHYSICAL GAME

Wolanin doesn't have an ounce of nasty in him and generally wastes his size. He isn't a fighter and his effectiveness as an open-ice hitter is reduced as he seems genuinely afraid he is going to hurt someone.

THE INTANGIBLES

Wolanin was rushed into the NHL as a highly regarded (first round, third overall in 1985) draft pick by New Jersey and his game has never developed as scouts anticipated it would. Wolanin was hampered by playing for two weak teams and he would have benefitted from playing with a veteran defenseman who would both get on his case and help him with the finer points of the game. Without that kind of assistance, it's likely he'll go into the books as a case of unfulfilled potential. He is a genuinely nice, bright, personable guy, but those qualities don't help him on the ice.

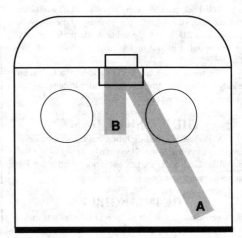

SAN JOSE SHARKS

DAVID BRUCE

Yrs. of NHL service: 3
Born: Thunder Bay, Ont., Canada; October 7, 1964
Position: Right wing/center
Height: 5-11
Weight: 185
Uniform no.:
Shoots: right

Career statistics:

GP	G	A	TP	PIM
155	24	20	44	259

1990-91 statistics:

GP	G	A	TP	+/-	PIM	PP	SH	GW	GT	S	PCT
12	1	2	3	+1	14	0	0	0	0	23	4.3

LAST SEASON

Acquired from St. Louis in expansion draft. Games played and all point totals were four-year lows.

THE FINESSE GAME

The Sharks plucked Bruce in the expansion draft hoping he will be able to finally make the jump to the NHL as a goal scorer. He is capable of good shooting accuracy, especially from the top of the circles in. If there is an opening, he's going to hit it.

His skating is only average, with more emphasis on his quickness than his speed. His play away from the puck is very good.

THE PHYSICAL GAME

Bruce is a willing physical player although it is not his strong suit. He will get involved, but doesn't have the size to play a solid hitting game. He accepts being hit and will hit.

THE INTANGIBLES

Bruce has been a high point producer in the minors, but hasn't been able to play in the NHL consis-tently. This will be his last stop to prove himself. He has to carry his goal scoring to the next level.

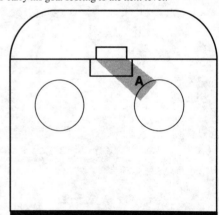

CRAIG COXE

Yrs. of NHL service: 4
Born: Chula Vista, Calif., USA; January 21, 1964
Position: Center
Height: 6-4
Weight: 220
Uniform no.:
Shoots: left

Career statistics:

GP	G	A	TP	PIM
225	12	31	43	694

1990-91 statistics:

GP	G	A	TP	+/-	PIM	PP	SH	GW	GT	S	PCT
7	0	0	0	-3	27	0	0	0	0	5	0.0

LAST SEASON

Acquired from Vancouver in expansion draft. Games played and all totals were career lows.

THE FINESSE GAME

Coxe is a clumsy skater with average puck skills. He doesn't get enough ice time to use those skills, so it's difficult to say how good he could get or if he could improve to the point where he could skate a regular shift.

Coxe could use his good size to jam the net, but in the past two seasons he has only played 32 games in the NHL, mostly because of his all-around deficiencies.

THE PHYSICAL GAME

Coxe is an enforcer, but one who loses his effectiveness because he doesn't play regularly. The high-priced players are smart enough to stay away from him—and he can't catch them—so all he does is cancel out the other team's lumbering guy. It's not much of a trade-off. The better enforcers, like Kevin Hatcher and Shayne Corson, will take someone valuable with them when they go (although, conversely, they are valuable to lose). Most of Coxe's battles are a waste of everyone's time including the two players involved. Coxe is not a good enough skater to be an effective checker either.

THE INTANGIBLES

Going to an expansion team which is stockpiling tough customers, Coxe will get his share of playing time. He needs to add another dimension to his game to be of any real use to a hockey club. The Sharks won't have much patience with him if he doesn't play much smarter. If he doesn't, he will enjoy his stay in Kansas City (the Sharks' minor league affiliate).

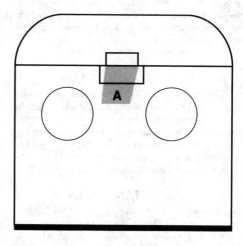

PAT FALLOON

Yrs. of NHL service: 0
Born: Foxwarren, Man., Canada; September 22, 1972
Height: 5-11
Weight: 192
Position: Center/right wing
Shoots: right

1990-91 junior statistics:

GP	G	A	TP	PIM
61	64	71	138	33

LAST SEASON

Drafted first round, second overall by San Jose.

THE FINESSE GAME

Falloon is an excellent skater who utlizes his speed and acceleration to pop into open ice for scoring chances.

In junior (where he played for the Spokane Chiefs of the WHL), Falloon demonstrated creative playmaking ability. He can give a soft or crisp pass to either side and can find and hit the open man. He stickhandles well. He was the most creative passer available in the 1991 draft. At the junior level, the game probably appears slow to him because he has the ability to recognize one play, seek a second option and still have time to go back to the first play. He will make the highest percentage play most of the time.

Falloon is a scoring natural with hard, accurate wrist and slap shots. He can play the point on the power play or work the puck low. He is aware of his defensive responsibilities and backchecks well, using his speed to recover from defensive mistakes. Falloon can play on both special teams. At the levels he has played so far, Falloon has few flaws.

THE PHYSICAL GAME

Falloon uses his body well along the boards and in the corners. He is aggressive but not a scrapper; he completes his checks solidly, although he is not a big thumper. He may have some trouble handling the bigger NHL checkers and will have to get stronger and quicker. He has the kind of work ethic that indicates he will put in the effort to fine tune his game.

THE INTANGIBLES

Falloon has been compared by some to Chicago's Jeremy Roenick. The Sharks could only hope. One asset for Falloon is all of the attention being paid to Eric Lindros. Falloon will be very unheralded for a No. 2 overall pick and will benefit from being able to break into the NHL with less pressure. He is a blue chip prospect. The concern with Falloon, as with all youngsters making the big jump, is how well his skills will translate in the majors. He is a good character player and a skilled one who will make the players around him better.

The Sharks also drafted Falloon's linemate, Ray Whitney, in the second round and they could become an impressive duo three or four years down the road. Falloon may be loaned to the Canadian Olympic team.

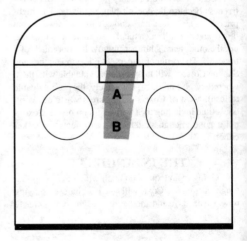

LINK GAETZ

Yrs. of NHL service: 0
Born: Vancouver, B.C., Canada; October 2, 1968
Position: Defenseman
Height: 6-2
Weight: 210
Uniform no.:
Shoots: left

Career statistics:

GP	G	A	TP	PIM
17	0	2	2	86

1990-91 statistics:
Did not play in the NHL

LAST SEASON

Acquired from Minnesota in dispersal draft. Suspended twice during the season for alcohol-related incidents.

THE FINESSE GAME

Well, folks, he's not nicknamed "the Missing Link" for nothing. Even when the North Stars were struggling through a terrible first half last season, Gaetz couldn't earn a spot in the lineup. His off-ice troubles are unfortunate because Gaetz is a blend of size and talent.

Gaetz is an excellent skater for a big man. He is a well-balanced skater with quickness. He handles the puck well and can rush with it or make hard, flat passes. He has a good shot from the point and has an understanding of the game to go along with his skills.

THE PHYSICAL GAME

In a widely publicized quote, Sharks scout Chuck Grillo called Gatz "one of the meanest kids living." He said that affectionately. Gaetz will hit anyone, anywhere, anytime—and had 222 PIM in 22 IHL games last season at Kalamazoo. He is a fierce competitor and fighter. Gaetz is a willing shot-blocker.

THE INTANGIBLES

The bottom line on Gaetz is whether he will grow up and have the proper mental approach to get along with his coaches and teammates and develop the consistency, concentration and focus to make it in the NHL. It's all up to him.

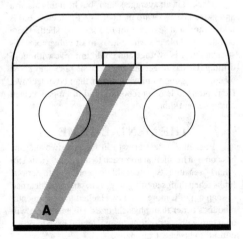

JEFF HACKETT

Yrs. of NHL service: 1
Born: London, Ont., Canada; June 1, 1968
Position: Goaltender
Height: 6-1
Weight: 175
Uniform no.:
Catches: left

Career statistics:

GP	MINS	GA	SO	GAA	A	PIM
43	2170	130	0	3.59	0	4

1990-91 statistics:

GP	MINS	GAA	W	L	T	SO	GA	S	SAPCT	PIM
30	1508	3.62	5	18	1	0	91	741	.877	4

LAST SEASON

Acquired from the New York Islanders in expansion draft. Missed eight games with a groin injury. First full NHL season.

THE PHYSICAL GAME

Hackett is a reflex goalie who relies too much on his reactions. He has to take a smarter approach to the game and learn to play his angles better and stay on his feet.

Hackett is an average skater, but he holds his arm and glove in a awkward manner—in tight, close to his body—and that leaves a lot of room top shelf. There and the five-hole are where he is most vulnerable. His stickhandling is average and could improve with more drilling. He has to get out and stop the puck and know where he's going to move it rather than be indecisive. He is prone to leaving rebounds and often gets beaten on the second shot.

THE MENTAL GAME

Hackett's fastest growth in the past two seasons has come in his mental approach to the game. He is still a fairly sensitive type, capable of getting into serious funks when things aren't going well, but he has learned to snap out of it more quickly. Hackett handles mental rebounds better than physical ones. His resilience will help him with a struggling team. He will have to prove himself to his new teammates.

THE INTANGIBLES

Hackett is eager to prove he can be a No. 1 goalie. While his game is still laden with flaws, he has a positive attitude and work ethic that can give him a chance at the NHL level. Hackett was a winner at the minor league level. He was a second-round draft pick of the Islanders in 1987, and could be the steal of the expansion draft for the Sharks.

BRIAN HAYWARD

Yrs. of NHL service: 9
Born: Georgetown, Ont., Canada; June 25, 1960
Position: Goaltender
Height: 5-10
Weight: 175
Uniform no.:
Catches: left

Career statistics:

GP	MINS	GA	SO	GAA	A	PIM
332	18770	1131	8	3.62	12	79

1990-91 statistics:

GP	MINS	GAA	W	L	T	SO	GA	S	SAPCT	PIM
26	1473	3.14	6	15	3	2	77	674	.886	2

LAST SEASON

Acquired from Minnesota in dispersal draft. Sat out part of season while with Montreal before being traded to Minnesota. All totals were seven-year lows except shutouts, which was three-season high.

THE PHYSICAL GAME

Hayward's experience shows in his technical approach to the game. He plays his angles well and moves economically. He doesn't flop. He doesn't scoot around the ice. He doesn't do too much.

Hayward may have trouble maintaining that cool with an expansion team. Where Montreal defensemen were expected to clear rebounds, Hayward may have to do it himself. Hayward is not a good skater and if he is relied upon to do more out of his net, he will become more vulnerable.

Hayward is not very quick with his feet and—unusual for a small goalie—he is weaker low than high. He sometimes stays too deep in his net and doesn't get the angle shut off completely.

THE MENTAL GAME

Hayward is a competitor with intense pride. He wants to prove himself as a No. 1 goalie and his mental toughness will be put to the test this season. He is consistent and steady and in the past always showed an ability to shake off bad goals or bad games.

THE INTANGIBLES

Hayward wanted out of Montreal because of his lack of playing time behind Patrick Roy. Be careful what you wish for, you might get it...After a brief stay in Minnesota, Hayward will learn whether 'tis better to open the bench door on a contending team than stopping pucks for a bad one. He is a steady goalie whose presence should help the young San Jose netminders.

TONY HRKAC

Yrs. of NHL service: 4
Born: Thunder Bay, Ont., Canada; July 7, 1966
Position: Center
Height: 5-11
Weight: 165
Uniform no.:
Shoots: left

Career statistics:

GP	G	A	TP	PIM
257	53	117	170	56

1990-91 statistics:

GP	G	A	TP	+/-	PIM	PP	SH	GW	GT	S	PCT
70	16	32	48	-22	16	6	0	0	0	122	13.1

LAST SEASON

Acquired from Quebec for Greg Paslawski on May 30, 1991. Was third on Nordiques in points. Games played matched career high.

THE FINESSE GAME

Hrkac is a high-tech player. He is a very good skater with quickness and is shifty with some very deceptive moves. He handles the puck well as he skates and has good hockey sense and hand skills.

Hrkac is a better playmaker than shooter. He has fairly good vision and is good tactically. He hasn't played consistently enough at the high level he has shown. He is creative.

Hrkac has a good shot from medium range but needs to shoot more. He doesn't always recognize the best percentage play. As a result, he will sometimes pass to a teammate who is in a worse shooting position than he is.

Hrkac needs to work to improve his defensive play.

THE PHYSICAL GAME

Hrkac is not a physical player. He is not afraid and accepts the hits in traffic but he doesn't dish things out. He is a small player and works better at darting into the holes. He will pursue loose pucks in traffic, but sometimes gets outmuscled.

THE INTANGIBLES

Hrkac has to be a first- or second-line center in order to succeed. Whether that has to do with his perceived importance to the team (and thus his self-worth) is a puzzle, but Hrkac just doesn't fit as a role player. So far in his career, he hasn't been given that opportunity full-time.

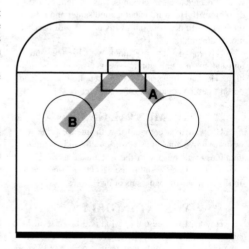

KELLY KISIO

Yrs. of NHL service: 9
Born: Peace River, Alta., Canada; Septmber 18, 1959
Position: Center
Height: 5-9
Weight: 180
Uniform no.:
Shoots: right

Career statistics:

GP	G	A	TP	PIM
572	178	324	502	590

1990-91 statistics:

GP	G	A	TP	+/-	PIM	PP	SH	GW	GT	S	PCT
51	15	20	35	+3	58	7	1	2	0	74	20.3

LAST SEASON

Acquired from the New York Rangers in expansion draft. Missed 18 games with a fractured right ankle. Missed five games with a hip injury. Missed four games with a groin injury. Missed one game each with a charley horse and abdominal strain. Underwent off-season groin surgery. Games played and all point totals were career lows for full season.

THE FINESSE GAME

Kisio has no overwhelming offensive skills, but he is imbued with incredible determination and a huge heart. Kisio is not a very good skater, but he gets to where he has to go on sheer willpower. He is always in motion and negates many icings by outhustling everyone else to the puck. He hustles back the other way as well, and is always in position to help out his defense.

Kisio does not have any frightening shots, but he is very poised in tight and will hold onto the puck and make the goalie commit. Most of his goals are scored from right in front of the net after a goalie is down. He has strong wrists and a good backhand.

Kisio has very good hockey sense and plays well on specialty teams. He needs to play with a strong finishing winger to make the most of the playmaking efforts.

THE PHYSICAL GAME

Kisio is persistent along the wall, always trying to get at the puck whether he is on his feet, his knees or his back. Opposing defenseman can't let up for a second because Kisio will grab that opening to get at the puck and move it, even though he is physically overmatched by most opponents. When his arms and stick are tied up, Kisio will still keep the puck alive by stepping on it with the toe of his skate blade and trying to move it to a teammate. Kisio couldn't care less how big the opposition is: he will have to be stopped by force, because Kisio won't give up on his own.

THE INTANGIBLES

A leader by example (he was captain of the Rangers prior to leaving that organization), Kisio is a smaller version of his new coach, Bob Gainey. If Kisio can stay healthy—a big if, because of the physical style he has to play to be effective—he will be a valuable addition to the Sharks.

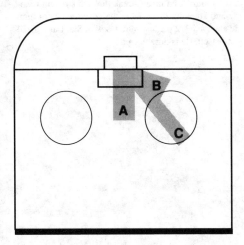

RICK LESSARD

Yrs. of NHL service: 0
Born: Timmins, Ont., Canada; January 9, 1968
Position: Defenseman
Height: 6-2
Weight: 200
Uniform no.:
Shoots: left

Career statistics:

GP	G	A	TP	PIM
7	0	2	2	2

1990-91 statistics:

GP	G	A	TP	+/-	PIM	PP	SH	GW	GT	S	PCT
1	0	1	1	-1	0	0	0	0	0	0	0.0

LAST SEASON

Acquired from Calgary in expansion draft.

THE FINESSE GAME

Lessard is a stay-at-home defenseman who has shown good offensive ability. He can get the puck out of his own end well by rushing or headmanning the puck. He does all the practical things a defensive should do. He is consistent in all three zones.

Lessard has developed his game by concentrating on the defensive basics first. He positions himself well. He is learning the game progessively and his offensive skills should surface as he becomes more comfortable.

THE PHYSICAL GAME

Lessard has major league size. He's tall and lanky and finishes all of his checks. He probably could develop more of a mean streak through strength training and knowing that's what the coach wants of him. He amassed 272 penalty minutes with Salt Lake (IHL) last season. He is durable and honest.

THE INTANGIBLES

Lessard will fill the role of a solid, defensive defenseman with offensive potential. He needs to show he can play at the NHL level.

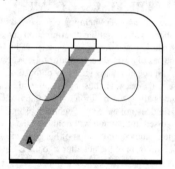

JEFF MADILL

Yrs. of NHL service: 0
Born: Oshawa, Ont., Canada; June 21, 1965
Position: Right wing
Height: 5-11
Weight: 195
Uniform no.:
Shoots: left

1990-91 statistics:

GP	G	A	TP	+/-	PIM	PP	SH	GW	GT	S	PCT
14	4	0	4	-1	46	0	0	0	0	24	16.7

LAST SEASON

Acquired from New Jersey in expansion draft.

THE FINESSE GAME

Madill is not a textbook player. He is a hard worker who has a future as a sanitation engineer—he loves picking up garbage around the net. He's been a goal scorer at every stage of his career. Even in the limited ice time he got with New Jersey last season he showed a good scoring instinct. With his willingness to crash and bang around the net, he will probably make a good power play man up front. Creative, he's not.

Madill's skating is what has held him back. He has worked hard at it, but remains very slow of foot. He does have good balance, which helps him in traffic.

THE PHYSICAL GAME

Madill is a pest, in the complimentary sense. He is always getting in someone's hair and he plays bigger than he is. He's not tough in the enforcer sense, but he will hit and antagonize people. He won't back down from anyone. Madill's balance is good and that helps him with his skating strength. Madill has battled a weight problem through most of his career (and will prbably continue to do so), so he must dedicate himself to conditioning.

THE INTANGIBLES

Madill is a self-made player. He's felt overlooked and neglected in the New Jersey system and is delighted to get his chance to play with the Sharks. Some players are timid about the spotlight; Madill is not shy about showing what he can do. He will do anything a coach asks.

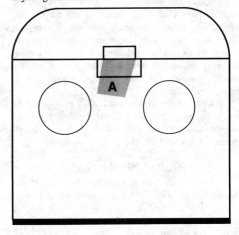

BOB MCGILL

Yrs. of NHL service: 10
Born: Edmonton, Alta., Canada; April 27, 1962
Position: Defenseman
Height: 6-1
Weight: 193
Uniform no.:
Shoots: right

Career statistics:

GP	G	A	TP	PIM
577	13	51	64	1600

1990-91 statistics:

GP	G	A	TP	+/-	PIM	PP	SH	GW	GT	S	PCT
77	4	5	9	+8	153	0	0	0	0	69	5.8

LAST SEASON

Acquired from Chicago in expansion draft. Games played was career high.

THE FINESSE GAME

McGill's greatest asset is his team play. He is willing to dive head first, feet first or mouth first in front of pucks.

McGill has a surprisingly good shot from the point, when he does get involved offensively. He played very little on the power play (only if everyone else was in the penalty box or exhausted). His point shot is reliable and low. Players will charge to the net knowing his shot is going to arrive. McGill himself doesn't gamble in beyond the blue line because he cannot recover quickly.

His skating is limited. He is slow of foot and he can be beaten wide. He also has to keep himself in good position because he can't play catch-up. McGill doesn't rush with the puck.

THE PHYSICAL GAME

McGill is a solid checker who is inhibited by his lack of skating ability. When someone does come into McGill's neighborhood, he will hit hard. He has cut down on bad penalties by playing better positionally and not running around as much.

THE INTANGIBLES

This will be the first time in his career that McGill will report to camp and not be on the bubble. He is advancing in years (he's 29) and it will be interesting to see how he reacts now that he has job security with an expansion team. McGill can't forget what's gotten him to the NHL. Going to the Sharks may add four years to his career.

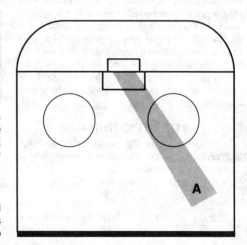

348

JAYSON MORE

Yrs. of NHL service: 0
Born: Souris, Man., Canada; January 12, 1969
Position: Defenseman
Height: 6-1
Weight: 190
Uniform no.:
Shoots: right

Career statistics:

GP	G	A	TP	PIM
6	0	0	0	16

1990-91 statistics:
Did not play in the NHL

LAST SEASON
Acquired from Montreal in expansion draft.

THE FINESSE GAME
More is an excellent blend of talent and meanness. Unfortunately, his mean streak sometimes overwhelms his game and he will simply lose it.

More skates with good balance and agility and skates well backwards, but he is not as strong on his skates as he should be and could benefit from training.

More has a very good shot. He possesses strong wrist and slap shots and shoots low and accurately. He is also a good passer and likes to get involved in the offensive flow. He headmans the puck well, controls the puck and rushes effectively. He also has a very good short pass game. He can play the point on the power play and be used to kill penalties. More has a lot of natural ability and may just need the right coach to bring his talents out.

THE PHYSICAL GAME
More makes solid contact with the body and likes to hit. His checks are take-outs. He clears the front of the net and uses his strength to good advantage. He plays a tough, physical game and earns himself a lot of room. More had 157 PIM in 57 games with Halifax (AHL) last season. He scored seven goals and had 17 assists.

THE INTANGIBLES
More is a first-round draft pick (Rangers, 10th overall in 1987) who is taking time to mature. He needs to develop a more stable approach to the game to make the most of his abilities.

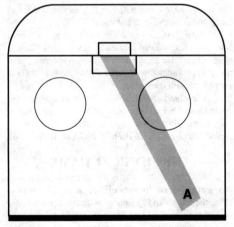

BRIAN MULLEN

Yrs. of NHL service: 9
Born: New York, N.Y., USA; March 16, 1962
Position: Left wing
Height: 5-10
Weight: 180
Uniform no.:
Shoots: left

Career statistics:

GP	G	A	TP	PIM
679	224	320	544	338

1990-91 statistics:

GP	G	A	TP	+/-	PIM	PP	SH	GW	GT	S	PCT
79	19	43	62	+12	44	4	0	3	0	188	10.1

LAST SEASON

Acquired from New York Rangers with future considerations for Tim Kerr, May 30, 1991. Was fourth on Rangers in assists, fifth in points. Goal total was four-season low. Missed one game with a hand injury.

THE FINESSE GAME

Mullen, a native New Yorker, has playground smarts. He has really nice offensive instincts (which will be missed by the Rangers) and is very creative. He has lovely hands and will use his backhand pass as much as his forehand, if not more.

Mullen gets his shot off quickly and he will shoot from anywhere—even scoring from so-called "impossible" angles. He has a good, accurate one-timer and at times has an uncanny sense of where the net is. He is very smart with the puck.

Defensively, Mullen is attentive away from the puck. One of his favorite plays is to lift an opponent's stick from behind, steal the puck and start a counterattack. He comes back deep in his zone to help out.

THE PHYSICAL GAME

Mullen is small but wiry and does not play a very physical game. He finishes off his check if his man is along the boards and he finishes with authority because of his good skating and balance. He will forge into traffic in the offensive zone, taking and giving whacks with his stick.

THE INTANGIBLES

Mullen is about the only offensively skilled player (except for unknown quantity Pat Falloon) on the Sharks and will be asked to carry the offensive load for the first time in his career. He has always played a supporting role, so this will be a season of adjusting for Mullen. He is a significant addition for San Jose.

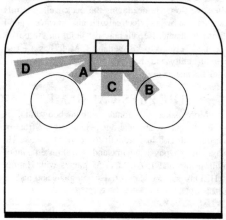

350

NEIL WILKINSON

Yrs. of NHL service: 2
Born: Selkirk, Man., Canada; August 16, 1967
Position: Defenseman
Height: 6-3
Weight: 180
Uniform no.:
Shoots: right

Career statistics:

GP	G	A	TP	PIM
86	2	14	16	217

1990-91 statistics:

GP	G	A	TP	+/-	PIM	PP	SH	GW	GT	S	PCT
50	2	9	11	-5	117	0	0	0	0	55	3.6

LAST SEASON

Acquired from Minnesota in dispersal draft.

THE FINESSE GAME

Wilkinson can either fight at the drop of a glove or make a slick play. Anything Wilkinson does is driven by his competitive nature. He is wiry and tenacious.

Wilkinson is a good skater who can get involved offensively. He handles the puck well, can rush it and is a good passer. He has a good shot from the point. As he develops more confidence he has the potential to become a front-line two-way defenseman. He will be given the chance to show his leadership qualities in San Jose.

THE PHYSICAL GAME

Wilkinson is a very big, physical defenseman who could get even stronger if he adds more upper-body strength (he is fairly light for his height, by NHL defense standards). Wilkinson plays a smart game, doesn't take many bad penalties and could develop a real physical presence on the ice.

THE INTANGIBLES

Wilkinson's game has developed very quickly in his two NHL seasons and the North Stars were unhappy about losing him. He is a very promising talent and it is revealing to note that when the Stars put added responsibility on him in the playoffs, he responded in a big way.

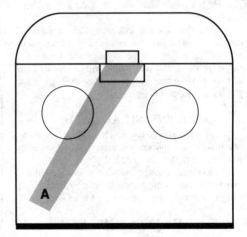

ROB ZETTLER

Yrs. of NHL service: 2
Born: Sept Iles, Que., Canada; March 8, 1968
Position: Defenseman
Height: 6-3
Weight: 190
Uniform no.:
Shoots: left

Career statistics:

GP	G	A	TP	PIM
80	1	12	13	154

1990-91 statistics:

GP	G	A	TP	+/-	PIM	PP	SH	GW	GT	S	PCT
47	1	4	5	-10	109	0	0	0	0	30	3.3

LAST SEASON

Acquired from Minnesota in dispersal draft.

THE FINESSE GAME

Zettler is a subtle player who does all the little things a good defenseman needs to do. He is the kind of player a coach won't notice until he is out of the lineup.

Zettler reacts well in offensive zone. He has a heavy and accurate shot and good hand-eye coordination. He is a good passer who can make soft and hard passes.

Zettler handles the puck well. He is capable of carrying it out of his own zone and is a good stick-handler. He plays well positionally and knows the defensive game. His plus-minus will always be high and he allows other people to play their game by playing as a support player.

THE PHYSICAL GAME

Zettler has gone to the limit to improve himself by becoming bigger, quicker and stronger with off-season workouts. Although his physical play is not his best asset, he is tough enough and is never intimidated. He may not initiate as often as he should. Zettler is good along boards but plays finesse style for his size.

THE INTANGIBLES

Zettler is a promising defenseman who will benefit from the ice time playing for an expansion team. He has a lot of desire and will always go the extra mile for his team. He will be a good partner for a more offensive-minded defenseman. Zettler is a solid character player and team man.

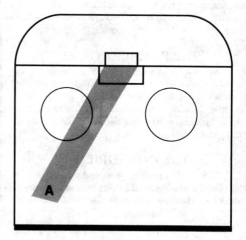

ST. LOUIS BLUES

BOB BASSEN

Yrs. of NHL service: 5
Born: Calgary, Alta., Canada; May 6, 1965
Position: Center
Height: 5-10
Weight: 180
Uniform no.: 28
Shoots: Left

Career statistics:

GP	G	A	TP	PIM
318	37	62	99	468

1990-91 statistics:

GP	G	A	TP	+/-	PIM	PP	SH	GW	GT	S	PCT
79	16	18	34	17	183	0	2	1	0	117	13.7

LAST SEASON

Claimed in waiver draft from Chicago Oct. 1.

THE FINESSE GAME

Bassen is a good skater, one of the people who reaffirms your faith in the waiver draft. He is quick. He has great lateral ability, good acceleration and can make quick starts and stops. Looks like a 5-10 bundle of fast-twitch muscles.

Bassen is only an average playmaker for a center, only average on faceoffs. He is not without hands, but is not really gifted with much of a touch. He is not a gifted passer, but he has a good sense of where to try to move the puck.

Bassen took the checker's role from Rick Meagher, plays mostly in defensive situations and does a good job killing penalties because he hounds the puck so well.

THE PHYSICAL GAME

Bassen is not big, but hits big. He really smokes people. He is intimidating on the forecheck, because he hits and hurts.

He is always in your face, driving you nuts, and he doesn't back down; he's always there with a jab or a yap and can be extremely annoying and distracting to the finesse guys who just want to score their goals and go home.

Bassen is not a stick man, but he's always with you to bump, get in the way, interfere and tick you right off.

THE INTANGIBLES

Bassen is not vocal, but plays every shift at high intensity, a character player who gets the most out of his abilities. Possibly the most Sutter-like non-Sutter on the Blues; the family grapevine (Daryl in Chicago to Brian in St. Louis), probably is why the Blues obtained him. They had nothing to lose, and gained, big time, by Bassen's addition to their roster.

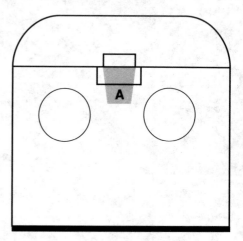

ROD BRIND'AMOUR

Yrs. of NHL service: 2
Born: Ottawa, Ont., Canada; August 9, 1970
Position: Center/left wing
Height: 6-1
Weight: 202
Uniform no.: 19
Shoots: Left

Career statistics:

GP	G	A	TP	PIM
157	43	67	110	139

1990-91 statistics:

GP	G	A	TP	+/-	PIM	PP	SH	GW	GT	S	PCT
78	17	32	49	2	93	4	0	3	0	169	10.1

LAST SEASON

Goal total dropped by nine from rookie season, penalty total more than doubled.

THE FINESSE GAME

At times, Brind'Amour seems overwhelmed by the pressures of the creativity that does not come naturally to him. He is a muscle player, a good finisher, more than a smooth, fluid setup man who can skate, then skate some more. He overhandles at times, gets a little tentative and out of synch because he may be thinking too much. But when his mind and body are working in unison, he is quite a player.

Brind'Amour can play a special-teams role because of his strength, his skating skills, his desire and his eagerness. He can pressure any puck carrier and can be a threat to convert any turnover with a high shot that is faster than many goalies' glove hands.

On the power play, Brind'Amour can get himself in position to score if Brett Hull hasn't scored already. He has no problem at all with the gritty going in front of the net. He can more than hold his own in those stampedes.

THE PHYSICAL GAME

Brind'Amour can crunch people. He's a Bryan Trottier type who isn't fancy, but will go through people to score a simple strength goal. Pretty much a straight-line guy, Brind'Amour gets the puck deep, finishes every check, and goes to the net.

THE INTANGIBLES

Brind'Amour is an extremely intense individual who puts a tremendous amount of pressure on himself. Sometimes players use that pressure as a normal buildup to performace; if they can control it, channel it properly, that pressure works to their benefit. If the pressure controls them, though, the opposite occurs, which summed up Brind'Amour's apparent sophomore slump. He never really got on track or put a stretch of solid games together.

It didn't help that he never really got a role. Was he the second center, once Oates returned? The first left wing? The second or third left wing? Was he a power-play guy? A faceoff guy? He was moved around and never really settled anyplace.

But he's very young. There is some maturing to be done. You could look at his face and see his frustration. He needs to relax, use the strength that is his asset, and leave the finesse to the people who have an easier time handling it.

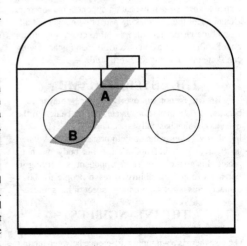

JEFF BROWN

Yrs. of NHL service: 5
Born: Ottawa, Ont., Canada; April 30, 1966
Position: Defenseman
Height: 6-1
Weight: 204
Uniform no.: 21
Shoots: Right

Career statistics:

GP	G	A	TP	PIM
352	75	192	267	242

1990-91 statistics:

GP	G	A	TP	+/-	PIM	PP	SH	GW	GT	S	PCT
67	12	47	59	4	39	6	1	0	2	176	6.8

LAST SEASON

Games played and goal totals were lowest in four seasons. Assists tied career high.

THE FINESSE GAME

Brown has a hard, accurate slap shot, which he does not get off quickly enough to qualify for the status of Al MacInnis or Doug Wilson. But he keeps it low, and when he gets it through, creates more than his share of rebounds and scrambles.

He has above-average skating skill and all the qualities of a well-rounded skating student. He can change direction easily, jump to an opening, control a point on the power play. But he doesn't always appear to be working at the top end; he can cover the same ground at three-quarter speed that others require all-out effort to attain.

Brown makes solid plays and approaches the attacking blue line in control of his speed—just in case he needs another gear to beat an opponent one-on-one. He enhances the playmaking aspect with splendid all-around ice vision that allows him to create something out of nothing with a deft pass to an opening that a wing can skate into and collect at full stride.

THE PHYSICAL GAME

Brown is not an overly physical player and, because he is a bit lackadaisical, can be beaten to the outside—which basically is scandalous, given his skating ability. He uses his body to protect the puck when he's carrying it, but doesn't use his body much to protect his goalie when some opponent is carrying it. For his size and his ability to reach people for body contacts, this is a disappointing aspect of his game.

THE INTANGIBLES

This player is among the most difficult to evaluate because there is a whopping difference between having effortless ability and having ability but not making a suitable effort.

Brown may be a natural athlete who can accomplish what he needs to do without being all flailing arms and churning legs, items which provide the APPEARANCE of effort. So it would be improper to criticize him on the simple cause that it looks like he may not be getting the most out of himself. His skills put him near the league's elite; his will remains at question more because of appearance than because of fact.

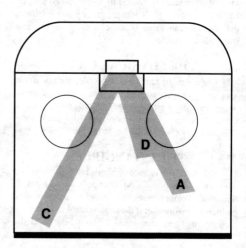

GARTH BUTCHER

Yrs. of NHL service: 9
Born: Regina, Sask., Canada; January 8, 1963
Position: Defenseman
Height: 6-0
Weight: 200
Uniform no.: 5
Shoots: Right

Career statistics:

GP	G	A	TP	PIM
623	33	111	144	122

1990-91 statistics:

GP	G	A	TP	+/-	PIM	PP	SH	GW	GT	S	PCT
82	6	16	22	-14	289	1	0	1	0	75	8.0

LAST SEASON

Obtained March 5 from Vancouver, along with Dan Quinn, for Sergio Momesso, Cliff Ronning, Geoff Courtnall and Robert Dirk. Goal total tied career high; point total was three-season high and within one of matching personal best.

THE FINESSE GAME

Butcher can give the intelligent pass, can be creative. He doesn't just whack the puck around the boards to get it out of the zone. He can handle the puck a little; he'll get it to the red line and get it in deep. Butcher doesn't operate at the speed of a Paul Cavallini, but he can gain the opposing blue line at times.

Butcher can make the touch pass or try the long, crisp breakaway pass, but mostly keeps the play simple, up the boards, and makes the proper choices that don't get him in trouble. He doesn't have great skills, but he has good ones.

Has good skating skills, but isn't the most agile guy in the league.

THE PHYSICAL GAME

Garth Butcher is mean every shift but also is very solid defensively. Last year's minus 14, it should be noted, included a minus 18 with Vancouver and a plus-four with sounder defensive execution in St. Louis.

Butcher is aggressive in eliminating time and space. He doesn't get knocked off the puck, but will do all he can to knock his adversary off it.

But perhaps the best feature of his game is his insistence in annoying you to the point of fury. He will do anything he can to antagonize you into taking a dumb penalty and get you off your game.

THE INTANGIBLES

The guy's no dummy. He knows that keeping the game simple will keep him in the league and make him valuable to his team.

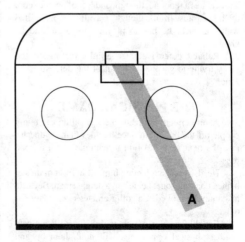

GINO CAVALLINI

Yrs. of NHL service: 7
Born: Toronto, Ont., Canada; November 24, 1962
Position: Left wing
Height: 6-1
Weight: 215
Uniform no.: 17
Shoots: Left

Career statistics:

GP	G	A	TP	PIM
460	95	130	225	429

1990-91 statistics:

GP	G	A	TP	+/-	PIM	PP	SH	GW	GT	S	PCT
78	8	27	35	4	81	3	0	2	0	131	6.1

LAST SEASON

Goal total was lowest in six seasons, but assist total was career best.

THE FINESSE GAME

Gino Cavallini lacks acceleration and lateral movement, but is a very strong straight-ahead skater. His balance is okay, but his agility is questionable and it is asking a lot for him to maneuver in confined areas.

Cavallini has a monster slap shot off the wing, but takes too long getting it off. Consequently, he ends up creating more of his points by going to the net. In tight, he has less-than-average ability; he might have an opening but drill the puck right into the goalie's pads. That creates a rebound, though, and lots of people score off his caroms. In all, though, Cavallini is not gifted with the puck; he has to play give-and-go, and he knows it.

Reliable defensively, Cavallini sometimes is too fancy trying to get the puck out of the defensive end zone.

THE PHYSICAL GAME

A very effective forechecker, Cavallini can bump people off the puck; but once he does that, he doesn't take the next step and find a teammate with a good pass.

He also good at planting himself in front of the net in the attacking zone; he ties up a defenseman. Because he cannot be moved, Cavallini creates open space for others.

Cavallini is not a fighter, but he will compete against physical opponents, will hold them up and bump them and will fight occasionally. He is tough because he's big; he doesn't create a lot of scoring chances with his talent, but he creates space with his strength.

THE INTANGIBLES

Gino Cavallini is a positive guy to have around; he accepts any role you give him. Intense. Works hard in practice. He is always riding the stationary bike, doing anything he can to get better. And he needs to maintain that approach to the job if he is going to keep his sweater.

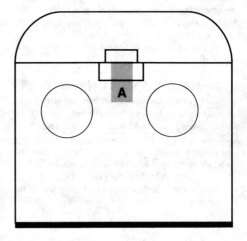

PAUL CAVALLINI

Yrs. of NHL service: 4
Born: Toronto, Ont., Canada; October 13, 1965
Position: Defenseman
Height: 6-1
Weight: 210
Uniform no.: 14
Shoots: Left

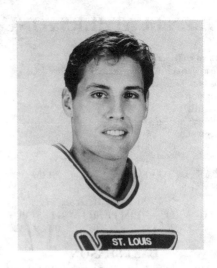

Career statistics:

GP	G	A	TP	PIM
290	28	96	124	483

1990-91 statistics:

GP	G	A	TP	+/-	PIM	PP	SH	GW	GT	S	PCT
67	10	25	35	19	89	3	0	0	0	116	9.9

LAST SEASON

Lost the tip of a finger after blocking slap shot by Chicago's Doug Wilson. Goal total was career high, PIM a career low.

THE FINESSE GAME

Because he has wonderful skating skills—balance, agility, acceleration, mobility forward and backward—Cavallini can play what seems to be some of the most reckless defense in the NHL.

Cavaliini has uncanny anticipation at both ends. He takes high-risk chances that pay off. You see the situation develop and know that if he doesn't intercept the pass he's trying to pick off, he's toasted for a breakaway. But he picks it off more times than not and turns that quick counter into offensive thrust.

An excellent poke-checker, Cavallini is a gambler in his use of the move, but backs it up with great puck sense. He will go for the poke—heaven help him if he misses it—then will make an instant transition from defense to offense, be off and gone.

Cavallini can make a rush with the best of them. He knows when to break for scoring holes as the fourth man in the rush or the defenseman who activates in the zone. Has ability to score with very good, accurate slap and wrist shots, but tries to score too much from the point instead of making better use of his teammates in front.

At times, Cavalllini also will overhandle at the attacking blue line. But even if he does, Cavallini also has the ability to gain the blue line and be creative after having done so.

THE PHYSICAL GAME

Cavallini doesn't bang, but he elminates along the boards and allows a teammate to come and take the puck. In front, he plays the puck rather than eliminate the man.

He can be an agitator and get under opponents' skin, but Cavallini is not a real physical player. Though talented in all aspects of the game, probably the one thing he doesn't do is punish people. He is more a finesse guy with great size than a physical player with hands, feet and intellect.

THE INTANGIBLES

Not a fiercely physical player, but he competes and likes to win. Cavallini is intense. He is gaining consistency, though there is still a ways to go.

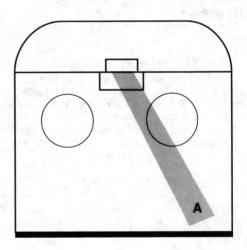

GLEN FEATHERSTONE

Yrs. of NHL service: 2
Born: Toronto, Ont., Canada; July 8, 1968
Position: Defense
Height: 6-4
Weight: 216
Uniform no.: 36
Shoots: Left

Career statistics:

GP	G	A	TP	PIM
144	5	29	34	371

1990-91 statistics:

GP	G	A	TP	+/-	PIM	PP	SH	GW	GT	S	PCT
68	5	15	20	19	204	1	0	1	0	59	8.5

LAST SEASON

Totals for goals, assists, points and PIM all were personal highs.

THE FINESSE GAME

An excellent skater with excellent lateral mobility for a big man, Featherstone is quick to accelerate, forward and backward.

His hands skills are nearly as strong. Featherstone is a very good passer and his shot is extremely hard, though not always accurate. He can wrist the puck and slap it, but his shot selection is not very good. When he's got time, and there's no screen in front of the goalie, he just throws a floater to the net; and when there's good traffic in front, he comes with the cannon that just bounces off somebody's head and goes into the crowd.

Featherstone holds the blue line as well as anybody and keeps the gap to the forwards closed. Positionally, he is strong; he might get over-aggressive in his challenges and get beat by good one-on-one players, but more of his errors are by comission than omission.

THE PHYSICAL GAME

It takes a while before Featherstone gets mad enough to fight, but when he does go, he handles himself well. He's mean, but not consistently; he isn't mean every shift, the way Scott Stevens can be. His hitting is just as erratic: some games, yes; some games, no. But when he does hit, Featherstone is able to hit hard, then recover and re-enter the play.

THE INTANGIBLES

A big kid, literally, Featherstone still has some maturing to do and needs to avoid emotional, "heat of battle" penalties. But he already has made himself better.

He is willing to work, to fulfill more potential than you might think. On a team with Scott Stevens, Jeff Brown, Paul Cavallini and Garth Butcher, Featherstone did not get all the ice time in the world.

When you rarely play higher than the No. 5 spot, you can't always just come off the bench confident that you won't make a mistake. You tend to play tentative; you don't want to make the mistake or take the penalty that could cost you the rest of the evening's ice time. With more playing time—and the accompanying increase in confidence—Featherstone should be, and probably will be, a very substantial NHL player. Because there didn't seem to be much chance he would get that ice time in St. Louis, it seemed a certainty he would make the most of his free-agent status and be with another team by the time the 1991-92 season began.

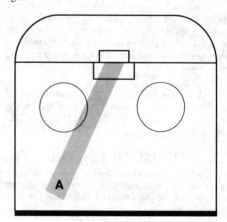

BRETT HULL

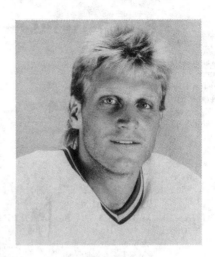

Yrs. of NHL service: 4
Born: Belleville, Ont., Canada; August 9, 1964
Position: Right wing
Height: 5-10
Weight: 201
Uniform no.: 16
Shoots: Right

Career statistics:

GP	G	A	TP	PIM
306	232	161	393	95

1990-91 statistics:

GP	G	A	TP	+/-	PIM	PP	SH	GW	GT	S	PCT
78	86	45	131	23	22	29	0	11	1	389	22.1

LAST SEASON

Was voted the Hart Trophy as league MVP after amassing a goal total that was third-highest in NHL history and improved his own one-season league record for right wings. Led league in power-play goals, game-winning goals, first goals (19) and shots. His 10-game goal streak was longest in league. His assist total was a career-high, PIM total a career-low for full season.

THE FINESSE GAME

Checking attention really doesn't matter. Hull has all the shots. He can score coming down the wing; he'll come off the wing, keep his feet moving and snap the puck; he'll score on the deke or on a wrist shot from 50 feet. He can one-time it, slap it, wrist it, and get every one of those shots off in an eyeblink. And he has the in-tight ability to roof a backhand.

Hull is confident where his shots are going. He always makes the goalie make a save. You never know what can happen, sometimes, when you just throw the puck at the net and turn it into the goalie's problem.

Hull is exceptional at getting himself in position to receive a pass. If the pass isn't perfectly accurate, Hull can bend his knees or extend his arms and still get off some kind of shot. He doesn't need it set up on a tee.

And he can return the favor with any pass that might be needed. Hull might be one of the best one-touch passers in the league. He also reads the play well and can give-and-go expertly.

He might give up something on defense to gain something on offense. If there's a puck up for grabs in a defending corner, Hull will anticipate possession and sprint toward the neutral zone for a breakaway pass, rather than charge toward the corner to help win the puck. Then again, the defensive corners are a long way from where he earns his millions.

THE PHYSICAL GAME

Hull is strong on his feet and shifty. He can deke outside/inside, inside/outside. Defensemen don't like

to give him much room, but if he can't go around them, Hull is more than strong enough to go over them or through them. They want to stand up, but he won't let them.

Hull is a power forward. He's a finesse shooter, but he's willing to be abused in front to score more goals. He will take more than he dishes out; he doesn't stick anybody or yap after whistles.

THE INTANGIBLES

The magic number is 100 goals in a season. He can do it. If Adam Oates is healthy all season and available to load Hull's gun, it should be a lock. If Hull takes the occasional long shift, not too many people are going to hold it against him.

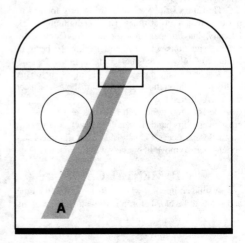

CURTIS JOSEPH

Yrs. of NHL service: 2
Born: Keswick, Ont., Canada; April 29, 1967
Position: Goaltender
Height: 5-10
Weight: 180
Uniform no.: 31
Catches: Left

Career statistics:

GP	MINS	GA	SO	GAA	A	PIM
45	2562	137	0	3.21	2	0

1990-91 statistics:

GP	MINS	GAA	W	L	T	SO	GA	S	SAPCT	PIM
30	1710	3.12	16	10	2	0	89	874	.898	0

LAST SEASON

Doubled games played total from rookie season, posted personal best pro goals against average, record highs in all three decision categories. Missed time due to knee injury in January.

THE PHYSICAL GAME

Joseph is more a pads goalie than anything else. He doesn't catch a lot of pucks, which is especially evident on the rebounds he permits off long shots he should be controlling.

Joseph has gotten by so far by playing deep in the net and depending on his reactions. Has started to come out more, but prefers to stay back, because that way, he isn't beaten on plays that get behind him. If he stays back, Joseph is closer to the posts, and on two-on-ones, he won't be out, flat on his belly and out of the play, while somebody is putting a tap-in into the unguarded net.

Because he stays back, teams tend to think they can beat him high. But Joseph is very quick in-close and teams find that by the end of the night, they have not been successful shooting there.

He isn't a strict V-goalie, isn't overly fond of it, but uses that setup at times. He isn't lightning-quick laterally, but compensates for that shortcoming by reading situations well and anticipating, so he is in better position when the puck comes to him.

Joseph sees the puck well and is improving on his ability to see through screens on point shots, an aspect that had bothered him.

He isn't too good with the puck and that weird cross-over of his hands to handle the puck doesn't help much. Joseph doesn't always make the right decision about where to move it, but he's working on it.

THE MENTAL GAME

A solid competitor who wants to play all the time and wants to be No. 1, Joseph has won because of his mental ability as much as his physical skills. He has excellent concentration and mental toughness. He isn't bothered by adversity, and he's had quite a bit of it, because of many injuries.

Bad goals do not weigh on him. The ones that have occurred have been mostly the result of inexperience. Some netminders let in a weak goal and go in the tank, others get mad and bear down after one; Joseph belongs to the latter category. And because of that, he can carry a team.

THE INTANGIBLES

Joseph made the climb from Tier II to the NHL in barely 2 1/2 seasons, so clearly there is potential.

362

DARIN KIMBLE

Yrs. of NHL service: 3
Born: Lucky Lake, Sask., Canada; November 22, 1968
Position: Right wing
Height: 6-2
Weight: 210
Uniform no.: 29
Shoots: Right

Career statistics:

GP	G	A	TP	PIM
131	11	12	23	576

1990-91 statistics:

GP	G	A	TP	+/-	PIM	PP	SH	GW	GT	S	PCT
61	3	6	9	-3	242	0	0	1	0	28	10.7

LAST SEASON

Obtained February 4 from Quebec for Herb Raglan, Tony Twist and Andy Rymsha.

THE FINESSE GAME

Kimble does have good thought processes, but needs playing time to flesh them out successfully. He has good instincts and a feel for the game, but needs to improve his physical and mental quickness to react more appropriately to what he sees.

Kimble needs to work on his skating. The agility just isn't there; his turns are cumbersome. His lateral movement and acceleration needs work. He takes a long time to start and to stop.

He can read the forecheck, he can read plays. It's just getting comfortable with the speed of the game.

Kimble has a good wrist shot but not much of a slap, because it takes him a while to get it off, and goalies can time it off the stick.

THE PHYSICAL GAME

Kimble's physical toughness is evident. He is willing to play his role and takes on all the heavyweights. His points come from going to the net.

He is not a stick man and does not take retaliatory penalties. He's a big farm kid who goes on guts and basic strength and more than gets by.

THE INTANGIBLES

If he had another half-step, or made better decisions, Kimble would keep people honest. But he tries to get fancy with limited skills. Kimble needs to learn his limitations and decide what he's going to do about them.

He needs confidence, needs time, needs ice time, and his conditioning needs work if he's going to play with the big boys and play like one. You have to learn the ins and outs of being a fourth-line player on a three-line team. But Kimble is intelligent, he doesn't take bad penalties and he has the potential to become a regular.

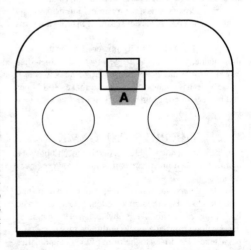

DAVE LOWRY

Yrs. of NHL service: 5
Born: Sudbury, Ont., Canada; February 14, 1965
Position: Left wing
Height: 6-1
Weight: 195
Uniform no.: 10
Shoots: Left

Career statistics:

GP	G	A	TP	PIM
343	60	51	111	611

1990-91 statistics:

GP	G	A	TP	+/-	PIM	PP	SH	GW	GT	S	PCT
79	19	21	40	19	168	0	2	5	0	123	15.4

LAST SEASON

Goal total matched prior season's, which was a career-high. Point total was NHL career high.

THE FINESSE GAME

Though he doesn't have great agility, Lowry is one of the fastest players in the game. He has better-than-average acceleration and positively exceptional speed, breakaway speed that especially comes into play while he is killing penalties.

Lowry has a good slap shot, but fires it with only average accuracy. He's an average finisher, but he's getting better and gaining confidence, which should provide great rewards as he warms to the role of checker/penalty killer. Rare is the checking forward who can convert a high percentage of the chances they create, but Lowry was a scorer in his junior days and could flirt with 30 goals per season if his touch returns in full.

Not an especially shifty player, if he beats you to the outside, it's with a change of speed, rather than power. Lowry has better-than-average hockey sense; he doesn't make fancy plays but he makes solid ones and he doesn't cough up the puck at the attacking blue line.

THE PHYSICAL GAME

Lowry is a not a fighter, in that he doesn't provoke them. But when push comes to shove, Lowry shoves back.

He prefers, though, to keep his gloves on; and when he does, Lowry is an excellent forechecker who is getting more involved physically. He separates defensemen from the puck with his insistence and persistence. He drives to the front of the net and defies defensemen to move him out of the space he has claimed.

THE INTANGIBLES

His curve definitely is on an upward sweep. Lowry had a very solid plus rating that more effectively underscored his checking skills and his ability to produce—at times outscoring the top opposition forwards he regularly is assigned to check.

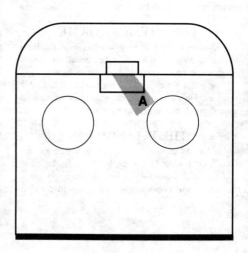

MARIO MAROIS

Yrs. of NHL service: 12
Born: Ancienne Lorette, Que., Canada;
December 15, 1957
Position: Defenseman
Height: 5-11
Weight: 170
Uniform no.: 44
Shoots: Right

Career statistics:

GP	G	A	TP	PIM
904	75	353	428	1674

1990-91 statistics:

GP	G	A	TP	+/-	PIM	PP	SH	GW	GT	S	PCT
64	2	14	16	17	81	0	0	0	0	59	3.4

LAST SEASON

Claimed from Quebec in waiver draft Oct. 1.

THE FINESSE GAME

Marois seldom gets involved offensively, but still has the ability to join the play if a high-percentage, high-reward situation arises. He used to try to carry the puck but would cough it up; now, if he has any doubts or there's any hint of danger, it's off the glass and out, off the boards and out. Marois doesn't overhandle; he gets it deep, and keeps the shifts short. He is less vigor, more smarts. He makes the correct decisions most of the time and uses experience as a guide for his anticipation. That's one reason he's still playing: He can read the situation and react to it ahead of time.

Marois passes the puck very well. He has a good shot from the point and he shoots with a purpose; he gets it on net and gives people a chance to tip it. And he doesn't get many blocked.

A player of only average speed—there are a lot of miles on those tires—Marois' lateral mobility is only fair and there still are times he gets his feet tangled.

THE PHYSICAL GAME

And Marois still has a bit of the mean streak he brought to his rookie season with the Rangers so many years ago. He's not going to fight, as he did then, because he is past that stage. But he will move people in front and do whatever body work has to be done.

THE INTANGIBLES

Marois plays the 5-6-7 role and accepts being out of the lineup at times. He has nothing left to prove, but that doesn't mean he has nothing left. He's excellent in the dressing room and is the creator of many off-ice team activities that keep the players close. He still enjoys the game, stays in shape and plays it simple.

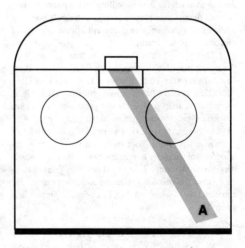

ADAM OATES

Yrs. of NHL service: 6
Born: Weston, Ont., Canada; August 27, 1962
Position: Center
Height: 5-11
Weight: 189
Uniform no.: 12
Shoots: Right

Career statistics:

GP	G	A	TP	PIM
387	102	314	416	124

1990-91 statistics:

GP	G	A	TP	+/-	PIM	PP	SH	GW	GT	S	PCT
61	25	90	115	15	29	3	1	3	0	139	18.0

LAST SEASON

Got a late start last season due to a stomach-muscle injury that needed time to heal but still finished second in NHL in assists. Assist total in 61 games was only 12 short of personal best set over 80 games the prior season. Goal, assist and point totals were career bests. Second on team in scoring.

THE FINESSE GAME

Oates knows the defensive game inside-out, knows the game without the puck. He might gamble too much to get the puck back, might take a high-risk chance at picking off a pass, but feels the risk is worth it, because he can make other teams worry when he has it.

Oates is used against the other team's top lines. He isn't used much for penalty killing, but is a threat when he's out there. Oates played defense extremely well one game as an emergency replacement after a number of ejections depleted lineup.

This player has brilliant vision from the point on the power play. No dummy, he always looks for Brett Hull, always sees Hull, always gets the puck to Hull.

Oates doesn't have an overpowering shot. He is more finesse than power. He has great moves in tight, but would much rather get an assist than a goal. And most of those assists are first assists. He is unselfish to a fault; you wish he'd shoot more just to keep defenses honest—they can try to take away his passing lanes if they know he's only going to shoot as a final option.

Oates has quick acceleration and is very agile. He can make plays while moving, he can make plays while sleeping.

THE PHYSICAL GAME

Not muscular, but strong, Oates will give you the shoulder, lift your stick off the puck. He is willing to hit and be hit, but is not physical by any means. Oates eliminates people in traffic, carries the puck into traffic, goes into traffic to get it.

Oates plays his size. He has wiry strength. He's not going to knock people off the puck, but he's going to manipulate them into the places he wants them to be. Then, once he has the puck and the room, he's going to try to make a pass that will put his teammate at best advantage.

THE INTANGIBLES

Oates has an excellent work ethic, and he makes his linemates better with his exceptional passing talents.

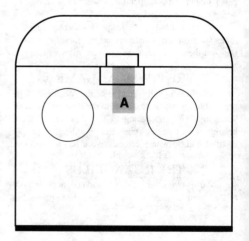

DAN QUINN

Yrs. of NHL service: 8
Born: Ottawa, Ont., Canada; June 1, 1965
Position: Center
Height: 5-11
Weight: 175
Uniform no.: 7
Shoots: Left

Career statistics:

GP	G	A	TP	PIM
591	221	337	558	407

1990-91 statistics:

GP	G	A	TP	+/-	PIM	PP	SH	GW	GT	S	PCT
78	22	38	60	-33	66	12	0	5	1	183	12.0

LAST SEASON

Obtained from Vancouver March 5 with Garth Butcher for Sergio Momesso, Geoff Courtnall, Robert Dirk and Cliff Ronning. Goal and point totals were six-season lows. Plus-minus was second worst in league; Toronto's Michel Petit was -34.

THE FINESSE GAME

Quinn has skills with the puck and can create offense if he plays with people who can convert his passes. He is a good skater, with speed to burn, plus balance and agility to match. He can put people into the clear with his passes and also can keep the puck to make the occasional one-on-one play against a lumbering defenseman he can victimize with darting moves.

Quinn has a scoring touch, because he gets his shots off quickly and sprays them to different locations. He will materialize in the scrambles in front of the net and will pay an occasional price to score.

THE PHYSICAL GAME

Quinn basically plays his size. He is not a physical player and is a liability on defense, which stems from a lack of strength and positional awareness more than from a lack of concern or effort.

THE INTANGIBLES

Quinn is in a peculiar position at St. Louis. He is creative, he can make a play, but doesn't have a lot of skilled people to pass to because of the people who play on the lines ahead of him. He was brought to St. Louis, basically, to add depth and provide the power-play skills that had been assigned Cliff Ronning; the Blues needed a specific person for a specific role. This year will provide a truer indication of whether he's up to the task.

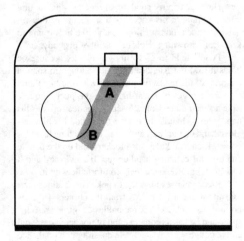

VINCENT RIENDEAU

Yrs. of NHL service: 3
Born: St. Hyacinthe, Que., Canada; April 20, 1966
Position: Goaltender
Height: 5-10
Weight: 181
Uniform no.: 30
Catches: Left

Career statistics:

GP	MINS	GA	SO	GAA	A	PIM
120	7100	396	4	3.35	3	10

1990-91 statistics:

GP	MINS	GAA	W	L	T	SO	GA	S	SAPCT	PIM
44	2671	3.01	29	9	6	3	134	1241	.892	0

LAST SEASON

Goals against average was best of his career, minutes played total was personal high. Victory total was one better than his prior career total for 72 decisions. His first season with a won-lost record above .500

THE PHYSICAL GAME

Riendeau is more of a traditional goaltender who plays his angles pretty well, challenges, reads and reacts to the play. A good skater and getting better, Riendeau gets to everything behind the net and can get across well on two-on-one situations.

He does a pretty good job of regaining his footing after dropping to his knees for a save, and he doesn't "swim" much, doesn't flop around like he's trying to keep from drowning. He's in control of his body.

People tend to go to his glove side, because he holds it low, but Riendeau is quick enough to snare a majority of the pucks people think will beat him there.

He can get better at handling the puck, though. Like his teammate, Curtis Joseph, Riendeau crosses his hand over to handle it. Rather than slide his blocker-glove hand up the shaft and using his catching hand for power, Riendeau keeps his blocker hand on the paddle and uses his catching hand up top. It's awkward and it eats time, but Riendeau feels comfortable with it.

Riendeau uses his stick to poke check and is alert to using it to cut off passes from the corners. He does not use his stick to hack the ankles of intruders to his space and he has a problem habit of not being prepared early enough with his stick. He doesn't put it on the ice until the shooter is in his windup and sometimes shooters fill that hole before he gets set.

THE MENTAL GAME

Riendeau is a competitor who makes the big save and he is getting mentally tougher. He fights through little injuries and adversities better than he did. Bad goals affected him in the past, but no more.

Riendeau has matured. He appears calm under pressure, which keeps his teammates under control during tense game situations.

THE INTANGIBLES

Riendeau likes to play on the road. He enjoys the challenge of a tough building.

He has trimmed nearly 20 pounds of his playing weight since arriving in St. Louis, adding quickness and conditioning. He has improved his skating, his conditioning and his confidence. He spends more time at his job and it has paid off handsomely.

SCOTT STEVENS

Yrs. of NHL service: 9
Born: Kitchener, Ont., Canada; April 1, 1964
Position: Defenseman
Height: 6-2
Weight: 215
Uniform no.: 2
Shoots: Left

Career statistics:

GP	G	A	TP	PIM
679	103	375	478	1780

1990-91 statistics:

GP	G	A	TP	+/-	PIM	PP	SH	GW	GT	S	PCT
78	5	44	49	23	150	1	0	1	0	160	3.1

LAST SEASON

His first season with the team after eight campaigns in Washington. Goal total was career low, so was PIM total.

THE FINESSE GAME

Stevens has quite a pair of hands, he can stickhandle and carry the puck. But gets in trouble when he tries to make things too fancy—especially in his defensive zone. He doesn't turn over the puck much in the neutral or attacking zones, but sometimes, he sets off scrambles in his end by overhandling, trying to beat too many opponents by carrying instead of passing the puck from harm's way.

A strong, agile skater in the forward and backward moves, Stevens adds good lateral mobility to his repertory.

He has a hard shot, but it isn't accurate. He tries too hard to score goals from the point and too rarely takes some steam off the puck so that teammates can tip it.

THE PHYSICAL GAME

Stevens' strength is a huge asset. He uses it to ward off checkers when he's carrying the puck. And he hits. He doesn't set a goal of one big hit per shift, but he's strong on the boards and he moves people in front.

Stevens blocks shots. He moves people in front. He's good one-on-one. He stands up and challenges. He can close people off before the blue line because he keeps a tight gap to the forwards.

Stevens has the ability to play the puck and the man; he'll try for a sweep check at the blue line, but will keep his body in position to continue the play if the sweep attempt fails.

THE INTANGIBLES

Scott Stevens provides top-notch two way defense, leads on and off the ice, works hard every practice and sets an example. He's tough. He competes every shift. He backs up his teammates. He makes others better by his physical presence. He's a very good all-around player who is very good at most things but isn't really great at any.

More important, he is less emotional now. He is aggressive with a purpose, not out of control. He was able last year to handle the ballyhoo over his contract and his arrival; with Hull getting the big numbers—and putting up the big numbers—it was much easier to come to St. Louis and establish himself.

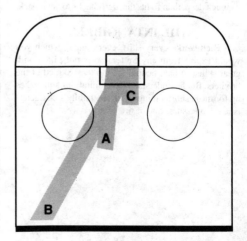

RICH SUTTER

Yrs. of NHL service: 7
Born: Viking, Alta., Canada; December 2, 1963
Position: Right wing
Height: 5-11
Weight: 188
Uniform no.: 23
Shoots: Right

Career statistics:

GP	G	A	TP	PIM
518	115	119	234	1058

1990-91 statistics:

GP	G	A	TP	+/-	PIM	PP	SH	GW	GT	S	PCT
77	16	11	27	6	122	0	2	2	0	130	12.3

LAST SEASON

Goal total was four-season high, PIM total a four-season low.

THE FINESSE GAME

Sutter can make plays, but simple plays. He doesn't saucer the puck to an open space the way an Adam Oates can. He has only average thought processes in terms of seeing the ice; he likes to keep it deep in the attack zone and keep it simple

Sutter does not create opportunities off the rush, he makes them off the forecheck. He gets himself in position to score, but isn't a great finisher.

Sutter is not an agile skater, but he's strong. He has the ability to forecheck because of his persistence. And at the other end, what he lacks in quickness in the defensive zone, he makes up for with smarts.

THE PHYSICAL GAME

A confrontational player, Sutter finishes every check emphatically. He goes to the net hard. He drives the puck deep, then fights through checks to get it back.

THE INTANGIBLES

Rich works every shift, every game, which you would expect from any Sutter. He is not gifted with great skills; in fact, he may be the least-skilled of the brothers. But he understands his limitations and makes up for those shortcomings with the family's characteristic relentlessness and desire.

And from all outward appearances, anyway, Rich Sutter did a good job of handling the fact that his big brother coaches the team. It did not seem to become an issue in the dressing room.

Sutter is good in the room. He plays hurt and, given the style he plays, that is often.

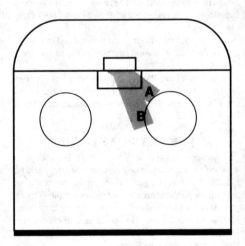

370

RON WILSON

Yrs. of NHL service: 11
Born: Toronto, Ont., Canada; May 13, 1956
Position: Center
Height: 5-9
Weight: 180
Uniform no.: 18
Shoots: Left

Career statistics:

GP	G	A	TP	PIM
642	88	178	266	313

1990-91 statistics:

GP	G	A	TP	+/-	PIM	PP	SH	GW	GT	S	PCT
73	10	27	37	-1	54	1	2	1	0	101	9.9

LAST SEASON

Goal total was highest in seven seasons, assists total highest in 10.

THE FINESSE GAME

Wilson possesses great quickness and speed, which makes him an above-average penalty killer and checking center. His skating is what allows him to play at a high level. He's quick on the forecheck, can play all situations and does well in one-on-one battles for loose pucks.

Shifty, with good offensive moves, Wilson beats people to the outside more with his change of pace than his dekes. His offense generally comes from a defensive posture, off sequences where he forechecks the puck into up-for-grabs status, wins it, then goes to work in deep.

Strength and mental skills are shortcomings. He is only average on faceoffs, and his hockey sense is only average.

THE PHYSICAL GAME

Not a banger, Wilson will hit and accept being hit; but it's not a huge part of his game because he is not a huge player. Wilson uses quickness, rather than muscle, to take the puck away from people.

THE INTANGIBLES

Wilson works and works, plays his role and uses his experience to make his skills greater.

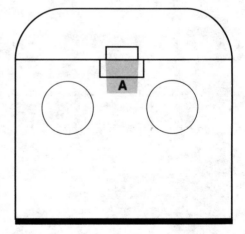

TORONTO MAPLE LEAFS

BRIAN BRADLEY

Yrs. of NHL service: 4
Born: Kitchener, Ont., Canada; January 21, 1965
Position: Center
Height: 5-10
Weight: 170
Uniform no.: 44
Shoots: right

Career statistics:

GP	G	A	TP	PIM
264	61	111	172	174

1990-91 statistics:

GP	G	A	TP	+/-	PIM	PP	SH	GW	GT	S	PCT
70	11	31	42	-9	62	3	0	3	0	116	9.5

LAST SEASON

Acquired from Vancouver for Tom Kurvers, January 12, 1991. Goal total was four-year low. Assist total was career high. Third on team in assists, fourth in points.

THE FINESSE GAME

Bradley has good speed but doesn't always realize how to use it to his best ability. He has great agility and acceleration, and can make a move inside or beat a defenseman wide. The problem comes from not always seeing which move to use at the right time.

Bradley has good hands and stick skills. He has started shooting more, overcoming a tendency to look for the perfect play, but he should get even more unselfish. He seems to lack confidence in his shot. He could become a more productive goal-scorer if he could master better use of his speed. He likes to lead the rush into the zone and could use his quickness to get into the holes for good scoring chances. He is also quick to jump on loose pucks.

Bradley seems to have good hockey sense and, with his hand skills, should be a better playmaker than he is.

THE PHYSICAL GAME

Bradley is a small forward and doesn't play a physical game. He is aware defensively, but can get pushed off the puck easily. Bradley could work a little harder in this department—not that we expect him to go challenging Scott Stevens—because it would help him develop a more consistent game if he nudged his involvement up a notch. He has the skating strength to do more than he has shown.

THE INTANGIBLES

Bradley made a splash when he first came to the Maple Leafs, then went into a prolonged slump. He asked for a trade if he couldn't get more ice time. If he couldn't fit in with Toronto, with their weakness at center, he may have a hard time fitting in anywhere else.

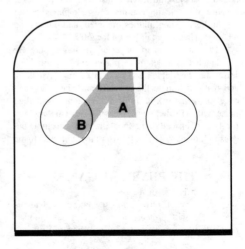

AARON BROTEN

Yrs. of NHL service: 10
Born: Roseau, Minn., USA; November 14, 1960
Position: Center
Height: 5-10
Weight: 180
Uniform no.: 21
Shoots: left

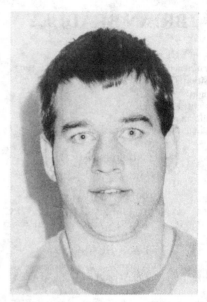

Career statistics:

GP	G	A	TP	PIM
723	181	325	506	427

1990-91 statistics:

GP	G	A	TP	+/-	PIM	PP	SH	GW	GT	S	PCT
47	11	8	19	+9	38	1	1	1	0	85	12.9

LAST SEASON

Acquired from Quebec with Michel Petit and Lucien DeBlois for Scott Pearson and Toronto's second-round draft picks in 1991 and 1992, November 17, 1990. Games played total was lowest in career for the former iron man (Broten once had a consecutive-games played streak of 318). Led team in plus-minus. Missed 33 games with a shoulder injury.

THE FINESSE GAME

Nothing about Broten shouts, but he adds to a team with his experience and quiet intelligence.

Broten is a good skater, not fast, but with close-in quickness and strength and balance. He is very low to the ice. He can turn sharply and can handle himself (and the puck) in traffic. He is also a good forechecker because of his skating and his reads. He played center for the Leafs when injuries mounted, and did a good job there. He does a fair job on faceoffs.

He is a very smart player on the power play. He was labeled as a defensive player once he left New Jersey, but the Maple Leafs recognized his playmaking and restored him to the special team (he is also an excellent penalty killer). Broten is a highly skilled passer with a feather touch. He will almost always look for the pass instead of the shot. His shot is accurate but doesn't fool many goalie. He won't force his way to the net.

THE PHYSICAL GAME

Broten is one of the best players for his size at keeping the puck alive along the boards and in his skates. He will protect the puck very well. Other players will takes runs at him and they roll off and

Broten cuts to the net with the puck. He is compact and was a very durable player until this season (well, you'd hurt too if Dave Manson fell on you). Broten will bump and get into people's way to slow them down.

THE INTANGIBLES

Always an underrated player because of his low-key style on and off the ice, Broten gives his all every night and a coach never has to worry about his preparation. Teams are naturally always looking to put youth in their lineup, but a player of Broten's experience is very valuable.

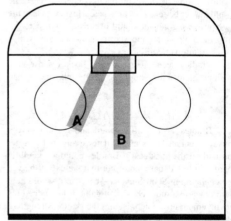

WENDEL CLARK

Yrs. of NHL service: 6
Born: Kelvington, Sask., Canada; October 25, 1966
Position: Left wing
Height: 5-11
Weight: 195
Uniform no.: 17
Shoots: left

Career statistics:

GP	G	A	TP	PIM
290	126	73	199	912

1990-91 statistics:

GP	G	A	TP	+/-	PIM	PP	SH	GW	GT	S	PCT
63	18	16	34	-5	152	4	0	2	0	181	9.9

LAST SEASON

Games played and points were highest totals in four seasons. Missed 12 games with a rib injury.

THE FINESSE GAME

Now that Clark seems to have recovered from a nagging back and knee injuries, he can go about putting his game back together. It's not a pretty game, but it's an effective one.

Clark played defense as a junior, and his rough and tumble style as a forward has needed some honing. Clark's game is founded on power, his sheer physical strength and willingness, which overcomes the lesser parts of his skating game. Clark is not very fast, agile or mobile, but he can steamroll right over opponents when he makes a beeline for the net.

Clark has a fantastic wrist shot but still takes a fraction too much time to get it away. He gets enough room from his reputation and if he starts making the most of it, he could return to the ranks of the 30-35 goal scorers. He does not use his teammates well and is not a good passer. Clark is a finisher. Let someone else do all the fancy work, and Clark can punctuate it.

Clark used to be quite dreadful defensively. He has improved this aspect of his game and plays better positionally instead of running all over the ice. He still won't be mistaken for a checking forward.

THE PHYSICAL GAME

Clark is a lightweight who will take on the heavyweights, but that bravery has taken its toll. Clark has to develop the smarts to realize when to hold back, because he is more valuable to the Leafs on the ice, and in one piece. He has established himself as a bona fide tough NHLer, and he has no need to go meeting every challenge flung at him. He can cut back on the fighting without neglecting the hitting that is a big asset to his game. Clark has started showing signs that he can control his emotions better.

Since Clark has had the kind of injuries that prohibited him from working out aerobically while he was recuperating, he was short on conditioning last year and tired easily.

THE INTANGIBLES

Clark played out his option last season, but the Leafs should do everything they can to make him financially happy. His health remains a question mark, but he is a team leader who is respected by his own teammates and by opponents. We have not seen the best of Clark yet.

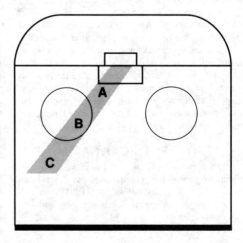

VINCENT DAMPHOUSSE

Yrs. of NHL service: 5
Born: Montreal, Que., Canada; December 17, 1967
Position: Left wing
Height: 6-1
Weight: 185
Uniform no.: 10
Shoots: left

Career statistics:

GP	G	A	TP	PIM
394	118	211	329	262

1990-91 statistics:

GP	G	A	TP	+/-	PIM	PP	SH	GW	GT	S	PCT
79	26	47	73	-31	65	10	1	4	0	247	10.5

LAST SEASON

Led team in goals, assists, points and shots. Second on team in power play goals. Second-worst plus-minus in NHL. All point totals were two-year lows.

THE FINESSE GAME

Damphousse has wonderful offensive instincts and the playmaking skills to complement them. He lacks, however, a killer instinct.

Damphousse is a skilled passer and he handles the puck well at varying speeds and when wheeling. He seems to love being a playmaker, and though he has shown he is a good shooter, he doesn't always make the smartest play selection. He has improved in his reading of plays, but he seems to lack natural goal-scoring instincts, although he works hard at getting into high percentage scoring areas. It's unlikely he'll score much more than 30 goals in a season.

Damphousse is a good skater who uses his agility well in the offensive zone and he can handle the puck while doing his zigs and zags. He has also learned to use his speed to get back on defense, and the Leafs used him to kill penalties on occasion.

Damphousse is growing into a better two-way player. Although his point totals tailed off last season, he played better hockey than he did the year before. His plus-minus was atrocious, but he played numerous games out of position (at center).

THE PHYSICAL GAME

Damphousse will take a hit to make a play, but bump and grind doesn't come naturally to him. He does not have much hockey strength and will lose most of the one-on-one battles. He is not aggressive and does not like to fight.

THE INTANGIBLES

Damphousse dazzled everyone in earning MVP honors in last season's All-Star Game. If all the pieces fit right, Damphousse could produce his first 100-point season this year. What's missing? A grinding center to play between him and Daniel Marois. Damphousse has done a lot of maturing in the past season, and has shown consistency and a desire to establish himself among the NHL's best.

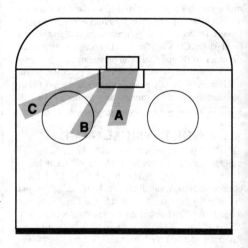

DAVE ELLETT

Yrs. of NHL service: 7
Born: Cleveland, Ohio, USA; March 30, 1964
Position: Defenseman
Height: 6-1
Weight: 200
Uniform no.: 4
Shoots: left

Career statistics:

GP	G	A	TP	PIM
535	103	234	337	573

1990-91 statistics:

GP	G	A	TP	+/-	PIM	PP	SH	GW	GT	S	PCT
77	12	37	49	-8	75	6	1	1	1	195	6.2

LAST SEASON

Acquired from Winnipeg with Paul Fenton for Ed Olczyk and Mark Osborne, November 10, 1990. Led team defensemen in scoring. Second on team in assists and points.

THE FINESSE GAME

Ellett is the kind of defenseman that a team relies upon to control a game, and the Leafs may have relied on Ellett too much last season. He is not a robust player and started wearing down late in the year, although he never complained nor asked the team to give him a lighter work load.

Ellett is an offensive defenseman who likes to start a play from his own end with a pass, then has the skating speed to jump up and get involved with the play. He is a heads-up passer and sees all his choices well. Ellett has a big slapshot and is a good point man on the power play, possibly one of the NHL's best. His shot is low and hard, and gets through, so forwards can charge for the net knowing the puck will arrive and the goalie will be forced to make a play.

Ellett is an excellent skater, and that is a key component of his game. He has very good lateral movement and is difficult to beat one-on-one. He has the skating speed to scramble back after making defensive mistakes—which he doesn't make that often; he pinches wisely and well and recognizes when to back off.

He can handle the puck well at speed and has good hands. He prefers the headman pass to rushing with the puck, but he is capable of either. Because of his skating ability and hockey sense, Ellett is developing into a fair penalty killer, certainly a player with shorthanded goal capabilities.

THE PHYSICAL GAME

Ellett is not going to overpower anyone. He plays well positionally and will make a hit, but he plays more of a containment game. He is very strong but doesn't have a meanness in him to be a punishing hitter. Because he is a finesse player, he is very good at working the puck out of a player's skates or a scrum in front of his net and moving it smartly up-ice. He plays a good transition game.

THE INTANGIBLES

Ellett is a good character player whose offensive skills are far superior to his defensive ones. He is improving defensively, however, and at 27, it isn't too late for him to become a better two-way player. He was only minus 4 in 60 games with the Leafs (second only to the departed Rob Ramage's plus 2 among team defensemen).

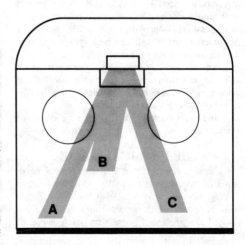

TOM FERGUS

Yrs. of NHL service: 10
Born: Chicago, Ill., USA; June 16, 1962
Position: Center
Height: 6-3
Weight: 210
Uniform no.: 19
Shoots: left

Career statistics:

GP	G	A	TP	PIM
635	215	314	529	458

1990-91 statistics:

GP	G	A	TP	+/-	PIM	PP	SH	GW	GT	S	PCT
14	5	4	9	-5	8	2	0	0	0	17	29.4

LAST SEASON

Missed 60 games with groin surgery. Missed five games with back and chest strain, and was in and out of the lineup with lingering soreness from his groin surgery. All totals career lows.

THE FINESSE GAME

All of Fergus's game is finesse, and almost all of it is contained in his arms and hands. There may be none better in the NHL at making the cup and saucer pass— a precise pass over a defender's stick that nestles on the tape of a teammate.

Fergus is also a very accurate shooter. He has a great shot with a snap or a wrist (note his very high shooting percentage) and can shoot or pass in traffic— although he would rather avoid it and operate in open ice. Fergus doesn't shoot often enough and sometimes overhandles the puck trying to make one more play. Overall, he has the abilities to become a team's No. 1 center, but he has never been able to put it all together on a consistent basis. His work ethic is suspect. He will reach loose pucks with his quick stick, but won't battle for possession in front of the net. You won't see him in the corners, either. He will hang back while a teammate fights it out to pry the puck away.

Fergus was always an average skater and he hasn't fully recovered from his surgery, which has slowed him down even more. He has good balance, but has lost some of his strength and mobility.

He has no interest or aptitude for the defensive aspect of the game, which will limit his future.

THE PHYSICAL GAME

Fergus plays far below his size. He has never played a physical game and will avoid it even more as he continues his comeback. With his skills, Fergus could have become an impact center, but more has always been expected of Fergus than he has delivered.

THE INTANGIBLES

Fergus has had his best moments playing between Vincent Damphousse and Daniel Marois, but following his severe injury last season, it's unlikely he will be able to come back with the same level of effectiveness. Most of Fergus's career has been the big tease. He has more talent than he has been able to use on a consistent basis. His health makes him even more of a longshot, although he did play well when he briefly returned for the end of the season.

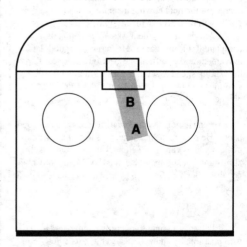

MIKE FOLIGNO

Yrs. of NHL service: 12
Born: Sudbury, Ont., Canada; January 29, 1959
Position: Right wing
Height: 6-2
Weight: 195
Uniform no.: 71
Shoots: right

Career statistics:

GP	G	A	TP	PIM
887	332	354	686	1862

1990-91 statistics:

GP	G	A	TP	+/-	PIM	PP	SH	GW	GT	S	PCT
68	12	12	24	+1	107	1	0	0	1	83	14.5

LAST SEASON

Acquired from Buffalo with future considerations for Brian Curran and Lou Franceschetti, December 17, 1990. All point totals career lows.

THE FINESSE GAME

Foligno has inner and outer strength—the inner to drive him as a team leader, the outer to power his gutsy game. There is no quit in him. He is not a big goal scorer (although he once had a 41-goal season), but it wouldn't be surprising if he came through with one more big productive season this year, if only to spite the Buffalo Sabres. Foligno can pound a shot from the top of the circles, but his favorite move is to come down the right wing and one-time a shot. He is also good at close range, scrapping for a loose puck.

Foligno earns himself a lot of space with his physical playing style, and he uses it wisely, seeing the openings. He makes very good passes in deep, especially quick touch passes.

Foligno is not a great skater, but he works so hard that his heart gets his feet where they have to go. He is very secure on a his blades and is an excellent corner-man because of that. He also knows what to do with the puck once he comes away with it, which makes him more of a force.

THE PHYSICAL GAME

Foligno is strong on his skates and is a physical specimen. His build is lean and sinewy, and he plays bigger than he is. He also plays younger than he is, with reckless abandon. When he hits, it hurts, and he hits at every opportunity. Foligno takes no prisoners at either end of the ice. With all of his experience, Foligno occasionally gets carried away with things and will take a bad penalty out of aggression.

THE INTANGIBLES

Foligno was a key acquisition for the Leafs, who have a short supply of leaders. Foligno is a gung-ho player with a great attitude on the ice and in the dressing room. His work ethic is to push himself to the limit, and that can't help but have a positive effect on his younger, more complacent teammates.

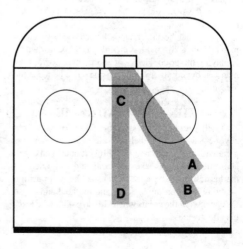

TODD GILL

Yrs. of NHL service: 5
Born: Brockville, Ont., Canada; November 9, 1965
Position: Defenseman
Height: 6-0
Weight: 180
Uniform no.: 23
Shoots: left

Career statistics:

GP	G	A	TP	PIM
330	28	95	123	541

1990-91 statistics:

GP	G	A	TP	+/-	PIM	PP	SH	GW	GT	S	PCT
72	2	21	23	-4	113	0	0	0	0	90	2.2

LAST SEASON

Games played and assist totals career highs. Assist total three-season high. Point total two-season high.

THE FINESSE GAME

The most difficult thing for Gill was to learn his limitations. He (and others) fancied himself as an offensive defenseman, but he just doesn't have the finesse or the offensive instincts of, say, teammate Dave Ellett. Once Gill learned he could be a valuable contributor defensively, he relaxed and had a satisfactory season.

Gill is a good skater, good enough to get involved offensively on a rush. He lacks lateral movement and has to concentrate to avoid getting beaten one-on-one. He has come to grips with the notion that he's not going to be deking people at the other end of the ice, either. He has good straightaway speed and can put on a burst to carry the puck out of the zone. He headmans the puck well.

Now that he understands he will be a two-goal man and not a 20-goal scorer, Gill has relaxed when he is playing the point. He is not an effective power play man yet, but could develop into one since he reads the ice well.

THE PHYSICAL GAME

Gill is either fearless or brainless. He will fight anyone—would you believe this 180-pounder has gone with Joe Kocur and Bob Probert and lived to tell about it? He always takes the body and while he isn't the hardest hitter because of his size, he will position his body between the attacker and the goal and finish his checks. On the nights when Gill doesn't hit, he loses his effectiveness.

THE INTANGIBLES

Gill struggled through his career while being shuffled from forward to defense. He appears to be getting comfortable in his defense role and, while it might not be saying much, was Toronto's best defenseman last season.

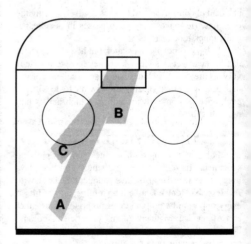

DAVE HANNAN

Yrs. of NHL service: 7
Born: Sudbury, Ont., Canada; November 26, 1961
Position: Center
Height: 5-10
Weight: 185
Uniform no.: 9
Shoots: left

Career statistics:

GP	G	A	TP	PIM
519	86	131	217	710

1990-91 statistics:

GP	G	A	TP	+/-	PIM	PP	SH	GW	GT	S	PCT
74	11	23	34	-9	82	0	1	2	0	72	15.3

LAST SEASON

Games played and point totals were five-season highs.

THE FINESSE GAME

Hannan is a good skater with average speed, but he is experienced enough to conserve his energy and turn on the quick spurts when he needs them. Hannan knows the ice well and doesn't run all over, but knows in which areas he can be most effective. Since he plays smart positionally, his skating flaws are not as glaring until he gets into a footrace with someone. He will beat a defenseman to a loose puck more on desire than outright quickness.

Most of what Hannan does is accomplished through hard work. He is a fair stickhandler, but not a good playmaker. Hannan is a determined forechecker and most of his points will come from his pressure.

Hannan is not a very good shooter and has a slow release. He will score most of his goals from scrambles around the net.

Hannan is a good defensive center and is reliable on faceoffs.

THE PHYSICAL GAME

Hannan lost a few pounds whle he was sick and surprised himself by finding he was a better player with the weight off. He should be a better conditioned athlete this year. Hannan plays bigger than he is, bumping bigger guys off the puck. He is reliable along the boards and will sacrifice his body to make the play.

THE INTANGIBLES

Hannan is a typical defensive forward who can get 10-12 goals a season. He is a hard worker and a good character man, but is an otherwise undistinguished player and is on the bubble in Toronto.

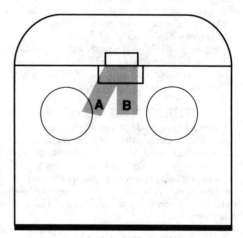

PETER ING

Yrs. of NHL service: 1
Born: Toronto, Ont., Canada; April 28, 1969
Position: Goaltender
Height: 6-2
Weight: 165
Uniform no.: 1
Catches: left

Career statistics:

GP	MINS	GA	SO	GAA	A	PIM
59	3308	218	1	3.95	0	6

1990-91 statistics:

GP	MINS	GAA	W	L	T	SO	GA	S	SAPCT	PIM
56	3126	3.84	16	29	8	1	200	716	.883	6

LAST SEASON

First full NHL season.

THE PHYSICAL GAME

Ing is an agile and acrobatic goalie who relies almost too heavily on his excellent reflexes. He plays too deep in his net, which means he gives the shooters a lot of room. He uses a butterfly style and has a very quick glove hand, but needs to learn to come out and play his angles better or the better NHL shooters will just deke him to the ice and beat him high.

Ing reads and anticipates plays well. He is a good skater with good balance, and has fair recovery time for a tall goalie. He is not as strong with his stick as he should be. He can stop the hard-arounds behind the net, but is limited with his passing and stickhandling.

Ing has good height but is on the lightweight size. He may be unwilling to bulk up for fear of losing some of his quickness, but he would be better off improving his technical game and adding some muscle.

THE MENTAL GAME

Ing has a good psyche, doesn't get too high or low emotionally. He can be pulled out of the net in a game and be put back in and not have his confidence battered. Ing has good concentration and can keep his eye on the puck through a crowd. Ing has his own way of doing things and doesn't like coaching advice on how to change his game, so any improvements will have to be self-generated.

THE INTANGIBLES

Ing is only 21 and has a fragile team in front of him. There is a lot of pressure in knowing that if you allow one bad goal, your team is already in a deep hole.

Unless the Leafs improve their team defense this season, Ing will be in for another difficult year and there is no telling how it will affect him. He will have to earn his No. 1 role in training camp, since the Leafs are not totally convinced he is better than Jeff Reese.

MIKE KRUSHELNYSKI

Yrs. of NHL service: 9
Born: Montreal, Que., Canada; April 27, 1960
Position: Center
Height: 6-2
Weight: 200
Uniform no.: 26
Shoots: left

Career statistics:

GP	G	A	TP	PIM
667	206	284	490	531

1990-91 statistics:

GP	G	A	TP	+/-	PIM	PP	SH	GW	GT	S	PCT
74	18	27	45	+1	58	3	2	1	1	109	16.5

LAST SEASON

Acquired from Los Angeles for John McIntyre, November 9, 1990. Third on team in points. Fourth on team in assists.

THE FINESSE GAME

Krushelnyski is a very deceptive skater, and has the kind of presence in the offensive zone that will draw two or three defenders to him and open up some ice for his linemates. Krushelnyski can go for the holes himself, with a long, ground-eating stride. He has good balance and can keep going with the puck or be ready to receive a pass. His agility helps him out of tight spots and he can get into position quickly for a play.

To complement his skating, Krushelnyski has good ice vision and soft hands for making and taking passes. He has a strong, accurate wrist shot which he doesn't unleash nearly often enough. He will also drive to the net in pursuit of a puck but will not go to the net without it.

Krushelnyski protects the puck well with his body. His strength and good hand-eye coordination make him a good face-off man.

THE PHYSICAL GAME

Krushelnyski has a lanky build and is strong, but doesn't get as involved as he should. Because Krushelnyski has some good finesse skills, maybe he thinks the grinding should be left to the less talented guys, and that limits him. Krushelnyski will take a hit to make a play, but he won't initiate. He has a long reach and good balance in traffic, so he can get checked and still make a good play. But Krushelnyski won't work too hard to get the puck back.

THE INTANGIBLES

The Leafs had hoped Krushelnyski could solve their center ice woes and move into the No. 1 slot, but they seem to be resigned to his being a third line center for Toronto. His contributions (probably 20 goals or so) won't match his potential. We noted Krushelnyski as an underachiever last season. Nothing has happened in the interim to alter that assessment, except for Krushelnyski's change of uniform. He hasn't changed his habits.

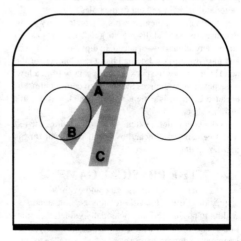

GARY LEEMAN

Yrs. of NHL service: 8
Born: Toronto, Ont., Canada; February 19, 1964
Position: Right wing
Height: 5-11
Weight: 175
Uniform no.: 11
Shoots: right

Career statistics:

GP	G	A	TP	PIM
511	169	218	387	419

1990-91 statistics:

GP	G	A	TP	+/-	PIM	PP	SH	GW	GT	S	PCT
52	17	12	29	-25	39	4	0	1	1	135	12.6

LAST SEASON

All point totals were five-year lows, due to Leeman missing 25 games with a shoulder injury.

THE FINESSE GAME

Leeman is highly skilled, with one of the best set of hands in the NHL. He is a naturally gifted athlete who could pick up any sport and play it well, but as is frequently the problem with the athletically blessed, Leeman doesn't always work as hard as he should to bump his game up to the next level.

He has explosive speed and is the kind of forward the opposing team is forced to key on. Leeman has very good agility and balance, but he is not a very strong skater and can be pushed off the puck when he tries to go into traffic. He has very good hand skills and is better at darting in and out of the holes.

Leeman complements his linemates very well. Because his hand skills are so good, he can pass in almost any situation—at speed, in dipsy-doodle moves and in give-and-gos. Leeman has a real hunger for the net. He one-times the puck well, especially from a low, wide position, and forces the goalie to commit himself, because Leeman is patient with the puck and doesn't rush his shots.

His talents don't extend to his own half of the red line. Leeman was benched by coach Tom Watt for his indifferent defensive play.

THE PHYSICAL GAME

Leeman is not a big guy and with his recent history of injuries, he will probably become even less willing to put himself into potentially vulnerable situations. This would mean quite a change in style for Leeman, an aggressive forward when it comes to pursuit of the puck in front of the goal. Leeman does not go to the boards well and does not use his body back on defense. He will also have to work hard on his off-ice conditioning to make up for time lost last season. Leeman can hold his own in a fight.

THE INTANGIBLES

Now that Leeman's off-ice problems (or more accurately, Al Iafrate) are resolved, he may come close to duplicating his 51-goal season if he can stay healthy. Leeman probably tied with Luc Robitaille and Gary Suter as the player most involved in unfounded trade rumors. If he doesn't return to 40-goal form this season, his rumor could become reality.

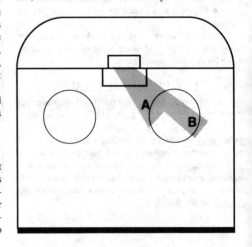

CLAUDE LOISELLE

Yrs. of NHL service: 9
Born: Ottawa, Ont., Canada; May 29, 1963
Position: Center
Height: 5-11
Weight: 190
Uniform no.: 15
Shoots: left

Career statistics:

GP	G	A	TP	PIM
483	79	103	182	895

1990-91 statistics:

GP	G	A	TP	+/-	PIM	PP	SH	GW	GT	S	PCT
66	6	11	17	-20	88	0	2	0	0	89	6.7

LAST SEASON

Acquired on waivers from Quebec, March 5, 1991. Games played and all point totals five-season lows.

THE FINESSE GAME

There are few subtleties to Loiselle's game. He is powered by his intensity (which in the past few seasons had been inconsistent) and his skating. Loiselle sets his skates wide apart and is hard to dislodge once he's planted by the net. His stance also gives him an advantage over bigger players with poorer skating technique.

Loiselle is a defensive forward with the capability to contribute more offensively than he has in recent seasons. Loiselle has good hockey sense, although his playmaking is more blue collar than creative. He has a very good shot on stride, which isn't seen often in a defensive player, and he can surprise goalies with it. More often, his goals come from pouncing on pucks around the net and forcing miscues with his in-your-face forechecking.

THE PHYSICAL GAME

On the nights when he shows up, Loiselle can be a gritty, aggravating forward who will smack anyone in his work along the boards. Because he has such good strength on his skates, Loiselle can outmuscle bigger players (he plays much bigger than his size) and can make a play with the puck once he gets it. He can be a nasty stick man. Loiselle has had a troublesome knee and needs to upgrade his conditioning.

THE INTANGIBLES

Three seasons ago, when the New Jersey Devils made their remarkable run to the 1988 Stanley Cup semi-finals, Loiselle was an underrated element of the overachieving team. He never regained that level of personal commitment, and injuries have intervened to make his even less of a force. He is a role player.

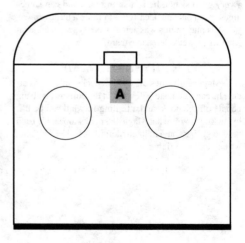

KEVIN MAGUIRE

Yrs. of NHL service: 4
Born: Toronto, Ont., Canada; January 5, 1963
Position: Right wing
Height: 6-2
Weight: 200
Uniform no.: 18
Shoots: right

Career statistics:

GP	G	A	TP	PIM
252	28	30	58	778

GP	G	A	TP	+/-	PIM	PP	SH	GW	GT	S	PCT
63	9	5	14	-10	180	1	0	0	0	52	17.3

LAST SEASON

Goal total career high. Games played and PIM two-season lows.

THE FINESSE GAME

No, that's not a misprint. Kevin Maguire, goon, scored nine goals and even saw time on the power play.

Don't expect Maguire to challenge Brett Hull for the Lady Byng Trophy this season. He has made some strides in his play by being a little smarter in the offensive zone. He's not a playmaker and lacks real scoring instinct, but he will go to the front of the net, set screens and hope something bounces in off him. He plays a basic dump and chase game, and while he is not a very good skater, he is a strong one, and can sometimes get in on a puck carrier and force a turnover.

His plus-minus was actually pretty respectable on what was a weak defensive team.

THE PHYSICAL GAME

Maguire finishes all of his checks, hitting whatever he can catch. He will work in the corners and bang people off the puck, and a trailing forward can benefit by picking up on what Maguire knocks loose. He tried hard to get back and help out defensively. He is a good, willing and able fighter.

THE INTANGIBLES

Maguire is an enforcer with sufficient skills to handle a regular role as a fourth-line winger.

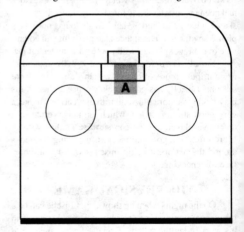

DANIEL MAROIS

Yrs. of NHL service: 3
Born: Montreal, Que., Canada; October 3, 1968
Position: Right wing
Height: 6-0
Weight: 190
Uniform no.: 32
Shoots: right

Career statistics:

GP	G	A	TP	PIM
222	91	69	160	270

1990-91 statistics:

GP	G	A	TP	+/-	PIM	PP	SH	GW	GT	S	PCT
78	21	9	30	-16	112	6	0	1	1	152	13.8

LAST SEASON

All point totals were three-year career lows. Tied for second on team in goals.

THE FINESSE GAME

Marois is a highly skilled finisher who was thrown off-kilter by the disuption of the Leafs' No. 1 line (with Tom Fergus and Vincent Damphousse). Marois knows where the net is and will score in a variety of ways. He has a move where he zooms in off the wing and tucks the puck upstairs after making the goalie commit. He gets in front of the net and causes havoc. He has very good hand-eye coordination and can release his shot quickly.

Marois has very good hockey sense and knows where to go on the ice to maximize his scoring opportunties. He can carry the puck through traffic and is very good at accepting the pass. He is patient with the puck. Marois is not a very good playmaker. He knows his job is to bury it.

Marois has very good skating ability, which ennables him to be in the right place at the right time. He cuts to the net with quick acceleration, and takes a check to complete the play. He can handle the puck in his skates. Marois is an asset to the power play.

On the downside, Marois is just brutal defensively.

THE PHYSICAL GAME

Marois has good size but plays smaller than he is. He is not very strong (some upper-body work would help) and gets outmuscled in the one-on-one situations where he can't use his speed to elude his shadow. Since he is so astute around the net, increased strength would also help him as a goal scorer.

THE INTANGIBLES

Marois may have suffered most from the constant shuffles Toronto was forced to do because of injuries at center. His slumps made him nervous and indecisive on the ice, since had never been through them at any level of hockey before. He will rebound strongly this season if the Leafs find a complementary center.

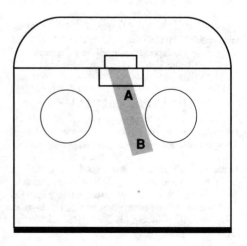

MICHEL PETIT

Yrs. of NHL service: 8
Born: St. Malo, Que., Canada; February 12, 1964
Position: Defenseman
Height: 6-1
Weight: 205
Uniform no.: 22
Shoots: right

Career statistics:

GP	G	A	TP	PIM
495	66	156	222	1144

1990-91 statistics:

GP	G	A	TP	+/-	PIM	PP	SH	GW	GT	S	PCT
73	13	26	39	-34	179	6	1	2	0	134	9.7

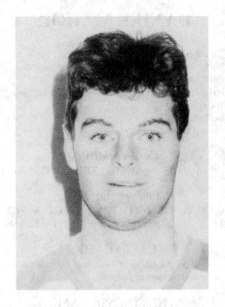

LAST SEASON

Acquired from Quebec with Aaron Broten and Lucien DeBlois for Scott Pearson and Toronto's second-round picks in 1991 and 1992, November 17, 1990. Worst plus-minus in NHL. Second among team defensemen in points and assists. Missed seven games with a sprained knee.

THE FINESSE GAME

All of Petit's tools are compromised by the lack of hockey sense necessary to put them to optimum use. He simply is not a smart player.

Petit's skating ability is above average. He has good balance, speed and agility, and certainly has the craft to be involved more in his team's attack. He will get a steady diet of points in the 35-40 range, but anyone breaking down the individual parts of his game would say he should be contributing more.

Petit has a very good shot but is not good offensively because he can't make the right play with it. He takes most of his shots from the point. He does not see the ice well, although he does pass capably when he sees the open man.

THE PHYSICAL GAME

Petit has a mean streak and plays tough at times, but inconsistently. He will take bad penalties because he lacks discipline. He will run around and get himself out of position to make a big hit, which he can do because he is big, strong and a good skater. He is a horse, with a good physique, and he has the stamina to handle as much ice time as the coach will give him. He is a crude player who annoys the opposition with some cheap play (he will use his stick). He is a willing fighter.

THE INTANGIBLES

Any coach who plays a preparation game will run out of patience with Petit, who can't respond because of his lack of hockey intelligence. Petit has played for four different teams in the last four seasons; each time he seems stunned by the trade because he perceives himself to be a better player than he actually is. Teams will keep giving him chances because of the talents he does have.

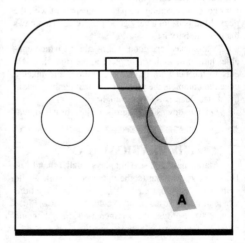

JEFF REESE

Yrs. of NHL service: 1
Born: Brantford, Ont., Canada; March 24, 1966
Position: Goaltender
Height: 5-9
Weight: 170
Uniform no.: 35
Catches: left

Career statistics:

GP	MINS	GA	SO	GAA	A	PIM
66	3266	230	1	4.23	2	10

1990-91 statistics:

GP	MINS	GAA	W	L	T	SO	GA	S	SAPCT	PIM
30	1430	3.86	6	13	3	1	92	695	.868	0

LAST SEASON

First full NHL season. Missed three games at the end of the season with two fractured transverse processes in his back.

THE PHYSICAL GAME

Reese started out as a blocky goaltender who was content to stand there, play his angles and let the puck hit him. He refined that game during last season, especially in the recognition of plays. He knows when he has to come out of the net to move the puck, and he is a fair skater and better stickhandler. He can use his stick to cut off plays around the net.

Reese no longer lets rebounds fall at his feet, but is adept at directing them into the corners. He is a small goalie with very good reflexes, although he is smart enough to work on his technique to take away as much of the net as possible. He challenges the shooter well. He is agile and mobile, and smothers the close-in plays immediately. He has a good hand and is effective with his blocker.

THE MENTAL GAME

Reese stays relaxed, alert and focused during games, in sharp contrast to his loose, off-ice demeanor. Reese doesn't play the style of game that can get a team fired up, but he is a cool player who can calm a frazzled team down. He has strong character and a positive attitude.

THE INTANGIBLES

Reese showed signs late in the season of being able to displace Peter Ing as the Leafs' No. 1 goalie, but his serious injury casts a shadow over that development. Reese has indicated a willingness to work and improve his technique, and has eagerly worked with a goaltending consultant to do so. If he doesn't make it in the NHL, it won't be for lack of desire.

DAVE REID

Yrs. of NHL service: 5
Born: Toronto, Ont., Canada; May 15, 1964
Position: Left wing
Height: 6-1
Weight: 205
Uniform no.: 14
Shoots: left

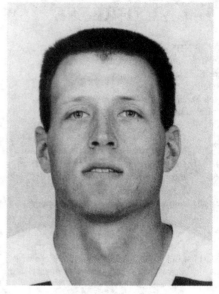

Career statistics:

GP	G	A	TP	PIM
311	61	79	140	88

1990-91 statistics:

GP	G	A	TP	+/-	PIM	PP	SH	GW	GT	S	PCT
69	15	13	28	-10	18	1	8	0	0	110	13.6

LAST SEASON

Led league in shorthanded goals. Goals were career high.

THE FINESSE GAME

Reid is a smart player who makes good use of his limited skills. At even strength, Reid is unremarkable. His skating is just above average (he has improved it) and he has some quickness.

Reid doesn't shoot as often as he should. He likes to wrist the puck from the left circle and also scores some goals from close in off of scrambles. As a playmaker, Reid has a tendency to hold onto the puck too long. He is not a very good puckhandler.

Reid's game goes up a notch when he is killing penalties, especially with the speedy Dave Hannan. Reid shoots well on stride when trying to score shorthanded, and he surprises goalies with it. Overall, he plays a smart game, but without much determination.

THE PHYSICAL GAME

Reid will not play a very physical game, but is a containment player who will step in the way of the pass. He doesn't check hard and doesn't even finish most of his checks. As he showed with his league-leading shorthanded goal total last season, Reid plays a good transition game and will go on the attack in a flash.

THE INTANGIBLES

More has always been expected of Reid than he has shown, mostly because of his size. He is little more than a defensive role player and a fourth-line checking forward, but a player who commands respect in shorthanded situations.

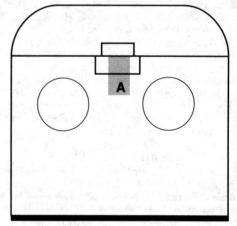

LUKE RICHARDSON

Yrs. of NHL service: 4
Born: Ottawa, Ont., Canada; March 26, 1969
Position: Defenseman
Height: 6-3
Weight: 215
Uniform no.: 2
Shoots: left

Career statistics:

GP	G	A	TP	PIM
278	11	36	47	556

1990-91 statistics:

GP	G	A	TP	+/-	PIM	PP	SH	GW	GT	S	PCT
78	1	9	10	-28	238	0	0	0	0	68	1.5

LAST SEASON

Led team in penalty minutes, which were a career high. Plus-minus was second-worst on team among defensemen.

THE FINESSE GAME

Richardson has outstanding skating ability for a big man. He skates backward quickly and has good acceleration in all directions.

Richardson has an average shot from the point. It is low and accurate, but he is not confident about using it. He is a good passer, but not a playmaker. He will make the safe outlet pass or he can rush the puck out of the zone, but he will pull up at the red line.

Richardson does not get involved offensively and needs to be paired with a more aggressive partner who will join the attack while Richardson stays at home. He shows a lot of indecision on the other team's blue line. He could show improvement in reading plays. Richardson used to get burned frequently by wrong decisions and he has become somewhat shy about challenging shooters.

THE PHYSICAL GAME

Richardson is a powerful hitter, one of the better open-ice checkers on the team. He hits cleanly and effectively, is strong in front of his net and in the corners and doesn't lose many one-on-one battles. His good lateral mobility also helps him avoid getting beaten when a skater is coming in one-on-one. Richardson clears the front of his net like a Hoover. He answers physical challenges, but doesn't like to fight. He plays well positionally.

THE INTANGIBLES

Richardson may miss Rob Ramage (gone to Minnesota in the expansion draft) since he was paired with the puck-carrying veteran for most of the season. He has served a tough four-year apprenticeship in Toronto. The next step for him will be to evolve into a player who acts rather than reacts. That may come as he gains more confidence.

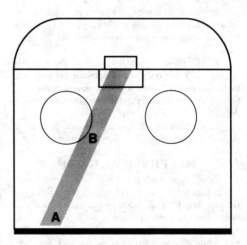

PETER ZEZEL

Yrs. of NHL service: 7
Born: Toronto, Ont., Canada; April 22, 1965
Position: Center
Height: 5-9
Weight: 200
Uniform no.: 25
Shoots: left

Career statistics:

GP	G	A	TP	PIM
487	154	272	446	301

1990-91 statistics:

GP	G	A	TP	+/-	PIM	PP	SH	GW	GT	S	PCT
52	21	19	40	-20	14	12	0	5	0	90	23.3

LAST SEASON

Acquired from Washington with Bob Rouse for Al Iafrate, January 16, 1991. Led team in power play goals and shooting percentage. Tied for second on team in goals. Games played and assist totals career lows. Missed two games with a bruised shoulder.

THE FINESSE GAME

Zezel combines toughness with excellent foot and hand skills. He is a strong, agile skater, with good balance, and his soccer background (he played professionally for the NASL) has given him nimble feet. As he rampages along the boards and behind the net, he will keep the puck alive with his feet, often kicking it to a teammate.

Zezel can juke with or without the puck. He is poised under pressure and is a good passer. He draws the attention of one or two defenders and finds the open man.

Zezel can score from all areas of the ice. His skating and lower body strength powers his slapshot. He has very strong wrists and is accurate with his shot. He will wait for a screen and has confidence handling the puck.

Zezel excels on both special teams, but his finesse skills really make him an asset on the power play.

THE PHYSICAL GAME

Zezel has a tough frame with very strong lower legs (a legacy from his soccer-playing days, perhaps). He gets into a tripod stance and is very difficult to budge from in front of the net. He is a very good forechecker because of his balance and strength. He will aggravate opponents by using his stick and then going and drawing a penalty with an artistically enhanced fall (i.e., a dive). Zezel has a tendency to let his conditioning slide.

THE INTANGIBLES

Zezel had his most productive season playing alongside Brett Hull in St. Louis. He won't be a 90-point man again, but he can be a good second-line center who will chip in with big goals. Zezel is a crunch time player whose only question mark is his inconsistent intensity. He has shown a good attitude since the move to his hometown.

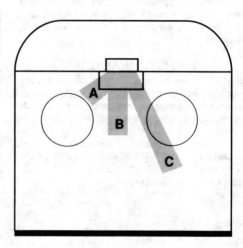

VANCOUVER
CANUCKS

GREG ADAMS

Yrs. of NHL service: 7
Born: Nelson, B.C., Canada; August 1, 1963
Position: Left wing
Height: 6-3
Weight: 185
Uniform no.: 8
Shoots: Left

Career statistics:

GP	G	A	TP	PIM
447	173	176	349	145

1990-91 statistics:

GP	G	A	TP	+/-	PIM	PP	SH	GW	GT	S	PCT
55	21	24	45	-5	10	5	1	2	2	148	14.2

LAST SEASON

Games played total was six-season low and marked third consecutive season of 65 games or fewer. PIM were a career low. Power-play goal total dropped by eight.

THE FINESSE GAME

Adams is a good open-ice skater and has some shifty moves. He is very mobile, can go inside/outside with the puck to set up his shots.

Adams likes to shoot, and is very accurate with the snap shot that he always uses over the slap. It takes less time to use that weapon, and it complements what speed he has, plus the feints, that force the goalies to react while in motion. He is not, however, a distance threat because the snap loses its effectiveness from long range.

Adams is an attentive checker, but as that is not a teamwide trait, has spent the last few seasons on the minus side of the ledger.

THE PHYSICAL GAME

An honest player, Adams stands up for himself. He maximizes his height by using his reach effectively to shield the puck, but also minimizes that asset with a basic lack of upper-body strength.

THE INTANGIBLES

Greg Adams is one of his team's top players, talent-wise, yet the respect is more within the Canucks' dressing room than in the quarters of the other teams in the league. He isn't THE Vancouver player that opponents worry about, Linden is.

But with more determination and grit, more impact, Adams could lift his team, help it set and attain loftier goals. He would have to stay in the lineup more to achieve that aim, however, and find some way to add bite to a quiet game.

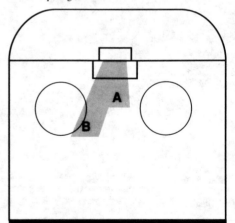

STEVE BOZEK

Yrs. of NHL service: 10
Born: Kelowna, B.C., Canada; November 26, 1960
Position: Left wing
Height: 5-11
Weight: 180
Uniform no.: 14
Shoots: Left

Career statistics:

GP	G	A	TP	PIM
583	156	159	315	282

1990-91 statistics:

GP	G	A	TP	+/-	PIM	PP	SH	GW	GT	S	PCT
62	15	17	32	-6	22	0	1	2	1	126	11.9

LAST SEASON

Goal total was within two of his five-season high. Of players who were with Canucks all season, only Trevor Linden (33) and Greg Adams (21) had more goals.

THE FINESSE GAME

Bozek is not going to score 30 goals, but will give an honest effort that accentuates his skating gifts.

Speed is the source of the offensive punch that will provide roughly a dozen goals per season. Bozek's wheels always are spinning at top speed, which can be good and bad. It can be good because Bozek's legs will carry him to the front of the net for scoring chances. It can be bad because Bozek is not overly adept at shifting gears and controlling his speed, so there are times when momentum carries him away from a scoring chance instead of into it.

He can play a fourth-line center's role in which he makes decent use of his wings and does a good job on faceoffs. Bozek's hands are better-suited to draws; they are not especially useful for finishing. He doesn't come close to finishing half the chances he creates by rushing the puck on offense or pressuring it on defense. Bozek does, however, play an alert role on defense. He looks around, reads the situation, pays attention, uses his smarts and speed to make himself a reliable penalty killer.

THE PHYSICAL GAME

Bozek is a plucky player who gets by with making the most of his ability. This extends to the physical aspect. He doesn't take shortcuts. He plays the body, battles for the puck along the wood. He scraps and yaps, stands up for himself, adding at least a physical element to what essentially is a finesse game.

THE INTANGIBLES

Bozek is a proven NHL role player who would be better-suited to playing a lesser role with a better team.

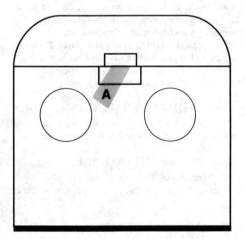

DAVE CAPUANO

Yrs. of NHL service: 2
Born: Warwick, R.I., USA; July 27, 1968
Position: Center/right wing
Height: 6-2
Weight: 195
Uniform no.: 28
Shoots: Left

Career statistics:

GP	G	A	TP	PIM
94	16	36	52	54

1990-91 statistics:

GP	G	A	TP	+/-	PIM	PP	SH	GW	GT	S	PCT
61	13	31	44	1	42	5	0	1	0	77	16.9

LAST SEASON

All offensive totals were career highs, as was penalty minute total.

THE FINESSE GAME

Capuano is an offensive specialist with quick moves which are effective enough to beat more than his share of defensemen one-on-one. He sees teammates well, is among the most skilled passers in the league, and his shots (snap and slap) are extremely strong.

It is difficult to characterize his skating. He has a big, long stride. He is not slow, but he doesn't have speed—yet he can score off a rush. Capuano has some quickness, some agility; turns don't exactly slow him down, but he isn't moving that fast in the first place. His checking isn't great, but he's a "plus" player on a disturbingly disappointing defensive team.

Capuano tends to be a perimeter player. There is a chance he has that tendency because his feet will not get him deep in the attacking zone. There also is a chance he prefers to be a perimeter player.

THE PHYSICAL GAME

Capuano is not afraid to take a hit, but is not going to initiate. He definitely is a finesse player with size.

THE INTANGIBLES

Capuano was the only Canuck to play three-fourths of his team's games and manage to finish "plus" for the season, so clearly, he is doing something right. He has some consistency troubles, though, and simply is not a factor every night, which is why his potential for 80-100 points may never be realized.

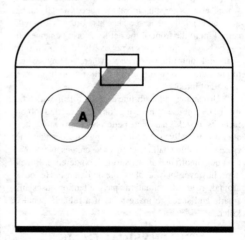

GEOFF COURTNALL

Yrs. of NHL service: 7
Born: Victoria, B.C., Canada; August 18, 1962
Position: Left wing
Height: 6-1
Weight: 190
Uniform no.: 10
Shoots: Left

Career statistics:

GP	G	A	TP	PIM
507	192	194	386	663

1990-91 statistics:

GP	G	A	TP	+/-	PIM	PP	SH	GW	GT	S	PCT
77	33	32	65	16	64	12	0	8	0	263	12.5

LAST SEASON

Obtained March 5, 1991, from St. Louis, with Sergio Momesso, Robert Dirk and Cliff Ronning, for Garth Butcher and Dan Quinn. Fourth consecutive season of 70 or more games played, 30 or more goals scored. Penalty minute total was five-season low.

THE FINESSE GAME

If you want blazing speed, if you want just about the NHL's top release from the left side, if you want a shot that can overwhelm a goalie's glove from the circle, you'll get it from Geoff Courtnall.

Courtnall skates, Courtnall shoots, Courtnall scores. He does not do a great deal else. Not many shadows can keep up with him; Courtnall knows how to use his speed to get open up the flank, and once he gets the puck, he is gone.

He can be a marvelous give-and-go player if a center on his team is capable of a good lead pass. The other key is to complement Courtnall with a checking right wing or a substantial, mobile defenseman. Courtnall has an idea about defense and certainly has the speed to get back on the play, but doesn't get it done all the time. There are times when he may be the first man on the puck, pressuring a defenseman; but if that defenseman's first pass gets past him, somebody else better be there to prevent a break.

THE PHYSICAL GAME

Courtnall simply is not a physical player. For a player of such speed, his legs do not seem to carry him as fast when they are heading toward contact situations. At the same time, he is not a player who will be intimidated to any great extent.

THE INTANGIBLES

There are two ways of looking at why Geoff Courtnall continually puts up numbers and never stays with a team very long. One way: he's a problem in the dressing room or infuriating to coaches because he has no interest in anything that doesn't involve scoring. Another way: he's a left wing who has speed and who scores, there aren't more than a dozen or so of them in a 22-team league, thus teams want him or will put up with his lack of physical presence.

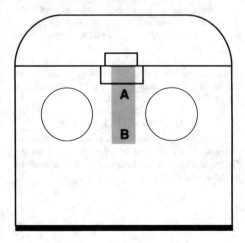

GERALD DIDUCK

Yrs. of NHL service: 6
Born: Edmonton, Alta., Canada; April 6, 1965
Position: Defenseman
Height: 6-2
Weight: 207
Uniform no.: 4
Shoots: Right

Career statistics:

GP	G	A	TP	PIM
377	30	72	102	685

1990-91 statistics:

GP	G	A	TP	+/-	PIM	PP	SH	GW	GT	S	PCT
63	4	9	13	-5	105	0	0	1	0	100	4.0

LAST SEASON

Obtained from Montreal, January 12, 1991, for fourth-round (1991) draft choice (Vladimir Vujtek of Czechoslovakia). Games played, assists and penalty minutes were four-season low.

THE FINESSE GAME

Skating is an asset for Diduck, who has good drive in his legs. He also has a very, very hard shot, which he gets off quickly and willingly sprays to every area of the rink. Sometimes, he even gets it on net. The shot is perplexing to goalies because it is not readable immediately off the stick; there is some kind of weird spin that makes it take longer for goalies to pick it up.

Diduck does not otherwise have especially good hands. His puck-handling game is not overly strong and neither is his vision of the ice. He does not make defensive decisions well and at critical times appears so intent on avoiding a mistake that he steers clear of the puck entirely.

He seemed to do a better job of tying the package together toward the end of the season in Vancouver, but the jury remained out as to whether he could continue the good work over a full season.

THE PHYSICAL GAME

Diduck is physically strong and uses it in his board work. He is a good fighter, but not a willing fighter, and he is inconsistent in the application of his strength/toughness.

THE INTANGIBLES

Diduck understands the game well, but struggles when the heat is on because he has a hard time handling pressure situations.

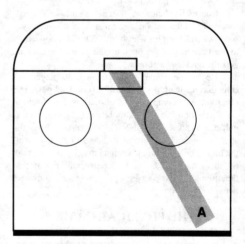

TROY GAMBLE

Yrs. of NHL service: 1
Born: New Glasgow, N.S., Canada; April 7, 1967
Position: Goaltender
Height: 5-11
Weight: 195
Uniform no.: 35
Catches: Left

Career statistics:

GP	MINS	GA	SO	GAA	A	PIM
53	2795	156	1	3.35	1	14

1990-91 statistics:

GP	MINS	GAA	W	L	T	SO	GA	S	SAPCT	PIM
47	2433	3.45	16	16	6	1	140	1156	.879	14

LAST SEASON

First full season in NHL.

THE PHYSICAL GAME

Gamble might be the textbook example of an unorthodox goalie. He is not quite a standup guy, not quite a butterfly guy. There are times when his stance is a truly ugly thing—hands way too low, shoulders way too far forward—but style is not remotely an issue to Gamble as long as some part of his body comes in contact with enough of the puck to keep it from going in the net.

His approach to the glove side is a puzzlment. He keeps the catching glove low, as though his intention is to give people a hole and try to get them to shoot there—then take away the shot. Gamble, though, keeps the hand low and DOESN'T take away the shot. People score there a lot.

Gamble is better low. He plays deep and uses his feet to take away the bottom corners, which is a byproduct of his agility more than his skating skill.

He does not seem very confident in his skating. Though it is a difficult play for any goaltender, Gamble seems to have a hard time with forwards walking out from the corner at his right. He needs to take a step out to the shooter, but hangs back—leaving room on the long side. Yet on stuff tries from his left, Gamble will use the pokecheck naturally; the same goes for breakaways.

Otherwise, his stick skills are limited. He does not handle the puck well and would be much better off stopping the puck, then turning it over to his defensemen.

THE MENTAL GAME

Gamble is a fiery, intense competitor who battles on every shot. He does not want to let you score. He is a streak player who will get roaring hot for stretches of four to six games but cannot sustain the heat beyond that.

THE INTANGIBLES

Injuries were a problem. Concussions, strep throat, leg and groin woes all cost him playing time, which may have had something to do with Gamble's inconsistency. And, though last season was the year of Ed Belfour and Mike Richter, goal remains an extremely difficult position for a first-year player—even a healthy one.

ROBERT KRON

Yrs. of NHL service: 1
Born: Brno, Czechoslovakia; February 27, 1967
Position: Center
Height: 5-10
Weight: 174
Uniform no.: 58
Shoots: Left

Career statistics:

GP	G	A	TP	PIM
76	12	20	32	21

1990-91 statistics:

GP	G	A	TP	+/-	PIM	PP	SH	GW	GT	S	PCT
76	12	20	32	-11	21	2	3	0	0	124	9.7

LAST SEASON

First in the NHL.

THE FINESSE GAME

If one aspect of his finesse skills surpasses all the others, it is Kron's ability to skate. He has quickness. He has acceleration. And he has exceptional lateral movement, which makes him a threat on almost every rush.

Many other players in the league can skate, but lose an edge on that speed because their hands cannot "keep up" with their feet—the puck slows them down, limits their game and their creativity because they simply cannot make the right play at speed. Kron is not in that group; his hands do not slow him. He is able to stickhandle at top speed and able to shoot at top speed, which forces defensemen to concede ground.

The Canucks are able to maximize Kron's assets by using him in more of a defensive role. He is all over the puck with his speed.

THE PHYSICAL GAME

A small player who tends to play to his size, Kron is willing to play in the rough going. He will work, hustle and scrap for the puck, but really is not a physical player. He simply does not have the heft or the instinct for physical play.

THE INTANGIBLES

Kron is an exciting player, but through no fault of his own is a symbol of a corner into which the Canucks have painted themselves. In Cliff Ronning, Igor

Larionov and Kron, there is speed but no size up the middle. Petr Nedved, a larger player, is a finesse guy, too. Strong centers do not grow on trees, but this center corps doesn't reach any of the higher branches.

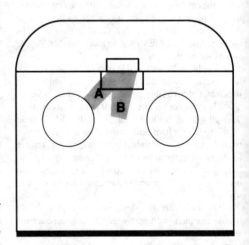

IGOR LARIONOV

Yrs. of NHL service: 2
Born: Voskresensk, Soviet Union; December 3, 1960
Position: Center
Height: 5-9
Weight: 165
Uniform no.: 18
Shoots: Left

Career statistics:

GP	G	A	TP	PIM
138	30	48	78	34

1990-91 statistics:

GP	G	A	TP	+/-	PIM	PP	SH	GW	GT	S	PCT
64	13	21	34	-3	14	1	1	0	0	66	19.7

LAST SEASON

Games played decreased by 10, points decreased by 10, power-play goals decreased by seven from rookie season.

THE FINESSE GAME

Larionov is an exquisitely skilled finesse player who still is seeking a translation of those eminent international assets into relevant NHL production. He is an agile, elusive skater who complements fancy footwork with a splendid pair of hands and a creative mind that still is trying to compress international-sized plays into NHL-sized rinks.

Larionov challenges his wingers to get to open ice. You know he will get them the puck if they get open, because Larionov has an exceptional passing touch; the problem is, he has lost a step. He cannot hold the puck forever and wait for the wings to break free. He will give defensemen trouble, though; for while they can step up to challenge the puck and expect to out-muscle him, they will be beaten if Larionov uses his balance and lateral mobility to dart around them.

He will not overpower a goalie with a shot. Larionov relies on accuracy, moves and a quick release for in-close scoring.

Larionov is extremely solid in his positional play, and his defensive play improved last season. He helps out in all areas of the ice but, naturally, is at a disadvantage in the strength matchups.

THE PHYSICAL GAME

Until two seasons ago, Larionov never had been asked to play a physical game, and age 29 was a bit late for a finesse player to commence so dramatic a change in style. Larionov accepted being hit while playing in the Soviet Union, he accepts being hit while playing in North America and got more involved last season than

in his rookie campaign. But the guy weighs 165-170 pounds; the best that can be hoped is a bit more involvement.

THE INTANGIBLES

The Canucks spent a lot of money, time and effort to bring him to the NHL and they are trying to be patient while he adjusts to North America. But 34 points is a tiny return on their investment, and they are more or less stuck with him, as you would be hard-pressed to find a team that would take him in a trade.

Larionov can run a power play, and he's not a bad checker, but for the money they spent, the Canucks have to be disappointed.

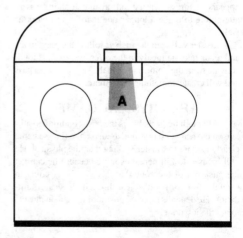

DOUG LIDSTER

Yrs. of NHL service: 7
Born: Kamloops, B.C., Canada; October 18, 1960
Position: Defenseman
Height: 6-1
Weight: 200
Uniform no.: 3
Shoots: Right

Career statistics:

GP	G	A	TP	PIM
529	53	200	253	451

1990-91 statistics:

GP	G	A	TP	+/-	PIM	PP	SH	GW	GT	S	PCT
78	6	32	38	-6	77	4	0	1	0	157	3.8

LAST SEASON

Assist total tied four-season high. Plus-minus declined by 10 goals.

THE FINESSE GAME

Lidster's hands are his main finesse asset, though his skating gets him to places where his hands can take over, and his hockey sense allows him to tie the package together neatly.

Lidster has speed, mobility, agility and balance and gets a lot out of himself. He is no Al MacInnis in terms of talent, and certainly he is no MacInnis from the standpoint of shooting—Lidster's shot does not compare at all—but he is better-than-average because of his intelligence. He will reach the loose pucks and do something with them beyond slapping them off the boards and out of the zone, and his heady play makes him a natural quarterback on the power play.

At times, it seems he thinks too much. Lidster appears to foresake a natural, available short pass in attempting to make a longer one that doesn't work as well.

Lidster will lead the rush or follow the play up ice and reads his role nicely in the offensive zone. He will activate from the point, step into the slot, pick up a pass and will create something from there.

THE PHYSICAL GAME

Although he probably is the best-conditioned athlete on the team and is strong as an ox, the finesse game clearly is more to Lidster's liking than the physical. He will be used to kill penalties more because he can get the puck out of the zone than because he is going to keep the front of his net clear through physical intimidation. He depends more on positioning than on muscle to get the job done.

THE INTANGIBLES

He's still a player teams want in a trade—a game, proven, veteran defenseman with offensive skills—yet Vancouver doesn't move him. He comes to play every night, but precisely what role he comes to play is anybody's guess. Is he a defensive stalwart? A power-play specialist? Trade bait?

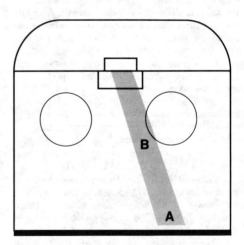

TREVOR LINDEN

Yrs. of NHL service: 3
Born: Medicine Hat, Alta., Canada; April 11, 1970
Position: Right wing
Height: 6-4
Weight: 205
Uniform no.: 16
Shoots: Right

Career statistics:

GP	G	A	TP	PIM
233	84	95	179	175

1990-91 statistics:

GP	G	A	TP	+/-	PIM	PP	SH	GW	GT	S	PCT
80	33	36	69	-25	65	16	2	4	1	229	14.4

LAST SEASON

For second time in three seasons, played all 80 games and scored at least 30 goals. Plus-minus declined by eight goals, shots figure improved by 58.

THE FINESSE GAME

Linden is powerful and uses his body to shield the puck, but is not an elite skater who can pull away from people or run over people. He is a strong skater, rather than a fleet one; a quick one rather than an agile one. His feet seem a touch heavy at times, but still Linden manages to stickhandle, stop, change directions and start again.

Coming off the right wing, Linden likes to use the wrist shot low to the far corner. The wrist shot is a good one, but he is slow in letting it go. Linden gets better results with his slap shot, which is hard and is released more quickly.

The center in him loves to pass, and does it rather well—the times when he looks up and sees a teammate instead of trying to make one-on-three plays. But there are times when he is utterly counfounding, as he foresakes a much better shooting chance to make a lower-percentage pass to a teammate. There are times Linden uses his strength to win a puck and take it to the net, there are times when he wins a puck and takes it AWAY from the net. There will be an alley to the cage from the corner, which a player his size should use, but Linden will be looking for others. Linden is not going to make the most of himself from the perimeter.

In the transition to defense, Linden locates his man quickly on transition and hustles back instead of coasting. His effort notwithstanding, minus 42 over two seasons demands improvement.

THE PHYSICAL GAME

Linden uses his size, strength and reach whenever possible. He goes right to the boards to hit or be hit, he forechecks, skates through checks to cycle out of the corners, works the goal mouth, wins faceoffs and drives to the net.

Other teams run Linden all the time, because when you stop him, you tend to stop the Canucks. But Linden is tough and mean. He commands respect from a reactive stance; he does not start trouble, but he more than has the wherewithal to finish trouble.

THE INTANGIBLES

He works so hard, wants so much for his team to win, that he ends up trying to do everything himself too much of the time. Linden's heart is in the right place, but his head may burst from all the pressure he places on himself.

No one disputes that if the Canucks are going to be a force in their division, Linden must become their Mark Messier. For Linden to reach that level would require more aggressiveness, more consistency, more power—less trying and more doing.

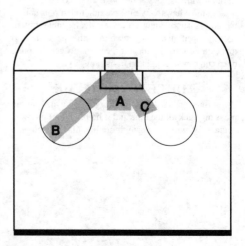

JYRKI LUMME

Yrs. of NHL service: 3
Born: Tampere, Finland; July 16, 1966
Position: Defenseman
Height: 6-1
Weight: 207
Uniform no.: 21
Shoots: Left

Career statistics:

GP	G	A	TP	PIM
166	10	56	66	118

1990-91 statistics:

GP	G	A	TP	+/-	PIM	PP	SH	GW	GT	S	PCT
80	5	27	32	-15	59	1	0	0	0	157	3.2

LAST SEASON

Goal output doubled career total. Assists total was career best. Was fourth on team in assists by players who were with Canucks all season.

THE FINESSE GAME

Lumme is the Canucks defenseman with the best all-around skills.

He is a good puckhandler who puts those skills to good use on the power play. His shot is okay, but he isn't going to overpower a goalie from the point. He had just one power-play goal and five overall because Lumme does not synchronize the shot well with the activity in front. He will shoot either too early, before teammates get to the front of the net for deflections or screens, or too late—after there is so much traffic in front the puck does not get through.

Lumme is a gambler on offense and defense. He has good-enough skating skills and mobility that he can recover position when he goes for a pinch and does not get the puck. On defense, he will challenge with the poke check at the blue line but does not always follow through with his body if the poke try fails.

Lumme has a very nice passing touch plus anticipation and a good view of the ice, which enables him to spot the open man and reach him with a pass. He also makes a good rush, but at times fails to get the puck deep and can be caught on transition.

THE PHYSICAL GAME

From the red line back, forget about it. Lumme plays the puck all the time and is no big fan of physical contact. He will take many more hits than he delivers.

THE INTANGIBLES

If you hit him all night, it will pay dividends, because he will give up the puck. But in a non-physical game, when he has time and space for skating and puck handling, Lumme can hurt you.

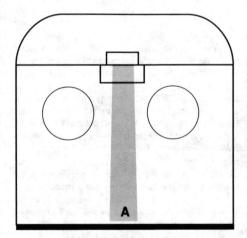

KIRK MCLEAN

Yrs. of NHL service: 4
Born: Willowdale, Ont., Canada; June 26, 1966
Position: Goaltender
Height: 6-0
Weight: 177
Uniform no.: 1
Catches: Left

Career statistics:

GP	MINS	GA	SO	GAA	A	PIM
193	10836	642	5	3.55	6	24

1990-91 statistics:

GP	MINS	GAA	W	L	T	SO	GA	S	SAPCT	PIM
41	1969	3.99	10	22	3	0	131	983	.867	4

LAST SEASON

Games played and minutes were four-season low, goals against was his worst as a regular.

THE PHYSICAL GAME

McLean is a very sound goalkeeper and fundamentally is as sound as there is in the league. He stands up well, he skates well, challenges aggressively on his angles, catches and controls a lot of high pucks. McLean has good movement side-to-side, very good balance and keeps his shoulders square with the puck.

McLean does a nice job when he drops to his knees. He covers the bottom half of the net and regains his footing quickly.

Also, McLean is especially skilled at moving the puck. He is up there with Ron Hextall in that regard, but is more selective in using that tool, more precise, and more effective with it.

He does have some holes, though, or did last year, anyway. A shot to the stick side was a free goal too many nights.

THE MENTAL GAME

McLean may get beaten more on the first shot of a game than any goalie in the league, and that can really set off a struggle in his head. Once he gets past the first few shots, McLean gains confidence—as does the team. If you don't get him early, you aren't likely to beat him at all.

THE INTANGIBLES

McLean is a much better goaltender than his statistics from last season would suggest, and there were a few nights last season when the Canucks only got him two or three goals of offensive support.

At the same time, there were a lot of nights when four goals weren't enough. If a low-scoring team such as the Canucks is going to have a four-goal night, a goalie has to make it enough to win more than McLean did in 1990-91.

So this will be a telling year for him. But the feeling here is that McLean will, uh, rebound.

SERGIO MOMESSO

Yrs. of NHL service: 7
Born: Montreal, Que., Canada; September 4, 1965
Position: Left wing
Height: 6-3
Weight: 215
Uniform no.: 27
Shoots: Left

Career statistics:

GP	G	A	TP	PIM
339	78	107	185	755

1990-91 statistics:

GP	G	A	TP	+/-	PIM	PP	SH	GW	GT	S	PCT
70	16	20	36	13	174	3	0	3	1	119	13.4

LAST SEASON

Obtained March 5, 1991, from St. Louis, with Geoff Courtnall, Cliff Ronning and Robert Dirk, for Garth Butcher and Dan Quinn. Though his game total declined by nine, his shot total dropped by 63. Plus-minus improved by 28 goals.

THE FINESSE GAME

Often on these pages, you will notice references to players who perform specific finesse functions well "...for a big man," as though there is little hope someone with size can do anything but bang. Momesso does more than a few things well.

He is a strong skater in the straightaways, an imposing sight as he powers up the wing, an impressive sight as he uses his agility to cut in occasionally from the flank. Momesso can handle the puck in traffic, can finish from close range, can make plays from the corners to spring teammates for scoring chances.

From longer range, his slap shot is extremely heavy—it knocks goaltenders backward—but Momesso takes quite a long time getting rid of it. And when he does, the spectators in the end-zone seats have just as much reason for concern as the goalies do.

The defensive aspect seems to be rounding into shape somewhat. Though he built a plus 12 record while spending the bulk of the year on an exceptional defensive team in St. Louis, Momesso also managed a plus 1 in 11 games for the Canucks, which is no small task.

THE PHYSICAL GAME

Momesso is a good banger who handles himself more than capably in front of the opposing net. He stands his ground and gets feet wide apart so defensemen have trouble moving him.

Momesso has a mean streak, but seems to pick his spots about displaying it—or seems unable to focus that concentration/mean streak for every game. That fact probably is what got him traded out of the Norris Division, where, when you're Momesso's size, you have to come to the rink good and angry every night.

THE INTANGIBLES

Every team wants a big, tough left wing who can fight, score and hit, a description that certainly suits Momesso. But has he, like Geoff Courtnall, been moved so often lately because he's so attractive as a player, or because he wears out his welcome?

Inconsistency on the finesse end is maddening, because he could achieve more than he does. Inconsistency on the physical end is maddening, because it makes you wonder if he wants to go through the aggravation of playing as big as he is.

Momesso could be the perfect bookend for Trevor Linden. The question is whether he can meet the challenge of giving Vancouver what it expects of him, what it needs—which is about 30 goals and 175 penalty minutes. If he doesn't produce that way, Momesso could end up not even being a perfect bookend for Gino Odjick.

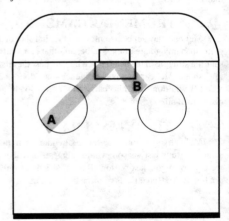

DANA MURZYN

Yrs. of NHL service: 6
Born: Regina, Sask., Canada; December 9, 1966
Position: Defenseman
Height: 6-3
Weight: 205
Uniform no.: 5
Shoots: Left

Career statistics:

GP	G	A	TP	PIM
396	30	87	117	679

1990-91 statistics:

GP	G	A	TP	+/-	PIM	PP	SH	GW	GT	S	PCT
29	1	2	3	-7	38	0	0	0	0	40	2.5

LAST SEASON

Obtained March 5 from Calgary Flames for Ron Stern, Kevan Guy and future considerations. Games played and all offensive figures were career lows.

THE FINESSE GAME

If you cannot skate the puck out of the zone—and believe us, Murzyn can't—then you have to be able to do other things. About the only thing Murzyn does especially well, other than make a nice pass occasionally, is shoot the puck.

Murzyn has a heavy shot from the point and gets it away quickly. He keeps it low and tipable. It's accurate, not wide. Shooting may be the thing he does best, yet he did it only 40 times in 29 games last year, 97 times in 78 games the year before.

Otherwise, things are only OK at best. Murzyn could be more alert, could do a better job positionally, be stronger on the puck, not give it away blindly. He does well killing penalties, as he has a good handle on things in front of the net and doesn't have to skate much; the other aspects become suspect because his skating does not support him. Motion and mobility are of utmost relevance in the current cycle of hockey evolution, and the inability to execute in those departments can create profound hardships for a player.

THE PHYSICAL GAME

Hockey is an amazingly judgemental sport, and the big guys always are judged the harshest, always held up to the highest (and generally the most unfair) standards. If they don't put people in hospitals, they are stealing their salaries, according to conventional thinking that says a player Murzyn's size should be an intimidating force.

Murzyn, however, is he-man big and Boy Scout polite. He performs the physical functions of defense—plays the body along the boards and in front of the net, blocks shots, uses his reach. If a guy 5-11 plays that way, you don't hear a peep; a guy Murzyn's size does it and the whole world gets on him.

THE INTANGIBLES

Is Dana Murzyn the Sergio Momesso of defensemen? He is big and strong, a player you would think teams want to keep—yet you're never surprised to see their names in the "Transactions" box on the sports page. Teams tend to give up on coaches every year or two; they seem to give up on Murzyn in roughly the same time.

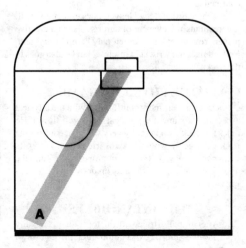

PETR NEDVED

Yrs. of NHL service: 1
Born: Liberec, Czechoslovakia; December 9, 1971
Position: Center
Height: 6-3
Weight: 178
Uniform no.: 19
Shoots: Left

Career statistics:

GP	G	A	TP	PIM
61	10	6	16	20

1990-91 statistics:

GP	G	A	TP	+/-	PIM	PP	SH	GW	GT	S	PCT
61	10	6	16	-21	20	1	0	0	0	97	10.3

LAST SEASON

First in NHL.

THE FINESSE GAME

Although at times last season he seemed indecisive as he attacked the blue line and seemed reluctant to move the puck to an open man, that was more attributable to inexperience and the attempt to make the perfect play. Nedved has good on-ice presence, knows where his teammates are, knows how to find them with the puck and should do a better job of it this season.

He has very good hands and good puck-handling ability, even in traffic. He has the puck a lot, it always seems to find him, and he makes better use of it than would be suggested by his six assists.

His skating could use a bit of work. Nedved did not display supreme speed consistently last year and does not have the best balance in the world, but he does have the agility to make a quick change of direction in a confined area.

If there is one thing Nedved does especially well, it is retaining the element of surprise. He is a creative player. You never know which play he might try next. Nedved likes the wrist shot in-close, but he also goes to the backhand.

THE PHYSICAL GAME

Once he feels more comfortable with the physical aspect of the game, his physical skills will flower. He hides the puck with his body very well and controls the puck very nicely with his skates. He can win faceoffs with consistency, but must improve at locking the opposing center out of the play on draws in the attacking zone.

THE INTANGIBLES

After initially trying to do too much, probably from the pressure of expectation after his high draft selection, Nedved finished very strongly—which probably is a truer indication of things to come from this extremely talented playmaker. It is going to take him another year at least to grow into a top-flight role on this team, to fill out physically and emotionally. But Nedved can only get better, and on talent alone, he will be a commanding commodity for the Canucks.

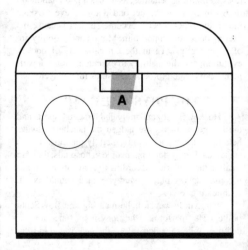

ROBERT NORDMARK

Yrs. of NHL service: 4
Born: Lulea, Sweden; August 20, 1962
Position: Defenseman
Height: 6-1
Weight: 200
Uniform no.: 6
Shoots: Right

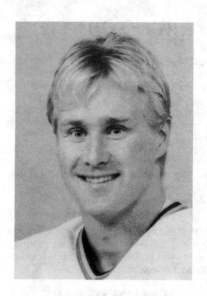

Career statistics:

GP	G	A	TP	PIM
236	10	52	62	254

1990-91 statistics:

GP	G	A	TP	+/-	PIM	PP	SH	GW	GT	S	PCT
45	2	6	8	-10	63	1	0	0	0	65	3.1

LAST SEASON

Assist and point totals were career lows.

THE FINESSE GAME

Nordmark plays a smooth, natural, flowing game that is so polished as to seem effortless and elegant while also being notably effective.

Skating provides the base. Nordmark is quick, mobile and agile; he covers a lot of ground laterally and, accordingly, plays with tremendous confidence at both blue lines.

Nordmark does a nice job moving the puck. He stays alert at all times, sees the good-percentage pass and gets the puck there crisply. He also has one of the hardest right-hand point shots in the league and absolutely does not use it enough. Nordmark has a bomb of a slap shot and exceptional one-timer skills that get the puck on net with accuracy and sting.

By natural extension, Nordmark moves up nicely with the play. He can start the transition game by forcing a turnover, then will move the puck ahead and follow the attack.

THE PHYSICAL GAME

A finesse player through and through, Nordmark prefers prudent

positioning to muscular might. He will jostle, rather than jolt—will bump rather than bang. Ulf Samuelsson he ain't.

THE INTANGIBLES

Nordmark seems a natural for the point on the power play but his scoring is not nearly the equal of his skill. He is mature enough, experienced enough and—above all—talented enough to be having much more of an impact on his team than he does.

GINO ODJICK

Yrs. of NHL service: 1
Born: Quebec, Canada; September 7, 1970
Position: Left wing
Height: 6-2
Weight: 220
Uniform no.: 29
Shoots: Left

Career statistics:

GP	G	A	TP	PIM
45	7	1	8	296

LAST SEASON

First in the NHL. Led team in penalty minutes. Was one of only two "original" Canucks players (not obtained by trade during season), to collect more than 100 PIM; Jim Sandlak had 125.

THE FINESSE GAME

Odjick's NHL ratio of penalty minutes to points last season was 37 to one, which you might think is a perfect summary of the relationship between his physical skills and his finesse skills. That point is argued by his two seasons of junior hockey at Laval, where the ratio was roughly 12 minutes per point his first year and was one-third lower, about eight minutes per point, his second season.

The suggestion, then, is more that Odjick spent last season paying his dues more than that he needs the three inches of height on skates to keep his knuckles from scraping on the ground. He is not an especially mobile player, but he does have some hand skills those moments he actually is wearing his gloves. Odjick can pull the puck in close to his body, fake past a guy and move up ice; the problems start after the fake has succeeded, as Odjick does not have the speed to pull away from anybody faster than Brad Marsh or Dave Marcinyshyn.

But nobody is suggesting this player is an offensive presence. He was a fifth-round pick, No. 86 overall in 1990, and there was only one player drafted lower (Washington's Peter Bondra at No. 156) who played as much of a role with his team as Odjick did with the Canucks. Still, Odjick will go in front for a scramble or a tip-in or a rebound, and is capable of finishing a play. He did have the seven goals with Vancouver and also had seven in 17 games—along with 102 more penalty minutes)—with Vancouver's Milwaukee affiliate in the IHL.

THE PHYSICAL GAME

Odjick knows his role, knows its impact on his staying with the team, and plays it to the best of his ability. He is tough, he plays tough, and he backs up that toughness willingly. Odjick is fearless on his own behalf and aggressive in backing up teammates who may need the room created by his physical assets.

Again, though, Odjick is not simply a cheese wheel on skates. When you get 296 minutes in penalties over 45 games, there are going to be some bad ones. But a very high percentage of the time, when Odjick goes to the box, he takes someone with him. He is smarter than you might think about the game situation and the importance of not making his team shorthanded.

THE INTANGIBLES

Odjick may have a struggle on his hands just to stay with the team this season. As big and tough as he is, the Canucks' No. 2 choice in Odjick's draft year was Shawn Antoski, a left wing who played on the right side at Milwaukee last year and got 17 goals to go with 330 penalty minutes. Still, Odjick was a fan favourite in Vancouver, it looked like his teammates really liked him, too.

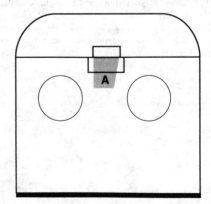

CLIFF RONNING

Yrs. of NHL service: 4
Born: Vancouver, B.C., Canada; October 1, 1965
Position: Center
Height: 5-8
Weight: 175
Uniform no.: 7
Shoots: Left

Career statistics:

GP	G	A	TP	PIM
191	60	77	137	46

1990-91 statistics:

GP	G	A	TP	+/-	PIM	PP	SH	GW	GT	S	PCT
59	20	24	44	0	10	7	0	2	0	113	17.7

LAST SEASON

Obtained March 5, 1991, from St Louis with Geoff Courtnall, Robert Dirk and Sergio Momesso, for Dan Quinn and Garth Butcher.

THE FINESSE GAME

Though faced with continually having to prove himself because of his stature, Ronning has had an unarguable ability to make things happen on the power play because of his quickness—mentally and physically—and his hands. He has superb operational skills from the hash marks near the boards, a formation more and more teams are using to vary their attacks if the point men are being closely marked.

Ronning can come off the wall and curl into the slot, he can pass to the corners or the point and then go to the net—if he can get through the traffic without being knocked down. His shot is only average, but Ronning is very quick to turn it loose.

Ronning is conscientious in attending to his defensive details, using his quickness and agility to swarm the puck whenever possible, using his smarts and anticipation to be in the right place at more than his share of right times.

THE PHYSICAL GAME

Ronning's scoring prowess never has been doubted, but when push has come to shove, his inconsistency and his lack of grit (or ability to overcome his size) ultimately has outweighed his tremendous ability to score in every league in which he has competed.

THE INTANGIBLES

Always a player of talent, Ronning was a man on a mission, a scrappy dynamo, in the playoffs last spring.

The question now is whether he is a late bloomer or a surprise who can broaden his contribution beyond power-play specialist.

In the playoffs you play for the fun and the challenge rather than the money; the REAL hockey is played in November, December and January, when each game is a grind and the consistent players earn their stripes.

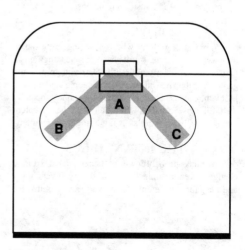

JIM SANDLAK

Yrs. of NHL service: 5
Born: Kitchener, Ont., Canada; December 12, 1966
Position: Right wing
Height: 6-4
Weight: 219
Uniform no.: 25
Shoots: Right

Career statistics:

GP	G	A	TP	PIM
351	74	73	147	485

1990-91 statistics:

GP	G	A	TP	+/-	PIM	PP	SH	GW	GT	S	PCT
59	7	6	13	-20	125	4	0	0	0	88	8.0

LAST SEASON

Games played was three-year low. Goal, assist and points totals were five-season lows.

THE FINESSE GAME

Sandlak's finest offensive weapon is his cannon of a slap shot, which he can blow past goalies from the back of the circle.

Otherwise, he does not have great hand skills. He is not going to see high-percentage passing plays evolving and he is not going to get the puck there a high percentage of the time. And he certainly is not going to beat people with his stickhandling.

Weaker still is Sandlak's skating. The lack of speed and mobility turns most of the rest of his game to powder. He can keep up with the play, but he can't catch people on the transition to defense.

THE PHYSICAL GAME

A big, strong player who is a willing, enthusiastic hitter when his game is at its best, but the banging is a part of his game only indirectly. He wants to play the game more than he wants to crunch people, and that is a problem, because he doesn't play the game especially well. Likewise, Sandlak will hit anything he can catch, but, slow as he is, Sandlak is not going to catch many.

THE INTANGIBLES

Sandlak probably would benefit most from a change in scenery, unless he wants to stay in Vancouver and play for a different coach every few months. He probably would be better-suited to life on a smaller rink (Boston, Buffalo, Chicago), where he can cover more ground, because the big ice eats him up. He probably would go to a new team and become the player the Canucks thought he was going to be.

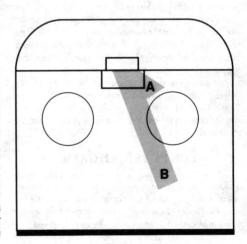

WASHINGTON CAPITALS

DON BEAUPRE

Yrs. of NHL service: 11
Born: Kitchener, Ont., Canada; September 19, 1961
Position: Goaltender
Height: 5-9
Weight: 195
Uniform no.: 33
Catches: Left

Career statistics:

GP	MINS	GA	SO	GAA	A	PIM
420	23776	1402	11	3.53	4	176

1990-91 statistics:

GP	MINS	GAA	W	L	T	SO	GA	S	SAPCT	PIM
45	2572	2.64	20	18	3	5	113	1095	.897	18

LAST SEASON

Set team record for goals-against average and save percentage. Led NHL in shutouts, finished second in goals-against and moved into fourth on team all-time victories list with 48.

THE PHYSICAL GAME

Beaupre is fast, but he isn't lightning. His positioning smarts and strong sense of anticipation put him in the right place, though, and experience allows him to just let the puck hit him. Strong legs and a powerful pushoff make him very quick on decked-pads saves off passes across the crease

Beaupre has a very quick glove, he makes the first save, he directs rebounds well. He can play a standup game, he can leave his feet; when he does, he recovers well. He uses the stick well to block passes and to direct the puck to his teammates

THE MENTAL GAME

Beaupre wants to come right back and stop a breakaway after allowing a soft goal. He wants to start the next game after a weak performance; he wants to start every game—period. But he also understands that whichever goalie is on a roll is the one who plays for the Capitals.

Beaupre uses his head more than in his younger years, when he was an out-of-control flopper. He uses it to maximize his assets and his positioning, doesn't suffer from paralysis by analysis. He wants to play, he wants to win, he wants to be better every day; he also knows he is susceptible to injury and fatigue, so accepts being rested in a positive way.

When the Capitals count on him, he's there. He will give his club a chance to win; he is like the "snooze" button on an alarm clock-radio: even if the team starts 10 minutes late, Beaupre reports on time and keeps the score manageable.

THE INTANGIBLES

Whatever success Beaupre has gotten, he has earned. He stopped flopping all over the place, learned his position, learned how it must be played in the NHL and learned how to use his assets to advantage—which has made him an eminently capable, and frequently outstanding, competitor.

PETER BONDRA

Yrs. of NHL service: 1
Born: Luck, Soviet Union; February 7, 1968
Position: Right wing
Height: 5-11
Weight: 180
Uniform no.: 12
Shoots: Left

Career statistics:

GP	G	A	TP	PIM
54	12	16	28	47

1990-91 statistics:

GP	G	A	TP	+/-	PIM	PP	SH	GW	GT	S	PCT
54	12	16	28	-10	47	4	0	1	0	95	12.6

LAST SEASON

Missed 12 games due to shoulder injury. Led Capitals rookies in scoring.

THE FINESSE GAME

Bondra has lots of speed and skating ability, but is not always in control of it. Sometimes it's lucky there are boards on the rink, or he'd be out in the parking lot. Still, he is a threat to score every time he's on the ice—every time he can get his shot under the crossbar and get it on net, that is.

Defensively, he needs work, as do most second-year pros. He doesn't read the play especially well deep in his zone, gets somewhat swallowed up by the transition from offense to defense—the challenge to identify his man, get tohim and stay with him. From the center line back, quick adjustments are needed and Bondra still is learning how to make them.

A left-hand shot on the right side, Bondra uses his hand and foot speed to cut in, slice across the top of the faceoff circles and fire a shot back against the grain.

THE PHYSICAL GAME

A willing, brave competitor, Bondra is built powerfully. He is strong enough to play a one-on-one game, but is not especially eager to. He pulls up a bit heading to the corners on offense; on defense, Bondra prefers to angle a player to bad ice and is not likely to finish his rival once the contact is available.

Bondra accepts being hit, but will not be intimidated; nor will he imtimidate anyone.

THE INTANGIBLES

Bondra enjoys Washington and is committed to doing the things necessary for becoming a quality NHL player. He wants to show his considerable technical skills and use them to put the opposition on the defensive virtually every shift.

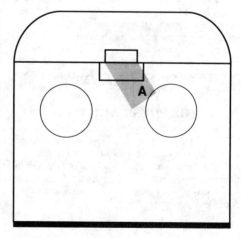

RANDY BURRIDGE

Yrs. of NHL service: 5
Born: Fort Erie, Ont., Canada; January 7, 1966
Position: Left wing
Height: 5-9
Weight: 180
Uniform no.:
Shoots: left

Career statistics:

GP	G	A	TP	PIM
259	108	115	223	275

1990-91 statistics:

GP	G	A	TP	+/-	PIM	PP	SH	GW	GT	S	PCT
62	15	13	28	+17	40	1	0	4	0	108	13.9

LAST SEASON

Games played, goals and points totals were lowest in four seasons. Tied for third on team in game-winning goals. Missed games with a right knee injury.

THE FINESSE GAME

Burridge is a typical, honest two-way player. He is built like a bulldog and that's the way he plays: tenacious behind and around the net. He would get more recognition if he finished off his plays better, but Burridge is the kind of player who can be relied upon to get big goals if not that many (four of his 15 this season were game-winners).

Burridge has a very good, quick wrist shot. It's sneaky fast and picks up speed like a rising fastball. He doesn't use it nearly enough, often trying to pick his spots instead of just getting the shots on net. Along the boards, he will keep the puck alive with his efforts.

Burridge minds his responsibility on defense, will take on checking assignments and is almost always a plus player. He is quick laterally, with short strides.

THE PHYSICAL GAME

Burridge is very good along the boards, because he is short and stocky and has a low center of gravity. Bigger defensemen have difficulty trying to pin him, and Burridge's good balance and agility help him in tight quarters. He is difficult to knock off the puck, but has to play a small man's game because he can get outmuscled one-on-one.

THE INTANGIBLES

Burridge has an upbeat personality and is a willing player who will play any role a coach asks.

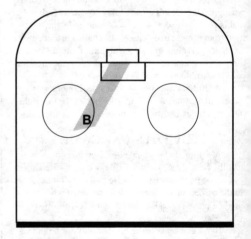

DINO CICCARELLI

Yrs. of NHL service: 10
Born: Sarnia, Ont., Canada; February 8, 1960
Position: Right wing
Height: 5-10
Weight: 175
Uniform no.: 22
Shoots: Right

Career statistics:

GP	G	A	TP	PIM
747	406	378	784	842

1990-91 statistics:

GP	G	A	TP	+/-	PIM	PP	SH	GW	GT	S	PCT
54	21	18	39	-17	66	2	0	2	0	186	11.3

LAST SEASON

Missed 21 games with a broken thumb, five more due to pulled groin. Had his fourth "minus" season in the past five and is minus-57 over those five campaigns.

THE FINESSE GAME

Ciccarelli is a very agile skater, which allows him to cover a tremendous amount of ground; and he covers the most territory in the attacking zone. He gets to the corners and scrounges for pucks, he goes in front for deflections and rebounds, he goes behind the net to kick the puck loose or to harry a defenseman. He plays like a man in a hurry.

Always in search of the game-breaking goal, Ciccarelli sprays shots from everywhere. He gets his shots off very quickly; the puck is on his stick, it's gone. He will score from the faceoff dots or the top of the right-wing circle. He will pay the price for the garbage goals in front. He will walk out from behind the net at times; at others, he will charge to the net from the slot.

Except for an occasional bomb of a shot from the wing, virtually all the scoring is of the in-close, bang-bang variety. Ciccarelli's hands are made for scoring, not carrying the puck or passing it; he wants no part of lugging it out of the defensive zone or the neutral zone. He needs to get open in a scoring area and play with a center who will get the puck to him.

His plus-minus figure last season was the second-worst of his career, a byproduct of a weak offensive year and of his line being outscored by the team against which it was matched.

THE PHYSICAL GAME

As a "little guy," Ciccarelli tries to take advantage of the referees, because a lot of defensemen are strong and are capable of dropping him with a crosscheck in front of the net. But the guy also dives so much it's ridiculous. It may even cost the Capitals power plays, because referees are so sick of the antics: if they see Ciccarelli on his belly, they figure he got there by self-propulsion.

The thing of it is, though, Ciccarelli also plays a physical game in front of the net—takes his whacks, gives them back, pays the price for his tip-ins and rebounds. A lot of those hacks don't get called, so the dives that lead to occasional power plays—he might dive six times in a game just to get one call at an important time—even out in the end.

THE INTANGIBLES

Ciccarelli plays a vital role on his team. He provides the game-breaking offense and takes it upon himself to read the way the game is going and to help control its ebbs and flows. If the Capitals need an emotional jolt, he might cause a confrontation with the other team's toughest player. If they need a power play, he will drop as though shot until the Capitals get one. He is a lieutenant to Dale Hunter in that business, but he is very good at handling the responsibility and he is willing to place himself at physical risk in order to get the job done.

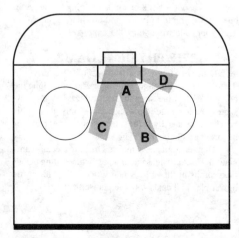

JOHN DRUCE

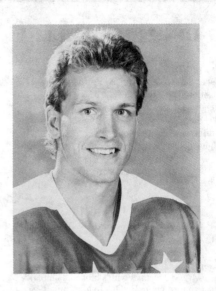

Yrs. of NHL service: 3
Born: Peterborough, Ont., Canada; February 23, 1966
Position: Left wing
Height: 6-1
Weight: 200
Uniform no.: 19
Shoots: Left

Career statistics:

GP	G	A	TP	PIM
173	38	46	84	160

1990-91 statistics:

GP	G	A	TP	+/-	PIM	PP	SH	GW	GT	S	PCT
80	22	36	58	4	46	7	1	4	0	209	10.5

LAST SEASON

Set career highs in all offensive categories. Finished fourth on team in goals and scoring.

THE FINESSE GAME

Another product of that fine junior finishing school in Peterborough, Druce brought two-way skills to the NHL and now is working toward a graduate degree in performance with the Capitals. He may be classified properly as a checker with scoring skills, a scorer with checking skills. Most of the time, you will find him in front of one net or the other, scrapping for whatever territory he can grab, carrying a defenseman or two on his back.

Druce's turns seems a little sluggish at times, as do his decisions the rare occasions when he's carrying the puck. When he decides to shoot, though, Druce takes only a tiny backswing on his half-slap shot, getting it away very quickly. He has the strength to score with a shot from the faceoff circle, but most of his scoring is done off the short game, off driving to the net to convert rebounds or to redirect an alley-oop pass. Druce isn't going to carry the puck much, isn't going to finesse it, but he IS going to bury it—and do whatever he can to keep your team from doing the same.

THE PHYSICAL GAME

Druce has to go where the traffic is. He thrives in the jostling, stop-and-go, rush-hour craziness along the boards. He has the strength for it, the balance on his skates, the leverage in his legs. Snow only gets on his britches if he has dived for some second-effort play, for he rarely gets knocked off his skates.

That tenaciousness makes Druce a special-teams natural. He challenges the first pass while killing penalties, camps in the areas where prices get paid on the power play and deals with the punishment.

Druce is a very good fighter, a left-hander, and will scrap when the fuse scorches the powder. Injuries to both wrists may hinder his punching power, but people who try to find out may be in for a surprise.

THE INTANGIBLES

Druce is a determined, mentally tough, dedicated team player who drove to prominence in the 1990 playoffs but played every night as though fighting for his job. He played the second half of the season with a wrist injury that prevented him from shooting and which would have sidelined most others, but he will not be stopped by such "minor" inconveniences. This player is emerging, growing more and more like his favorite player, Bob Gainey.

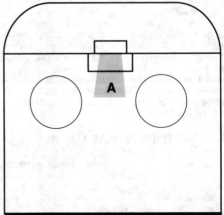

KEVIN HATCHER

Yrs. of NHL service: 6
Born: Detroit, Mich., USA; September 9, 1966
Position: Defenseman
Height: 6-4
Weight: 225
Uniform no.: 4
Shoots: Right

Career statistics:

GP	G	A	TP	PIM
451	82	171	374	674

1990-91 statistics:

GP	G	A	TP	+/-	PIM	PP	SH	GW	GT	S	PCT
79	24	50	74	-10	69	9	2	3	0	267	9.0

LAST SEASON

Led team in scoring and set personal bests for all major offensive categories. Set club records for points by a defenseman and shots.

THE FINESSE GAME

Lots of broad strokes paint the portrait of Hatcher's fine finesse game. He can shoot, he has a range of skating speeds—all of them powerful. He has soft hands for giving and accepting passes, he has size and reach and range, and uses all to solid advantage. He can go end-to-end, using his body beautifully to shield the puck, or he can play give-and-go and sprint for the holes. He can lead a rush or join it.

Adding the texture of finer, subtler strokes would hoist him from very good to exceptional.

Hatcher has a strong shot from the point, as his size and his goal total would suggest, but there are times when he seems to aim too much for the corners instead of just air-mailing a grenade toward the crease. He doesn't always keep his stick on the ice while defending against a rush, which eliminates any chance of a poke check or a pass interception. He is a good, but not a great, passer.

Any team in the league gladly would suffer those minor flaws.

Hatcher struggles a bit in his turns and pivots, he compensates by using his reach and following with his body. If he gets caught occasionally on transition, after one of his frequent rushes leads to a turnover, Hatcher simply puts his head down and skates as hard as he can and will use his giant stride to catch people from behind.

THE PHYSICAL GAME

Hatcher finishes just about every check, challenging his body to play strong 30 minutes a night. He will leave his position to bang, which opens various cans of defensive worms, but he'll probably grow out of that habit, too.

He is a mean hitter, a defiant antagonist in front of his own net. He stops people dead along the wall, leans on them, nullifies their hands and smushes their faces against the glass. To beat him, it's your quickness against his reach and strength and mass, a matchup very few forwards can win.

THE INTANGIBLES

Hatcher is huge enough to block out the sun, physical enough to punch out your lights, strong enough to run you over, balanced enough to beat you at either end of the ice. He has an imposing impact on the game and on his team, which depends on him entirely too much. In his game now, the steps ahead will be smaller and more difficult to earn.

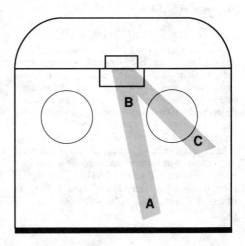

DALE HUNTER

Yrs. of NHL service: 11
Born: Petrolia, Ont., Canada; July 31, 1960
Position: Center
Height: 5-10
Weight: 198
Uniform no.: 32
Shoots: Left

Career statistics:

GP	G	A	TP	PIM
838	221	461	682	2471

1990-91 statistics:

GP	G	A	TP	+/-	PIM	PP	SH	GW	GT	S	PCT
76	16	30	46	-22	234	9	0	2	0	106	15.1

LAST SEASON

Tied for the team lead in power-play goals. Amassed more than 200 penalty minutes a fourth consecutive season

THE FINESSE GAME

Hunter uses his hands and his head to make up for the fact that his legs don't carry him as well as they once did.

A skater of only acceptable speed, Hunter still prefers to make a pass than to take a shot on goal. For the number of opportunities he creates, Hunter should shoot more; of the goals he does score, a high percentage are ones for which he has paid some type of price—deflections, rebounds, loose pucks, etc.

Hunter is extremely alert away from the puck, especially in the defensive zone. He does not leave his position to charge after it unless he thinks he can win it. Moreover, he will secure a teammate's checking responsibility until that teammate can regain position. And on faceoffs, Hunter has no peers in the Washington dressing room—a factor which makes him a critical component onspecial teams.

THE PHYSICAL GAME

Hunter will try to beat you one-on-one with his leg strength, his upper body strength or his mental strength. He must go through an awful lot of elbow pads, because they're always bonking off someone's nose or chin in the heavy traffic around the net and in the corners—areas where Hunter spends most ofthe game.

Hunter's physicality is an asset on the power play, as he is always camping in front of the net, scrapping with a defenseman, and distracting the goaltender from his appointed task. It takes a heckuva crosscheck to knock him off his feet once Hunter takes his "tripod" stance—feet spread wide apart, weightplanted on his stick.

THE INTANGIBLES

Hunter is a guy you want on your side. He will get your whole team mad at him. He will get your whole family mad at him. He will cheap shot any opponent if the chips are on the line and his team needs to win. Let the moralists debate his methods; there is no doubting his ability to lift his team's heart and confidence and hope.

But there also is no question this type of play has taken a toll on him. He cannot summon such efforts as often as in the past. He did it in Game 4 of the first round against the Rangers last spring and the Rangers never recovered; it is doubtful he could have mustered another such performance before Game 7, say. But what better time?

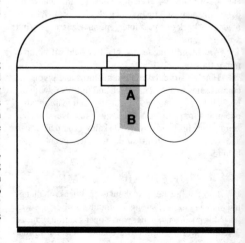

AL IAFRATE

Yrs. of NHL service: 7
Born: Dearborn, Mich., USA; March 21, 1966
Position: Defenseman
Height: 6-3
Weight: 220
Uniform no.: 34
Shoots: Left

Career statistics:

GP	G	A	TP	PIM
502	87	177	264	670

1990-91 statistics:

GP	G	A	TP	+/-	PIM	PP	SH	GW	GT	S	PCT
72	9	23	32	-16	237	2	1	1	0	106	8.5

LAST SEASON

Obtained from Toronto January 15, 1991 for Peter Zezel and Bob Rouse. Set a personal career penalty mark.

THE FINESSE GAME

A powerful, intimidating skater with exceptional acceleration, Iafrate will be just as happy to go over or through an opponent as around one. He has the ability to skate the puck out of trouble, rather than simply slap it off the glass; he can lead a rush or join it and is fast enough to get back in position if there is a turnover. He is smooth, fleet and agile going backward as well.

His hands are just as skilled and are driven by the desire not just to score, but to drive the puck through the goalie if need be—to drive it through the net, too. He can handle the puck, is almost cocky with it, which steers him into occasional trouble. Sometimes he gets so carried away with the rush, Iafrate loses a view of the whole picture and can't regroup mentally in time; but improving on-ice vision helps him spot the open man and reach him with a pass.

Iafrate can surprise a goaltender with a wrist shot, overpower a goalie from the point with a bomb of a slap shot. He keeps the drives low and on-target, which avoids making his teammates duck.

On defense, Iafrate can be considered improving. He read and reacted to plays better under the Capitals' more disciplined defensive system, but still has a way to go before his defensive skills catch his offensive ones.

THE PHYSICAL GAME

Iafrate is fairly physical most of the time and VERY physical when he wants to be. He takes the man with authority as often as possible; he can hurt when he hits, but still should be considered a finesse player with size and physicality rather than a physical player with finesse skills.

Iafrate will reach a boiling point. He will fight.

THE INTANGIBLES

Iafrate had to be the Top Gun on defense in Toronto; in Washington, he can let Kevin Hatcher be the lightning rod. It should be a perfect situation for Iafrate; and while nobody is handing him a Norris Trophy, there is a chance of one for him some day if he adds more layers to his defensive game and starts feeling better about himself.

Sometimes Iafrate tries to do too much, which is understandable, since his hockey gifts are so substantial and varied. But his talent was wasted in Toronto and the feeling here is that a full season in a more positive environment will bring out the best in him.

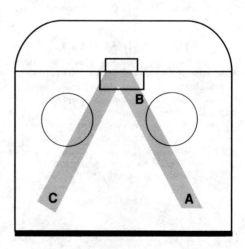

421

CALLE JOHANSSON

Yrs. of NHL service: 4
Born: Goteborg, Sweden; February 14, 1967
Position: Defenseman
Height: 5-11
Weight: 205
Uniform no.: 6
Shoots: Left

Career statistics:

GP	G	A	TP	PIM
280	26	128	154	122

1990-91 statistics:

GP	G	A	TP	+/-	PIM	PP	SH	GW	GT	S	PCT
80	11	41	52	-2	23	2	1	2	0	128	8.6

LAST SEASON

Set career-highs in goals, assists and points.

THE FINESSE GAME

Johansson makes marvelous, controlled turns into the puck and gathers speed as he reaches it so he can accelerate to top gear by the time he collects the disc. Rather than rush it, though, Johansson will make an outlet pass—then REALLY turn on the speed, powering into the clear for a return pass so he can attack the blue line with speed and make something happen.

The smoothness and elegance of his skating become especially useful for Johansson whenever there are fewer than 10 skaters on the ice. He is a perfect special-teams or four-on-four player because he exploits that extra room.

An unselfish player, Johansson virtually always looks to pass before he looks to score. Johansson gets solid wood on his one-timers, and though the odd one gets up near his teammates' helmets, a far greater percentage of the shots are low, hard and accurate.

Johansson is solid defensively. He reads the rush, sees the potential troubles well in advance, and reacts intelligently.

THE PHYSICAL GAME

Johansson plays the man with good success. He is strong enough on his skates and mobile enough to reach his man. A thick upper body provides strength that matches his leg drive and allows him to take the body well. Moreover, the hits are clean.

He doesn't punish anybody, though. He ties up opponents in front of the net, grabs sticks, blocks shots, gets the job done.

THE INTANGIBLES

Johansson handles pressure situations extremely well and wants to be out there with the game on the line. The trouble is self-confidence and assertiveness. He can be a force instead of just a factor.

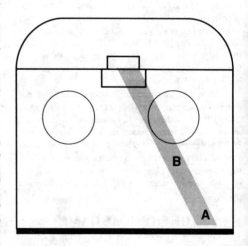

DIMITRI KHRISTICH

Yrs. of NHL service: 1
Born: Kiev, Soviet Union; July 23, 1969
Position: Center/left wing
Height: 6-2
Weight: 190
Uniform no.: 29
Shoots: Right

Career statistics:

GP	G	A	TP	PIM
40	13	14	27	21

1990-91 statistics:

GP	G	A	TP	+/-	PIM	PP	SH	GW	GT	S	PCT
40	13	14	27	-1	21	1	0	0	1	77	16.9

LAST SEASON

Signed with Capitals December 11, 1990, from Sokol Kiev of Soviet Union National League.

THE FINESSE GAME

Khristich is rather a lumbering skater who is strong on his skates, but not fast. His acceleration is very limited; he doesn't explode to the puck so much as he treks toward it.

At times Khristich will force a rush, rather than looking to give-and-go. He likes one move where he slides the puck to the defenseman's left, then tries to step around, to the right, before reclaiming the puck. He has good instincts. He will try certain plays, simply to see if they work. Khristich likes to score, wants to score, and will try a number of methods to achieve the objective. He will shoot off the back foot, set up a screen and use it, or will use a quick release to whip a quick, accurate snap shot of deceptive speed from the top of the circle.

Khristich is alert defensively and is an asset on penalty killing. He played center in the Soviet Union, where the center has the "high" (defensive) responsibilities under their system. So Khristich knows what to do in the checking role and can handle it well against the opposition's first or second lines.

THE PHYSICAL GAME

Khristich is not a banger, but he is strong, he will bump and doesn't shy away from the boards at all. In fact, he likes the boards and traffic and is very aggressive in his pursuit of loose pucks. He uses his body mass to advantage along the boards and in the corners.

THE INTANGIBLES

Khristich adjusted to the North American game very quickly. He has great desire and determination to become a star here and he owns the mental toughness to act on his wish. He is popular with his teammates, likes to hang around with them, and eagerly participates in team functions off the ice. There is a fine up-side to his NHL future.

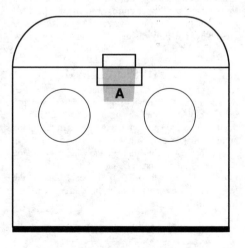

NICK KYPREOS

Yrs. of NHL service: 2
Born: Toronto, Ont., Canada; June 4, 1966
Position: Left wing
Height: 6-0
Weight: 195
Uniform no.: 9
Shoots: Left

Career statistics:

GP	G	A	TP	PIM
110	14	13	27	278

1990-91 statistics:

GP	G	A	TP	+/-	PIM	PP	SH	GW	GT	S	PCT
79	9	9	18	-4	196	0	0	3	0	60	15.0

LAST SEASON

Set career highs in games played, goals, assists, points and penalty minutes.

THE FINESSE GAME

Kypreos is not blessed with great speed; his feet do not move as fast as his head, which basically reduces his finesse game to corner work—he is a powerful skater with good endurance for long scrums—and an occasional shot. He needs to get in close to the net to score, using an accurate, heavy shot to drive the goaltender back or create a rebound.

But the foot speed troubles him in the transition to defense. His turns are only average and he doesn't skate out of them, he glides, which tends to put him a step behind when the puck turns over. The way he reads plays could also use improvement; Kypreos needs to see the play, identify the man he should be covering, and get to him quicker than he has in the past.

THE PHYSICAL GAME

Kypreos has size and strength, which he uses effectively in the corners and the boards, and has unmistakable hand skills with his gloves on. He pays the price to get the puck and may be underrated for his ability to make a play with it once obtained.

Kypreos will come in from the wing, break to the net and put a lot of pressure on a defenseman to stop him. In tight, he will muscle for the puck, take all the hits. And if push comes to punch, he is a very good left-handed fighter.

THE INTANGIBLES

Kypreos understands the game and works hard at it, plays his fourth-line role well because he plays under tight emotional control at all times. He is intense, full of energy, good in the dressing room, and a force on the bench when spirits are sagging. He got nine goals in VERY limited ice time as a fourth-line player and could move up to the third line (with 15-goal potential), if the improvement continues.

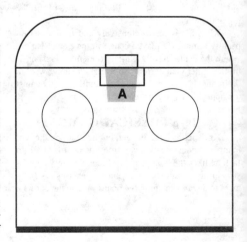

MIKE LALOR

Yrs. of NHL service: 6
Born: Buffalo, N.Y., USA; March 8, 1963
Position: Defenseman
Height: 6-0
Weight: 200
Uniform no.: 26
Shoots: Left

Career statistics:

GP	G	A	TP	PIM
379	7	64	71	427

1990-91 statistics:

GP	G	A	TP	+/-	PIM	PP	SH	GW	GT	S	PCT
68	1	5	6	-23	61	0	0	0	0	49	2.0

LAST SEASON

Plus-minus was career-worst. Goal was first in 139 games.

THE FINESSE GAME

One thing Lalor does extremely well is make a good first pass out of the defensive zone. He identifies the best option very quickly and gets the pass to his teammate sharply, tape to tape. After the goaltender stops pucks that have been driven around the boards, Lalor is smart enough not to overhandle the puck or try to carry it; he moves the puck, so it's into the Washington zone, then it's out of the zone.

Basically, Lalor must play that way, because his other hand and foot skills are very limited. He is not a quick skater, does not have a strong pushoff and does not generate skating power. He is not very agile or mobile or good on the turns. As a result, Lalor becomes something of a gambler; he looks to intercept a pass, but has a difficult time recovering if the interception is not made.

He will, however, sneak into the slot if the percentages are very highly in his favor for a scoring chance. He keeps his point shot low and accurate, but takes a while to get it off.

THE PHYSICAL GAME

Lalor's skating deficiencies make it difficult for him to get to the people he wants to hit. He ends up lunging, which throws off his balance; and when he reaches them in the corners, he is not strong enough to seal them off, bring them to a complete stop, unless they want to be stopped. He is not a punishing hitter.

The shortage of range makes him rather tentative, for if he commits to the corner to hit somebody, he's in trouble if the player he's chasing makes a pass to the area Lalor just left. More often than not, Lalor just stays in front of the net and his partner ranges from one corner to the other. That places stringent demands on the other defenseman, but it identifies Lalor's limitations and helps him play within them.

Lalor, then, does what he can. He hits whatever he can reach and he stands up for his teammates as well.

THE INTANGIBLES

The top defensemen have two-way skills, the lower-ranked defensemen at least tend to play the body or have some above-average attribute. Lower-ranked defensemen who were minus 23 last season may simply have had a tough year . . . or they may have a tough time hanging onto their jobs if someone younger/better comes along.

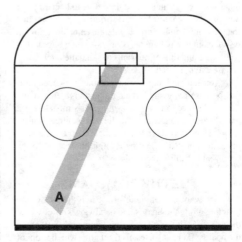

ROD LANGWAY

Yrs. of NHL service: 13
Born: Formosa; May 3, 1957
Position: Defenseman
Height: 6-3
Weight: 218
Uniform no.: 5
Shoots: Left

Career statistics:

GP	G	A	TP	PIM
909	51	265	316	807

1990-91 statistics:

GP	G	A	TP	+/-	PIM	PP	SH	GW	GT	S	PCT
56	1	7	8	12	24	0	0	0	0	32	3.1

LAST SEASON

Missed 24 games due to back problems. His games played were a career low and the seventh straight season in which he was unable to play all 80. Was a "plus" player for thirteenth consecutive season and is +279 for his career.

THE FINESSE GAME

Langway has played so many seasons in the league because he doesn't get fancy. Clearly an advocate of the KISS approach to the game, (Keep It Simple, Stupid), Langway loves to use the strong-side boards for his clearing passes if he has time, and goes hard around the weak-side boards if he's under pressure.

At the same time, some of his best passes are the backhand five-footers that help a teammate get the puck out of trouble—which is the only aim Langwaybrings to the rink.

Other times, Langway will fire a breakaway pass up the middle just to keep the opposition's defense honest. It's worth an icing. If they have to keep one eye out for a Washington forward sprinting up the middle, looking for a bomb, opposing defensemen are going to be reluctant to pinch up the boards—which buys Langway space and time if he wants to skate the puck out . . . a rare event, indeed.

You can put Langway with an inexperienced partner, because Langway has the range and the reach and the intelligence to cover the youngster's mistakes. He may have to concede some turf to younger, faster forwards, he may have to meet their charges deeper in his zone, but that's fine; he'll angle those kids to the corner and swallow them whole.

THE PHYSICAL GAME

Langway, of mammoth strength, is the king of the bear hug along the boards and he always knows where the referee is. If the referee is on Langway's left, along the boards, Langway uses his right arm (which is out of sight) like a vise to grab the opposing player. Similarly, he is a master of grabbing the stick of an opponent; and because he is smart enough to keep skating when the opposition player skates, the clear case of holding is less-easily detected.

He is the best on the team at taking the body, at controlling and containing an opponent. Forwards don't dictate position to Langway as often as Langway dictates it to them. And on penalty killing, Langway is a tower of strength due to his anticipation and knowledge of the game, his physical nature in tying up people in front and his shot-blocking skills.

THE INTANGIBLES

Langway still loves the game, still wants to play it, is still a plus player, is still a leader. He can continue to play a critical role on the team, if his battered body doesn't fall completely apart, for two more seasons.

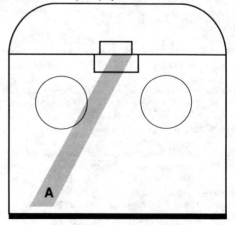

MIKE LIUT

Yrs. of NHL service: 12
Born: Weston, Ont., Canada; January 7, 1956
Position: Goaltender
Height: 6-2
Weight: 195
Uniform no.: 1
Catches: Left

Career statistics:

GP	MINS	GA	SO	GAA	A	PIM
642	37032	2149	24	3.48	12	20

1990-91 statistics:

GP	MINS	GAA	W	L	T	SO	GA	S	SAPCT	PIM
35	1834	3.73	13	16	3	0	114	786	.855	0

LAST SEASON

Failed to record at least one shutout for first time in his NHL career.

THE PHYSICAL GAME

Liut perfectly complements the Washington style, as he is a solid first-stop goaltender. He uses the butterfly style, deploys his long legs to maximize coverage of the corners. After all these years, the legs remain quick.

But all tall goalies have a difficult time climbing back up and Liut—thoughabove-average—is no exception. While first saves are a strength, second shots are a problem if the rebound bounces into a danger zone. And while the butterfly is used to Liut's advantage, people very often find room at the corner above his glove.

Liut's stick work has improved. When he broke into the pro game, goaltenders hardly ever had to leave the net; now, they have to leave the net, stop the puck and clear it. More mobility is being asked of him now than ever and the adjustment has not been an easy one, because Liut feels far more secure in his crease area than out of it.

It doesn't help, either, that he "changes hands" to shoot, as Jon Casey does in Minnesota and Curtis Joseph does in St. Louis. That is a time-consuming, awkward maneuver and he does not do it as well as either of those Norris Division counterparts.

THE MENTAL GAME

A strong, intelligent individual, Liut has spent a tremendous amount of time studying the game and coming to grips with its technical and tactical aspects—adding his own layers of experience to the foundation of knowledge. He reads situations and knows the whole playbook—knows where all of his players shouldbe while reacting to those situations. Sometimes they aren't there, though, and Liut doesn't always adjust well.

And he still is good for a freebie every once in a while. Concentration should be a strength for a player of his tenure, yet sometimes it just vanishes for a moment. A high-scoring team can afford such lapses, but the Capitals have to work so hard to score most nights that a soft goal against can be deflating. If the bad one comes early, Liut fights the puck all night.

THE INTANGIBLES

Liut still can outplay some NHL goalies and the feeling here is he will be asked to outplay Washington goalies when he faces the Capitals with some new team. Don Beaupre is the No. 1 guy there and Washington needs to find out about whether the kids in their system—Olaf Kolzig, Byron Dafoe, Jim Hrivnak—finally are ready to play. Liut bought Washington the time to give these kids seasoning.

ALAN MAY

Yrs. of NHL service: 2
Born: Barrhead, Alta., Canada; January 14, 1965
Position: Wing
Height: 6-1
Weight: 200
Uniform no.: 16
Shoots: Right

Career statistics:

GP	G	A	TP	PIM
150	12	16	28	525

1990-91 statistics:

GP	G	A	TP	+/-	PIM	PP	SH	GW	GT	S	PCT
67	4	6	10	-10	264	0	0	0	0	64	6.1

LAST SEASON

Led team in penalty minutes for second consecutive season.

THE FINESSE GAME

A skater with good quickness, some speed and above-average balance, May has a good, heavy shot which he can fire from the wing, but he needs time to get it off. In tight, though, the hand skills just aren't there; he tries too hard and gets too little done.

May gets to the net, where a player his size can excel, but seems to place a higher premium on getting involved with a defenseman—freeing the puck and theroom for a teammate—than having his stick on the ice and hacking at the rebounds that often seem to land at his feet. A heads-up player, May should look down occasionally.

There are similar difficulties in the corners; he might force a loose puck, then struggle with the decision about what to do next.

THE PHYSICAL GAME

Some players tailor their games around their skating; May uses his foot skills to maximize the physical game that is his meal ticket.

He does some nice work along the boards. In the corners and along the boards, May bends at the waist, makes opponent lean on him, but keeps a channel clear to kick the puck free. As first man in on the forecheck, May's balance allows him to deliver a big hit and remain on his feet.

Moreover, he has decent agility, and he doesn't need a 40-acre field to make a simple turn out of the corners—though he does give up valuableacceleration by gliding through his turns instead of skating through them.

May is a very smart fighter. Though not quite of heavyweight stature, he will throw with both hands and handle himself well. And while his penalty-minute total is extremely high, May very rarely leaves his team shorthanded; if he goes to the box, an opponent virtually always goes with him.

THE INTANGIBLES

A hard worker, an intense player and a strong individual, May tries to stay at the top of a limited, but necessary, game. There is room for growth here. He is working on making better decisions, better plays out of the corners and has a great desire to improve.

For now, though, he remains mostly the Capitals' intimidator, or their response to attempts at intimidation by the opposition.

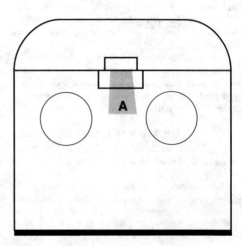

KELLY MILLER

Yrs. of NHL service: 6
Born: Lansing, Mich., USA; March 3, 1963
Position: Left wing
Height: 5-11
Weight: 196
Uniform no.: 10
Shoots: Left

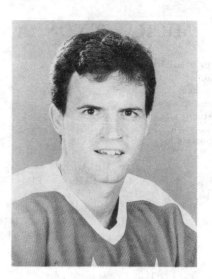

Career statistics:

GP	G	A	TP	PIM
474	99	140	239	260

1990-91 statistics:

GP	G	A	TP	+/-	PIM	PP	SH	GW	GT	S	PCT
80	24	26	50	10	29	4	2	3	1	155	15.5

LAST SEASON

Tied Kevin Hatcher for team lead in goals. Set career highs for goals, assists and points. Played all 80 games for second consecutive season. Was third on team in plus-minus.

THE FINESSE GAME

Strong skating skills and quickness, plus boundless energy and intensity make checking Miller's claim to fame. He loves to spend the night along the walls, hacking at the puck. It's safe there, so that's where Miller stays—other than an occasional attempt at a spin-o-rama move from the left-wing boards, which virtually everybody knows about and virtually nobody falls for anymore. Brother Kevin does it much more effectively.

His goals result from hard work, from turnovers, from slam dunks, from scrambles his forechecking likely helped create. At equal strength, he's always out against the opposition's top forwards; during shorthanded situations, Miller is always harrying the first pass with his great speed and endless willingness to use it.

THE PHYSICAL GAME

Miller likes to carry across the blue line with speed, then cut toward the net, leave a drop pass, and drive to the cage, all but putting his head or shoulders into the defenseman with him and carrying him along for a ride. That opens nice space for the players on his team, but it also opens a huge hole for the players on the other team if they get to the puck first and counterattack. Should that occur, though, Miller will kill himself getting back into the play.

Miller persists and persists. He wants to get the big hit, wants the puck—especially if you have it.

THE INTANGIBLES

We will not play ostrich here: Last season, HSR told you Miller "will score no more than 20 goals a season..." Well, you messed up, you trusted us. He scored more than 20 goals.

Miller's goal total last season finally reflected some reward for his hard work, some return on the investment of energy and will. He is in the top one percent of the league's all-out-effort players. He is relentless in pursuit of the puck, unstoppable in his drive to succeed and improve. He can demoralize you with his work ethic, with his utter refusal to accept anything that does not involve winning. This guy does not lose; you may be better than he is one night, you may beat him one night, but don't count on it happening again.

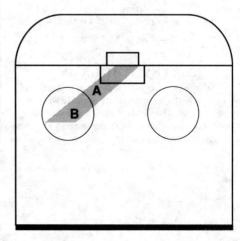

MICHAL PIVONKA

Yrs. of NHL service: 5
Born: Kladno, Czechoslovakia; January 28, 1966
Position: Center/Left wing
Height: 6-2
Weight: 198
Uniform no.: 20
Shoots: Left

Career statistics:

GP	G	A	TP	PIM
352	102	156	258	187

1990-91 statistics:

GP	G	A	TP	+/-	PIM	PP	SH	GW	GT	S	PCT
79	20	50	70	3	34	6	0	4	0	172	11.6

LAST SEASON

Set career highs for assists and points.

THE FINESSE GAME

Pivonka skates superbly, takes a quality wrist or slap shot, handles the puck well and is aware of what is happening on the ice. A fine playmaker, he will not challenge a defenseman physically, but will shield the puck with his body and force the defenseman to concede the time and space needed to make the play Pivonka wants to make.

Pivonka favors coming across the blue line, drifting to the left-wing circle to make the defenseman cross-over and stride, then snap off a shot from the circle, somewhere between the outer rim and the dot. Other centers would get to the circle, then try to take the puck to the net and challenge the defenseman even more, but that is not Pivonka's game.

Pivonka does a pretty good job defensively and is improving all the time. But he still has trouble making defensive decisions—identifying the open man and covering him—when the other team cranks up the tempo in the Capitals' defensive zone. He is comfortable killing penalties, though, with his size, strength, quickness and durability being the major assets in that area.

THE PHYSICAL GAME

Pivonka does not mind the physical going, but it is not high on his list of favored activities. He will take a hit and give one, but tends to stay in the safer, more user-friendly areas around the perimeter—which is one reason he doesn't score more goals.

THE INTANGIBLES

Pivonka can do better than 70 points. His challenge is to determine whether he wants the 80 or 90 points his size and athletic skills could produce.

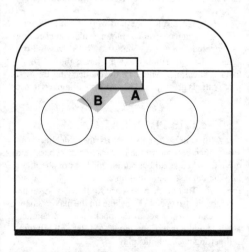

MIKE RIDLEY

Yrs. of NHL service: 6
Born: Winnipeg, Man., Canada; July 8, 1963
Position: Center
Height: 6-1
Weight: 200
Uniform no.: 17
Shoots: Left

Career statistics:

GP	G	A	TP	PIM
461	175	252	427	233

1990-91 statistics:

GP	G	A	TP	+/-	PIM	PP	SH	GW	GT	S	PCT
79	23	48	71	9	26	6	5	4	0	155	14.8

LAST SEASON

Was second on team in points, third on team in goals and assists. Scored 20 goals or more for sixth consecutive season.

THE FINESSE GAME

Ridley is one of those rare individuals who may be faster with the puck than without it. He seems to relish the challenge of doing something creative, making something out of nothing; the challenge gets his legs and hands and mind going faster than when someone else is carrying it. His one-on-one game runs off that internal electricity, which also energizes the extremely powerful lower body which provides his skating power and balance.

Ridley has extremely fast hands and does not believe in wasting time. He gets the puck and releases it when a shot is available, surprising goaltenders with his quick release. He can score from the top of the circle but also likes to take the puck deep; he will carry into traffic and handle the puck in tight—making himself the eye of a storm he creates.

Ridley is very responsible defensively and is an extremely effective penalty killer who uses his speed and smarts to challenge and pressure the opposition power play. He forces puck carriers to make decisions, then is off on the counter-attack if a turnover ensues. And he will look to score, not simply dump the puck down ice.

THE PHYSICAL GAME

Something about his carriage makes you think this is not a strong guy, except that perception is utterly and completely incorrect.

Ridley plays a physical game, drives defensemen back off the blue line. He drives to the net and he uses

his body nicely to shield the backhand as he mushes onward. He will give a big hit if the opportunity arises and it will be the other guy who goes to the ice.

THE INTANGIBLES

Ridley puts tremendous pressure on himself to be the best player possible. He is intense, emotional, sensitive and demanding of himself—which might be surprising to the people who look at him and constantly see a poker face. They are wrong to underestimate his drive; the guy wasn't even drafted, yet he made himself an all-star and made it look easy.

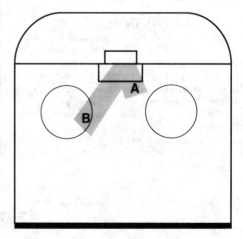

KEN SABOURIN

Yrs. of NHL service: 1
Born: Scarborough, Ont., Canada; April 28, 1966
Position: Defenseman
Height: 6-3
Weight: 205
Uniform no.: 8
Shoots: Left

Career statistics:

GP	G	A	TP	PIM
55	2	8	10	153

1990-91 statistics:

GP	G	A	TP	+/-	PIM	PP	SH	GW	GT	S	PCT
44	2	7	9	15	117	0	0	0	0	23	8.7

LAST SEASON

Obtained from Calgary January 24 for Paul Fenton.

THE FINESSE GAME

Sabourin will not be mistaken for Paul Coffey. His feet are big and heavy; agility and mobility are not a strong point. His stride is well short of power, though for a plodder, Sabourin skates backward effectively and gets to the corners fairly well.

Sabourin has a good reach and uses it intelligently to compensate for his foot skills—or the lack thereof. He is good at deflecting passes, but tends to overhandle them once he makes the steal, instead of getting the puck and sending it someplace.

Other hand skills? Nope. Not yet. His passes are on the too-soft side, as is his shot, which is accurate, but underpowered.

THE PHYSICAL GAME

Since his skating skills are so limited, it is Sabourin's strength that allows him to play in the league. But even that needs work. For a guy his size, not too many opponents get pinned or dropped in the corners, because Sabourin sets too high a target and doesn't use his stick as an effective checking/pinning tool.

When backed to the wall, Sabourin will fight; but he is more of a calculating disturber who will rub his glove in a guy's face or get into the yapping contests, but not do a great deal else.

THE INTANGIBLES

Sabourin still is adjusting to the speed of the NHL game, which means his playing time will be limited to careful placement against third- and fourth-line players until he proves trustworthy against higher-caliber competition. He'll have to work extra hard just to keep his spot as sixth/seventh on the depth chart.

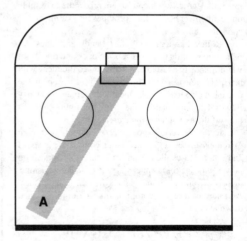

DAVE TIPPETT

Yrs. of NHL service: 7
Born: Moosomin, Sask., Canada; August 25, 1961
Position: Left wing
Height: 5-10
Weight: 180
Uniform no.: 14
Shoots: Left

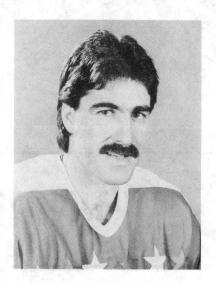

Career statistics:

GP	G	A	TP	PIM
544	81	129	210	205

1990-91 statistics:

GP	G	A	TP	+/-	PIM	PP	SH	GW	GT	S	PCT
61	6	9	15	-13	24	0	0	2	0	68	8.8

LAST SEASON

Obtained from Hartford October 2, 1990 for Capitals' sixth selection in 1992 draft.

THE FINESSE GAME

Because of his size and the accompanying problems in strength matchups, penalty killing and defense are Tippett's top areas—last season'splus-minus notwithstanding. Though he has had only one "plus" season in his career, checking guys tend to take that kind of hit, because they do not score much themselves while playing against the lines which are the opposition's top point producers.

Tippett does not have an overpowering shot or great hands in tight; he's going to muscle in an occasional loose puck, or hack in a rebound off a scramble. His attributes tend to show more when he doesn't have the puck. He skates well, with speed and more quickness than agility, he reads and reacts, and that plays into his penalty-killing strengths.

THE PHYSICAL GAME

Tippett does not have great size, but he is extremely competitive. He takes hits, and gives them, and willingly goes into the corners with players much larger than himself (which happens to be a high percentage of the league).

Because people tend to throw him around, Tippett draws his share of penalties. He will keep his legs going, force people to hold him or tackle him.

THE INTANGIBLES

Tippett brings his team experience, enthusiasm and intensity. His work ethic sets a good example for the younger players who tend to forget that persistent effort tends to overcome sporadic talent.

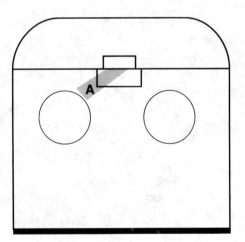

WINNIPEG JETS

SCOTT ARNIEL

Yrs. of NHL service: 9
Born: Kingston, Ont., Canada; September 17, 1962
Position: Left wing
Height: 6-1
Weight: 188
Uniform no.: 11
Shoots: Left

Career statistics:

GP	G	A	TP	PIM
701	144	186	330	579

1990-91 statistics:

GP	G	A	TP	+/-	PIM	PP	SH	GW	GT	S	PCT
75	5	17	22	-12	87	0	0	1	1	91	5.5

LAST SEASON

Goal production dropped 12, to a nine-season low. Point total also was a nine-season low. Plus-minus declined by 16 goals.

THE FINESSE GAME

A few seasons ago, a national hockey publication threw into a computer all the heights, weights, ages and annual production figures of all the players in the NHL, then came up with a "Mister Average." Arniel ended up as the typical forward, and his skills fit in just about perfectly with that general profile.

Arniel understands the defensive aspects of the game and uses his skills, which are average, to transact the business at hand. He can skate, can get where he's going, but he doesn't make you go, "Wow! Look at that Arniel motor!" He forechecks and kills penalties and is average, maybe a bit above, in dispatch of his duties.

We are not talking great hands, great hockey sense, great vision of the ice. He was getting 40 or 50 points a year and scoring in the teens, which was fine—in fact, probably above average for a checking left wing. Then he was made redundant in Buffalo by Dave Snuggerud, who does the same things, but does them better and faster and is a little younger.

THE PHYSICAL GAME

Above average some nights, below average on others. When he's involved and hitting and working the boards and making plays and blocking shots and is into the game, Arniel might even be above average. When he is not involved, simply getting caught along the boards, Arniel is just kind of sleepwalking—not getting the most out of whatever skills he has.

THE INTANGIBLES

In Buffalo, Arniel solidified the third line/checking line, which was asked to accept all the opponent's top offensive players as the assignment for the night. Back in Winnipeg for a second tenure, Arniel's role did not seem as well defined and his play suffered. The funny thing was, he might have been the perfect guy to play with his good buddy, Dale Hawerchuk; instead, Arniel ended up in the package the Sabres put up to get Hawerchuk.

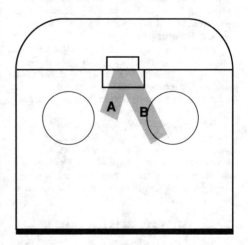

BRENT ASHTON

Yrs. of NHL service: 12
Born: Saskatoon, Sask., Canada; May 18, 1960
Position: Left wing
Height: 6-1
Weight: 210
Uniform no.: 7
Shoots: Left

Career statistics:

GP	G	A	TP	PIM
872	256	310	566	532

1990-91 statistics:

GP	G	A	TP	+/-	PIM	PP	SH	GW	GT	S	PCT
61	12	24	36	-10	58	1	0	2	0	107	11.2

LAST SEASON

Missed six games due to groin injury, 13 games because of a broken jaw. His worst year for goals and assists since 1983-84, his lowest for games played since 1979-80.

THE FINESSE GAME

Speed, balance and a variety of shots comprise Ashton's bag of finesse tricks. He will use the wrist shot or the snap, surprising goalies as often as possible from his favorite short-range scoring areas. He will get it off quickly and accurately, and makes regular use of the backhand as well; he uses the backhand so much, it might just be easier to play on the right side, a la Brian Mullen.

For all his skills, though, Ashton seems to out-think himself—especially on the many breakaways his speed creates—and misses a number of chances for every one or two he puts into the net.

Because of his hand speed, Ashton often is trusted with faceoffs while the Jets are short a player. He is, however, unquestionably a wing; a center who overhandles the puck as much as Ashton does would not last long with even the most tolerant, patient linemates.

Season after season, Ashton has shown the knack for scoring upwards of 20 goals, which is part of the reason he has played for so many NHL teams. It remains extremely difficult to find left wings who have some speed and can score; Ashton is such a player, even if last year's statistics certainly do not suggest as much.

THE PHYSICAL GAME

Ashton has size and uses it in very quiet ways. While some players make a big show of leaving their feet to check an opponent, and others will crunch a guy, then wind up in a pile in the corner, Ashton simply hits, keeps his footing, and skates away. He doesn't make a big show, doesn't go down. So he gets the job done in a subtler fashion.

But he is far more a finesse player with size than a physical player with skill.

THE INTANGIBLES

Scoring is the thing Ashton does best. Playmaking is for playmakers, not for him; Ashton is the finisher, and it is fine with him if everybody else is the starter.

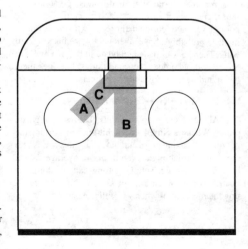

RANDY CARLYLE

Yrs. of NHL service: 15
Born: Sudbury, Ont., Canada; April 19, 1956
Position: Defenseman
Height: 5-10
Weight: 200
Uniform no.: 8
Shoots: Left

Career statistics:

GP	G	A	TP	PIM
967	146	489	635	1332

1990-91 statistics:

GP	G	A	TP	+/-	PIM	PP	SH	GW	GT	S	PCT
52	9	19	28	6	44	2	0	1	0	89	10.1

LAST SEASON

Missed five games due to foot contusion, six due to groin strain, six due to triceps strain, but still was the only "plus" regular on the team. Games played total was lowest since 1977-78, yet his goal total was a three-season high.

THE FINESSE GAME

Carlyle obviously does not dominate on offense any more, but he works hard all the time and retains his enthusiasm for the game. He takes those assets, combines them with a very good view of the ice, and tempers them with the anticipation on which he must depend to survive these nights against 20-year-old kids with rockets on their feet.

The years of experience have not been wasted. Carlyle is very savvy in defensive situations around the net and will not get sucked into any adventures behind the cage unless there's a good chance he can seal the puck off for a faceoff or get it clear. On offense, he can still bring it from the point with some steam.

The opportunities are rarer, though. Carlyle must watch younger defensemen handle the evening's chores against the first and second opposing lines. His minutes come against the third- and fourth-liners, whose games are rougher around the edges and whose skills are more vulnerable to his wiles.

THE PHYSICAL GAME

Carlyle always has his stick on you. He's tapping at your ankles, he's hooking your elbows to get you off balance, he's hacking at your stick to knock the puck free. The stick is Carlyle's range-extender now, making up for legs that don't get him to places right away, and he uses it effectively.

THE INTANGIBLES

Carlyle remains competitive, and bare-headed, at age 35. He spends more and more time on the sidelines as the Jets look at players who can provide the team with the spirit and skill and leadership Carlyle offers.

It is a compliment to Carlyle that they have not been able to phase him out completely, a sad commentary on the team that a 35-year-old can still make their lineup and be their only plus regular.

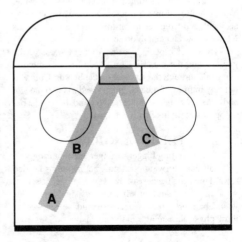

DANTON COLE

Yrs. of NHL service: 1
Born: Pontiac, Mich., USA; January 10, 1967
Position: Center/right wing
Height: 5-11
Weight: 189
Uniform no.: 24
Shoots: Right

Career statistics:

GP	G	A	TP	PIM
68	14	12	26	24

1990-91 statistics:

GP	G	A	TP	+/-	PIM	PP	SH	GW	GT	S	PCT
66	13	11	24	-14	24	1	1	1	1	109	11.9

LAST SEASON

First in NHL.

THE FINESSE GAME

Cole has decent hands, some quality moves and is fairly strong on his skates. He can score goals or he can hold onto the puck and make plays from the perimeter. Cole is not always willing to take punishment and drive to the net, though; and when he plays center, he seems to have a difficult time locating his linemates.

Cole is responsible defensively, good positionally and not too bad on faceoffs, but strength is an issue. His game falters when he tries to grind or grab a player and stop him from moving.

THE PHYSICAL GAME

There is some softness in Cole's physical game. You've got to go into traffic once in a while, even by accident, and Cole seems, at this early moment of his NHL career, reluctant to do so.

He is not especially eager to fight wars for the puck behind the net. He won't keep his legs moving and battle through the gauntlet on the boards. Cole will not stay in front of the net, either; he darts into the slot and darts back out. When he has to grind, he grinds; but it does not seem his favorite activity.

THE INTANGIBLES

Cole is getting bigger, stronger and maturing, and plays all three forward positions, but he seems headed toward the wing because of the way Winnipeg is set up. As a right-hand shot on left wing, his shooting angles would be more open and Cole would be relieved of those physical matchups in the defensive slot.

At center, he isn't going to play ahead of Thomas Steen or Ed Olczyk, unless Olczyk is moved to the wing. So, barring injury or trade, Cole will be no higher than a No. 3, and he won't have either quality minutes or quality linemates.

On the flank, at least, he'd be a depth wing with some skill who could step in as No. 2 center for a week if there's an injury. At this stage of Cole's development, a steady diet of play against No. 2 centers would wear him down.

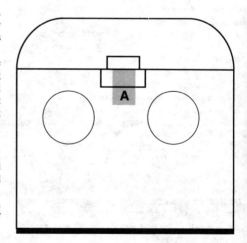

SHAWN CRONIN

Yrs. of NHL service: 2
Born: Flushing, Mich., USA; August 20, 1963
Position: Defenseman
Height: 6-2
Weight: 210
Uniform no.: 44
Shoots: Right

Career statistics:

GP	G	A	TP	PIM
128	1	9	10	432

1990-91 statistics:

GP	G	A	TP	+/-	PIM	PP	SH	GW	GT	S	PCT
67	1	5	6	-10	189	0	0	0	0	40	2.5

LAST SEASON

Penalty minutes dropped by 54 from his rookie season, offensive production improved by one goal, one assist; plus-minus improved by six.

THE FINESSE GAME

With his odd, knock-kneed style, Cronin isn't much of a skater. People can, and do, blow past him to the outside because he has trouble turning in that direction.

Cronin is not an especially disciplined player. He runs all over the place in the defensive zone, looking for people to hit. But he ends up covering people who are not in a position to do any particular offensive damage.

When he gets the puck, Cronin tends to over-carry it. The hands and the head are not connected real well for finesse situations.

THE PHYSICAL GAME

The physical game—punching people, intimidating, being an enforcer—makes up virtually all of Cronin's contribution. And on a team comprised of so many solid finesse players as Winnipeg, he plays an important role in keeping the ice safe for his much more skilled teammates.

Cronin unmistakably is a top heavyweight puncher. The question is, What happens if Cronin can't find anyone to fight? If opposing teams keep sending out skilled players who can skate and make plays, then Cronin, in a way, has done his job. So does he dress for 80 games and never touch the ice?

THE INTANGIBLES

Cronin has a tremendous work ethic. He will do anything to improve the limited skills he has and to stay in shape for his limited role. But the roster reduction to 17 skaters may make it extremely difficult to get Cronin into the lineup on a lot of nights against better skating, less physical teams.

There is always a sweater available for a tough guy; but the game is reaching a point where the tough guy better be able to do some good things with his gloves on. Cronin isn't at that level yet, and he's 28 years old.

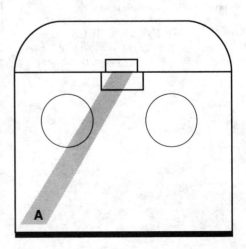

GORD DONNELLY

Yrs. of NHL service: 8
Born: Montreal, Que., Canada; April 5, 1962
Position: Right wing/defense
Height: 6-1
Weight: 202
Uniform no.: 34
Shoots: Right

Career statistics:

GP	G	A	TP	PIM
382	22	29	51	1383

1990-91 statistics:

GP	G	A	TP	+/-	PIM	PP	SH	GW	GT	S	PCT
57	3	4	7	-13	265	0	0	0	0	35	8.6

LAST SEASON

Goal total matched prior season. PIM increased by 43. Plus-minus worsened by 16 goals.

THE FINESSE GAME

Donnelly plays better on defense than at wing because he's better with the play coming at him. He moves the puck well, he knows when to move it— which in his case is as soon as possible—and he sees the ice better from the defensive posture.

But that's about it, finesse-wise. He can put one skate in front of the other going forward, one skate behind the other going backward. The trouble starts when there's any variation on that theme.

THE PHYSICAL GAME

Donnelly is tough and aggressive, and he'll do what the team asks, which is punch faces. He is enormously strong, which is an asset when he is trying to pry people's helmets off their heads.

THE INTANGIBLES

Players get to be 29 and try to get by doing less; Donnelly still tries to do what he can. He remains good insurance on the road against stiffer teams. He still knows his job, and he does it.

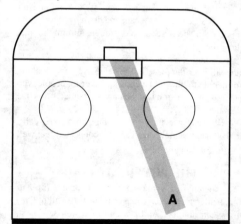

PAT ELYNUIK

Yrs. of NHL service: 2
Born: Foam Lake, Sask., Canada; October 30, 1967
Position: Right wing
Height: 6-0
Weight: 185
Uniform no.: 15
Shoots: Right

Career statistics:

GP	G	A	TP	PIM
229	90	104	194	197

1990-91 statistics:

GP	G	A	TP	+/-	PIM	PP	SH	GW	GT	S	PCT
80	31	34	65	-13	73	16	0	4	1	150	20.7

LAST SEASON

Had second straight season of 30 goals or better and led team in goal production, power play goals and shooting percentage. Played 80 games a second consecutive season.

THE FINESSE GAME

A perfect complement for Thomas Steen, Elynuik is an agile skater who maneuvers himself into goal-scoring position and finishes plays extremely well. The Jets' big-goal, big-game player, Elynuik has the good sense to keep his forehand alive all the time; he will criss-cross with Steen, then stay prepared for the set-up pass Steen is only too happy to throw across for a one-timer. Or he will come into the play late, after Steen has driven the defense back, and shoot off the drop pass. Elynuik must work extra hard to get there for the play, as he is more agile that fast. His outside speed is debatable, he is not exceptionally quick, but he compensates at least to some degree with smart shot selection and accuracy; he didn't even average two shots per game, while Detroit's Sergei Fedorov needed 259 shots for 31 goals last season, the Rangers' John Ogrodnick required 250 and Montreal's Stephane Richer 221.

Elynuik does virtually all his scoring from between the faceoff dots. He can bury a chip pass from behind the net and ram in a one-timer on a pass across the slot. He doesn't have the puck much and he doesn't have it long; Elynuik gets the puck, shoots it, buries it.

THE PHYSICAL GAME

Elynuik's output is more remarkable because he won't linger around the goal crease, won't always face the shooter and try to deflect point shots and is not a physical player. Elynuik does not have much one-on-one power, isn't much of a banger, but he is not an incomplete player. He works the corners well and prides himself on his defensive play, but his game is based much more on his hands than on his bulk.

THE INTANGIBLES

It would not be fair to link Elynuik's scoring strictly to Steen, any more than it was fair to label Chicago's Steve Larmer as merely a co-efficient of Denis Savard or to call Jari Kurri a creation of Wayne Gretzky. Rather, Elynuik is an accomplished scorer in his own right, one who can make the most of a setup man. He is a 40- or 50-goal scorer waiting to happen; a bit more physical gusto would improve the chances.

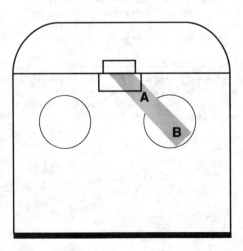

BOB ESSENSA

Yrs. of NHL service: 3
Born: Toronto, Ont., Canada; January 14, 1965
Position: Goaltender
Height: 6-0
Weight: 160
Uniform no.: 35
Catches: Left

Career statistics:

GP	MINS	GA	SO	GAA	A	PIM
111	6053	328	6	3.25	5	8

1990-91 statistics:

GP	MINS	GAA	W	L	T	SO	GA	S	SAPCT	PIM
55	2916	3.15	19	24	6	4	153	1496	.898	6

LAST SEASON

Shutout total tied for second in NHL behind Don Beaupre's five. Games played figure came within one of matching prior career total.

THE PHYSICAL GAME

Essensa is a big, boring, butterfly goalie who lets his size and smarts be assets. He isn't a great athlete and he used to get caught in between: people would shoot while Essensa was in the process of dropping to his knees. He is more a standup goaltender now, but when he drops, he drops right away and is in better position for the initial shot.

Recovery remains a bit of a problem, because there are times when he goes down too much. He has to anticipate, read the play, use his size and let the puck hit him.

Essensa does not use his stick a great deal, does not handle the puck very well, and you aren't going to be excited by the way he moves. But he's going to be there when it counts. He can come out of nowhere to make a stop. He's pretty good at controlling his rebounds, pretty good at controlling the tempo of the game, and he has a better-than-average glove hand.

THE MENTAL GAME

Essensa's biggest asset is his composure. He never gets rattled and can go five, six or seven games without giving up a weak goal. Essensa has always been a goalie who finds a way to win.

THE INTANGIBLES

Essensa is getting better, developing into a consistent NHL goaltender. His six NHL shutouts are five more than Ron Hextall has managed over more than twice as many career games, so he must be doing something right. He is a goalie who makes the simple play, who can be trusted with a big game.

442

DOUG EVANS

Yrs. of NHL service: 5
Born: Peterborough, Ont., Canada; June 2, 1963
Position: Left wing
Height: 5-9
Weight: 185
Uniform no.: 39
Shoots: Left

Career statistics:

GP	G	A	TP	PIM
260	33	67	100	331

1990-91 statistics:

GP	G	A	TP	+/-	PIM	PP	SH	GW	GT	S	PCT
70	7	27	34	-1	108	1	0	0	1	70	10.0

LAST SEASON

Career high for games played in a one season. Goal total tied second best career figure and was within three of prior campaign's total.

THE FINESSE GAME

Evans was a 100-point player in the minors, but he is a different player now. He is a role player for whom 40 points would be an extremely successful season, because generally, he doesn't play with people who are scorers. Other times, though, he has teamed with Thomas Steen and Pat Elynuik, complementing their offensive skills with his defensive strength and willingness to mix it up.

Evans' points are going to come from a defensive posture, from an occasional shorthanded goal (he kills penalties well), from hounding people off the puck on the forecheck, using his surprisingly good hockey sense to spot an open man and having his teammate convert the turnovers into goals.

THE PHYSICAL GAME

Evans seems completely clear on the reality of hockey life that when you're a "little" guy, you have to do more to stay at the game's top level. So he goes to the net (though he rarely gets the puck there). He gets involved physically as much as possible. He uses every weapon available to make himself useful.

That extends to fighting. Evans could be likened to a good club middleweight. He ties a lot of the scraps, but he doesn't lose many, doesn't get thrown around and makes sure to show up for the next one.

THE INTANGIBLES

There is nothing fancy about Doug Evans. He is not big, he is not quick, but he's going to make the other team very nervous because he is a complete pest and he gives nobody any respect at all unless they earn it. He has a good head but not great skills. He is going to do anything he can to win, and he will do anything to help his teammates. He may be a fourth-liner on the ice, but he is much closer to a first-line player in the dressing room.

As an aside, Evans went back and spent a third year in junior hockey as a 20-year-old at Peterborough, giving himself the benefit of another year of discipline and finishing school under coach Dick Todd. It may be the reason he is a credible NHL player today, albeit usually as a fourth-line left wing.

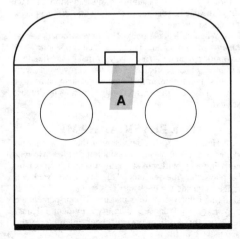

PHIL HOUSLEY

Yrs. of NHL service: 9
Born: St. Paul, Minn., USA; March 9, 1964
Position: Defenseman
Height: 5-10
Weight: 185
Uniform no.: 6
Shoots: Left

Career statistics:

GP	G	A	TP	PIM
686	201	433	634	410

1990-91 statistics:

GP	G	A	TP	+/-	PIM	PP	SH	GW	GT	S	PCT
78	23	53	76	-13	24	12	1	3	0	206	11.2

LAST SEASON

In his first season with team, led Jets in scoring and notched at least 20 goals for fifth consecutive season. Was only player who was with Jets all season to take more than 200 shots on goal.

THE FINESSE GAME

Far more an offensive than defensive defenseman, Housley relies on exceptional skating skill to dance the puck out of the defensive zone. He uses his speed to sprint to the corners, makes tight turns to dart away from checkers and accelerates out of the curves to reach daylight. But Housley often throws caution to the wind on loose pucks that other people seem to reach first at the boards or in the corners, then is out of position when passes go to the goalmouth.

Owner of every finesse skill in the book, Housley can lead the rush or move into a play quickly. When he's carrying the puck, Housley can gain the blue line with speed and make something happen, yet he's fast enough to catch virtually anyone from behind if there's a turnover and he is caught on the transition. He can move the puck or can make exciting one-on-one plays, going end-to-end.

When he has the puck, Housley is remarkable at making something out of nothing. It can appear he's out of options, then he'll find a hole or make one, like O.J. Simpson with a football. He can run a power play with the best point men in the league, but also can run it productively out of the right wing circle, as he did last season.

THE PHYSICAL GAME

Housley is less a defenseman than a wing who skates backwards when the situation dictates. He will not win many battles of strength or size, which is why he plays the finesse game. Housley uses speed and range to invade the puck carrier's space, challenge his skills and hurry him into making a poor-percentage play. Excellent balance and agility is evident in Housley's use of reach on sweep check attempts at the defensive blue line.

He's a rover; he's everywhere. Housley will dart in front of a pass, pick it off and start a counter-attack. Rather than physically engage a forward in front, he will try to nullify an opponent by tying up the player's stick. More of a stick checker, he will skate with an opponent and eliminate him if possible, but is not capable of doing it with any authority.

That cuts into his minutes played. Housley can't always match up with the top opposing lines if they have a physical wing crashing the net, and his size makes it intellectually irresponsible to attempt to play a grinding game.

THE INTANGIBLES

Do not mistake the often reckless style he plays for a lack of intensity. This is a player who enjoys the game, who would be just as happy playing shinny on a pond, but one who can also channel his energy into crackling displays of skill.

Dependable from a health standpoint, Housley never has missed more than eight games in a season. Fine defensemen can't help you win if they're always hurt, and Housley is a fine defenseman...as long as it is a free-skating game.

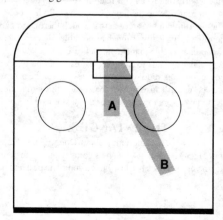

PAUL MACDERMID

Yrs. of NHL service: 7
Born: Chesley, Ont., Canada; April 14, 1963
Position: Right wing
Height: 6-1
Weight: 205
Uniform no.: 23
Shoots: Right

Career statistics:

GP	G	A	TP	PIM
486	90	114	204	972

1990-91 statistics:

GP	G	A	TP	+/-	PIM	PP	SH	GW	GT	S	PCT
69	15	21	36	-6	128	3	0	1	0	94	16.0

LAST SEASON

Missed six games due to lower back spasms. Games played total was his lowest in NHL since 1984-85. Penalty minutes were his fewest in any full NHL season.

THE FINESSE GAME

MacDermid is not a great skater, though his legs do carry him to collisions with various opponents. He doesn't have great speed or great hands; he has about average speed and acceptable hands, and he has a decent release on his shot.

But most of the time, MacDermid does not touch the puck for the sake of offense and he does not play the game for the sake of finesse. He plays it to send people flying; he plays it to score the second-effort goals that require driving to the net and fighting off a check and jamming the goalie into the cage with the puck, if that is what it takes.

Away from the puck, MacDermid is well aware of the requirements of the defensive zone and will pick up the open man.

THE PHYSICAL GAME

This is a grinding, hard-nosed right wing who is extremely effective at the game of disrupting the opposing defense. He spends as much of the game as possible behind the opponent's net or in the corners. He's got some size and will hit, but he does not seem to do it all the time. He keeps his legs moving, though; sometimes, it will require two opposing players to stop him in the corners.

THE INTANGIBLES

While the consistency of his work ethic is evident, the consistency of his overall performance remains a goal for MacDermid. He will get the team about a dozen goals a year, whether the team needs them or not.

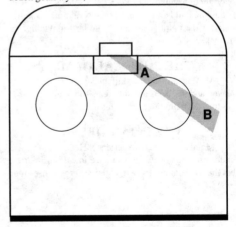

MOE MANTHA

Yrs. of NHL service: 11
Born: Lakewood, Ohio, USA; January 21, 1961
Position: Defenseman
Height: 6-2
Weight: 210
Uniform no.: 22
Shoots: Right

Career statistics:

GP	G	A	TP	PIM
639	81	285	366	493

1990-91 statistics:

GP	G	A	TP	+/-	PIM	PP	SH	GW	GT	S	PCT
57	9	15	24	-20	33	4	1	2	0	102	8.8

LAST SEASON

Goal total tied his best over past five seasons. Plus-minus declined by 28 goals from prior campaign.

THE FINESSE GAME

Mantha can skate a little, carry the puck a little, can skate it out of his defensive zone and dump it across the red line. He can survive with those skills in the Smthe Division, where teams generally don't send two forecheckers to smoke defensemen against the glass and throw the puck up for grabs, but he had a hard time dealing with those circumstances in Philadelphia.

Mantha will get you some points on the power play, though with such other defensemen as Fredrik Olausson, Phil Housley and Teppo Numminen, another man for the point seems to be the last of Winnipeg's many needs.

THE PHYSICAL GAME

Mantha is more a skill player than a physical player, and his skills are not great. Too many forwards get too much time in front of his net.

THE INTANGIBLES

Mantha does have experience. He has some poise under fire. He is veteran insurance in case of injuries, but that is about all. Even if Winnipeg mostly uses four defensemen and spots a third pair against the other team's weakest forwards, they'd have to be better off bringing a kid into that role rather than stay with a journeyman who's 30 and probably making more money.

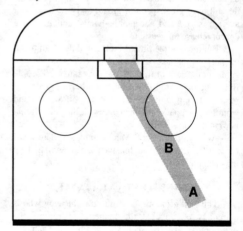

BRYAN MARCHMENT

Yrs. of NHL service: 1
Born: Toronto, Ont., Canada; May 1, 1969
Position: Defenseman
Height: 6-1
Weight: 198
Uniform no.: 3
Shoots: Left

Career statistics:

GP	G	A	TP	PIM
37	2	4	6	121

1990-91 statistics:

GP	G	A	TP	+/-	PIM	PP	SH	GW	GT	S	PCT
28	2	2	4	-5	91	0	0	0	0	24	8.4

LAST SEASON

Split season between Jets and their Moncton (AHL) affiliate.

THE FINESSE GAME

Marchment's offensive skills have not fully developed, owing at least partially to skating weaknesses that prevent him from changing directions especially well. But the Jets have plenty of guys who can move up with the play; Marchment's deployment will be as a defensive player who can add a strong defensive element for an offensive-minded partner.

THE PHYSICAL GAME

Though his range is limited, Marchment throws the kind of checks that makes people do cartwheels on the ice. He is a solid banger who plays the body at every opportunity and who should get even better once he gains some savvy. He put opposing players out of four consecutive games with hits last season, and all the hits were legal.

THE INTANGIBLES

His training habits are something of a problem—he arrived as a big kid with a bad body. But he is a prospect who gave enough positive signs last year, and who this season should break through for his first full shot at the big boys.

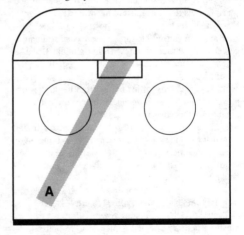

DAVE MCLLWAIN

Yrs. of NHL service: 4
Born: Seaforth, Ont., Canada; June 9, 1967
Position: Right wing
Height: 6-0
Weight: 190
Uniform no.: 20
Shoots: Right

Career statistics:

GP	G	A	TP	PIM
230	51	47	98	150

1990-91 statistics:

GP	G	A	TP	+/-	PIM	PP	SH	GW	GT	S	PCT
60	14	11	25	-13	46	2	2	2	0	104	13.5

LAST SEASON

Missed two games due to sprained wrist, missed 16 due to knee sprain, two due to coach's decision. Goal production dropped by 11, plus-minus worsened by 12.

THE FINESSE GAME

McLlwain has quick feet which generate the speed he uses to create most of his offensive moments. He is agile in the sense that he picks up speed by crossing over during his turns, as opposed to being a power skater who accelerates in a straight line. Because he can dart and chase—he is fast, especially to the outside, but not overly strong on his skates— McLlwain gets most of his points from being the first player in the zone for forechecking pressure and making plays off turnovers.

McLlwain would have more points if his offensive instincts and skills were sharper. For the amount of speed he has, the amount of penalty killing he does, one shorthanded goal speaks for itself and for his shot, which is not a feared weapon.

McLlwain makes better use of his hands on faceoffs, which he wins with regularity. He is especially trustworthy on defensive-zone draws, as his is mostly a defense-oriented game; he is responsible in his checking and can carry out defensive assignments well.

THE PHYSICAL GAME

Rather than hit, McLlwain tends to rub people out along the wood. He doesn't really plow for the puck in the trenches; he'll use his stick to probe the puck from a forest of ankles, and occasionally will do something with it. He is fairly scrappy, but is not going to fight or take a lot of aggression fouls.

THE INTANGIBLES

McLlwain is an enthusiastic player, a No. 2 or 3 center who will get you a goal here and there, win his fair share of faceoffs, kill penalties and underwhelm offensively.

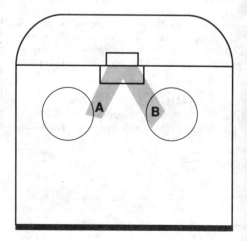

TEPPO NUMMINEN

Yrs. of NHL service: 3
Born: Tampere, Finland; July 3, 1968
Position: Defenseman
Height: 6-1
Weight: 190
Uniform no.: 27
Shoots: Right

Career statistics:

GP	G	A	TP	PIM
228	20	71	91	84

1990-91 statistics:

GP	G	A	TP	+/-	PIM	PP	SH	GW	GT	S	PCT
80	8	25	33	-15	28	3	0	0	0	151	5.3

LAST SEASON

Goal and assist totals dropped three and seven, respectively, from prior season.

THE FINESSE GAME

It is a pleasure to watch Numminen skate. He has a long, graceful stride and an effortless shift from forward skating to backward skating and up again. He may take some extra time making decisions with the puck in the attacking zone, especially on the power play; but he is far more automatic—and more persistently correct—making decisions in the defensive and neutral zones, which is why he is a good penalty killer.

Numminen looks to pass first, looks to carry second as a method of clearing the puck from his defensive end. In center ice, he does not hesitate for an instant if the situation calls for the puck to be drilled around the boards and into the attacking zone. Though European players tend to want to make a play at the blue line, Numminen wants to make the play that will work for his team. The main thing to him is that the puck keep moving, a critical line of thought for a skating team such as his.

Numminen gets lot of shots on the net. But he gets few goals because the shot is not exactly a bomb and because he does not work the puck in closer if people are conceding the territory. He gets few assists, because few teammates are willing to go to the net to look for garbage goals from his rebounds.

THE PHYSICAL GAME

Numminen is not a very physical player. He likes to skate with the puck, likes to skate without it, but aggressive contact puts him off.

He does not deal well with opposition forwards crashing the net while a puck is on the way from the point; he still tends to fish with his stick for the pucks in the corners, rather than go in, drop a guy and pick up the puck.

THE INTANGIBLES

A rotten year does not by any means make Numminen a rotten defenseman. It does, however, make him an intriguing player to watch in 1991-92. After a tentative first year, Numminen mounted a solid sophomore season that pointed toward a lot more promise than he kept last season.

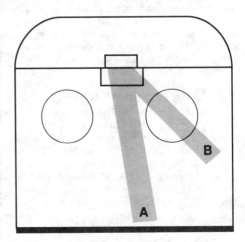

449

FREDRIK OLAUSSON

Yrs. of NHL service: 5
Born: Vaxsjo, Sweden; October 5, 1966
Position: Defenseman
Height: 6-2
Weight: 200
Uniform no.: 4
Shoots: Right

Career statistics:

GP	G	A	TP	PIM
333	48	161	209	130

1990-91 statistics:

GP	G	A	TP	+/-	PIM	PP	SH	GW	GT	S	PCT
71	12	29	41	-22	24	5	0	0	0	168	7.1

LAST SEASON

Third straight season with 40 or more points and 70 or more games played. Plus-minus was worst of any player with Winnipeg all season.

THE FINESSE GAME

Olausson is an exceptional puck handler and shooter, a powerful skater who simply can pull away from people with the strength of his stride and with his speed. He is so agile, he steps away at the last instant and makes people miss checks on him when they seem to think they have him lined up.

Olausson's work ethic is the mainspring. He will skate back hard to collect the puck behind the net, will make a crisp outlet pass to a teammate at the hash marks, then really will take off to join the attack and maintain a small gap to the forwards.

Olausson has a very good head for situations, plus hands that enable him to move the puck to the right places. He joins the rush well, he sneaks in the back door well and he is extremely capable of running the power play. He uses a strong half-slap shot from the point, gets it off quickly, and keeps it low to facilitate deflections and create rebounds.

THE PHYSICAL GAME

Olausson plays the hard minutes, against the opposition's top line. He will take the hits, make a few, but he isn't as chippy as, say, a Gary Suter is for Calgary. The stick check still is his first option, though he plays the body more as a last resort.

An intelligent player who gets by despite a lack of size, Olausson is not tough on the road. And when the score is out of reach, he tends to leave early. Still,

Olausson gets to the front of the net, good body position; and while he won't knock down too many forwards, he does not have too many problems with a physical game and he accepts being hit.

THE INTANGIBLES

Olausson went for goal scoring last season and produced, but at great cost to his overall game. Last season was Olausson's first as a "minus" player, it will be interesting to see how he responds. He needs to be in better shape and to get his focus back if he is to retain his status as the club's No. 1 defenseman.

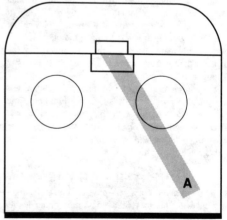

ED OLCZYK

Yrs. of NHL service: 7
Born: Chicago, Ill., USA; August 16, 1966
Position: Center
Height: 6-1
Weight: 200
Uniform no.: 16
Shoots: Left

Career statistics:

GP	G	A	TP	PIM
536	207	297	504	523

1990-91 statistics:

GP	G	A	TP	+/-	PIM	PP	SH	GW	GT	S	PCT
79	30	41	71	-27	82	14	0	2	2	226	13.3

LAST SEASON

Had highest goals-per-game ratio, one every 2.35 games, of any player on Jets. Marked fourth straight year of 30 goals or better, though point total declined for third successive season.

THE FINESSE GAME

Olczyk handles the puck well enough and has adequate-enough skating skills to play the one-on-one game he relishes—creating one-on-one situations whenever possible. A straight-line power center, Olczyk will power past a defenseman, will shoot, will go to the net and, on rare occasion, will carry an opponent with him.

But all that leaves his wings precious little to do; they can look for some rebounds, they can hope for an occasional pass from behind the net or from up high, near the blue line. Or they can watch Olczyk carry the mail, which generally is the case.

The offensive game Olczyk likes to play is an effective goal producer. Olczyk can score off the wing or make the plays in front; he will scramble into the slot for a snap shot off a loose puck or plant outside the crease, looking for tips and screens.

Defense is the weakest aspect of Olczyk's game. That is understandable to a degree, because Olczyk always has been called upon to lead his team's attack rather than contribute from a two-way standpoint. But he seems to do a lot of star-gazing in the neutral zone when he should be picking up a man.

THE PHYSICAL GAME

Olczyk recognizes there are times when you have to collide with somebody, but isn't keen on those situations when he may end up getting as much as he's giving. If a stick check isn't enough to slow down his man, Olczyk has been known to give up on the play. He puts the stick on his man instead of taking one or two extra steps and putting his shoulder into him. His errors are by omission, not comission.

As a consequence, Olczyk's size generally gets wasted and his team's chances of winning are not as greatly enhanced by his appearance as they should be. He had 16 even-strength goals and was minus 27, he was "even" after a 90-point season a few years ago, which more than makes clear Olczyk could be a lot more involved in a lot more areas of the ice.

THE INTANGIBLES

Olczyk is Winnipeg's one-man line, much in the manner of a Pat LaFontaine with the Islanders. A distributing center, a playmaker, would have more assists than Olczyk—even if he plays on a line with people who don't finish well—which is why the Jets are giving serious consideration to playing him on right wing.

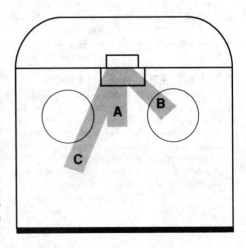

MARK OSBORNE

Yrs. of NHL service: 10
Born: Toronto, Ont., Canada; August 13, 1961
Position: Left wing
Height: 6-2
Weight: 205
Uniform no.: 12
Shoots: Left

Career statistics:

GP	G	A	TP	PIM
679	183	274	457	826

1990-91 statistics:

GP	G	A	TP	+/-	PIM	PP	SH	GW	GT	S	PCT
55	11	11	22	-11	63	1	1	2	1	87	12.6

LAST SEASON

Obtained November 10 from Toronto, with Ed Olczyk, for Dave Ellett and Paul Fenton. Missed 21 games due to broken thumb. Plus-minus declined by 13 goals.

THE FINESSE GAME

Osborne is a powerful player who has speed with the puck as well as without it. He plays into those skating skills by making intelligent use of the give-and-go; he might grab a puck off the boards and carry it a short distance, but he'll use that time to locate someone jumping into the play for a short, quick lead pass.

A dependable scorer whose output was hampered by a hand injury last season, Osborne can drive a slap shot past a goalie from the faceoff circle or he can get his nose dirty and score the grungy stuff off snap shots from the slot. He will use his strength to gain position for the short-game plays, use his mobility and power for drive on the rush.

Osborne also pays attention to the defensive aspect and generally is a plus player. He'll scrap for the puck, though for balance reasons he is not as effective flat-up against the wall as he is when he's the second man—the guy hacking the fellow who's flat-up along the wall.

THE PHYSICAL GAME

Osborne is not a fighter; never has been, really. But he is accomplished at the art of the two-hander, from the more-subtle chop at close range (right above the cuff of the glove, where there's no padding) to the full-out, home run swing. And he is not reluctant to use whichever is needed to mark out his turf.

Osborne finishes his checks with authority when he can. If he gets there late, or the shot at a big hit has passed, he will at least get a piece of the guy or retain body position so he is between the player and the puck.

THE INTANGIBLES

Osborne is a quality individual of intelligence and integrity. Certainly he has battled adversity with an assortment of debilitating injuries, certainly he has paid the price for success. It is more those qualities that have led him to so many teams than that his prior teams were unhappy with his output.

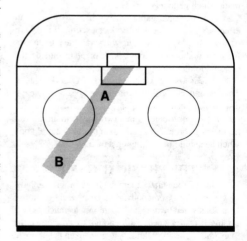

THOMAS STEEN

Yrs. of NHL service: 10
Born: Tocksmark, Sweden; June 8, 1960
Position: Center
Height: 5-10
Weight: 195
Uniform no.: 25
Shoots: Left

Career statistics:

GP	G	A	TP	PIM
725	205	436	641	603

1990-91 statistics:

GP	G	A	TP	+/-	PIM	PP	SH	GW	GT	S	PCT
58	19	48	67	-3	49	7	0	3	0	125	15.2

LAST SEASON

Broken ankle cost him 21 games, but goal total was higher than it had been in five of the past six seasons.

THE FINESSE GAME

Steen's foot speed, hand skills and mental dexterity allow him to play the game at a high tempo. An exceptional puck handler, he is more of a playmaker than a goal scorer, a player equally likely to get the puck and move it or get the puck and carry it—but one who all too rarely gets the puck and shoots it. Steen loves to criss-cross with a wing, isolate a defenseman and create the two-on-one game he plays so well. If his wing gets open, Steen will find a way to get him the puck for a good shot.

Steen's technical skills are exceptional, and his ice awareness is exactly what you would except from an elite European athlete. He needs very little room to change directions and start a new move immediately. On offense and defense, he sees and reacts to things other players don't even imagine. That vision is useful especially on the power play, which Steen can run capably from the right wing faceoff dot. He will create open space, then decide whether it would be better if he used it or a teammate did, and the decision is the correct one an extremely high percentage of the time.

Though only average on faceoffs. Steen is sound defensively. He plays every inch of the ice, and does it without letting up because of extremely good stamina.

THE PHYSICAL GAME

Steen is a willingly physical player from the standpoint of accepting physical contact or eagerly entering into it, and plays off the hits as well as anybody. He commands a tremendous amount of respect for the punishment he takes in the course of a game and his refusal to be intimidated by it.

Steen will steer the puck into the heaviest traffic. He will grind and cycle along the boards and in the corners. He keeps his legs going and is an extremely difficult player to cover. Plus, if you pay too much checking attention to him, one of his linemates will sprint into the open.

THE INTANGIBLES

This is Winnipeg's finest all-around player, one who improves the players around him. He is determined. He plays hurt. He is a tremendous competitor who despises losing. He takes tremendous pride in his performance. He is a major force whenever he's on the ice.

The only concern is that last season was the second straight under 60 games-played. At age 31, the sun may be starting to set.

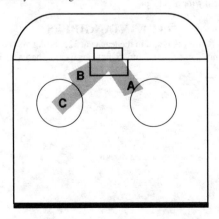

PHIL SYKES

Yrs. of NHL service: 7
Born: Dawson Creek, B.C., Canada; March 19, 1959
Position: Left wing
Height: 6-0
Weight: 175
Uniform no.: 17
Shoots: Left

Career statistics:

GP	G	A	TP	PIM
404	75	83	158	447

1990-91 statistics:

GP	G	A	TP	+/-	PIM	PP	SH	GW	GT	S	PCT
70	12	10	22	-9	59	0	2	0	1	65	18.5

LAST SEASON

Games played was a six-season high, as was goal total. Assist total was four-season high.

THE FINESSE GAME

Though his reputation is that of a guy who can check the other team's top right wing and do a good job, Sykes tends mostly to just race around and gravitates to open ice even when placed in that checking role. There are nights you don't see a whole lot of him when the clubs are at five skaters per side.

Sykes has a wiry build. He has some speed and quickness, which suits his "role," but he is best used for penalty killing or under any conditions when fewer than 10 skaters are on the ice.

THE PHYSICAL GAME

Sykes' physical willingness outstrips his finesse skills. Sykes can still put his stick in a guy's ribs and hang on for a free ride or scrap around for the puck if it isn't in a part of the ice where it would be extremely risky for him to go.

THE INTANGIBLES

Sykes is still in the league at 32, scoring his six or nine or 12 goals and convincing people he can still play, so he must be doing something right. He would be the perfect candidate to go someplace in the waiver draft, but there won't be one for a few years—by which time he should be well into his next career.

RICK TABARACCI

Yrs. of NHL service: 1
Born: Toronto, Ont., Canada; January 2, 1969
Position: Goaltender
Height: 5-10
Weight: 185
Uniform no.: 31
Catches: Right

Career statistics:

GP	MINS	GA	SO	GAA	A	PIM
25	1126	75	1	3.99	1	8

1990-91 statistics:

GP	MINS	GAA	W	L	T	SO	GA	S	SAPCT	PIM
24	1093	3.90	4	9	4	1	71	570	.875	8

LAST SEASON

First NHL season.

THE PHYSICAL GAME

Tabaracci doesn't quite seem comfortable with the first tenet of goaltending philosophy, which is, "Let the puck hit you." Tabaracci would prefer to wriggle and jump so that his body or stick hits the puck and he looks great in all the photographs. He comes out nicely on his angle to challenge the shooters, but then he's scrambling, reacting, swimming around, almost challenging himself to make the most difficult saves on the easiest shots. Tabaracci wants to be an acrobatic, heroic goaltender, and virtually is the complete opposite of his far calmer (and more effective) counterpart, Bob Essensa.

Tabaracci has two tremendous assets to complement his agility and quickness. He is an excellent skater, which is a part of the entire physical package, and he really can handle the puck. Except, again, Tabaracci overdoes it instead of making that ability something his team can use positively. He can put the puck in the press box if he wants, but not many teammates can reach it there.

Sometimes Tabaracci combines his skating and athletic skills. He likes to go behind the net and hit people.

THE MENTAL GAME

Tabaracci can be great one night, an unknown quantity the next. All physical aspects play off the mental game in his case, and it takes a great deal of time for most goaltenders to grab an emotional handle on the tremendous mood swings they must confront almost daily. Tabaracci is not yet at that stage; he cannot maintain his concentration yet on a consistent basis.

THE INTANGIBLES

Tabaracci has the athletic skills to succeed at NHL level, but the discipline is not yet there. He needs to play more in control so that, by extension, the entire team would be more composed in the defensive zone. The style he plays may have been suited to success in juniors, but it does not translate especially well against players of far greater skills at this level.

INDEX OF
PLAYERS